Professional
IE4 Programming

Mike Barta
Jon Bonnell
Andrew Enfield
Dino Esposito
Brian Francis
Richard Harrison
Alex Homer
Stephen Jakab
Sing Li
Shawn Murphy
Chris Ullman

Wrox Press Ltd.®

Professional IE4 Programming

© 1997 Wrox Press

Published by Wrox Press Ltd. 30 Lincoln Road, Olton, Birmingham, B27 6PA
Printed in USA

ISBN 1-861000-70-7

Credits

Authors
Mike Barta
Jon Bonnell
Andrew Enfield
Dino Esposito
Brian Francis
Richard Harrison
Alex Homer
Stephen Jakab
Sing Li
Shawn Murphy
Chris Ullman

Additional Material
Dan Kohn

Editors
Anthea Elston
Jeremy Beacock

Index
Simon Gilks

Technical Reviewers
Jon Bonnell
William Buxton
Diane Castillo
Andrew Enfield
Brian Francis
Richard Harrison
Stephen Jakab
Rick Kingslan
Sing Li
Shawn Murphy
Tony Pittarese
Larry Roof
David Steinmetz
Nick Temple
Omar Khan

Cover/Design/Layout
Andrew Guillaume
Graham Butler

Cover photo supplied by The Image Bank

About the Authors

Mike Barta

Subject file for Mike Barta
While the full details are somewhat obscured, some pertinent facts have emerged during our investigation. The subject is in his twenties. He has been seen lurking in the Redmond, WA area for several years now, and it is said he is in program management. Prior to this he has spent time as a mismanager, an itinerant student of Slavic languages, a 'media professional' and a professional eavesdropper in military employ. His strange appreciation for rainy days might be attributable to Seattle childhood. These observations are based partially on hearsay, veracity is suspected thereby.
This is an unsecured line.

Jon Bonnell

Jon Bonnell is a full time programmer and program manager, and has been for seven years. Before that it was formal education and high school, but there has always been a computer influencing his life. Jon spends his free time doing this: writing books, articles, etc. When his wife lets him and he can wrestle the computer away from his three-year old son, he logs on the Internet and tries to keep up with the myriad of changes that occur there, every day. Since that's almost impossible, he gets discouraged and plays a quick game of Quake or works on one of many programming projects he has cluttering up his hard drive that he never finds time to complete.

Andrew Enfield

Andrew Enfield is currently finishing an undergraduate degree in Computer Engineering at the University of Washington. He has co-authored three books with Wrox Press and very much enjoys the writing and school lifestyle. When he's not writing, coding, studying, or living in labs on campus he likes to travel, read, watch baseball, and take long walks in beautiful, green, and wet Seattle. In the last year he's camped in New Mexico and Arizona, visited Boston and California, and ventured out on a three-month jaunt to Europe and the Middle East. That makes it four down, with three continents to go!

Dino Esposito

Dino Esposito is a trainer and a consultant who specializes in Windows and COM programming. He works for Infomedia Communications, writing and teaching seminars on Win32 programming, VB, and HTML. Has an extensive experience developing commercial Windows-based software, especially for the photography world. He's a regular contributor to Microsoft Interactive Developer and Windows Developer's Journal and writes occasionally also for Windows Tech Journal. Dino lives in Rome (Italy) with his wife Silvia and can be contacted at desposito@infomedia.it.
To Silvia, with all my love.

Brian Francis

Brian is a Senior developer with NCR's Human Interface Technology Center in Atlanta, Georgia. At the HITC, Brian is responsible for prototyping and developing advanced applications that apply superior human interface as developed at the Center. His tools of choice include Visual Basic, Visual C++, Java, and all of the Microsoft Internet products. Brian has developed and deployed Multimedia Kiosk applications, Computer-based Training applications, and other advanced user interface prototypes for the past three years. *All my love and thanks go to my wife Kristi, without whom my life would not be complete. Thank you for always being there for me and for supporting me in of my writing adventures.*

Richard Harrison

Richard is a Microsoft Certified Solution Developer (MCSD) and a senior consultant for a major global IT services company. He has recently been specializing in Microsoft Internet architectures and helping organizations to use these technologies to build mission critical Web solutions.

About the Authors

Alex Homer

Alex is a software consultant and developer, who lives and works in the idyllic rural surroundings of Derbyshire UK. His company, Stonebroom Software, specializes in office integration and Internet-related development, and produces a range of vertical application software. He has worked with Wrox Press on several projects.

Stephen Jakab

Stephen Jakab has experience in writing custom solutions for corporate companies. He worked on the Consort II car fleet management system written in CA Clipper, and as a Microsoft Certified Professional he now concentrates on VB and ASP Internet/Intranet Web projects with the SQL Server backend. While he's not working, he enjoys many sports, reading and travelling. This year, he's been to the US, Canada and has recently returned from Hungary. *Thanks to all my good Friends around the globe: Valérie, Christine, Rehéma, Phil and my Friends in Hungary. Your friendship means the world to me.*

Sing Li

Bitten by the computer bug since 1978, Sing's first computer was a Netronics ELF single-board computer with 256 bytes of memory. Adopting a 'Java Way of Life', Sing is a founder of microWonders, a product development and consulting firm. He is an active author, consultant and entrepreneur, Sing has written for popular technical journals, and worked in diverse technical areas spanning Computer Telephony Intergration, Internet and Intranet system designs, distributed architectures, digital convergence, embedded systems, and cross-platform software design.

Shawn Murphy

Shawn is currently an independent Internet developer and consultant working in the Los Angeles area where he is also studying architecture at the University of Southern California. He writes articles for IEWorld (http://www.ieworld.net) an on-line journal that is dedicated to the latest in Internet Development and Microsoft technologies. His experience in web technologies ranges from HTML to client and server-side code and web application development. He has also worked as a contractor for companies ranging from nursing homes to Microsoft's Internet Gaming Zone.

Chris Ullman

Chris Ullman is a computer science graduate who has not let this handicap prevent him becoming a programmer fluent in Visual Basic, Java, SQL and Dynamic HTML. When not cutting up pictures by old masters to re-assemble them as dynamic jigsaws on his preferred browser, he's either found down his local soccer ground urging on his favorite team, Birmingham City, or at home trying to prevent his two new kittens from tearing up the house, or each other. *All my love to Kate, who's always there to give me support and a home and usually tries to look interested when I explain the latest Internet based technology.*

'Our thanks to all the research and development staff at Microsoft, especially Garth Bruce, Rich Rollman, David Wascha and Omar Khan, who assisted by supplying the nuggets of hard-to-find information just when we needed them during the writing of this book.'

Table of Contents

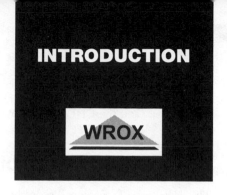

So, can *you* remember those dark and distant days (say, around eighteen months ago) when Web browsers were simple applications, and there were lots of different ones to choose from? In those far-off times, all the browser had to do was take a text file sprinkled with HTML tags, and render it so that it looked a bit like a page of text. OK, so there may have been a few images as well, and it also had to cope with hyperlinks to other pages, but life was–relatively–simple.

Of course, in those days, Microsoft had only just noticed that the Internet existed. Yet now, less that two years later, we've got a brand new version of their Web browser–Internet Explorer 4. And to say that it's changed is certainly an understatement. Comparing it with version 1, or the equivalent Web browsers of that time, is like saying that your wristwatch has the same bits inside as the Hubble Telescope. Yes, they do both work in the dark–but there's not much else you can compare.

So it is with Internet Explorer 4. On the outside it looks reassuringly familiar. There are all the bits you would expect around the edge of the window, including the obligatory animated logo in the top right-hand corner. But once you start to investigate what it can do, and see some of the effects it can achieve using things like Dynamic HTML, Data Binding, Cascading Style Sheet Filters, Webcasting and the Active Desktop, you soon start to see that this isn't just evolution–it's revolution.

What is this Book about?

This book is all about Internet Explorer 4. We're going to explore all the exciting new technologies that are now part of the browser, and show you some of the amazing things you can do with it. We'll also look at the background to Internet Explorer, to see how it fits into the rest of Microsoft's server-based technologies.

The technologies we'll be covering fall reasonably neatly into categories:

- ▲ Dynamic HTML–the changes to the browser that enable the contents of the page to be changed dynamically using script written within the page.

- ▲ Data Binding–which allows pages to be created that act like database forms, displaying data from a database and enabling it to be updated on the fly.

- ▲ Multimedia and Filters–new ways that HTML styles and browser-embedded objects can produce really professional graphics and sound effects.

- ▲ Client/Server Programming–a brief look at some of the new ways that the browser and server can work together using scripting at both ends of the network link.

- ▲ The Active Desktop–a comprehensive examination of the way that the browser and Windows operating system have merged to produce a smoother and more intuitive Web environment.

- ▲ Webcasting–the ability to turn your IE4 client, into the equivalent of a TV set, allowing you to download updates to web pages, without having to type so much as a URL.

On top of all this, we've provided a comprehensive reference section that covers the two major scripting languages–JavaScript and VBScript–the Dynamic HTML Document Object Model, Cascading Styles and Style Sheets, and the CDF/OSD Active Desktop.

Who is this Book for?

This is a Wrox 'Professional' series book, and so we won't be wasting your time by trying to teach you everything from scratch. We appreciate that most, if not all, of the professional Web page authors and developers who take up Internet Explorer will be reasonably familiar with ordinary HTML, basic programming concepts, and the simple constructs of the two main browser-specific languages.

That's not to say that we're forgetting about the newcomer to the Web. Part 1 of this book describes Dynamic HTML and CSS from the ground up, and also includes a chapter that shows you just how scripting can be used in Web pages. Don't worry, you won't find an abstract approach here. Like all Wrox books, this one is written by programmers, for programmers. It's full of practical techniques that you can develop from yourself.

However the real value will undoubtedly come from Parts 2,3 and 4 of this book. Part 2 is an in depth examination of data binding with the Tabular Data Control and also provides two case studies for the developer to dissect. Part 3 details advanced programming techniques, which is where we look at how to program the multimedia controls and filters in IE4. However we also take a look at other interesting elements in the component library, Scriptlets and how Dynamic HTML can be used with a dynamic server-side scripting technology, namely Active Server Pages. The final part of the book looks at the active desktop and the concept of webcasting. We don't discuss how to use Active Desktop Items and Channels, this is self-evident for the experienced developer, we show them how to program Active Desktop Items and Channels, for themselves.

There are also plenty of solid code examples, case studies that produce real, practical, applications, and reference material both throughout and at the end of the book. This means that you can use it both as a primer to learn the new techniques, and as a reference for the future-as you develop your skills and your Web sites, you can keep coming back to learn more.

We also publish a companion book to this one, which covers Dynamic HTML from a reference point of view. You might find it useful, as it contains a huge reference section that lists all the various HTML tags, properties, methods and events. Look out for Instant IE4 Dynamic HTML Programmer's Reference, ISBN 1-861000-68-5.

What you'll Need to Use this Book

It probably sounds banal to spell out what you need to use this book, but you really don't need much at all. Here's the full list of requisites:

Internet Explorer 4, including the Active Desktop Extensions. You can download IE4 from Microsoft's Web site at `http://www.microsoft.com/ie`. When you install it, make sure that you also install the Active Desktop extensions–unless you don't intend to implement anything from Part 4 of this book.

A text editor, such as Windows NotePad. Any text editor will do, though one that provides line numbers is useful. You can use a word processor, such as Microsoft Word, as long as you remember to save the files as plain text.

Most of the examples you'll see in this book can be run locally, from your hard disk. However, some of the case studies, and the client/server examples that use Active Server Pages, require an HTTP link to a **Web server**. Windows NT4 Server, Microsoft Personal Web Server, or Peer Web Server will do fine, or a server from any other supplier that implements Active Serve Pages.

You may also wish to develop your pages within a specialist environment, such as Microsoft Interdev, FrontPage, or a similar application like HoTMetaL Pro or other Web page creation software. At the time of writing, no single one of these provided all the features for creating Dynamic HTML pages that are dynamic (if you see what we mean), although the beta of FrontPage 98 did go some way to addressing this.

In other words, you still need to get in there and work that code by hand. But, let's face it, that's what learning to program is all about. Feel free to use any tool you like that saves time creating the basic structure of the page. What we're interested in is bringing it to life with scripting and all kinds of other new techniques.

Where you'll Find the Sample Code

Our prominent presence on the Web provides you with assistance and support as you use our books. Our main US-based site is at `http://www.wrox.com`, and it provides details of all our books. There is also a mirror site at `http://www.wrox.co.uk` that may be more responsive if you're accessing it from Europe. For our Internet-related books, we also have a special site that provides examples, and from where you can download code to run on your own machine. This is at `http://rapid.wrox.co.uk`.

Conventions

We have used a number of different styles of text and layout in the book to help differentiate between the different kinds of information. Here are examples of the styles we use and an explanation of what they mean:

Advice, hints, or background information comes in this type of font.

> **Important pieces of information come in boxes like this**

▲ **Important Words** are in a bold type font

▲ Words that appear on the screen in menus like the <u>F</u>ile or <u>W</u>indow are in a similar font to the one that you see on screen

▲ Keys that you press on the keyboard, like *Ctrl* and *Enter*, are in italics

▲   Code has several fonts. If it's a word that we're talking about in the text, for example, when
discussing the **For...Next** loop, it's in a bold font. If it's a block of code that you can type
in as a program and run, then it's also in a gray box:

```
<STYLE>
… Some VBScript …
</STYLE>
```

▲   Sometimes you'll see code in a mixture of styles, like this:

```
<HTML>
<HEAD>
<TITLE>Cascading Style Sheet Example</TITLE>
<STYLE>
style1 {color: red;
    font-size: 25}
</STYLE>
</HEAD>
```

▲   The code with a white background is code we've already looked at and that we don't wish to
examine further.

These formats are designed to make sure that you know what it is you're looking at. I hope they make life
easier.

Tell Us What You Think

We've worked hard on this book to make it useful. We've tried to understand what you're willing to
exchange your hard-earned money for, and we've tried to make the book live up to your expectations.

Please let us know what you think about this book. Tell us what we did wrong, and what we did right.
This isn't just marketing flannel: we really do huddle around the email to find out what you think. If you
don't believe it, then send us a note. We'll answer, and we'll take whatever you say on board for future
editions. The easiest way is to use email:

feedback@wrox.com

You can also find more details about Wrox Press on our web site. There, you'll find the code from our
latest books, sneak previews of forthcoming titles, and information about the authors and editors. You can
order Wrox titles directly from the site, or find out where your nearest local bookstore with Wrox titles is
located.

Customer Support

If you find a mistake, please have a look at the errata page for this book on our web site first. Appendix I outlines how can you can submit an errata in much greater detail, if you are unsure. The full URL for the errata page is:

`http://www.wrox.com/Scripts/Errata.idc?Code=0707`

If you can't find an answer there, tell us about the problem and we'll do everything we can to answer promptly!

Just send us an email to `support@wrox.com`.

or fill in the form on our web site: `http://www.wrox.com/Contact.stm`

Getting Started with IE4 and Dynamic HTML

Internet Explorer 4 adds a whole range of new features to the concept of the Web browser. One of the most exciting and the most visible of these, especially as far as traditional Web page authoring goes, is the provision of a more exposed document object model. Previously, browsers hid most of the content of the page from the author, and from any script within the page. Once the page was rendered on the screen, so that the user could read it, the majority of its contents had to remain static. Only by using add-ins, like embedded ActiveX controls or Java applets, could the page start to come to life.

Now, by exposing almost all the contents of the page—through a wholesale rebuilding of the browser and document object models—Microsoft have provided an environment where the page can be changed in almost any way, while it is loaded and being viewed. The possibilities for exciting and dynamic pages are now limited only by the imagination of the author, rather than by the browser's ability to manipulate the content.

On top of this, the full adoption of the Web standards for cascading style sheets has provided far more control over the way a page can be organized, and brings new opportunities for creating the kinds of effects previously only obtainable with a desktop publishing-style application.

Microsoft group all these new techniques under the heading of Dynamic HTML. In this first part of the book we'll take a brief tour of all the new features in IE4, and then show you how to get started learning about it, and developing with it.

Introducing
Internet Explorer 4

During a keynote speech at COMDEX in 1990, Bill Gates – Chairman and CEO of Microsoft – announced the concept of "Information at Your Fingertips" and gave his vision of the future. He painted a picture of the consequences that desktop computer technology would have in many areas of everyday life. Four years later, Bill Gates gave another COMDEX speech updating his original theme. While he talked about the effects of the recent rapid changes in the technology, there was still no reference to what no doubt will cause the biggest revolution in the IT industry since the PC – the Internet.

It wasn't until December 1995 that Microsoft publicly acknowledged the significance of the Internet and announced an overall Internet strategy. Later, in March 1996, Microsoft delivered a promise to produce a comprehensive set of Internet technologies, products and tools at their Professional Developers Conference. While Microsoft joined the Internet game relatively late, they rapidly gained momentum and have since released an incredible range of innovative Internet products. These products have provided users rich Internet experiences and organizations the mechanisms to develop high impact, secure and mission critical Internet solutions.

One of the most powerful and compelling pieces in the Microsoft Internet jigsaw is Internet Explorer – a Web browser offering users an increasingly sophisticated medium for experiencing the Internet. It wasn't until Internet Explorer 3.0, Microsoft's first ActiveX compliant browser, that there was serious competition for the market leader Netscape's Navigator. However it caught up very fast. IE3 came with a host of other client Internet applications for communications and collaboration with others. Internet Explorer version 4.0 (IE4 for short) takes it one step further. Without a doubt, the power of IE4 provides the potential to forever change the direction of Internet development. In this chapter we'll give you a quick introduction, in no particular order, to all of the new technologies that go into making up IE4.

- **Browser integration with the Desktop** – these blur the boundary between desktop, network and Internet.

- **Webcasting and Offline Browsing** – allows you to subscribe to web sites and then have updates automatically downloaded to your cache allowing you to browse them off line.

- **The Active Desktop** – turns the Windows desktop into a web page.

- **Multimedia Controls** - methods of enhancing the sound and graphics on your web pages without requiring third party add-ins.

- **Tools for Communication** – there are packages for e-mail, newsgroups, multi-user conferencing facilities and facilities for live download of audio and video.

- **Dynamic HTML** – an upgraded version of the language, that allows dynamic manipulation of elements on a web page, without the need for a page refresh.

We'll also take a look at the underlying ActiveX technology that provides much of the power in Internet Explorer 4.0, but first we'll begin by looking at what precipitated the need for a new version of the browser.

A Document-centric Computing Environment

The great leap forward in IE3 was that, in addition to handling standard HTML documents, the ActiveX technologies enabled IE to be a universal client capable of handling a broad variety of document types. This provided the first step in Microsoft's move towards a document-centric computing environment (as opposed to the traditional application centric approach).

IE3 still left a gap in Microsoft's aim of the seamless browsing of resources across the desktop, the LAN and the Internet. At this time, we accessed local and LAN resources with the Windows Explorer and Internet resources with the Internet Explorer. The basis of the next release of Microsoft IE was to address this goal by integrating their browser technologies with the operating system and Windows shell to provide a single view of all resources irrespective of where they were located.

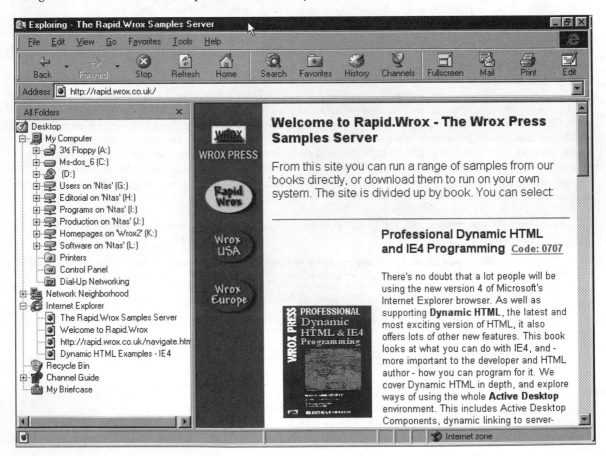

Originally targeted for a later IE5 release was the implementation of Dynamic HTML, the W3C extensions to standard HTML to allow complete control over the complete page to provide totally interactive applications. However, the decision was made for the IE4 release to be delayed, and for it to include this important functionality.

IE4 will provide the user interface for the next generation of the windows operating systems – Windows NT 5.0 and Windows 98. We'll now take a brief look at the significant features of IE4.

Browser Integration with the Desktop

When we first install IE4, an option to install full integration with the Windows shell is given. If this option is selected, we get a number of changes that blur the current boundary between the desk, network and Internet, the most noticeable including:

▲ **Single explorer** – enhances the Windows Explorer to provide a single application that provides both file / directory management and Internet document browsing.

▲ **Consistent navigation** – users now navigate resources in a consistent manner irrespective of whether they are located on the desktop, LAN or Internet.

▲ **Start bar menu** – has been changed to include direct access to Web favorites and extensions to the Find to search on the Internet

▲ **Web view** – provides a new view allowing the contents of a folder to be displayed as an HTML page. This is accessible via a Customize This Folder wizard accessible from the View menu which leads the user through the creation of a Web View.

▲ **Task bar extensions** – currently takes the CoolBar style with a series of bands and can include an Address bar and QuickLinks for quick access to the Web. Bands can be dragged away from the task bar and docked to an edge of the screen; also users can create their own task bar bands of the following types:

> Folder band – references a system folder and works like a traditional toolbar
>
> HTML – the contents of a web page is hosted within the band
>
> Custom code – functionality written in any language is hosted within the band

The new task bar extensions can be viewed at the foot of the screen, just right click on the mouse button and select Toolbars from the menu to switch them on.

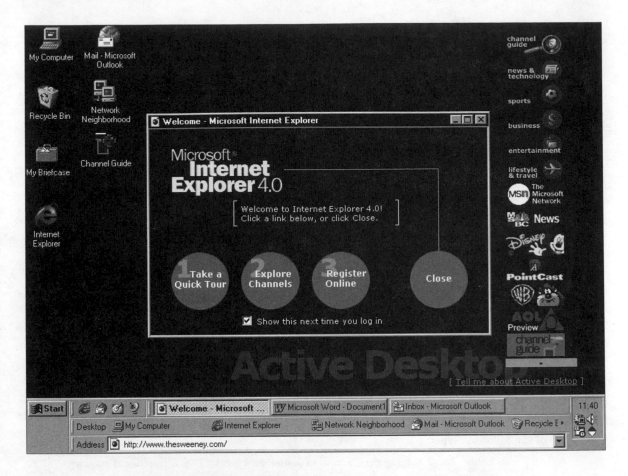

Webcasting and Offline Browsing

One of the aims of IE4 was to reduce the time and the associated costs of browsing the web, yet increase productivity. This is achieved by:

▲ 'Push' technology or **Webcasting**

>   Channels

>   Subscriptions

▲ Offline Browsing – downloaded content can be read when it's convenient

Webcasting

Webcasting is the automated delivery of up to date information for selected sites. The information is downloaded from a page, to the user's cache. This reverses the role of IE4, since previously the user would actively have to search the web for the information required. Now it's possible to tell IE4 what information you require and then get IE4 to do the hard work for you. This new model of retrieving information is termed 'push' technology, as the server is now appearing to transmit or broadcast the information to the receiver (IE4), which assumes a role similar to a television or radio. There are two methods for achieving this.

Channels

Channels allow a user to enable a frame on the Active Desktop to receive Web content. A number of leading Web content providers will offer channels that will deliver in-depth, up-to-the-minute content for a number of different chosen topics, e.g. news, sport, entertainment etc. With IE4 you already get MSN, NBC news, Disney, Pointcast channels and a channel guide as standard on the Internet Explorer channel bar. When looking at channels, the browser assumes a special full-screen format to aid viewing:

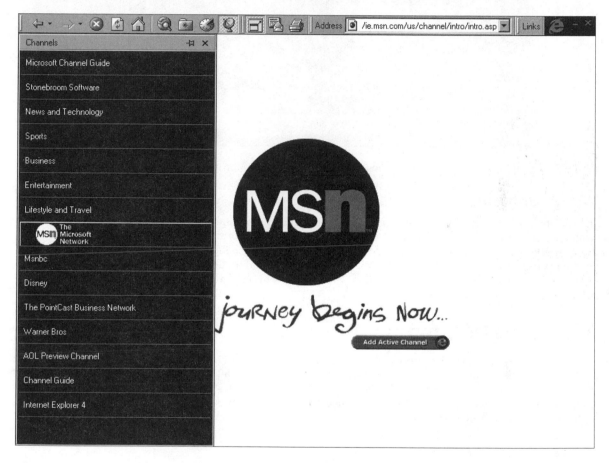

It's also possible to create your own channels. This is done with the aid of a Channel Definition File (CDF), which determines the hierarchical organization of the channel and the updating schedule. CDF is effectively a mini HTML-like language that has been defined in a meta-language XML (eXtensible Markup Language). The creator of a channel provides a list of URLs in the CDF that describe what content IE4 must retrieve. This is downloaded to the local cache and then displayed in the channel frame. This whole process is covered in detail in Chapter 16, together with a case study which puts together a sample channel in Chapter 17.

Subscriptions

Subscriptions are a mechanism to avoid the wasted time spent checking lists of favorites site to determine if any updates have been made and to allow offline browsing.Users may subscribe to a Web site to schedule the regular automatic download of any changes to the pages. If any changes are detected, then the user can be notified with an icon change (on the Task Bar or Favorites menu), or by the delivery of an email message. When you add a favorite to your folder, you are now asked whether you wish to just add the item to your folder, subscribe to the site, or even download the page for the purposes of offline browsing.

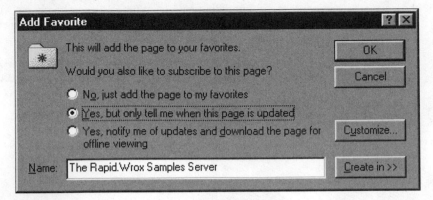

You can also update your subscriptions manually from the options on the IE4 Favorites menu.

Offline Browsing

Previously a lot of user time was often spent just retrieving information rather than actually reading the material. IE4's offline browsing facilities solve this problem, which previously required the user having to be connected to the network to be able to read Web content. Subscribed content can now be downloaded and users can disconnect and still work with the cached information. This optimizes Internet connect time and gives user the freedom to read the pages when convenient, i.e. while traveling on a plane or train when they cannot have a live connection

The Active Desktop

Prior to IE4, the Windows desktop had been used to display a favorite bitmap picture and locate a series of shortcut icons for quick access to applications and documents. Available customization options of the desktop had been limited to a few aesthetic choices. IE4 now provides the **Active Desktop** where this area can come alive by having access to the same functionality as any Web page–HTML, Scripting, Java applets, ActiveX controls and floating frames.

Active Desktop Items

Active Desktop Items are just small sized web pages embedded in floating frames or document division elements. These frames include the content specified by a URL shortcut. They are very similar to channels but differ because they are intended as brief headlines and links. The items are only meant to be entry points on the desktop into more detailed information. Here's a customized desktop item, which provides links to Dynamic HTML examples from our Instant IE4 Dynamic HTML programmer's reference:

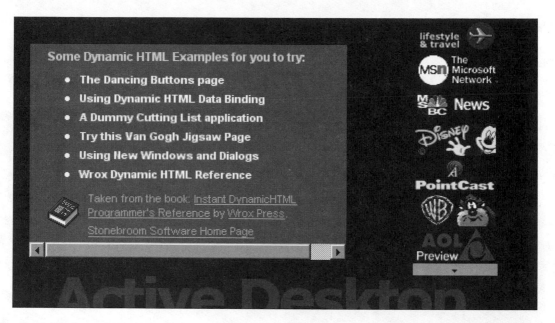

It's downloadable from the site `http://www.stonebroom.com`, if you follow the Dynamic HTML link on the default page. Locate the Add to Active Desktop option at the foot of the page, and then click to add the item to your desktop.

Active Desktop Items are resident on the desktop and can be moved and resized as required by the user by dragging handles that appear whenever the mouse cursor is moved over the item. Other examples of Desktop Items include:

- News tickers/stock market updates
- Frequently accessed Web applications/sites, such as, a company intranet
- Notifications/pop up messages
- Web channels with 'pushed' content
- Access to search engines

Desktop Items can either be added by users to the desktop or created by specifying either a Web site (i.e. a URL) or a picture. These items complement Active Channels so that you can place links to your channels, within your desktop item. All Desktop Items are added to the IE4 subscription folders and the content is automatically refreshed whenever an update is detected.

Active Themes

The Active Desktop will provide a great opportunity for Web authors to create imaginative and useful desktop components. Part of the Windows 95 Plus Pack included Themes–a series of bitmaps, cursors, icons and sounds providing a consistent theme to the desktop. Microsoft will be releasing Active Themes 2.0, a hypertext version of this original product.

Channel Screen Saver

IE4 provides a Channel Screen Saver that can be enabled by selecting the Screen Saver tab in the Display properties – accessed either via the control panel or from the menu obtained by right clicking the desktop. The Screen Saver can be configured to display subscribed and favorites sites for a predetermined time.

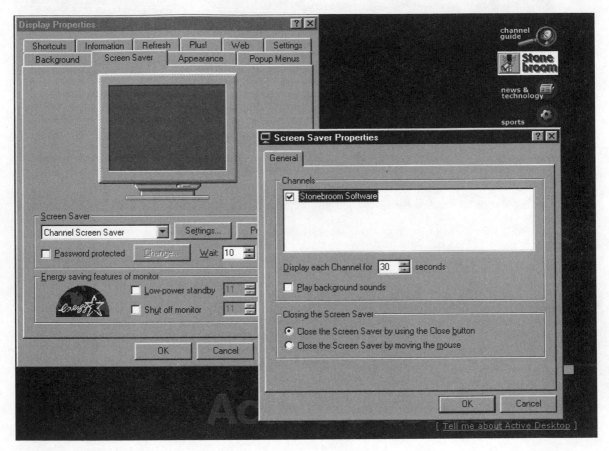

Multimedia controls

Microsoft already distributes a set of high level APIs and programming tools known as **DirectX**. These aim to standardize the way in which all multimedia will be developed. In IE4, components of DirectX are included. The first is **DirectAnimation** which provides rich animation features and strong integration with Dynamic HTML.

DirectAnimation

DirectAnimation is comprised of four multimedia ActiveX controls that can provide powerful Web page effects in a fashion that uses up minimal bandwidth and does not require excessive scripting.

- **Structured graphics** – provides vector graphics that can be scaled, rotated and filled. Since it's very time and memory consuming to manipulate photographic images (JPGs) or even graphic images such as GIFs, IE4 provides these as a low memory consuming alternative, which has the added benefit of being much easier and quicker to manipulate.

- **Sprite** – can be used to create animated images and you can control their playback at a very fine level of detail. Sprite controls can move over backgrounds and they look after the restoration of the original background underneath after the control has moved.

- **Path** – allows you to moves objects dynamically on a web page over time, following a pre-defined path. These paths can take on many shapes such as ovals, rectangles, polygons or even spline curves.

- **Sequencer** – allows you to control the sequence in which other controls are used and the timing of when actions such as scripts or methods of ActiveX controls are called.

Here is an example of the structured graphics control in action that consists of a Stop Sign image that rotates along its three axes, and some text that scales dynamically:

You will need to view the page at `http://rapid.wrox.co.uk/books/0707` *in order to actually see the animation take place.*

DirectShow

The second component of DirectX that is included with IE4, is known as DirectShow. This is a media architecture which provides audio or video playback from the Internet. DirectShow supports all of the most common multimedia types including MPEG, AVI, WAV and QuickTime. The way to make use of this architecture within IE4 is via the ActiveMovie Control. This can be used to add multimedia support to all of your applications and can be manipulated via a programming language such as Visual Basic or Visual C++. Here's an example that uses the Active Movie Control to play a video clip.

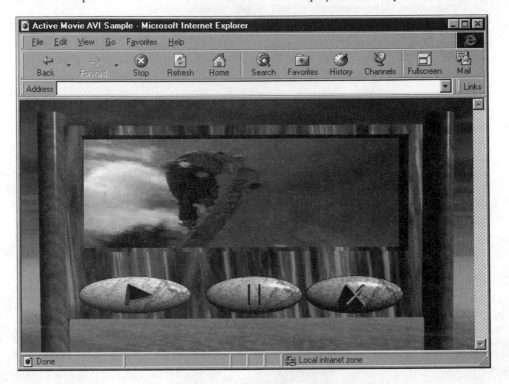

Filters

IE4 also provides two sets of multimedia effects that have been added to cascading style sheets. Originally, in Platform Preview Release one, they were also implemented as ActiveX controls, but since Platform Preview Release two it has become possible to use them within Cascading Style Sheets instead. These effects are known as filters and there are two different types.

- **Visual Filters** – a collection of effects allowing you to alter the appearance of graphics and text, such as by flipping an image upside down, or by making text appear to glow, for example. The results of this filter persist.

- **Transition Filters** – a collection of effects allowing you to make graphics and text appear/ disappear in a variety of patterns and these come into effect over a specified period of time.

Here's a screenshot demonstrating a visual filter which makes the text appear to glow:

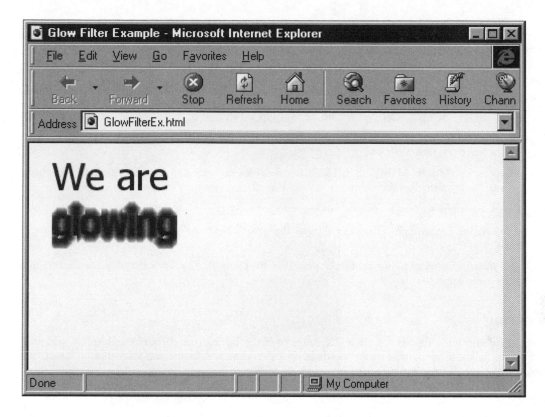

You can find this example page at `http://rapid.wrox.co.uk/books/0707`.

We look at all four of the Direct Animation controls, the Active Movie control and multimedia filter effects in detail in Chapters **11** and **12** of this book.

Communication Tools

Some additions to IE4, which can be optionally installed, are a set of tools for communication and collaboration that can be tightly integrated with other items on the Active Client. These include:

▲ Outlook Express for messaging (Email and newsGroups)

▲ NetMeeting for conferencing and application sharing

▲ NetShow for the receipt of video and audio broadcasts

We're not going to cover Outlook Express or NetMeeting within this book since they can't be accessed or controlled from a web page. However we do look at NetShow in Chapter **13**, in our overview of components, because this is scriptable from a web page. As this is a basic overview of all IE4's new features, we will very briefly touch upon what each of the products can do.

Outlook Express

Outlook Express provides support for the common messaging protocols (POP3, SMTP, NNTP, LDAP and IMAP) and a number of productivity features. Features include:

- ▲ Hierarchical folders for both email and newsgroups
- ▲ Support for multiple mail server and newsgroup servers
- ▲ Facilities to format messages using HTML, enabling the rich formatting that we are accustomed to with Web pages
- ▲ Support for **Secure MIME** (S/MIME) that enables messages to be encrypted (using public/private keys) and digitally signed
- ▲ Inbox assistant so that messages can be automatically moved, copied or forwarded
- ▲ Support for Lightweight Directory Access Protocol (LDAP) to provide access to white pages servers
- ▲ Support for the messaging protocols provided by Outlook Express can be incorporated into your own applications.

NetMeeting

NetMeeting provides multi-user conferencing facilities over the Internet or corporate enterprise and enables users at remote locations to participate in meetings as if everyone was at the same location. This obviously cuts down on the much time wasted spent travelling to meetings. Features include:

- ▲ A text based chat application allowing multiple users to hold conversations
- ▲ Facilities for Internet telephony and video conferencing allowing users to talk face-to-face in real-time
- ▲ The ability for all conference participants to see the same view of an application running on one machine, for example, watching a PowerPoint presentation or discussing a problem around an electronic whiteboard

The conferencing facilities provided by NetMeeting are open and extensible, and can be incorporated into your own applications. A NetMeeting Software development Kit is available from Microsoft.

NetShow

The NetShow client component is an important part of IE4 and is used for receiving and playing the broadcasted show. Features include:

- ▲ Delivery of audio, illustrated audio (synchronized sound and image) or video content in real time
- ▲ The show is played as received and unlike some previous multimedia Web technologies it avoids the frustrating delays of users having to wait for the complete file to be received before commencement
- ▲ NetShow provides a high quality playback yet uses sophisticated compression algorithms reducing storage requirements and network bandwidth

- Simple integration with IE4 provides high impact and exciting Web pages – alternatively, the show can be played in its own external frame

- Hyperlinks can be included in the show's visual images

Dynamic HTML

IE4 delivers the next generation of Web Browser technologies including Dynamic HTML. Dynamic HTML is a collection of HTML and CSS specifications from W3C, forming part of the new HTML 4.0 standards, which provide the ability to dynamically update the contents and styles of a Web page without refreshing the page.

While Dynamic HTML still supports many of the tags and attributes available with the previous generations of browsers, what's new is that full access to all items in the browser is available from a scripting language. This also means that web pages designed for Dynamic HTML will degrade gracefully on earlier browsers such as IE3. It frees the user from the straitjacket of static pages, by providing many new features. The most significant of these are:

- All of the elements on the page are now accessible to the scripting languages and also, with some extra effort, so is any software component that has been installed on the desktop.

- Extensions to the browser object model, in particular the `document` object, mean that there's far more hooks for the scripting languages to use.

- Extensions to style sheets to bring support in style sheets in line with the CSS1 recommendations.

- Dynamic redrawing of any page or section of a page, without the need for a full-page refresh.

- Absolute positioning of elements on the screen with x and y type coordinates, including a third dimensional coordinate, the `zindex`, which allows a desktop publishing format of layout.

- New event handling techniques, including a facility called **event bubbling** that reduces the amount of script code previously required. When an object is notified of an event it can either process it or delegate the processing to the parent object.

On top of this, most of IE4's new features, such as multimedia controls, are directly programmable with Dynamic HTML, and we'll spend the rest of the first section of the book getting you up to speed with it.

Dynamic HTML in action

While we shall be delving deeper throughout this book into Dynamic HTML technologies and the associated programming techniques, we'll now take a look at an example which demonstrates the following capabilities:

- **Dynamic styles** – the menu options are displayed in a frame on the left hand side of the display and, as the mouse pointer hovers over the option text, the menu text changes color and adopts additional decoration

- **Dynamic content** – help text is displayed in a frame at the base of the display and, as the mouse pointer hovers over various items, the help text is updated

▲ **Absolute positioning** – the home page title text is displayed twice using two colors with the second copy slightly out of phase from the first. This gives a shadow effect and the impression of three dimensions

▲ **Multimedia controls** – a music control is used to play some Beethoven style music and a visual effect control is used to invert the logo whenever the mouse pointer hovers over it

▲ **Data binding** – we use the Microsoft Tabular Data Control (TDC) to retrieve information (a list of Wrox book titles) from a text file and insert the information in a table on the Web Page

The example is available from the Wrox web site at `http://rapid.wrox.co.uk/books/0707`. The opening page provides an ordinary looking two frame page, but the frame on left contains a menu which reacts dynamically to user interaction by highlighting an item when the mouse pointer moves over it.

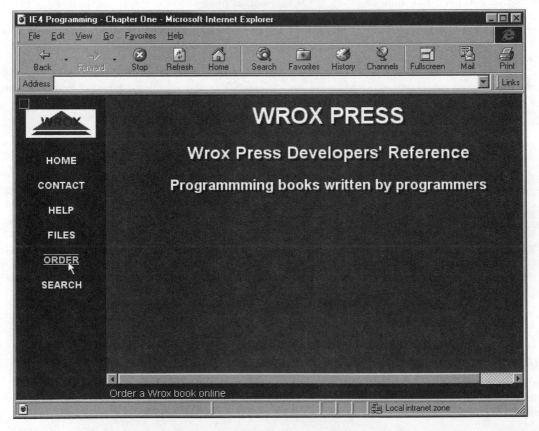

If you click on the Order item, you'll be able to see data binding in action. The resulting list of books is dynamically generated from the database, and you can create an order for several books client-side, in the same way as you can with a CGI script or Active Server Pages and server interaction.

Take some time to browse the source code as well, from the View Source option, because while you might not understand it all yet, it demonstrates that many of the pages were generated with relatively little code.

Scriptlets

A late addition to IE4 was the innovation of scriptlets. These are reusable components that have been created in Dynamic HTML. These components are scripts that are written by the developer according to certain criteria. They can be added to web pages, with the `<OBJECT>` tag, in the same way that ActiveX controls and Java applets can. They can be written in either JavaScript or VBScript, but aren't limited to just these two languages. Effectively, by embedding a scriptlet within a page, you are embedding a browser within a browser. These may not seem like an overly useful thing to do, but when you realize that you can follow these principles to embed a browser within any application from Word to Access, by using ActiveX, you can then see how almost any application can suddenly be Internet enabled. We devote a chapter to Scriptlets later in the book–Chapter 14.

Internet Client SDK

A really great resource for IE4 developers is the Internet Client Software Development Kit (SDK). This is a collection of related documentation, samples and tools for use with IE4. You'll find lots of material in particular for Dynamic HTML, channels, the active desktop and the different components that go to make up IE4. In its entirety it takes up about 80 MB, which is a massive download in anyone's books, but it's meant for several different audiences and consequently is available in separate sections, which the user can choose to download. The Active Setup process allows you to select just the parts you need and is available from `http://www.microsoft.com/msdn/sdk/inetsdk/asetup/default.asp`

You should at least consider installing some of the controls in the Component Library as some of them aren't even included in the full installation of IE4, such as the Chat Control that we talk about later in the book, in Chapter 13.

Activating the Internet

Of course, a large part of IE4's strength is derived from the way it harnesses existing web integration technologies. One of the primary strengths of the web is its ability to be viewed from many different platforms, the same code being executed successfully on rival platforms. Two differing, but not necessarily mutually exclusive, visions of how this can be achieved are ActiveX and Java. IE4 is designed to be able to execute both Microsoft's own ActiveX technology and Sun's Java. We'll take a little time to examine both of these technologies now as they form a vital part of the future of the web and their support was central to IE4's design.

ActiveX

ActiveX has to be one of the most misunderstood and ambiguously used expressions in the Internet technology arena. When Microsoft released their first set of Internet tools in March 1996, they announced **ActiveX** technology – which in all truth was just a new marketing name for their existing **OLE** technology. ActiveX (or 3rd generation OLE technology) is a framework that allows software components to co-operate even if they have been written by different vendors, at different times using different tools and different languages, and if the objects are located in the same process, same machine or distributed over multiple machines. Put simply, ActiveX provides the **software plumbing** between software objects and insulates the component developer from such complexities.

Many people get confused because ActiveX actually encompasses a number of technologies and is not just one thing. Each ActiveX technology defines the interfaces between the objects to implement the particular technology. For the Internet, examples include:

- **ActiveX Documents** – enables the browser to support non-HTML documents
- **ActiveX Scripting** – enables script logic, included with a downloaded Web page or a server-side ASP page, to be executed
- **ActiveX Controls** – provides a method of packaging client components for reuse across platforms and development environments which can then be dynamically downloaded as needed and used within a web page
- **ActiveX Server Components** – enables the Web Server (IIS and ASP) to interface to server software components

To most users, ActiveX is transparent, and they just see the effects of these technologies—it is irrelevant to them whether it is ActiveX or black magic that is operating behind the scenes. However, it is different for the developer, and we shall see later how the Internet ActiveX technologies provide a powerful environment for creating interactive Web content.

Underneath ActiveX is the generic **Component Object Model** (COM) which defines the binary interface between objects. The original specification of COM always allowed for co-operating objects to be located on different machines, but this was not implemented until Windows NT 4.0 and was then called **Distributed COM** (DCOM). Because of this, in reality DCOM and COM are now the same animal. This is all we really need to know about COM/DCOM, although they will be mentioned throughout the book.

There does exist a small anti-ActiveX camp (with members typically having investments in alternative technologies!), that are concerned this will make the Internet as Windows-centric as today's desktops. However, since ActiveX is the most advanced component software platform around, there is no doubt that it will build on its current momentum and play a major role in the next wave of Internet application development.

Corresponding to Microsoft's recent focus on Internet technology is their aim of embracing industry standards and support openness. The ActiveX technologies have been given to an independent consortium called The Active Group and Microsoft has been working with a number of third parties to support ActiveX on non-Windows platforms including UNIX and Apple Macintosh. NCompass Labs, `http://www.ncompasslabs.com`, have an ActiveX Plug-in for the Netscape Navigator browser.

Let's now see ActiveX in action.

ActiveX Documents

As part of their move towards seamless browsing, ActiveX Documents are fundamental to Microsoft's aim to achieve a document-centric world rather than the current application-centric notion. ActiveX Documents are based on the previous OLE DocObjects technology that allowed in-place activation or **visual editing.** For example, an MS Excel spreadsheet embedded in a MS Word document could be edited directly within the Word frame, with the menus and toolbars adapting to make available the Excel facilities.

If you look at the size of the IE4 executable, **IEXPLORE.EXE**, you will see it is so very small for an application that is as rich in functionality as IE4. In fact, this executable is just a simple process that loops to handle windows messages and provide a container for ActiveX Documents. Normally IE4 displays

HTML – this is handled by a software component providing Web Browser support and using the IE4 container for displaying the page. The Web browser functionality is provided by an object implemented in `SHDOCVW.DLL`.

As IE4 is an ActiveX Document container, it can support any applications that support the interfaces (i.e. methods, properties and events) that are defined by the ActiveX Document specifications. This includes the Microsoft Office products and other application vendors that are rapidly supporting this technology. This means that as we navigate the numerous resources within an Intranet, we no longer need to invoke separate word processors, spreadsheets, etc. to access the various items of information, IE4 can do it for us:

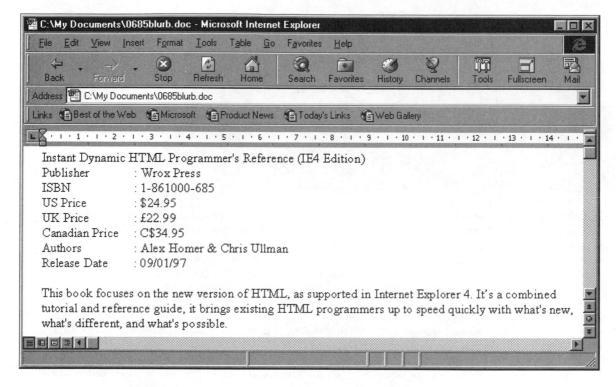

ActiveX Scripting

Scripting is an easy way to make our Web pages come alive and allows the browser to interact with the user and software components (i.e. trap events, invoke methods and access properties). It involves incorporating high level script commands into the HTML document that automatically get invoked by the browser when loaded or by the user clicking on something.

Rather than just develop script processing for IE4, Microsoft has used ActiveX to provide a flexible architecture for adding any scripting language to an application. ActiveX Scripting allows **script hosts** to invoke scripting services within **script engines**. Further the hosts and engines can be from different software vendors and can implement different languages, since the plumbing between the two is handled by COM/DCOM. The ActiveX Scripting specifications define the interfaces that a script host and script engine must support. The script language, syntax and execution rules are defined by the vendor of the script engine. All script logic is interpreted on the fly by the script engine, there is no concept of compiling the scripts. This is shown as follows:

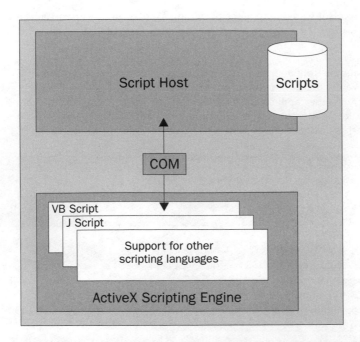

IE4, ASP and Visual InterDev are examples of script hosts, but you can now easily add scripting to your own applications. **VBScript** and **JScript** are examples of script languages, but again, you can also develop your own. VBScript is a subset of Visual Basic for Applications (as used by the Microsoft Office Products) which in turn is a subset of the popular Visual Basic programming language. JScript is Microsoft's implementation of the Netscape's JavaScript, although Microsoft and Netscape are currently working on standardizing their versions of JavaScript.

The real power of scripting comes with the ability to interact with other objects. This enables accessing an object's properties, invoking methods and detecting events, and of course all this happens using COM/DCOM under the covers. Accessible objects are either:

- Intrinsic (built-in) objects exposed within the script host – often referred to as an **object model**.

- Executable software components: packages of reusable code that usually serve a specific function and don't have to be resident on the browser, and can therefore be downloaded when needed.

Client-side scripting can be inserted into an HTML page using the `<SCRIPT>` tags pair, and so can be incorporated within minimal impact. To identify the script language, the `LANGUAGE` attribute is used, as shown in the following template.

```
<HTML>
<HEAD>
    <TITLE>Document title
    </TITLE>
    <SCRIPT LANGUAGE="VBSCRIPT">
            Client-side VBS scripting logic
    </SCRIPT>
</HEAD>
<BODY>
</BODY>
</HTML>
```

If you wish your page to viewed normally in older browsers that cannot process script as well, then you can hide the script within HTML comment tags `<!--` and `-->`.

The client-side scripting can interface to all element objects in a web page (e.g. tags, images, text, etc.), browser objects (e.g. windows, frames, history, etc.) and 'talk to' any object that has been included in the page. From this, we can see that scripting is what really enables the *Dynamic* in Dynamic HTML. We can now change any part of the Web page as a user interacts with the page, as demonstrated in our Wrox Press orders example earlier.

While there are third parties supplying alternative scripting languages (e.g. Perl etc.), most people will use one of the two Microsoft supplied core options, VBScript or JScript – but which is best? Well the truth is that there is very little difference in between the capabilities of the two. Both languages are capable of being used by those with minimal programming experience. At the time of writing, IE3/IE4 are the only browsers that support VBScript. Thus, if you are aiming for mass penetration on the Internet then you should probably restrict the scripting to JavaScript, although to remain functional on both IE and Netscape browsers you will require a lot more than just one simple JavaScript program, because the two implementations of Dynamic HTML are so different. If you are developing for an Intranet, where you have control over the infrastructure and can enforce IE4 as the browser of choice, you can choose to use VBScript.

Active Server Pages and Scripting

Active Server Pages (ASP) is a technology that provides a server-side application framework. You may wonder why we're discussing a server-side technology in a books focussed primarily on the client-side. This is because ASP provided a robust object model that also allowed the web page developer to do things dynamically. Later in the book we will take a look at how can combine the two technologies, but first we need to take a brief look at what ASP can do.

ASP allows executable script logic to be embedded within an HTML page. It enables the scripting to interface to a number of internal objects, which automatically handle many of the menial tasks, and so simplifies the script logic. ASP uses server-side scripting to dynamically create HTML responses. The content generated is typically based on the following features:

- ▲ User's identity
- ▲ Parameters in the HTTP request
- ▲ Interacting with other objects (e.g. ASP objects, multi-tier client/server business objects, middleware to access databases and legacy systems, BackOffice components, etc.).

ASP provides a number of built-in objects and useful components. The built-in objects simplify many of the common server-side tasks, such as handling the HTTP request/responses, the user's session and the Web environment.

Server-side scripting is inserted in an ASP file using either the `<SCRIPT>` tags pair or `<%` and `%>` delimiters. To distinguish client-side from server-side scripting, the latter's `<SCRIPT>` tag should include the `RUNAT="SERVER"` attribute and value. For example:

```
<HTML>
<HEAD>
    <TITLE>Document title
    </TITLE>
    <SCRIPT LANGUAGE="VBSCRIPT" RUNAT="SERVER">
            Server-side VBS scripting logic
    </SCRIPT>
    <SCRIPT LANGUAGE="VBSCRIPT">
            Client-side VBS scripting logic
    </SCRIPT>
</HEAD>
<BODY>
    <% Server-side VBS scripting logic %>
</BODY>
```

Script that runs on the server can always run VBScript, because it has to be running on IIS which is a Microsoft Product. The script which runs on the client(browser) has to be either JavaScript or VBScript, depending on the browser or preference.

Prior to scripting, all user interactions had to be handled by communication with the Web Server. Script logic now enables client-side processing to occur and can help to avoid some of the time-consuming communication with overburdened servers. It should be noted that the ASP server-side scripting is not exposed in the generated HTML file, where as client-side scripting could be inspected by simply viewing the HTML source code. This means that if you are concerned about the people copying your clever code or seeing your confidential business rules then you should engage such logic in the server. In practise, you will find that both server-side and client-side scripting have specific uses and that the design of your Web application will require a combination of the two.

ActiveX Controls

An ActiveX Control is a software component that gives a specific item of functionality to a parent application (i.e. an ActiveX Control container). IE4 is an application that can host such ActiveX Controls within a Web page. The forerunners to ActiveX Controls were OLE Controls (for 32 bit applications) and the original, but limited, VBX controls (for 16 bit Visual Basic applications only).

ActiveX Controls expose properties and methods and can fire events, using COM/DCOM under the covers. The combining of this with ActiveX Scripting provides our goal of user interactivity. For example, clicking a button would fire the associated event and could cause a script to invoke a method on a control, which may then effect the results seen in the Web page. ActiveX Controls cannot directly communicate with each other. However, this can be achieved via script logic.

ActiveX Controls can contain sophisticated logic and add features to Web pages that could never be achieved with standard HTML even with scripting. It is estimated that there are over 1,000 commercial ActiveX Controls on the market; examples of cool controls include:

- ▲ Citrix WinFrame Control – enables a Windows application to be run on the server but displayed in a Web page `http://www.citrix.com`

- ▲ Black Diamond Surround Video – provides facilities for 360-degree images that can be panned by mouse movement `http://www.bdiamond.com`

- ▲ MacroMedia ShockWave – provides extensive facilities for creating web based animations `http://www.macromedia.com`

- ▲ The ActiveX site – provides access to a large library of ActiveX controls from a wide variety of vendors `http://www.activex.com`

One great advantage that ActiveX Controls provide is that they are automatically downloaded and installed, as needed. If a Web page references an ActiveX Control that is either not installed or is out of date, the deployment of the control is automatically handled by a helpful facility within IE4 called the Internet Component Download Service (ICDS). ICDS is also responsible for handling the **Authenticode processing**. Authenticode is Microsoft's and Verisign's Digital Signing system. It provides a mechanism to digitally sign and authenticate code to independent vendors. It will present the user with a certificate dialog highlighting details of the component's origin and can be used to hold vendors accountable to their software, whenever it causes problems:

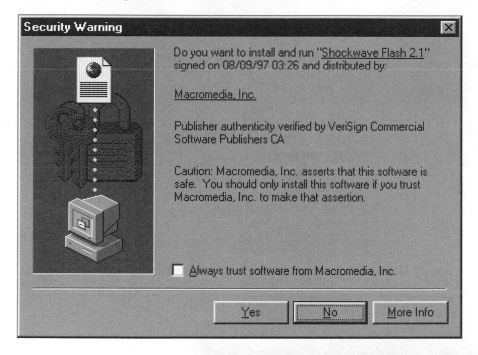

Or alternatively, IE4 will flag a problem, such as the control being unsigned or not in the exact format as when released by the author. If this last case happens, it could mean that the control has been tampered with and isn't safe to use.

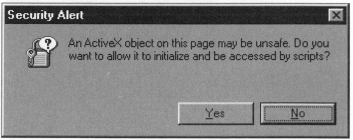

ActiveX Controls are compiled into native machine code. This means that if you intend to support multiple target client platforms you must produce a separate version for each. You should also remember that code size is important as many users connect to the Internet using slow modems, and might not be patient enough to wait for a fat control to arrive.

The OBJECT Tag

An ActiveX Control is embedded into an HTML page by specifying a number of attributes between the `<OBJECT>` tag pair. For a visual control, this will be displayed in the page at the point where the tag is placed. Every ActiveX Control is uniquely identified by a sequence of numbers called a **Class ID** or **Globally Unique Id** (GUID). For example, the Class ID of the Microsoft NetShow Client Control is `{2179C5D3-EBFF-11CF-B6FD-00AA00B4E220}`. Since it is obviously not possible to remember such sequences for the numerous controls that are available, we need a quick way finding the Class ID.

One easy way is to use the Insert ActiveX Control facility in the Microsoft FrontPad (that ships with full installation of IE4) & FrontPage HTML editors. By selecting this menu option, the user is able to select an ActiveX Control from all controls installed in the Registry, and this will automatically insert the `<OBJECT>` tags with the appropriate Class ID. This automatic insertion is very useful since the nature of Class IDs tend to make typos frequent; it is very easy to key a wrong digit and not realize it until the control fails to instantiate.

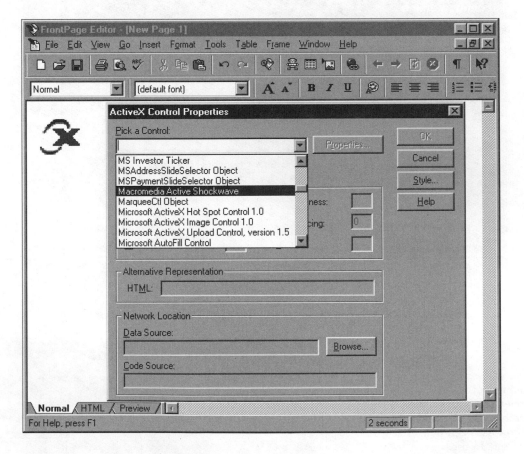

Control properties are specified using the **<PARAM>** tag that takes two attributes – **NAME** and **VALUE**, for the property name and the value to initialize the property to. The following example shows what the code for a Tab control looks like:

```
<HTML>
<HEAD>
<TITLE>Tabs</TITLE>
<SCRIPT LANGUAGE="VBScript">
    <!-to be added -->
</SCRIPT>
</HEAD>
<BODY bgcolor=cyan>
<OBJECT ID="TabStrip1" WIDTH=69 HEIGHT=107
 CLASSID="CLSID:EAE50EB0-4A62-11CE-BED6-00AA00611080">
    <PARAM NAME="ListIndex" VALUE="3">
    <PARAM NAME="BackColor" VALUE="16776960">
    <PARAM NAME="Size" VALUE="1834;2822">
    <PARAM NAME="Items" VALUE="One;Two;Three;Four;">
    <PARAM NAME="TabOrientation" VALUE="2">
    <PARAM NAME="MultiRow" VALUE="-1">
    <PARAM NAME="TipStrings" VALUE="One;Two;Three;Four;">
    <PARAM NAME="Names" VALUE="One;Two;Three;Four;">
    <PARAM NAME="NewVersion" VALUE="-1">
    <PARAM NAME="TabsAllocated" VALUE="4">
    <PARAM NAME="Tags" VALUE=";;;;">
    <PARAM NAME="TabData" VALUE="4">
    <PARAM NAME="Accelerator" VALUE=";;;;">
    <PARAM NAME="FontCharSet" VALUE="0">
    <PARAM NAME="FontPitchAndFamily" VALUE="2">
    <PARAM NAME="TabState" VALUE="3;3;3;3">
</OBJECT>
</BODY>
</HTML>
```

*Remember that the **<OBJECT>** tag attributes, including **<PARAM>** are all editor generated and you wouldn't have type these in yourself.*

The tab control is inserted in the page as follows, but if you click on it, there is no response:

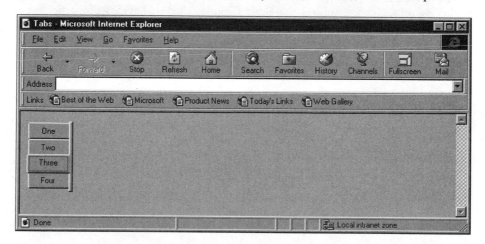

This is because an important attribute in the `<OBJECT>` tag is the `ID` that is used to provide an easier name to reference the control; in particular it is used by the scripting language to apply any logic to the object. We have to first set the `ID` in the HTML:

```
...
<BODY bgcolor=cyan>
<OBJECT ID="TabStrip1" WIDTH=69 HEIGHT=107
 CLASSID="CLSID:EAE50EB0-4A62-11CE-BED6-00AA00611080">
...
```

in order to be able to reference it within a scripting language and therefore get the tab control to respond to each tab that is selected:

```
<SCRIPT LANGUAGE="VBScript">
Sub TabStrip1_Click(Index)
select case Index
  case 0  msgbox "one"
  case 1  msgbox "two"
  case 2  msgbox "three"
  case 3  msgbox "four"
end select
end sub
</SCRIPT>
```

The `<OBJECT>` tag can include a **CODEBASE** attribute to specify the location of the control and the required version. If the control has not been previously installed or it is out of date, the ICDS uses the **CODEBASE**'s URL to retrieve and install the control. For example

```
CODEBASE="http://activex.microsoft.com/controls/iexplorer/timer.ocx#
          Version=4,70,0,1161">
```

Managing Downloaded ActiveX Controls

Until IE4 there was no smart way of managing the numerous ActiveX Controls that were downloaded and installed. It was possible that controls could be installed, used only once, and then would become redundant wasting disk space. With IE4, downloaded controls are installed in a folder called Downloaded Program Files within the Windows folder. When this folder is viewed via the Windows Explorer, a shell extension provides special functionality to manage the content. Each installed control is represented by an icon. By right clicking on an icon, a control can either be uninstalled or have its properties inspected.

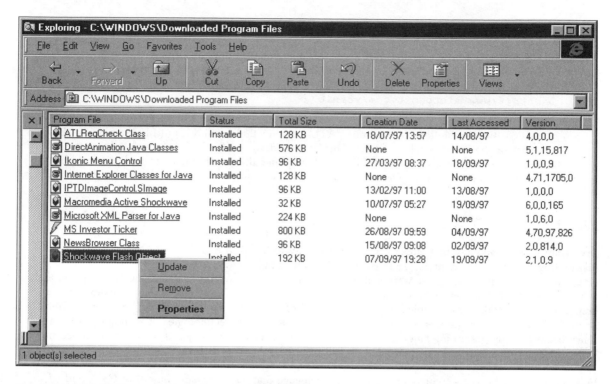

You have three different choices of view, which supply general information such as the Class ID, Dependency Information and Version Information:

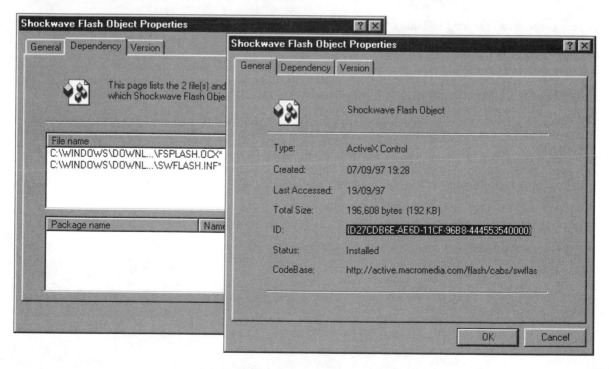

To create ActiveX Controls, the developer has several options, including the following:

▲ Visual Basic – from version 5, VB can create ActiveX controls; furthermore, there is a free version, VB Control Creation Edition (VB CCE), that is limited to just the creation of ActiveX Controls and can be downloaded off the Microsoft Web site, `http://www.microsoft.com/vbasic/`

▲ Visual C++ – provides three frameworks for creating controls: Microsoft Foundation Classes (MFC), the Active Template Library (ATL) or from the ActiveX Controls Framework (BaseCtl –part of the Internet Client SDK). The latter is designed for building very light controls but requires expert knowledge of OLE. MFC simplifies the development of such controls but, compared to other two, generates bulky code and requires the MFC libraries to be installed.

Java

Java is another technology that aims to bring interactivity to the Web and networks by dynamically distributing executable content as required. It originated from Sun Microsystems, `http://java.sun.com/`. They were working on a language that would be cross platform capable and, at the same time, help them to propel their products in the market. They recognized its suitability as a language for embedding executable logic within an HTML page for processing by a Java enabled Web Browser. While the term Java encompasses a number of Sun owned technologies, it is frequently used to refer to the Java programming language. This is distinct from JavaScript which is very loosely based on Java and C++, and is used in scripting and should not be confused with Java.

Java is a simplified object-orientated programming language that was originally based on C++, and so looks familiar to C++ programmers. However, the Java designers removed some of the C++ features that can cause developers problems and stop code from being robust.

A Java program is compiled into **Java byte code** – while this is an optimized format, it is not native CPU machine code. Java Byte code is executed by an interpreter called a **Java Virtual Machine** (JVM)which converts byte code, on the fly, into native machine code. Some JVMs include a **just-in-time** (JIT) compiler that speeds up the processing by keeping a copy and reusing translated codes. Alternatively, some vendors have produce native compilers that directly generate native machine code for the target platform. Like most operating system vendors, Microsoft developed a Java VM for their Windows operating systems and then licensed the name from Sun.

A Java program running in a Web Browser is called an **Applet** and is referenced in the HTML page with the `<APPLET>` tag. Java applets can be anything from games, business resources, and complex multimedia effects to simple animations and scrolling logos, or even dynamic menus, such as the one featured at `http://java.sun.com`:

A Java program running standalone is called an **Application**. A great advantage of a Java program is that it is portable – it can run on platforms that support the Java VM. Java is sometimes summarized as *"Write Once – Run Anywhere"*.

A lot of effort has been made to ensure that Java Applets are safe and cannot cause malicious damage to a client machine. Typically, the JVM uses the sandbox security model to ensure this doesn't happen. By sandbox we mean a model which restricts access to potentially dangerous parts of the operating system – you don't want an applet to be able to wipe your hard disk. The Microsoft JVM supports the Authenticode mechanism and allows trusted Applets the freedom to access certain system resources.

Many people question whether Java is better than ActiveX – in truth, both have their strengths and weaknesses. While many view the technologies as competing, Microsoft has embraced the idea that Java and ActiveX complement each other. The Microsoft JVM is actually an ActiveX control that can expose public variables and functions, as shown in the following diagram. This enables an Applet to co-operate with a Web Browser scripting language. Furthermore, the Microsoft JVM provides full support with COM/ DCOM allowing the two different technologies to integrate seamlessly.

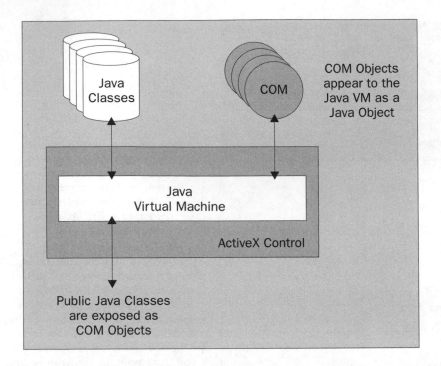

Microsoft's Java development tool is called Visual J++. In addition to the standard JAVA classes found in the AWT, IE4 comes with Microsoft's **Application Foundation Classes** (AFC), so saving the trouble of the classes having to be downloaded each time. The AFC is a set of powerful class libraries that expand upon the standard Java offerings to provide user interface capabilities that have the visual quality that Windows users are accustomed to. AFC is designed to run on all platforms supporting a JVM except for two classes that are Internet Explorer specific and are used for data binding.

It's not really appropriate to go much further into Java in this introduction as we won't be using it in the book. If you wish to know more, then look out for *Beginning Java*, by Wrox Press *ISBN 1-861000-27-8*.

Summary

In this chapter we have taken a quick look at the new features that make up IE4. The six most significant features are the shell extensions, the active desktop, multimedia controls, webcasting technology, the communication tools suite and Dynamic HTML. As the way in which IE4 communicates with Web servers is crucial to its operation, we also took the time to look at the technology that Microsoft has now delivered to provide the Active Platform. We finally took a very brief overview of an alternative web integration technology, Java.

As this book is all about IE4 programming, we won't be really be considering the new extensions to the shell or the communication tools suite (except for NetShow) as they aren't really programmable. Instead, we will be concentrating solely on the other four features, starting with Dynamic HTML. This is the language that enables many of the new features and so it's important to know it in some detail. This text will help you to wind your way through the complexities and subtleties of this emerging technology, and show you what can be done with the features found within Microsoft's Internet Explorer 4.0.

Formatting with Style Sheets

The more popular HTML has become, the more page designers accustomed to a finer level of control over the appearance and location of each element have chafed at the limitations imposed by the language. The World Wide Web Consortium's (W³C's) solution was to develop a specification for a new addition to HTML called style sheets. Over the last year both Netscape and Microsoft have adopted W³C consortium's standard (more or less), paving the way for web pages that can be laid out as precisely as magazinesand other printed materials. For those with programming experience, style sheets allow HTML elements to be placed with the same precision as elements on Visual Basic forms – an improvement, but they still don't offer the fine level of detail that might be required.

With the introduction of Dynamic HTML, the functionality of style sheets has been extended allowing developers to gain increased control over the positioning of elements, via the provision of x and y type coordinates which are calculated in pixels. Also, it is now possible to alter properties of elements on a page dynamically, and for the positions to be altered without a page refresh. Indeed style sheets now form the main method for connecting your scripts to the elements on the page. However, we won't be covering style sheets and scripting until Chapter 5. Although many of the more advanced Dynamic HTML effects, such as element movement require this, this chapter provides a quick overview of style sheets and demonstrates how useful style sheets can be on their own.

In this chapter we'll be talking about:

- What exactly style sheets are and why we need to use them.
- How they provide for formatting and positioning in Dynamic HTML.
- How to add style information to HTML tags.
- The new `style` object.

What is a Style Sheet?

A style sheet is a series of style rules that can be linked to elements in an HTML document. IE4 implements style sheets through the use of **Cascading Style Sheets** (CSS). Cascading Style Sheets were developed by W³C to provide a standard for effective markup, layered text and images, and exact positioning of items. IE4 and Dynamic HTML build on the W³C CSS specification to enable faster and more interactive Web pages. What exactly are the advantages of learning yet another addition to HTML?

Benefits of Style Sheets

HTML in its pre-web form was designed to enable only the meaning of text phrases to be defined – any mention of formatting was explicitly left out. The idea was that each viewer of an HTML page would be free to set the specific formatting they preferred for each functional element. Users with high resolution color monitors could view their pages one way, and those with monochrome text only displays could view them in another.

The web adopted HTML, which quickly evolved, and browser manufacturers soon began to add additional capabilities to existing tags and even new tags themselves to enable web authors to add formatting to their pages. As quickly as these tags proliferated, they detracted from the content/formatting division so important to HTML. But, while these tags gave some improved control over the appearance of HTML, they weren't enough to remedy the problem, since authors continued to replace lengthy blocks of text with graphics when they weren't able to create the effect they wanted with new tags.

Fortunately, style sheets overcome these problems while at the same time adding even more features: everything a layout artist could want. However, they still give the user some control over the browser presentation of different HTML.

General HTML Benefits

Style sheets enable the separation of content and formatting in HTML documents. In fact, styles can be so separate from the HTML pages that use them that we can even define them in another file. With styles characterized in a separate file, they can easily be applied to more than one document – a great advantage.

Wherever we define as our styles, we know that they won't alter the text in any way. This means that people with text-only browsers (and browsers that don't support style sheets) will still be able to see all of the content – it just might not look quite as good.

But these advantages wouldn't mean anything at all if the first purpose of style sheets, to give web developers greater control over the appearance of their pages, wasn't met. As we'll see, style sheets do indeed make pages with all kinds of objects possible in any location we desire.

New Uses for Dynamic HTML

All of this is great, but you need to consider how style sheets apply to the topic at hand. If text and other elements are statically placed when the page is loaded, can we really call it Dynamic HTML? We don't need to argue about this point, because our elements aren't statically arranged – they can be moved and their display properties can be changed. These features are all due to the object model, styles and script code. Before we get into a description of how style sheets work and how they relate to Dynamic HTML, let's get a small taste of what they can do for us.

A style sheet example

The screen shot of the browser below shows what we can do with a normal HTML page and a few style declarations.

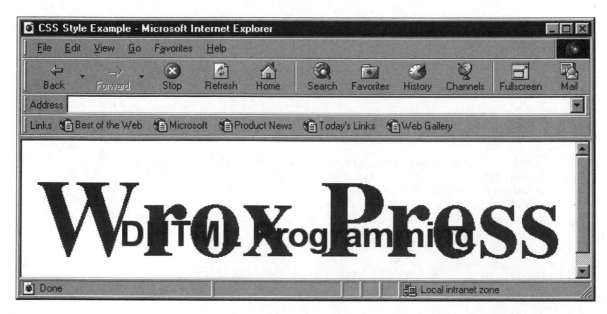

Without style sheets this sort of page would have been impossible to create without using a graphic... not any more! Here's the HTML code for this page:

```
<HTML>
<HEAD>
<TITLE>CSS Style Example</TITLE>
<STYLE>
<!--
BODY        {font-family: Times;
    font-size: 125;
    font-weight: bold;
    color: red }

.layer      {font-family: Arial;
    font-size: 40;
    font-weight: bold;
    color: blue;
    margin-top: -75px }
-->
</STYLE>
</HEAD>
<BODY>
<CENTER>
Wrox Press
<DIV CLASS=layer>DHTML Programming</DIV>
</CENTER>
</BODY>
</HTML>
```

If you ignore the information between the **<STYLE>** and **</STYLE>** tags and **<DIV>** and **</DIV>** tags the page consists simply of two lines of text – Wrox Press and DHTML Programming. Obviously, the work must be done by the new HTML in the page. All body text has been defined as being in the Times font face, 125 points large, bold, and colored red. Our Wrox Press line of text is displayed in this base body style. We've also defined another style and called it `layer` (an additional style like this is also known as a 'class'). This extra style uses the Arial font and sets the top margin for any text displayed with this style as 75 pixels **above** the normal font baseline. DHTML Programming is displayed using the `layer` class.

The end result of this work is that the second line of text is displayed in a different color and size, and 75 pixels above where it would be placed normally – which puts it immediately in the middle of the first line of text we displayed.

> In order for Internet Explorer 4.0 to use any style sheet information when rendering the page you must have style sheets turned on. This is the default setting of Internet Explorer 4.0, but in case you've turned style sheets off, you can turn them back on by opening the View menu, choosing Options…, and switching to the Advanced tab. To turn on style sheets make sure the checkbox next to the Use Stylesheets option (listed under Browsing) is checked.

We'll be covering all of this and more in detail over the rest of this chapter.

Style Sheet Capabilities

We've been alluding to the capabilities of style sheets for the last three pages, but apart from the first example, we haven't talked exactly about how style sheets extend HTML. This section of the chapter will spell out the capabilities of style sheets.

While we call the different style sheet elements 'properties' we don't use them in exactly the same way we use properties of objects. In our example, we set the **BODY** text properties like this:

```
BODY        {font-family: Times;
    font-size: 125;
    font-weight: bold;
    color: red }
```

As we'll see later in this chapter when we talk about the **style** object, this is clearly a different way of doing things than we use for objects. With objects we refer to a property by appending a period and the property name to the name of the object instance, like this:

```
MyTextObject.fontFamily = "Times"
MyTextObject.fontSize = 48
```

Although it's a semantic difference and not important for understanding the capabilities of style sheets we should keep this in mind while we learn about the different style properties that we can use.

Formatting Properties

The appearance of elements is of course a primary concern of ours, and numerous properties of this type can be set through the use of style sheets. In this section we'll talk briefly about the different style properties that can be used to change the formatting of an element (be it a block of text, an image, or whatever).

The style sheet reference in Appendix E provides you with more information about each style property,
including the values they can assume and their applicability to different elements.

Font Properties

These properties are used primarily with groups of text. They control every possible element of the
appearance of a block of text.

Property	Description	Possible Values
`font-family`	name of a specific or generic font family	specific (`Arial`, etc.) generic (`serif`, etc.)
`font-style`	changes in font style	`normal`, `italic`, `oblique`
`font-variant`	changes in font appearance	`normal` or `small-caps`
`font-weight`	the weight of the font	`normal`, `bold`, `bolder`, `lighter` or numeric values `100-900`
`font-size`	size of the font	in absolute or relative units
`font`	allows setting of all font properties at one time	all of the above

As we'll discuss in more detail later in this chapter, one of the ways of adding style information to tags is
simply to include a **STYLE** attribute in the HTML tag itself. We can specify multiple style sheet elements
by delimiting them with a semi-colon. This is the format we'll generally use for our examples. For
example, to set the font of a single **<H1>** element to 48 point Times New Roman italic, we could use this
HTML:

```
<H1 STYLE="font-family:Times New Roman; font-size:48pt; font-style:italic">This is a
stylish heading</H1>
```

This code produces a heading that looks like this (see for yourself – just add the above code to a page
with an **<HTML>** and **<BODY>** block):

Multiple fonts can be specified for the `font-family` property. Browsers can then use the first font on the list that is available on the machine in question. Font names should separated with commas.

For example, suppose we would like to display our text in the Arial Black font, but aren't sure that all of our users will have this font installed on their machines. We could specify Arial Black first in the `font-family` string, followed by another serif font that is more common, like Arial. With this arrangement we'll get Arial Black if it's installed, but our text will still look good if Arial Black isn't on the machine. This is how we would do it:

```
<H1 STYLE="font-family:Arial Black,Arial; font-size:24pt">This heading uses Arial
Black</H1>
<H1 STYLE="font-family:Arial; font-size:24pt">This heading uses Arial</H1>
```

The code is rendered by the browser like this (on a machine that has both Arial Black and Arial installed):

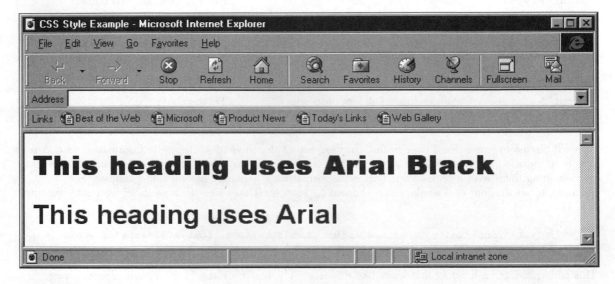

Text Properties

While you're setting the traits of your font, you might also want to set the properties of the text you'll display with this font using the many different text properties that style sheets provide.

Property	Description	Possible Values
`word-spacing`	distance between words	numeric value
`letter-spacing`	distance between letters	numeric value
`text-decoration`	special appearance of the text	`underline`, `overline`, `strikethrough`
`vertical-align`	vertical positioning of an element in the line	`baseline`, `sub`, `super`, `top`, `text-top`, `middle`, `bottom`, `text-bottom`, or percentage

Property	Description	Possible Values
`text-transform`	capitalization of the text	`capitalize`, `uppercase`, `lowercase`, `none`
`text-align`	alignment of the text	`left`, `center`, `right`, `justify`
`text-indent`	indentation of the text	numeric or percentage
`line-height`	height of the line	numeric of percentage

These properties are useful if you want to control your text like you can in a desktop publishing program. As the power of these properties demonstrate, the change from the old HTML to style-sheet enhanced HTML is nothing short of amazing.

We've always been able to center HTML using the `<CENTER>` tag. Style sheets allow us to control the justification of our text more robustly, with the `text-align` property. As an example of some of the things that the text properties can do, take a look at the browser in this screen shot:

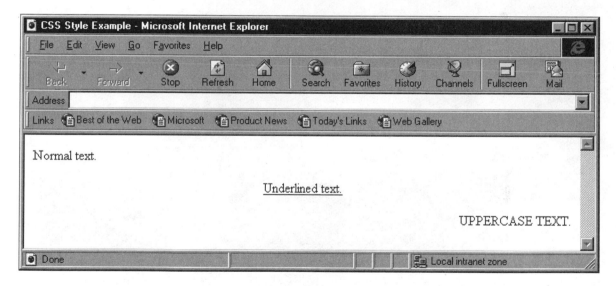

This page was created with just these three lines of style sheet HTML:

```
<P STYLE="text-align:left">Normal text.</P>
<P STYLE="text-align:center; text-decoration:underline">Underlined text.</P>
<P STYLE="text-align:right; text-transform:uppercase">Uppercase text.</P>
```

With this we can begin to see how style sheets now give users of HTML the same power previously only existed in word processors and page layout programs.

Color and Background Properties

Property	Description	Possible Values
color	color of the element	color name or RGB value "#RRGGBB"
background	background of the element scroll value, position value	color value, URL location, repeat value,

The `color` property is simple but useful – just specify a color and the element is displayed in this color. `Background` is equally useful, but more complicated because of its wide variety of options. The background of an element can be set to a solid color, an image, or a combination of both. Images can be set to repeat and/or scroll with the document. So if we wanted the code to set the background of the `<BODY>` tag to have a default color of red, but to also have the Wrox logo repeating down the y-axis of the page, underneath some text, it would be fairly simple to achieve:

```
<BODY STYLE="background: url(wrox.gif) red repeat-y">
This is some example text
</BODY>
```

The resulting screen would look like this:

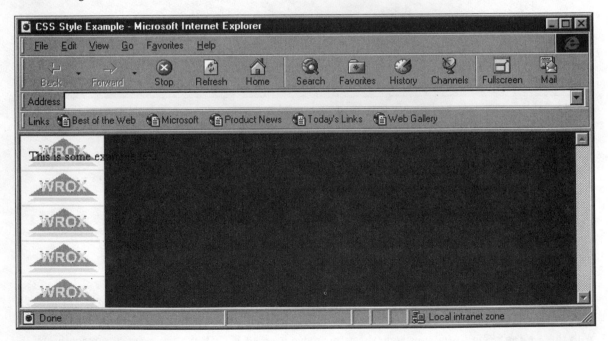

Supplementary Background Properties

In addition to the basic `background` property, style sheets in Internet Explorer 4.0 support a number of properties that address specific elements of the background, like `background-image`, `background-color`, and so on.

```
background-attachment          background-color

background-image               background-position

background-repeat
```

While the `background` property can be used to set all of these attributes at one time, with these properties you can modify a part of the background without having to set each element. So you could you create the last example by setting each supplementary background property as follows:

```
<BODY STYLE="background-image: url(wrox.gif); background-color: red; background-
repeat: repeat-y">
This is some example text
</BODY>
```

Border Properties

Using these properties, each side of the border around the element can be set with a style and width value.

Property	Description	Possible Values
`border-top`		
`border-right`		
`border-left`	Sets the width, color, and style	
`border-bottom`	properties of the border around	
`border`	the element	
`color`		any color value
`width`		numeric
`style`		`thin`, `medium`, `thick`

Supplementary Border Properties

The `border` property has additional properties in the same way that `background` does.

```
border-color                   border-style

border-right-width             border-left-width

border-top-width               border-bottom-width
```

Positioning Properties

Specifying exactly the formatting of text or an element is one part of style sheets. To compliment this feature we also have the ability to position each element precisely on the page.

Positioning attributes of style sheets will apply to much more than just text. In Dynamic HTML many page elements, from headings to images, can have a `style` property that includes the positioning properties we're going to discuss in this section. And, as you'll see shortly, those elements that don't include their own style properties can be wrapped in a container that does include style information, and they can be moved and positioned in this way.

Intrinsic Positioning Properties of the Element

The properties in this category control properties inherent to the element, that is, properties that are more important to the element and whatever it contains or displays than they are to the page or container that hosts the element.

Property	Description	Possible Values

`margin-top`
`margin-right`
`margin-left`
`margin-bottom`
`margin`
	size of the margin for the current element (creates a minimum distance between this element and any others)	`auto`, numeric, percentage (of parent element's value)

`padding-top`
`padding-right`
`padding-left`
`padding-bottom`
`padding`
	amount of space between the border and the element	`auto`, numeric, percentage (of parent element's value)

`float`	controls which side text flows around an element	`left`, `right`, `none`
`clear`	controls whether text is allowed to flow around an element	`left`, `right`, `none`, `both`
`width`	horizontal size of the element	`auto`, numeric, percentage
`height`	vertical size of element	`auto`, numeric, percentage
`visibility`	whether or not the element is currently displayed	`visible`, `hidden`
`overflow`	determines how text that overflows the height or width is displayed	`none`, `clip`, `scroll`

Both the `margin` and `padding` properties allow us to control how the contents of an element are positioned inside the box created by the border (whether or not the border is actually visible). These properties work in tandem with the `left` and `top` properties we'll talk about in a second. `Clear` and `float` control if and how text is allowed to flow around the element, respectively, and `height` and `width` are self-explanatory.

The Visibility Property

`Visibility` is a new property added to the style sheets implementation in Internet Explorer 4.0. Using this property we can place an element on a page, but make it invisible. This might not seem too interesting until you consider the fact that script code on the page can change this property dynamically and so hide and display elements depending on other actions in the page.

Here's a simple page that shows something we'd never see with regular HTML. With this page loaded into our browser, we can press the spacebar repeatedly and make the sole header on the page appear and disappear at will.

```
<HTML>
<BODY>

<H1 ID="MyHeader" STYLE="visibility:visible; text-align:center">Phantom Header</P>

<SCRIPT LANGUAGE="VBScript">
Sub Document_onKeyPress
    If MyHeader.style.visibility = "hidden" Then
            MyHeader.style.visibility = "visible"
    Else
            MyHeader.style.visibility = "hidden"
    End If
End Sub
</SCRIPT>

</BODY>
</HTML>
```

The script code we've written is fired when a key is pressed – it's the job of the **document** object's
onKeyPress event to inform us when this happens.

> *We'll talk about the document object in more detail in chapter 4 and cover scripting in chapter 5.*

Our code checks to see if the **visibility** property of the header is currently set to **hidden** or
visible, and it then toggles this property to the other setting, making the header disappear and reappear.

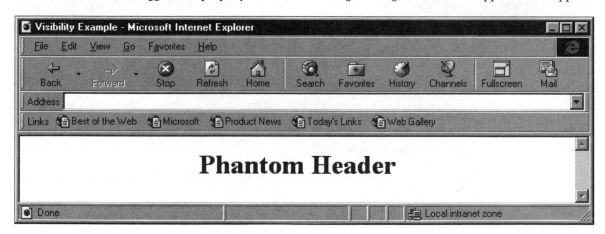

The Overflow Property

Another new property included with IE4's implementation of style sheets is **overflow**. Based on the
setting of this property to **none**, **clip**, or **scroll**, the contents of a text element will be allowed to
overflow without scrolling, will be clipped to the size of the element, or will be clipped but be scrollable.

The Margin Property

Using the margin properties we just described, it's possible to position an element anywhere on the page, however, using the method can lead to some confusing results. `Margin` lets us adjust the current element relative to where it would be displayed normally. Unfortunately, this means that if we change the order that the elements are placed in the HTML file we can completely change how the page looks.

We can see an example of this phenomenon if we go back our first example in this chapter and swap two of the lines around.

```
...
Wrox Press
<DIV CLASS=layer>DHTML Programming</DIV>
...
```

```
...
<DIV CLASS=layer>DHTML
Programming</DIV>
Wrox Press
...
```

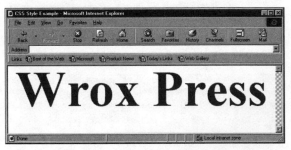

We defined the style we use to display the string DHTML Programming as having a margin-top property of -75 pixels. This works in the way we want it to as long as the text that uses this second style is placed after the first bit of text in our HTML file. If we switch it we get completely different results: the DHTML Programming text completely disappears from page!

Clearly this is undesirable. Ideally, we'd like to be able to specify the position of each element so our formatting is maintained even if the order of our tags in the HTML source changes.

Page/Container Location Properties

When IE3 was released in the summer of 1996 the W3C was still working hard on developing a specification for absolute positioning of HTML elements. If you used Microsoft's HTML Layout Control with IE3 you were treated to a preview of this technology (and you shouldn't be surprised to see that a lot of your old code should work as styles with IE4).

IE4 implements this specification without a control. It uses the details of this specification to provide web authors with the capability to place elements at any location on the HTML page, as well as enabling objects to move dynamically after the page is displayed, as we'll see when we start to talk about scripting.

Property	Description	Possible Values
`position`	specifies how the top and left properties should be interpreted for element positioning	`relative`, `absolute`, `static`
`left`	the left position of the element with respect to its container	numeric value
`top`	the top position of the element with respect to its container	numeric value
`z-index`	the position of the element above and / or below other elements	numeric value

`Left` and `top` are reasonably intuitive. They specify the leftmost and topmost positions of the element with respect to its current container and depending on the current setting of the `position` property. The container can be an entire page or a subset of the page called document division.

What `left` and `top` actually do depends on the `position` property of the element. If `position` is set to `relative`, then `left` and `top` offset the current element from the position it would reside in without any extra code. The `absolute` setting ignores any previous HTML and just places the element in the position specified (relative to the upper left-hand corner of the current container location coordinates of 0,0).

Any elements placed with `absolute` 'disappear' from the HTML source as far as the layout of subsequent elements are concerned. The HTML rendering engine doesn't reserve any space on the page for elements positioned with `absolute`, it places all subsequent elements in the location they would be in if the `absolute` element(s) wasn't a part of the page. Finally, if we omit a `position` property in our style, or just don't use styles at all, the default is `static`; this setting just causes the element to be placed in the position it would be without style sheets.

The `z-index` property provides analogous formatting, but in the 'third dimension'. Strictly, it's a form of **2.5D** control. Another way to put it is that `z-index` controls the layout of elements, one on top of the other Elements with higher `z-index` values overlap elements with lower `z-index` values. Elements placed later in the HTML source and lacking a `z-index` value will overlap identical elements placed earlier.

A Positioning Example

Now, let's pause from our descriptions for a moment to show an example of most of the positioning topics we're covering in this section.

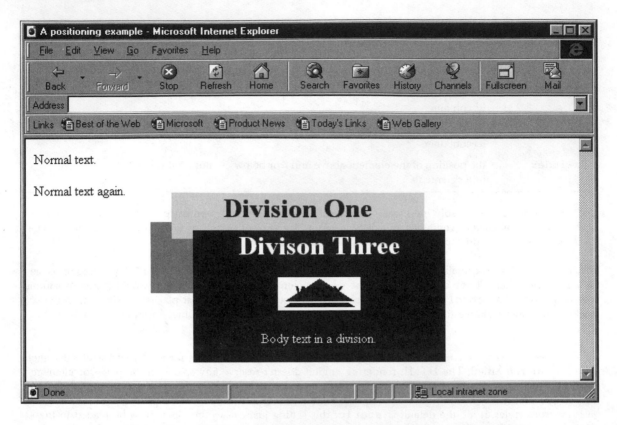

You can run this page from our Web site at: `http://rapid.wrox.co.uk/books/0707`

The text for this page contains two different paragraphs and a few document divisions created with the `<DIV>` tag. Here's the source:

```
<HTML>
<HEAD>
<TITLE>A positioning example</TITLE>
</HEAD>
<BODY>

<P>
Normal text.
</P>

<DIV STYLE="background:yellow; position:absolute; left:175; top:65; width=300; z-
index:-1; text-align:center">

<H1>Division One</H1>
</DIV>

<DIV STYLE="background:orange; position:absolute; left:150; top:100; width=100;
height:85; z-index:-2">
</DIV>
```

```
<DIV STYLE="background:purple; position:absolute; left:200; top:110; width=300;
height:150; color:white; text-align:center">

<H1>Divison Three</H1>
<IMG SRC="wrox0.gif">
<P STYLE="position:relative">Body text in a division.</P>
</DIV>

<P>
Normal text again.
</P>

</BODY>
</HTML>
```

The Document Division Tag

A `<DIV>` tag creates a division of the page that, while it inherits formatting information from the document or other containing tag, is considered a separate element for positioning purposes. This means that each document division created with `<DIV>` can be located on the page with top and left properties. It also means that elements placed inside a division use the coordinate system of the division so they can be positioned with respect to the division and will move when the division moves. Think of a `<DIV>`...`</DIV>` block as being a separate page that can be moved and positioned on the main HTML page we reference in the address bar of the browser. We'll see how the `<DIV>` tag is used in this example and then cover it again in detail in a few pages.

Absolute Positioning of Divisions

We'll cover the three squares shown in the browser window. Each of these squares is created with a separate `<DIV>` tag. Here's the HTML code for the first square (the one that holds the text 'Division One'):

```
<DIV STYLE="background:yellow; position:absolute; left:175; top:65; width=300; z-
index:-1; text-align:center">

<H1>Division One</H1>
</DIV>
```

The `STYLE` parameter specifies all of the formatting for this element. The `background` property sets the color of the block to yellow and the `text-align` property centers whatever elements are placed inside the division. We've talked about these properties already... what about the new positioning properties? We're using `position:absolute` for this division, so we know that the division will be offset 175 pixels right and 65 pixels below the top-left-hand corner of the container – which is the page itself in this case. We set the width of the division to 300 pixels and let the browser determine the height by omitting the `height` property. Finally, we place the division at the `z-index` level of -1. This means that the division will be behind page elements that don't have their `z-index` set explicitly (these elements are at a `z-index` of 0). The `<H1>` tag that displays 'Division One' is placed before the closing `</DIV>` tag and we're done.

The next division is identical except that it's orange instead of yellow, is placed at a slightly different position, and contains no text. Again, we use `position:absolute` so our `top` and `left` properties will be with respect to the page. Setting the `left` property to less than the first division means that the division will be placed 25 pixels to the left of the first division. The division is moved down on the page since its `top` property is greater than the `top` property of the first division.

```
<DIV STYLE="background:orange; position:absolute; left:150; top:100; width=100;
height:85; z-index:-2">
</DIV>
```

We've neglected to mention the **z-index** of the division up until this point. Normally elements that are placed later in the HTML source are rendered on top of earlier elements – but in this case our second division is placed behind the first division. Why? The answer is in our **z-index** property. Since it's set to -2, this element is rendered behind the first division (with a **z-index** of -1) and also behind all other divisions and elements (which have the default **z-index** setting of 0).

Our third division is created like the first two and it shows up on top of both of them (it's at the default **z-index** level of 0).

```
<H1>Divison Three</H1>
<IMG SRC="wrox0.gif">
<P STYLE="position:relative">Body text in a division.</P>
```

The interesting thing about this block of HTML is how the header, image, and paragraph are rendered. With this code each element is rendered in order and the appropriate amount of space is reserved by the browser for the header, the graphic, and the text. Since each of these elements is inside the **<DIV>**… **</DIV>** block they're located using the division as the container. The paragraph uses the **position:relative** style although this isn't explicitly necessary in this case. The paragraph would be placed at the same location in this code if we allowed the position attribute to default to **static**.

Now, let's change the above image code to this code instead:

```
<IMG STYLE="position:absolute; left:0; top:0" SRC="wrox0.gif">
```

Here we're using the position attribute to specify that the **<IMG>** tag should be placed **absolute**ly inside the division.

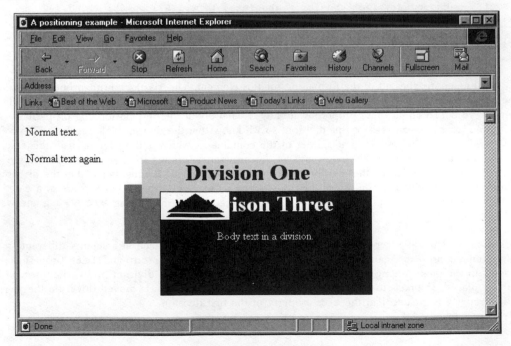

By specifying the coordinates 0,0, the image gets placed at the top-left hand corner of the division. Notice also that the paragraph is placed closer to the header in this case. This happens because the browser doesn't reserve space for elements placed with absolute positioning. The normal `relative` and `static` elements are placed without regard to any elements positioned with `position:absolute`.

This same concept also explains the last part of our example. Notice that the two bits of normal text are placed before and after the HTML that creates the divisions we have just considered.

```
<HTML>
<BODY>

<P>
Normal text.
</P>

...

<P>
Normal text again.
</P>

</BODY>
</HTML>
```

While the bit of text that says Normal text again is placed at the end of the HTML page it's still rendered by the browser at the top of the page (immediately underneath the first normal text block). We used `position:absolute` with all three of our divisions and so the rest of the page text is laid out as if the divisions didn't exist, and, as we would expect, our text blocks are placed next to each other.

Numeric Units with Style Sheets

As you've seen, a large number of style sheet properties accept a 'numeric value' as their parameter. However, the style sheet specifications allow us to specify our numbers with several different units.

The table below shows the different units we can use when providing a numeric value.

Unit	Description	Category
em	height of a single character in the current element	relative
ex	height of the letter x in the current element	relative
px	pixels	relative
in	inches	absolute
cm	centimeters	absolute
mm	millimeters	absolute
pt	points (72 points per inch)	absolute
pc	picas (1 pica = 12 points)	absolute

The actual syntax we use is simple: just append the unit abbreviation to the number.

```
letter-spacing:12px
margin-left:2in
```

With the units in the **relative** category, the browser actually calculates the value based on the current settings of the page or screen (for pixels). This means that elements set with these designators will change with different pages or computer systems. For these elements, the browser calculates the amount of space using characters from the current element. This is true except for one case: when these units are used with the `font-size` property. Instead of using the size of the current element, the value is calculated using characters from the parent element. So, for example, if we set the `font-size` property of a heading with a relative designator the browser will use the font size of the body element (or other containing element if it lies between the heading and the body of the document).

Percentage values are, in most cases, relative to the `font-size` of the current element. Child elements that inherit a value set with a percentage inherit the value itself, not a percentage of a percentage. Consequently a changed parent font-size property doesn't propagate through to the child.

Using Style Sheets

So we know what style sheets can do for us, but we haven't talked about how we can actually add them to our pages. There are several different ways to provide style information and an equal amount of latitude when it comes to reapplying style information to different but similar tags.

Specifying Properties and Values

To indicate to the HTML engine our setting for a property we simply use this syntax:

`TAG {property:value}`

We'll see an actual example of this in the next paragraph. We can specify additional property values by adding new text and separating them with a semi-colon. We can also set the property values for more than one tag at time; for this purpose we use a comma as a delimiter.

For example, first, set the body text to the Arial font:

```
BODY {font-family:Arial}
```

Then set all of the headings to be green:

```
H1, H2, H3, H4, H5, H6 {color:green}
```

Finally, define emphasis text as bold 24-point Times:

```
EM {font-family:Times; font-size:24pt; font-weight:bold}
```

And that's all there is to setting style sheet properties – we just put whatever property we'd like to set together with the value and associate this combo with a tag.

The <DIV> Tag

We looked at this briefly earlier in the chapter, but it's now time to consider it in more detail. We use <DIV>...</DIV> blocks to create what we'll call a **document division**. We can think of a division as a separate part of the HTML page – in effect, an HTML page in itself, inside a top level page and displayed in the same browser window.

We can have any number of divisions in a page, and each division has its own set of style properties that can be used to position the division anywhere on the page, down to the pixel. Divisions have a z-index property and can overlap each other. Text or other elements inside a division automatically take the font, color, and other settings from their parent division, allowing us to set the formatting properties of objects (like small blocks of text) that might not have their very own set of style properties.

Finally, when using <DIV> with absolute position, it's important to remember that the <DIV> tag starts a new coordinate system that is relative only to the HTML placed within the <DIV>...</DIV> block.

The <DIV> tag is one of the most useful single tags in Dynamic HTML programming and you'll get very familiar with it as you read and use the rest of this book.

Incorporating Styles into a Page

Once we've decided how we want our page to look and know what our style tags will look like, we need to take the final step and apply this information to the page. Just as we can't add script code to the page without enclosing it in a variety of <SCRIPT> tags, we can't add style sheet information without some sort of structure. There are a few different ways to add styles to a page, and they each have their own set of advantages and disadvantages.

The Single <STYLE> Tag

Our first example of style sheets uses probably the most intuitive method of adding style information. With this method, we open a <STYLE> tag, provide all of the formatting information for our page (according to the syntax we just laid out), and then close the tag. Usually, we'll place this <STYLE> block in the header of the HTML document, as we did in the first example.

```
<STYLE>
<!--
BODY        {font-family: Times;
    font-size: 125;
    font-weight: bold;
    color: red }

.layer      {font-family: Arial;
    font-size: 40;
    font-weight: bold;
    color: blue;
    margin-top: -75px }
-->
</STYLE>
```

This makes sense, but it does have a few limitations. Most importantly, this technique requires that we hardcode the style information into every single HTML file that needs it. If we need to change one small bit of the formatting for our pages, then we have to manually open, edit, and save each file. Also, in addition to being difficult to change, information repeated in many documents needs to be downloaded repeatedly, and this consumes time and server/network resources.

We also need to remember to enclose our style information inside the HTML comment tags `<!--` and `-->` so that browsers that don't understand style sheets won't attempt to display the information inside of our `<STYLE>` tag as text.

Using <STYLE> with Individual Tags

For quick and easy addition of style information we can add styles directly to almost all elements on the page.

```
<H1 STYLE="color:purple; font-size:100">A Big Ugly Heading</H1>
```

This biggest advantage to this method is its flexibility. Style information can be added to individual elements, and it will only affect the specific instance of the element it's added to. In this example, we'll only change one `<H1>` tag, not all of the first-level headers. This ability makes it even more useful when we're using just a bit of style information for the sake of scripting.

However, we still haven't done anything about the problem of repeating identical style information across pages. To fix that we'll need to use one of the next two methods.

The <LINK> Tag with Style Sheets

If we have a set of style information that we'd like to apply to multiple pages (or even think we might want to, someday) then we can save this information in a separate file. Adding these styles to a new page is now no more complicated than adding a single `<LINK>` tag to each page that should incorporate the style information:

```
<LINK REL=STYLESHEET TYPE="text/css" HREF="http://yourserver/yourpath/style.css">
```

This tag can be placed in the `<HEAD>` of the document, in the same location where we've been placing all of the in-line style information.

The `HREF` attribute should be changed to point at the appropriate style sheet, which should incorporate style information in exactly the same format as we saw when we used the `<STYLE>` tag – just omit `<STYLE>` and `</STYLE>`:

```
BODY        {font-family: Times;
    font-size: 125;
    font-weight: bold;
    color: red; }

.layer      {font-family: Arial;
    font-size: 40;
    font-weight: bold;
    color: blue;
    margin-top: -75px }
```

Using @import

There is another way to automatically apply style sheets and still keep the file sizes down, the **@import** notation. This functions in a very similar way to using **LINK** and **HREF**, except that the URL of the style sheet is specified within an **@import** line.

```
<HTML>
<HEAD>
<TITLE>CSS Style Example</TITLE>
<STYLE>
@import URL("http://rapid.wrox.co.uk/books/0707/style.css");
</STYLE>
</HEAD>
<BODY>
<CENTER>
Wrox Press
<DIV CLASS=layer>DHTML Programming</DIV>
</CENTER>
</BODY>
</HTML>
```

This notation tells the browser to get the style sheet **style.css** from the server at **rapid.wrox.co.uk**. If we place the **@import** line between **<STYLE>** tags in the **<HEAD>** of our document, the style will be automatically retrieved and applied before our document is displayed. These are the preferred methods of incorporating style sheets using IE4: it's easy, and they maintain all of the advantages we gain from using style sheets.

More Style Sheet Features

We've already established how useful style information is to designing HTML pages, and we've talked about a multiplicity of different ways to add style information to a page. We're now going to cover two additional and very useful features of specifying style information.

Simple Inheritance

Tags enclosed in other tags inherit the settings of the outer tags. You might have seen this phenomenon if you've experimented much with style sheets, although you might not have recognized it as such.

For example, suppose we've defined the **<H1>** style like this:

```
H1 {font-size:48; font-family:Arial}
```

In the course of writing the HTML for the page that uses this style we use an **<EM>** tag **inside** a **<H1>** block:

```
<H1>Here's my <EM>important</EM> heading</H1>
```

We wouldn't be very happy if the word **important** reverted to some other style, such as the body text style. However, because embedded tags inherit the style properties of the tags enclosing them, the text inside the **<EM>** tag is rendered as bold in 48 point Arial – because it's enclosed in an **<H1>** tag.

It is important to know that the **<EM>** tag will only inherit the properties of the **<H1>** tag if it hasn't already had its own style defined. If you think about this approach you'll see that it makes a lot of sense.

In effect, the style sheet engine standardizes everything that you do not specifically define. This works well in practice – as you'll see when you start writing HTML pages that use style sheets heavily.

Contextual Selectors

But this isn't all there is to inheritance! Style sheets even give us the ability to specify that certain instances of certain tags should look a specific way. If we've set all **<H1>** tags to the color green and all **<EM>** tags to yellow, we can use what is known as a contextual selector (because the selector depends on the context it's used in) to stipulate additional behavior for a given tag.

With the two declarations above, an **<EM>** tag inside of a **<H1>** tag would be rendered as yellow. However, with the following simple declaration we can require that all **<EM>** tags inside **<H1>** tags be colored purple instead:

```
H1 EM {color:purple}
```

This declaration only affects **<EM>** tags inside **<H1>** – it leaves every other combination alone.

Classes

Another interesting kind of syntax we're going to cover here is known as a style sheet **class**. This technique allows us to assign names to modifications of basic styles and then use them in much the same way we would use a normal style.

Suppose we usually would like our first level headings to be displayed in black 24 point Arial type. From our previous discussions we know that we can accomplish this with the style sheet declaration of:

```
H1 {font-family:Arial; font-size:24pt; color:black}
```

Now further suppose that occasionally we'd like the **<H1>** tag to take on a slightly different appearance – maybe we want it to be a larger point size, but in all other respects we'd like it to remain the same. Using a class in our style sheet declarations, we can accomplish this easily:

```
H1.second {font-size:48pt}:
```

Now we can use both the original declaration and the subclass in our HTML:

```
<H1>First heading</H1>
<H1 CLASS="second">First large point heading</H1>
```

Another way to accomplish this task would be to use an in-line **<STYLE>** tag for each heading that we wanted to appear red:

```
<H1 STYLE="font-size:48pt">Another large point heading</H1>
```

As we'll see shortly when we talk about how properties take precedence over each other, the large point size specified in the heading tag itself will override the other **font-size** specified in the top-level set of styles.

Conflict Resolution (What does 'Cascading' mean anyway?)

With all of these different ways to specify what elements should appear like, how does the style sheet engine determine which declaration wins if more than one declaration could apply to a given element?

The answer is in the title of the specification we've spent so much time discussing in this chapter: **Cascading** Style Sheets. In a nutshell, the title indicates an important and special property about style sheets, which is that if more than one style attempts to format an element at the same time the style that actually formats the element will be determined based on a concrete set of rules.

Specifying Your Own Style Sheet

There's one other source of style sheet information that we haven't considered yet. In addition to the different styles we can specify in the source of our page or in a linked style sheet, the browser user can also define their own style sheet. In general the values in this sheet will be overridden by any style values in a page. The rationale behind this practice is that any style information in a page is important enough to display, but pages without style sheets can still be prettied up by following user preferences.

Setting a default style sheet is easy to do with IE4. Select the Internet Options menu item from the View menu, and then click on the Accessibility... button. In the Accessibility dialog, check the Format documents using my style sheet checkbox and fill in the path or use the Browse... button to specify the location of your own personal style sheet.

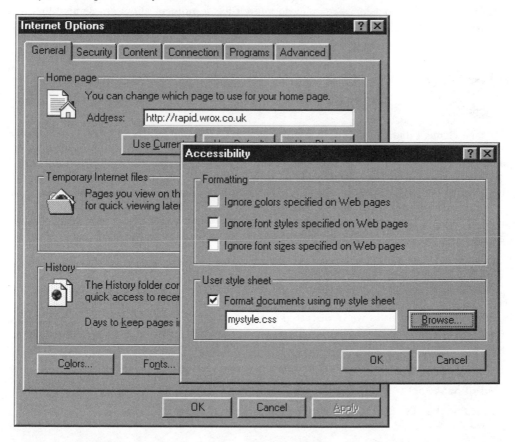

Rendering the Page: Resolving Style Conflicts

When a style sheet enabled browser downloads a page it runs through the following steps to determine which (if any) style information should be used to format each element:

▲ Parse the page and consider all elements. If an element (including its parents) contains no style information, then use the user defaults that were set via style sheet or browser options. If parent elements contain style information use this data instead of the default values.

▲ If a conflict exists, the values are sorted again so that values set by the author of the page rank higher than default values set by the browser user.

▲ If we still have not resolved all conflicts, sort the values by their specificity to the situation. A value that applies only to the situation at hand will override a value that applies in a more general case.

With the information from this section (and the style sheet reference, Appendix F, in the back of the book) you can write HTML pages that look great because they contain specific formatting and layout information.

The Style Object

Before we finish up with the chapter, we're going to talk for just a moment about an element that isn't officially a part of the style sheet specification, but is very important to our use of style sheets in Dynamic HTML.

The Style Object

First, we should explain **why** you'd use the **style** object when writing Dynamic HTML script code...

Any HTML page element that can take a style property has a corresponding **style** object. This object is of no importance while we're writing the page layout and text itself, but plays a vital role when we come to write code. In short, if we want to do anything to a page element dynamically, we'll use the underlying **style** object to do it. Want to change the color of a list item as the mouse moves over it? Write to the **color** property of the list item's **style** object. Curious about the size of the heading elements on the page? Read from each heading's **style.fontsize** property. Need to move an element after the page has been loaded and displayed? Use the **top** and **left** properties of that element's **style** object. You get the idea, and you'll surely be seeing many examples using the style object throughout the rest of this book.

The Style Object's Interface

The **style** object has a very long list of properties. Fortunately, they're all easy to categorize as they mimic the different style properties we've discussed in this chapter.

background	backgroundAttachment
backgroundColor	backgroundImage
backgroundPosition	backgroundPositionX
backgroundPositionY	backgroundRepeat

border	borderBottom
borderBottomColor	borderBottomStyle
borderBottomWidth	borderColor
borderLeft	borderLeftColor
borderLeftStyle	borderLeftWidth
borderRight	borderRightColor
borderRightStyle	borderRightWidth
borderTop	borderTopColor
borderTopStyle	borderTopWidth
clear	clip
color	cssText
cursor	display
filter	font
fontFamily	fontSize
fontStyle	fontVariant
fontWeight	height
left	letterSpacing
lineHeight	listStyle
listStyleImage	listStylePosition
listStyleType	margin
marginBottom	marginLeft
marginRight	marginTop
overflow	paddingBottom
paddingLeft	paddingRight
paddingTop	pageBreakAfter
pageBreakBefore	pixelHeight
pixelLeft	pixelTop
pixelWidth	posHeight
position	posLeft
posTop	posWidth
styleFloat	textAlign
textDecoration	textDecorationBlink
textDecorationLinethrough	textDecorationNone
textDecorationOverline	textDecorationUnderline

```
textIndent                    textTransform

top                           verticalAlign

visibility                    width

zIndex
```

From time to time we see a very slight change as hyphenated properties lose their hyphens when translated into a property of the style object. For example, the style sheet **font-size** property corresponds to the style object's **fontsize** property. Other than this difference, the list of properties is identical.

With this discussion of the **style** property we can revisit the code we wrote earlier in the chapter to make a header disappear and reappear:

```
<H1 ID="MyHeader" STYLE="visibility:visible; text-align:center">Phantom Header</P>

<SCRIPT LANGUAGE="VBScript">
Sub Document_onKeyPress
    If MyHeader.style.visibility = "hidden" Then
            MyHeader.style.visibility = "visible"
    Else
            MyHeader.style.visibility = "hidden"
    End If
End Sub
</SCRIPT>
```

You can understand now exactly what we're doing in this code. The header object we created with a normal **<H1>** tag and gave the ID of **MyHeader** exposes a **style** object. Our code uses the **visibility** property of this **style** object to hide and show the header.

Summary

In this chapter we talked about one of the most important additions to Internet Explorer which is utilized by Dynamic HTML. While style sheets were present in IE3, it's only in IE4 that virtually of the CSS1 standard has been implemented. Style sheets give us the ability to precisely display and position elements on our pages, and are a key to creating dynamic pages with scripting.

Specifically we learned in this chapter that:

- ▲ Style sheets have tremendous importance for Dynamic HTML: they're the mechanism we use to change the appearance of HTML elements dynamically.

- ▲ Several kinds of style information, such as positioning or fonts, can be added to HTML pages in a number of different ways.

- ▲ The **style** object makes the different style properties of elements available to script code.

Over the rest of the book you'll be seeing the objects and concepts we talked about in this chapter again and again. As we cover the rest of the fundamentals of dynamic HTML, we'll see how style sheets can be used to connect script to the elements in this page. When tied together with script code and the browser object model, the full functionality of style sheets are revealed. We'll cover this over the next few chapters, but first we need to look at the browser object model.

HTML Formatting and the Browser Object Model

After our brief introduction to style sheets in the last chapter, we're now ready to dig into one of the main foundations of Dynamic HTML: the **browser object model**. Netscape 2 was actually the first browser that provided a documented object model, which allowed users to access both the browser environment and page contents with scripting code. However certain contents of the page such as text and images weren't accessible, until the advent of Dynamic HTML. If we are going to be able to program the object model using Dynamic HTML, then we need to understand the whole hierarchy of objects inside the browser first and what they all do.

So we're going break our discussion of the object model into two chapters. In this, the first, we'll discuss exactly what the object model is and why it's so important to Dynamic HTML programmers. From this introduction, we'll move on to the programmatic representation of the browser itself. The actual discussion of how we can manipulate elements on the web page, via the object model, won't be dealt with until the next chapter.

In this chapter, we're going to cover::

- The purpose of the browser object model and its overall organization.
- Properties, methods, and events of the top-level **window** object.
- Window's subsidiary objects: **history**, **location**, **navigator**, **screen**, and **event**.

Since we haven't had an opportunity to talk in-depth about writing script code inside HTML pages, we'll refrain from giving detailed code examples in these chapters. The foundation of everything we do with Dynamic HTML is the object model; these two chapters provide a basis for everything we'll write about in this book. The fact that we're talking about the object model before we talk about scripting is logical too: it's important to talk about the objects that we can manipulate through code before we talk too much about the script code itself. While we won't explicate page after page of code in these chapters, we'll spend plenty of time talking about what the objects can do.

The Organization of the Browser Object Model

While it is possible to write good Dynamic HTML code without a basic understanding of how the objects provided by the browser interact, knowledge of the object model makes this a lot easier.

What is the Browser Object Model?

In short, the browser object model is the interface between the code we write to control or react to the browser and the internal workings of the browser itself. This level of abstraction allows us to manipulate the browser without worrying about how the instructions we give are carried out. In effect, the guts of the browser become a 'black box'–we perform some action and get a result, but we don't need to know how our input is translated into output by the browser.

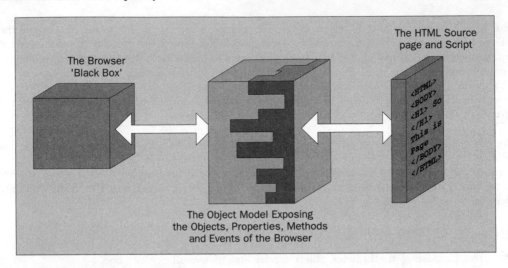

However, in many cases we do need to know information about the task itself, or we might need to instruct the browser to perform a task or know when a task has been undertaken or completed. For example, the specific code that the browser uses to decide exactly which pixels are turned on and off is of little concern to us. However, we'll often find other information extremely useful. For instance, we might want to instruct the browser to navigate to a list of different page based on an entry in a form on the current page. We might also want to respond to the loading of a new page, for example, perhaps we'd like to display a dialog that grabs the user's attention the first time they've seen our page. The browser object model gives us the ability to write code that will accomplish all of these tasks.

Objects

The object model provides us with an interface to the browser that masks us from what actually goes on beneath the hood of the browser, such as how browser operations are accomplished. This interface is embodied in the set of objects that make up the object model. But what actually is an object in computer terms?

While an object can be anything from an apple to a television in the real world, to keep things simple, in computer terms, we shall just consider an object to be a combination of data and code. Objects are self-contained parts of a program, which carry out specific functions. The data and code associated to the object define everything that the object represents (state) and what it can do (behavior). The characteristics or *blueprint* of an object is specified by a **class** definition. An object, of which there may be many, is a created **instance** of a class, just as an instance of a cake can be created from a recipe. IE4 is made up from many interrelated objects and indeed even the whole browser itself is considered an object.

An Object's Interface

All object models, including the browser object model, are made up of a set of interconnected and interrelated objects. Fortunately for us, while these objects might represent anything, they all operate in the same way to a script developer. It's this similarity that makes objects so powerful. Our script code can access every object with similar syntax, without regard for what the object represents. Furthermore, code can only interact with objects in predefined ways–through **properties**, **methods**, and **events**. A standard way of communicating is a key concept in any set of objects.

Properties

A property of an object is an attribute that somehow reflects the current state of the object. As an example, suppose we were working with a `Car` object. This object might have properties with names like *NumberOfDoors*, *BodyStyle*, *CurrentSpeed*, and *LightsOn*. Some properties can only be read–they can't be changed. Others can be read and written. Many of the `Car` object properties are read-only; that is, they were set when the car was built and can't be changed (at least without a lot of work!). Other properties, like *CurrentSpeed* and *LightsOn*, can be changed or retrieved; these properties are read/write properties.

While we've said many times that we won't provide any more than the most rudimentary code in these chapters, it's important to understand on the simplest scale how properties are called. Assuming we had an instance of our object called *MyCarObject*, we could display the read-only properties we invented in the previous paragraph in VBScript like this:

```
MsgBox MyCarObject.NumberOfDoors
MsgBox MyCarObject.BodyStyle
```

Setting read/write properties is equally as simple:

```
MyCarObject.CurrentSpeed = 55
MyCarObject.LightsOn = True
```

We can read these variables in the same manner that we access read-only variables:

```
MsgBox MyCarObject.CurrentSpeed
MsgBox MyCarObject.LightsOn
```

Methods

Properties are great if we're only interested in finding out what state an object is in or in changing a discrete characteristic of an object. Fortunately we have methods to help us out of this situation. In short, objects provide methods so that they can be instructed to carry out certain predefined operations. Our `Car` object could have methods like *SpeedUp*, *SlowDown*, *TurnRight*, *TurnLeft*, and *Stop*. These methods could take any number of parameters (perhaps the miles per hour to change speed or the degrees to turn). We use methods to influence the current state of the object.

Calling methods with VBScript is simple:

```
MyCarObject.SpeedUp 20   'speed up 20mph
MyCarObject.TurnLeft 90  'turn left 90 degrees
```

Events

Both properties and methods are things that we, as an outside force, do **to** an object. Events, in contrast, are things that an object does to its container or host. More specifically, they're entities that allow us to respond to some condition or state inside an object. A *Car* object might have, among other things, a *FuelLow* event that would be raised when the fuel level in the car fell below some level, a *FuelEmpty* event raised when the fuel tank was empty, and a *Collision* event–which we hope we never see!

There are a few different ways to connect code to events with VBScript. In our simple examples we'll use the same style that Visual Basic uses:

```
Sub MyCarObject_FuelLow
    ...            'switch the fuel-low light on
End Sub

Sub MyCarObject_Collision
    ...            'call the insurance company
End Sub
```

Collections

The final object concept we need to understand before digging into the object model is the idea of a collection–an easy way to group related objects together so they can be on as a unit. A car rental agency might keep a few collections of *Car* objects around. These collections might be called names like *AvailableCars*, *RentedCars*, and *WreckedCars* (these cars would probably have seen at least one *Collision* event). Collections are objects in their own right, and they have their own properties to show the status of the collection (like *Length*–the number of elements in the collection). They can also have their own methods and events, which will operate on the collection as a whole.

The Object Model in Action

Having looked at the basic objects, we need to know more about what exactly the browser object model enables us, as developers, to accomplish. What kind of access does it provide to the operation of the browser or to the HTML pages currently or previously displayed? What can you do with the object model to create new and exciting web pages and web applications? To discover the answer to these questions, we need to talk about the objects in the object model.

The Object Model Diagram

This diagram is intended to give you a feel for each object's place in the object model. There are a lot of different objects in the diagram, but don't worry as we'll be spending most of this and the next chapter going over them all so you can understand their use throughout the rest of the book and apply them in your own code.

The object model shows the 'hierarchical' relationships between different objects. The connections between the objects in model are arranged in a hierarchy because one object can often contain one (or more) of another object, rather like a parent having one or more children. There are also a number of important objects (like the **style** object that we talked about in the last chapter) that aren't an intrinsic part of the model at a high level, but are very important when we get into actually working with objects that the model provides.

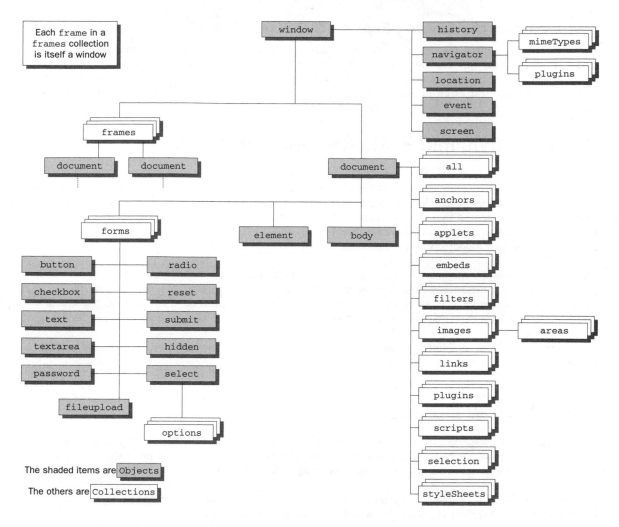

As you can see, the top-level object is the **window** object. This is the parent object of the entire model–we can think of all the other objects as being children of **window**. This object **contains** the focus of the next chapter, the **document** object–think of it in the same way as the browser window contains the HTML document.

The **window** object also contains a collection called **frames**. Each object in the **frames** collections represents a frame currently displayed in the browser. In addition to **document** and **frames**, the **window** object also **exposes** (makes available to the programmer) five separate objects: **history**, **navigator**, **location**, **event**, and **screen**. We'll talk more about these objects in this chapter and leave the rest of the **document** object's descendants (like the numerous collections) until the next chapter when we talk more about the **document** object.

While we've made the point (over and over again!) that the **window** object is the top-level object in the hierarchy, we need to modify our thinking just a bit when we work with frames. As we'll see in more detail a bit later in the chapter, each frame contains its own **window** object, with its own set of objects, properties, methods, and events.

Changes from the Internet Explorer 3.0 Object Model

If you have some experience with the Internet Explorer 3.0 object model you'll see many similarities between this diagram and the one you might be familiar with for Internet Explorer 3.0. You'll also notice a few differences. The basic layout of the object model hasn't changed, however, you'll see a lot of new objects, like **event** and **screen**, as well as a large number of new **document** collections. We'll cover each of these objects in turn in this and the next chapter.

The Wrox Dynamic HTML Reference Database

As you can start to appreciate when you begin to digest the diagram on the previous page, the Dynamic HTML object model encompasses nearly every part of the browser and displayed HTML document. This makes logical sense: we know that we can use Dynamic HTML to modify almost every part of the browser and the page and that the object model is the sole conduit between our code and the browser. From this follows the reasonable conclusion that the object model must expose all of this extensive functionality through its objects and collections.

The pages that follow explain what each object can accomplish and how the objects relate to each other. We talk about the most important properties, methods, and events. However, to save you from paging through endless amounts of material while you're trying to read and understand, we've placed the extensive reference section with descriptions of every interface element at the end of this book in Appendix D.

The same information, including any updates are available in a snazzy and easy to use Access 97 format database on the Wrox web site at **http://rapid.wrox.co.uk**.

The Window Object

The **window** object represents the browser itself. Since we start IE4 to view HTML documents and perform any other task using the browser it makes sense that the **window** object's properties, methods, and events concern themselves with the state and operations of the browser.

The **window** object has properties, methods, and events of its own as well as subsidiary objects. We'll cover the intrinsic interface elements below before moving onto the objects.

Properties

The following properties are available for the **window** object:

Property	Description
clientInformation	A reference that returns the **navigator** object for the browser
closed	A true or false value that indicates whether a window is closed
defaultStatus	The text that is displayed in the browser's status bar by default
dialogArguments	Returns arguments that were passed into a dialog window, as an array

Property	Description
`dialogHeight`	Sets or returns the height of a dialog window
`dialogLeft`	Sets or returns the x coordinate of a dialog window
`dialogTop`	Sets or returns the y coordinate of a dialog window
`dialogWidth`	Sets or returns the width of a dialog window
`document`	Read-only reference to the **window.document** object
`event`	Read-only reference to the global **event** object
`history`	Read-only reference to the **window.history** object
`length`	Returns the number of elements in a collection
`name`	The name of the window object
`navigator`	Read-only reference to the **window.navigator** object
`offScreenBuffering`	Specifies whether or not to use off-screen buffering for the document
`opener`	A reference to the window object that opened this window object
`parent`	A reference to the parent of the current window object (for use with frames)
`returnValue`	Allows a return value to be specified for the event or dialog window
`screen`	Read-only reference to the global **screen** object
`self`	A reference to the current window
`status`	Text displayed in the browser's status bar
`top`	A reference to the top-most window object (for use with frames)

> When using property, method or event names in JavaScript, you must be very careful, as JavaScript is case sensitive, so while `defaultStatus` would be a correct reference, `defaultstatus` would return an error. In VBScript however, either version would be acceptable!

The **opener**, **parent**, **self**, and **top** properties are useful when we write code that deals with more than one **window** object. As we'll discuss when we talk about the **frames** collection below, multiple **window** objects can come about when the page we're displaying has multiple frames and when we've explicitly created new windows with the **open** method (which we'll also discuss shortly).

The **dialogArguments**, **dialogHeight**, **dialogLeft**, **dialogTop** and **dialogWidth** properties can all be used to set the various properties of a dialog window, these are only available for Windows created using the **showModalDialog** method. We take a look at dialogs later in this chapter.

The other two useful properties are **defaultStatus** and **status**. Both of these properties control what is displayed in the status bar of the browser, when the page is first displayed and afterwards respectively.

Methods

While the properties of the `window` object are useful, in contrast to what you might see for many other objects, they aren't as numerous or wide-ranging as the window's methods:

Method	Description
`alert`	Displays an Alert-style dialog with a message and an OK button
`blur`	Causes the browser window to lose the focus and be placed at the back of the list of all non-minimized windows
`close`	Closes the current browser window
`confirm`	Displays a Confirm-style dialog with a message and OK and Cancel buttons
`focus`	Causes the window to gain focus (useful when used with references to other browser windows that don't have the focus)
`navigate`	Causes the browser window to navigate to the URL specified after the method name
`open`	Opens a new browser window using the options specified
`prompt`	Displays a prompt-style dialog box with an input text box and OK and Cancel buttons
`scroll`	Scrolls the window to the x and y position specified after the method name
`setTimeout`	Sets a timeout to execute a specific piece of code after a specified time interval
`clearTimeout`	Turns off a timeout that was set with the `setTimeout` method
`setInterval`	Sets an block of code that will execute repeatedly every x milliseconds
`clearInterval`	Turns off an interval that was set with the `setInterval` method
`execScript`	Executes a script (default language is JavaScript, not VBScript)
`showHelp`	Displays an HTML help window as a dialog
`showModalDialog`	Displays a new HTML window modally

Dialogs

The `window` object provides three methods that can be used to display dialogs commonly used for simple messages, confirmations, or prompts. The `alert` method displays a dialog with a text message and a single OK button; use it to give the user a message. `Confirm` is identical to `alert` but the dialog includes an additional Cancel button. Finally, the `prompt` method displays a dialog with a single line text box that can be used for input. These events are most useful when used with a scripting language (like JavaScript) that doesn't include basic dialogs in the language. VBScript provides more powerful equivalent statements that can be used instead of these methods.

The code next to each dialog below is all that is necessary to generate the displayed dialog.

Note that while **alert,** **confirm,** *and* **prompt** *are all methods of the* **window** *object, we haven't prefaced our calls with a '***window.** ' *We can do this because* **window** *is the default object for any script code. If we don't give the name of an object, the script interpreter will assume that we're calling a method or accessing a property of the* **window** *object.*

```
alert "This is an alert dialog"
```

```
confirm "This is a confirm dialog"
```

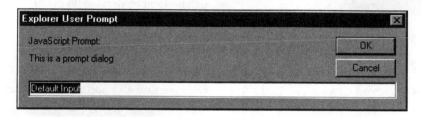

```
strReturnValue = prompt "This is a prompt dialog", "Default Input"
```

We'll usually use the **prompt** method when we care about what the user chooses. In our example above we've saved the text entered by the user in the string variable called **strReturnValue**. We can then use this variable to change the way the rest of our script code executes.

New Windows (Open, ShowModalDialog, and ShowHelp)

One of the most powerful methods in the Internet Explorer 3.0 object model was **open**, allowing new instances of Internet Explorer to be opened at will with a highly customizable list of features. Fortunately for us as developers, IE4 expands even further on this ability with more configuration options and the new **showModalDialog** method.

Open

The open method is called with this syntax:

```
Set objMyWindowRef = window.open (URL, name, features)
```

In this line of code, all three parameters are strings. URL is the only required argument – it specifies the URL of the document to be displayed in the new window. Name can be used to name the window, although this isn't as much use to us as the reference to the newly created window object that the open method returns to us. If we specify the name of a window that already exists, open will bring this window to the foreground instead of creating a new window. In our example line of code we're saving this reference in a variable called objMyWindowRef. Since this variable is a reference to another window object, any of the properties or methods we've talked about in this chapter can be used with this reference in the same way that we've used them with the window object where our code is executed.

The last parameter, features, is what gives us the fine level of control over the appearance of the new window. The following table shows the attributes that can be set with the features parameter.

Attributes	Values	Description
channelmode	yes | no | 1 | 0	Show channel controls
directories	yes | no | 1 | 0	Show directory buttons
fullscreen	yes | no | 1 | 0	Maximize new window or leave default size
height	*number*	Height of new window in pixels
left	*number*	Left position on desktop (in pixels)
location	yes | no | 1 | 0	Show the URL address text box
menubar	yes | no | 1 | 0	Show the default browser menus
resizeable	yes | no | 1 | 0	Window can or cannot be resized by user
scrollbars	yes | no | 1 | 0	Show vertical and horizontal scrollbars
status	yes | no | 1 | 0	Show the status bar at the bottom of the window
toolbar	yes | no | 1 | 0	Show the default browser toolbars
top	*number*	Desktop position (in pixels) of the new window
width	*number*	Width of the new window in pixels

The features string is formed by concatenating the values we would like to set with delimiting commas. Here's an example that opens the Wrox site and saves the window reference in a variable called objWinRef:

```
set objWinRef = window.open ("http://www.wrox.com", "MyWindow", "toolbar=no, left=150,
top=200, menubar=no, systemMenu=no")
```

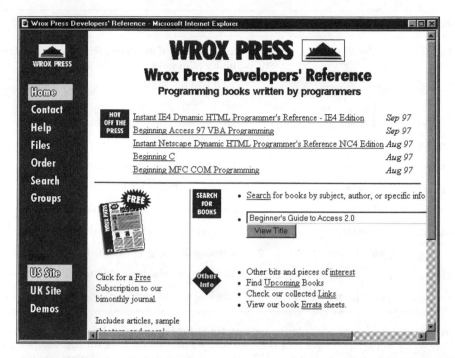

The **open** method returns a reference to the window that it opens. What does this mean? If we save the reference in a variable, like we do in the above example where it's saved in the variable called **objWinRef**, then we can control the window after it has been opened. To do this we use the same **window** object methods we've been talking about in this chapter. For example, to close the window in the same block of code that opened it, we would simply use this line of code:

```
objWinRef.close
```

Any of the other **window** methods and properties can also be used.

ShowModalDialog

The **showModalDialog** method is similar to **open** but has a few differences. It takes a feature string built the same way we build an **open** feature string, except that some of the options are different with a modal dialog.

Attributes	Values	Description
border	**thick	thin**	Size of border around window
center	**yes	no	1	0**	Center the dialog window with respect to the browser window that opens it
dialogHeight	*number & units*	Height of the dialog window in style sheet units specified
dialogLeft	*number & units*	Left position of the dialog window with respect to the desktop (in style sheet units specified)

Table Continued on Following Page

Attributes	Values	Description
dialogTop	*number & units*	Top position of the dialog window with respect to the desktop (in style sheet units specified)
dialogWidth	*number & units*	Width of the dialog window in style sheet units specified
font	*CSS string*	Default font and style for the dialog
font-family	*CSS string*	Default font for the dialog
font-size	*CSS string*	Default font size for the dialog
font-style	*CSS string*	Default font style for the dialog
font-variant	*CSS string*	Default font variant for the dialog
font-weight	*CSS string*	Default font weight for the dialog
help	yes | no | 1 | 0	Display the help button in the dialog title bar
maximize	yes | no | 1 | 0	Display the Maximize button in the title bar
minimize	yes | no | 1 | 0	Display the Minimize button in the title bar

Since we can now use CSS font attributes in our feature string, we have to format the string a bit differently. Instead of using equal signs and commas like we did with the **open** method, we'll create our features string in the same style as we create CSS formatting, using colons and semicolons.

Compare these strings:

```
strOpenFeatures = "toolbar=no, left=150, top=200, menubar=no, systemMenu=no"

strModalFeatures = "font-size:10;font-family:Times;dialogHeight:200px"
```

Since we're using CSS formatting, we need to remember to specify the unit for the size and position attributes. This is why we said **dialogHeight:200px** in the above example.

The method displays a new browser window, but makes this window modal to the browser it is shown from. This means that the user won't be able to switch back to work in the original browser until the modal browser instance is dismissed. It also means that any script code in the original browser stops execution while a modal dialog is displayed.

Modal dialogs look different to windows created with **open**. As we can see in the screen shot below, there is a lack of a system menu icon and minimize/maximize buttons of the type we'd see with an **open**-created window. How do we show a modal dialog? The next line of code creates the dialog shown in the screen shot. The first argument is simply the filename of the page to display. We've seen the third argument before also, when we worked with the **open** method (but remember that the table above shows the differences in what we can use with non-modal and modal windows). We'll talk about the second parameter in this call in just a few seconds.

```
DialogRef = showModalDialog ("blank.htm", 0, "toolbar=no")
```

This method can be very useful. Suppose we'd like to prompt our users for some information, but find the basic dialog we get with the **prompt** method too limiting. To display a custom prompt from our script and not take any action until the viewer of our page has responded to the prompt, we can create an HTML page that implements the prompt and then display the page using the **showModalDialog** method. For example, suppose we'd like to ask the user to choose between three different options. We would first create an HTML page that showed these options, perhaps using a set of radio buttons, and then we would show this page with the **showModalDialog** method. Our code would stop while the dialog was displayed, and when our code continued we could use the value that the user selected to determine how to proceed.

Since we now have the same ability to choose specific positions (using style sheets) as we do with environments like Visual Basic, we can use prompts and other specific forms in the same way that we use forms with Visual Basic and other rapid-application development tools.

As we saw above, the **showModalDialog** method takes a second parameter called **arguments** instead of **name**. We'll often want a way to pass information to the dialog, and to do this we can use the **arguments** string. Inside the code that may reside in the dialog's HTML page (remember, the page is created with HTML like any other we're using) we can access the **arguments** string and take appropriate action. For example, suppose we create an HTML page that contains a set of radio buttons, but we want to display different information in the text of the radio buttons each time the dialog is shown. If we wrote the code for our dialog so that it took the text from the **arguments** string, then changing the radio buttons would be a simple matter of changing the call to **showModalDialog**.

Finally, we've said that **showModalDialog** doesn't return a reference to a window like **open** does. Why? First of all, a reference wouldn't be much use to us, since, by definition, the code that creates a modal dialog stops until the dialog is dismissed. A reference to a non-existing window wouldn't do us any good! Secondly, since modal dialogs will often be used to create custom prompts, we want a way to return information from the dialog to the calling code, like the **prompt** dialog does.

For these reasons **showModalDialog** returns a string that can be set in the code that resides on the calling page.

ShowHelp

Online help is a necessity in today's computer applications. Since DHTML gives web authors the foundation they need to write full-featured applications with all the features and perks a native Windows application can provide, it's not surprising to see efforts to make it possible to provide online help in a web environment also. Microsoft has created a standard called HTML Help that allows help information to be displayed in a browser window that looks similar to the Help Topics window that Windows applications like Word and Excel display today.

IE4 is, in fact, one of the first HTML Help hosts. To see it, load up IE and click on the Content and Index menu item in the Help menu.

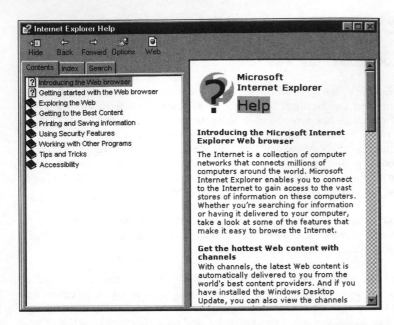

If you right click on the right-hand pane of the new dialog you'll see the familiar View Source option in the menu that proves that what you're seeing is indeed an HTML page.

So how does the **showHelp** method work anyway? It takes the URL of an HTML Help page, as well as a second optional parameter where arguments that control how the page is displayed can be specified.

For example, if we have an HTML Help page called **MyHelp.htm**, then we'd show it with this simple line of code:

```
showHelp "MyHelp.htm"
```

Timers

Using the **setTimeout, clearTimeout, setInterval**, and **clearInterval** methods of the **window** object we can automatically execute any code we've written after some time interval (that we set) has elapsed.

SetTimeout and ClearTimeout

setTimeout takes the name of a function, and a time value in milliseconds. After the time value has passed, the function is called automatically.

For example, the following code calls a routine named **TimerFunc** after 5000 milliseconds (5 seconds):

```
TimeoutID = Window.setTimeout ("TimerFunc",5000)
```

Once you've started a timer with **setTimout**, you may find that you want to cancel it so the function specified in the **setTimeout** call is not executed. This is where the **clearTimeout** function comes into play, assuming you've saved the return value of the **setTimeout** function, a number. In the line of code above we've saved our return value in a variable called **ID**, and it's this variable that we'll use in our call to clear the timer:

```
Window.clearTimeout TimeoutID
```

If you call `clearTimeout` with an ID value that doesn't exist, nothing will happen and any timers you have active will continue to work.

SetInterval and ClearInterval

The `setInterval` and `clearInterval` methods are new to IE4. They're called just like `setTimeout` and `clearTimeout`; the only difference is that the function specified in the call executes repeatedly, instead of just once, until the page is unloaded or the `clearInterval` method is called.

The following line of code starts the process of calling `TimerFunc` every 1 second.

```
IntervalID = setInterval("TimerFunc", 1000, VBScript)
```

To stop the repeated calling of this function, we'd just use this line of code:

```
clearInterval IntervalID
```

Window Control (focus, blur, scroll)

If we have a reference to a window, we can use the `focus`, `blur`, and `scroll` methods to control the instance of the browser. Firing the `blur` method causes the browser in question to lose the focus and be placed at the back of any non-minimized windows; the window that was immediately behind the browser before it lost focus is made the active window. After we've `blur`red a window, we can bring it back to the forefront by using the `focus` method.

The scroll method should be called like this:

```
windowref.scroll x, y
```

where **x** and **y** are pixel values that the top left corner of the document should be scrolled to.

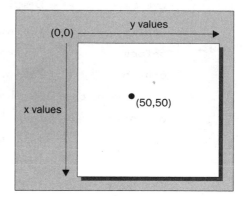

The top left hand of the document is defined to be point (0, 0), so:

```
scroll 0, 0
```

tells the browser to scroll the current document to the position it was displayed at originally. This line of code:

```
scroll 50, 50
```

scrolls the document to a position 50 pixels down the page and 50 pixels to the right. We'll use this method to do things like ensuring that a certain portion of the page is displayed in the viewer's copy of IE4.

Navigate

We've covered more than a several methods over the last couple of pages. Fortunately, the final **window** method we'll cover is much simpler. **Navigate** is powerful – it's used to load a different page into the current browser window. Calling it is simply a matter of specifying the method name and a URL string as the only parameter, like this:

```
navigate "http://www.wrox.com"
```

Using just a few lines of code with the **prompt** and **navigate** methods we can point a user's browser to a completely different site based their response to a simple question:

```
W3Cdhtml = prompt("Do you like IE4 - enter yes or no", "yes")
If W3Cdhtml = "yes" then
    navigate "http://www.microsoft.com"
Else
    navigate "http://www.netscape.com"
End If
```

Using the **navigate** method is the same thing as setting the **href** property of the **location** object, as we'll see in a bit when we cover **window**'s child objects.

Events

The **window** object contains the HTML document and has top-level events that make sense for this purpose:

Event	Description
onblur	Fired when the window object loses the focus
onfocus	Fired when the window object gains the focus
onhelp	Fired when the user presses the *F1* or *Help* key
onbeforeunload	Fired before the browser window is closed
onresize	Fired when the browser window is resized
onload	Fired when the HTML text for the page has finished loading
onunload	Fired just before the page is unloaded
onscroll	Fired when the user scrolls a page or element
onerror	Fired when an error occurs loading a document or image

OnLoad, OnUnload, onBeforeUnload

These events are very useful for executing any code that needs to coincide with the loading or unloading of the browser. **onLoad** is fired when the HTML for the current page has been downloaded, but may fire before all images, controls, or applets have finished loading.

The `onUnload` event is not only fired before the browser navigates to a new page, but also immediately before the browser is shut down (which is understandable, because the page is indeed being unloaded in preparation for application shutdown).

Finally, `onBeforeUnload`, fires before the page is unloaded. This event is only used during data binding and it allows you to validate entries in a field, before they're sent to a server, or pop a message box up. Its uses are discussed in the data binding section of the book in Chapter 8.

OnFocus and OnBlur

When the user of the browser switches to another application or instance of IE4, `onBlur` is fired. Any code placed in this event will be executed before the switch to the new window is made. The converse of `onBlur` is `onFocus`. This event is fired in the current browser when the user switches **back** to the browser window from another application. While `onFocus` and `onBlur` existed in the Internet Explorer 3.0 object model for some form elements, their appearance in the object definition for the `window` object didn't happen until IE4.

OnResize

This event is rather simple compared to some of the other events we've just finished considered. When the browser window is resized, this event is fired.

OnHelp

If a user presses *F1* (or another key that happens to be mapped to online help), the window's `onHelp` event is fired. This gives the developer control over what will happen if a person browsing their page requests help. The code for this event could redirect the user to one or more help pages on the same or another server on the internet/intranet. The new page can be displayed in a new window, in a modal dialog, or in the same browser window by using the `open`, `showModalWindow`, or `navigate` methods of the `window` object, respectively.

OnScroll

If not all of the display is visible to the user, and the user has to scroll the display to view it in its entirety, then an `onscroll` event is generated.

OnError

This is one of the most useful events. It can be used if an error occurs during the download of a page or image. It can be used to determine whether an error occurred to the connection or whether the download was actually aborted. The user can allow for this eventuality within script and decide whether to get the script to try and download the information again, or display an appropriate message and take corrective action.

The frames Collection

The last major element of the `window` object, aside from its descendant objects, is the `frames` collection. This collection exists to give a developer access to all of the frames in any frameset currently displayed in the browser.

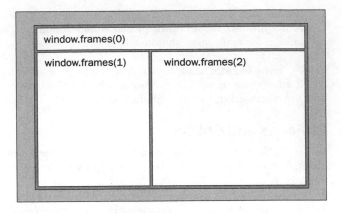

The **frames** collection is indexed from 0 so that a three-frame frameset, like the one that follows, has three elements in the **frames** collection, numbered from 0 to 2. It's important to note that this three-element collection is only seen from the top-level window–more about this in a second.

Each frame is a **window** object itself, and each frame reference returns a reference to a **window** object. All we need is a reference to a **window** object to enable our use of the properties and methods we've spent the last few pages discussing. It shouldn't be surprising then that the **frames** collection allows us to control each frame in a frameset as if we're controlling a separate window. In fact, this is exactly what we're doing. Each element in the **frames** collection is a reference to a new **window** object.

Accessing Collection Members by Index and Name

For example, this code changes the URL of the bottom left-hand frame in the frameset above:

```
window.frames(1).navigate "http://bossman"
```

In the above example we're referencing the frame object we want 'by index' which means we're using a number that refers to the frame. We can also access members of the **frames** collection (and other collections) 'by name' if we've specified an ID or name attribute when we created the element of the collection. For example, if the frameset with an index of 1 was named **leftHandFrame**, we could also access it with this code:

```
window.frames("leftHandFrame").navigate "http://bossman.com"
```

These naming methods work identically–they both return a reference to the same frame.

As we'll see when we talk about scripting in chapter six, we also have the **For Each** construct available to us for use with collections. We use **For Each** to iterate through each element in a collection.

The Frame as a Window Object

Now back to that cryptic statement about the top-level window that I made a second ago... The only other confusing aspect about the **frames** collection also arises from the fact that each frame is a **window** object in its own right. Think about the world from the point of view of the frame in our example indexed with the number 1. It doesn't contain any additional frames (although it could – its page would need to contain a **<FRAMESET>** tag with one or more **<FRAME>** tags). No contained frames means that the **frames** collection of the **frame(1)** should be empty, and this is exactly what we see if we query the **length** property of the collection in code. Its own **frames** collection has zero elements, but the page containing it owns three frames.

So how do we access another frame from our code in **frame(1)**? Remember the **top** and **parent** properties of the **window** object? These properties are the key to working with multiple frames in the browser object model. Before we can reference **frame(0)** or **frame(2)** from **frame(1)** we need to get a reference to the top-level **window** object so we can use its **frames** collection. This task is just as simple as using the code from **frame(1)**:

```
parent.frames(0).method
parent.frames(2).method
```

In this case, since we're only moving up a single level, **parent** and **top** return a reference to the same **window** object.If we were to work with a set of nested frames, we'd see that **top** always returns a reference to the top-most **window** object, while **parent** just returns a reference to the **window** object that is immediately above itself.

Generally we'll stick to using **parent** instead of **top** to avoid problems when our pages are viewed from another site. If a user browses to our framed pages from another site that uses frames then **top** will return a reference to the top-level frame from the first site. In this instance, assuming that **top** and **parent** are identical breaks our code.

Children of the Window Object

Despite the fact that we've spent some time on the intrinsic **window** elements, we still have a lot of browser functionality that we haven't covered yet. Instead of adding numerous new methods, properties, and events to the **window** object, the designers of the object model decided to group pieces of related functionality together into new objects and to make these objects children of the **window** object. As we'll see in a moment, these objects represent things like history list of the browser, the location currently shown, and information specific to the browser like its version and display properties. We'll cover each of these subsidiary, but still important, objects over the next few pages.

The Location Object

When we learned that the **navigate** method of the **window** object could be used to display a new URL, we alluded to a child object, called **location**.

The **location** object represents the current URL displayed by the browser. As you might expect, **location**'s properties give information about the URL and its methods allow us to modify the browser's current location, but in a rather different way than we do with **navigate**.

Properties

The properties of location reflect every last thing we could ever hope to know about the link the browser is currently displaying. The following table describes each property and gives the value that the property would return for a URL of **http://www.wrox.com:80/dhtml/book.htm?abc**.

Property	Value	Description
href	http://www.wrox.com:80/dhtml/book.htm?abc	Complete URL
protocol	http:	The protocol of the URL
host	www.wrox.com:80	Hostname and port number
hostname	www.wrox.com	Name of host
port	80	Port number (default is 80)
pathname	/dhtml/book.htm	Path after the host property
search	?abc	Any value after a '?' in the URL
hash	(nothing in this example – would contain any anchor specified with #)	Any value after a '#' in the URL

In our example we haven't specified that we want to jump to any bookmark that might exist in the document. To jump to the anchor named **two**, we'd use an address similar to this:

```
http://myserver/location.htm#two
```

In this case the **hash** property of the location object would contain the string '**#two**'.

If you look at the values for these properties a little closer, you'll see that the **href** property includes the information in all of the other properties. The browser parses the full **href** string and fills in the appropriate information for each property, saving us the trouble of interpreting the full string ourselves and making it easier to find any specific piece of information we might need without having to write explicit script code.

The other thing about the **href** property is how it's dynamically tied to the browser. Read the **href** property and nothing special will happen; change the **href** property and the browser will display the new page. Changing the browser's current URL in this manner is exactly the same as using the **window.navigate** method.

Methods

In the old Internet Explorer 3.0 object model, the **location** object had no methods. This has changed with IE4. We now have three methods that give us a bit more control over the browser's current location.

Method	Description
assign	Loads the page specified, equivalent to changing the **window.location.href** property
reload	Reloads the current page and displays any changes to the HTML source
replace	Navigates to the URL passed as a parameter and replaces the current page in the history list with this new page

With **assign** we can navigate to another page by passing the URL of the page when we call the method, like this:

```
location.assign("http://www.microsoft.com")
```

Using the **reload** method we can refresh the contents of a page we're viewing. While Internet Explorer 3.0 didn't have this method, we could achieve the same affect using the **go** method of the **history** object with a parameter of 0. This was an often-requested feature, and so it was given its own method in IE4.

Replace, on the other hand, is a completely new method that enables functionality we didn't have at all with Internet Explorer 3.0. The immediate effect is no different to the user than changing the **href** property or using the **navigate** method of the **window** object: the page the browser is displaying changes. The difference lies in what is added (or in this case not added) to the history list of the browser. When we change pages in a conventional manner, each new page is added to the end of Internet Explorer's history list, forming a queue of visited pages. In contrast, if we use **replace** to change our location, the current URL is overwritten by the new URL and won't remain in the history list.

The History Object

The **history** object contains information about all of the different URLs that a client has visited, stored in the history list of the browser.

Method	Description
back	Takes an integer and moves back this many places in the history list
forward	Takes an integer and moves forward this many places in the history list
go	Takes a string that represents all or part of a URL and attempts to move to this URL in the history list (also takes a positive or negative integer)

The **forward** and **back** methods work identically. Each method takes a positive integer and moves the specified number of places forward or back in the history list. The **go** method works similarly if the argument you pass is an integer. In this case a negative integer will move backwards and a positive integer forwards. With IE4 you can also pass the go method a string representing all or part of a URL. If this URL exists in the history list, the browser will display the page.

History's only property, **length**, shows the number of elements in a collection.

If you attempt to move past either the beginning or end of the history list with any of these methods, the browser won't raise an error. Instead you'll just be left at the page at the beginning or end of the history list

The **history** object can be used to create a very useful part of most web pages: a back button or link that doesn't require a hard-coded URL. Instead, we can just execute either of the following lines of code whenever the link or button is pressed:

```
history.back 1
```

or:

```
history.go -1
```

Both lines of code use the **history** object to move to the previous page in the history list.

The Navigator Object

Using the **navigator** object we can retrieve information about the capabilities and nature of the browser that is executing our code. If we'd like to execute different code for different browsers, this is the object for us.

Properties

Instead of describing what each of the properties do, it's easier to use some and demonstrate them by querying some of the recent release of Microsoft and Netscape browsers using this JavaScript code:

```
alert(navigator.appName);
alert(navigator.appVersion);
alert(navigator.appCodeName);
alert(navigator.userAgent);
alert(navigator.cookieEnabled);
```

The following table shows the values that IE4 returned:

Property	Value
appName	Microsoft Internet Explorer
appVersion	4.0 (compatible; MSIE 4.0; Windows NT)
appCodeName	Mozilla
userAgent	Mozilla/4.0 (compatible; MSIE 4.0; Windows NT)
cookieEnabled	True

For comparison here's the Navigator 4.02 values:

Property	Value
appName	Netscape
appVersion	4.02 [en] (WinNT; I; Nav)
appCodeName	Mozilla
userAgent	Mozilla/4.02 [en] (WinNT; I; Nav)
cookieEnabled	undefined

The values for Navigator 3.01:

Property	Value
appName	Netscape
appVersion	3.01 (WinNT; I)
appCodeName	Mozilla
userAgent	Mozilla/3.01 (WinNT; I)
cookieEnabled	True

And also the values for Internet Explorer 3.01:

Property	Value
appName	Microsoft Internet Explorer
appVersion	2.0 (compatible; MSIE 3.01; Windows NT)
appCodeName	Mozilla
userAgent	Mozilla/2.0 (compatible; MSIE 3.01; Windows NT)
cookieEnabled	True

The **appName** and **userAgent** properties (and their derivatives **appVersion** and **appCodeName**) reflect the browser that is executing the script code.

> *In case you haven't heard the explanation behind the Mozilla code name yet… it goes like this: Marc Andreesen who helped to develop the Mosaic browser while in college, once he left, founded Netscape, and started work on a browser that should 'beat its chest and smash Mosaic. '**Mo**saic + Godzilla = Mozilla. Get it?*

Methods

There are two methods of the **navigator** object.

Methods	Description
javaEnabled	Returns true or false depending on whether a Java VM is installed or not
taintEnabled	Returns false, included for compatibility with Netscape Navigator – the title seems to be Microsoft's little joke!

Collections

There are two collections of the **navigator** object as well.

Collections	Description
plugins	An alias for the collection of all the **<EMBED>**ded objects in the page
mimeTypes	Collection of all the document and file types supported by the browser

The Screen Object

If you're curious about the capabilities of the display your code is executing on or if you want to change the display of your page depending on the pixel and color resolution the browser is running at then the **screen** object provides you with the capability to accomplish these tasks.

Property	Value
width	returns the width of the user's display, in pixels
height	returns the height of the user's display, in pixels
updateInterval	sets or returns the interval between screen updates
bufferDepth	returns or changes the color depth of the off-screen bitmap buffer
colorDepth	returns the currently supported color depth for the browser

height and **width** simply return the height and width of the screen. These are useful when creating new browser windows as they can be used to help decide where the new window should go. You can also use them to change the size of the existing display.

The **colorDepth** property tells us how many bits per pixel the browser currently has available for displaying different colors. With one bit per pixel we can display $2^1 = 2$ different colors, with 4 bits per pixel we can display $2^4 = 16$ different colors, and so on. Most displays today have at least 256 colors per pixel available and some may have over 16 million different colors. One immediate use for this property is in determining how many different colors to use on our page or in graphics that we might display. If a display can only handle 16 colors, and we have a 16 color and 16 million color JPEG to choose from the **colorDepth** property can allow us to give the high resolution image only to the person with the high resolution monitor. To do this in code we'd just need to change the URL of the **<IMG>** tag to point to the correct graphic.

In this case, our code would look something like this:

```
<SCRIPT LANGUAGE="VBScript">
If screen.colorDepth > 4 Then
    document.writeln "<IMG SRC=""manycolor.jpg"">"
Else
    document.writeln "<IMG SRC=""fewcolor.jpg"">"
End If
</SCRIPT>
```

This code block tests the value of the **colorDepth** property and then outputs a string to the browser that either references the **manycolor.jpg** file if the display is capable of more than 2^4 or 16 colors or the **fewcolor.jpg** file otherwise. The next chapter talks more about the **document.write** method that we're using in this example to create HTML as the page is loaded.

Using the read/write **bufferDepth** property, we can instruct the browser to buffer all input off-screen before display with whatever color depth we desire–it's as simple as setting **screen.bufferDepth** to the number of pixels you'd like. **bufferDepth** can handle values of 0 (the default), 1, 4, 8, 15, 16, 24, and 32, as well as -1 (indicating that buffering should always be performed at the screen depth). Yes, this means that if you've always wanted to know what your pages looked like with two colors you now have your chance! When the **bufferDepth** property is set to the default of 0, the browser may buffer the input, but it isn't required to do so.

The Event Object

The **event** object is a subsidiary object of **window**, but we won't spend too much time covering it here. Instead, we'll wait for chapter 5 when we talk more about scripting, as this is when the properties will come in to use – in conjunction with the events that have been triggered by the browser and identified in the scripting code.

The objects we've talked about so far generally have reflected concrete parts of the window or browser. Many of them can't even be changed, and they're all around at all times for querying if not modifying. The **event** object, in contrast, is a much more ephemeral beast. It furnishes specific information about the event last fired by the browser and can and will be very different from one instant to the next. The different properties of **event** tell things like the state of the *Ctrl*, *Alt*, and *Shift* keys when the event was first fired, whether or not any mouse buttons were pressed, and so on.

Property	Value
altKey	The state of the *Alt* key
button	The mouse button(s), if any, that was (were) pressed to fire the event
cancelBubble	Stops the current event from bubbling up the hierarchy
clientX	The x coordinate of an element, excluding borders, margins, scrollbars etc
clientY	The y coordinate of an element, excluding borders, margins, scrollbars etc
ctrlKey	The state of the *Ctrl* key
fromElement	Specifies the element being moved from (for **onmouseover** and **onmouseout** events)
keyCode	ASCII code of the key being pressed (if a key has been pressed)
offsetX	the x coordinate of the mouse pointer when an event occurs, relative to the containing element
offsetY	The y coordinate of the mouse pointer when an event occurs, relative to the containing element
returnValue	Sets the return value for the event

Property	Value
screenX	The x coordinate of the mouse pointer when an event occurs, relative to the screen
screenY	The y coordinate of the mouse pointer when an event occurs, relative to the screen
shiftKey	The state of the *Shift* key
srcElement	The deepest element that the event occurred over
srcFilter	Specifies the filter that caused the element to produce an **onfilterchange** event
toElement	Specifies the element being moved to (for **onmouseover** and **onmouseout** events)
type	Returns the name of the event as a string, without the **on** prefix, such as **mouseover** instead of **onmouseover**
x	The horizontal position of the mouse in window coordinates (pixels)
y	The vertical position of the mouse in window coordinates (pixels)

This object is extremely useful when we write script code and perform exotic sounding things like 'event-bubbling'. However, we'll avoid discussing any of the properties until Chapter 5 of this book, as you'll need to understand how events can be caught by your scripting code first.

Summary

In this chapter we've gained a thorough introduction to three of the most important parts of Dynamic HTML: the browser object model, the **window** object, and most of **window**'s child objects. We looked at the reasons why the browser object model is important to Dynamic HTML programmers although held back from giving complex examples of how it can be manipulated via script code. We looked at how the object model is use to hide us from the internal operations of the browser itself. We considered the top level object, **window** and looked at its most significant properties, methods and events. We finally looked at all of the child objects of **window** to round off this chapter.

Specifically, we learned that:

- ▲ The browser object model is the interface between our script code and the browser itself.

- ▲ Through the properties, methods, and events of the different objects in the object model, we can find out about objects, tell them to perform tasks, and be notified when something happens to the object.

- ▲ The **window** object is the top-level object in the object model, and, while it has a lot of significant elements, this doesn't necessarily make it the most important object we'll use in Dynamic HTML programming.

- ▲ A number of child **window** objects allow us to do things like access the browser's history list, find out information about the browser's version and display properties, and more

With this foundation in the object model, we're ready to move on to discuss the most important child of the **window** object, the **document** object. In the next chapter we'll be able to find out why this provides Dynamic HTML programmers with the functionality needed to manipulate individual elements on the web pages, such as text and graphics, something that was never possible in previous Internet Explorer releases.

The Document Object

We spent the previous chapter talking about many of the objects that make up the browser object model. We included a detailed discussion of the **window** object and its children. In fact, we covered everything barring the **document** object. This is the object that represents the HTML document in the browser window. We've kept discussion of this object separate, because it is arguably the most important object in the IE4 object model. Not only can you retrieve information about the web page displayed in the browser window, via the different properties and methods of this object, but you can also now modify the elements on the page, such as the text and graphics.

This forms a radical new innovation in HTML, and is part of the reason behind the new language being christened Dynamic. Previously pages were static in that, once they had been created, there was nothing the user could do change them without a page refresh. However it's the changes to the **document** object that now allow the user to manipulate the different elements on screen, such as dragging and dropping images or simply animating them. All of these properties and methods have now become alterable with scripts. Another change is a separate object, **textRange**, can be used in conjunction with the document object to allow the user cut and paste blocks of text and even move them about the page, as though they were using a word processor. It allows a new flexibility in web pages, unheard of even in Internet Explorer 3.

In this chapter we'll talk about:

- ▲ How the **document** object fits into the overall browser object model
- ▲ The direct properties, methods, and events of the **document** object
- ▲ The many different types of collections used by **document** to provide access to the elements of the HTML page
- ▲ Managing blocks of text with Dynamic HTML's **textRange** object and the new text properties
- ▲ Using the **selection** object

As before, we won't use this chapter to explain how to write large blocks of script code that use the **document** object or its important members. We also won't give detailed syntax recitations–you can find these in reference section D, on the browser object model. Instead, we'll show why the **document** object is so important, and how traits of its elements can be used together with the rest of the object model to fully utilize Dynamic HTML.

Document and the Browser Object Model

In the IE3 object model, **document** was significant, but the magnitude of its importance has increased greatly with the advent of Dynamic HTML. Before, we could only change the text of the page as it was loaded, and the only parts of the page that could respond to events and be controlled by script code were form elements. As we've seen from the new features we've introduced already, Dynamic HTML is completely different. HTML pages can now be truly dynamic–the pages themselves can change while displayed in the browser. The model's **document** object has changed to make this possible.

An Overview of the Document Object

The document object encapsulates the HTML page currently in the browser and its properties and collections represent each and every last element on the page.

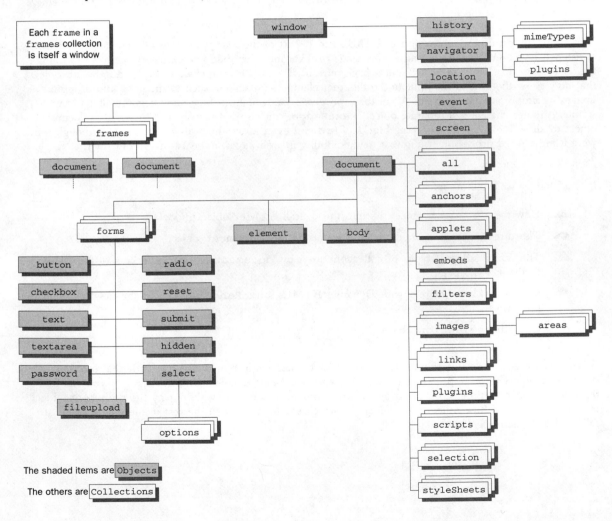

In the diagram above, you see the **document** object at the center with its children arranged about it. It has a host of properties, methods, and events that relate to the HTML page, as a whole, just as the **window** object's interface includes objects that relate to the window.

The children of the **document** object include the **selection** object and a number of collections representing sets of objects that abound on a typical HTML page, like **anchors**, **links**, and **images**. The **all** collection is a set of all of the elements and tags within the body of the document—we devote a whole section to discussing this important (and somewhat out of the ordinary) collection. The diagram is rounded out by the **forms** collection and a few representative **element** objects.

> *An **element** object is simply an HTML form element, and, not surprisingly, we see that the **forms** collection has **elements** beneath it. With these **element** objects we can do things like stopping the submission of a form, as you'll see later in the chapter.*

Changes from the Internet Explorer 3.0 Document Object

While the purpose and importance of the document object has intensified with Dynamic HTML, the actual object model doesn't look much different. The main differences are the addition of many new collections (the old object model had only **anchor**, **links**, and **forms**, **elements** and **scripts** collections) and the **selection** object. As small as these changes may seem, it is these new collections, along with additional properties, methods, and events for objects all across the board, produce a completely new environment for HTML authors and script developers.

Document's Place in the Browser Object Model

From a glance back at the browser object model diagram in the last chapter you can see that the **document** object assumes a position completely out of proportion with its small size on that diagram. You might remember that we have a separate **document** object for each **window** object we can access in script code. This means that when a page without any frames is displayed in our browser, we'll have one **window** object and one **document** object. Also, each frame in a frameset has its own **window** object, and, subsequently, its own **document** object. Each **window** has its own associated **document** object, and a **document** can't exist without a **window** object.

The diagram to the right shows what a page with two frames looks like to the browser object model.

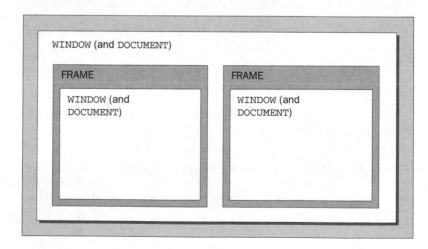

The top-level `window` object contains two child `window` objects, so we total three `window` objects all together. Since a `window` always has a `document` object attached, we also have three `document` objects.

The Document Object

As we did with the `window` object, we'll talk about the `document` object's interface before we spend time with the subsidiary collections and other objects that complement the features of `document`.

Properties

`Document`'s properties range from the file information for the current page's HTML file to domain and HTML cookies associated with the URL.

Property	Description
`activeElement`	A reference to the element that currently has the focus
`alinkColor`	The color for active links on the page (active links are links that are currently being clicked)
`bgColor`	The color of the page background
`body`	Read-only reference to the document's `body` object (defined by the `<BODY>` tag)
`cookie`	The cookie (if any) associated with the currently displayed page
`domain`	The root domain of the current document (discussed below)
`lastModified`	The last modified date of the file
`linkColor`	The color of unvisited links on the page
`location`	The location of the current page (can be set to redirect the browser)
`parentWindow`	The parent window that contains the document
`readyState`	The state of downloaded objects on the page
`referrer`	The URL of the page that referred to this page (the last clicked page)
`selection`	Read-only reference to the document's selection object
`title`	The title of the page as set by the `<TITLE>` tag
`url`	The uniform resource locator of the currently displayed document
`vlinkColor`	The color of visited links on the page

While many of these properties are rather self-explanatory, there are a few that deserve a comment or two, and we'll discuss these properties in more detail later. We'll talk about `readyState` and `activeElement` first, then cover the `cookie` property, domains, and document colors.

Page Status

The two new **readyState** and **activeElement** properties provide functionality we didn't have with Internet Explorer 3.0 and can be extremely useful when writing Dynamic HTML code.

readyState

As we saw in the last chapter, the **window** object's **onLoad** event is fired when the base HTML for the page has been downloaded and displayed. However, **onLoad** doesn't give us any information about the state of the objects and images on the page. Often we don't want to execute certain portions of script code unless we're sure that the objects we will be working with have completely downloaded and are operational.

Now, with the **readyState** property of the **document** object, we can check the page's objects download status. This property can return up to four different values depending on the state of the document, and these values are outlined in the table below. In a few pages when we move onto events, we'll see the important and complementary **onReadyStateChange** event that is fired whenever this property changes.

Value	Description
uninitialized (0)	Objects aren't created
loading (1)	Objects are currently loading
interactive (2)	Objects can be interacted with, but aren't fully loaded yet
complete (3)	Objects are fully loaded and can be interacted with completely

The page level **readyState** property is a compilation of the individual **readyState** properties of Java applets, images, controls, and script blocks on the page. Each of these elements has their own **readyState** property that can return any of the four values mentioned above. Each element is responsible for providing its own response to this query–the object model just forwards it along to the developer. The descriptions of each event are the guidelines that an applet or control author should follow when deciding what to return as their component is downloaded and initialized.

To check the download status of the whole page we can use a simple block of code like this:

```
fReady = document.readyState

If fReady = 3 Then
     'Code for fully loaded page
Else
     'Code for page still loading
End If
```

If we're waiting to perform some task when the page has reached a certain state, we can also use the **onReadyStateChange** event.

activeElement

Via the **activeElement** property, a script can access the element that currently has the focus. This property provides a reference to this element, so any of its properties can be accessed or its methods invoked. For example, we can use the **ID** or **name** property of the element (depending on which one it has) properties to determine exactly which element is selected. For example, the following two lines of code display the current element's name or ID in a message box:

```
MsgBox document.activeElement.name
MsgBox document.activeElement.ID
```

The Cookie Property

Cookies are items of information held by the browser and transmitted to the server as part of the request for each page. Web sites and pages can use the cookie they receive from a browser to determine if the browser that is accessing the site has visited before, and, if it has things like what pages were viewed, what items might have been purchased at the site, and so on. Because cookies are domain-specific we know that the browser will only transmit cookies placed by site **www.xyz.com** back to site **www.xyz.com** (the specific path within a domain can also be set). This security measure prevents other sites from accessing a cookie that has been placed on the browser by a different site.

Using the **cookie** property we can read and set the cookie associated with the page. Normally, a cookie is made up of a set of key / value pairs, like this:

```
MyKey1=MyValue1, MyKey2=MyValue2
```

After retrieving the cookie into a local variable, we only need to use the scripting language's string manipulation functions to retrieve any portion of the cookie that we desire.

Cookies can also be used solely on the client-side to exchange information between pages, store configuration options used by the page to determine how to display itself, and to initialize script variables to the state they were in when the page was last viewed. By setting the **cookie** property of the document with a key / value pair that holds a variable name and its value, we can retain the contents of variables across pages. This method only works with text and numerical values—it doesn't work with object references—but it can still be very useful.

To save a variable we need a line of code like this, where **VariableName** is the name of the variable we're saving and **VariableValue** is the value:

```
document.cookie = VariableName & "=" & VariableValue
```

To read this variable back (on the same or other page) we'll use the VBScript **Instr** and **Mid** functions to determine where the variable exists in the cookie string. The following code finds the value for a variable whose name is stored in the variable **VariableName**.

```
iVariableLocation = Instr(document.cookie, VariableName)
sShortString = Right(document.cookie, Len(document.cookie) -    iVariableLocation + 1)
iNextSemicolon = Instr(sShortString, ";")

'if we don't find a semi-colon we need the last element of the cookie
If iNextSemicolon = 0 Then iNextSemicolon = Len(sShortString) + 1

'check for empty variable
If iNextSemicolon = (Len(VariableName) + 2) Then
    'variable is empty
    VariableValue = ""
Else
```

```
    'calculate value normally
    iValueLength = iNextSemicolon - (Len(VariableName)) - 2
    VariableValue = Mid(sShortString, (Len(VariableName)) + 2, iValueLength)
End If
```

This code uses **Instr** to find the location of the variable and **Right** to chop off anything on the left of the relevant part of the cookie string. This shortens the cookie string to something a bit more manageable. We then use **Instr** again to find the location of the next semi-colon–this lets us rule out the right most part of the cookie string and use **Mid** to find the actual value of the variable. If we don't find a semi-colon we know that the value we're looking for is the last value in the cookie string and we can adjust our search accordingly.

After this lengthy bit of code we can display the value of the variable with this code:

```
MsgBox VariableValue
```

> *This code was based on a sample on the Microsoft VBScript site at* **http://www.microsoft.com/vbscript/us/samples/cookies/extcookie.htm**. *The sample at this site includes more robust error checking.*

Domains

With the additional abilities of IE4 has come the need for greater security. We know that script code in one frame of a frameset can access the elements of another frame, which raises the question of when and how we should restrict access from one frame to another. Therefore IE4 won't allow script code from a page that originates in one domain to access a page that comes from a different domain. We can see the current domain by using the **document** object's **domain** property.

A domain is the first part of the address used to access a page. Code that resides in a page that originates from the main Wrox site has a domain of **www.wrox.com**. Code on a page from this site would be able to access other pages from the Wrox site, but wouldn't be able to access any pages from the **www.microsoft.com** site.

The above restriction can even come into play when developing pages at home on a single computer if you're running a web server for testing purposes. The **domain** properties of a page served from a local web server and on a page accessed via the file system (**C:** instead of **http://**) will be different. Script code on a page that comes from the file system will be restricted from accessing properties on the pages that came from the local web server or vice-versa.

Document Colors

Before style sheets, the major source of control HTML authors had over the color of the text and links on the page was via HTML attributes of the **<BODY>** tag. These color attributes can be used to set the page's foreground and background colors, as well as the colors of the links on the page. Not surprisingly, the color properties of the document object reflect these HTML attributes.

The **fgColor** and **bgColor** properties reflect and change the foreground and background colors respectively. Also **aLinkColor**, **vLinkColor**, and **linkColor** set the link colors for the page. Internet Explorer 3.0 only implemented **vLinkColor** and **linkColor** – it did nothing with active (currently clicked) links. IE4 fully implements this concept, and so we can see the effect of setting all three of the link color properties.

The following HTML code first creates a button element called **btnColors**. The script following the HTML is only run when the button is clicked. This code allows the viewer of the page to change any of the document colors.

```
<INPUT TYPE="BUTTON" NAME="btnColors" VALUE="Colors">

<SCRIPT LANGUAGE="VBScript">
Sub btnColors_onClick
    document.bgColor = prompt("Enter bgColor", document.bgColor)
    document.fgColor = prompt("Enter fgColor", document.fgColor)
    document.vLinkColor = prompt("Enter vLinkColor", document.vLinkColor)
    document.aLinkColor = prompt("Enter aLinkColor", document.aLinkColor)
    document.linkColor = prompt("Enter linkColor", document.linkColor)
End Sub
</SCRIPT>
```

Here we use **prompt** method of the window object (covered last chapter) to ask the viewer to enter values for each of the **document** object properties. The first parameter to **prompt** is the text that should be displayed in the dialog. In our code we're just informing the viewer which color they're changing. The second **prompt** parameter is the default value that will be returned if the user just presses the OK button. In our example we set this value to the current value of the color by reading the appropriate property.

You can see this demonstrated on a color selector page on the Wrox site at `http://rapid.wrox.co.uk/books/0707/`. *It can be used to find the hexadecimal values for any color under the sun.*

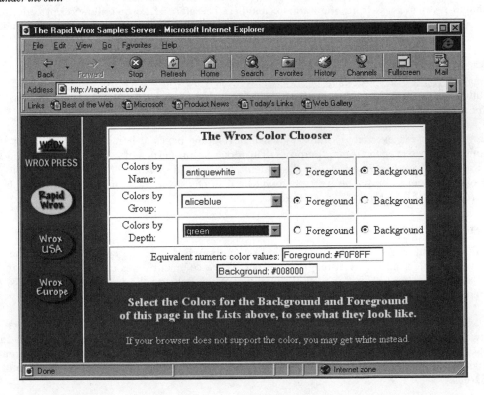

In general, any values set with a style sheet will override document's color properties. For example, suppose we set the color of one heading to green with a style sheet but leave other headings alone, and then later change the `fgColor` of this single heading to red. All of the headings except for the one we explicitly specified to be green will change to red.

Methods

The `document` object also supports a wide variety of methods that can do everything from creating HTML elements on the fly to opening new browser windows.

Method	Description
clear	Clears the document stream of all text
close	Closes the current document stream, forcing display
createElement	Creates the element specified by the tag passed as a parameter
elementFromPoint	Returns a reference to the element and the **x** and **y** coordinates passed as parameters
execCommand	Executes a command over the selection or range
open	Opens a document stream to collect the output of **write** and **writeln** methods
queryCommandEnabled	Whether or not a specified command is available
queryCommandIndeterm	Whether or not a specified command is in an indeterminate state
queryCommandState	The current state of the command
queryCommandSupported	Whether or not the specified command is support
queryCommandText	The string associated with a command
queryCommandValue	The value associated with the command
write	Writes text to a document stream
writeLn	Writes text terminate by a new-line character to the document stream

Again, we'll cover the most interesting of these methods. We've given some details of the syntax of the most important methods below, but for full details you should refer to reference section D on the object model.

Creating and Referencing Objects

`createElement` and `elementFromPoint` are completely new methods to IE4 and can be considered truly "dynamic".

createElement

This method can be used to dynamically create an `<IMG>`, `<OPTION>`, or `<AREA>` tag by passing the tag as a parameter.

Using this method we can, for example, dynamically changing the contents of a `<SELECT>` list box by adding new `<OPTION>` tags–something we couldn't hope to do without Dynamic HTML.

To see this in action, load the following page into your browser.

```
<HTML>
<BODY>

<CENTER>
<SELECT ID="MyCombo" SIZE=10>
    <OPTION VALUE="1">Element 1
    <OPTION VALUE="2">Element 2
</SELECT><P>
<INPUT TYPE="BUTTON" NAME="btnAdd" VALUE="Add OPTION">
</CENTER>

<SCRIPT LANGUAGE="VBScript">
Sub btnAdd_onClick
    Set objNewEl = document.createElement("OPTION")
    objNewEl.text = prompt("Enter element text")
    objNewEl.value = prompt("Enter element value")
    MyCombo.add objNewEl
End Sub
</SCRIPT>

</BODY>
</HTML>
```

You will see a button and a list box containing two entries. Press the Add OPTION button, answer the prompts, and then see that the new element is dynamically added to the `<SELECT>` list box.

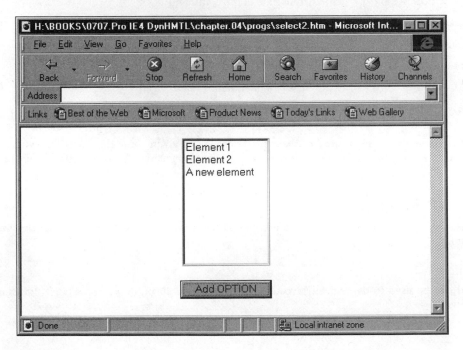

You can run this code on the Wrox Rapid site at http://rapid.wrox.co.uk/books/0707

The code in this example is simple. We use the **createElement** method to give birth to a new option object and we save a reference to this object in the **objNewEl** variable. After this step the rest of our code uses **prompt** to ask the viewer for the text and value portions of the new element. Finally, we pass the object reference stored in **objNewE** to the add method of the **<SELECT>** element to get the new element to show up in our list box.

elementFromPoint

The **elementFromPoint** method takes a set of x and y coordinates and returns a reference to the element at this point.

Given two variables, **xVal** and **yVal**, that store the pixel coordinates we want to find the element for, this line of code is all that is necessary to print out the name of the tag that creates the element:

```
set objCurrent = document.elementfrompoint (xVal, yVal)
MsgBox objCurrent.TagName
```

Since **elementFromPoint** just returns a reference to the element, we can call any of its methods or access any of its properties: the possibilities are enormous

Inline HTML Generation

Any script code that resides outside of a function or subroutine will be executed as the HTML for the page is parsed. Using the document methods **open**, **write**, **writeln**, and **close**, we can generate new HTML as the page is loaded.

To create inline HTML as the page is parsed, we **open** a document stream by calling **document.open**. After the stream is ready for input, we can write to it with **write** and **writeln**. **write** and **writeln** are identical for almost all HTML. Carriage returns have no effect on HTML source unless they're located inside a **<PRE>...</PRE>** block; **writeln** only causes different behavior if it is used inside a **<PRE>** tag (or with script code – see below). Once we've finished creating our HTML code, we can close the document stream with the **close** method. The Internet Explorer documentation recommends using **open** and **close** with **write** and **writeln** although it isn't strictly necessary to produce working code – **write** and **writeln** will work identically without these method calls.

Let's revisit the **screen** object example we saw in the last chapter. That example and the following code, both use the **writeln** method to generate the HTML source for an image tag:

```
<SCRIPT LANGUAGE="VBScript">
If screen.colorDepth > 4 Then
    document.writeln "<IMG SRC=""manycolor.jpg"">"
Else
    document.writeln "<IMG SRC=""fewcolor.jpg"">"
End If
</SCRIPT>
```

When the page is parsed, the **colorDepth** property of the **screen** object is checked and only the appropriate **<IMG>** tag is added to the document stream. We need to remember the difference between **write** and **writeln** when using these document methods to generate HTML. While white space isn't generally important to HTML, it is **very** important to script code. The difference between the following two blocks of code is great—one causes an error and one works!

```
MsgBox "First string"
MsgBox "Second String"
```

```
MsgBox "First String"MsgBox "Second String"
```

Finally, let's cover the **clear** method. Although this method is documented, it doesn't do anything on IE4. Netscape Navigator invented this method, but, according to the Microsoft documentation, its implementation is too flaky to be emulated. Calling **open** again after **open** has already been called (but before calling **close**) should clear the document stream, although this operation is also unreliable - both in Navigator and IE4!

The Query Methods and execCommand

The six methods that begin with QueryCommand, like **QueryCommandText** and **QueryCommandValue**, and the **execCommand** method, are designed to be used when the browser is being controlled by an external application or when it is embedded as part of an external application. In this book, we've focused on IE4 from the inside out, so we won't concern ourselves with these methods. We can do everything we want with just the internal object model's properties, methods, and events.

Events

Finally we need to consider the **document** object's events.

Event	Description
onafterupdate	Fired when the data transfer from element to provider (the data source) is complete
onbeforeupdate	Fired immediately before changed data is transferred from an element to a provider (when an element loses focus or the page is unloaded)
onclick	Fired when the mouse button is clicked on the document
ondblclick	Fired when the mouse button is double clicked on the document
ondragstart	Fired when the user first starts to drag an object
onerror	Fired when an error loading a document or image arises
onhelp	Fired when the *F1* key (or another key mapped to online help) is pressed
onkeydown	Fired when a keyboard key is pressed (before **onkeypress**)
onkeypress	Fired when a keyboard key is pressed and continues to fire if it is held down(after **onkeydown**, before **onkeyup**)
onkeyup	Fired when a keyboard key is released
onload	Fired when the document has completed loading
onmousedown	Fired when a mouse button is pressed
onmousemove	Fired when the user moves the mouse over the document
onmouseout	Fired when the mouse leaves an element

Event	Description
`onmouseover`	Fired when the mouse first moves over an element
`onmouseup`	Fired when the mouse button is released
`onreadystatechange`	Fired when the **readystate** property has changed
`onselectstart`	Fired when the user first starts to select the contents of an element

Many of the **document** object's events support the script concept called **event bubbling**. This means that we can write a handler at the document level for an event like **onClick** that might be fired by a number of different elements on an HTML page. If the child object that actually raises the event doesn't handle it completely, it can pass it along to the **onClick** events of its parent objects. The **document** object is the last object in what might be a relatively long chain of objects that can handle an event. We'll talk more about event bubbling in the next chapter.

Mouse and Keyboard Events

Most of the mouse and keyboard events are pretty self-explanatory. Click a mouse button and get an **onClick** event, double click a mouse button and get an **onDoubleClick** event (and an **onClick** event first!), and so on.

When using the keyboard events it's important to remember the order that the three events are fired. Pressing a key first causes the **onKeyDown** event to fire, followed by **onKeyPress**, and finished up with **onKeyUp**.

The **onMouseOver** and **onMouseOut** events are relevant for objects contained in the HTML page. These events can be used, in conjunction with the **event** object's **toElement** and **srcElement** properties, when working with dragged elements. They can also be used, like the **onMouseMove** event can, to change an element when the mouse is moved over it.

Page Condition Events

These events give information about two new features included with Internet Explorer: the ability to check the download status of page elements, and data-binding.

onReadyStateChange

The **onReadyStateChange** event fires whenever the **readyState** property of the **document** object changes. This event doesn't include any parameters but the current page condition can be checked by simply reading from the **readyState** property.

As discussed earlier in this chapter, **ReadyState** can hold these four different values: **uninitialized** (0); **loading** (1); **interactive** (2); and **complete** (3).

Sometimes we want to execute certain code when the **readyState** property changes. If we're waiting for all of the elements on the page to finish loading we'll want to execute code when **readyState** changes to 3. To do this in code we'd write an event handler looking like this:

```
Sub Document_onReadyStateChange
    If readyState = 3 Then
        'execute code for fully loaded page
```

```
        End If
    End Sub
```

Data Binding

The `onBeforeUpdate` and `onAfterUpdate` events are relevant to HTML elements that are bound to data sources using IE4's data-binding functionality. We won't even begin to cover this important and very useful topic right here; this is best left until the next section of this book.

Collections

While the aforementioned properties, methods, and events are useful, you'll have noticed that none of them provide explicit access to the actual elements on the page. However we've been billing the main advantage of the `document` object as the unique ability to manipulate every page element with Dynamic HTML. It's the collections that provide the much-needed access. Previously, we only had access to a few of the collections on the page, but now we have access to much more of the document via the large number of new `document` object collections.

Collection	Description
`all`	All the tags and elements in the document
`anchors`	The anchors in the document
`applets`	The applets in the document
`embeds`	The `<EMBED>` tags in the document
`forms`	References to the forms in the documents
`frames`	The same frames collection available via the window object
`images`	The images in the document
`links`	The hyperlinks in the document
`plugins`	The same collection as the embed collection
`scripts`	The `<SCRIPT>` sections in the document
`stylesheets`	The style objects defined in the document

These collections work the same way as the `frames` collection. Each collection exposes a `length` property that holds the number of elements currently in the collection and each element is accessible either by index or by name. For example, suppose we'd defined the first link on a page with this HTML:

```
<a href="http://myserver/page1.htm" id="linkone">Page 1</a><p>
```

To obtain a reference to the first link on the page and to print the `href` property we could use either of the following lines of code:

```
msgbox document.links(0).href
```
or
```
msgbox document.links("linkone").href
```

All of the collections that the **document** object exposes work like this–they can be accessed by a numeric index or by the name of the element as defined in the HTML.

Page Text: The All Collection

The **all** collection can provide access to all the elements on a page. Once we have a reference to an object we can access any of its properties (like its **style** object), call its methods, or even dynamically generate event handlers.

If, for example, we wanted to find out the type of tag that created the first element on the page we could use the following code:

```
document.all(0).tagName
```

If you start your HTML documents with the **<HTML>** tag, the above line of code will return HTML.

Why would we want to do this, especially if we already know that the first element in our document is **<HTML>**? The answer is that we wouldn't use the **all** collection in exactly this way–we would, however, use it to obtain a reference to other elements on the page. Each page is likely to have a large number of elements, and the **all** collection exposes every one of them.

Obviously counting and trying to remember the exact index of each element we might want to work with can be cumbersome, especially when even small pages can have 20 or 30 elements. This sort of situation is another where using the ability to index elements by name can prove helpful.

As another quick example, suppose we've named a paragraph **myp**, like this:

```
<p id="myp">Some text</p>
```

Then we could use this code and the **style** object that we talked about in Chapter 2 to change the color of the paragraph's text:

```
document.all("myp").style.color = "red"
```

We'll be using the **all** collection repeatedly throughout the rest of the book.

Using Forms

The ability to access individual form elements isn't new to Dynamic HTML, but it's still one of the most important uses for the document object and will remain so indefinitely, as forms are one of the best ways to collect information from a user.

A **<FORM>** tag is a container for HTML form elements like buttons, **<SELECT>** list boxes, and text areas. We can access each form on a page with the **forms** collection of the **document** object.

Each form element has an **elements** collection that contains a reference to each form element *in the form*.

> *Note that we can also use form elements outside of a form – in fact, if we specify any form elements outside of a <FORM> tag, then we'll access them via the* **all** *collection, without using* **forms**.

Once we obtain a reference to the specific form we want, through the forms index or name, we can access any form elements inside the form.

For example, to retrieve the value of a text input element called **mytext**, in a form named **myform**, we'd use this code:

```
msgbox document.forms("myform").elements("mytext").value
```

While other page elements beside form elements can reside inside a form, we can't use the **elements** collection to access them because it only holds references to form elements. We can, however, reference any non-form elements inside a form with the **all** collection.

Using Default Properties

While the above code works correctly, we can also use a shortcut known as a **default property** and simply write:

```
msgbox document.forms("myform").mytext.value
```

This line of code doesn't use the **elements** collection, it just refers directly to the default property of the form object – the **elements** collection. Default properties don't need to be referenced–they're assumed if no property is named.

We should also note that we further streamlined this line of code by assuming the default object of the browser object model, **window**. The following line of code works identically to the previous code:

```
msgbox window.document.forms("myform").mytext.value
```

Following this concept to its logical end we can say that since the default property of the document object is the **all** collection, both of these lines of code will work identically:

```
msgbox document.myform.mytext.value
msgbox document.all("myform").mytext.value
```

Form Element Objects

In our code above, we used the **value** property to print out the contents of text box. But there's a lot more to forms than just text boxes. In order to use these objects to their fullest, we need to know more about the interface each object exposes.

With Internet Explorer 3.0, the interface for even the most complex object (the text input area) was simple enough to only total just above ten properties, methods, and events. In Internet Explorer 4.0, the range is hugely expanded. We could list each element here, in a huge table with columns for properties, methods, and events, but you'll find that this information is more readily accessible in the reference sections of this book and the reference database found on the web site at **http://rapid.wrox.co.uk/books/0707**.

Manipulating the Content of the Page

Probably the biggest conceptual change in Dynamic HTML is the new ability to manipulate the actual text on the page and to respond to mouse clicks and selection of different sections of text.

Why Do We Need to Change HTML Dynamically?

We've seen already the parts of the object model that allow us to do things like moving an image from place to place by changing the properties of its `style` object. For example, this code moves the image with the name `MyImg` 100 pixels to the right and down from its current position, when the image is clicked on:

```
<HTML>
<BODY>
<IMG ID="MyImg" SRC="wrox.gif" STYLE="position:absolute;left:100px;top:100px">

<SCRIPT LANGUAGE="VBScript">
Sub MyImg_onClick
    MyImg.style.posleft = MyImg.style.posleft + 100
    MyImg.style.postop = MyImg.style.postop + 100
End sub
</SCRIPT>
</BODY>
</HTML>
```

What we haven't explored yet is how to change the actual text of the page, without reloading anything! This ability means we can do almost anything to an HTML page, including changing the text of headings and paragraphs, adding new elements (like images) to the page, and changing the formatting of any element on the fly.

For example, if we have a page that contains a list created using `<OL>` and `<LI>` tags, we might want to show that the mouse is over a certain list element by highlighting that element with a larger font and a different color.

Since we've talked about style sheets, we know that the difference between a normal list item and a bigger list item shown in a different font is the simple addition of a `STYLE` attribute.

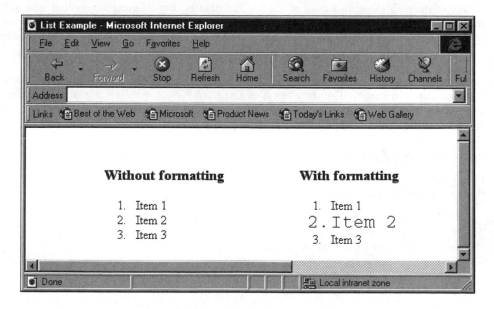

The HTML for the first list looks like this:

```
...
<OL>
<LI>Item 1
<LI>Item 2
<LI>Item 3
</OL>
...
```

While the second list is displayed with this code:

```
...
<OL>
<LI>Item 1
<LI STYLE="font-size: 24px; font-family:courier">Item 2
<LI>Item 3
</OL>
...
```

One method of creating a dynamic list involves changing the HTML of the page so that when a mouse is moved over a list item, the HTML code of the page changes from the first, non-stylized, block into the second stylized block. Before Dynamic HTML, this was impossible. But not anymore, and in this section of the chapter we'll introduce the objects and techniques we need to perform these tasks.

We can manipulate text in two basic ways: by using the new text properties that most HTML elements now possess, and with the new `textRange` object. We'll talk about both of these methods, and also about the `selection` object that provides a link to the selected text on a page, in this section.

The New Text and HTML Properties

HTML is a way of defining the appearance of a document that is already quite segmented into individual pieces; likewise, the organization of these components is also well defined. Each HTML element we type in when we create a page has its own set of rules and characteristics. Depending on how we set these attributes, we can hopefully produce documents to look the way we want.

With this fundamental nature of HTML in mind, the first method we have at our disposal to change the contents of a page comes naturally. The developers of Dynamic HTML have created four new properties that reflect the text and HTML of an element. These properties, `innerText`, `outerText`, `innerHTML`, and `outerHTML`, can be examined and changed by script code.

The Properties: An Example

We'll delve into the details of the new properties in just a moment, but, before we do that, we'll give an example of what they return for a simple paragraph.

```
<HTML>
<HEAD>
<TITLE>Test Properties Page</TITLE>
</HEAD>
```

```
<BODY>
<H3>The contents:</H3>
<P ID="MyText">The <i>quick</i> brown fox <b>jumps</b> over the lazy dog.</P>
<INPUT TYPE="BUTTON" NAME="Button1" VALUE="Click Me">

<SCRIPT LANGUAGE="VBScript">
Sub Button1_onClick
    msgbox "innerText: " & document.all("MyText").innerText
    msgbox "outerText: " & document.all("MyText").outerText
    msgbox "innerHTML: " & document.all("MyText").innerHTML
    msgbox "outerHTML: " & document.all("MyText").outerHTML
End sub
</SCRIPT>
</BODY>
</HTML>
```

If you run this page in IE4, click the button and then make a note of the four message boxes that pop up in turn on your screen. These four properties can be examined for a majority of the elements on any page, and they can be set to modify the pages' appearance.

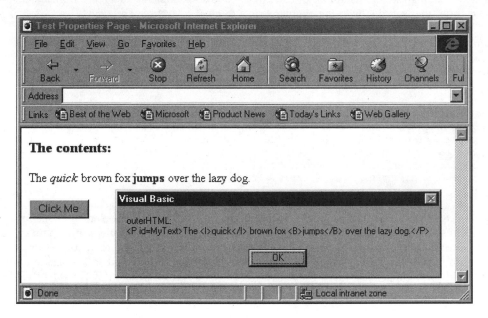

The following table summarizes the results for the HTML paragraph block `<P ID="MyText">The <i>quick</i> brown fox <b>jumps</b> over the lazy dog.</P>`:

Property	Result
`innerText`	The quick brown fox jumps over the lazy dog.
`outerText`	The quick brown fox jumps over the lazy dog.
`innerHTML`	The `<i>`quick`</i>` brown fox `<b>`jumps`</b>` over the lazy dog.
`outerHTML`	`<P ID="MyText">`The `<i>`quick`</i>` brown fox `<b>`jumps`</b>` over the lazy dog.`</P>`

113

As you saw, the two HTML properties returned text that included at least some HTML tags, while the two text properties just returned plain, unadorned, text. The major difference between the two text properties and the two HTML properties is that one set ignores any HTML tags, while the other maintains the HTML to see (and to modify). Depending on what our script code is accomplishing, one set of properties will usually be more useful than the other.

You might have noticed and wondered why we have both the **innerText** and **outerText** properties, when they returned the same result. We'll talk about this in more detail in the next section.

innerText and outerText

These properties disregard completely the HTML that is used inside whatever text block they refer to. In the example above, we saw that both the italic block and the bold block didn't show up when we queried **innerText** and **outerText**. In a moment we'll talk more about the HTML properties that retained the HTML code causing the italic and bold formatting.

Setting one of the text properties in code causes the element to be updated with whatever text we specify. For example, executing the following line of code in the above example would replace (instantaneously!) the sentence about the lazy dog with the simpler string **Dynamic HTML is Cool!**:

```
document.all("MyText").innerText = "Dynamic HTML is Cool!"
```

If you'd like to see this yourself, just add this line to the code block that is executed when the button is clicked:

```
Sub Button1_onClick
   document.all("MyText").innerText = "Dynamic HTML is Cool!"
      msgbox "innerText: " & document.all("MyText").innerText
      msgbox "outerText: " & document.all("MyText").outerText
      msgbox "innerHTML: " & document.all("MyText").innerHTML
      msgbox "outerHTML: " & document.all("MyText").outerHTML
End sub
```

The **innerText** and **outerText** properties ignore all HTML code inside an element. This means that we can't use either of these properties to set any HTML formatting. For example, setting **innerText** to the string **Dynamic HTML is <b>Cool</b>!** would cause the (probably unintended) result that the string in the browser's page displayed on the screen would include the **<b>** and **</b>** tags, but wouldn't include any bold formatting. We'd see Dynamic HTML is <b>Cool</b>! instead of Dynamic HTML is **Cool**!. If we need to set (or maintain) existing formatting, we need to use **innerHTML** or **outerHTML**.

The Difference Between innerText and outerText

While both of these properties return the same thing when their values are queried, they behave differently when they're used to set text. We lose any internal HTML when we set the **innerText** property, but we maintain whatever HTML we've used to create the element that we're manipulating in the first place. With **outerText** we ignore both the internal HTML and the creating HTML.

Why is this so important? In our example above, we used this HTML to create the paragraph block:

```
<P ID="MyText">...</P>
```

The line about the jumping fox is just the contents of the paragraph block, the paragraph that was created with this HTML. We could have displayed our sentence without specifying a paragraph block named **MyText**, but if we'd done things this way we wouldn't have been able to manipulate or read any properties associated with this paragraph. We have to name a block of text something before we can do anything with it.

This is where **innerText** and **outerText** differ. **innerText** replaces internal HTML, but does nothing with external HTML like the paragraph block. In contrast, **outerText** replaces **all** HTML used with an element.

What this all means is that setting **outerText** to a string like `Dynamic HTML is Cool!` would replace:

```
<P ID="MyText">The <i>quick</i> brown fox <b>jumps</b> over the lazy dog.</P>
```

with the string:

`Dynamic HTML is Cool!`

It would be as though the **MyText** paragraph never existed–we wouldn't be able to retrieve or set any properties of **MyText**, because the **MyText** object would be gone! Whatever text we set **outerText** to would still exist, but our reference to the text would be lost. If your Dynamic HTML code depends on being able to manipulate a certain named portion of the page (as most text code does) you need to be vigilant that you don't misuse the **outerText** property and destroy the link to your text.

innerHTML and outerHTML

The **innerHTML** and **outerHTML** properties differ from the corresponding text only properties in one major way: they maintain the HTML used internally and also to create the element in question.

This means that we can use the next line of code to change the text **and** include HTML formatting:

```
document.all("MyText").innerHTML = "Dynamic HTML is <b>Cool</b>!"
```

Changing **innerHTML** like this would result in the expected Dynamic HTML is **Cool**! in the browser window.

But we're not limited to just changing formatting options. We have access to anything HTML allows, and this means that we can do things like adding a new image or changing an image (by changing the SRC attribute), modifying existing links, creating new links, creating new paragraphs, or headers, or form fields, and so on.

The **outerHTML** property shares the same similarity to **innerHTML** as **outerText** shares with **innerText**: instead of just referring to the enclosed text of whatever element we're manipulating, we have access to the entire text, including the HTML used to create the element. Because the HTML properties display the existing HTML in addition to allowing it to be changed, we see a difference between the return values of **innerHTML** and **outerHTML**. In our example above this is what the two properties returned:

```
innerHTML    The <i>quick</i> brown fox <b>jumps</b> over the lazy dog.
outerHTML    <P ID="MyText">The <i>quick</i> brown fox <b>jumps</b> over
             the lazy dog.</P>.
```

We still need to be careful when using `outerHTML` because it allows us to change the name of an element that we might already in our code, but at least we can change it any way we want (which can be useful sometimes) instead of losing it entirely.

Tag Support for Text Manipulation Properties

In all of our example code up until this point we've used a paragraph element created with `<P ID="...">` and `</P>` tags. But `<P>` isn't the only HTML tag that supports the properties we've been talking about.

In our introductory discussion a few pages back we talked about dynamically changing `<LI>` elements when the mouse moved over them. We could accomplish this by setting the `style` object of the list item, but we could also achieve the same result using the text and HTML properties we've been talking about in this section. This is easy to do because `<LI>` supports `innerText`, `outerText`, `innerHTML`, and `outerHTML`. So to change the style of a list item we just need to obtain a reference to the item in question and modify the HTML accordingly, using `innerHTML` and `outerHTML`.

For example, this code changes the font and size of a list item when the mouse first moves over it:

```
...
<SCRIPT LANGUAGE=VBScript>
Sub document_onmouseover
    If window.event.srcelement.tagname = "LI" then
            strCurrentText = window.event.srcelement.innerHTML
            window.event.srcelement.outerHTML = "<LI STYLE=""font-size:24px;font-
family:courier"">" & strCurrentText
        end if
end sub
</SCRIPT>
...
```

In short, the `document_onmouseover` event is fired when the mouse is moved over any element. Any time the `onmouseover` event fires, a reference to the element that was moved over is stored in the `srcelement` property of the `window.event` object. We check to see that the element moved over is a list item, and, if it is, we first get the current text of the list item (including any formatting) using the `innerHTML` property. Then we set the `outerHTML` property with a new `STYLE` attribute and the text that we obtained from `innerHTML`.

If this seems a little confusing right now, don't worry. We'll talk more about this in Chapter 10 when we give the full code for this example. The point we want to make clear now is that most HTML elements now possess at least some of the four text and HTML properties that allow them to be read and changed by script code. Not all of the HTML elements support all of the four properties we've been talking about, but you'll usually find that even the limited elements support enough of the properties to be useful. What's more, if you find an element that doesn't, you're free to use the `textRange` object that we talk about in a moment. It can do everything the new text properties can do, and it can do it anytime and anywhere on a page.

We won't list the specific properties every single element supports here, but we do provide a full reference in the Wrox Dynamic HTML database you can download from the Wrox web site at **http://rapid.wrox.co.uk/books/0707.**

The New InsertAdjacent Methods

Along with these four new properties, we also have access to two new methods that are supported by many of the HTML properties used in most documents. These methods, `insertAdjacentText` and `insertAdjacentHTML`, can be used to easily insert new text and HTML into an existing document.

The difference between the methods is similar to the difference between the text and HTML properties we've been discussing: `insertAdjacentHTML` inserts HTML code and renders it correctly, while `insertAdjacentText` assumes that anything it adds is just text. This means that any HTML code added with `insertAdjacentText` won't be rendered as HTML–it will remain as straight text, so don't use `insertAdjacentText` to add anything that needs to be rendered by Internet Explorer's HTML engine!

Furthermore, these methods can add text and/or HTML in four locations with respect to the element we're working with. These locations are summarized in the table below:

Location	Description
`BeforeBegin`	Before the beginning of the element's opening tag
`AfterBegin`	After the element's opening tag, but before the enclosed text of the element
`BeforeEnd`	Before the element's closing tag, and after the enclosed text of the element
`AfterEnd`	After the ending of the element's closing tag

The methods can be called like this:

```
MyText.insertAdjacentText("Text to insert", "AfterBegin")
MyText.insertAdjacentHTML("<B>HTML</B> to insert", "BeforeEnd")
```

The second parameter to each call is the string location (one of the four choices out of the above table) where the text or HTML should be added.

Details of the TextRange Object

While we can change the actual text on the page with the `innerText`, `outerText`, `innerHTML`, and `outerHTML` properties, as well as the `insertAdjacentText` and `insertAdjacentHTML` methods, we can also change the text on the page with the `textRange` object. This relatively complex object, once mastered, will provide us with all the control over the HTML document text we could want or need.

You can think of a `textRange` object as a black box that contains some selection of HTML text on the page. The box exposes properties and methods that allow us to find out information about and manipulate the text it contains. Also, if our text range represents text actually on the page (in contrast to a text range we've created but that hasn't been displayed) then we can think of the `textRange` object as being a placeholder for that section of text. If we change the text in the range this new text will replace whatever was displayed before–and the page will be updated the instant we change the text!

It's important to remember that a `textRange` object is just a reference to a certain section of text. The element objects that expose properties like `innerText` and `innerHTML` represent the actual element on a page. If we manipulate a paragraph we've called `MyText` (perhaps gained by using syntax like `document.all("MyText")`) then we're manipulating the actual element.

In contrast, with the `textRange` object, we have a reference to a specific block of text, but any manipulation we do goes on via this reference, and not directly. A `textRange` object can be shifted to a completely different block of text easily, using methods we'll cover shortly, but a reference to an element like a paragraph is constant (as long as the element isn't removed from the page or moved by removing and then adding again!).

We won't be giving much in-depth `textRange` code in this section of the book, but we will return to the topic in chapter 10 with an in-depth `textRange` object example.

TextRange Properties

After we've created a `textRange` object (we'll talk about how to do this in a moment), we'll have access to two properties. The `text` property returns (what else?) the text of the range, devoid of HTML tags and any other additional text or code. In contrast, the `htmlText` property returns everything that would be displayed if the source of the page were viewed, including all enclosed HTML tags, any script code, and so on.

Property	Description
`htmlText`	Returns the HTML source as a valid HTML fragment
`text`	Returns the plain text contained within the text range

The diagram below shows graphically how the two properties of the `textRange` object work.

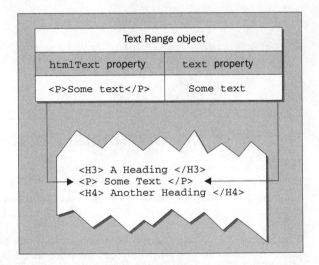

While these two properties could be considered simple, the same can't be as easily said when we talk about the methods of the `textRange` object.

TextRange Methods

As you can see from the table, the `textRange` object boasts more methods than almost any other object we've considered up to this point.

Method	Description
collapse	Shrinks a text range to the start or end of the current range
compareEndPoints	Compares two text ranges and returns a value indicating the result
duplicate	Returns a duplicate of the current textRange object
execCommand	Executes a command over the range
expand	Expands a range by character, word, sentence, or story (fully containing all partially contained units)
findText	Changes the text range to refer to the specified text in the range (if found)
getBookmark	Sets string to a unique value to identify that position in the document
inRange	Returns whether or not the specified range is within or equal to the current range
isEqual	Returns whether or not the specified range is equal to the current range
move	Moves the text range to cover a different portion of document text
moveEnd	Grows or shrinks the range from the end of the range
moveStart	Grows or shrinks the range from the beginning of the range
moveToBookmark	Moves the range to enclose a previously stored bookmark value
moveToElementText	Moves the range to enclose the text in the specified element
moveToPoint	Moves and collapses the range to the x,y point specified
parentElement	Returns a reference to the parent element that completely encloses the current range
pasteHTML	Pastes text and HTML into the current text range
queryCommandEnabled	Whether or not a specified command is available
queryCommandIndeterm	Whether or not a specified command is in an indeterminate state
queryCommandState	The current state of the command
queryCommandSupported	Whether or not the specified command is supported
queryCommandText	The string associated with a command
queryCommandValue	The value associated with the command
scrollIntoView	Scrolls the text range into view in the browser
select	Makes the active selection equal to the current text range object
setEndPoint	Sets the end point of the range based on the end point of another range

These methods can be categorized (at a general level) into methods that select a section of the text on the page, methods that provide information about the text range, and methods that actually change the text in the object or influence the browser's display of the text. The queryCommand methods along with execCommand are provided for use by applications that control or contain Internet Explorer. This topic is beyond the scope of this book, so we won't spend any more time talking about these methods here.

Obtaining a TextRange

Before we can manipulate a range of text or find out anything about it, we have to create a `textRange` object.

How do we do this? The most common way to create a `textRange` object is to use the `createTextRange` method of one of the elements that support it. We can also use the selection object's `createRange` method to create a range from whatever is currently selected on the screen. If we have a `textRange` object already, we can use the object's own `duplicate` method to create a copy of the range.

createTextRange

The most common way to create a new text range is to use the `createTextRange` method of the `document`'s `body` object. Since the body object represents the entire body of the HTML page (everything contained between the `<BODY>` and `</BODY>` tags), a text range created like this starts life containing everything in the document outside of the page's header text. Using the text position methods we'll cover shortly, this text range object can then be pointed at any subset of the page.

The code used to call this method looks like this:

```
TextRangeObj = document.body.createTextRange
```

While the `createTextRange` method of the `body` object will probably be used most of the time, three other objects currently provide `createTextRange` methods. These elements are the `<BUTTON>`, `<TEXTAREA>`, and `<INPUT TYPE=TEXT>`.

Every visible element supports a property named `isTextEdit`. This property returns true if the element in question supports the `createTextRange` method (so only `<BODY>`, `<BUTTON>`, `<TEXTAREA>`, and `<INPUT TYPE=TEXT>` return true at this time).

The Selection Object's createRange Method

As we'll see in a moment, the `selection` object reflects whatever text is currently selected. The `selection` object's `createRange` method returns to us a `textRange` object that reflects whatever text is currently selected. We'll postpone our discussion of `selection` for a minute, and talk more about the `selection` object in the last major section of this chapter.

The TextRange duplicate Method

Once we have a `textRange` object, the `textRange` object's `duplicate` method can be used to make a copy of the text range. This method is easy to call—we simply provide the name of the variable that will hold the reference to the copy of the range, like this:

```
newRange = oldRange.duplicate
```

Now that we know how to create a text range, we're ready to move onto the methods that allow us to change the position of the range on the page.

Changing the Page Position of a TextRange

The `textRange` object includes a lot of methods that we can use to modify the text that a text range contains. We should clarify that what we're talking about here isn't changing the actual text contained in a text range (we'll talk about how to do this in a moment), but instead changing the start and end positions of the range so that the range contains a different set of text.

To do this we can use the `collapse`, `expand`, `findText`, `move`, `moveStart`, `moveEnd`, `moveToBookmark` (and `getBookmark`), `moveToElementText`, `moveToPoint`, and `setEndPoint` methods.

The collapse and expand Methods

With `collapse` we can move the `textRange` object to the beginning or end of a currently selected text range. If we had a `textRange` object that contained all of the text in a heading on our page, calling `collapse` would reduce the text contained to 0 characters. It would also move the location of the object to either the beginning or the end of the current text range, depending on the parameter we had passed to the `collapse` method. To call `collapse`, we just pass `true` (to move to the beginning of the range) or `false` (to move to the end) when we call the method, like this:

```
CurrentRange.collapse(true)
```

This method is useful when we want to insert new text before or after a block of text on the page. To do this, we first obtain a `textRange` object representing the block of text that is before or after the text we want to insert, and then call `collapse` from this `textRange`.

The `expand` method (as well as some of the move methods) requires that we specify the unit that we want to move or expand by.

Unit	Description
`character`	A single character
`word`	A single word
`sentence`	A single sentence
`textEdit`	The start or end position of the original range

`expand` simply takes a unit parameter and returns true or false depending on whether or not it was able to expand the range to include the specified unit.

```
bReturnValue = objCurrentRange.expand("character")
```

The Six move Methods

With the six methods that begin with the word move, we have fine control over the exact contents of the text range.

Each of the `move`, `moveStart`, and `moveEnd` methods take a number and a unit, in the same style as the `expand` method. The `move` method collapses the given range and then moves the empty range the number of units specified. The `moveStart` and `moveEnd` methods move the beginning or ending position of the text range respectively. All three of the methods return a number that indicates how many of the specified units they were able to move the range. In all cases, negative numbers move the position of the text range in the opposite direction and the number 1 is assumed if no number is specified.

```
iUnitsMoved = objCurrentRange.move("word")
iUnitsMoved = objCurrentRange.moveStart("sentence",5)
iUnitsMoved = objCurrentRange.moveEnd("textEdit",-10)
```

The **getBookmark** method returns a unique string whose sole use is as a parameter to the **moveToBookmark** method. When we have a bookmark, we can simply call **moveToBookmark**, passing our string as the only parameter, and the browser will move the current text range to enclose the part of the page that was previously selected when **getBookmark** was called.

```
strBookmark = objCurrentRange.getBookmark
bReturnValue = objCurrentRange.moveToBookmark(strBookmark)
```

If we have a specific element that we'd like to enclose in a **textRange** object, then we can use the **moveToElementText** method. This method takes a reference to an element, and moves the current range so that it completely envelops the given element.

```
objCurrentRange.moveToElementText("MyElementName")
objCurrentRange.moveToElementText(document.all.links(3))
```

Finally, the **moveToPoint** method modifies the current range yet again, this time turning it into an empty range at the x and y position (relative to the top left corner of the page) specified in the call to the method.

```
objCurrentRange.moveToPoint(100,100)
```

The **moveToPoint** empty range, like the one created with the **move** method, can then be modified using other position-changing methods.

The findText and setEndPoint Methods

The last two methods we haven't talked about do a bit more than the move and **collapse/expand** methods. **findText** actually searches the given range for text we specify and **setEndPoint** uses another range to move one the current range's start or ending point.

To call **findText**, we just pass whatever string we're searching for as the only parameter. If the search is successful, the current text range is changed to encompass the found text, and the method returns true.

```
ReturnValue = objCurrentRange.findText("Text to find")
```

In comparison, the **setEndPoint** method moves a single starting or ending point, depending on the string specified in the method call. The four available strings are **startToEnd**, **startToStart**, **endToStart**, and **endToEnd**. When calling **setEndPoint** we also specify the other text range that the given point should be taken from.

```
objCurrentRange.setEndPoint("StartToStart", objOtherRange)
```

TextRange Attributes

Along with the `text` and `htmlText` properties the `textRange` object also provides methods that provide more information about the relationship of the range to other ranges and the `textRange` object itself.

First, there are the `inRange` and `isEqual` methods that tell whether a specified range is within (`inRange`) or equal (`isEqual`) to the current range. Both of these methods return a Boolean value indicating whether or not the specific test returned true or false.

```
bReturnValue = objCurrentRange.inRange(ObjOtherRange)
bReturnValue = objCurrentRange.isEqual(ObjOtherRange)
```

The `parentElement` method returns a reference to the HTML element that completely encloses the current range.

```
objElement = objCurrentRange.parentElement
```

Finally, `compareEndPoints` compares the specific end point of the current range and another range passed as a parameter. It takes two parameters: which end points to compare, specified with one of the same four strings as `setEndPoint` uses, and a reference to the other range. `compareEndPoints` returns −1, 0, or +1 depending on whether the end point is less than, equal to, or greater than the other end point.

```
iReturnValue = objCurrentRange.compareEndPoints("EndToStart", objOtherRange)
```

Changing Text Dynamically with pasteHTML

Now we know how we get a `textRange` object, how we change what it refers to, and how to find information about the object itself, we can look at how we can change the actual text in the range. Because we can change the HTML of any block on the page, we can add or change anything, at anytime, once the page is loaded.

The method we use is `pasteHTML`. This is one of **the** methods that make the text on the page truly dynamic when we're using `textRange` objects.

With `pasteHTML`, we can add any new HTML text to the page that we desire. Since `pasteHTML` is a method of the `textRange` object, we obviously need to start with a text range. We pass a string (which can include HTML) as an argument and this string replaces whatever text occurs in the selected `textRange`.

```
objCurrentRange.pasteHTML("New text that will replace whatever text objCurrentRange
used to hold."
```

If we want to insert text, but not replace anything, we should use the `collapse` method to reduce the `textRange` object we are using. It now contains zero characters but resides at the correct location for our new text to be added when we call `pasteHTML`.

The Visible TextRange: scrollIntoView and select

`textRange` also provides two other methods that change the display of HTML.

`scrollIntoView` scrolls the browser window in whatever manner is necessary so that the contents of the `textRange` object from which it is called are displayed. The `select` method visibly highlights the contents of the `textRange` on the screen, and this brings us to the last object we're going to talk about in this chapter, the `selection` object.

The Selection Object

As soon as we start working with text on the page, the text that is currently selected can become useful–the `selection` object provides our interface to this important part of the page.

When you're working with `selection` don't forget that the object is a property of the `document` object. This means that you can only refer to any property or method of the `selection` object after adding the string `document.` to the front, like this:

```
document.selection.clear
```

If you forget to do this, the browser will assume you're referring to a separate object variable you created yourself, and your code will fail with an Object required: 'selection' error.

The Methods of Selection

Selection isn't too complicated–it only has three methods.

Method	Description
clear	Deletes the currently selected text from the document
createRange	Creates and returns a `textRange` object containing the currently selected text
empty	Sets the currently selected text to nothing but leaves all page text intact

The `createRange` method returns a ready-to-use `textRange` object that responds to all the properties and methods we've just finished discussing.

If you expect `clear` to set the current selection to nothing you'll be surprised when the currently selected text disappears from the page when you execute `clear`. This isn't an error–it's what the `clear` method is documented as doing. In effect, this is identical to using the `createRange` statement to obtain a range containing the current selection and then using `pasteHTML` with an empty string. In both cases the selected text is deleted from the document.

Instead of `clear`, the method we can use to set the current selection to nothing is called `empty`. Calling this deselects anything currently selected and sets the `selection.type` property to `None`.

You'll notice that there is nothing among these three methods that allows us to select a block of text. To do this we need to first obtain a `textRange` object containing the text we want to select and then use the `select` method of our new `textRange` object.

Finally, while it's not a method, selection's only property, `type`, deserves a mention. `Type` returns either `Control`, `None`, `Table`, or `Text`, depending on what is currently selected.

Summary

The most useful object in the browser object model that we've discussed over the last two chapters is the **document** object.

In this chapter we learned about:

- The place the **document** object holds in the browser object model as the most important descendent of the top-level **window** object and that it's properties, methods, and events, are critical for Dynamic HTML programming.

- The **document** object's interface including detailed passages on the most important intrinsic properties, methods, and events.

- The critical **all** collection provided by **document** and how we can use it to obtain a reference to nearly every element on a page.

- The relationship the four new element properties, **innerText**, **outerText**, **innerHTML**, and **outerHTML**, have to the page, and how they can be used to modify our documents dynamically.

- Using the **textRange** object to create and modify the HTML page on the fly.

- How the **selection** object works closely with ranges of text.

With this background, we're fully prepared to cover scripting. In the next chapter you'll see the objects and style sheet information we've covered put to use with code to produce real examples of Dynamic HTML.

Dynamic HTML Scripting Basics

"Why should we use scripting in our web page design?" That's a good question. Of course we can design our HTML pages without any scripting whatsoever. People have been designing web pages without the benefits of scripting for quite some time. So why use scripting at all?

Scripting gives us the ability to manipulate content and react to user input. We can customize each page in a site without actually creating multiple pages. Scripting can also be used to interact with the user, validate data before sending it to the host, and much more besides. In fact, the advent of Dynamic HTML gives developers the power to create animation, motion, and change content right within the page, after it has been downloaded to the browser.

However before we can even consider how to do these type of things, we need to understand how and where to place a script within our HTML code, how to connect it our code and how to ensure that it executes at the correct times. Also we need to consider the two types of scripting language, the differences between them and how you indicate to IE4 which language you are going to use. From there we'll take a look at how scripts can be called up in response to browser or user generated events. We'll examine how IE4 gets information back from events and how it determines what to do with the information. Finally we link all of these concepts together in one large example, where we create an application not unlike IE4's own toolbar!

In this chapter we are going to learn how to:

- ▲ Where to place scripts within your code
- ▲ What an event is
- ▲ How to get IE4 to respond to events
- ▲ How to create element objects
- ▲ How to connect to objects
- ▲ How to change content without calling the server

This chapter will provide a fast overview of these topics as we've already laid much of the groundwork for Dynamic HTML scripting in the previous chapter.

What is Script?

Scripting is not a new concept. For years scripting languages were used to enhance operating systems. UNIX has Perl and REXX. Even MS-DOS had its *Batch* programming language that could be thought of as a scripting language.

Applications started using embedded programming languages to allow the user to manipulate the application or document. For example, Microsoft Word includes a subset of the Visual Basic programming language, Visual Basic for Application (VBA) which provides scripting language capabilities. VBA is used in most of the Microsoft Office applications and also in other, non-Microsoft, applications.

Within the last few years scripting has also been added to web browsers, giving them the ability to manipulate text within a web page or validate user input. Currently there are two scripting languages available for use with Internet Explorer, VBScript and JScript.

Microsoft has recently implemented an interface called the ActiveX Scripting architecture that allows developers to create their own scripting languages so this may change. In fact, Sun Microsystems is currently working on their own scripting language that may be implemented on Microsoft's Internet Explorer browsers in the future.

> *Visual Basic Scripting Edition (VBScript) is a subset version of Microsoft Visual Basic. Visual Basic is the development language of choice in most corporate Management Information Systems departments.*

> *JScript is Microsoft's implementation of Netscape's Javascript. Javascript is based very loosely on C and the Java programming language.*

Scripting has been present in both Internet Explorer and Netscape Navigator/Communicator since version 3. Internet Explorer 4 supports both JScript, and VBScript, while Communicator 4 only supports JavaScript (without the aid of a proprietary add-in). As this is a book about IE4, we'll be using examples in both VBScript and JScript. There is a full reference to the two languages at the back of the book.

Where Do You Place Your Script?

Scripting code is placed in the page within the HTML `<SCRIPT>` and `</SCRIPT>` tags. These tell the browser that the code between the tags is to be interpreted and executed as the page is loaded. Inside the opening `<SCRIPT>` tag, we use a **LANGUAGE** attribute to tell the browser which interpreter to use. If omitted, the browser will assume it's JavaScript, and getting it wrong will provoke error messages as the page loads.

```
...
<SCRIPT LANGUAGE=VBSCRIPT>
   ... VBScript code goes here
</SCRIPT>
...
```

```
...
<SCRIPT LANGUAGE=JAVASCRIPT>
   ... JavaScript code goes here
</SCRIPT>
...
```

The script section can be placed almost anywhere in the page. The favorite position is often at the end, so that the rest of the page is loaded and rendered by the browser before the interpreter loads and runs the code. However, if we are using the code to insert something into the page, like the time and date, we need to place the `<SCRIPT>` section in the appropriate position within the HTML source.

```
...
<H3>The date and time is
<SCRIPT LANGUAGE=VBSCRIPT> document.write(Now) </SCRIPT></H3>
<P>
...
```

This causes the browser to execute the VBScript **Now** function and pass the result to the **write** method of the **document** object. This method writes the information into that page at the point where it's called, so the result is something like this:

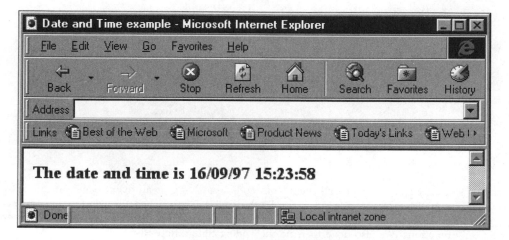

If this page is loaded into a browser that doesn't support VBScript, the code itself will simply be displayed as text on the page. The traditional way to prevent this is to enclose the contents of the `<SCRIPT>` section in a comment tag. Non-script enabled browsers will then ignore it, while browsers that do support scripting will still be able to interpret and execute it (unless of course they only support JavaScript, in which case the script will be ignored).

```
...
<SCRIPT LANGUAGE=VBSCRIPT>
<!-- hide from older browsers
   ... script code goes here
-->
</SCRIPT>
...
```

Of course, we're aiming our page at Dynamic HTML-enabled browsers, and support for a scripting language is a prerequisite for this anyway. However, it doesn't hurt to hide the scripting in case the page is loaded by an older browser—even though it will probably still look odd because the browser won't support the other layout features of Dynamic HTML either.

Creating Script Routines in a Page

The other technique you need to be familiar with is how we create separate code routines in a page that are *not* executed as the page is loading. Much of the dynamic nature of modern web pages is down to script code that reacts to **events** occurring within the browser. Changing the contents of a page by executing script as it is loading does provide a dynamic page, but doesn't provide the true dynamic page refresh that we're seeking.

To prevent VBScript code being executed as the page loads, we place it inside a **subroutine** or a **function**. The only difference is the way they are defined in the script, and that a function produces a value that gets passed back to the code that called it. As far as this book is concerned, we'll mainly be using subroutines.

```
<SCRIPT LANGUAGE=VBSCRIPT>

Sub MyNewRoutine()
   .. VBScript code goes here
End Sub

Sub window_onLoad()
   .. VBScript code to run when the window object gets an 'onLoad' event
End Sub

Function GetAnyNumber()
   .. VBScript code goes here, including setting the return value
   GetAnyNumber = 42
End Function

</SCRIPT>
```

These routines will only run when we call them from code elsewhere, or an event occurs in the browser that calls them automatically. In the second example, the code will run when the window has finished loading a new page, for example. In JavaScript, things are slightly different, because it doesn't support subroutines, only functions. We also have to write the code a little differently:

```
<SCRIPT LANGUAGE=JAVASCRIPT>

function MyNewRoutine()
{
   .. JavaScript code goes here;
}

function window_onLoad()
{
   .. JavaScript code to run when the window object gets an 'onLoad' event;
}

function GetAnyNumber()
{
   .. JavaScript code goes here, including setting the return value;
   return 42
}

</SCRIPT>
```

JavaScript requires the code in a routine to be enclosed in curly braces, and each line within a function to be separated by a semicolon.

What can Script do?

Scripting, in conjunction with IE4's object model, can be used to do any number of things. In fact, with IE4 and its enhanced abilities, one could write an entire application without any other programming language. Scripting is the link that binds the object model and user input together. Throw in additional ActiveX controls or other programming constructs and you can create practical applications. Just by accessing the object model with scripting we can create dynamic content in our documents.

As previously mentioned, we can change the actual text in the page without retrieving another page from the server, a very time and resource intensive process. We can manipulate elements on the page, such as images or links, by changing their color, content, or position. We can even add additional elements to a page after the page has been loaded. But while we've looked at techniques for doing each of these things separately, it's time now to see all of this put together in one large example. This screenshot shows a fully implemented toolbar:

Later in this chapter we're also going to create a toolbar like the one implemented in Internet Explorer. In IE4, buttons highlight when the mouse pointer passes over the toolbar, ToolTips popup to explain the function of the button and we can even drag the toolbar and dock it elsewhere on the page. This is a perfect example of what can be done by utilizing scripting within Internet Explorer 4.0 and we will create an element like this in its entirety before completing this chapter. However we need to look at the concept of events in IE4. It's events which make your browser react when you move the cursor over a button, it's events that cause your program to execute when you click on the button.

What are Events?

Whenever you carry out an action in Windows, such as clicking on a window with the mouse, dragging an icon from one side of the screen to the other, the operating system raises an **event**. This is simply a signal that something has happened. Windows examines the event to decide what caused it, and what to do about it. This isn't always as simple as it may seem. For example, the user may have clicked on a window that was not currently active (i.e. not part of the application they were working with).

In this case, Windows has to work out where the mouse pointer is on the screen and which application is under the pointer, bring this application's window to the front, and tell the other application that it is no longer the active one. And this is only a simplified view. In reality there will be a lot more happening 'under the hood'—a stream of messages is being sent to all the applications by the operating system. Each application can choose to either do something about the message, or simply ignore it.

However, some events may not be aimed at any application in particular. For example pressing a key when Microsoft Word is active will normally cause that character to appear in the page. But if there is another application running at the same time, and the key-press is *Alt-Tab*, Windows brings up its own task-switching window instead of passing the event onto Word.

Events in Dynamic HTML

In the case of the browser and Dynamic HTML, this constant barrage of messages provides a way for us to react to things that are going on in the browser. We can link code in our pages to the events that are occurring, and use them to interact with the viewer of our pages.

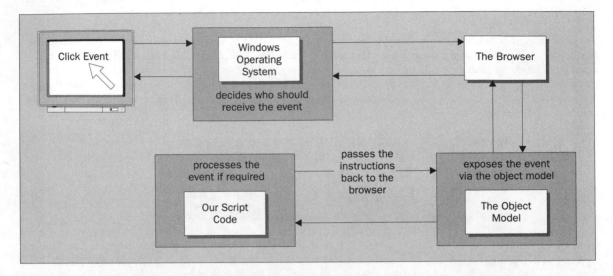

For example, just clicking the mouse button creates several events—descriptively named `onmousedown`, `onmouseup`, and `onclick`. Each message is collected by the Windows operating system, which then decides what to do with it. If the user pressed the mouse button while the pointer was on the screen over the browser window, Windows sends a message to the browser. It includes information on which button was pressed, what other keys were held down, and where the pointer was on the screen.

The browser then decides if it is going to handle the event. If they clicked on one of the browser toolbar buttons, it just gets on and does whatever is required—perhaps printing the page, refreshing it, or loading the user's Home page. If, however, the click was over the page itself, the browser then **exposes** it, by passing it on to our script code via the browser's object model. At this point, we can react to the event ourselves if we want to.

The reverse path is taken if we actually do decide to respond. The instructions in our code are passed back to the browser via the object model. It decides what effect this will have on the page and tells Windows. Windows then updates the screen to show the new page. The great thing is that, as Dynamic HTML programmers, all we have to do is decide which events to respond to, and what instructions to give the browser. Everything else is looked after automatically.

Reacting to Browser Events

To be able to react to an event, we have to be able to detect it happening. If we don't react to it, the browser will just carry on regardless—perhaps carrying out some action of its own. And even if we do decide to react, we can still let the browser carry out the original task as well. If this sounds confusing, think about the following example.

When we have a Submit button on a page, and the user clicks it, the browser sends the information from all the HTML control elements on the form to the server. However, it also provides an event that we can react to, called **onsubmit**. If we want to, we can react to this event, have a look at what the user entered, and decide if we want to submit the form or not. If we don't, we can instruct the browser to ignore the event, as though it never happened. We'll explore this in more detail later in the chapter.

Connecting Script to Events

So, we're now getting to the crux of the matter. All we have to do is capture the event, by connecting our code to it, and then decide how to react to it ourselves. The first step, then, is to understand how we can connect code to an event.

There are 39 different events that the browser exposes to our script—but for any one element in the page, only a limited number of these are available. For example a heading in the page, such as **<H2>Some Text</H2>**, only provides 14 events, while an image tag **<IMG>** provides 25 different ones. And to make matters more complicated, the ways in which VBScript and JScript handle events are different as well!

Event Handling in VBScript

In VBScript, we have four ways of connecting our code to an event. The main one we've used so far is to create a subroutine or function whose name is a combination of the *element* name and the *event* name. To react to a click on some heading text, we can use:

```
<H2 ID=MyHeading> Some Text </H2>
...
<SCRIPT LANGUAGE=VBSCRIPT>
  Sub MyHeading_onClick()
    MsgBox "You clicked me!"
  End Sub
</SCRIPT>
```

Alternatively, we can create a routine with almost any name, and link it to the event and the element by declaring the name of the routine in the element tag. And we don't need an **ID** in this case:

```
<H2 LANGUAGE=VBSCRIPT ONCLICK="MyClickCode"> Some Text </H2>
...
<SCRIPT LANGUAGE=VBSCRIPT>
  Sub MyClickCode()
    MsgBox "You clicked me!"
  End Sub
</SCRIPT>
```

Another way is to use 'inline' script code, which does away with the need for a separate code routine. We simply write the code inside the tag, as the value of the event name attribute. Notice how we have to use single quotes inside the **ONCLICK** attribute, because this itself is a string:

```
<H2 LANGUAGE=VBSCRIPT ONCLICK="MsgBox 'You clicked me!'"> Some Text </H2>
```

The final method is to use a different script section for each event. This is done by identifying the element and the event in the **<SCRIPT>** tag:

```
<H2 ID=MyHeading> Some Text </H2>
...
```

```
<SCRIPT LANGUAGE=VBSCRIPT FOR=MyHeading EVENT=ONCLICK>
  MsgBox "You clicked me!"
</SCRIPT>
```

Event Handling in JavaScript

In JavaScript (or Microsoft's implementation of JavaScript, called **JScript**), we don't have as many options for connecting events to our code. And the two things we have to watch out for are that JavaScript only supports functions, and the language interpreter is case-sensitive in all browsers.

The most usual way of making the connection between the function and the element is by defining the name of the function in the element tag itself. Notice that we need **MyClickCode()**, not just **MyClickCode**, to satisfy the JavaScript syntax requirements. We also have to use the browser's built-in **alert** dialog, rather than **MsgBox**, which is part of VBScript:

```
<H2 ONCLICK="MyClickCode()"> Some Text </H2>
...
<SCRIPT LANGUAGE=JAVASCRIPT>
function MyClickCode()
  {
    alert("You clicked me!");
  }
</SCRIPT>
```

This is fine for connecting script to specific elements in the page, but what about when we want to connect event handlers to the document itself? In this case, we simply put them all in the **<BODY>** tag:

```
<BODY ONMOUSEMOVE="MyMouseMoveCode()" ONCLICK="MyClickCode()">
```

We can also use inline code, within the element tag. This time, we're using the alternative **LANGUAGE** description of **JSCRIPT**:

```
<H2 LANGUAGE=JSCRIPT ONCLICK="alert('You clicked me!');">Some Text</H2>
```

And because JavaScript is the default language in the browser, we can omit the **LANGUAGE** attribute if we want to, making our code more compact:

```
<H2 ONCLICK="alert('You clicked me!');"> Some Text </H2>
```

Finally, we can create the separate **<SCRIPT>** sections for each event, just like we did for VBScript. However, this time, we have to make sure that the name of the event is all lower-case:

```
<H2 ID=MyHeading> Some Text </H2>
...
<SCRIPT LANGUAGE=JAVASCRIPT FOR=MyHeading EVENT=onclick>
  alert("You clicked me!");
</ SCRIPT>
```

Handling Window Events in JavaScript

We've seen how we can place event handler declarations, such as **onmousemove**, in the **<BODY>** tag of the document to cause them to occur at **document** level. The other situation is how we handle events at **window** level. In Internet Explorer, we can place the event handler declarations on the opening **<HTML>** tag:

```
<HTML ONMOUSEMOVE="MyMouseMoveCode()" ONCLICK="MyClickCode()">
...
</HTML>
```

Alternatively, we can use a technique similar to the VBScript method of naming an event handler in line with the ID of the element and the event name. This time, we separate the two with a period (full stop) rather than an underscore. For example, the following are both supported in IE4—but bear in mind that this is not the generally accepted method for connecting events and their code. (It works because the functions are themselves actually stored as properties of the element object).

```
<H2 ID=MHyeading > Some Text </H2>
...
<SCRIPT LANGUAGE=JAVASCRIPT>
function MyHeading.onclick()
  {
    alert("You clicked me!");
  }
</SCRIPT>
```

The same works for the main browser objects as well, such as the **document** and **window**:

```
<SCRIPT LANGUAGE=JAVASCRIPT>
function window.onload()
  {
    alert("I've just loaded!");
  }
</SCRIPT>
```

*The **LANGUAGE** attribute in a script or element tag can take one of four values. **VBSCRIPT** and **VBS** both instruct the browser to pass the script to its VBScript interpreter, while **JAVASCRIPT** or **JSCRIPT** pass it to the Internet Explorer JScript interpreter. Omitting the attribute altogether sends the script to the JScript interpreter by default.*

Canceling an Event Action

Some events, such as **onsubmit**, allow us to provide a return value that controls how the browser behaves. As you'll recall, to return a value in VBScript we have to use a **function** rather than a **subroutine**. In JavaScript, everything is a function anyway. This example uses JavaScript, and defines a form section with a single text box named **Email**, and a Submit button:

```
<FORM ID=MyForm ONSUBMIT="return CheckAddress()"
      ACTION="http://www.somesite.com/scripts/doit.asp">
  <INPUT TYPE=TEXT ID=Email>
  <INPUT TYPE=SUBMIT>
</FORM>

<SCRIPT LANGUAGE=JAVASCRIPT>
function CheckAddress()
{
  strAddress = document.forms["MyForm"].elements["Email"].value;
  if (strAddress.indexOf("@") != -1)   // contains @ somewhere
```

```
        return true
    else
    {
      alert("You must supply a valid email address.");
      return false
    }
  }
</SCRIPT>
```

This code uses the **indexOf()** function to find the position of the first **@** character in the string the user enters into a textbox named **Email** on the form. If there isn't a **@** character in the string the function returns **-1**. In this case, we can assume it's not a valid email address, display a message, and cancel the submission of the form by returning **false**. Notice that we have to use the **return** keyword in the element's **ONSUBMIT** attribute as well, so that the result is fed back to the browser's own form submission code:

```
<FORM ID=MyForm ONSUBMIT="return CheckAddress()"
    ...
```

You can also see how we have to use the browser's object model to get at the text in the text box. The string we want is the **value** property of the element object named **Email** in the **elements** collection of the form named **MyForm**, which is stored in the **forms** collection of the **document** object. (We could have started with **window.document**, but—as you'll recall—the **window** object is the default anyway).

Instead of returning a value from the function directly, we can also cancel the default action for any event by setting the **returnValue** property of the **event** object.

Responding to Events

Now that we've found ways of connecting our code to an event, we can start to write the code that instructs the browser—and tells the browser what we want to do. In general, this involves three tasks—getting information about the event, finding out about the element the event occurred for, and carrying out the task. This is where the links between our code and the elements in the page (as exposed by the object model) come into play.

Getting Information about an Event

All the ways you've seen here of connecting code to an event were equally valid in earlier releases of browsers that supported scripting (though the heading element didn't expose its events—only a very limited subset of controls did this previously). Dynamic HTML also adds another way of getting information about an event.

In Chapter 3, we briefly mentioned the **event** object, which is part of the new object model and a subsidiary object to the top-level **window** object. The **event** object is constantly being updated to include information about each event that occurs in our page—it is global to all events in this sense. So, when an event occurs we can query the **event** object's properties to learn more about the event.

Mouse Information and the Event Object

As you've seen in Chapter 3, the **event** object provides a whole range of properties that tell us about an event that has just occurred. We simply query these properties inside our event handler to find the information we need to make a decision on what to do. Here's how we can query the properties of the **event** object to get information about the mouse button that was pressed, and the position of the moue pointer when the event occurred:

```
...
<H2 ID=MyHeading> Some Text </H2>
<SCRIPT LANGUAGE=VBS>
Sub MyHeading_onmousedown()
  strMesg = "You clicked the "
  If window.event.button = 1 Then strMesg = strMesg & "left "
  If window.event.button = 2 Then strMesg = strMesg & "right "
  If window.event.button = 4 Then strMesg = strMesg & "middle "
  strMesg = strMesg & "button, at position x = " & window.event.x _
          & ", y = " & window.event.y
  strMesg = strMesg & Chr(10) & "and you held down the "
  If window.event.shiftKey Then strMesg = strMesg & "Shift key "
  If window.event.ctrlKey Then strMesg = strMesg & "Ctrl key "
  If window.event.altKey Then strMesg = strMesg & "Alt key "
  MsgBox strMesg
End Sub
</SCRIPT>
...
```

Here's the result, when the *Shift* key is held down while clicking on the heading:

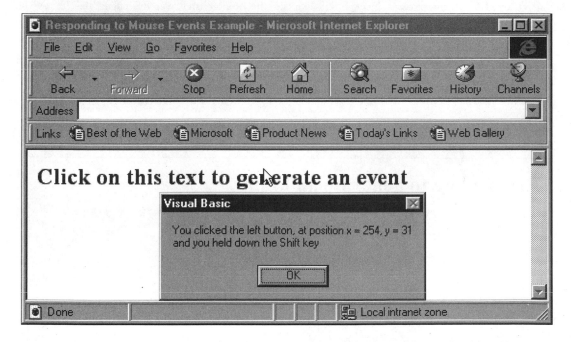

> Notice that in this example, we've preceded the `event` object with the default `window` object. This is not necessary in JavaScript (or JScript), but must be done in VBScript to prevent a clash between the `event` object and the VBScript `event` keyword.

Key-press Information and the Event Object

If we query the **event** object for a key-press event, we can use the same techniques as we did for a mouse event to find out where the mouse pointer is, and use the **shiftKey**, **ctrlKey** and **altKey** properties. However, more than that, we can use the **keyCode** property to find out which key was pressed. In this example, we're reacting to the **onkeypress** event of the **document**:

```
Sub document_onkeypress()
   strMesg = "You pressed the " & Chr(window.event.keyCode) & " key, " _
           & "which has an ASCII value of " & window.event.keyCode
   strMesg = strMesg & Chr(10) & "while holding down the "
   If window.event.shiftKey Then strMesg = strMesg & "Shift key "
   If window.event.ctrlKey Then strMesg = strMesg & "Ctrl key "
   If window.event.altKey Then strMesg = strMesg & "Alt key "
   strMesg = strMesg & Chr(10) & "The mouse pointer is at position " _
           & "x = " & window.event.x & ", y = " & window.event.y
   MsgBox strMesg, vbInformation, "The Event object parameters"
End Sub
```

Here's the result. Look where the mouse pointer is in the screenshot, and at the values of the mouse position retrieved from the **event** object. It still works if the pointer isn't over the page:

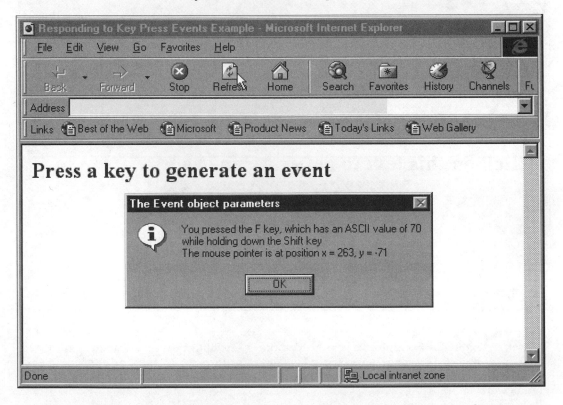

Both of the pages demonstrating the **event** *object,* **mouse.htm** *and* **key.htm**, *can be run directly from our Web site at:* **http://rapid.wrox.co.uk/books/0707**

Examining the Source of an Event

Often the first step in reacting to an event is to find more out about the event itself, and the element it occurred for. We've seen how we can find out more about the actual event from the **event** object. The next question is; how do we find out more about the element that originally raised the event?

Examining an Element's Properties

Every element in a page has a set of **properties**. For example, this **<H2>** heading has an **align** property, which indicates how we aligned the text when we created the page in HTML:

```
<H2 ALIGN=CENTER> Some Text </H2>
```

We can query the element's **align** property in code using the **Me** keyword (which provides a reference to the element that the event is bound to) like this:

```
Sub MyHeading_onclick()
  MsgBox Me.align
End Sub
```

> *In JavaScript or JScript, the equivalent to* **Me** *is the keyword* **this**.

In this case, our heading will have the value **center** for its **align** property. (Notice that the value is returned in lower case). This is one useful way in which Dynamic HTML exposes the properties of the elements within the page, and allows them to be changed in our code. There is a whole range of different properties available for different element tags, depending on which HTML attributes are valid for that tag.

An **<IMG>** tag has (amongst many others) the **width**, **height** and **src** properties—while the **<BODY>** tag can have **aLink**, **bgColor** and **scroll** properties. Updating the properties, as you would expect, causes the change to appear dynamically on the page where appropriate.

> *One point you need to watch out for is that many elements return an empty string as the value of a property that has not been set explicitly. For example the default alignment of a* **<H2>** *tag, if no* **ALIGN** *attribute is included, is* **left**. *However the* **align** *property in this case returns an empty string.*

Amongst the standard properties of all elements is the **id**. As you've seen, we use the **id** property, which we define in the **ID** attribute of the tag, to give an element a unique name that we can use to refer to in our script code:

```
<H2 ID=MyHeading> Some Text </H2>
```

We can always retrieve this value using **Me.id**, though you'll see other ways of identifying elements later on.

Element Properties vs Style Properties

While setting the attributes of an element is an accepted way to control its alignment, appearance, etc., there is another way. All the visible elements on a page also have a **style** object, and this can be used to control the way the element appears—as well as or instead of the traditional attributes of its HTML tag.

We met the **style** object in Chapter 2 and you should remember that we can use it to set, retrieve and change style properties for elements in our code, from the font size and font color, to the positioning of the text and graphics on the page.

```
<H2 ID=MyHeading STYLE="font-family:Arial; color:red; font-size:48">
  Some Text
</H2>
```

We can align our text heading in the same way, and in fact this is the technique recommended by W3C for the upcoming version 4.0 of the HTML standards:

```
<H2 ID=MyHeading STYLE="text-align:center"> Some Text </H2>
```

Once we've applied a style property like this, we have to remember to query the element's **style** object to get the value—in this case the **textAlign** property:

```
Sub MyHeading_onmousedown()
  MsgBox Me.style.textAlign
End Sub
```

Here's the equivalent in JavaScript:

```
<SCRIPT LANGUAGE=JAVASCRIPT>
function MyHeading.onmousedown()
  {
    alert(this.style.textAlign);
  }
</SCRIPT>
```

Remember that when we align text using a **STYLE** attribute like this, the **align** property of the element returns an empty string unless it's also been set to a specific value.

Event Bubbling

One major topic that makes Dynamic HTML different from scripting in earlier versions, either with VBScript, JavaScript, or any other language, is the way that the browser manages the events that are occurring in the page. This is known as **event bubbling**. The best way to explain event bubbling is with an example. Take a blank HTML document and place a division on it. Now, within that division, place an image. With Internet Explorer 3.0, if the user clicked on the image there was an **onClick** event generated for that image, and that was all. With event bubbling an **onClick** event is generated for the image, but if that event is not canceled by the code it is passed to the container for the image, in this case the division. If the event is still not handled it is passed on to division's container, the document.

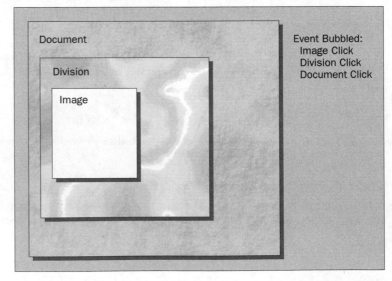

There are two main advantages of using event bubbling:

▲ **Using a Single Event Handler:** can help to minimize the code we write. Think about what happens when we have a lot of similar elements on the page that all need to respond to the same event, e.g. being clicked on. We only need one event handler to handle the events for many similar items, as long as we identify each of the elements on the screen in a unique way.

▲ **Using Containers in Dynamic HTML :** In HTML, when we create a list of items in the page, we can group them together in **<UL>** or **<OL>** tags, or group images inside a <DIV> tag. We can then move and manipulate many items as though they were all one item. We can then place containers within containers of the list items and then trap the event at any one point between the item that generated the event and the document object. This again minimizes the amount of code we need to write.

We'll now take a closer look at the sequence of things that happen to an event, enabling it to be handled by any element in the hierarchy between the original element and the document object.

The Event Object's Control System

When an event occurs in a page, the **event** object gets first look at it, and decides which element should receive it. Take the situation shown below where we have a **<H3>** heading inside a **<DIV>** document division on the page:

```
<DIV ID=MyDiv STYLE="background-color=aqua">
<H3 ID=MyTitle> Click Here To Fire An Event </H3>
</DIV>
```

When the **event** object receives an **onclick** event, it looks to see which element the mouse pointer was over at the time. (If two elements are overlapped, it uses the one with the higher z-index). If it was the heading line (which has the **ID** of **MyTitle**), it looks for a routine connected to this event, and—if it finds one—executes it:

```
Sub MyTitle_onclick()
  ...
End Sub
```

Bubbling Events to the Container Element

However, it doesn't stop there. It now looks to see which element is the **container** of the heading tag. In our case, it's the **<DIV>** tag named **MyDiv**, so it runs the **onclick** event code for this as well:

```
Sub MyDiv_onclick()
  ...
End Sub
```

This process continues while there are containers available. In our case, the only remaining one is the document itself, so it looks for the equivalent event code for this and executes it:

```
Sub document_onclick()
  ...
End Sub
```

Now that all the elements support events, this is particularly helpful.

Finding the Source Element

OK, so we can react to an event by using a handler that collects the event when it gets down to the `document`, or down as far as the element's container. One thing that we generally need to know is where it actually came from—in our toolbar example, we'll need to know which button has been pressed. This is where the `srcElement` property of the `event` object comes in.

The srcElement Property in Action

Inside any event routine, we can retrieve the object that was 'topmost' and active when the user clicked the page, or when the event occurred, from the event object's `srcElement` property. Let's consider a page that has a document division on it, and a heading within the document division, as follows:

```
<DIV ID=DivTag STYLE="position:absolute; left:100; top: 100; height:100; width: 300;
background: yellow">
<H3 ID=Heading1>A heading inside the Div Tag</H3>
</DIV>
<SCRIPT LANGUAGE=VBSCRIPT>
Sub document_onclick()
  set objItem = window.event.srcElement
  msgbox objItem.id
End Sub
</SCRIPT>
```

If you click on the heading tag inside the document division on the page, the topmost element is the heading tag and the Heading tags `id` is returned. If you click on the division, but not the heading, the topmost element is the division and the division's `id` is returned. If you click on the blank page, there is no topmost element so nothing is returned, and the event goes straight to the document.

The cancelBubble Property in Action

Another thing is that we sometimes want to be a little more selective about the way we react to an event. For example, we may want most of the elements on a page to react to an event, but for one or two particular ones not to. In cases like this, we can use the `event` object's `cancelBubble` property to give us that extra control.

All we do is create an event handler that reacts to the event for just this element. Normally, once the code in this event handler has finished executing, the event will be bubbled up the object hierarchy to the next container, or to the top-level document object. To prevent this, all we have to do is set the `event` object's `cancelBubble` property to `True`.

For example, if we wanted to do this for an element with the `ID` of `picture`, we just need to add the `cancelBubble` property assignment to the `onclick` event handler of that element:

```
Sub picture_onclick()
   'some code to react to the onclick event
   'now stop the event being bubbled to any other event handlers
   window.event.cancelBubble = True
End Sub
```

This breaks the chain of events, and the `document` object will not receive this `onclick` event. Of course, we can set the `cancelBubble` property in any of the events in the chain, and stop the processing at any point we choose. There's not much point in doing it in the `document` event handler, which is at end of the chain, and we can't stop the first event handler from running because this is our first chance to set the `cancelBubble` property.

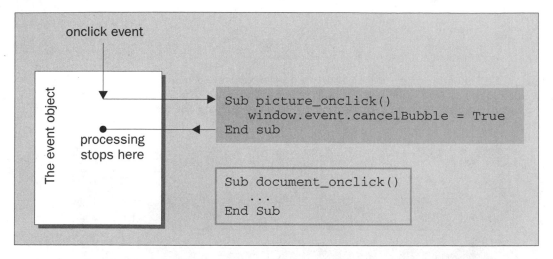

The fromElement and toElement Properties

There are another two other properties that are useful for finding out what's going on in a Dynamic HTML page. As the mouse moves into and out of elements, it fires the `onmouseover` and `onmouseout` events. These are useful for updating the object that the event is fired for, but not much use in telling us about what's going on in other elements.

By adding a line to the `onmouseover` code, we can display the value of the `event` object's `fromElement` or `toElement` property as an event is received. The useful one here is `fromElement`, which returns a reference to the element that the mouse was leaving when the event was fired:

```
Sub MyList_onmouseover
   ...
   window.status = window.event.fromElement.id
End Sub
```

The returnValue Property

Earlier in this chapter, we saw how some events allow us to handle them with a `Function` rather than a `Subroutine`, and prevent the browser's default action taking place by setting the return value of the function to `True`. The example we looked at was a form submission, and we found that we could use this method to prevent the browser's default action of sending the data in the form to the server.

The `event` object in Dynamic HTML allows us to use another technique. All we have to do is set the `returnValue` property of the `event` object to `False`. This cancels the default action. For example, here's a page containing an `<A>` tag, which jumps to our home page when clicked:

```
...
<A ID=MyLink HREF="http://www.wrox.com">Wrox Press Limited</A>
```

```
<SCRIPT LANGUAGE=VBSCRIPT>
Sub MyLink_onclick()
  If MsgBox("Go to our site?", vbYesNo + vbQuestion, "Jump?") = vbNo Then
    window.event.returnValue=False
  End If
End Sub
</SCRIPT>
...
```

Clicking on the link in the page runs the **MyLink_onclick()** event handler code, which displays a message box asking the viewer to confirm their action. If they select No, we just have to set the **returnValue** property to **False**, and the browser ignores the jump, as though they hadn't clicked it in the first place.

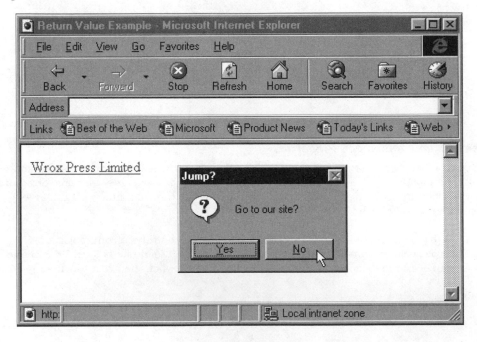

Notice how we've used the built in VBScript constants to define the **MsgBox** *function parameters. You'll find a list of these in appendix* **B**, *at the back of this book.*

Putting It All Together

Now we've seen how IE4 handles scripts and events, and how we can bubble events from one element to another, we can create a toolbar, which handles each of the different events generated by the user in a unique way. For example we'll display a tooltip for onmouseover, or execute the corresponding code for onclick. We'll gradually build up the features of the toolbar throughout the rest of the chapter, starting with the creation of the element itself.

Creating an Element Object - the ID attribute

In HTML we use tags to create elements within the page. When scripting was first introduced to the world of HTML, we learned to access elements within the document by referencing their name.

```
<DIV ID="toolbar"> … </DIV>
```

By adding the ID field to a tag we add a reference to the element that scripting can access. The above HTML sample provides the page with the ability to reference the HTML within the DIV tags. In this case we would reference the **toolbar** object. For example, we could move the toolbar object by assigning its left property a value: **toolbar.style.posleft = 0**.

Since we're going to develop the toolbar mentioned earlier, let's start with the initial layout. The toolbar should be separated from the rest of the page so that it can be an independent object. To do that we will use the DIV tag. This defines a division in the HTML that can be grouped together. We'll create the rest of the toolbar in a standard HTML table so that it can be grouped together in one HTML object.

```
<HTML>
<HEAD>
    <TITLE>Dynamic HTML Toolbar</TITLE>
</HEAD>

<BODY>
<!-- Start Toolbar HTML -->
<DIV ID="toolbar">
    <TABLE ID="tbstrip" WIDTH=1280 HEIGHT=28 VALIGN="CENTER" CELLSPACING=0
CELLPADDING=0 BGCOLOR="SILVER">
    <TR>
            <TD  ID="tbback" WIDTH="100%" BGCOLOR="SILVER" VALIGN="CENTER"
BACKGROUND="wroxbg.gif" >

                    <IMG ID="baricon" SRC="bar.gif" BORDER=0>

                    <IMG ID="btnup1" SRC="new.gif" BORDER=0>
                    <IMG ID="btndn1" SRC="newdn.gif" BORDER=0>
                    <IMG ID="btnup2" SRC="open.gif" BORDER=0>
                    <IMG ID="btndn2" SRC="opendn.gif" BORDER=0>
                    <IMG ID="btnup3" SRC="delete.gif" BORDER=0>
                    <IMG ID="btndn3" SRC="deletedn.gif" BORDER=0>
            </TD>
    </TR>
    </TABLE>
</DIV>
</BODY>
</HTML>
```

All source and images can be retrieved from the download page on the Wrox website, `http://` `rapid.wrox.co.uk/books/0707.` *This example is* `preliminary.html`*.*

We can see the starting layout of the toolbar, but we're not there yet. All the buttons, raised and normal, are being displayed, but there's a gap between the sides of the window and the toolbar.

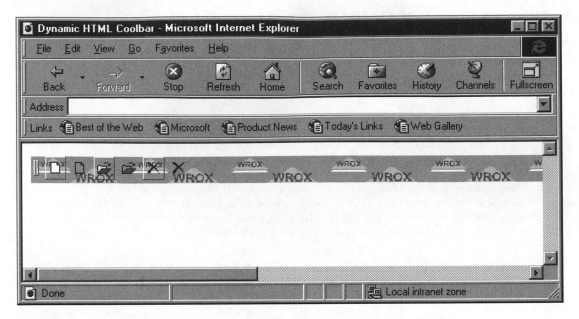

To take care of this we will have to use rules from Cascading Style Sheet (CSS) Positioning.

CSS Positioning

As we have seen in chapter 2, CSS gave us the ability to layout a page in much the same fashion as a graphic designer does. We could finally place page elements in exact locations within the page. Text could even be positioned in such a way as to overlap other text and create unique views. CSS provided us with a way to show/hide elements and control the positioning of elements within a web page. Not only can it control the left and top positioning, but, with enhancements implemented in IE4, also the z-order or the layers in which the elements are displayed within the page.

Knowing this let's change our original code listing so that the toolbar will be positioned correctly within the page. First, it makes sense that the toolbar itself, the original `<DIV>` tag, should be absolutely positioned. We need our elements within the toolbar to have their own coordinate system, so making the `<DIV>` tag absolutely positioned will supply its child elements, the buttons, with their own coordinate system, separate from the toolbar's positioning within the page.

Second, it also makes sense to position each of the buttons at absolute coordinates within the toolbar. Each button, or image, needs to be at a specific location so that it will be positioned correctly on the toolbar.

There is one other thing about CSS positioning that needs to be covered and that is the concept of **display**. CSS gives the ability to show and hide elements within the page. To make a long explanation short, by specifying `display:none` you can cause an element to be treated as if it is not even in the page. This not only hides the element from view, but from the HTML rendering as well. We will set the "raised" graphics on our toolbar to `display:none` for this reason. We will amend our code accordingly.

```
<HTML>
<HEAD>
    <TITLE>Dyanmic HTML Coolbar</TITLE>
</HEAD>

<BODY>
<!-- Start Toolbar HTML -->
<DIV ID="toolbar" STYLE="position:absolute;Top=0;left=0">
<TABLE ID="tbstrip" WIDTH=1280 HEIGHT=28 VALIGN="CENTER" CELLSPACING=0 CELLPADDING=0
BGCOLOR="SILVER">
    <TR>
            <TD ID="tbback" WIDTH="100%" BGCOLOR="SILVER" VALIGN="CENTER"
                BACKGROUND="wroxbg.gif" >

            <IMG ID="baricon" SRC="bar.gif"
                STYLE="position:absolute;HEIGHT=26;TOP=0">

            <IMG ID="btnup1" SRC="new.gif"

            STYLE="display:none;position:absolute;LEFT=15;HEIGHT=26;TOP=0"
                        BORDER=0 >
            <IMG ID="btndn1" SRC="newdn.gif"
                STYLE="position:absolute;LEFT=15;HEIGHT=26;TOP=0" BORDER=0 >
            <IMG ID="btnup2" SRC="open.gif"

            STYLE="display:none;position:absolute;LEFT=50;HEIGHT=26;TOP=0" BORDER=0 >
                <IMG ID="btndn2" SRC="opendn.gif"
            STYLE="position:absolute;LEFT=50;HEIGHT=26;TOP=0" BORDER=0 >
                <IMG ID="btnup3" SRC="delete.gif"

            STYLE="display:none;position:absolute;LEFT=85;HEIGHT=26;TOP=0"
                BORDER=0 >
                <IMG ID="btndn3" SRC="deletedn.gif"
            STYLE="position:absolute;LEFT=85;HEIGHT=26;TOP=0" BORDER=0 >
            </TD>
    </TR>
    </TABLE>
</DIV>
</BODY>
</HTML>
```

Please note that the following code is available in `toolbar1.html`, *available from our web site at http://rapid.wrox.co.uk/books/0707*

This amends the positioning so there's now no unsightly gap between the window edges and our toolbar. It also hides three of the buttons from view.

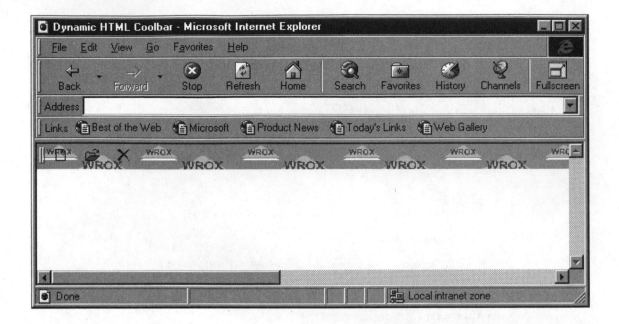

Events in the Toolbar

Now that we've completed the HTML code, it's time to make the page reactive. We need to respond to what the user is doing. Look at the toolbar on Internet Explorer. When the mouse moves over a button, the image raises up and highlights. IE4's scripting model has an event, **onMouseOver**, which signals when the mouse is being moved over an element.

For example, if we wanted a message to display when the mouse passed over an image whose **ID** was **image1**, we would add the following code to our page:

```
<SCRIPT LANGUAGE="VBScript">
<!--
    Sub image1_OnMouseOver()
            MsgBox "You passed over the picture!"
    End sub
-->
</SCRIPT>
```

Likewise, with the **onMouseOut** event, it would seem then a simple task to make our code respond to the mouse moving over our buttons. When the mouse moves over the button, raise it, when the mouse moves out of the range of our button, lower it.

But how do we raise and lower a button? This is where the style object comes in. We just need to manipulate the style object's display property to hide the image we don't want to display and display the other one. By setting the **style.display** property to an empty string, blank, we show an item. By setting the display property to **none** we hide it. Actually, the element is not only hidden but also ignored by the browser. As far as the browser is concerned the element will not generate events and not effect any other element on the page.

```
<SCRIPT LANGUAGE="VBScript">
<!--
    Sub btndn1_onMouseOver ()
            btndn1.style.display = "none"
            btnup1.style.display = ""
    End sub

    Sub btnup1_onMouseOut ()
            btnup1.style.display = "none"
            btndn1.style.display = ""
    End sub
-->
</SCRIPT>
```

We just repeat this for each button. Now we need to respond to the user clicking one of our buttons using the **onClick** event, which is fired every time the user clicks on an element.

```
<SCRIPT LANGUAGE="VBScript">
<!--
    Sub btnup1_onClick()
            MsgBox "Clicked Button 1"
    End sub
-->
</SCRIPT>
```

Now we could just repeat this section of code for each button as well, but this would make for a very long section of code, just for the toolbar. Instead we can return the concept of event bubbling and we can finally see how it can save us a lot of effort in this case.

Event Bubbling in the Toolbar

Let's start with the **OnMouseOver** event. Since we want to respond to all events within the toolbar, but ignore other events, we will only want to look at events generated within the toolbar element and its children. Practically speaking, we want to trap the **Document_onMouseOver** event.

The first thing you need to do when trapping an event is to determine what element generated the event. To do this we ask the event object which element generated the event. This is where **srcElement** property we looked at earlier comes into play. It contains a reference to the element that generated the event. We need to assign this value to an object variable that we can use. In this case the object which we are assigning to the object variable is an element on the HTML page.

```
Sub Document_onMouseOver()
    set obj = window.event.srcElement
end sub
```

As before, if the user passes over one of the down images, we want to raise it. The element object has an ID property, this is the ID that we assigned to it. All we need to do, then, is confirm that the user has passed over a down, or flat, button and respond accordingly.

```
Sub Document_onMouseOver()

    set obj = window.event.srcElement
    Select Case Left(obj.ID,5)
    Case "btndn"
            obj.style.display = "none"
            document.images("btnup" & Right(obj.ID,1)).Style.display = ""
            cancelEvent
    end select
end sub
```

In this example, we look at the text of the element's ID field. If it starts with the letters **btndn**, which conforms to our naming convention, then the user passed over a non-highlighted button, so we should highlight it. We first turn the button off. Since **obj** is just a reference to the original element, **obj** has a style property just like the original **btndn** object that was created. Next, to turn on the highlighted button we must reference it in the images collection of the document object.

A collection is like an array of objects, but it has one additional feature, and that is the ability to reference the objects by a key field. In the case of the scripting object model, all objects within a collection are referenced by the ID of the object or by its ordinal position within the collection. In this case we want to reference the **btnup** element that corresponds to the **btndn** element we just hid.

Finally, we cancel the event. You must remember to cancel the event, once you've handled it, or it will continue to 'bubble up' until it has passed to through all container objects. The code for the **cancelEvent** routine is straightforward.

```
Sub cancelEvent()
    window.event.returnValue = false
    window.event.cancelBubble = true
end sub
```

Now that we've seen how to handle events and program for event bubbling, let's finish the **onMouseOver**, **onMouseOut**, and **onClick** events for the button bar and together with the **cancelEvent** procedure, the basic implementation of the toolbar will be complete. It is important to note that the following script together with will replace any previous scripting code that we've created.

```
<SCRIPT LANGUAGE="VBScript">
<!-

NumberOfButtons = 3
    'Designates how many buttons are on the
    'coolbar

Sub Document_onMouseOver()

    set obj = window.event.srcElement
    Select Case Left(obj.ID,5)
    Case "btndn"
            ' The mouse moved over one of
            ' the DOWN buttons so switch
            ' it with the correct UP button
```

```vbscript
                    obj.style.display = "none"
                    document.images("btnup" & _
                            Right(obj.ID,1)).Style.display = ""
                    cancelevent

            Case "btnup"
                    ' Its ok to move over an up
                    ' button we just want to
                    ' ignore this move but there is no
                    ' need to bubble up the event

                    cancelEvent
            Case else
                    ' The mouse moved over something
                    ' else on the page or coolbar.
                    ' Obviously the mouse is nolonger
                    ' over a button so replace all
                    ' UP buttons with DOWN buttons.

                    for iIndex = 1 to NumberOfButtons
                            document.images("btnup" & _
                                    Cstr(iIndex)).Style.display = _
                                    "none"
                            document.images("btndn" & _
                                    CStr(iIndex)).Style.display = ""
                    Next
            end select
    end sub

Sub Document_onMouseOut()

    set obj = window.event.srcElement
    if Left(obj.ID,5)="btnup" then
            ' The mouse is moving out
            ' of the range of an UP button so
            ' put it back down. This event does
            ' not fire if the user
            ' moves the mouse quickly,
            ' that is why the MOUSEOVER event is
            ' used above.

            if document.images("btnup" & _
                    Right(obj.ID,1)).Style.display _
                    = "" then
                            obj.style.display = "none"
                            document.images("btndn" & _
                            Right(obj.ID,1)).Style.display= ""
                    cancelEvent
            end if
    end if

end sub

Sub Document_onClick
    set obj = window.event.srcElement

    ' If the user clicked on one of the
    ' UP buttons then do the appropriate
    ' action.
```

```
      if Left(obj.ID,5)="btnup" then
            Select Case Right(obj.ID,1)
            Case "1"
                    Msgbox "New Clicked!"
            Case "2"
                    Msgbox "Open Clicked!"
            Case "3"
                    MsgBox "Delete Clicked!"
            end select
            cancelEvent
      end if
end sub

Sub cancelEvent()
    ' Cancels a "bubbleup" event.
    ' This informs the
    ' system that the event has
    ' been handled and does
    ' not need to be passed on
    ' to other controls or the browser.

    window.event.returnValue = false
    window.event.cancelBubble = true
end sub
-->
</SCRIPT>
```

The code can be found in the file toolbar2.html on the samples page at http://rapid.wrox.co.uk/books/ 0707.

Getting More Advanced

It raises and lowers buttons. It responds to clicks. It's a toolbar!

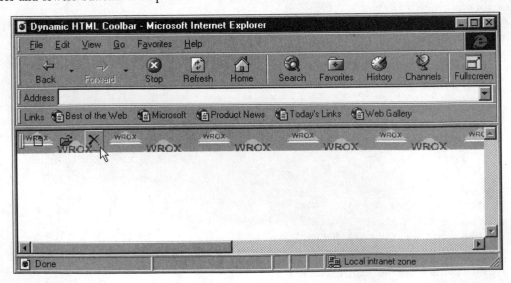

But toolbars can do so much more. Look at MS Word '97. If we hover over a button it displays a tooltip. We can drag the toolbar from side to side, or reposition it anywhere on the screen. And if we leave MS Word '97 and come back at a later time, the toolbar is positioned exactly where we left it.

Creating a Tooltip

Creating a tooltip is simple—we just display a given message over our toolbar. But let's make this a little more dynamic. First, we need to add a tooltip element to the page. Let's place it directly after the toolbar element, after the `</DIV>` statement.

```
<DIV ID="tooltip" STYLE="background:cornsilk; position:absolute; top=0; left=0;
height=15; width=75; font-size:12; display:none">
 
</DIV>
```

The reason we define the tooltip outside of the toolbar element is that we want to place the tooltip over the toolbar, quite possibly displaying the tooltip outside of the area of the toolbar. Also, the tooltip's initial display is set to none as we don't want it shown.

Now, let's analyze how a tooltip reacts. A tooltip only comes up after someone has hovered over an element for a given period of time. Also, a tooltip hides itself if the mouse moves again. So how do we generate an event that happens after a timed delay? The object model provides us with a method to generate timed events.

SetTimeout and ClearTimeout

The SetTimeout method allows the HTML developer to create his/her own timed events.

```
TimerID = setTimeout(event ,delay, [language])
```

▲ *event* - is the name of the subroutine or function that you wish to have the timeout method call

▲ *delay* - is the time, in milliseconds, to delay before establishing the event. One half of one second would be 500 milliseconds.

▲ *language* - is the language that was used to define the method or function that is being called. If the language parameter is not specified the default, JScript, is used.

SetTimeout is a function. It returns an ID that references the timed event that we have just created. To use it, first, we will need to setup a subroutine that displays the tooltip and we'll call it ShowTooltip. We'll pass it a number corresponding to the tooltip we wish to display.

```
Sub ShowToolTip(xWhich)

    ' Event just fired to display the tooltip.
    ' Position it over the correct button and
    ' change the tip to the appropriate text.

tooltip.style.posleft=toolbar.style.posleft+_
        document.images("btnup" & _
                xWhich).Style.posleft + 5
```

```
tooltip.style.postop=toolbar.style.posTop _
        + document.images("btnup" & _
                xWhich).Style.postop + _
                document.images("btnup" & _
                xWhich).Style.posheight
tooltip.style.display = ""

Select Case xWhich
    Case "1"
            Tooltip.innerText="Start it"
    Case "2"
            Tooltip.innerText="Open it"
    Case "3"
            Tooltip.innerText="Delete it"
end select
end sub
```

Notice that we position the tooltip by manipulating its style object, specifically the **posleft** and **postop** properties that represent its left and top coordinates. We get these coordinates by adding the left and top values of the toolbar to the left and top values of the button element whose tip we are displaying. The reason for this is that all elements of the toolbar are in their own coordinate system, separate from the document's coordinate system. Therefore, the coordinates of the button would not represent the button's true positioning on the screen. Remember, the toolbar is defined as having position:absolute. After positioning the tooltip element we then display it, simply by settings its display property to an empty string.

The innerText property used in the example was covered in the last chapter. Basically the method allows the HTML to extract text from the page itself and then change that text to something else. In our example we are changing the blank space   stored in the tooltip element to the text specified. Now that we have the **ShowToolTip** routine complete we just need to set the timer so that it will display. We'll do this in **onMouseOver** event when we enable the highlighted button image.

```
Case "btndn"
    ' The mouse moved over one of
    ' the DOWN buttons so switch
            ' it with the correct UP button

    obj.style.display = "none"
            document.images("btnup" & _
                Right(obj.ID,1)).Style.display = ""
            cancelevent

    ' Turn on the ToolTip timer
    ToolTipId = setTimeout("ShowToolTip(" & _
            Right(obj.ID,1) & ")",500,"VBScript")
Case "btnup"
```

We pass the number on the button ID to the **ShowToolTip** event and set the timer to initialize after one half of one second or 500 milliseconds. Also, we specify that the language being used is VBScript and not the default JScript. ToolTipId needs to be defined as a global variable because we will need this value to turn off the timed event in the case of the mouse moving. It is very simple.

For instance, when the mouse moves we want to stop the tooltip from coming up, but only if it isn't moving on a button. We just need to modify the three events we've already defined: **onMouseOver**, **onMouseOut**, and **onClick**.

154

```
Sub Document_onMouseOver()

    set obj = window.event.srcElement
    Select Case Left(obj.ID,5)
    Case "btndn"
            ' The mouse moved over one of
            ' the DOWN buttons so switch
            ' it with the correct UP button

            obj.style.display = "none"
            document.images("btnup" & _
                    Right(obj.ID,1)).Style.display = ""
            cancelevent
            ' Turn on the ToolTip timer
    ToolTipId = setTimeout("ShowToolTip(" & _
                    Right(obj.ID,1) & ")",500,"VBScript")

    Case "btnup"
            ' Its ok to move over an up
            ' button we just want to
            ' ignore this move
    Case else
            ' The mouse moved over something
            ' else on the page or coolbar.
            ' Obviously the mouse is nolonger
            ' over a button so replace all
            ' UP buttons with DOWN buttons.

            for iIndex = 1 to NumberOfButtons
                    document.images("btnup" & _
                            Cstr(iIndex)).Style.display = _
                            "none"
                    document.images("btndn" & _
                            CStr(iIndex)).Style.display = ""
            Next
            tooltip.style.display = "none"
            clearTimeout(ToolTipID)
    end select
end sub

Sub Document_onMouseOut()

    set obj = window.event.srcElement
    if Left(obj.ID,5)="btnup" then
            ' The mouse is moving out
            ' of the range of an UP button so
            ' put it back down. This event does
            ' not fire if the user
            ' moves the mouse quickly,
            ' that is why the MOUSEOVER event is
            ' used above.

            if document.images("btnup" & _
                    Right(obj.ID,1)).Style.display _
                    = "" then
                            obj.style.display = "none"
                            document.images("btndn" & _
                            Right(obj.ID,1)).Style.display = ""
```

```
                    tooltip.style.display = "none"
                    clearTimeout(ToolTipID)
                            cancelevent
                    end if
        end if

end sub

Sub Document_onClick
        set obj = window.event.srcElement

        ' If the user clicked on one of the
        ' UP buttons then do the appropriate
        ' action.

        if Left(obj.ID,5)="btnup" then
                Select Case Right(obj.ID,1)
                Case "1"
                        Msgbox "New Clicked!"
                Case "2"
                        Msgbox "Open Clicked!"
                Case "3"
                        MsgBox "Delete Clicked!"
                end select
        tooltip.style.display = "none"
        clearTimeout(ToolTipID)
                cancelevent
    end if
end sub
```

All code, up to this point, can be viewed in `toolbar3.html` *and can be found on the web site at http:/
/rapid.wrox.co.uk/books/0707*

The toolbar now has tooltips. It's almost a fully fledged toolbar.

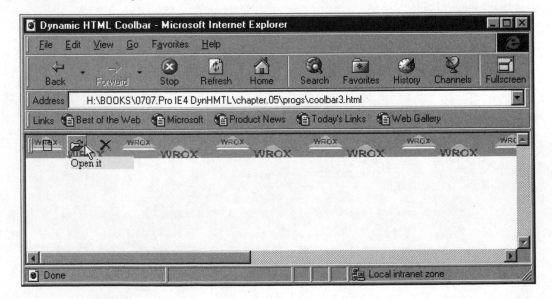

Positioning the Toolbar

Well, it looks like it's almost done. In fact, we could stop here. The toolbar responds to clicks, mouse movement, and even generates tooltips to give the user some aid in using the element, but our definition included one more thing: repositioning.

Really, this is nothing new. We want to capture an event that tells us that someone is attempting to drag the toolbar. Dragging involves mouse movement and holding down the mouse button. One thought would be to use the onmouseover event, but this doesn't inform us that the user is holding down the button. We don't want to drag the element every time the mouse is moved only when the mouse button is held down on the element we named baricon, the double-lined bar at the beginning of the toolbar.

The Event Object Properties

So we need to respond to this event by positioning the toolbar element at the same x,y coordinates. To simulate the slide from side to side that toolbars do, we'll just narrow our focus. If the **y** coordinate of the mouse-position doesn't change by too much we will leave our toolbar at the top of the screen, giving the bar a "snap to" effect. Also, when we do drag our toolbar we need to shrink its width so that it appears to "float" like other toolbars when dragged.

Sliding the toolbar is rather simple. As you would expect, just set the posLeft property of the toolbar to the value returned by **x**. The trick is that the mouse can move faster than the browser can report the event. This causes the mouse pointer to move out of the bounds of the toolbar. To compensate for this we will set a state variable, `DraggingToolbar`, to designate that the toolbar is being dragged.

```
Dim DraggingToolBar

Sub Document_onMouseDown
Dim obj
    ' If the mouse button is pressed down
    ' over the "baricon" image then
    ' start a drag

    set obj = Window.event.srcElement
    if obj.ID = "baricon" then
            DraggingToolBar = True
            toolbar.style.zIndex = 1
            cancelEvent
    else
            DragginToolBar = False
    end if

end sub

Sub Document_onMouseMove
dim iIndex
dim x, y
    ' If the mouse is moved and
    ' the toolbar is in drag mode
    ' then the user is attempting a drag.

    if DraggingToolBar then
            x = window.event.x
            y = window.event.y
```

```
            Position_Toolbar x, y

            cancelEvent
      end if

   end sub

   Sub Document_onMouseUp

      ' If the toolbar is being dragged and
      ' the mousebutton is released then
      ' stop dragging mode.

      if DraggingToolBar then
            DraggingToolBar = False
            cancelEvent
      end if

   end sub

   Sub Position_Toolbar(x, y)
   dim iIndex

      ' Set the posleft position of the toolbar relative
      ' to the position of the "baricon" image

      if x - baricon.style.posleft - 7 > 0 then
            toolbar.style.posLeft = x - baricon.style.posleft - 7
      end if

   end sub
```

OK, now the toolbar slides back and forth. To implement a drag we just need to set the **posTop** to the **y** coordinate that is passed to the onmousemove event. Since it wouldn't make sense to drag the toolbar but keep it the width of the screen, we need to resize it and make it look like a windowed object.

First, we need to add two more global variables to the routine, one that represents the number of icons on the toolbar and the other that represents the width of the icons. These numbers will be used to determine the width of the toolbar when it is being dragged.

```
<SCRIPT LANGUAGE="VBScript">
<!--
    ' Global constants for toolbar element

NumberOfButtons = 3          'How many buttons are
                             'we displaying
-->
</SCRIPT>
```

Using these two values, we'll implement the logic for dragging the toolbar.

```
Sub Position_Toolbar(x, y)
dim iIndex

    ' Set the posleft position of the toolbar relative
    ' to the position of the "baricon" image

    if x - baricon.style.posleft - 7 > 0 then
            toolbar.style.posLeft = x - baricon.style.posleft - 7
    end if

    ' if the mouse y-position is more than 3/4 of the height of the
    ' toolbar, then resize the toolbar to look like a floating window
    ' otherwise "snap" the toolbar to the top margin of the window

    if y > (tbstrip.style.posHeight * (3/4)) then
            tbstrip.border=5
            tbstrip.height=38
            tbstrip.bordercolor = "00008B"
            tbstrip.style.posWidth = _
                    document.images("btndn" & NumberOfButtons).Style.PosLeft _
                    + document.images("btndn" & NumberOfButtons).width + 20
            toolbar.style.posTop = Y - (tbstrip.style.posHeight / 2)
            for iIndex = 1 to NumberOfButtons
                    document.images("btndn" & iIndex).Style.PosTop = 5
                    document.images("btnup" & iIndex).Style.PosTop = 5
            next
    else
            tbstrip.border = 0
            tbstrip.height=28
            tbstrip.style.posWidth = 1280
            toolbar.style.posTop = 0
            for iIndex = 1 to NumberOfButtons
                    document.images("btndn" & iIndex).Style.PosTop = 0
                    document.images("btnup" & iIndex).Style.PosTop = 0
            next
    end if

end sub
```

We've used another element that we originally setup in the HTML code, the **tbstrip. tbstrip** is the reference to the TABLE element that makes up the toolbar. We need to resize the table when it is being dragged so that it appears as a window. Also, you'll notice that we manipulate its border property, making it 5 pixels wide while being dragged and turning the bordercolor to a dark blue. Manipulating elements through scripting in Internet Explorer 4.0 is straightforward. This completed example can be found in the toolbar4.html sample file.

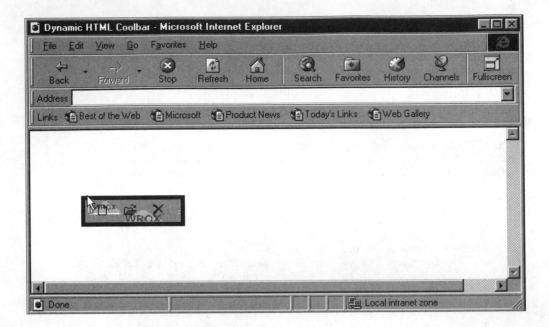

Saving the Positioning - Cookies

All that is left is to save the position of the toolbar so that a return visit to the page will display the toolbar in the same position that the user has chosen. We can accomplish this with a cookie. A cookie is a piece of data that is stored on the browser's computer that can be retrieved by a script capable browser or the server. To save cookie information you just assign a string to the **document.cookie** property. For example, **document.cookie = "MYNAME = John Doe"**.

Cookies, also, have an optional expiration that can be assigned to them, if no expiration is assigned the cookie is discarded when the browser session is stopped. Expiration dates must be formatted in standard time format. For example, to expire a cookie on Dec 31, 1997 you would include the following in your string: EXPIRES=Friday, 31-Dec-1997 23:59:00 GMT.

Let's put the following code in our project.

```
Sub window_onunload
Dim CookieString

    ' When the current HTML page unloads or changes to another page
    ' save the current top and left properties of the toolbar so that
    ' it can be repositioned correctly when the user comes back
    ' to this page.
```

```
   Document.Cookie = "TBLEFT=" & toolbar.style.posleft & _
          ";EXPIRES=Friday, 31-Dec-1997 23:59:00 GMT"
   Document.Cookie = "TBTOP=" & toolbar.style.postop & _
          ";EXPIRES=Friday, 31-Dec-1997 23:59:00 GMT"

end sub
```

The `window_onunload` event tells the script that the page is being unloaded. Either the browser is being shut down, or another page is being loaded. Hence, it only makes sense that we store the current settings of the toolbar just before unloading the current page. Likewise, it would make sense to setup the toolbar as soon as the page is loaded into the browser. We can use the `window_onunload` event for this purpose.

```
Sub window_onload
Dim CookieString
Dim HoldString

    ' Reloads the position that the toolbar was in when the page
    ' was last viewed.

    CookieString = Document.Cookie
    if InStr(CookieString,"TBLEFT")=0 then
          toolbar.style.posleft = 0
          toolbar.style.postop = 0
    else
          HoldString = Mid(CookieString,InStr(CookieString,"TBLEFT=")+7)
          if InStr(HoldString,";") then Holdstring = _
                      Left(HoldString,InStr(HoldString,";")-1)
          toolbar.style.posleft = HoldString
          HoldString = Mid(CookieString,InStr(CookieString,"TBTOP=")+6)
          if InStr(HoldString,";") then Holdstring = _
                      Left(HoldString,InStr(HoldString,";")-1)
          toolbar.style.postop = HoldString
    end if

    Position_Toolbar toolbar.style.posLeft, toolbar.style.posTop

End Sub
```

You probably noticed that the last line of the above code calls our Position_Toolbar procedure. Remember, anytime we can lower the amount of code in our HTML document, the faster it will download to the browser. Moving code that is reused into one common procedure is a perfect way of lowering your code size.

One thing to remember is that the `document.cookie` does not return the expiration date, only the variables that you passed to it. Also important to note, is that the 'cookie' is returned in one long string, even though it was established with two calls to the function. Make sure to include unique variable names so that you can properly parse the data from the string.

Summary

Scripting has always been useful for enhancing our HTML pages but now, with the release of IE4, it has become a tool for developing tools within our HTML pages. As we've seen, scripting can now manipulate elements within a page, respond to many more events within that page, and even control the layout of the page after the page has been loaded.

We covered quite a few points in brief that will be covered in more detail in later chapters. The most important points are:

- ▲ We can add scripts to our HTML code in many different ways.

- ▲ We can create code elements from HTML tags that use CSS-Positioning allowing them to be manipulated.

- ▲ Elements respond to events through event handlers. By default, any generated events bubble up the browser object hierarchy, but can be turned off explicitly.

- ▲ We can position elements within their own coordinate systems.

- ▲ We can respond events generated by the user, such as mouse movement, mouse clicks, and loading and unloading the page.

- ▲ We can save and retrieve data to remember what the user had done last time he visited our page and redraw our page accordingly.

At the end of this first section you should now have a good feel for Dynamic HTML and the IE4 object model. In the next section, we're going to be moving swiftly onwards to some of IE4's more advanced databinding features, and looking at some detailed case studies of those features in action.

Working With Databases

PART
2

In this section of the book we're looking at what is destined to become one of the cornerstone applications of Dynamic HTML–database access. Since the earliest days of computing, application analysts and corporate Management Information System(MIS) personnel alike have been in search of a holy grail known as "ubiquitous instant corporate data access". The idea is simple–to enable the timely access of the corporate data assets in a customized, controlled, secure and flexible manner, for everyone who needs it. What is not simple, however, is the means by which this can be achieved.

Most people have heard the terms 4GL, client/server computing, data access middleware, decision support systems, and data warehousing. These are all current attempts to provide components that facilitate this elusive "ubiquitous instant corporate data access". Many of the solutions are single-vendor products (i.e. mainframe, mini or RDBMS centric) and prohibitively expensive–scoring poorly on the cost-effectiveness scale.

The explosive growth of the Internet, combined with the subsequent phenomenon of the application of Internet technology to the corporate network (often called the Intranet), has provided the catalyst for a new approach to this data access problem. Data access on the web is instant, and most of the web based access technologies are free, or still relatively inexpensive. The ease with which HTML pages can be put together, even by authors with minimal programming training, provides a panacea for customized, controlled, access to "back-end" data. Furthermore, there is a growing trend for software vendors to add new Intranet features to their existing products. This trend will greatly facilitate technology integration in heterogeneous environments.

Now, Dynamic HTML provides one of the most promising, flexible, and cost-effective solutions to the classic data access problem through **Data Binding**–the subject of the next four chapters.

An Introduction to Data Binding

In the introduction to this section of the book, we talked about the problems of accessing databases in a way that provides "ubiquitous instant corporate data access". Although this is a universal concept across the Internet, as more sites start to be powered by a back-end database, we must step back a little to understand where the new techniques of data binding actually come from.

We'll take a detour from the innovative but free-wheeling world of the Internet, to venture into the more serious and disciplined world of corporate business computing on the Intranet. We need to do this because many of the design decisions made by Microsoft for Dynamic HTML data binding are based on the requirements of the corporation, as much as the global Internet user. Their approach to Dynamic HTML data access has evolved from techniques applied to business data networks. Even if you are Internet bound, and currently do not care too much about Intranets, please bear with us–many of the following ideas and techniques can be creatively applied on the Internet as well. This is especially true with the merging of the two realms in the exciting new world of e-commerce and the "extranet", as you'll see in this and subsequent chapters.

This first chapter is designed as an introduction to the whole subject of data binding, and so we'll be taking an overview of the way it fits together. Then, we'll move on to look at some of the simplest ways it can be applied. In the remaining three chapters of this part of the book, we'll be expanding and developing on these simple beginnings to provide you with a full understanding of it's amazing capabilities.

So, in this chapter, we'll be examining:

- ▲ Where and how the concepts of Dynamic HTML data binding arose
- ▲ What Dynamic HTML data binding actually is, and how it works in overview
- ▲ The elements that support data binding, and the new attributes that enable it
- ▲ The two generic presentation formats used in data binding
- ▲ An introduction to the data source objects that link data to the page
- ▲ A look at the simplest of these data source objects, the Tabular Data Control

By the end of the chapter, you will appreciate some of the advantages of Dynamic HTML data binding, and understand how it works in outline. You'll also see the simplest of the data source controls in use. But first, we'll look at where data binding came from.

The Data Access Evolution Cycle

Let's attempt to appreciate why we needed Dynamic HTML data binding. The answer can be found in the historical evolution of data access. In a nutshell, the task of corporate data access, and database management, can be summarized as consisting four functional parts or "layers". These layers, from the lowest to the highest, are:

- **Physical data storage and management**
  This layer deals with the actual storage of the data on physical medium, such as a disk drive or tape. The actual organization and management of the data (i.e. mapping to disk files, file formats) also belongs to this layer.

- **Logical relationship and integrity management**
  This layer deals with the logical data items, and how they are related to each other—frequently, patterns of relationships would surface during analysis of the data organization. It also contains provisions to enforce these relationships during data entry and modification.

- **Designer/Business Logic enforcement**
  This deals with the "real-world" application of the data items. During the process of system design and analysis, rules and relationships reflecting business practices or anticipated system behavior are identified. This layer implements the logic to enforce these business logic rules and relationships.

- **Presentation for end-user data access and modification**
  This layer provides what the end-user will actually see and work with. From a user point of view, this *is* the application. This layer hides the details of all the lower layers from the user, and gives them an interface to work with. This interface is typically very specific to the tasks required to be performed, as well as providing any alternate presentation of the underlying data required.

Implementations of the Functional Model

The root of the data access problem centers round the simultaneous sharing of one or more data sources amongst potentially many users, each with diverse requirements. We'll step back in time to observe how this problem has been solved, and see the how layers of responsibility have been handled by various system architectures.

Mainframe Based Centralized Access

In the beginning of interactive computing, there were mainframe computers and dumb access terminals. Databases were all kept on the mainframe, and the dumb terminals were used to "timeshare" the expensive mainframe resource. All of these early terminals were text based, and many supported a "form" mode—which allowed the data-entry operator to enter data into a form painted by instructions sent from the mainframe. Once the form was completed, the operator could hit a "submit" key, which sent the data to the mainframe for validation and further processing.

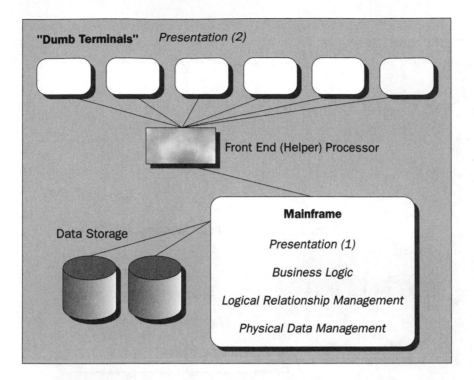

Some later terminals also provided minimal validation of the entered data, based on a template sent with the form from the mainframe. This early model of data access is centralized. The data management is handled by the mainframe, while the presentation task is shared between the mainframe (1) and the dumb terminals (2)–a set-up that bears some resemblance to modern client/server technologies.

UNIX, Smart Terminals, and More Centralized Computing

Next, the minicomputers and UNIX-based super-microcomputers took over small business computing. The dumb terminals continued to triumph, and amazingly became even dumber along the way. Thanks to higher speed interconnection between the CPU and the terminals, many of them didn't actually have to support forms (saving significant cost). Since every single character typed on every terminal was intercepted by the centralized computer, it was possible to generate the form display and manage the data entry operation entirely from the central computer.

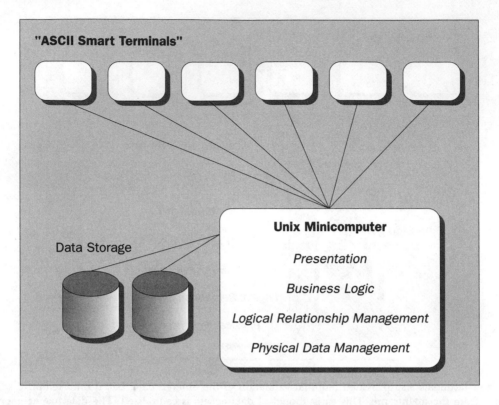

Although many terminals of this generation were called "ASCII/ANSI smart terminals", because they contained microprocessor technologies and accepted "macro" programming, operationally they were actually dumber than their predecessors. This era of data access was even more centralized, as both data management and presentation were handled by the centralized computer. During this period, many of the less critical data management functions shifted from mainframe control to minicomputer (or super-micro) control. Minicomputers during this era typically use proprietary components, while super-micros use commodity off-the-shelf parts.

Graphical User Interface Hiding Centralized Data Access

With UNIX came the first widely adopted attempt at a Graphical User Interface–known as X-Windows. The X-Windows model, introduced by MIT, takes a completely GUI workstation-centric computing point of view. When first introduced it also challenged conventional wisdom, by reversing the accepted definition of client versus server. The X-Clients were non-graphical programs that ran on the computing server, and which managed the data and access logistics.

Meanwhile, the X-Servers (servers designed to display the graphics) were fully graphical, mouse based, display and entry 'X-Terminals' which could handle graphical primitives. The connection between the UNIX based server machines (hosting the X-Clients) and the X-Terminals (hosting the X-Server) was a high speed LAN connection (typically Ethernet). Thanks to this speed, our centralized data management and presentation architecture was given a new life in a graphical world.

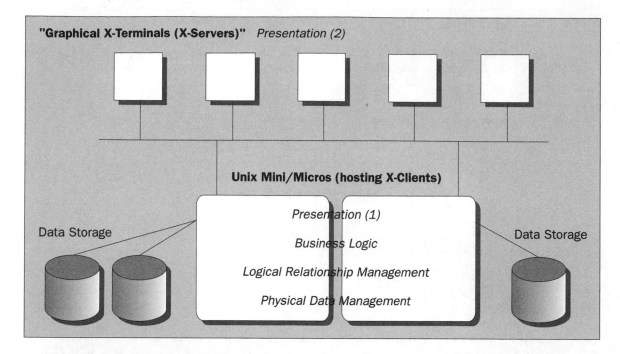

Even though the LAN provided an opportunity to distribute the data access and management workload amongst multiple servers, such an architecture was typically not taken advantage of by software in this fast-growing and highly profitable era. Instead, each X-Terminal was typically given separate access to multiple monolithic data servers, one in each window.

Microcomputers As Terminal Emulators

Next came the powerful microcomputers, ready to ruin it all. Initially, these were limited to terminal emulation mode—they could emulate the early dumb mainframe terminals (i.e. IBM 3270), the later ASCII/ANSI smart terminals (i.e. VT220 or WYSE 50), and X-Terminals (by executing an X-Server over a graphical operating system such as Windows). Indeed, early versions of most of the current major database systems all used the PC in this way.

Attempts to Decentralize: Client/Server Computing

Shortly after their introduction, however, power users discovered that their LAN interconnection and PCs were severely under-utilized when acting as dumb terminals. In answer to their demands, and in an attempt to reduce the cost of computing in general, the database industry entertained a new mode of computing known as **client-server**.

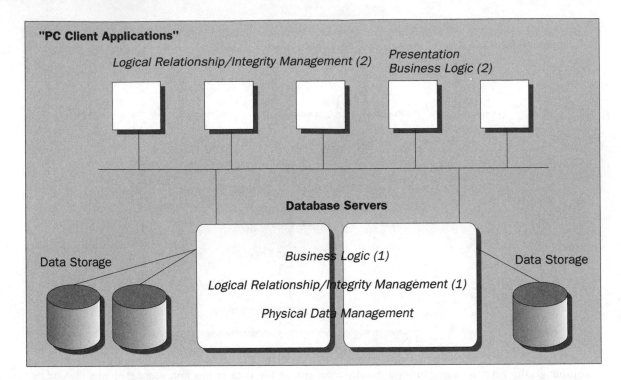

This was the first real step towards true "smart terminal" computing. In client/server computing (at its simplest, also known as two-tier computing) the centralized server still maintains most of the control over data management and data access. However, the client—or smart PC terminal—will completely handle the presentation task, and also perform some intelligent data validation. As a matter of fact, this was the first architecture in the evolution where the centralized data server usually *did not* have a hand in the presentation layer. In many cases, even some of the business logic and integrity management functions were moved onto the (unfortunately less reliable) client PC. This also marked the beginning of the application of a true distributed processing model to microcomputer data processing.

The Web: Back to Centralized Computing with a Twist

Just as client/server computing was gathering steam, and new "fourth generation" tools were becoming available to automatically generate the presentation code for the PC client, along came the Internet. Having realized that the lack of centralized control over presentation was not desirable, the web model of "thin client everywhere" became very appealing to modern-day database designers. Recent industry-wide audits of MIS bottom-lines revealed alarmingly high cost of ownership associated with the decentralized microcomputer based client/server computing model. This further reinforced the need for a more centrally controllable architecture.

In fact, the PC web terminal (known today as a browser) is graphical, and is smarter than ever. It doesn't just display characters and primitive macros like UNIX terminals, or graphical primitives like X-Terminals. It can also provide forms (thanks to standard HTML), do any sort of custom data validation (thanks to scripting), and execute custom macros (using scripts downloaded with the page). It will even change the behavior and appearance of the data it displays, based on instructions received (using, for example, Java and ActiveX controls and now, Dynamic HTML).

As a matter of fact, the entire behavior of the (browser) terminal is completely customizable. The back-end server has control over how the data access, management, and presentation duties should be split between the database server and the PC web terminal. Notice that our data access model has traveled full circle–back to an apparently centralized control model. This time, however, the control emanates from a "back-office", which consists of multiple special purpose servers (i.e. database server, mail server, SNA server, etc.) connected by a network. This back-office architecture can often be a distributed one as well:

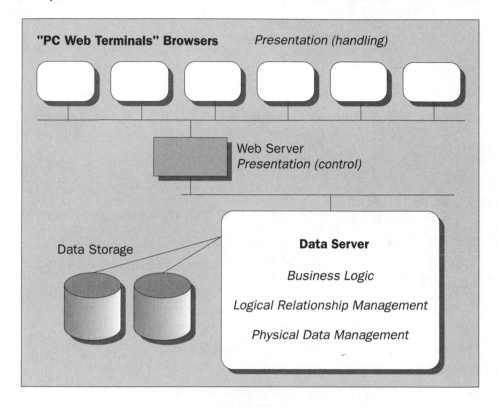

Ironically, while all of this was going on, very little has happened to all those critical data stores that were left managed by mainframe computers. To involve this legacy data in typical data access scenarios, new multi-tiered computing architectures were devised. In this new model, the presentation is controlled by the client, the "logic" (sometimes called the "business rules") is encapsulated in objects running on their own servers, while the data access is performed by the corresponding database servers (either new or legacy). This topology is frequently referred to as the "three tier" client/server computing model.

Dynamic HTML and Data Binding – Accelerating the Evolution

Dynamic HTML and its data binding extensions are instrumental in making this web revolution practical. Data access applications can be authored using Dynamic HTML data binding so as to provide the desired centralized control, without sacrificing client side responsiveness and flexibility. Server interventions can be minimized, while a larger portion of the data access, validation, and management work can be intelligently offloaded to the smart client browser. This can all be achieved while maintaining full control in the back-office. The heavily componentized architecture of the new Internet Explorer 4 makes it ideal as a "PC Web Terminal" client, or as the presentation front-end for a multi-tiered object-based data access application. .

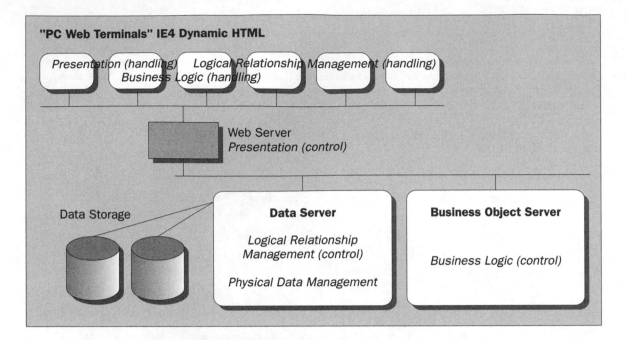

This chronology brings us right up to date, and we can now start to examine the latest marvel in the evolution of networked data access. A Dynamic HTML based data access solution can be:

▲ Highly cost effective

▲ A more efficient solution than standard HTML-based methods

▲ Superior in performance terms to a server based solution

▲ Completely complementary to any other data access solution available

▲ Potentially vendor-independent, enabling best-of-breed technology selection

▲ A natural lead into an "extranet" model, providing access to agencies external to the corporation, through the extension of a secure Intranet

And of course, the data access and data presentation techniques are also generally applicable outside of the corporate enterprises–in the Internet at large.

Data Binding – The Basic Principles

The most natural way for Dynamic HTML to work with data sources is through a mechanism referred to as **data binding**. If you've used any relational database Rapid Application Development (RAD) products before, such as Oracle Forms, PowerBuilder, Microsoft Access, Borland Delphi, or even Microsoft Visual Basic, the overall concept of data binding will probably be familiar.

With data binding in Dynamic HTML, specific data items originating from a data source (i.e. a database server) are "bound" to visual HTML elements. The control then acts as the interface to that particular field, or column of data, in the data source. It displays the current value from a particular record in that source table, and can be used to change the value in certain circumstances. The web page designer (or application designer) can code the association between a data item from a data source by using a selection of existing HTML controls and elements, and new attributes for these elements.

The Overall Structure and Components

Consistent with the componentized, object oriented architecture of IE 4, data binding uses a series of components to provide the link between the data source and the visible element on the page:

The **data source object** is required to be a client side ActiveX control (or Java Applet). It provides the bridging between the visual HTML elements participating in data binding, and the actual data source (usually remote). The data source object works intimately with the actual server side data source, and the pair can implement custom and intelligent caching schemes to improve data access efficiency and responsiveness. Sometimes referred to as a *data provider*.

The **data consumers** (in Microsoft's terminology) are the visual elements in the page that participate in data binding, such as HTML control elements like **<INPUT>** and **<SELECT>**, or non-control elements such as **<A>** and **<MARQUEE>**.

Let's look at an example of how this works. The following is a diagram of an HTML page, with three **<INPUT>** text fields bound to data originating from remote data source, through a client side data source object:

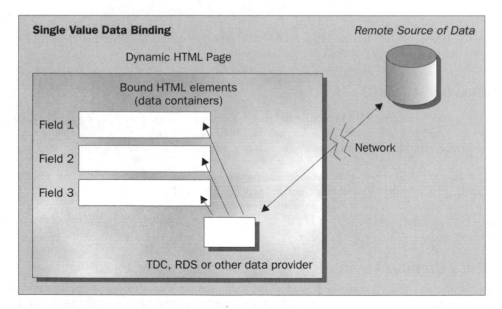

175

The Data Source Object

IE4 itself includes two data source objects with the standard distribution. They are:

- ▲ **TDC** – the Tabular Data Control, for accessing simple flat-file data sources
- ▲ **RDS** – a complex front-end control to access Microsoft's Remote Data Services

If neither of these fits the task in hand, it's possible to create you own data source object based on the COM specifications and using the interfaces provided by OLE-DB. This subject is outside the scope of this book, however.

Tabular Data Control (TDC)

The TDC object works with "databases" that are in the form of delimited ASCII data in text files, and it provides read-only access. It downloads and caches the entire data file on the client, and requires no subsequent server access. If your application can live with a read-only, static view of the data, this control should be your first choice since it is both lighter weight and substantially easier to setup and program.

Remote Data Service (RDS)

The RDS object works with a variety of server side data sources through ODBC, and without custom client-side software installation or consumption of excessive client resources. It manages a dynamic client-side recordset cache, and tunnels all requests and data transfer through HTTP. If your application requires data entry, modification or update this is your only choice at present, unless you create your own control object. It's also the one to use if your application requires read-only access to dynamically changing back-end databases since this is also your only built-in choice.

As you can clearly see, the TDC and the RDS controls address very different audiences. Most of the time, it is a very easy selection, driven by application requirements.

The Data Consumers

We'll now examine the "bindable" HTML elements, and see in outline how data binding affects each them. All of the elements listed below support single-valued data binding, and can also be used inside the template of a repeated table binding—you'll meet these two presentation formats in a while.

Some of the elements provide a read-only presentation, while others are read/write and allow the source data to be updated. In addition, some of the elements support HTML Rendering, where any HTML tags within the data are rendered as such by the element. Elements that don't support HTML Rendering will just display any HTML content as text, showing the tags themselves. Again, we'll examine what this means in more depth later on.

The New Data Binding Attributes

Each of the elements that supports data binding also has some new attributes to enable and control this feature. The new attributes are `DATASRC`, `DATAFLD`, `DATAFORMATAS`, and `DATAPAGESIZE`. Only the `<TABLE>` element supports `DATAPAGESIZE`. However, the other data binding elements support one or more of the other three attributes.

Attribute	Description
DATASRC	A string value, which must begin with the '#' character. This attribute identifies the data source object used for data binding, typically an ActiveX control (i.e. TDC or RDS), through its ID. The initial configuration of the data source object would control the actual source of the data (for example, a CSV file or a remote database).
DATAFLD	A string value identifying the field within a data record that is bound to this HTML element.
DATAFORMATAS	A string value that indicates the type of data contained in the field. This is always used in conjunction with the DATAFLD attribute and currently can be "text", "html", or "none". The value of "html" tells IE4 to parse the data as HTML before displaying it to the end user. The value of "none" leaves the data supplied in its raw, long integer form.
DATAPAGESIZE	A numeric value. This is an optional attribute useful only for repeated table binding presentation (covered later). It controls the number of visible records (rows) displayed within a bound HTML table.

An example binding of a <TABLE> element using the DATASRC attribute may look like this:

```
<TABLE ID='tblMyList' DATASRC='#tdcFruit'>....... </TABLE>
```

Here, we are binding the table tblMyList to the data source object with the ID of tdcFruit. When we come to bind a <DIV> or other element, we also have to specify the DATAFLD attribute:

```
<DIV ID='divCustName'  DATASRC='#rdsCust' DATAFLD='CustName'>
```

In this case, we are binding the divCustName (a <DIV> element) to an RDS data source object with the ID of rdsCust. The field in the database being bind to the <DIV> element is named CustName. When we use an element that supports HTML rendering, we can include the DATAFORMATAS attribute to specify how we want the data to be displayed:

```
<SPAN ID='spnDesc' DATASRC='#rdsBooks' DATAFLD='booklink' DATAFORMATAS='html'>
```

In this case, we are binding the <SPAN> element spnDesc to an RDS data source object with the ID of rdsBooks, on the field named booklink. However, we know that the value of the booklink field is actually HTML code. The above binding will cause this HTML code to be rendered into the page within the position occupied by the <SPAN> element.

These attributes have been submitted by Microsoft to the W3C for consideration for inclusion into the Dynamic HTML standard. Regardless of what name changes they may end up making during the required ratification process, the basic, very simple, data binding mechanism will probably remain very similar.

The Data Bindable HTML Elements

The elements that support data binding, and the attributes they accept, are:

Element	Capability	HTML Rendering	DATASRC	DATAFLD	DATAFORMATAS
<A>	Read only	✗	✓	✓	✗
<APPLET>	Read/Write	✗	✓(1)	✓(1)	✗
<BUTTON>	Read only	✓	✓	✓	✓
<DIV>	Read only	✓	✓	✓	✓
<FRAME>	Read only	✗	✓	✓	✗
<IFRAME>	Read only	✗	✓	✓	✗
<IMG>	Read only	✗	✓	✓	✗
<INPUT>	Read/Write	✗	✓	✓	✗
<LABEL>	Read only	✓	✓	✓	✓
<MARQUEE>	Read only	✓	✓	✓	✓
<OBJECT>	Read/Write	✗	✓	✓(2)	✗
<SELECT>	Read/Write	✗	✓	✓	✗
<SPAN>	Read only	✓	✓	✓	✓
<TABLE>	Read only	✗	✓	✗	✗
<TEXTAREA>	Read/Write	✗	✓	✓	✗

(1) Used in the **<PARAM>** tag within the **<APPLET>** tag.
(2) When used in the **<OBJECT>** tag binds the default property of the object. When used in the **<PARAM>** tag (within the **<OBJECT>** tag) it can bind a specific property instead.

The <A> Element

When bound to a data field, the **HREF** attribute is affected. This means that the **DATAFLD** attribute actually replaces the **HREF** attribute in the tag, and should correspond to a valid URL for the anchor. Binding to the **<A>** element in a repeated table can be useful for data fields which are URL links. Here's an example:

```
<TABLE DATASRC="#wroxBooks">
  <TR>
   <TD><DIV DATAFLD="bookISBN"></DIV><TD>
   <TD><A DATAFLD="relatedLinks"><DIV DATAFLD="bookName"></DIV></A><TD>
  </TR>
</TABLE>
```

This will provide a table with two columns. The first one has the ISBN number, the second has a hyperlink with the books name visible, and will take the user to a page with more information on the book when clicked. The **<A>** element provides a read-only binding.

The <APPLET> Element

The **DATASRC**, and **DATAFLD** attribute may be applied to an embedded Java applet, for binding the value of a data field from a data source object to a JavaBean property. This binding can be associated via the **<PARAM>** tag. For example:

```
<APPLET CODEBASE="http://www.wrox.com/java/"
  CODE="ShowNumber.class"  WIDTH=251 HEIGHT=125>
  <PARAM NAME="num" DATASRC="#mySource" DATAFLD="input">
</APPLET>
```

This will bind the **input** field from the current record of the **mySource** data provider to the **num** property of the JavaBean-compatible applet.

When the current record changes in a single-valued data binding, the corresponding JavaBean property of the applet will be modified. The applet may then react to the change (changing its appearance, etc.). The current Java VM implementation does not issue a notification event when the bound property value is changed during applet operation. This means that IE4 must poll the applet's bound property value every time the current record changes.

The **<APPLET>** element can also be used inside a template for a repeated table binding. Because multiple instances of the applet will be created, one for each template/row, you must make sure that the applet will work when instantiated multiple times on the same page. The **<APPLET>** element provides a read/write binding.

The <BUTTON> Element

The **<BUTTON>** element supports data binding on the text that it displays on the face of the button, and provides HTML rendering of that data. The text on a bound button's face will change when the bound data changes. The **<BUTTON>** element provides a read-only binding.

The <DIV> Element

With the **<DIV>** element, the **DATASRC** and **DATAFLD** attribute can be used to bind it to a data field from a data source object. It provides a mean of injecting almost any text or rendered HTML into a page—by using the **DATAFORMATAS="html"** attribute to bind the **<DIV>** tag to a chunk of HTML code supplied from a field in a database. This chunk of HTML code is interpreted "on the fly" as the value of the underlying data field changes.

This can be a simple, yet very powerful, technique for rendering HTML code directly driven from a database. For example, the following will render some HTML from a database:

```
<DIV DATASRC="#WroxList" DATAFLD="randHtml"> DATAFORMATAS="html"</DIV>
```

In a single-valued binding, changes to the current record will cause re-rendering of the **randHtml** field. For example, if the value of **randHtml** changes from:

```
<A HREF="http://wrox.com/listing.htm"> Click Here </A>
```

to:

```
<IMG SRC="mypicture.gif">
```

then the corresponding display will change from a hyperlink to a graphic picture. The **<DIV>** element provides a read-only binding.

The <FRAME> Element

The <FRAME> element supports data binding on the HREF attribute. This means that the source URL (i.e. the address of the content) of a frame can be obtained dynamically from a data source. One requirement for <FRAME> data binding is that the data source object must be defined in the <HEAD> section of the HTML file containing the frame. The <FRAME> element offers a read-only binding.

The <IFRAME> Element

The <IFRAME> element binds identically to the <FRAME> element. However, it does not have the requirement for the data source object to be defined in the <HEAD> section. The <IFRAME> element provides a read-only binding.

The <IMG> Element

The SRC attribute of the <IMG> element can be bound to a data field using the DATASRC and DATAFLD attributes. The data field must contain a valid URL string suitable for the SRC attribute (i.e. a URL pointing to a valid GIF or JPG file). Data binding an <IMG> element allows for dynamic changes to the displayed graphic, in line with the context of the current database record. This is a powerful technique for creating database driven, on-line catalogs. The <IMG> element provides a read-only binding.

The <INPUT> Element

The <INPUT> element represents data entry controls that are typically used in forms. Since they can be used to alter the value of the bound data, they also generate notification events for updateable elements. However, the TDC is read-only, so in this case the <INPUT> element can be used for data viewing only. With the RDS object, read/write support is possible, and the following descriptions assume this type of data source.

An <INPUT> element can be of four types. The following is a list of the types and how they are affected by data binding attributes:

Textbox – TYPE="text"
This is the most common <INPUT> type. It presents a text edit field, which will initially contain the value of the DATAFLD field. When dealing with an data source object which supports updates, any change made to the value of the edit by end user will be reflected in the bound field value.

Radio Buttons – TYPE="radio"
All radio buttons in the same grouping must have the same NAME attribute. Any of the radio button <INPUT> elements may specify the DATASRC and DATAFLD attributes. For a data source object that permits updating, when the user selects a radio button in the group, the bound data field's value will change to corresponding VALUE of that button. This is useful for data fields with enumerated values (i.e. Boolean Yes/No fields):

```
<INPUT TYPE="radio" NAME="WantOnList" VALUE="yes"
       DATASRC="#wroxSurvey" DATAFLD="onList"> Yes <P>
<INPUT TYPE="radio" NAME="WantOnList" VALUE="no"> No <P>
```

Checkboxes – TYPE="checkbox"
Checkboxes are only used for Boolean value entry when used in conjunction with data binding. They should be bound to data fields with Boolean type value using the DATASRC and DATAFLD attributes. The VALUE attribute of the data bound checkbox should be either True or False to avoid unexpected type conversion. Use TYPE="radio" or the <SELECT> element for enumerated values entry. A checkbox example for a Boolean data field named WillCall is:

```
<INPUT TYPE="checkbox" DATASRC="#WroxAnswer" DATAFLD="WillCall"> Call for delivery.
```

Non-visible controls – TYPE="hidden"

Hidden `<INPUT>` elements are read-only data bound fields. You can use the `DATASRC` and `DATAFLD` attributes to bind the element, and then access the element's `TEXT` attribute programmatically through scripting.

The `<INPUT>` element offers a read/write binding.

The <LABEL> Element

The `<LABEL>` element support the binding of the label's displayed text to a data field. Custom formatting of the text can be effected using the `DATAFORMATAS="html"` attribute, and providing HTML formatting with the text from the data field. The `<LABEL>` element should not be used in repeated table binding, and offers read-only binding.

The <MARQUEE> Element

The `<MARQUEE>` element can be bound to a data field. The value of the data field will replace any content of the static `<MARQUEE>` specification in the original HTML page. To display varying HTML formatted text in the `<MARQUEE>` we can use the `DATAFORMATAS="html"` attribute when binding the data. The `<MARQUEE>` element provides a read-only binding.

The <OBJECT> Element

If the `DATASRC` and `DATAFLD` attributes appear in the `<OBJECT>` element definition, the data field will be bound to the **default** property of the embedded OLE object. For example, an OCX representing a text entry box will typically have the `text` property as the default. Obviously, there can be only one default property, and it is generally the "obvious" value for a visual control. If the `DATASRC` and `DATAFLD` attributes appear in the `<PARAM>` elements within the `<OBJECT>` tag. However, they can be used to bind the data source to any specific property. This later behavior is similar to that of the `<APPLET>` element as described earlier, and–like the `<APPLET>` element–the `<OBJECT>` tag provides a read/write binding.

The <SELECT> Element

With data binding, the `<SELECT>` element can be used only in the "single entry" selection mode (i.e. when there is no `MULTIPLE` attribute included in the definition of the element). Typically, the `<SELECT>` element appears to the user as a selectable list or combo box, and is usually associated with a collection of `<OPTION>` elements. However, the binding is only applicable to the equivalent of the `selectedIndex` property, and not the actual `<OPTION>` elements themselves. In effect, it just reflects the selected item in the list, where the `<OPTION>` contents have been previously created using HTML (or server-side processing techniques).

When the bound `<SELECT>` element is initially displayed, the value selected will reflect the original value of the data field. This is only true if one of the `<OPTION>` element's `TEXT` attribute actually match the field's value–otherwise, it will be blank. Once bound, the user selecting an entry in the list or combo box will result in an update to the data source object's recordset, changing the value of the bound field. The `<SELECT>` element provides a read/write binding.

The <SPAN> Element

The `<SPAN>` element is functionally identical to the `<DIV>` element as far as data binding is concerned. The `DATAFORMATAS="html"` attribute can be used to cause dynamic interpretation of data fields containing HTML. However, the `<SPAN>` element cannot contain any HTML block-level elements (i.e. ones with an open and close tag), which is where the `<DIV>` element is required instead. The `<SPAN>` element provides a read-only binding.

The `<TEXTAREA>` Element

The `<TEXTAREA>` element has identical data binding behaviour as the `<INPUT TYPE="text">` element, but provides a multi-line edit for display and modification of a bound data field. The `<TEXTAREA>` element provides read/write binding.

Data Presentation Formats

So far, we've considered the two topics of the data source object and the data consumer, or bound elements. The third topic we need to cover briefly in this introduction is the way that the data is presented. There are two general presentation formats for data binding supported in the IE4 Dynamic HTML implementation. They are:

- ▲ Single-valued data binding (or current record data binding)
- ▲ Repeated table data binding (or tabular data binding)

IE4 data binding allows us to present data in both the tabular presentation format and the single-valued format, or a combination of both on the same page. Both formats are the standard presentation format for applications developed using conventional database RAD tools, and Access database programmers will recognize these as "datasheet" and "form" views. Dynamic HTML pages can, potentially, replace the RAD front-end development systems that we've come to know and love.

Single-Value Data Binding

The simplest presentation format (at least in theory) is single-value data binding. This is the model we looked at when we introduced the data source objects:

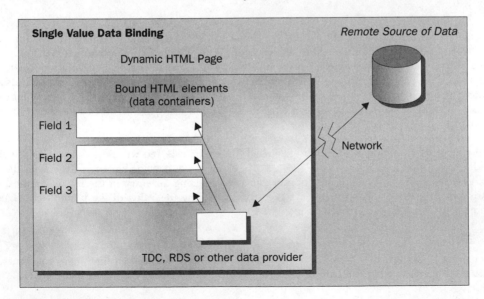

Each bound element on the page is connected to a particular field in the data source, although there is no reason why more than one element can't be bound to any single field. The element displays the value of the data in the current record. It's this notion of a **current record** that makes single-value data binding more complex, however. The page (and the programmer) have to be able to control which record is the current one.

The Concept of a Current Record

The concept of a current record is indispensable in the case of the single-valued data binding presentation. The current record is essentially the record which the user is currently viewing. Furthermore, if the data source object supports data modification and the application needs to modify the underlying database, the current record is used to perform programmatic modification to the underlying database, one record at a time. We will be taking a look at some database update examples in the RDS chapter, later in the book.

A more comprehensive definition of the current record is the record in a recordset which is being worked on, or viewed, at any moment in time. Several methods of the recordset object—move, `moveFirst`, `moveLast`, `moveNext` and `movePrevious`—provide generic navigation capability through the records in the recordset, thus changing which is the current record.

A recordset object can only have one current record at any moment in time, and in fact it's possible for it to have *no* current record (when the current record is at the BOF or EOF special position or the current record has been deleted by another user). This can also be true, for example, when a data source object's recordset contains no data, and therefore the resulting recordset is empty. If you have a Visual Basic or Microsoft Access background, all this should already be familiar to you.

We'll be looking at an example of implementing single-value data binding later in this chapter.

Tabular or Repeated Table Data Binding

While the second type of presentation, tabular data binding, is harder to explain, it's generally easier to implement. Again, you'll be seeing an example towards the end of this chapter. The principle is that of "table view" or "datasheet" view in a database—being able to see a listing of the records on the page.

In fact this is the format mostly used for viewing information, such as over the Web or on an Intranet. It makes it easy to assimilate the range of values, or to scroll through and find a particular record. Under the hood, it works in a similar way to single-value data binding, except that now the data source object supplies data that is used to fill a column of a table on the page, rather than a single element.

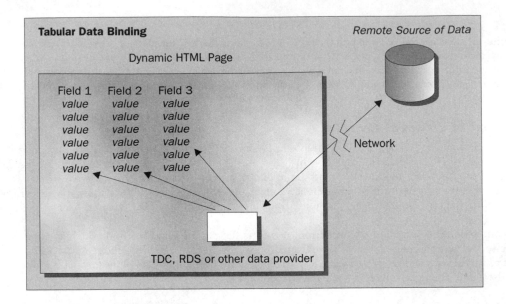

Defining a Tabular Data Binding Template

The trick with tabular data binding, like many server-side technologies in use at present, is to define a 'template' in HTML that is used over and over again, once for each row in the table. We can also add header and footer roes to the table, using the **<THEAD>** and **<TBODY>** elements to define where they start and end:

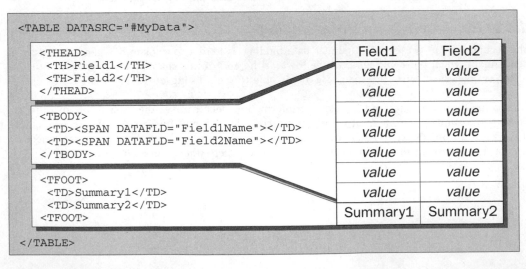

The optional **<THEAD>** and **<TFOOT>** sections are displayed only once. The **<TFOOT>** section can even be placed immediately after the **<THEAD>** section in the source, and before the **<TBODY>** section. Note that the presence of **<TH>** tags, rather than **<TD>** tags, has no effect on the layout of the table rows—only the formatting of the text in the heading cells. It's the **<THEAD>** tags that control how the actual heading row appears.

The **<TBODY>** section of the code forms a template, and the HTML here is repeated automatically by the browser as it builds the visible page—once for each record in the source recordset. However, this automatic repetition of the table rows for each record means that we can have a situation where there are hundreds (or even thousands) of rows in our table. Obviously, we need some way of controlling and managing the number of rows within our page.

Paging Data in a Table with Tabular Binding

When used in data binding, the HTML **<TABLE>** element exposes two methods through the object model: **nextPage** and **previousPage**. These can be called from a script in the page to control how the table presents the data from the source recordset. If the **DATAPAGESIZE** attribute is not set, all the records from the data source will be displayed in a bound table, and **nextPage** and **previousPage** have no effect.

However, if we specify the maximum number of rows to include in the table using the **DATAPAGESIZE** attribute, we can use the two methods to 'page through' the data, displaying each page of records at a time. IE4 looks after this automatically, and when we get to the last page it adjusts the table size to accommodate just the remaining number of records. The **DATAPAGESIZE** attribute can only be used with the HTML **<TABLE>** element.

An example of its use is:

```
<TABLE ID='tblMyList' DATASRC='#tdcFruit' DATAPAGESIZE="10">.......</TABLE>
```

This causes the table **tblMyList** to display only 10 rows at a time from the **tdcFruit** data source object. A button can be created that uses script to advance to the next 'page' of data:

```
<BUTTON ID='btnMoreBut' ONCLICK='tblMyList.nextPage()'> More.. </BUTTON>
```

This simply calls the **nextPage** method of the table element **tblMyList**. Likewise, we can use the **previousPage** method to go back a page.

The Format of Data Within a Repeated Table

Repeated table data binding places no unreasonable restriction on what can be contained in the template. As long as the HTML elements in the template can be bound to data fields (i.e. they will act as data consumers), they can be included as part of the template. This includes HTML elements such as **<A>** elements, **<IMG>** elements, **<MARQUEE>** elements, and even custom objects via the **<OBJECT>** and **<APPLET>** elements. Each of these elements are affected by the data it bound to in a different fashion. For example, binding a data field to an **<IMG>** element provides a URL pointing to an image to be displayed by the **<IMG>** element.

And, of course, we can include HTML tags or element styles to change the appearance of the text or other content as required. For example, this excerpt from a **<TABLE>** template consists of **<DIV>** elements bound to fields, and the font face and size are set by a **<FONT>** tag in each cell:

```
<TR>
   <TD> <FONT SIZE="1" FACE="Verdana">  <DIV DATAFLD="Fruit">  </TD>
   <TD> <FONT SIZE="2" FACE="Arial">    <DIV DATAFLD="Family"> </TD>
   <TD> <FONT SIZE="3" FACE="Wingdings"> <DIV DATAFLD="Shape">  </TD>
</TR>
```

Data Binding in Summary

To summarize, we now know that data binding is the relationship between visual HTML elements on a Dynamic HTML page and a data source, arbitrated by a client-side data source object. The things in Internet Explorer 4 and Dynamic HTML that make all this possible include:

▲ Two built-in data source objects supplied and installed with IE4–the TDC and RDS

▲ Implementation of certain HTML elements that can act as data consumers

▲ Four new data binding HTML attributes for these particular elements

▲ The specification of two different data binding presentation formats

▲ Implementation of object model access to all of the above, providing complete application design flexibility

To better understand how to make Dynamic HTML data binding work for us, we'll look at some examples–beginning first with a thorough examination of the Tabular Data Control. We'll defer discussion of the more complex Remote Data Service control for a later chapter.

The Tabular Data Control (TDC)

The TDC is just about as simple a data source provider as you can get. It provides read-only access to a data file that is in delimited text format. One of the most frequently used delimited text file format is called Comma Separated Values (CSV) format. The following is a sample of such an input file, named `fruits.txt`:

```
"Fruit","Family","Shape"
"Honeydew","Melon","round"
"Water Melon","Melon","oval"
"Grape","Misc","oval"
"Orange","Citrus","round"
"Grapefruit","Citrus","round"
"Honeydew","Melon","Duplicate"
```

Note that the first row contains the field names, and each of the subsequent rows contains data for a record with fields separated by commas. When working with the TDC, we aren't limited to using the comma as the delimiter. We can, as you'll see later, specify that any other character be used as the delimiter–by setting the `FieldDelim` property of the control. First, we'll see how we incorporate a TDC onto our Dynamic HTML page.

Embedding the TDC in a Page

The TDC control can be embedded into an HTML page using the `<OBJECT>` tag. The following code shows how this is done:

```
<html>
<head>
</head>
<body>
```

```
<object id="tdcFruit" width=1 height=1
        classid="CLSID:333C7BC4-460F-11D0-BC04-0080C7055A83">
  <param name="DataURL" value="fruit.txt">
  <param name="UseHeader" value=True>
  <param name="FieldDelim" value=",">
  <param name="Sort" value="Fruit; -Shape">
  <param name="Filter" value='Family = "Melon"'>
</object>
</body>
</html>
```

If we load this page into IE4, we'll be disappointed–since the page is blank. This is only to be expected, since we have yet to bind any visual HTML elements to the TDC. We'll add some code to bring this page alive in a later section.

Setting the TDC Parameters

It's evident in the above code that many of the properties of the TDC control can be initialized using the `<PARAM>` tags. In our case, we set the `DataURL`, `UseHeader`, `FieldDelim`, `Filter` and `Sort` properties. The first three of these properties control how the data source control actually reads the contents of the file:

Property	Description
DataURL	A string value. The URL to the actual data file, which can be on a different server. Note that the particular URL is reloaded each time this property is changed.
UseHeader	This is a Boolean property. If `True`, it indicates that the first line of the data file should contain field names. If `False`, field names default to "`Column1`", "`Column2`", etc.
FieldDelim	A character value. Default to a comma for CSV data files. Can be set to any other ASCII character, indicating the field delimiter in that particular file.

The other `<PARAM>` tags in the example above deal with the sorting and filtering of the data.

Sorting the Data

Sorting of the data managed by the TDC is controlled by a single property called `Sort`. In the example code above, we used:

```
<param name="Sort" value="Fruit; -Shape">
```

to set the `Sort` property of the TDC so that it will first sort the data in ascending order on the `Fruit` column, with a secondary sort of the `Shape` field in descending order.

Property	Description
Sort	A string value. Specifies which fields are involved in the sort, as well as the sort order (ascending or descending) for these fields. If the `Sort` property is set to " ", sorting is disabled for the TDC instance. Otherwise, the string should contain a list of names of fields to be sorted on, in order, separated by semicolons. If the name of a field is prefixed by a minus sign, that column will be sorted in descending order.

187

If we are accessing and changing the value of the **Sort** property programmatically via scripting, we must call the TDC's **Reset** method to cause the bound HTML elements to update their values.

Filtering the Data

Like sorting, filtering is also controlled by a single property, called **Filter**. In our example, we used:

```
<param name="Filter" value='Family = "Melon"'>
```

to set the **Filter** property to **Family = "Melon"**. This means that only fruits belonging to the melon family will be available through the TDC data source object instance.

Property	Description
Filter	A string value. Specifies the conditions that the TDC data will be filtered on. If the Sort property is set to **" "** sorting is disabled for the TDC instance, and all rows of data will be available through data binding. Otherwise, the string should contain an expression involving one or more fields.

The **Filter** expression can contain field names, the comparison operators (=, <, >, <=, >=, and <>), and constants (string or numeric). If the expression contains sub-expressions, they should be placed in parenthesis. Only the **"&"** (AND) and **"|"** (OR) operators are allowed when combining sub-expressions. A constant string with an asterisk as the last character, i.e. **"abc*"**, has the special property of wildcard matching–**"abc*"** will match any string beginning with **"abc"**.

Some valid expression examples are:

```
(Family = 'Melon') & (Calories < 10)
((Score > 100) & (Name <> 'dum*')) | (Score < 10)
```

As with **Sort**, we must call the **Reset** method of the TDC after changing the **Filter** property. This will allow proper refresh of any bound visual elements with the filtered data. Having seen the most frequently used properties of the TDC, let's complete our coverage by taking a look at rest of the TDC methods and properties.

TDC Methods

The TDC has only one published method, **Reset**:

Method	Description
Reset	Should be called when any one of either **Sort** or the **Filter** property has been changed. This will cause the new **Sort** or **Filter** to take effect. Any bound visual data element will be updated if necessary. The entire data file may be re-read if the **DataURL** property has been changed.

Other TDC Properties

Here are the remaining, less frequently used, TDC properties:

Property	Description
AppendData	A Boolean value. This property has effect only if **DataURL** (the data source) is changed and the **Reset** method is called. In this case, if the **AppendData** property is also **True**, the data cached from the previous **DataURL** will not be deleted. Instead, the new data will be appended to the cached data. This means that the new **DataURL** must contain data with the same fields as the original **DataURL**.
CharSet	A string value indicating the character set of the data file, used for international support. It defaults to **"Latin1"**. Changing this value after the TDC has initialized has no effect on the data—you must change **DataURL** and call **Reset** if a dynamic change of **CharSet** is desired.
EscapeChar	A character value. The character used in "escaping" the special meaning of characters used in the data file. For example, the comma in a CSV file is special because it is treated as the delimiter. Any special characters that follow the **EscapeChar** are treated as regular text, so if the dollar "**$**" character is set in **EscapeChar**, the string "**$,**" (dollar followed by comma) will be treated as a regular comma character (i.e. not a field delimiter) in a CSV file. The default is a null string, which means there is no escape character
Language	A string value. indicating the language used in the data file. The default is **"eng-us"**. This is used in the internationalization of applications, and affects display formatting for things like the decimal separator, etc.
RowDelim	A character value, indicating the character used to delimit the end of a row (record). Default is the **newline** character—the row delimiter used in the CSV format.
TextQualifier	A character value, indicating the character used to enclose the data in text fields. Default is the double quote (**"**) character. Many CSV file generators will delimit text string using this character, and this allows for including the comma character inside the text string.

TDC Events (or lack of)

The TDC itself does not issue any events of its own. This is largely due to its simple nature, as well as to it being a read-only data control. In a later chapter, when we examine Remote Data Service control, we'll see how custom events from the RDS can be used in data validation and management of bound visual HTML elements.

This concludes our examination of the TDC as an ActiveX control, and is an opportune time to find out how to bind such a control to data consuming visual HTML elements. We will be going through a non-trivial case study using the TDC in the next chapter. For the moment, these simple examples apply some of the TDC properties we've discussed in this section, together with the data binding elements and formatting techniques we studies earlier in the chapter.

A Repeated Table Data Binding Example

Our earlier code sample simply placed the TDC object into our page, and set its properties to allow bound elements to display the sorted and filtered contents of the **fruit.txt** database:

```
<html>
<head>
</head>
<body>
<object id="tdcFruit" width=1 height=1
        classid="CLSID:333C7BC4-460F-11D0-BC04-0080C7055A83">
  <param name="DataURL" value="fruit.txt">
  <param name="UseHeader" value=True>
  <param name="FieldDelim" value=",">
  <param name="Sort" value="Fruit; -Shape">
  <param name="Filter" value='Family = "Melon"'>
</object>
</body>
</html>
```

Adding the Table Definition

However, there weren't any bound elements in the earlier example, so we'll add some now. First, we define the table we're going to use to display the data:

```
...
<body>
<table style="width:450" datasrc="#tdcFruit">
```

Note how the **DATASRC** attribute is used to form this binding, placing a hash sign in front of the data source object's **ID**. Next, we display the heading row for the table, containing the field names:

```
<thead>
 <th width="150">Fruit</th>
 <th width="150">Family</th>
 <th>Shape</th>
</thead>
```

Now, for each row, we build a template that tells IE4 how to generate each data row. It contains a **<DIV>** element for each field–note how the **DATAFLD** attribute is used to bind each **<DIV>** element to the associated field. We do not specify the **DATASRC** attribute for the **<DIV>** elements, because a row in a table inherits the **DATASRC** attribute from the enclosing table:

```
<tbody>
 <tr>
  <td>
   <font size="2" face="arial">
   <div datafld="Fruit" style="text-align:center">
   </font>
  </td>
  <td>
   <font size="2" face="arial">
   <div datafld="Family" style="text-align:center">
   </font>
  </td>
  <td>
   <font size="2" face="arial">
   <div datafld="Shape" style="text-align:center">
   </font>
  </td>
```

```
    </tr>
   </tbody>
  </table>
  <object id="tdcFruit" width=1 height=1
     classid="CLSID:333C7BC4-460F-11D0-BC04-0080C7055A83">
     ...
  </body>
  </html>
```

Viewing the Result

If we now load this page into IE4, we can see the data from the TDC displayed in our repeating table:

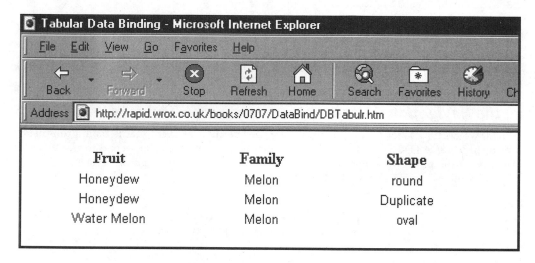

You can run or download this example, **DBTabulr.htm**, *from our Web site at* **http://rapid.wrox.co.uk/books/0707**

We've created a template row from which the data bound table element will repeatedly generate a new row instance for us corresponding to each available record in the TDC. By changing the `<PARAM>` initialization values for the TDC's `Sort` and `Filter` property, we can make this page to display different data.

A Single-Value Data Binding Example

As we have shown in the previous example, the repeated table (or tabular) data binding presentation format allows us to display several records at a time from a data source object. Let's now modify this example to create a single-valued data binding presentation.

Modifying the HTML Source

The first step is to replace the bound table with a normal "unbound" one. We'll be using it here simply to control the layout of the page. It is not involved in the actual data binding process—we do not have any `DATASRC` attribute on the table:

```
...
<body>
<table style="width:400">
```

Our table will contain the single valued data fields, and their associated labels, so that the final result will resemble a database-style form:

```
<tr>
 <td width="150">Fruit</td>
 <td><input type="text" datasrc="#tdcFruit" datafld="Fruit"></td>
</tr>
<tr>
 <td width="150">Family</td>
 <td><input type="text" datasrc="#tdcFruit" datafld="Family"></td>
</tr>
<tr>
 <td width="150"><b>Shape</b></td>
 <td><input type="text" datasrc="#tdcFruit" datafld="Shape"></td>
</tr>
```

Adding the Navigation Buttons

For each field, we create a label then an `<input type='text'>` element that is bound to a field from the current record in the TDC. The first is bound to the `Fruit` field, and the second to the `Family` field. For the last row of the table, we define two buttons—one for advancing through the data records provided by the TDC, the other one for moving back:

```
<tr>
 <td width="50%"><button onclick="movePrev()"> Prev </button></td>
 <td align="right"><button onclick="moveNext()"> Next </button></td>
</tr>
</table>
```

The remainder of the page is the definition of the TDC, but this time we've removed the `Sort` and `Filter` parameters so that there are more records in our example page to scroll through:

```
<object id="tdcFruit" width=1 height=1
    classid="CLSID:333C7BC4-460F-11D0-BC04-0080C7055A83">
<param name="DataURL" value="fruit.txt">
<param name="UseHeader" value=True>
<param name="FieldDelim" value=",">
</object>
</body>
<html>
```

Adding the Navigation Script

Finally, we write the two VBscript functions required to move backwards and forwards through the records. Note that we are actually using the recordset sub-object from the TDC. All data source providers expose this object through inheritance. We will have a lot more to say about recordset objects when we get to Remote Data Services description in later chapters. For now, we only have to know about the `EOF` and `BOF` properties, and the `movePrevious` and `moveNext` methods:

```
<script language="vbscript">
```

```
<!--
Sub movePrev
 if (tdcFruit.recordset.BOF = false) then
  tdcFruit.recordset.movePrevious()
 end if
end sub

Sub moveNext
 if (tdcFruit.recordset.EOF = false) then
   tdcFruit.recordset.moveNext()
 end if
end sub
-->
</script>
```

The **moveNext** method advances the current record to the next record in the recordset, and **movePrevious** moves it back to the previous one (pretty obvious stuff!). There are two special positions at the beginning and the end of the records in a recordset, which do not point to any actual data. If the current record is at the "Beginning Of File" position, i.e. before the first actual data record, the **BOF** property will be true. If the current record is at the "End Of File" position, i.e. after the last actual data record, the **EOF** property will be true.

If **moveNext** is called with **EOF** already **True**, an error will occur. Similarly, if **movePrevious** is called with **BOF** already true, an error will also occur. To avoid these errors, we check the state of the **BOF** and **EOF** properties before we call the **movePrevious** and **moveNext** methods.

Viewing the Result

Here's the result in IE4, showing the values of the first record in our database file. Try clicking on the Prev and Next buttons repeatedly to traverse all the records in the CSV file, and notice what happens at the beginning and end of the set of records. You get a blank record, and at this point the BOF or EOF property (as appropriate to the direction you're moving) is True. As you saw earlier, further clicks on the buttons will have no effect, because we've guarded against this causing an error in our script.

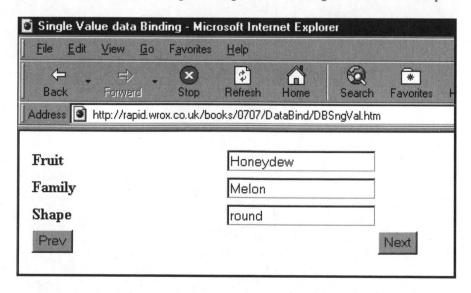

You can run or download this example, DBSngVal.htm, from our Web site at
`http://rapid.wrox.co.uk/books/0707`

Summary

This concludes our initial analysis of Dynamic HTML data binding. In it, we've taken a whirlwind tour of the history of data access to get us insight into why a shift towards Dynamic HTML based, multi-tiered client/server architecture is a natural inevitable part of the business computing evolution.

Dynamic HTML data binding is implemented through the connection of visual HTML elements (**data consumers**) to a **data source object**. This object is typically an ActiveX control, although it could also be a Java applet or a custom object. IE4 comes natively with two data source objects: the **Tabular Data Control** (TDC) and the **Remote Data Service** control (RDS).

The TDC is a simple yet versatile read-only data source object that manages data from delimited text files. We examined all the available methods and properties of the TDC, and saw how they apply in data binding scenarios. We also constructed simple TDC based example pages which supported both **single-value** and **repeated table** (tabular) data binding. From these examples, we learned the programming techniques, and the application of each type of binding. We also briefly saw that the **recordset object**, and the concept of a **current record**, are at the heart of single-valued binding.

Finally, we examined all the HTML elements that can participate in data binding and found out how they are affected by the operation. With all the basics under our belt, we are ready to undertake a case study in the next chapter. This is a chance to apply most of what we have learnt, and will document the construction of a non-trivial data binding application based on the TDC.

Case Study: A Searchable Booklist

In the previous chapter, we learned the basic techniques of data binding in Internet Explorer 4, and examined the Tabular Data Control (TDC) in detail. We'll now design and build a non-trivial data binding application using the TDC, as a case study. This will give you some hands-on experience with data binding, and a thorough understanding of what the TDC actually does.

The application we will look at is an on-line facility for looking up books that have been published by Wrox Press to date. It will allow us to search for and list the books according to various criteria. Our approach to the problem will be highly systematic, and we'll complete the application through two iterations.

In the first one, we'll create a working application using the most direct means. In the second iteration, we'll add some additional capabilities that demonstrate advanced techniques in Dynamic HTML data binding programming. By the end of the chapter, you'll be comfortable with programming data binding applications using Dynamic HTML, and especially familiar with the possibilities that the TDC offers.

So, the chapter will cover:

- The design aspects that we need to consider before we start
- The outline plan for the application, including the visual appearance
- Coding the main frames page, and the other pages to fill each frame
- A look at the shortcomings of our application, and of the TDC object
- Some improvements to the application, and workarounds for the shortcomings

First, let's look at the design issues that are involved.

Designing the BookList Application

To clearly show that designing a Dynamic HTML mini-application is similar to designing any database application, we'll go through the case study by first stating the problem we have to solve, and then following a three step design-and-build process:

- High level design
- Detailed logic design
- Coding the pages

The Problem Statement

In this case study, we are going to create a "quickly downloadable" mini-application which allows the end user to find information about the books that Wrox Press publishes. The goal is to keep the download time short and the load on the server light, making the application responsive and scalable to a very large number of users.

For each book that Wrox publishes, our database stores the following information:

- Title
- ISBN number
- Author(s)
- Subject matter
- Series (branding) it belongs to

The web application we create will enable a flexible look-up based on any one of the above attributes. We'll also provide the ability to browse through the complete list of the books, sorted on any one of these attributes. As a sneak preview, here's what the completed application will look like, so that you can see how it develops as we work through the chapter.

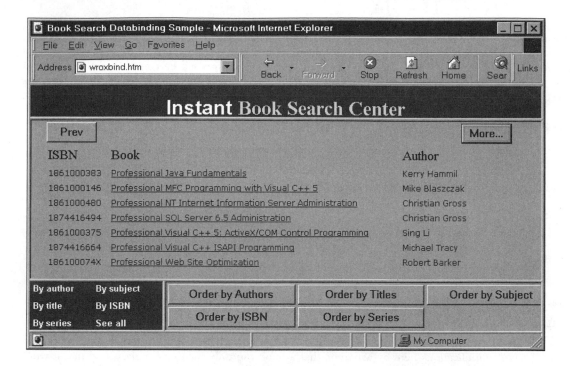

This is the final version of the application, as it appears after the second iteration of our design. Both this, **BookList2**, *and the first example (***BookList1***) can be run directly from our Web site at* **http://rapid.wrox.co.uk/books/0707**, *or downloaded from there for you to examine and run on your own system. To start either application once you have downloaded the samples, open the page* **wroxbind.htm** *from the respective folder.*

High Level Design

In this phase, we'll analyze the problem statement, take a look at the available data schema, sketch out how the user interface will look, and then plan the flow of user interaction.

Analyzing the Problem

The requirement to be "quickly downloadable" and "server light" makes this a natural Dynamic HTML data binding application. The "built-in" data source object, in this case the TDC, provides client-side data handling that we get for free as part of the IE4 distribution—no additional ActiveX control downloading is required by the user. All our code and data will be pure text, with no fancy graphics, which can improve download speed since it lends itself to router or modem based data compression.

Since IE4 allows the end-user to interact with the page before all the data is downloaded, the final application can be very responsive. All of the data manipulation and handling happens on the client-side, so the perceived performance of the application is not hampered by a slow-link to the network. Furthermore, once the TDC data file is on the client, the application won't be constrained by a server that suffers a high workload, since all the server is required to do is supply the few remaining text-only pages for each frame.

The Data Schema

A simplified data schema for the database is a single table with the following fields:

Field	Description
Author	The name of the author, first name followed by last name.
Title	The title of the book as published.
ISBN	The ISBN number.
Subject	Technical subject category that the book belongs to.
Series	The series the book belongs to (i.e. Beginner, Instant, Professional, etc).
URL	An optional URL for more information on the book. (not used initially)

We have made simplifications here by assuming that a book can only have one author, and that it will belong to only one subject category. In a later section of this chapter, we'll attempt to provide a more advanced treatment of these issues.

Sketching the Layout

We intend to divide the web page into four distinct areas. Using HTML frames, we will be using a "divide and conquer" approach to simplify the construction of this mini-application. The layout of the final application will look like this:

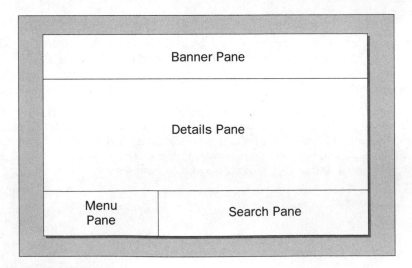

Notice that there are four distinct panes (or frames):

`Banner Pane`	A static pane using Dynamic HTML styles to display the title.
`Menu Pane`	A pane for the user to select the search criterion. We'll be using Dynamic HTML to make the selection interactive here.
`Search Pane`	Depending on the selected criterion, this pane will allow the user to enter the specific details of the specific search criterion. For example, the user can enter the actual ISBN number once "ISBN" has been clicked on the Menu Pane.
`Details Pane`	This pane is non-interactive, and shows the result of the search in tabular presentation format.

Planning User Interactions

A typical user interaction with the application will involve three steps:

- Select the search criterion from the Menu pane.
- Enter the search criterion details in the Search pane, and press a button in this pane to start the search.
- View the result of the search in the Details pane.

We've decided to place both the Menu pane and Search pane at the bottom of the screen, to give a "dashboard" feel to the application.

Detailed Logic Design

In this phase of the design, we'll plan how to proceed with the coding and implementation of the application. As any HTML scripting (or Dynamic HTML Scripting) programmer will attest, the language and layout of scripting code can be quite difficult to maintain once the project gets large. It does not have the modular organization of formal languages such as C/C++, and variable scoping is ad-hoc, and does not follow any formal definitions.

On top of this, the typical intermingling of the script with the HTML code only makes matters worse. In short, it was never meant to be used for the manual coding of complex applications. And yet, Dynamic HTML is definitely heading in the direction of encouraging the construction of "ever so complex" web applications! What's going on?

The answer from Microsoft and Netscape is "automated code generation tools". And indeed, with Netscape's Visual Javascript tool, and the soon-to-be-available Visual development tool from Microsoft for Dynamic HTML, there may be no need in the long term to code raw Dynamic HTML. In the meantime, however, we must be prepared to deal with the problem ourselves. One way we try to help as publishers is to provide generically applicable sample code on our Web site for you to easily adapt to your specific needs.

Divide and Conquer Using Frames

One specific decision we've already made is to use frames to reduce the overall complexity of the coding. A generally available methodology to reduce the immediate complexity of a problem is through divide-

and-conquer techniques—split the problem into smaller chunks and solve each part separately. By using HTML frames, we can divide the complex requirement of the application into separate (though not actually independent) modules, and attack the design and coding of each module separately.

In our case, the center of attention is the Details pane, because it's here that the output of the search is displayed. What the end-user is viewing, of course, is actually a data bound table. The filter criterion of this table is changed in line with the user's entry in the Search pane. The actual content of the Search pane frame itself changes, depending on the search criterion selected on the Menu pane. For example, if the user clicks on the By Author link in the Menu pane, a new HTML page is loaded into the Search pane which allows them to enter an author's name, and then activate the search by pressing a button. We chose this approach to simplify the code that is not directly relating to data binding.

So we can switch different HTML pages with different search criterions into the Search pane. Each of these HTML pages can contain different code that modifies the filtering conditions of the TDC data provider object, which is embedded in the Details pane. And now that we've got round to the Details pane, we know that the table in this pane is bound to an instance of the TDC. Therefore, the programming exercise is really reduced to setting appropriate parameter values for the TDC, depending on the search options selected.

Parameterizing the TDC

Let us look at each of the search options, and the parameters that we will be using in each case. Note that we are using string concatenation to build the filter criterion, and using single quotes to delimit the user input:

Search Option	Parameter settings required
`By Author`	Request author name from user, set: `Filter = "Author = " + <user input>`
`By Title`	Request title from user, set: `Filter = "Title = " + <user input>`
`By ISBN`	Request ISBN from user, set: `Filter "ISBN = " + <user input>`
`By Subject`	User selects a subject from a list of available subjects, set: `Filter = "Subject = " + <user input>`
`By Series`	User selects a series from a list of available series, set: `Filter ="Series = " + <user input>`

To handle the case when the user selects All, we just need to set `Filter` back to an empty string and—depending on which sort order button the user presses—sort the data appropriately:

Sort Selected	Parameter settings required
`By Author`	`Sort = "Author; Title"` Primary sort is on the author field, ascending; secondary sort is on the title ascending
`By Title`	`Sort = "Title"` Sort is just on the title field, ascending;

Sort Selected	Parameter settings required
By ISBN	Sort = "ISBN" Sort is just on the ISBN field, ascending;
By Subject	Sort = "Subject; Title" Primary sort is on the subject field, ascending; secondary sort is on the title, ascending
By Series	Sort = "Series; Title" Primary sort is on the series field, ascending; secondary sort is on the title, ascending

The Data File

The actual data file we will be using is a CSV file suitable for TDC access. You can find the file in the samples as **bookinfo.txt**. Here is an excerpt from the file:

```
Author,Title,ISBN,Subject,Series,Url
Bruce Hartwell,Instant PowerBuilder Objects,1861000065,Powerbuilder,Instant,h123.htm
Ivor Horton,Beginning Visual C++ 5,1861000081,Visual C++,Beginning,h124.htm
Oleg Yaroshenko,Beginner's Guide to C++ 2nd Edition,186100012X,C++,Beginning,h125.htm
Mike Blaszczak,Professional MFC Programming with Visual C++ 5,1861000146,Visual
C++,Professional,h126.htm
Rockford Lhotka,Instant Visual Basic 5 ActiveX Control Creation,1861000235,Visual
Basic,Instant,h127.htm
Ivor Horton,Beginning Java,1861000278,Java,Beginning,h128.htm
Sing Li,Professional Visual C++ 5: ActiveX/COM Control Programming,1861000375,Visual
C++,Professional,h129.htm
Kerry Hammil,Professional Java Fundamentals,1861000383,Java,Professional,h123.htm
Alex Homer,Instant VBScript,1861000448,Internet,Instant,h130.htm
Alex Homer,Instant ActiveX Web Database
Programming,1861000464,Internet,Instant,h131.htm
```

Notice the standard CSV convention, and the first line containing all the field (column) names.

Coding the Dynamic HTML Solution

With the detailed design and pseudo-coding out of the way, we're now ready to get our hands dirty and actually code some Dynamic HTML pages.

Implementing the Base Page

The base page contains the **<FRAMESET>** specification which lays out the four panes we defined earlier. It's the initial page of our application, and is named **wroxbind.htm**. The frameset has 3 rows. With the first row taking 50 pixels, the last row 75 pixels, and the middle (Details pane) using the rest:

```
<html>
<head>
<title>Book Search Databinding Sample</title>
</head>
<frameset rows="50,*,75">
```

The first row contains **banner.htm**, our Banner pane implementation. We disable scrolling for this frame. The second row contains **wroxbook.htm**, which is our Details pane implementation. Here we've left scrolling enabled, because the tabular list can often be more than a full frame

```
<frame src="banner.htm" scrolling=no noresize>
<frame src="wroxbook.htm" name="detail_pane" marginwidth=20>
```

The third row consists of two columns. The first is 200 pixels wide, with scrolling disabled, and is our Menu pane implementation, **menu.htm**. The second column is our Search pane, also scrolling disabled, which can house any of 6 different HTM files depending on the menu selection. By default, it contains the Search by Title implementation, **search_t.htm**:

```
<frameset cols="200,*">
  <frame src="menu.htm" scrolling=no noresize>
  <frame src="search_t.htm" name="search_pane" scrolling=no noresize>
</frameset>
</frameset>
</html>
```

Here's what the finished product looks like:

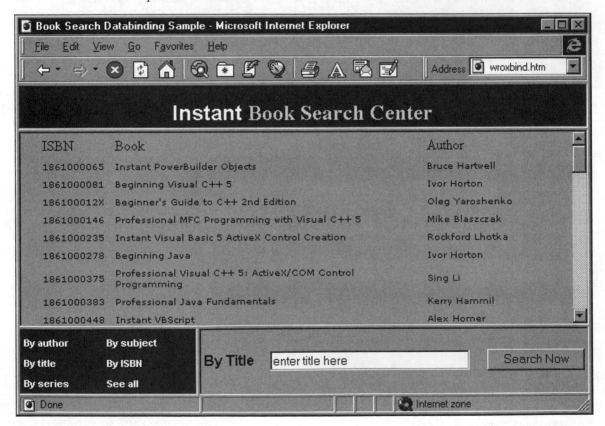

This example, BookList1, can be run directly from our Web site at http://rapid.wrox.co.uk/books/0707, or downloaded from there for you to examine and run on your own system. To start the application once you have downloaded the samples, open the page wroxbind.htm from the BookList1 folder.

Implementing the Banner Frame

The Banner Frame is implemented in **banner.htm** and uses simple CSS styling to set the title. The code is extremely straightforward:

```
<html>
<head>
<title>Book Search Databinding Sample</title>
<style>
<!--
 H2 {color:yellow; font-family: times,serif ; font-weight:bold}
-->
</style>
</head>
<body bgcolor="red">
 <center>
  <H2>
    <span style="color:white; font-family: arial,san-serif">Instant</span>
    Book Search Center
  </H2>
 </center>
</body>
</html>
```

It provides a simple yet attractive heading to our application:

Implementing the Details Frame

The Details pane is where all the data filtering action takes place. We have an embedded TDC with a repeated table binding on this page. The implementation displays only three columns: **ISBN**, **Title**, and **Author**, in the table–which is bound to the TDC that has **id='tdcBooks'**. The code for this data bound table is highlighted below, and can be found in the **wroxbook.htm** file:

```
<html>
<head>
<title>Wrox Book List</title>
</head>
<body bgcolor=#BBBBFF>
<div>
<table id="Data" width="100%" cellpadding="3" datasrc="#tdcBooks" >
  <thead>
    <td>ISBN</td>
    <td>Book</td>
```

```
      <td>Author</td>
    </thead>
    <tbody>
      <tr>
        <td width="75">
          <font size="1" face="verdana"><span datafld="ISBN"></span></font>
        </td>
        <td width="400">
          <font size="1" face="verdana"><span datafld="Title"></span></font>
        </td>
        <td width="150">
          <font size="1" face="verdana"><span datafld="Author"></span></font>
        </td>
      </tr>
    </tbody>
  </table>
</div>
```

The instance of the TDC comes immediately after the table definition, in the form of an **<OBJECT>** tag. The actual source of the data is set in the **DataURL** property as our data file **bookinfo.txt**. We also set the **FieldDelim** property to **","**, although this is not strictly necessary since it is the default. We indicate that the first row in the data file contains field names by setting **UserHeader** property to **True**.

```
<!-- This is a Tabular Data control. It can be used to feed text-based data into -->
<!-- HTML fields that are set up with datasrc/datafld attributes                 -->
<object id="tdcBooks" width=100 height=51
    classid="CLSID:333C7BC4-460F-11D0-BC04-0080C7055A83">
<param name="FieldDelim" value=",">
<param name="DataURL" value="bookinfo.txt">
<param name="UseHeader" value=True>
</object>
</body>
</html>
```

When the table is populated with data, it looks like this:

1861000146	Professional MFC Programming with Visual C++ 5	Mike Blaszczak
1861000235	Instant Visual Basic 5 ActiveX Control Creation	Rockford Lhotka
1861000278	Beginning Java	Ivor Horton
1861000375	Professional Visual C++ 5: ActiveX/COM Control Programming	Sing Li
1861000383	Professional Java Fundamentals	Kerry Hammil
1861000448	Instant VBScript	Alex Homer
1861000464	Instant ActiveX Web Database Programming	Alex Homer
1861000480	Professional NT Internet Information	Christian G

Implementing the Menu Frame

For the Menu Frame, we show off some Dynamic HTML scripting by temporarily enlarging the selection as the user moves the mouse over the selection matrix. We take advantage of the layout alignment on the left and bottom for the fonts and create a usable selection box.

This is the code which implements the menu. It can be found in `menu.htm`. Because we know that every selection there will be used to load a page into the Search frame, rather than this frame, we've set the default `target` frame using a `<BASE>` tag. Now all pages will load into the Search pane, so that we can switch in different HTM files depending on the user's selection:

```
<html>
<head>
<title>Book Search Databinding Sample Menu</title>
<base target="search_pane">
```

Next, we create two styles: `a.Reg` (for regular size), and `a.Big` (for bigger size) to contain the deselected and selected font attributes respectively. Also, because each menu selection is actually a hyperlink created with an `<A>` tag, we create a style using `text-decoration:none` for this, which will disguise the hyperlink by making the annoying underline go away:

```
<style>
<!--
  a.reg      {background:red; color:white; font-family:arial,san-serif;
               font-weight:bold; font-size:8pt;}
  a.big      {background:red; color:blue; font-family:arial,san-serif;
               font-weight:bold; font-size:10pt;}
  A:link     {color:white; text-decoration:none}
  A:visited  {color:white; text-decoration:none}
  A:active   {color:yellow; text-decoration:none}
-->
</style>
```

Now we can create the body of the page, and lay out the six selection elements in our menu using a table. To save repetition, we've omitted some code from this listing. Note that since each item is actually an `<A>` tag hyperlink, we take advantage of this by specifying the `HREF` as the corresponding file for the Search pane. And because we set the default `target` frame to the Search frame earlier, the new file will be loaded into the correct frame:

```
<body bgcolor=red leftmargin=0 topmargin=0>
 <table width=190 leftmargin=0 topmargin=0>
   <tr>
     <td width="50%" height="33%">
       <a class="reg" onmouseover="MouseOver()" onmouseout="MouseOut()"
          href="search_a.htm">By author</a>
     </td>
     <td>
       <a class="reg" onmouseover="MouseOver()" onmouseout="MouseOut()"
          href="search_s.htm">By subject</a>
     </td>
   </tr>
   ...
```

```
     remainder of menu hyperlinks go here
     ...
   </table>
   </body>
   </html>
```

You can also see that for each one we set the default style `class` to `reg`, and manually set the `onmouseover` and `onmouseout` event handlers to our own `MouseOver()` and `MouseOut()` routines. These are in the `<SCRIPT>` section of the page:

```
<script language="vbscript">
<!--
Sub MouseOver()
  set obj = window.event.srcElement
  obj.className = "big"
  cancelEvent
end sub

sub MouseOut ()
  set obj = window.event.srcElement
  obj.className = "reg"
  cancelEvent
end sub
```

These two functions, which is called by the `onmouseover` and `onmouseout` events of all the menu elements, essentially change the appropriate element's style to the class `big` when the mouse moves onto it, and back to `reg` when it moves off again. They do this by identifying the source element of the event using the `srcElement` property of the `event` object, and then changing its style `class` by assigning a new value to the `className` property. The final line calls another routine that we've included in the script section, `cancelEvent`:

```
Sub cancelEvent()
  window.event.returnValue = false
  window.event.cancelBubble = true
end sub
-->
</script>
```

This is a simple utility function that prevents event bubbling once we have handled the event ourselves. It also sets the `event` object's `return` property to `false`, which disables the default action of the source HTML element. And that's it for the menu frame. Next, we'll take a look at each of the Search frame pages that get loaded when a menu item is selected.

Implementing the Search Frame Pages

In the following discussion, you should be able to see how the implementation follows the pseudo-code design we completed during the high level design phase. There are six pages that can be loaded into the Search pane, and we'll examine each one separately:

- Search by Author
- Search by ISBN
- Search by Title

▲   Search by Series

▲   Search by Subject

▲   View and Sort all Records

The Search by Author Page

This page, `search_a.htm`, allows the user to enter an author's name, and view all the books by that author. It contains a text box and a button that starts the search. Here's the code:

```
<html>
<head>
<title>Book Search By Author</title>
<style>
<!--
  body {background:pink; color:black; font-family:arial,san-serif;
        font-weight: bold;font-size: 10pt;}
-->
</style>
</head>
<body leftmargin=0 topmargin=0>
 <table height=70 >
   <tr>
     <td width=100><b>By Author</b></td>
     <td width= 250>
       <input name="srchentry" size=30 type="text" value="enter author name here">
     </td>
     <td><input name="srchbut" type="button" value="Search Now"></td>
   </tr>
 </table>
</body>
</html>
```

This is the result, a simple page that has the default prompt in the text box when first opened:

The **<SCRIPT>** section of the page consists of a single routine, which runs when the Search Now button is clicked:

```
<script language="vbscript">
<!--
sub srchbut_onclick()
  dim SrchString, MyDataCtrl
  SrchString = srchentry.value                    'get the value from the text box
  set MyDataCtrl = top.detail_pane.tdcBooks    'get a reference to the TDC object
  if ((SrchString <> "enter author name here") and (SrchString <> "")) then
    MyDataCtrl.Filter = "Author =" + SrchString 'set the Filter property
    MyDataCtrl.Reset                    'and reset the control to display the results
  end if
```

```
    end sub
    -->
    </script>
```

Other than checking to make sure that the user has actually entered something to be searched on, the implementation is a direct translation of steps of the "search by author" pseudo-code we covered during design. Our code sets the corresponding value of the **Filter** property of the TDC in the Details pane, and calls its **Reset** method to cause the bound table to be updated.

The Search by ISBN Page

The Search by ISBN page, **search_i.htm**, allows a search to be made using a book's ISBN number. As you'd expect, the code that creates it is almost identical to the Search by Author example above. This much was evident even back in the pseudo-coding stage. The major changes are highlighted below:

```
...
<table height=70>
  <tr>
    <td width=100><b>By ISBN</b></td>
    <td width= 250>
      <input name="srchentry" size=30 type="text" value="enter ISBN here">
    </td>
    <td>
      <input name="srchbut" type="Button" value="Search Now">
    </td>
  </tr>
</table>
...
...
sub srchbut_onclick()
  dim SrchString, MyDataCtrl
  SrchString = srchentry.value
  set MyDataCtrl = top.detail_pane.tdcBooks
  if ((SrchString <> "enter ISBN here") and (SrchString <> "")) then
    MyDataCtr.Filter = "ISBN = " + SrchString
    MyDataCtrl.Reset
  end if
end sub
...
```

The final page looks like this:

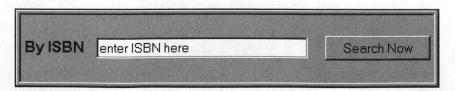

The Search by Title Page

Again, implementation of the Search by Title page, **search_t.htm**, is very similar to the Search by Author and Search by ISBN. The lines with the major changes are listed next:

```
...
<title>Book Search By Title</title>
...
<td width=100>
   <b>By Title</b>
</td>
<td width= 250>
   <input name="srchentry" size=30 type="text" value="enter title here">
</td>
...
if ((SrchString <> "enter title here") and (SrchString <> "")) then
   MyDataCtrl.Filter = "Title = " + SrchString
...
```

Here's what the finished Search by Title page looks like:

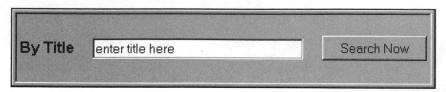

The Search by Series Page

The Search by Series page, `search_r.htm`, breaks the monotony a little. Since we know what the options are when selecting a series, we offer them in a **<SELECT>** HTML element, instead of a simple text box:

```
...
<table height=70 >
  <tr>
    <td width=100><B>By Series</B></td>
    <td width= 250>
      <select name="series">
        <option selected>Beginning
        <option>Instant
        <option>Revolutionary
        <option>Professional
        <option>Masterclass
      </select>
    </td>
    <td>
      <input name="srchbut" type="button" value="Search Now">
    </td>
  </tr>
</table>
...
```

We provide all the **<OPTION>** tags using in-line code in this example. In the Remote Data Service case-study (in a later chapter) we'll see more flexible technique for creating options in a list box or combo box. The script section of the page is also different now, because we need to use the selected value from the combo box to set the **Filter** property of the TDC:

```vbscript
<script language="vbscript">
<!--
sub srchbut_onclick()
  dim SrchString, MyDataCtrl
  select case series.SelectedIndex
    case 0: SrchString="Beginning"
    case 1: SrchString="Instant"
    case 2: SrchString="Revolutionary"
    case 3: SrchString="Professional"
    case 4: SrchString="Masterclass"
  end select
  set MyDataCtrl = top.detail_pane.tdcBooks
  if (SrchString <> "") then
    MyDataCtrl.Filter = "Series = " + SrchString
    MyDataCtrl.Reset
  end if
end sub
-->
</script>
```

Once we've got the search string from the combo box, we apply it to the **Filter** property. Notice that this time we don't have to check for an empty string. We're selecting the first item in the list when the page is first loaded, and the user can only change his to a different one, they can't select an "empty" item. Here's the final page:

The Search by Subject Page

The Search by Subject frame, **search_s.htm**, also uses a **<SELECT>** element, because we know what all the possible subjects are. The problem here is the even longer list of **<OPTION>** tags, and the though that we'll have to decode the user's selection in our routine later on. First, however, here's the changes to the HTML part of the page:

```html
...
<title>Book Search By Subject</title>
...
  <tr>
    <td width=100><B>Select Subject</B></td>
    <td width= 250>
      <select name="subject">
        <option selected>Visual C++
        <option>Delphi
        <option>C++
        <option>C
        <option>Visual Basic
        <option>VBA
        <option>SQL
        <option>QBasic
        <option>COBOL
```

```
              <option>Foxpro
              <option>Assembly
              <option>Powerbuilder
              <option>Java
              <option>Access
              <option>Office
              <option>Exchange
              <option>NT
              <option>IIS
              <option>UNIX
              <option>Paradox
              <option>SQL Server
              <option>Pascal
              <option>Internet
         </select>
      </td>
   ...
```

So, how are we going to decode the user's selection into string without a huge **Select..Case** statement? Easy, we use the fact that the **<SELECT>** element has its own **options** collection, containing all the **<OPTION>** tags in the list. We get the index of the selected option from **subject.selectedIndex** as before, and use it as the index to the **options** collection. Once we've pinned down the option we want, we retrieve its **text** property:

```
sub srchbut_onclick()
   dim SrchString , MyDataCtrl
   SrchString = subject.options(subject.SelectedIndex).text
   set MyDataCtrl = top.detail_pane.tdcBooks
   if  (SrchString <> "") then
     MyDataCtrl.Filter = "Subject = " + SrchString
     MyDataCtrl.Reset
   end if
end sub
```

Here's the final Search by Subject page:

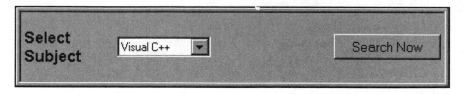

The View All and Sort by Selected Field Page

Finally, for a frame that is quite different in construction, we'll look at the All menu selection page. This is the file **search_1.htm**, and it basically consists of five buttons:

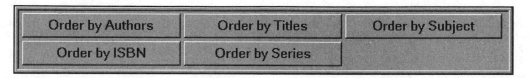

The HTML code uses a table to align the buttons on the page. Note that one of the more reliable way to create fixed width buttons (i.e. all the same size) is to use the `width` property of the `style` object associated with the HTML element:

```
<table>
  <tr>
    <td width="33%">
      <input name="buta" type="button" value="Order by Authors"
             style="width:190">
    </td>
    <td width="33%">
      <input name="butt" type="button" value="Order by Titles"
             style="width:190">
    </td>
    <td>
      <input name="buts" type="button" value="Order by Subject"
             style="width:190" >
    </td>
  </tr>
  <tr>
    <td width="33%">
      <input name="buti" type="button" value="Order by ISBN"
             style="width:190">
    </td>
    <td width="33%">
      <input name="butr" type="button" value="Order by Series"
             style="width:190">
    </td>
    <td></td>
  </tr>
</table>
```

In the script section, the first thing we have do once the page has loaded is set the filter on the TDC to `""`. This effectively removes the current filter, and allows all the records to show in the bound table–something the user will expect to happen. They'll still be displayed in the order previously selected with one of the Search pages, however:

```
<script language="vbscript">
<!--
Dim MyDataCtrl                              'create a global variable, and
Set MyDataCtrl = top.detail_pane.tdcBooks  'set it to refer to the TDC object

Sub window_onload()                         'runs when the page has finished loading
   MyDataCtrl.Filter = ""                   'remove the current filter
   MyDataCtrl.Reset                         'and reset the control
End Sub
```

Now we need to react to the user clicking one of the buttons. In each case, we just need to set the appropriate sorting order, with a primary and secondary sort in some cases, then `Reset` the control to display the records in the new order. You can verify each of the `Sort` property settings we're using against the pseudo-code we came up with during the earlier design phase:

```
Sub buta_onclick()     'runs when the 'Sort By Authors' button is clicked
   MyDataCtrl.Sort ="Author; Title"
   MyDataCtrl.Reset
End Sub
```

```
Sub butt_onclick()     'runs when the 'Sort By Titles' button is clicked
   MyDataCtrl.Sort ="Title"
   MyDataCtrl.Reset
End Sub

Sub buts_onclick()     'runs when the 'Sort By Subject' button is clicked
   MyDataCtrl.Sort ="Subject; Title"
   MyDataCtrl.Reset
End Sub

Sub buti_onclick()     'runs when the 'Sort By ISBN' button is clicked
   MyDataCtrl.Sort ="ISBN"
   MyDataCtrl.Reset
End Sub

Sub butr_onclick()     'runs when the 'Sort By Series' button is clicked
   MyDataCtrl.Sort ="Series; Title"
   MyDataCtrl.Reset
End Sub
```

This concludes the design and coding of our first data binding case study. Although simple, it serves to demonstrate the versatility of the Tabular Data Control in handling client-side data presentation.

Improving our Application

You can probably see quite a few areas for enhancement already, most notably some variation of combining the sorting and searching capability. Feel free to modify and experiment to your heart's content—we'll be looking at two enhancements a little later in this chapter. For now, let us take a hard look at some of the rigid restrictions imposed by the TDC, and see how we can work round them.

TDC Limitations: What's Wrong with BookList?

Serious practitioners of database design probably have already noticed some major limitations of the TDC based BookList sample. In fact, these reflect inherent weaknesses of the TDC when dealing with certain database applications scenarios. The most glaring limitations are:

- An inability to deal with one-to-many data relationships
- A limited set of filtering criterion options
- Data remains static (or stagnant) throughout the session

Let's take a look at each of these limitations in turn.

Working with One to Many Relationships

In creating our data file, `bookinfo.txt`, we made a couple of simplifying assumptions. The first is that a book can only have a single author (which is definitely not true, as this very book is written by a group of authors). The second is that a book will only belong to one `Subject` category. Again, this is not always true—a book on ActiveX C++ programming definitely qualifies as an Internet book, as well as a C++ book.

The fact that a book can have many authors, and a book can belong to many subject categories, are examples of one-to-many relationships. Inherently, the TDC cannot deal efficiently with this kind of data relationship.

We could imagine in a 'real' database that the data file would contain one row for each author of the book, in other words repeating the 'book' record as many times as required:

```
...
Stephen Jakab,Instant Visual Basic 5 ActiveX Control Creation,1861000235,Visual
Basic,Instant,h123.htm
Darren Gill,Instant Visual Basic 5 ActiveX Control Creation,1861000235,Visual
Basic,Instant,h123.htm
Dave Jewell,Instant Visual Basic 5 ActiveX Control Creation,1861000235,Visual
Basic,Instant,h123.htm
Andrew Enfield,Instant Visual Basic 5 ActiveX Control Creation,1861000235,Visual
Basic,Instant,h123.htm
...
```

What's wrong with this scenario? If the user now does a title search, an ISBN search, or a series search (all one-to-one relationships), they will end up seeing multiple entries for the same book in the Details pane.

Getting Around One to Many Relationships

Is there no way to use TDC with one-to-many relationships? Not exactly. One solution is to use different data files for each search criteria. For example, if we create the multiple author data file, as detailed above, and called it **bookinfa.txt**, we can modify **search_1.htm** simply by writing:

```
sub srchbut_onclick()
  dim SrchString, MyDataCtrl
  SrchString = srchentry.value
  set MyDataCtrl = top.detail_pane.books
  if ((SrchString <> "enter author name here") and (SrchString <> "")) then
    MyDataCtrl.DataURL="BOOKINFA.TXT"
    MyDataCtrl.Filter = "Author = " + SrchString
    MyDataCtrl.Reset
  end if
end sub
```

Of course, we must now also change all the other **search_*x*.htm** files to reset the **DataURL** back to **bookinfo.txt** again. For example, we must add the following to **search_t.htm**:

```
sub srchbut_onclick()
  dim SrchString, MyDataCtrl
  SrchString = srchentry.value
  set MyDataCtrl = top.detail_pane.books
  if ((SrchString <> "enter title here") and (SrchString <> "")) then
    MyDataCtrl.DataURL="BOOKINFO.TXT"
    MyDataCtrl.FilterColumn = "Title = " + SrchString
    MyDataCtrl.Reset
  end if
end sub
```

While we will be able to achieve the desired effect using this technique, it is very inefficient. For example, we will need another special data file to deal with the "one-book-to-many-subjects" case. What's more, every time a user changes from Search by Title, ISBN or Series (one-to-one) to Author or Subject (one-to-many), a completely new data file needs to be downloaded across the network.

In our case, this will happen three times before all the data files are cached locally. Even if we were to use three separate TDC objects to do the job, each of them will still need to download and cache its data file—again requiring substantial extra download time. If the set of data is very large, this is an unacceptable solution. In these cases, we will have to resort to more powerful data source objects such as the RDS, which we'll be covering in the next two chapters.

Limited Filter Criterion Capabilities

In many situations, the end-user may not know the exact information when searching. Unfortunately, the capabilities of the TDC's `Filter` property, and its list of relational operators, is very limited. We can test for =, >, <, >=, and <=. We can also combine multiple comparisons using the "`&`" and "`|`" operators. These are very precise operators and are quite meaningless for most non-numeric data searches.

What would be much more useful are some sort of "wildcard" processing, and fuzzy operators such as "like" and "sounds like". While the expression parsing mechanism does recognize an asterik "`*`" at the end of the property as a trailing wild-card, this is rather restrictive for many purposes. Furthermore, there is no way of performing functional operations on the data fields during comparison, such as applying the `InStr` or `indexOf` functions. While we can certainly use script in the page to do a record by record comparison to find the appropriate record, such an exercise completely defeats the purpose of using data binding to simplify and speed up data manipulation and presentation.

Unfortunately, there is no solution for these shortcoming when using the TDC. We must resort to more "powerful" data source objects, such as the RDS, if more sophisticated filtering is needed. Incidentally, the source code for the TDC is included with the Internet Client SDK for IE4, so if your knowledge of C++ is up to it, it's possible to extend the capabilities of the TDC yourself.

Static or Stagnant Recordsets

Another less obvious limitation of the TDC as a data source object is the fact that the data source is fixed. That is, the TDC's recordset will never change. After all, it is a text file residing on some server (or on the local cache). This means that changes and modifications made to the data source may not be instantly available to the user of the TDC.

There is no general solution for dealing with stagnant recordsets and the TDC. What you could do, though, is to minimize the lag between data update and TDC viewing. The best way to do this is to dynamically generate the CSV file from a live data source whenever the TDC page is accessed. This will ensure that the TDC is working with the most recent copy of the data available.

Such a scheme can be implemented using a combination of TDC and Active Server Pages (a server side processing technology). In essence, the actual URL, referring to the ASCII file that is hosted by the TDC, will be extracted dynamically by ASP from a back-end database each and every time, depending on user selection. This adds tremendous flexibility to the static data TDC solution. Chapter 12 illustrates some of the techniques for using Active Server Pages in conjunction with Dynamic HTML.

If using TDC is not mandatory for your application, a "real-time" client-based view of a data source can be achieved using the Remote Data Service control object instead. Coding and configuration for such a setup is substantially more complicated, but we'll examine its capabilities in the next two chapters.

More Improvements to the Booklist

Before we leave the topic of the TDC, let's make two final improvements to the BookList example. The first will illustrate a technique that you may find yourself using often in conjunction with the TDC–adding hyperlinks to the entries in a list. The second, coming later, shows how we can add table paging to our example, making it easier to scroll through the data that having one monolithic list of items.

Incorporating HTML On-the-Fly from A Data Source

Looking at the Details pane of our example, it would be nice if the book title was actually a hyperlink, leading to a page displaying the book cover image and details about the book. Although we won't actually design this new page, we will show how to include the hyperlink. This is what we're aiming for:

ISBN	Book	Author
1861000065	Instant PowerBuilder Objects	Bruce Hartwell
1861000081	Beginning Visual C++ 5	Ivor Horton
186100012X	Beginner's Guide to C++ 2nd Edition	Oleg Yaroshenko
1861000146	Professional MFC Programming with Visual C++ 5	Mike Blaszczak
1861000235	Instant Visual Basic 5 ActiveX Control Creation	Rockford Lhotka
1861000278	Beginning Java	Ivor Horton
1861000375	Professional Visual C++ 5: ActiveX/COM Control Programming	Sing Li

But how can we do it? The title link is bound to the TDC's **Title** field. The secret lies in the use of the often-ignored data binding attribute: **DATAFORMATAS**. Let's first look again at a few lines from the original **bookinfo.txt** file:

```
Author,Title,ISBN,Subject,Series,Url
Bruce Hartwell,Instant PowerBuilder Objects,1861000065,Powerbuilder,Instant,h123.htm
Ivor Horton,Beginning Visual C++ 5,1861000081,Visual C++,Beginning,h124.htm
Oleg Yaroshenko,Beginner's Guide to C++ 2nd Edition,186100012X,C++,Beginning,h125.htm
Mike Blaszczak,Professional MFC Programming with Visual C++ 5,1861000146,Visual
C++,Professional,h126.htm
```

This is bound into the table in the Details page, **wroxbook.htm**, using the HTML code:

```
<tr>
  <td width="75">
    <font size="1" face="verdana"><span datafld="ISBN"></span></font>
  </td>
  <td width="400">
    <font size="1" face="verdana"><span datafld="Title"></span></font>
  </td>
  <td width="150">
```

```
      <font size="1" face="verdana"><span datafld="Author"></span></font>
    </td>
  </tr>
```

Notice that the **Title** field contains a text string that is the book title. What we would like to do is to have the string contain a complete HTML hyperlink definition. In other words, we need a **bookinfo.txt** file that looks like this:

```
Author,URLTitle,ISBN,Subject,Series,Url,Title
Bruce Hartwell,"<A HREF=""h123.htm"">Instant PowerBuilder Objects</
A>",1861000065,Powerbuilder,Instant,h123.htm,Instant PowerBuilder Objects
Ivor Horton,"<A HREF=""h124.htm"">Beginning Visual C++ 5</A>",1861000081,Visual
C++,Beginning,h124.htm,Beginning Visual C++ 5
Oleg Yaroshenko,"<A HREF=""h125.htm"">Beginner's Guide to C++ 2nd Edition</
A>",186100012X,C++,Beginning,h125.htm,Beginner's Guide to C++ 2nd Edition
Mike Blaszczak,"<A HREF=""h126.htm"">Professional MFC Programming with Visual C++ 5</
A>",1861000146,Visual C++,Professional,h126.htm,Professional MFC Programming with
Visual C++ 5
```

Here, we've added a **URLTitle** field, which contains a complete hyperlink bracketing the title, while retaining the **Title** field as the last row. Let's look at how we can change the Details page **wroxbook.htm** to use it:

```
<tr>
  <td width="75">
    <font size="1" face="verdana"><span datafld="ISBN"></span></font>
  </td>
  <td width="400">
    <font size="1" face="verdana">
    <span datafld="URLTitle" dataformatas="html"></span></font>
  </td>
  <td width="150">
  <font size="1" face="verdana"><span datafld="Author"></span></font>
  </td>
</tr>
```

We've changed the binding of the title from the old **Title** field to the new **URLTitle** field, and added **DATAFORMATAS="html"** to tell IE4 to interpret the data field and render it as HTML, not just text. The reason why we kept the original **Title** field is for the search operations. If we were to simply change the original **Title** field to the new URL format, the end-user will not be able to do a Search by Title successfully, because of the additional HTML code in the field.

Adding Paging To Repeated Table Binding

When a user selects the All menu option, they are presented with a tabular listing of all the books—and it is significantly longer than the Details pane is capable of displaying. With the current design, the user will get a scroll bar in the Details pane, and have to use this to scroll through the resulting book list.

You'll recall that, in the last chapter, we talked about the **dataPageSize** property and the **previousPage** and **nextPage** methods that provide us with the capabilities to display the bound table as a set of 'pages'. We'll revamp our BookList example to use table paging instead of the scroll bar to display the results.

The final application will display only 7 lines per page, and provide two buttons that are used to navigate between the 'pages' of items in the table:

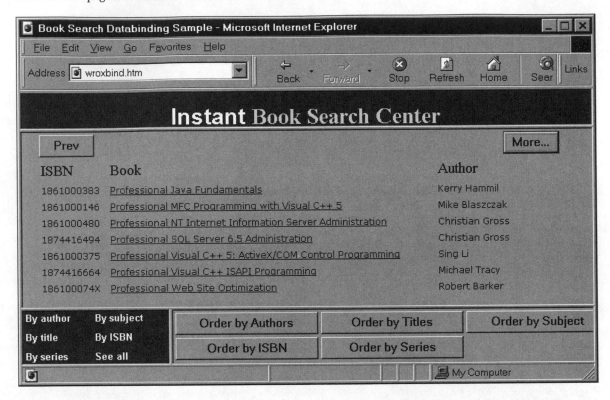

This example, `BookList2`, *can be run directly from our Web site at* `http://rapid.wrox.co.uk/books/0707`, *or downloaded from there for you to examine and run on your own system. To start the application once you have downloaded the samples, open the page* `wroxbind.htm` *from the* `BookList2` *folder.*

To set the table to display only seven lines, we just need to modify the `<TABLE>` tag in `wroxbook.htm`, adding the `datapagesize` attribute:

```
<table id="tblData" ... datasrc="#tdcBooks" datapagesize="7">
```

Using a Global Page Size Variable

However, it would be nice to make future changes to the actual number of lines as easy as possible. We're going to create a variable named `MaxRecords` at the beginning of the page, assign the required number of lines to it, then refer to the variable rather than a specific number in our code throughout the page. To make the variable global and accessible from anywhere in the page, we place it outside any `Sub` or `Function` sections:

```
<script language="vbscript">
<!--
Dim MaxRows    'number of rows per page in table
MaxRows = 7
```

The next part is to get this value into the **dataPageSize** property of the table. The easiest way is to assign it during the window's **onload** event:

```
Sub window_onload()
   tblData.dataPageSize = MaxRows      'set table page size
End Sub
```

However, the setting of the property will only take place after the page has finished loading, and by then the TDC will have filled the table. If we don't set a **dataPageSize** in the HTML attribute for the table, it will fill with all the records. This is a waste of processing effort, so instead we set it to **1** in the HTML so that initially only one record appears. The **onload** event occurs very soon afterwards, and re-renders the table to display the correct number:

```
<table id="tblData" ... datasrc="#tdcBooks" datapagesize="1">
```

We also need to lay out the Prev and More buttons, using a table that is inserted before the existing bound table:

```
<table width="100%">
  <tr>
    <td width="50%">
      <button id="butPrevButton" onclick="GoPrevPage()"> Prev </button>
    </td>
    <td align="right">
      <button id="butNextButton" onclick="GoNextPage()"> More... </button>
    </td>
  </tr>
</table>
```

The nextPage and previousPage Problems

Notice in the previous example that, as we only want to execute the **nextPage** and **previousPage** functions from these buttons, we may have been tempted to code them as:

```
<button onclick="tblData.previousPage()"> Prev </button>
```

and

```
<button onclick="tblData.nextPage()"> More... </button>
```

This would call the page navigation routines of the bound table directly, and would work to a certain degree. However, simply adding the buttons to the page like this is not a bullet-proof enough technique.

First, if the user is at the very first record and presses Prev twice, or is at the last and presses More twice, an error occurs. This is because the recordset is being advanced past the **BOF** or **EOF** positions. Secondly, the two buttons are always there—visible—even if the display is showing only a single record, or even no records at all. Again, pushing the buttons in these cases causes an error. These two situations are unacceptable in a real application.

The nextPage and previousPage Cure

It turns out, as we've discovered, that IE4's native support for robust paging is minimal. We need to provide our own. Therefore, we'll add some more code to our routines to ensure that the Prev and More buttons appear (i.e. are visible) only if there are more records to navigate in the appropriate direction. This way, we can be sure that pressing either button will not cause an error. Because they'll only be visible at the appropriate times, we don't have to worry about paging beyond the beginning or end of the table.

To enable hiding of the buttons programmatically, we add the **visibility** property to the **style** object by including it in the element's style attribute. When the page first loads, the two buttons are hidden. And of course, we include an **id**, so that we can refer to them later to show or hide them:

```
<button id="butPrevButton" onclick="GoPrevPage"
        style="width:75;visibility:hidden"> Prev </button>

  . . .
<button id="butNextButton" onclick="GoNextPage"
        style="width:75; visibility:hidden"> More... </button>
```

Next, we must determine exactly when each button should be shown, and when they should be hidden. The rules are simple enough, though carrying them out is—as you'll see—a little more complex. We need to show the Prev button only when the first record displayed in our table is *not* the first record in the entire available data set. IE4 will automatically page back **dataPageSize** records. If there are less than **dataPageSize** previous records, it will just go back to the first one in the available set of records.

Similarly, we only want to display the More button if there are more records available after the last one displayed in the table. Again, IE4 will page forward **dataPageSize** records, and display the next **dataPageSize**, or just the remaining records if there are less that **dataPageSize** left.

So we need two items of information to decide which buttons to show:

- ▲ The total number of records available in the entire data set.
- ▲ The absolute record number (in respect to the entire data set) of the first record currently displayed in our table

Getting the Total Number of Available Records

Like any experienced programmer, we'll start with the easy one. A data bound table object exposes it's **recordset** object (as we saw in the previous chapter), and this has the **recordCount** property—which gives thus the number we need directly:

```
tdcBooks.recordset.recordCount    'the total number of available records
```

Getting the Number of the First Displayed Record

Now the hard bit. To find the absolute record number of the first record displayed in our table, we have to go back a little, and understand how IE4 exposes the elements in the page. You'll recall that the **all** collection of the **document** object contains all the elements in the page, and can be referenced through each element's **id** property. In this second example application, we've added an **id** to the table row tag that creates out data bound table:

```
<tbody>
  <tr id="rowData">
    <td width="75">
      <font size="1" face="verdana"><span datafld="ISBN"></span></font>
    </td>
    <td width="400">
      <font size="1" face="verdana">
      <span datafld="URLTitle" dataformatas="html"></span></font>
    </td>
    <td width="150">
      <font size="1" face="verdana"><span datafld="Author"></span></font>
    </td>
  </tr>
</tbody>
```

However, the **<tbody>** part of a data bound table is just a template for the actual table that's displayed. There could be none, one, or several rows created in the page from this HTML source. Each one will have the same **id** property, **rowData**. When the **all** collection (or any other collection for that matter) contains multiple entries with the same key–in our case the **id**–each set of repeated items becomes a sub-collection within the all collection. referring to the item will return one of three possible values:

▲   **null** – there are no elements with that **id**

▲   a numeric value – there is exactly one element with that **id**

▲   a collection – there are several elements with the same **id**

This makes accessing the element difficult. If it's **null**, we can't access it at all. If its a number we just access it as normal:

```
document.all.rowData
```

and if it's a collection we need to access it using a secondary index. In this last case, we reference the first element with this **id** using:

```
document.all.rowData(0)
```

Microsoft document a function written in JScript that returns **true** only if the element is a member of a collection (i.e. there are multiple instances), or **false** if there is none or one instance. We can modify this function to return a value that indicates the number of rows in our table, and drop it into our page as a separate script section to use it in our code as required:

```
<script language="jscript">
function checkRowData() {
  if (document.all("rowData") == null)
    {return 0;}
  else if (document.all("rowData").length != null)
    {return 2;}
  else
    {return 1;}
}
</script>
```

Using the Table's Rows Collection

This seems a lot of work just to decide how many rows there are in our table, and it turns out that there's a much easier way. All **<TABLE>** elements have an associated **rows** collection, which contains a reference to each row in the table–including those in the header, body and footer sections. Like all collections, this has its own **length** property, reflecting the total number of rows.

So, we just need to read this property and subtract one for the header row that we always have present, even if there are no data rows:

```
NumRows = tblData.rows.length - 1          'number of data rows
```

So now we have a simple way of deciding how many rows there are in our data bound table.

Deciding Which Buttons to Display

Finally, we're in a position to decide which buttons to display. The rules are:

- If there are no rows, don't display either button.

- If there is only one row, but there are more than 7 records, display only the Prev button.

- If there are several rows, and the first row doesn't contain the first record, display the Prev button.

- If there are several rows, and the last row doesn't contain the last record, display the More button.

We use a routine called **SetButtons** that will determine when each button should be visible, and set it appropriately:

```
Sub SetButtons()
  NumRows = tblData.rows.length - 1                 'number of data rows
  if NumRows = 0  then                              'no records to display
    butPrevButton.style.visibility = "hidden"       'so hide the Prev button
    butNextButton.style.visibility = "hidden"       'and hide the More button
  elseif NumRows = 1  then                          'only one row in table
    if tdcBooks.recordset.recordCount > MaxRows then 'previous records exist
      butPrevButton.style.visibility = "visible"    'so show the Prev button
    else                                            'no previous records
      butPrevButton.style.visibility = "hidden"     'so hide the Prev button
    end if
    butNextButton.style.visibility = "hidden"       'and hide the More button
  else
    if rowData(0).recordnumber = 1 then             'displaying the first record
      butPrevButton.style.visibility = "hidden"     'so hide the Prev button
    else
      butPrevButton.style.visibility = "visible"    'else show the Prev button
    end if
    if (tdcBooks.recordset.recordCount - rowData(0).recordnumber) < MaxRows then
      butNextButton.style.visibility = "hidden"     'hide the More button
    else
      butNextButton.style.visibility = "visible"    'else show the More button
    end if
  end if
End Sub
```

This routine first finds out the number of rows being displayed. If there are none, **NumRows = 0**, we hide both buttons. If there's one row, and there are more than **dataPageSize** records, we know that we only need a Prev button. Otherwise, if there are several rows, we check the first row of the bound table—accessed through **rowData(0)**—to see if it contains the very first record of the TDC's recordset. If it does, we hide the Prev button since there's no where to go backwards. Otherwise, we set it to **visible**.

We also check the first row of the bound table and see if it is **dataPageSize** records or less from the end of the TDC's record set. The number of records in the TDC is obtained through the **recordCount** property of the TDC's recordset object, as we saw earlier. If it is, we are at the end of the record set and the More button should be hidden.

Doing the Paging

Now we have determined how to tell which buttons should be visible or invisible, we need to figure out when we are actually going to call this routine. Again, this proves to be more tricky than meets the eye. Obviously, we must call it every time we go backwards or forwards in the record set. This means that the **onclick** handler function for the buttons should call the **SetButtons** function. However, it turns out that this cannot be done directly—you'll see why shortly. In the meantime, the actual code to handle **onclick** for the buttons looks like this:

```
Sub GoPrevPage()
  tblData.previousPage()
End Sub

Sub GoNextPage()
  tblData.nextPage()
End Sub
```

The **GoPrevPage** function is called when the Prev button is clicked, and it calls the table's **previousPage** method to show the previous **dataPageSize** records. Likewise, the **GoNextPage** function, which runs when the More button is clicked, just calls the table's **nextPage** method. Although these methods automatically page the table to show the next or previous set of records, they don't do anything about displaying or hiding the buttons—this is the responsibility of the **SetButtons** routine. So when and how does the **SetButtons** routine get called?

Coping With Asynchronous Table Updating

We need to run the **SetButtons** routine once the table has been rendered. This will be "some time later" after the user clicks the button. It is this "some time later" that makes all the difference in the world. Thanks to the asynchronous updating of the table provided by data binding, if the **onclick** handlers were to directly call **SetButtons()**, the bound table might not yet have been fully updated. This means that the button visibility determination would give the wrong results.

Using the onreadystatechange() Event

To get round this re-rendering synchronization problem, we use the **onreadystatechange()** event for the bound table. The idea is to react to the table's **onreadystatechange()** event, which occurs during and after the table is re-rendered—each time the table's **readyState** property changes. By looking out for the special value **"complete"** for the table's **readyState** property, we know that all the rows have been rendered:

```
Sub tblData_onreadystatechange()
  If tblData.readyState = "complete" And tblData.dataPageSize>1 Then SetButtons()
End Sub
```

This simple routine automatically takes care of all the problems of setting the button visibility at the correct times. We've made both the buttons hidden in the source HTML of the page, so neither will be visible when the page is loaded. However, as soon as the table has been rendered—and every time it is re-rendered—the `onreadystatechange()` event occurs and the table's `readyState` property is continuously updated until the data transfer and rendering is complete. At this point, our `SetButtons` routine will display the appropriate buttons. Of course we only need to do it when the `dataPageSize` property has been set to `MaxRows`, and not when the page first loads and it is still 1.

This completes our coverage of enhancements to the BookList sample. The complete source code, including the on-the-fly HTML generation and table paging, can be found in the `BookList2` samples directory.

Summary

Using Dynamic HTML data binding, and the Tabular Data Control, we have designed and built a complete on-line book search application. Along the way, we have seen how repeated table data binding works in IE4, and studied in detail how to use the TDC in data binding applications. TDC provides fast, efficient, and scalable access to simple and relatively small data sets.

In retrospect, we identified the major deficiencies of the TDC and provided potential workarounds for each one. We surmised that if all of the shortcomings must be addressed in our application, we would be better served by moving to a more powerful data source object such as the RDS.

Finally, we turned our attention to the book search application again with an eye on opportunities for enhancement. We showed how to use the `DATAFORMATAS` attribute to incorporate on-the-fly HTML code, driven from a data source object. We also showed how to add paging to a data bound table with the `dataPageSize` attribute, and the `nextPage()` and `previousPage()` methods. We saw how complex the apparently simply paging enhancement can become.

At this point, we have a full understanding of how data binding works in IE4 using repeated table (or tabular) data binding techniques. It's an ideal time for advancing to the next level. In the next chapter, we'll see how the new Remote Data Service and it's associated Advanced Data Control enable us to break through all the barriers we've come across—and access any data, anywhere.

Databinding with RDS/ADC

During our examination of the TDC as a data source control, we identified several of its limitations. They included its inability to deal with one-to-many relationships, inability to update data and the provision of a stagnant data set–i.e. the inability to reflect real time change in the data source. Despite these limitations, there are a very large number of common data access problems on the Internet or an Intranet that can be solved with a simple TDC-based solution. After all, using a sledgehammer to crack a walnut is not always the optimal solution.

However, in this chapter, we'll meet the sledgehammer–the "other" data source control included with Internet Explorer 4. The data source object is called the **Advanced Data Control** (Version 1.5 to be precise) or ADC, and is part of the wider technology known as the **Remote Data Service**, or RDS.

Unlike the TDC, the RDS/ADC combination gives us real access to "live" databases. It also has no problem dealing with data that has complex relationships, including the one-to-many case that the TDC cannot handle. The only drawback to using the ADC is the complexity introduced by the existence of a real database, rather than the TDC object's flat file data source.

We'll begin with a quick coverage of the ADC as a data source control, contrasting it quickly with the TDC that you're now familiar with. Then, we'll go on to look at some examples of how it can be used, examining its data update capability, its ability to deal with complex data relationships, and its ability to reflect real-time data change from a data source. In short, this sample will show the ADC under bright lights–overcoming all the identified limitations of the TDC.

So, this chapter will cover:

- What the RDS/ADC data access technology is, and what it provides
- How we use RDS in its simplest form, with a tabular data binding
- How we use RDS with single-value data binding, and update the source data
- Some examples of RDS in use in different types of application

It's a long yet exciting journey, so let's get started right away.

Introducing RDS/ADC Data Binding

First, you need to understand that the ADC participates in Dynamic HTML data binding in the exact same manner as the TDC. That is to say, we can use the data binding attributes **DATASRC**, **DATAFLD**, **DATAFORMATAS**, and **DATAPAGESIZE** in exactly the same way as we have with the TDC in the two previous chapters.

All the Dynamic HTML elements that support data binding can be bound to an ADC using single-valued data binding, and the repeated table binding presentation works in the same way as we're used to. In effect, it's just the **data source** that has changed, and nothing else. The elements in the page will accept data from, and can be bound to, **any** data source-they're not particular in this respect.

What is the Remote Data Service?

So, all we have to worry about in theory is the techniques of working with the data source object itself, such as setting the properties and calling its methods. However, RDS is a considerably more complex method of providing data, and so, although we don't need to worry about re-learning the techniques of data binding at Dynamic HTML language level, we do need to know a lot about the data source control itself, and how we use extra abilities of the bound elements in the page to get the most from it.

The Remote Data Service uses the ADC data source object as the primary client side component for a data access, although it's not limited to just this one. Other suppliers can create their own components to interact with RDS if they wish. In fact, RDS is such a complex system that we will defer a detailed discussion of how it works until the reference section at the end of this book. For now, we will focus on how the ADC, its client component, can be used in client-side data binding applications.

The RDS Data Access Tiers

Without going into a lot of detail, the operation of the RDS/ADC is consistent with the three-tier client/server architecture that we discussed in Chapter 6. In fact, the ADC object is only one piece of the puzzle. On the client-side, it provides a data binding capability to all HTML elements that support this. The complete picture involves several other components, as shown in the following diagram:

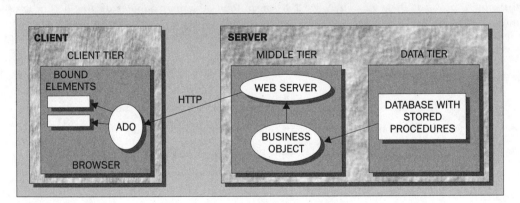

The data actually originates from a **server data source** (which can be any database, but in most cases will be an ODBC compliant data source). The data is fetched from the data source by a middle tier **business object** running on the server, which then passes it via the **Web server** to the ADC in the client tier for presentation in the bound HTML elements.

> *Check out Appendix G for a technical overview of how RDS works, and how the different layers provide a wide-ranging solution to existing Web-based data access problems.*

The Advantages of RDS

As we said before, the TDC and the RDS/ADC package are very much alike when it comes to data binding behaviors.

The overwhelming benefits of an RDS-based solution are that it:

- can work with complex data relationships, including the one-to-many link
- can reflect changes to data in the database in real time, as soon as it is changed, and even in multi-users scenarios
- can update the data in the source database in real time
- requires no database access middle-ware installation, other than IE4
- requires no configuration at the client side
- can rapidly change the source of the data without reconfiguring client
- is highly efficient for both viewing and modifying data
- supports asynchronous operation, enabling rapid application load times
- works directly with any ODBC compatible data source, and with other through OLE-DB

So RDS actually overcomes *all* of the handicaps of the TDC that we met in the previous chapters. To prove the point, in the first example of this chapter, we are going to take a page from our TDC BookList case study, and see how we can convert it to RDS operations–and do it live!

Working with RDS Data Binding

To show you how easy RDS is to use, we'll first walk through some modifications to the case study from the previous chapter. Then, we'll look at how a single-value data binding application might work using RDS. After that, we'll talk about some of the background theory that you'll need to become familiar with as you start to develop your own applications.

Configuration of the Server

Unlike the TDC data source we've used so far, which only required the data files and HTML pages to be placed on the server, RDS involves some setting up before it will function. It will also only work if the pages are accessed via HTTP, and not as files on the local system or over the network using the `file://` protocol. The examples in this chapter assume that server configuration required to use RDS is already completed. In the next chapter, we'll be examining a real application built with RDS, and show you step by step how you accomplish this configuration on your own server.

From TDC to ADC, and Back to TDC

If we load the Details page of the BookList example we used in the previous chapter into the browser (as an independent web page) we get the following:

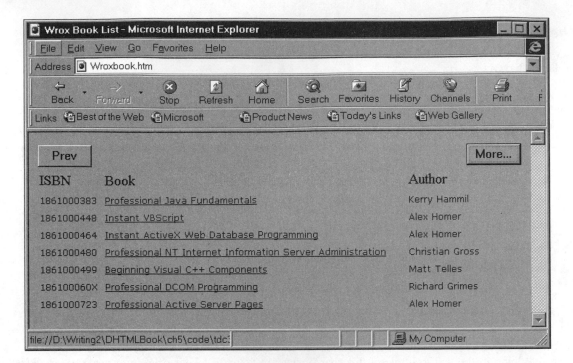

The list is displayed a page at a time, and we can move through the bound table using the buttons-as we did in the actual case study. Using just this page as the basis of our discussion allows us to avoid the complexity of the other frames, and just focus on how we can change over from TDC data binding to RDS. The source code for this example can be found with the other samples in the folder `/DataBind/Ch08_Tdcadc`.

Defining the BookList Database

As we have mentioned before, RDS provides us with data from remote databases, in real time. This means that the data source we will be using is no longer as simple as the text file of the TDC case study. Instead, we need a real database, whose structure must mirror our data file. This is the table within the database, named BOOKINFO:

Field Name	Type (Size)	Description
ID	integer	A unique serial number for the book, providing a key for the record.
Author	text (80)	The name of the author.
URL Title	text (255)	An HTML fragment containing the title and the link to the title. Typically an `<A HREF="link">"title"</A>` element.
ISBN	text (10)	The ISBN number of the book.
Subject	text (30)	The subject that the book covers.
Series	text (30)	The Wrox series that the book belongs to.
URL	text(150)	The URL of a link to the description of the book.
Title	text(100)	The title of the book.

Adding The TDC/RDS 'Switching' Button

What we will do is add another button on the page, which will allow the user to switch between using RDS and TDC to access the data. Clicking the button will toggle the actual data source bound to the table from ADC to TDC and vice versa:

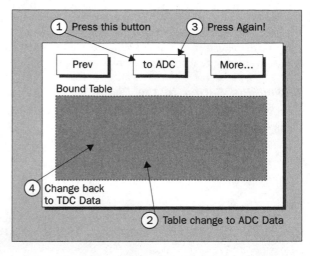

The New Switching Code

In this instance, thanks to the similarity between the RDS and TDC methods of tabular data binding, the task is almost trivial. The first modification we make is to add an instance of the ADC object, placing it just below the TDC that is already there. The new code is highlighted below:

```
<object classid="CLSID:333C7BC4-460F-11D0-BC04-0080C7055A83"
        id="tdcBooks" width=1 height=1>
<param name="FieldDelim" value=",">
<param name="DataURL" value="bookinfo.txt">
<param name="UseHeader" value=True>
</object>
<object classid="clsid:BD96C556-65A3-11D0-983A-00C04FC29E33"
        id="adcBooks" height=1 width=1>
<param name="Server" value="http://rapid.wrox.co.uk" >
<param name="Connect" value="DSN=0707WXBKDB" >
<param name="SQL" value="select * from BOOKINFO;">
</object>
</body>
</html>
```

Connecting to the Data Source

The three properties of the ADC object we're setting here (using **<PARAM>** tags) are **Server**, **Connect**, and **SQL**. Between them, they determine the actual recordset that we will be working with via RDS. In this case, the server that will host our RDS connection is **http://rapid.wrox.co.uk**. Obviously, in your own applications, you'll need to change this to point to your own server.

The **Connect** property describes a data source on the server. We can specify this in a number of ways, including the path to it, the user ID and password required to access it, and the various parameters that control that access, such as the **timeout**. A far easier method, ideally suited to the anonymous access we would expect to use in most of our Internet-based applications, is to use a Data Source Name (DSN). This is defined by the ODBC Manager program on the server, and uniquely identifies the database itself, and controls how access to it is made. You'll see how to set up a DSN in the next chapter. Here, we're using that we've one named **0707WXBKDB**.

The `SQL` property contains the query whose result we will be using in our display. Instead of specifying the query directly like this, we could instead identify the name of an existing query or stored procedure on the database that we wanted to use. In our case, to make this roughly equivalent to the TDC example, we simply select all the fields from the `BOOKINFO` table. We could be more efficient and just select the fields that are displayed in the table. When the number of rows in the table is large, this optimization will make a significant difference in the interactive response time of the application.

Adding the Button to the Page

Next, we modify the page itself to add the button, in between the existing Prev and More buttons. The change to the code looks like this:

```
<td width="50%">
  <button id="butPrevButton" onclick="GoPrevPage()"
        style="width:75;visibility:hidden"> Prev </button>
</td>
<td>
 <button id="butConvert" onclick="ConvertNow()"
        style="width:85;visibility:visible">to ADC</button>
 </td>
<td align="right">
   <button id="butNextButton" onclick="GoNextPage()"
        style="width:75;visibility:hidden"> More... </button>
</td>
```

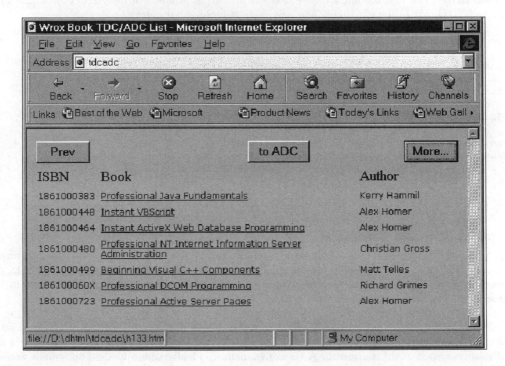

Handling the onclick Event

When this button is clicked, we want to switch the table contents to the ADC from the TDC, and then back when it's clicked again. We also need to change the text label of the button from "to ADC" to "to TDC". Here's the routine named **ConvertNow()**, which is executed for the **onclick** event of the new button. It changes the **innerText** property of the button to place the new caption on it, then changes the **datasrc** property of the bound table:

```
Sub ConvertNow()
  if butConvert.innerText = "to ADC" then
     butConvert.innerText = "to TDC"
     tblData.datasrc = "#adcBooks"
     PendButton()
  else    ' back to TDC
     butConvert.innerText = "to ADC"
     tblData.datasrc = "#tdcBooks"
     PendButton()
  end if
End Sub
```

That's all there is to it. The way that the TDC performs data binding to HTML elements is exactly the same as the ADC under RDS. The **PendButton()** subroutine is called just in case we are in the middle of paging data when the "convert" button is pressed, to determine which of the Prev and Next buttons need to be shown for the new recordset.

Using Multiple ADC Objects with RDS

This example is a simple one, but imagine now that you have multiple data sources to access, each with its own data source object in the page. Using RDS and ODBC, you may have an Oracle™ data source, an SQL Server data source, an IBM DB2™ mainframe data source, plus, of course, a TDC data source with simple flat-file data as well if you like.

It's easy to see how an example such as the one we've just seen can easily be modified to handle this (provided we have ODBC drivers for all the data sources at the server). The **only** change required at the client end is to point the **DATASRC** attribute at the corresponding ADC object, using script connected to a button or other control.

We can even programmatically modify the **Server**, **Connect**, and **SQL** properties of one single ADC to make this happen, instead of having several objects. Instant client access to multiple heterogeneous data sources, without code download and client configuration, is finally a reality!

Switching the Bound DATASRC On the Fly

This brings up an interesting topic-dynamic modification to bound data elements. Certainly, in our case, we found that when we modify the **DATASRC** attribute of the bound HTML table element, the table re-binds to the new **DATASRC** and behaves as expected. As a matter of fact, you'll find that in most cases, things work as expected.

For any bindable elements participating in single-valued binding, even one that is programmatically created (i.e. using **CreateObject()**, as discussed in Appendix **G**), visible binding results as soon as both the **DATASRC** and **DATAFLD** attribute have been completely specified. If one of these attributes is not yet specified, the element will not show any visible binding.

In tabular data binding, any bindable element that is in the row template (generally the `<TBODY>` section of a table), the rows (and thus the table) will show visible data binding as soon as the `DATAFLD` attribute is fully specified, providing that the `DATASRC` attribute is already fully specified in the surrounding `<TABLE>` element. For example:

```
<tbody>
  <tr id="rowData">
    <td width="75">
     <font size="1" face="verdana">
      <span datafld="ISBN"></span>
     </font>
    </td>
    <td width="400">
     <font size="1" face="verdana">
      <span datafld="URLTitle" dataformatas="html"></span>
     </font>
    </td>
  </tr>
</tbody>
```

All rows inherit the `DATASRC` attribute from the table in a tabular (repeated table) binding.

Finally, as in our example, you can modify the `DATASRC` attribute on a bound table in a repeated-table binding, as well as or instead of the `DATAFLD` attribute. No data will be displayed in the table until the `DATASRC` element is fully specified in the `<TABLE>` element, even if all the rows have fully specified `DATAFLD` attributes.

The contents of a bound table do not change automatically when you change the row template from script while the page is loaded. If you want to change the actual visual composition of a row of a bound table (i.e. the bound HTML elements that make up a row), it is necessary to:

▲ set the `DATASRC` attribute of the enclosing `<TABLE>` element to `" "`, thereby breaking the binding. IE4 will display a blank table momentarily

▲ modify the contents of the row template using the object model

▲ set the `DATASRC` attribute of the enclosing `<TABLE>` back to the original value, thus re-establishing the binding against the new table

For all intents and purpose, the momentary switch to a non-bound state is so brief that the end user will see an instantaneous change.

Protecting the Data Source

One potential problem of RDS is the fact that it supports automatic data update of the source data from script at the client side. Just because your page doesn't actually change the data (we'll see how it's done in the next example), doesn't mean to say that all the pages that access the data source won't.

Remember, the user can view the source HTML of the page they have loaded, and see not only the details of the tables and fields, but also the server name and the value of the `Connect` property. This might even contain the user ID and password details, so you present them with the opportunity to create their own pages using data binding that can update the data source. This means that you need to consider securing it if you want to prevent it being changed.

Creating Read-Only Data Sources

When the data source is connected through ODBC, we can protect the data source directly at the ODBC manager level. During the setup of a Microsoft Access ODBC data source, the following screen is used to select the location of the MDB file:

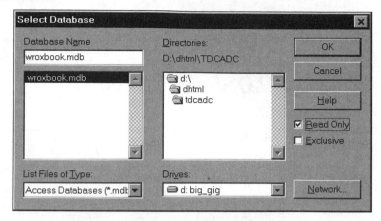

By setting the Read Only checkbox here, we prevent the data source from being written to by any page. This means its `Connect` values can be casually passed on in web pages, without any risk of malicious tampering with the actual source data. As a bonus, it also allows RDS to perform some optimization (since it doesn't need the ability to update this data source) when it communicates between the client and server.

Of course, we can also use the features of the actual data source in many situations, by adding "rules" to the database. This topic is, however, outside the scope of this book.

Updating the Data Source with RDS

Now that we are convinced that RDS is really quite a lot like using the TDC when scripting and DHTML authoring, we'll examine some of the differences. So far, we've only used **tabular data binding**, which is inherently a read-only presentation of the data. One of the major reasons for using RDS instead is that it supports a read/write capability–it can update the data source on the server from a client-based Web page. This requires **single-value data binding** techniques, which we also examined in Chapter 6.

First, we'll show you how we can use RDS in a classic single–valued binding form, and update the source data. Then we'll move on to see how we can use some of its more advanced features to perform data validation as well.

Single-Value Data Binding with RDS

The following example application is a page that allows us to modify, add, and delete records in an employee database. Here is what the user interface looks like–the source code for this example can be found with the other samples in the folder **/DataBind/Ch08_Adcmod**:

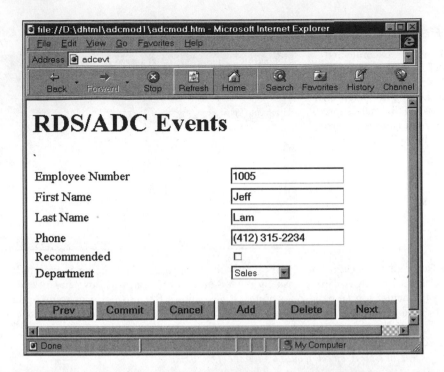

The Prev and Next buttons traverse through all the employee records in the database, and at any time–while a record is displayed–we can modify its content by using one of the **updateable** bound HTML elements. The Add button can be used to create a new blank employee record in the database, and the Delete button will delete the record currently displayed from the database.

Local Data Caching

If this sounds like a lot of activity will be occurring over the network, don't panic. RDS caches the data set that it extracts from the data source on the client machine. If you set up the ADC object to fetch all the employees that live in Kentucky, for example, they will be fetched from the database on the server and cached as a local recordset by the browser. All you are doing while the page is open is changing the contents of this local cache.

This allows highly interactive yet efficient data manipulation, and also permits cancellation of the modifications should the user change their mind. In our example, no changes to the data are sent to the server until the Commit button is pressed. If the Cancel button is pressed instead, all the changes to the database will be cancelled since the last data commit (or since the beginning of the application if Commit has not being pressed).

The Employee Database

Again we need a database to act as the source of the records. Obviously, it is not set up to be read-only in this case since the application will be updating it. The database definition is:

Table Name: `Employee`

Field Name	Type (Size)	Description
`FirstName`	Text (30)	The first name of the employee.
`LastName`	Text (30)	The last name of the employee.
`Phone`	Text (20)	The business phone number of the employee.
`Dept`	Text (10)	The department that the employee works in.
`Recommended`	Boolean	Indicates whether the employee is recommended for performance awards.

In this example, we assume that the user will only be entering employees that are either from the Sales or Accounting department into this database. Notice that the final field is of type `Boolean` (`True/False`), which provides us with the ideal opportunity to use a checkbox control, rather than the more usual text and list boxes we've used in earlier examples.

The Employee Database Application

Now let's look at how the application is constructed, and see what more we need to do beyond the basic single-value binding techniques we used with the TDC in Chapter 6. Here is the HTML that creates the main section of the page. This section creates the first four textboxes, setting the `datasrc` of each to point to an ADC object named `adcEmp`, and the `datafld` to point to the appropriate field in the database:

```
<html>
<head>
</head>
<body>
<H1>RDS/ADC Single-Valued Binding</H1>
<table style="width:600">
 <tr>
  <td width="300">Employee Number</td>
  <td>
    <input id="txtEmpNum" type="text"
          datasrc="#adcEmp" datafld="ID">
  </td>
 </tr>
 <tr>
  <td width="300">First Name</td>
   <td>
    <input id="txtFirst" type="text"
          datasrc="#adcEmp" datafld="Firstname">
  </td>
 </tr>
 <tr>
  <td width="300">Last Name</td>
  <td>
   <input id="txtLast" type="text"
          datasrc="#adcEmp" datafld="Lastname">
  </td>
 </tr>
```

```
<tr>
 <td width="300">Phone</td>
 <td>
  <input id="txtPhone" type="text"
         datasrc="#adcEmp" datafld="Phone">
 </td>
</tr>
...
```

This code looks very similar to the TDC singled-valued binding example we saw in Chapter 6. Note, however, that the `<INPUT>` elements are handling both display *and* update of the data in this case. However, you can't tell just from the code.

Updateable Binding with a Checkbox Control

The `Recommended` field in the database is of type Boolean, and is presented as an updateable checkbox. This is one of the new bindable HTML elements that we discussed in Chapter 6:

```
...
<tr>
 <td width="300">Recommended</td>
 <td><input id="chkRec" type="checkbox"
            datasrc="#adcEmp"  datafld="Recommended"></td>
</tr>
...
```

If the value of `Recommended` is `False`, the checkbox will not be checked. If it is `True`, it will be checked. Since the field is updatable, the user can also click on the checkbox to cause the underlying field value to change from `True` to `False`, and vice versa.

Updateable Binding with a Combo Box Control

The `Dept` field is a text value, but here is presented as an updateable `<SELECT>` element. This is an easy task in our case, since it can only be Accounting or Sales.

```
...
<tr>
 <td width="300">Department</td>
 <td>
  <select id="selDept" datasrc="#adcEmp" datafld="Dept">
   <option value="Accounting">Accounting
   <option value="Sales">Sales
  </select>
 </td>
</tr>
</table>
...
```

Here, we set the `<OPTION>` tags of the `<SELECT>` element to reflect the two possible department choices. If the database ever contains another value other than Accounting or Sales, the display for the corresponding Dept field in the record will be blank. And because it's a combo box in the page, the application itself will never allow anything else to be entered in this field.

This is a perfect example of how client-side data binding can be less than secure, however. If the user creates a page that has a normal text box for this field, they will be able to enter any old values. This is where the rules within the database itself, on the server, will need to come into play to protect against incorrect entries.

Adding the Navigation Buttons

The next section of the page lays out the button bar in another table, and associates an action with each button, as we'll see in a while:

```
<table>
 <tr>
  <td>
   <button onclick="movePrev()" style="width:90">
     Prev </button>
  </td>
  <td>
   <button onclick="submitChanges()" style="width:90">
    Commit </button>
  </td>
  <td>
   <button onclick="cancelUpdate()" style="width:90">
    Cancel </button>
  </td>
  <td>
   <button onclick="adcEmp.recordset.AddNew()" style="width:90">
    Add </button>
  </td>
  <td>
   <button onclick="adcEmp.recordset.Delete()" style="width:90">
    Delete </button>
  </td>
  <td>
   <button onclick="moveNext()" style="width:90">
    Next </button>
  </td>
 </tr>
</table>
```

Finally, here is our **adcEmp** ADC object. Remember that the **Server** value in the **<PARAM>** tag needs to reflect your own RDS server. The **SQL** value here simply selects all fields from the **Employee** table. This is fine, since we are updating all the fields of a record at once:

```
<object classid="clsid:BD96C556-65A3-11D0-983A-00C04FC29E33"
        id="adcEmp" height=1 width=1>
  <param name="Server" value="http://rapid.wrox.co.uk">
  <param name="Connect" value="DSN=0707WXUPDB">
  <param name="SQL" value="select * from Employee;">
</object>
</body>
</html>
```

The Script That Makes It Work

As it stands, opening the page will display the values of the first record in the control on the page. Like the TDC, the ADC control provides access to the underlying ADO **recordset** object. Its this that enables us to access and update the data source programmatically. The first step is to understand the script code we'll need to make the page actually perform. Essentially, we have the following button actions to manage:

Button	Action	Description
Prev	Call our own **movePrev()** subroutine.	Move back one record and update the display.
Commit	Call our own **submitChange()** subroutine.	Commit to the server all the changes we have made so far.
Cancel	Call our own **cancelUpdate()** subroutine.	Revert back to the original values, canceling all pending changes since the last commit.
Add	Call the **AddNew()** method of the recordset managed by the ADC.	Add a new record, and display this blank record for immediate data entry.
Delete	Call the **Delete()** method of the recordset managed by the ADC.	Delete the currently displayed record from the database.
Next	Call our own **moveNext()** subroutine.	Move forward one record and update the display.

Notice that (only) the Add and Delete button **onclick** events directly call methods of the **recordset** object. These methods, however, do exactly what we need–adding or deleting a record in the local cached copy of the source data. The other buttons have routines we've created ourselves for their **onclick** handlers, because we need to combine several scripting actions.

Moving To The Previous And Next Record

In the **movePrev()** and **moveNext()** subroutines, we can use the **movePrev()** and **moveNext()** methods of the recordset object. However, we also need to handle the boundary conditions, i.e. when the current record is at the beginning or end of the recordset:

```
sub movePrev
 if (not adcEmp.recordset.BOF) then
  adcEmp.recordset.movePrevious()
 end if
end sub
```

```
Sub moveNext
 if (not adcEmp.recordset.EOF) then
  adcEmp.recordset.moveNext()
 end if
end sub
```

Committing The Changes To The Server

In the **submitChanges()** routine, which runs when the Commit button is clicked, we call the ADC's **submitChanges()** method, but we also need to refresh the ADC so that the recordset reflects what's actually in the database on the server. This includes any changes that other users have made while we've been working with a cached recordset:

```
sub submitChanges()
 adcEmp.submitChanges()
 adcEmp.refresh()   'reflect server's database content
end sub
```

This is all that's required to tell RDS that we want to update the data on the server. It just gets on and does it by uploading the changes we've applied to the cached recordset, and applying them to the database.

In the same way, we call the ADC's **cancelUpdate()** method to handle the Cancel button's **onclick** event, and call **Refresh()** to get the latest recordset contents from the server:

```
sub cancelUpdate()
 adcEmp.cancelUpdate()
 adcEmp.refresh()      'reflect server's database content
end sub
```

Validating the Data on the Client

If you have coded any data entry applications in the past, there will no doubt be a few questions in your mind now. What if you want to do some field-by-field data validation? What if you want to enforce certain relationship constraints between fields? What if the user simply exits the application, or navigates to another page, while modified data still exists in the local data cache? We'll answer these questions, and more, in this section.

Handling Events In The Employee Application

Let's assume that any employee number between 2000 and 3000 should only refer to an employee that works in the Accounting department. We want to enforce this when the user enters new data, and when they modify existing records. In particular, we want to make sure that:

- whenever the Department is changed in the combo box, the employee number is validated. If the selection is changed to Accounting, the Employee Number must be between 2000 and 2999.

- after the Employee Number has been filled in, the department is validated. If the employee number is between 2000 and 2999, we must set the Department field to Accounting, otherwise we set it to Sales.

- when the user closes the application or navigates to another page, we should warn them that cached data may not be saved.

The new application will still look the same, and the changes will only become obvious as it is used–the source code for this example can be found with the other samples in the folder **/DataBind/ Ch08_Adcevt:**

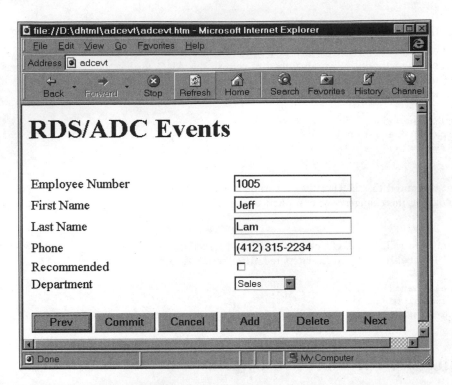

Translating Rules into Event Handlers

We'll summarize all the events that are available later in this chapter. In the mean time, we can lay out just the events we'll need to use, and create some rules (as 'pseudocode') defining how we'll be handling these events.

When the value in a bound control changes, that control fires a series of events. These include the **onbeforeupdate** and **onafterupdate** events. We'll use the **onbeforeupdate** event for our **selDept** combo box to check that the employee number in the **txtEmpNum** control is within the bounds we specified earlier. Because the event occurs before the change is applied to the cached recordset, we can cancel the change if it is invalid:

```
selDept_onbeforeupdate

if selDept=Accounting then
{
 if val(txtEmpNum) not between 2000 and 2999 then
   {
   cancel the event and prevent change
   }
}
```

When the employee number is changed in the **txtEmpNum** control, we need to check-and possibly change-the selection in the **selDept** control. We won't be attempting the cancel the change in the **txtEmpNum** text box, so we can use the **onafterupdate** event instead of **onbeforeupdate**. This occurs after the change has been applied to the cached recordset:

```
txtEmpNumt_onafterupdate

if val(txtEmpNum) is between 2000 and 2999
{
    selDept = Accounting
}
  else
{
    selDept = Sales
}
```

The final event we'll react to is the **onbeforeunload** event for the page itself, as exposed by the **document** object. This can't be cancelled, for security reasons, so we can't actually stop the user changing to another page-at which point the cached data is lost. We can, however, warn them that some data may not be saved. Alternatively, we could just submit the changes to the data anyway, before the page is unloaded. Our application provides a warning instead:

```
document_onbeforeunload

{
  alert with a warning message
}
```

The Changes to the Application Code

Now, all that's left is to actually code these event handlers. Here is the code we've used for the **selDept_onbeforeupdate** event. We use the object model to obtain the currently selected value in the Dept selection box. If it's Accounting and the employee number is out of range, we cancel the event and prevent it from bubbling further up the object model:

```
function selDept_onbeforeupdate()
 curNo = CInt(txtEmpNum.value)
 if (curNo >= 2000) and (curNo < 3000) then
  if selDept.options(selDept.selectedIndex).text <> "Accounting" then
   window.event.returnValue = false   'cancel the update to the data
   window.event.cancelBubble = true
  end if
 end if
end function
```

The event handler for the **txtEmpNum_onafterupdate** event (for the Employee Number field) simply checks the value entered by the user. If it's in the correct range for the Accounting department we set the combo box to Accounting, otherwise, we set it to Sales:

```
function txtEmpNum_onafterupdate()
 curNo = CInt(txtEmpNum.value)
 if (curNo >= 2000) and (curNo < 3000) then
  selDept.selectedIndex = 0
 else
  selDept.selectedIndex = 1
 end if
 window.event.returnValue = true
end function
```

Finally, if the user navigates to another page, we handle the `document_onbeforeunload` event and pop up an alert box to let the user know data may be lost:

```
function document_onbeforeunload()
 alert "You may lose data, please check that all data is saved."
end function
```

Summary of RDS/ADC Usage

In the example so far in this chapter, we've seen the basic ways that RDS can be used with the ADC object to access, display, and manipulate server-side databases. Before we look at a more complex example, we'll summarize the properties, methods and events provided by this exciting new technology.

RDS/ADC Properties Summary

The following is a list of the exposed properties and methods from the ADC. You'll notice a degree of similarity to those exposed by the TDC. This makes migration and scripting simple.

Property	Description
connect	*String*. Sets the database name against which the query and updates should be applied, as well as identifying the data source.
executeOptions	*Integer*. Can contain one of: 0 – no option set, operation may be synchronous or asynchronous. **adAsyncExecute** – specifies that query executes asynchronously. **adAsyncFetch** – specifies that data fetch executes asynchronously. Values can be combined o specify asynchronous fetch and execute.
filterColumn	*String*. The name of the column within the recordset to be used in the filtering operation.
filterCriterion	*String*. The relational operator used in filtering, can be one of =, <>, <, >, <= or >=.
filterValue	*String*. Value to compare the field against during filtering. Used in conjunction with **filterColumn** and **filterCriterion**.
recordset	Read-only reference to the object's recordset, as returned from a remote database query.
sourceRecordset	Write-only property of type **recordset** used to replace the control's recordset with another during runtime.
server	A string property containing a URL or host-name. Identifies the host on which the Web server supporting RDS is running.
state	*Integer* (read-only). Indicates the state of the ADC, can be one of: **adStateClosed** – the ADC's recordset is closed. **adStateOpen** – the ADC's recordset is open, ready for access. **adStateConnecting** – this state will never occur and is provided for completeness-connection is always synchronous.

Property	Description
	adStateExecuting – asynchronous executing is in progress. **adStateFetching** – asynchronous data fetching is in progress.
sortColumn	*String.* Name of the column for the data to be sorted on.
sortDirection	*Boolean.* Sort order of the column specified in **sortColumn**. **True** means ascending, **False** means descending.
SQL	*String.* The SQL query used to retrieve the recordset.

The 'named' values in the table can be found in the **adcvbs.inc** *file supplied with IE4. You'll find more information in Appendix* **G**.

RDS/ADC Methods Summary

The RDS/ADC object provides methods to control display and updating of the cached data, and commit of the data to the server:

Method	Description
cancel	Cancels the current asynchronous action, and resets the **state** property to **adStateClosed**.
cancelUpdate	Cancels any pending data update by reverting the data values in the recordset back to the values from the last call to **refresh**. All bound HTML elements will now display the previous value.
createRecordset	Creates a disconnected, empty recordset. Typically used in custom data access scripting.
refresh	Completely refreshes the cached recordset by re-querying the remote data source. Update any bound HTML elements with the new values.
reset	A client-side only cache-based refresh operation that creates no traffic to the server. Used to apply a sort or filter to the cached data after setting the appropriate properties of the control. There must be no pending updates when called. Accepts an optional *Boolean* argument. If this is **True** or omitted, the filter operation will be performed on the current set of data, even if it has been filtered already. If **False** the current filter is removed and the new filter applied to the complete set of cached data.
submitChanges	Send any pending changes in the local disconnected cached recordset to the remote database.

The 'named' value in the table can be found in the **adcvbs.inc** *file supplied with IE4. You'll find more information in Appendix* **G**.

RDS/ADC Events Summary

Unlike read-only data source objects such as TDC, the ADC can be used to update databases. To provide application level control that we frequently need to validate input or enforce certain constraints between values of fields, the ADC control exposes several events.

Some of these events are associated with the data source object itself (i.e. the ADC), while others are associated with the bound element (i.e. an `<INPUT>` object). There are also others that are associated with the entire `document` object during data binding. First, here's a list of the events and the associated objects. Each one is examined in more depth after the list:

Event	Associated Object
onbeforeupdate	The data-bound HTML element (i.e. `<INPUT>`, `<SELECT>`, etc.).
onafterupdate	The data-bound HTML element (i.e. `<INPUT>`, `<SELECT>`, etc.).
onrowexit	The data source object (i.e. the ADC).
onrowenter	The data source object (i.e. the ADC).
onerrorupdate	The data source object (i.e. the ADC).
ondatasetchanged	The data source object (i.e. the ADC).
ondataavailable	The data source object (i.e. the ADC).
ondatasetcomplete	The data source object (i.e. the ADC).
onbeforeunload	The document object associated with the data binding page.

The onbeforeupdate Event

This is fired by the data-bound HTML element before it loses the focus. This could happen via a user-initiated focus transfer (i.e. pressing the *Tab* key), or when the page is unloading. This event can be cancelled by setting the `window.event.returnValue` property to `false`. This will abort the focus transfer and any change to the data. Validation of the data in the element is typically performed here. Elements such as checkboxes and radio buttons will fire `onbeforeupdate` immediately upon change, rather than at focus transfer time.

The onafterupdate Event

This is fired by a data bound HTML element after the data has been transferred to the data source object, and cannot be cancelled. It will only fire if `onbeforeupdate` has not previously been canceled by its own event handler. The `onafterupdate` event is useful for setting the value of a related field based on the value entered into the current one. The input can be assumed to be valid since the `onbeforeupdate` event handler had been called and returned successfully.

The onrowexit Event

This is fired just prior to the transition between rows (or records) in the recordset, and is not cancelable. This can be used for per-record validation, record mirroring, or per-record resource de-allocation. The event will fire even if record position is changed via scripting. Note that both the `onbeforeupdate` and the `onafterupdate` events of *all* bound elements associated with the row will have already been fired before this event fires. Don't confuse the name of the event with rows in an HTML table—the *row* refers to a row of data within a data table.

The onrowenter Event

This is fired just before the user gets control of the current record, and after all this record's data fields have been loaded into the bound HTML elements from the cached recordset. This event is not cancelable, and will fire even if the current record position is changed via scripting. It is good for a per-record data preparation (i.e. other elements on the page may depend on the value of a combination of fields), or per-record resource allocation.

The onerrorupdate Event

This is fired if IE4 encounter problem transferring data from the bound HTML elements to the data source object (i.e. the ADC). This can occur, for example, if an `<INPUT type="text">` element contains the wrong type of data for its bound field. Normally an error message would be displayed by IE4. This event can be canceled by setting `window.event.returnValue` to `false`, and in this case the error message will not be displayed. This event will only fire if it is caused by user interaction-it will not be fired if an error in transfer is caused through scripting.

The ondatasetchanged Event

This is fired when the data object in the page has a new set of data available. This may be because a filter or sort has been applied, or just as the data set is fetched in the normal state of operation. Although it indicates that a recordset is available (through the `recordset` property) it doesn't mean the entire set of data has been received–it may only be the meta information that defines the recordset. In future versions of RDS, where data source objects will be able to support more than one concurrent recordset, the `window.event.qualifier` property will return the name of the recordset that has changed. This event may not occur if the page does not contain at least one element bound to the ADC.

The ondataavailable Event

This is fired each time a 'batch' of records are received from the server. The number of times it fires depends on the connection, server efficiency, size of recordset, and other associated factors. It can be used monitor for new data while the browser carries on with other tasks. This event may not occur if the page does not contain at least one element bound to the ADC.

The ondatasetcomplete Event

This is fired when the data recordset being fetched from the server is complete. This may not be all the data that was requested, if the server or connection has timed out or an error has occurred. The `window.event.reason` property returns a value indicating why the event occurred, and can be `0` – completed successfully, `1` – download was aborted by the user, possibly by clicking the browser's Stop button, or `2` – an error of some type occurred during the transfer. This event may not occur if the page does not contain at least one element bound to the ADC.

The onbeforeunload Event

This is the only data update event which fires for the `document` object. It occurs when the user attempts to leave the current page if it has any updateable data bound elements, and cannot be canceled. Since the page is associated with a local data cache, which will be lost when the page is unloaded, this is a good place to remind the user that they may loose data as they navigate beyond the current page. The same event will fire if the user attempts to close IE4 down while a data update page is active.

Note that the `onbeforeupdate`, `onafterupdate`, and `onerrorupdate` events are only fired if the data in the element is changed by the user directly. Programmatic change of the element's value (for example, via scripting) does not cause any of these events to fire.

Other Non-Data Binding Events

Other than the events above, there are also many element-specific events which deal with the content of the element, and not necessarily with data binding. For example, the `onchange` event occurs for any combo box, irrespective of whether it's data bound. It can be used in either situation, though this event can't be cancelled to prevent changes to the source data when it is data bound.

When Does Each Event Fire?

Many applications will depend on the events we've been discussing for validation and data pre-processing. A fixed, specified, and reliably reproducible ordering of events is essential for application stability. For example, if we cannot count on the `onload` event to be the first one after a page loads, there is no way to perform initialization of our application. Problems typically arise, and working programs will break, if the underlying event order should ever change. Having said all this, let us take a look at the currently specified ordering of the data update events:

1 The user makes a modification to the content of a data bound element and moves the focus out of it- logically committing the change.

2 The element fires the `onbeforeupdate` event.

3 The element transfers its data to the bound data source object, i.e. the ADC.

4 If there is a problem in the data transfer, the data source object fires the `onerrorupdate` event, and no more related events will be fired. However, if there is no error in the transfer, the element fires the `onafterupdate` event.

5 The element fires its own `onchange` event if supported, signifying that data has changed.

6 The data source object (i.e. the ADC) fires an `onrowexit` event if the change means that a different record becomes the current one.

7 The element fires its own `onblur` event.

8 The element that receives the focus, if applicable, fires its own `onfocus` event.

9 If a different record has become the current one, the data source object fires the `onrowenter` event.

After all this dry detail, it's now a good time to put some of these properties, methods and events to use in an example that explores some of the possibilities of RDS and the ADC data source object.

A Real RDS Data-Update Example

This is an opportune time to use RDS in a real application, and fulfill our initial objective of overcoming the limitations of the TDC. We're looking for an application that shows how RDS can be used to:

▲   add and update data on the data source

▲   access data through one-to-many relationships

▲   reflect changes in the data source in real-time

Simultaneous Multiple Read/Write Access

One other advantage that our application might reveal is the situation where we have multiple concurrent users. In database technician's lingo, database clients which perform database read are called **readers**, and ones which modify database contents are (you've guessed) called **writers**. Most typical database access applications are of the 'multiple-readers to single or multiple-writers' type.

To give an ADC a run for its money, we seek a multiple-readers/multiple-writers application. When we take this model to its limit, every single user is both a reader and a writer, and every single user is interested in every single database change made by all other writers. Indeed, this sounds like a very intense scenario for a database to handle, especially if the users write to the database frequently.

What does the database application become under this situation? Interestingly enough, almost like an Internet "chat" application.

The ADC TinyChat Application

We'll build a single-page TinyChat application using Dynamic HTML data binding, plus our new friends RDS and ADC. Unlike other chat-type applications, which require extensive programming, this one is almost trivial to code–relying heavily on the data presentation and update capabilities of Dynamic HTML data binding and RDS.

Here's what our final TinyChat application looks like in use. The source code for this example can be found with the other samples in the folder **/DataBind/TinyChat**.The client area of the browser is divided into two frames. The top one is the message frame, and the bottom one is the message entry frame:

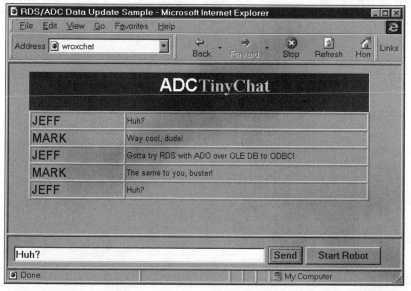

Using the TinyChat Application

To use TinyChat, the participant simply types into the message entry text box within the lower Entry frame, and then clicks the Send button. The message is sent to the server, and is immediately displayed in the Message frame of all the users. Messages from all participants are displayed to all users in real time, together with their user name. The following diagram illustrates this flow of actions:

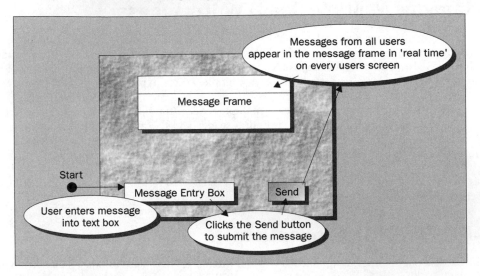

Note that two out of three of our design goals are already met by TinyChat. First, it definitely updates the remote data source–with the new message. Secondly, it's definitely reflecting real-time data changes–every user on the system can see every data update.

The Data Structure of TinyChat

To implement TinyChat using an ODBC backend database, we define two tables. One contains the user's name and a numeric ID; the other contains the actual messages. Since a single user can enter many messages during a session, this satisfies the last goal of our design, showing that ADC will handle the one-to-many data relationship we require.

These are the two tables:

Table Name: **USERS**

Field Name	Type (Size)	Description
UPDATED	Counter	System generated sequence number.
UID	Integer	The numeric ID of the user.
LOGIN	Character(30)	The login name of the user.
PASSWORD	Character(30)	The user's password (not used in TinyChat).
LASTLOG	DateTime	The time of their last login (not used in TinyChat).

Table Name: WORKMSG

Field Name	Type (Size)	Description
SERIAL	Counter	A system-generated sequence number.
MESSAGE	Character(65)	The message text sent by the user.
UID	Integer	The ID of the user who sent the message.
POSTTIME	DateTime	The time of the posting (local to the client).

You can create the tables above in your database using the corresponding data types. In SQL Server, substitute the **TIMESTAMP** type for the system counter. We've supplied a script named **maketables.sql** in the samples for this book that will create the tables for you in SQL Server.

Notice that we rely on the **SERIAL** field of the **WORKMSG** table to order the message. When the application is simultaneously accessed by clients from different time zones (or just with different clock settings on their machines), the **POSTTIME** field is not a reliable source for message ordering.

Implementing the TinyChat Application

We make use of two instances of the ADC object in the implementation of TinyChat. Both of them will be in the Message frame page **msgframe.htm**. The first is bound to a table, which displays the messages from the server, and is refreshed periodically to ensure all new updates are visible. The second is used programmatically through scripting only, and not data bound to any HTML elements. It is used to add a new message to the database when the user presses the Send button. The following diagram shows how the two ADC objects work together to implement the application.

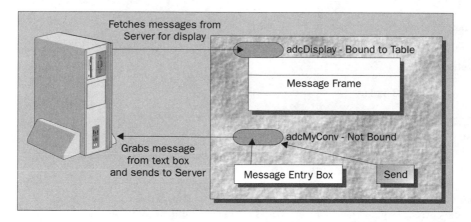

Handling One-to-Many Data Relationships

In order to show the user name next to the message in the data bound table, we must work with a one-to-many relationship (through an SQL join). Here we can see that a single user in the **USERS** table can be linked to many messages in the **WORKMSG** table:

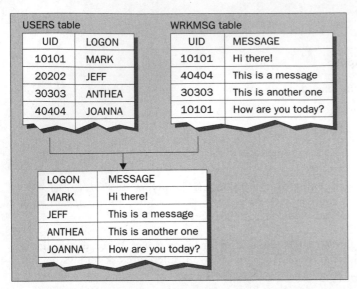

To achieve the result we want, we need to link the two tables together on the UID field. The SQL statement we'll be using is:

```
select LOGIN,MESSAGE,SERIAL
from WORKMSG,USERS
where WORKMSG.UID=USERS.UID
order by SERIAL;
```

Specifying the Parameters for the ADC Objects

We are now ready to decide on the parameters for the two ADC objects that will be embedded in the **Message** frame page:

ADC #1 (bound to a table, and used for displaying the messages)

Parameter	Value
ID	AdcDisplay
Connect	DSN=0707WXUPDB (substitute your own data source name)
Server	http://rapid.wrox.co.uk (substitute your own server name)
SQL	Select LOGIN,MESSAGE,SERIAL from WORKMSG,USERS where WORKMSG.UID=USERS.UID order by SERIAL

Notice that we need to ensure the displayed message are listed ordered by the **SERIAL** field in order to maintain time-correct sequencing of the messages on every client display. **SERIAL** is the server-generated sequence number for the messages.

ADC #2 (not data bound, and used via scripting only to add a new message)

Parameter	Value
ID	AdcMyConv
Connect	DSN=0707WXUPDB (substitute your own data source name)
Server	http://rapid.wrox.co.uk (substitute your own server name)
SQL	Select * from WORKMSG

In both of these, we're assuming a Data Source Name 0707WXUPDB has been set up to point to the database on the server. You'll need to change this to suit your own server configuration, and we'll show you exactly how to do this at the beginning of the next chapter.

Writing the Code for TinyChat

The coding of TinyChat is extremely straightforward. The main file **wroxchat.htm** contains the frameset definition. Remember to change the server name to point to your own server:

```
<html>
<head>
<title>RDS/ADC Data Update Sample</title>
<script language="vbscript">

'define and set global variables for database connection
'change these to suit your own installation and server name
Dim MyServerName, MySystemDSN
MyServerName = "http://pentium100"
MySystemDSN = "DSN=0707WXUPDB"

Dim myUID, refreshInterval, robotRate
myUID = 20202
refreshInterval = 5
robotRate = 3
</script>
</head>
```

The user ID **myUID** defines which user will show up as the author of the message sent. You can create several copies of **wroxchat.htm** (with different names and user IDs) to test the application in multi-user mode. They can even be run simultaneously on one a single machine. The **refreshInterval** is a number in seconds between refresh of the message table in the message frame. The **robotRate** (in seconds) is used by the "robot" message generator (described later), to determine how frequently to generate a message.

Finally, here is the actual frameset definition. The page has two frames, the top one is the message frame holding the page **msgframe.htm**; the bottom one is the entry frame which holds the page **msgentry.htm**, and occupies 60 pixels vertically:

```
<frameset rows="*,60">
  <frame src = "msgframe.htm" name="frmMessage" >
  <frame src="msgentry.htm"  name="frmEntry">
</frameset>
</html>
```

The Message Frame Page

The message frame page, `msgframe.htm`, is where the core of the chat logic is implemented. In it are the two ADC objects. However, the first part simply defines the styles for the page, then the data bound table that will display the messages:

```html
<html>
<head>
<title>Message Frame RDS/ADC Sample</title>
<style>
<!--
 H2    {color:yellow; font-family:times,serif; font-weight:bold}
 body {background:pink; color:black; font-family:arial,sans-serif;
        font-size:10pt;}
-->
</style>
</head>

<body>
<table width="100%"  bgcolor="red">
 <tr>
  <td width="100%">
   <center><h2>
   <span style="color:white; font-family:arial,sans-serif">ADC</span>
   TinyChat</h2></center>
  </td>
 </tr>
</table>
<table width="100%" id="Coll" border="1" datasrc="#adcD">
 <tr>
  <td width="150">
   <span datafld="LOGIN"></span>
  </td>
  <td>
   <span datafld="Message" style="font-size:8pt"></span>
  </td>
 </tr>
</table>
```

This is the table bound to one of the ADCs in the page. We display the user name (from the LOGIN field) and the contents of the MESSAGE field. You'll recall that these two fields actually originate from two separate tables, but are brought together through an SQL join via the ADC's SQL parameter. This is what the final table looks like, with five messages displayed:

ADCTinyChat	
JEFF	Huh?
MARK	Way cool, dude!
JEFF	Gotta try RDS with ADO over OLE DB to ODBC!
MARK	The same to you, buster!
JEFF	Huh?

The next part of the page defines the two ADC objects, and a hidden text box named **txtHid**, which is bound to the second data source object **adcC**:

```
<input type=text id=txtHid datasrc=#adcC datafld=UID style="visibility:hidden">

<! the data source object to poulate the table >
<object classid="clsid:BD96C556-65A3-11D0-983A-00C04FC29E33"
        id="adcD" height=1 width=1>
</object>

<! the data source object to send new messges with >
<object classid="clsid:BD96C556-65A3-11D0-983A-00C04FC29E33"
        id="adcC" height=1 width=1>
</object>
```

Working With Unbound Data Source Objects

OK, so why do we need a hidden text box? In fact, this is an extremely important point when you come to design your own applications that use data binding in IE4. The data source object may not work quite as you expect if there are no elements in the page that are bound to it. Even though your code may set the correct **Server**, **Connect** and **SQL** properties, you may not get a recordset back from it.

Almost certainly, this means that the events you are expecting to be able to use in your code, like **ondatasetchanged()**, **ondataavailable()**, and **ondatasetcomplete()** will not occur. Your page will just sit and look at you. However, when you come to access the recordset (which doesn't exist) the error messages start to appear. A popular one is a message telling you that "the data source is not open". This is why we've included the hidden bound text box on our page.

The Message Page Script

The two data source objects have no parameters set in the HTML, so the first job is to set these using the information we stored in the frameset page of our application, **wroxchat.htm**. This is the parent window for out two frames, so we can refer to the variables and code routines there using **parent.MyServerName**, etc. We create global variables and use them as references to the ADCs, so that we can get at them from other routines in the page:

```
<script language="vbscript">

dim adcDisplay, adcMyConv
set adcDisplay = document.all("adcD")
set adcMyConv = document.all("adcC")

function window_onload()
   'connect up the data source objects
  adcMyConv.Server = parent.MyServerName
  adcMyConv.Connect = parent.MySystemDSN
  adcMyConv.SQL = "select * from WORKMSG;"
  adcDisplay.Server = parent.MyServerName
  adcDisplay.Connect = parent.MySystemDSN
  adcDisplay.SQL = "select LOGIN,MESSAGE,SERIAL from WORKMSG,USERS " _
                & "where WORKMSG.UID=USERS.UID order by SERIAL;"
  dummy = window.setInterval("adcDisplay.Refresh()", _
                             parent.refreshInterval * 1000)
end function
```

We could also use `top.myServerName` *etc., but this would mean the page would not work if, for some reason, it was loaded inside another frameset. This might happen if someone links to our page from* **another** *site, for example. For this reason, it's best to be specific about which window or frame in the hierarchy you actually are referring to.*

The last line of the `window_onload()` routine sets an interval timer going, which will fire regularly based on the `refreshInterval` we specified in the frameset page–every five seconds. When it fires, it executes the refresh method of the first ADC, which is bound to the messages table. The source on the server will be re-queried, and the table updated with any new messages from any user.

Scrolling the Latest Message Into View

The only thing now is that the user will not see the latest updates if the number of messages exceeds a "framefull". To get round this, we respond to the data source object's `ondatasetcomplete()` event which occurs once all the data has been retrieved. Remember, the process is asynchronous, and so the script in our page will continue to run while the data is being fetched. The event tells us that the update is complete.

To bring the last records into view, we can use the `scrollIntoView` method of the data source object. It's actually invisible, of course, but is embedded directly after the end of the messages table in the page. By supplying the parameter `false` to the `scrollIntoView` method, we indicate that the element should be displayed at the bottom of the window (in this case our frame). The end result is that the latest update will always be shown after a `refresh`:

```
Sub adcD_ondatasetcomplete()
  adcDisplay.scrollIntoView(false)
End Sub
```

Sending a Message

The final code in the page is used to add a new message to the table. It isn't actually run from within this page, but it allows us to access the embedded ADC more easily if we put the code here. Of course, we could have put the code and the ADC in the "Send Message" frame instead. In fact, we'll be calling it from there, as you'll see later.

All the code has to do is manipulate the recordset created by the `adcC` ADC. This is the ADC that doesn't need to be bound to any visible element on the page, because we're only using it to manipulate the recordset. Remember, however, that we had to include a hidden bound element so as to ensure that the recordset was created. Here's the routine `sendALine` that accepts a message as a parameter `myLine`, and adds it to the database:

```
function sendALine(myLine)
  adcMyConv.recordset.MoveLast
  adcMyConv.recordset.AddNew
  adcMyConv.recordset.Fields("MESSAGE")=myLine
  adcMyConv.recordset.Fields("UID")= parent.myUID
  adcMyConv.recordset.Fields("POSTTIME")=Now()
  'add any other required fields here
  adcMyConv.SubmitChanges
  adcDisplay.Refresh
end function
</script>
```

It's simple a matter of moving to the end of the recordset, adding a new record, filling in the field values, and calling the **submitChanges** method of the ADC to make the changes final. This will also cause the new message to be reflected in the display of all other users when each one is updated next time.

> *For a complete reference of the* **recordset** *object and its properties and methods, see Reference section* **G**.

The Message Entry Frame and The Robot

The other frame in our application is the message entry frame. It contains one **<INPUT>** field text box, and two buttons:

In our design of the application, we didn't actually mention the "robot". Its purpose is to help during testing. After playing with TinyChat for a little while, you'll realize that testing it by yourself is quite boring. You really need a server on an Intranet or the Internet, and some very patient friends. Instead, the "robot" fills the role. It issues a chat message to the server at specified intervals (as stored in the **robotRate** variable in the **wroxchat.htm** main page). This allows us to start up several copies of TinyChat (each with a different **myUID** value), and have them "chat" with each other automatically.

The first part of our "Send Message" page creates the styles and lays out the elements in a table. The Send button calls the routine **sendALine** when clicked, and the Start Robot button calls the **robotClick** routine:

```html
<html>
<head>
<title>Send Message Frame - RDS/ADC Sample</title>
<style>
  body {background:pink; color:black; font-family:arial,sans-serif;
        font-size: 10pt;}
</style>
</head>
<body>
<input type="text" size="50" id="txtEntry">
<button onclick="sendALine()"> Send </button>
<button id="btnRobot" onclick="robotClick()"> Start Robot </button>
```

The Message Entry Code

To actually send a message, we just have to call the routine we've already seen in the "Details" page. The button on our "Send Message" page doesn't actually do this, event though the name of the routine is the same. It calls the copy of the **sendALine** routine that is local to the page, which in turn calls the copy of the routine in the other frame's page.

We reference this using **parent.frmMessage**, where **frmMessage** is the name we gave to the upper "Details" frame when we created the frameset in the **wroxchat.htm** main page. We also send the value of the text box **txtEntry** as the parameter. This is the text of the message to add to the database:

```
sub sendALine()
 parent.frmMessage.sendALine(txtEntry.value)
end sub
```

Programming The Robot

The `myCount` variable is used to indicate the sequence number of the message being sent, and the `myRobot` variable is used for turning on and off the robot feature. When the Start Robot button is clicked, we set a timer to call the `robot()` function regularly, and save the timer identifier in the `myRobot` variable. We also change the label of the button from Start Robot to Stop Robot. If the user clicks the button again, we clear the timer interval and toggle the button label back to Start Robot:

```
Dim myCount
Dim myRobot
myRobot = 0
myCount = 1

function robotClick()
  if myRobot= 0 then
    myRobot = window.setInterval("robot()", parent.robotRate * 1000)
    btnRobot.innerText = "Stop Robot"
  else
    myRobot = window.clearInterval(myRobot)
    myRobot = 0
    btnRobot.innerText = "Start Robot"
  end if
end function
```

To create message automatically is now a trivial task. The `robot()` function just builds a string for the message text, puts it into the text box, and calls the `sendALine` routine:

```
function robot()
  txtEntry.value = "Robot generated message number" & CStr(myCount) & "!"
  myCount = myCount + 1
  sendALine()
end function
```

Unfinished Business: The Maintainer

The TinyChat application works fine, but if you leave it running long enough with a few keen users, the database will completely eat up your available disk space. You will also discover that the lengthening list of message seems to take forever to refresh in the messages table. What is required is a "maintainer" application that will keep only the most recent messages visible. Thanks again to the power of Dynamic HTML and ADC, we've created this very simply–you'll find it in the sample files as `maintain.htm`:

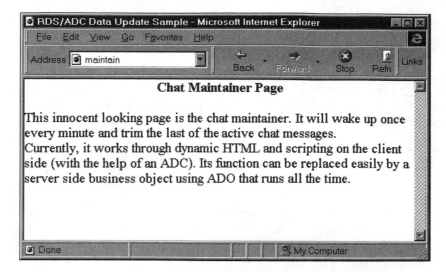

This application should be running all the time while TinyChat is operating. It simply sleeps for 60 seconds, then checks the message database and deletes all messages except for the most recent.

The Maintainer HTML Code

Here's the HTML code, including the hidden text box that ensures data binding takes place. There's one single ADC object, and we'll be manipulating the recordset using script to delete the extra records:

```
<html>
<head>
<title>RDS/ADC Data Update Sample</title>
</head>
<body leftmargin=0 topmargin=0>

<center><b>Chat Maintainer Page</b></center>
<p>This innocent looking page is the chat maintainance utility....</p>

<object classid="clsid:BD96C556-65A3-11D0-983A-00C04FC29E33"
        id="adcChop" height=1 width=1>
  <param name="Server" value="Your_Server_Name">
  <param name="Connect" value="DSN=Your_DSN">
  <param name="SQL" value="select * from WORKMSG order by SERIAL;">
</object>
<input type=text id=txtHid datasrc=#adcUpdate datafld=MESSAGE
        style="visibility:hidden">
```

The Maintainer Script Section

The script section defines global variables for the number of records to leave, and the interval between removing extra ones. In the `window_onload` routine, we just need to start an interval timer running, which will call the refresh method of the ADC every `timeBetweenChop` seconds:

```
<script language="vbscript">
dim recordsToLeave, timeBetweenChop
recordsToLeave = 5
timeBetweenChop = 60
```

```
function window_onload()
  d = window.setInterval("adcChop.refresh()", timeBetweenChop * 1000)
end function
```

To remove the extra records, we react to the **ondatasetcomplete()** event, which occurs after the refresh is completed. If the refresh didn't complete successfully, i.e. there was an error or it was aborted by the user, we don't do anything. We can check the result by examining the **window.event.reason** property, which will be zero if all went well:

```
sub adcUpdate_ondatasetcomplete()
  if window.event.reason = 0 then   'completed OK
    set rsChop = adcu.recordset
    if (rsChop.recordCount - parent.recordsToLeave) > 0 then
      rsChop.moveLast
      for i = 1 to (parent.recordsToLeave)
        rsChop.movePrevious
      next
      while not rsChop.BOF
        rsChop.delete
        rsChop.movePrevious
      wend
      rsChop.close
      set rsChop = nothing
      adcu.submitChanges
    end if
  end if
end sub
```

The remainder of the function first checks that there are some records to remove, then moves to the end of the recordset and counts backwards the number of message records to keep. Then it's just a matter of deleting the earlier ones by using the recordset's **delete** method, and moving back a record. It's as easy as that.

> *When we delete a record, the current record pointer becomes undefined, and we need to issue a* **movePrevious** *(or* **moveNext***) instruction to move to the previous or next valid record.*

Improving TinyChat

With a reasonable SQL Server based installation, you should be able to run up to a hundred or so users without major performance degradation-not bad for a handful of Dynamic HTML scripting. We've implemented a specially adapted version of the application on our samples server that you can try. Check out **http://rapid.wrox.co.uk/books/0707** and follow the link to see it in action.

Some obvious improvements you might like to make to your own implementation of TinyChat are:

▲ an additional frame listing the names of the current users, allowing filtering (squelch) of message based on active users

▲ allow retrieval of user information (real name, address, etc)

▲ implement multiple "forums" through additional message tables

▲ implement a maintainer which copies chat message to an archive, rather than deleting them

▲ implement color highlighting of user messages

▲ implement multimedia "alerts" when buddies comes on-line

All of these improvements are relatively easy to implement, and make great Dynamic HTML data binding programming exercise. We won't cover them here, as they don't add any extra value to our discussion of RDS.

Trying Out the Applications

In this chapter, we've shown you several different application build around the Remote Data Service (RDS) and the client-side Advanced Data Object (ADC). Unlike the stand-alone Dynamic HTML client-side coded examples we've met in earlier chapters, these require quite a bit of configuration before they can be run on your own server. We have implemented two examples of RDS on our Rapid.Wrox samples server, and the source code for all of the examples you've seen in this chapter is included in the sample files you can download from:
`http://rapid.wrox.co.uk/books/0707`.

In order to set up these examples on your own server, you will need to install the RDS Server Distribution kit (version1.5 or later). You'll also need an RDS 1.5-compatible ODBC data source, for example either Microsoft Access or SQL Server should work fine. You'll also need to create the appropriate System Data Source Names for the data source's `Connect` property-including the user ID and password if these are required to access the database:

```
<PARAM NAME="Connect" VALUE="DSN=DSNName;UID=userid;PWD=password;">
```

In the next chapter, we have a detailed case study of a more complex application built using RDS. In it, we'll show you how to create a System DSN, and lay out in more details the requirements for using RDS on your own system.

Summary

In this chapter, we've examined the second data source object provided as part of the IE4 distribution – the **Advanced Data Control**. This is part of the larger technology umbrella called Remote data Service, a new way of providing a live data connection over HTTP between the serve and client systems. In Reference section **G** of this book, you'll find a detailed exploration of RDS as a whole, and see how it interfaces with the systems at each end of the network.

Here, however, we examined the properties and methods supported by the ADC, and deployed it in a series of applications that demonstrated its capabilities. Of these, the TinyChat application shows how RDS and the ADC object completely overcome all the restrictions of the Tabular Data Control we used in the previous two chapters. With it we could add and update data on the data source, access data through one-to-many relationships, and reflect changes in the data source in real-time

So, the overwhelming benefits of an RDS-based solution are that it:

- can work with complex data relationships, including the one-to-many link
- can reflect changes to data in the database in real time, as soon as it is changed, and even in multi-users scenarios
- can update the data in the source database in real time
- requires no database access middle-ware installation, other than IE4
- requires no configuration at the client side
- can rapidly change the source of the data without reconfiguring client
- is highly efficient for both viewing and modifying data
- supports asynchronous operation, enabling rapid application load times
- works directly with any ODBC compatible data source, and with other through OLE-DB

In the next chapter, we will deploy the RDS framework once again, in a more involved Dynamic HTML data binding case-study.

A Database Case Study using RDS

CHAPTER 9

To round off this section of the book, we'll finish up with another case study. This is a moderately complex application that reflects the kind of thing you could encounter in a real-world assignment. We'll take one of the sources of reference that Wrox make available to their readers, and put it on the Internet for instant access worldwide.

The reference material we'll be using is a database called the **Wrox Dynamic HTML Reference Database**, which contains a cross-referenced list of all the objects and tags supported by Microsoft Internet Explorer 4—and presents them in an easy to use way. However, the database is stored in Microsoft Access format, and so our task is to take this information, and present it in real time in a format that allows it to be viewed in a browser over the 'Net.

This kind of task is one that is ideally suited to Remote Data Service (RDS) technology. The ability of RDS to provide an invisible middle-ware link between a Web browser and the server over HTTP means that, as far as we are concerned when building the application, the data could just as well be on the system's local disk.

In an Intranet solution, RDS also provides a neat way to get rid of the format-specific front end application (in this case Access 97), and integrate the information from a database into the rest of your browser-hosted corporate information system. This not only reduces cost, because you need to buy fewer application licenses, but also provides an extra level of security, and simplifies installation concerns. What's more, the application-independent nature of the information you provide means that the next two steps in opening up your Intranet—as an Extranet to specific customers, or globally over the Internet as a whole—are a lot simpler.

In this case study, we'll see:

- What the Wrox DHTML Reference Database looks like in Access
- What our Web-based solution can do, and how it's used
- The structure of the Access database, and the modifications required
- The way we designed our application, from the ground up
- How we implemented the design in the browser using RDS

To start with, then, let's see what the Wrox Dynamic HTML Reference Database looks like in Access.

What is the Wrox DHTML Database?

We designed and built the Wrox Dynamic HTML Reference Database both as a resource for our readers, and for use within our own organization as a quick and easy way to get listings of the events, properties, methods and collections supported by each browser object and each HTML element. First you select whether you want to see browser objects or elements, and then select the appropriate one from a drop-down list:

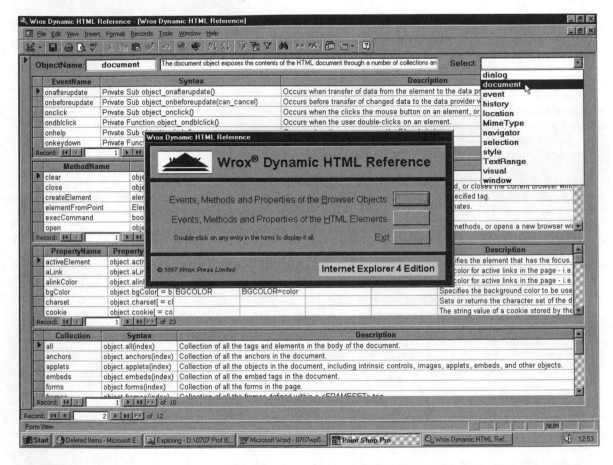

For each browser object or HTML element, there are up to four tables displayed within the main window. These show not only the names of the supported events, properties, methods and collections, but their syntax, description, and equivalents where appropriate. As you can see, this makes an ideal source of data for our case study application.

Before we start to look at how the Web-based version of this application was designed and built, we'll show you how to install it on your system, and what the final result looks like. That way, you'll more easily be able to follow the discussions on the structuring and implementation that follow.

Setting Up and Using the Application

Unlike the simpler case study we looked at in Chapter 7, this one can't be installed just by copying the files onto your server. RDS requires a combination of components to be installed and working at both ends of the HTTP link, before the connection to a database will work. However, much of the work on the server you'll only need to do once—and the client end (IE4, including the RDS and ADC components) looks after itself. If you aren't able to set up the sample files on your own system, you can run the application directly from the samples menu page on our Web site at `http://rapid.wrox.co.uk/books/0707`.

The Application Requirements

To use Remote Data Services, you will need the hardware and software listed below. In particular, notice that the Remote Data Services software for the server will need to be downloaded from Microsoft and installed. This is not part of the default Windows NT Server installation, and requires Service Pack 3 and the subsequent fixes to have been installed first. The Microsoft site at `http://www.microsoft.com/ntserver/` provides links to the download and information areas for all the products you may need.

Server Requirements

▲ An Operating System that supports the version 1.5 (or later) Remote Data Service Server components. This will probably be Windows NT Server 4, Windows NT Workstation 4, or Window 95. You must install the NT Service Pack 3 and the subsequent fixes before installing RDS on NT

▲ Internet Information Server 3.0 or later, with Active Server Pages, installed and verified (ASP is required by RDS to work properly)

▲ The ODBC 3.0 or later drivers installed and tested. These should already be installed with Service Pack 3

▲ Microsoft Remote Data Service – Server Distribution 1.5 or later, installed and verified on the machine. At the time of writing, this could be downloaded from: `http://www.microsoft.com/msdownload/rds/rdsdownload.htm`

▲ The TCP/IP network protocol installed, configured and tested

Client Requirements

▲ Microsoft Internet Explorer 4, installed and tested.

▲ If the client and server are different machines, you must also have TCP/IP configured and tested to connect them. A link over the Internet or your local network can be used

Setting up the WroxDHTML Application

When you unzip the samples zip file downloaded from our server, remember to select the 'Restore Directories' or 'Use Store Folder Information' option in your zip manager program to recreate the correct directory structure. Then simply create a new directory under your Web server's `WWWRoot` directory, and copy all the files from the `WroxRefDB` folder of the samples zip file into it.

Configuring The ODBC Data Source

Since the RDS server components will be accessing the data source through ADO over OLE-DB/ODBC, you must configure the database as using the appropriate ODBC driver. This can be done from the ODBC icon in Control Panel:

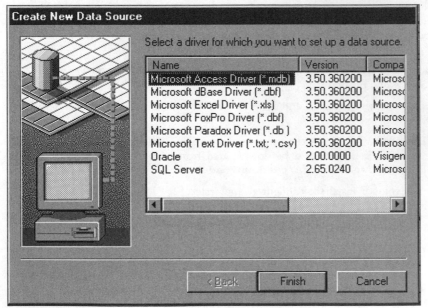

In the System DSN tab of the main dialog , click Add... to open the Create New Data Source dialog. Select Microsoft Access Driver (*.mdb):

Click Finish to open the driver-specific setup dialog. Enter the Data Source Name to use for the database, and a Description. Our Dynamic HTML sample pages assumes a Data Source Name of 0707WXREFDB, but you can change this if you wish:

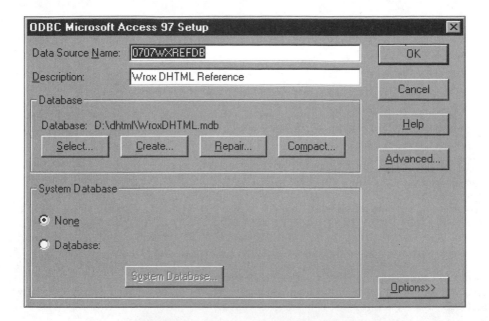

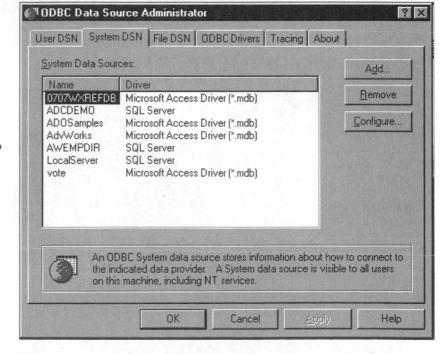

Next, click Select and use the Browse dialog that appears to select the location of the **WroxDHTML.mdb** file you copied onto your server. Then close the driver setup dialog, and you'll see the new System DSN. Remember to change this if you move or delete the database in the future.

The final task is to identify your server in the application, so that the RDS object in the browser knows where to look for the data source. As you've seen in the previous chapter, the RDS component has a **Server** property, which we set to point to the server that will be at the other end of the data link.

In our application, we've provided this name in the top-level frameset page **wroxdhtm.htm** as a global variable, and each of the other pages uses this to set the correct **Server** property value before they attempt to make a connection:

```
<html>
<head>
<title>Dynamic HTML Reference RDS Databinding Sample</title>
</head>

<script language=vbscript>
   'define and set global variables for database connection
   'change these to suit your own installation and server name
   Dim MyServerName
   Dim MySystemDSN
   MyServerName = "Server_Name_Goes_Here"
   MySystemDSN = "0707WXREFDB"
</script>
```

You will need to edit this to point to the server where you installed the RDS server components for your application—either by supplying the DNS name, such as **http://rapid.wrox.co.uk** or the IP address, such as **http://194.74.60.252**. If you used a different System DSN in the previous section, you will also need to change the value in the following line as appropriate.

That completes setup of the sample, and you can now start up Internet Explorer 4 on the (client) machine and try out the application.

Using the WroxDHTML Application

Here's the equivalent to our Access-based database, **WroxDHTM.htm**, running in Internet Explorer 4. In the lower right frame, you can see a combo box containing all the browser objects. In the screen shot, we've selected the navigator object, and the left-hand frame shows a list of the properties and methods that it supports. Notice that the **navigator** object doesn't support any events:

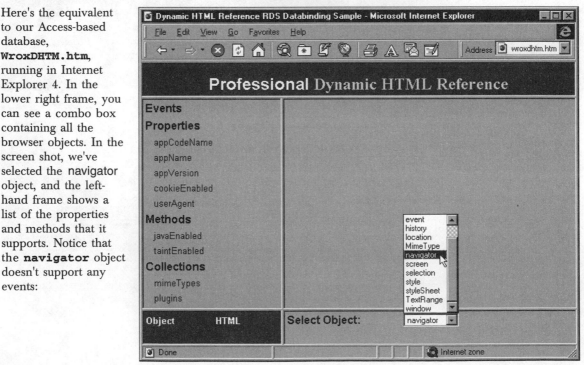

We can switch to viewing HTML elements, rather than browser objects, using the menu in the lower left frame. Like the BookList sample we created back in Chapter 7, this uses Dynamic HTML to highlight the options as the mouse pointer moves over them:

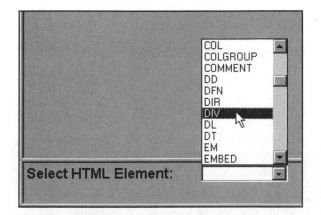

When we select HTML, instead of Object, the lower-right frame changes to display a combo list containing all the HTML tag names. Here we're selecting the DIV element:

Now, the left-hand frame displays a list of the events, properties and methods that **DIV** supports. In this frame, we can click on any of these to display details of it in the main frame on the right:

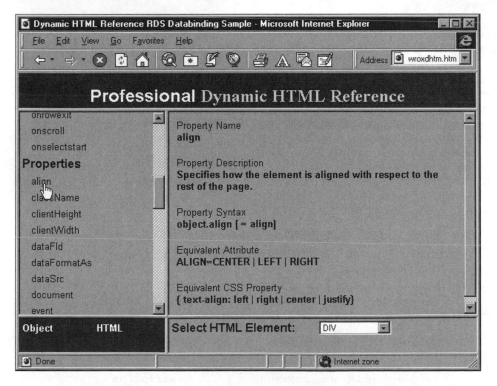

So, our implementation is different, in that we don't use several repeated and scrollable tables in a single page like the Access version. However, it provides all the same abilities, using a point and click interface, within the browser.

Designing the WroxDHTML Application

So, the next step is to look at how we went about designing the application. We'll do this in three steps:

- ▲ The specification of the task ahead
- ▲ The high-level design
- ▲ The detailed design

The Specification

Our Dynamic HTML Reference Database contains an exhaustive list of all the Dynamic HTML objects in the object model, as well as every HTML tag that is available via Internet Explorer 4.0. For every tag or object, it tracks all its properties, methods, events, and contained collections, if applicable. Created in Microsoft Access, the database already has a set of forms which can be used directly (in Microsoft Access) to browse through the data.

> *You can download the Access 97 version of this database from our Web site at*
> ***http://rapid.wrox.co.uk/books/0707*** *if you wish.*

For users who want to use the database occasionally, or who may not have Microsoft Access installed, this format of distribution is not too useful. Our task is to bring the information in the database to such a user, and the end result should be an "instantly download" Web application that can be used to access the database information at anytime, by anyone with Internet Explorer 4.0. Given this ease-of-access, developers can bookmark the database page, and return to it quickly on an as-required basis. Whenever we update it here at Wrox, the new information will be immediately available (without downloading the entire database). Although it sounds formidable, our implementation, as presented in the following pages, actually fulfills this lofty objective.

The Access Database File

The actual database file, `WroxDHTML.mdb`, is in Access 97 format and contains fourteen tables. Six of these contain the actual information, and the other eight are used to link the tables together. The six main tables are:

Table	Description	Fields
`Objects`	Information on all of the **objects** in the IE4 Dynamic HTML object model.	`OID` (unique ID), `ObjectName`, `Description`
`HTMLTags`	Information on all of the **HTML tags** recognized by Internet Explorer 4.0.	`TID` (unique ID), `TagName`, `Description`

Table	Description	Fields
Properties	Information on all the **properties** supported by the objects and HTML tags in the object model. It also has fields for the matching attribute names and the associated CSS information.	PID (unique ID), PropertyName, PropertySyntax, AttributeName, AttributeValue, CSSName, CSSValue, Description
Methods	Information on all the **methods** supported by the objects or HTML tags in the object model.	MID (unique ID), MethodName, Syntax, Description
Collections	Information on all **collections** contained by the objects or HTML tags in the object model.	CID (unique ID), CollectionName, Description
Events	Information on all **events** supported by the object or HTML tags in the object model.	EID (unique ID), EventName, Description

The Link Tables

The other eight tables provide the links between the six we've seen above. To see why these are necessary, consider a small section of two of the tables. Here, we've got part of the **Objects** and **Events** tables:

Objects Table

OID	Object Name	Description
21	document	xxxxxxxxxxx
22	history	xxxxxxxxxxx
23	location	xxxxxxxxxxx
24	window	xxxxxxxxxxx

Events Table

EID	Event Name	Description
14	onclick	xxxxxxxxxxx
15	ondblclick	xxxxxxxxxxx
16	onfocus	xxxxxxxxxxx
17	onhelp	xxxxxxxxxxx

Link Table

OID	EID
21	14
21	15
21	17
24	16
24	17

We know that an object can support several events, and that each event can be supported by several objects. This is the classic **many-to-many** database relationship situation, and is solved in the usual way in our database by these link tables. In the case of our **Objects** and **Events** tables, the link table contains a record for each link between an object and an event:

By examining the **IDs** in the left column for an object, and in the right column for an event, you can see that the **document** object supports the **onclick**, **ondblclick** and **onhelp** events, while the **window** object supports **onfocus** and **onhelp**. Reading the other way, the **onhelp** event is supported by the **document** and **window**, while the **onclick** event is only supported by the **document** (in our sample of the table). Now we have two **one-to-many** links, rather than one **many-to-many** link:

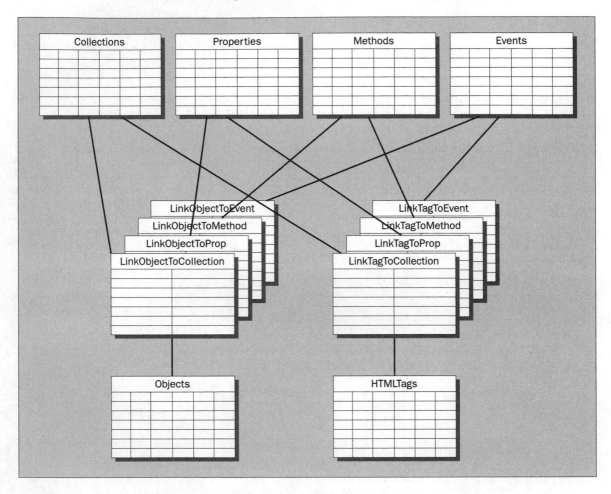

As well as the tables above, the database also contains many forms. These forms are used in maintaining the database and for presenting a search and browse interface for the users of the database (when used within Microsoft Access). These forms aren't of importance to us, since we will be replacing them with our web application.

High Level Design

Given the problem, and the existing database, we can now approach the high level design of our application. As with our previous case study, we would like to keep the design to one quickly downloadable HTML page, and use multiple frames within it. Let's take a stab at the data requirements, the visual layout of the application, and the planned user interaction.

Data Schema

Since the database is provided to begin with, there is no need to create any new data schema. However, since a lot of the linking of information is done with tables that contain only the ID values of the items, rather than their text names, it means that we have to link the tables together to get the information we want. Unlike the TDC we used earlier, the RDS object–and its underlying ADO data handling model–can do this.

However, since we will place the control inside Web pages at the other end of the network, we need to think about efficiency. In all cases of data middle-ware, it's a good idea to execute as much work as possible within the database, and only transport the necessary information over the network. We will create some queries within the database that simplify the manipulation will be necessary when we code the Dynamic HTML pages. The goal should be to make the coding as simple and easy to maintain as possible.

A Microsoft Access database can readily be accessible through ODBC, and we decided to use the Microsoft ODBC data provider for OLE-DB to make the database available to the RDS on the server side. This means that we can keep the Microsoft Access database at the server end, and allow users to get at the database data over the Internet via the pages that we will design. All this is done without any additional ActiveX control or database middle-ware for the user to download.

The following diagram shows the high level three-tiered data flow:

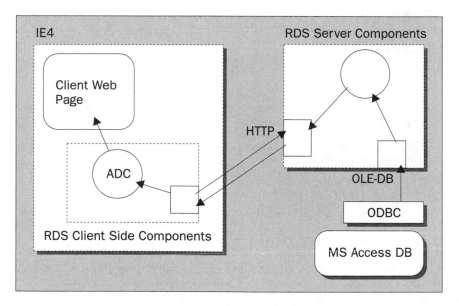

Of course, it's also possible to produce this kind of application as a server-only solution, using a package such as Active Server Pages. Such a solution can even be designed to be browser independent. We have decided to take a data binding plus RDS approach for the following reasons:

- To become familiar with RDS operation over the Internet
- To allow for future extension of more dynamic behavior on the client side
- To work on a solution that can potentially be more scalable (by lightening the load on the server) for the long term

Sketch The Interface Layout

The layout of the application is divided up into five different panes, providing the same "divide and conquer" technique used in the BookList sample back in Chapter 7:

Banner pane, not named, displays page banner.htm	
Selection pane, named "detail_sel" displays page proplist.htm	Details pane, named "detail_pane" displays page details.htm
Menu pane, displays menu.htm	Search pane, named "search_pane" displays pages search_o.htm or search_h.htm

This corresponds to the actual application we saw at the start of the chapter.

Planning User Interactions

In order to locate detailed information on a Dynamic HTML element or an object in the object model, the typical user interaction will be:

- ▲ Select either HTML (for HTML elements) or Object (for objects in the DHTML object model) from the Menu pane

- ▲ Select any of the objects or HTML elements displayed in a drop-down list within the Search pane (depending on the selection made in step 1)

- ▲ Select a property, event, method or collection in the Selection pane to see the details in the main Details pane

Detailed Design Considerations

Having completed the high level design, we now move on to the design details. Here, we will need to map out the way we will be accessing data, how the code will work in the application, and how we will be using RDS in our pages.

Microsoft Access as an ODBC Data Source

Making the database available on the server is as simple as configuring the ODBC data source using the ODBC applet in the control panel, as we saw earlier. Since we are working with the ODBC data provider for OLE-DB and using an Access database, we require the database to be physically located on the same server machine as the Web server (IIS), and with a complete IIS/RDS server components installation. If the database was in SQL Server, it can be resident on another server on the network.

Creating Data Views Using Access Queries

To make the design of the complex Selection pane a little simpler, we need to create eight queries within the Dynamic HTML Reference Database—one for each of the link tables. Effectively, we are combining the information from the tables at both ends of the link to replace the IDs in the link tables with the text of the items. Working with joins on a scripting level can make code very complex, so, instead, we combine them ahead of time using a query. In essence, these queries act as custom views on the database, and we can access them directly just as if they were native data tables. Here's one of the queries, which links the **Objects** and **Events** tables together.

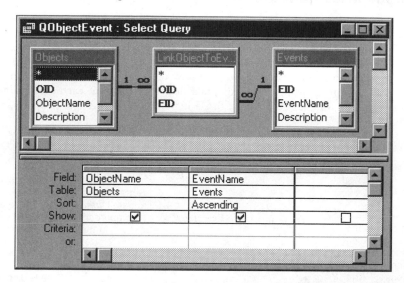

As you'll recall from our earlier discussions, the **LinkObjectToEvent** table contains only the unique **ID**s of the objects and events. Our query, **QObjectEvent**, provides the names instead. We can use this query in our code to get lists of the actual event names for any particular object.

279

In all, there are eight of these queries. We've
named them in a particular way, so that we can
easily refer to them in code—as you'll see later.
Each one provides a data set containing the text
of the items instead of the `ID`s:

`QObjectProp`	`QTagProp`
`QObjectMeth`	`QTagMeth`
`QObjectEvent`	`QTagEvent`
`QObjectColl`	`QTagColl`

Separating the Code Into Frames

According to the visual layout and the user interaction anticipated during the high level design, we can
now describe the scripting that will need to be done during implementation for each pane. Again, notice
how HTML frames really help to reduce the coding complexity as a whole.

We already defined the layout of the frames, and we've seen how the application works. We can now be
more specific about the individual routines in each frame, and how they relate to each other. This is a
graphical map of the way the user will work through a single iteration of viewing one property, method,
event or collection:

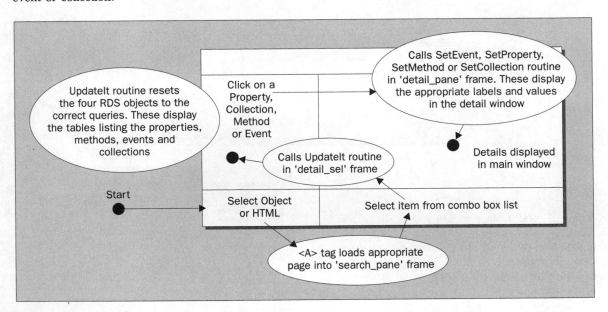

Some of the things to note are that we intend to create the lists for the Search pages' combo boxes
dynamically, using the information in the database. Secondly, we'll need to use more than once instance of
the client control for RDS (the actual ADC component), because we'll have several pages that need to use
data binding techniques. In fact, the left-hand Selection frame requires four controls, one for each table of
properties, events, methods and collections.

A Tally of the ADCs

The design seems to be heavily dependent on the use of RDS/ADCs, so let's take a tally of these, and see
the associated SQL queries that we'll use with them on a frame-by-frame basis:

Frame	ADCs	Description
Banner	0	Not Applicable
Menu	0	Not Applicable
Search (Object)	1	Supply `<SELECT>` element with list of objects using `"select ObjectName from Objects order by ObjectName"`
Search (HTML)	1	Supply `<SELECT>` element with list of HTML elements using: `"select TagName from HTMLTags order by TagName"`
Selection	4	Display four bound tables containing lists of matching properties, methods, events and collections, using dynamically created SQL `select` queries that depend on whether Object or HTML tag is selected in the Search pane.
Details	1	Display the detailed description of a property, method, event, or collection using dynamically created SQL `select` queries that depend on the item clicked in the Selection pane.

Well, that's more than enough design and planning to start with. We'll get down next to coding the actual application and bringing the concepts to life.

Building the WroxDHTML Application

It's time to take the detailed design and put it into real HTML and scripting code. The following pages show how each frame is coded according to our design. We'll look in turn at:

- ▲ The main frameset page, **wroxdhtm.htm**, which loads the other pages
- ▲ The top, window-width Banner page, **banner.htm**
- ▲ The Object or HTML selector page, **menu.htm**
- ▲ The two combo-box equipped Search pages, **search_o.htm** and **search_h.htm**
- ▲ The left-hand Selection page, **proplist.htm**
- ▲ The main Details window page, details.htm

The Main Frameset Page

The base frame is designed to be faithful to the high level design. We create a total of five frames (or panes). Here again is the outline plan:

The code that implements it can be found in **wroxdhtm.htm**. The frameset consists of three rows, the first and last rows have a height of 50 pixels. The first row contains only the banner frame, with scrolling disabled, while the second row of the frameset consists of two separate frames. The left frame is the Selection frame, fixed at a width of 200 pixels, and the Details pane occupies the remaining space. Both of these panes can contain a large list of information, therefore scrolling is not disabled. Finally the last row is divided up to provide the Menu frame on the left, and the remaining is reserved for the Search frame. We disable scrolling in both of these frames:

```
<html>
<head>
<title>Dynamic HTML Reference ADC Databinding Sample</title>
</head>
<frameset rows="50,*,50">
  <frame src="banner.htm" scrolling=no noresize>
  <frameset cols="200,*">
    <frame src="proplist.htm" name="detail_sel" marginwidth=5 noresize>
    <frame src="details.htm" name="detail_pane" marginwidth=10 noresize>
  </frameset>
  <frameset cols="200,*">
    <frame src="menu.htm" scrolling=no noresize>
    <frame src="search_o.htm" name="search_pane" scrolling=no noresize>
  </frameset>
</frameset>
</html>
```

This page also contains the script we saw earlier, where you need to change at least the **MyServerName**, and possibly the **MyServerDSN**, values to suit your setup if you are installing the files on your own server:

```
<script language=vbscript>
  'define and set global variables for database connection
  'change these to suit your own installation and server name
  Dim MyServerName
  Dim MySystemDSN
  MyServerName = "Server_Name_Goes_Here"
  MySystemDSN = "0707WXREFDB"
</script>
```

The Banner Frame Page

The page for the top Banner frame is **banner.htm**. As with the BookList case study, we lay out the title of the application using a Cascading Style Sheet definition. The code that implements it is:

```
<html>
<head>
<title>Dynamic HTML Reference ADC Databinding Sample</title>
<style>
 H2 {color:yellow; font-family:times,serif; font-weight:bold}
</style>
</head>
<body bgcolor="red">
<center><H2><span style="color:white; font-family:arial,sans-serif">Professional</
span> Dynamic HTML Reference</H2></center>
</body>
</html>
```

Professional Dynamic HTML Reference

The Menu Frame Page

Again, we use the same technique as the BookList case study to create our Menu page. The only difference here is that we only have two selections, instead of five. The code can be found in **menu.htm**, and the first part defines the styles that will change the items from small to large text as the mouse passes over them:

```
<html>
<head>
<title>Dynamic HTML Reference ADC Databinding Sample Menu</title>
<base target="search_pane">
<style>
<!--
  A.reg      {background:red; color:white; font-family:arial,sans-serif;
              font-weight:bold; font-size:10pt;}
  A.big      {background:red; color:blue; font-family:times,serif;
              font-weight:bold; font-size:20pt;}
  A:link     {color:white; text-decoration:none}
  A:visited  {color:white; text-decoration:none}
  A:active   {color:yellow; text-decoration:none}
-->
</style>
</head>
```

Notice also the **<BASE>** tag that points to the Search pane, so that the appropriate Search page will be loaded there automatically. Again, we use actual HTML hyperlinks to represent the selections, but hide the typical underline associated with them by using the **text-decoration:none** style property. The remainder of the HTML source is:

```
<body bgcolor=red leftmargin=0 topmargin=0>
```

```
<table width=190 leftmargin=0 topmargin=0>
  <tr>
    <td>
      <a class="reg" onMouseOver="MouseOver()" onMouseOut="MouseOut()"
         href="search_o.htm">Object</a>
    </td>
    <td>
      <a class="reg" onMouseOver="MouseOver()" onMouseOut="MouseOut()"
         href="search_h.htm">HTML</a>
    </td>
  </tr>
</table>
</body>
```

The Menu Page Script

This works in the same way as the BookList menu page, by swapping the CSS class from **reg** to **big**, and vice versa, thereby highlight the corresponding selection.

```
Sub MouseOver()
  set obj = window.event.srcElement
  obj.className = "big"
  cancelEvent()
End Sub

Sub MouseOut()
  set obj = window.event.srcElement
  obj.className = "reg"
  cancelEvent()
End Sub
```

As before, we have a **cancelEvent()** routine which we call to cancel event bubbling (by setting the **cancelBubble** property to **true**), and to avoid any unanticipated side effects by disabling the default behavior (by setting the **returnValue** equal to **false**):

```
Sub cancelEvent()
  window.event.returnValue = false
  window.event.cancelBubble = true
End Sub
```

The Search Frame Pages

While looking deceptively simple, and similar to the Search page of the BookList case study, our WroxRefDB Search pages are substantially more sophisticated. We found in the Chapter 7 case study that it was hard work typing in the list of **<OPTION>** tags, and that this only provided a static set of options. In our case, we would like to read them from the database each time, and thereby always have an updated list.

To achieve this, the list of objects or HTML elements is not hard-coded. Instead we use an instance of the RDS object to create the list each time the page is loaded.

The Search by Object Page

The Search by Object page, `search_o.htm` looks like this:

The first part of the page is the HTML preamble, and the definition of our RDS object. Notice that we've placed it in the **<HEAD>** section of the page to ensure that it's fully loaded before the remainder of our page loads:

```
<html>
<head>
<title>Reference by Objects</title>
<style>
  body {background:pink; color:black; font-family:arial,sans-serif;
        font-weight: bold;font-size: 10pt;}
</style>
<object classid="clsid:BD96C556-65A3-11D0-983A-00C04FC29E33"
        id="adco" height=1 width=1>
</object>
</head>
```

You'll notice that we aren't setting any of its properties with **<PARAM>** tags here. You'll see why shortly. The next step is to lay out the text label Select Object: and the **<SELECT>** HTML element. The list of **<OPTION>** tags will be filled dynamically via scripting, but while the page loads we'll include the option Initializing.. so that users know something is happening. At the end of the table is a hidden text box bound to the ADC object. You'll recall from the previous chapter that we need to include this to force the data binding events to occur correctly:

```
<body leftmargin=0 topmargin=0>
<td width=150 align=center>
  <B>Select Object:</B>
  </td>
  <td width>
   <SELECT id=selo size=1 style="width:150">
    <OPTION> Initializing ..
   </SELECT>
   </td>
  </tr>
</table>
<input type=text id=txtBound datasrc=#adco datafld=ObjectName
       style="visibility:hidden">
```

Following this text box is the script section of the page. In it we set a variable reference to the ADC object, and then set its properties using the values stored in the main frameset page:

```
<script language="vbscript">
 'set parameters of ADC while page is loading
 'using values in frameset page
 dim mydac 'global reference to ADC object
 set myadc = document.all("adco")
```

```
myadc.Server = parent.MyServerName
myadc.Connect = "DSN=" & parent.MySystemDSN
myadc.SQL = "select ObjectName from Objects order by ObjectName"
```

Looking at this code, you can see that the first step is to create a reference to the RDS object in the variable **myadc**, and then set the **Server**, **Connect** and **SQL** properties. We pull the first two from the frameset page using the reference **parent**, which refers to the top-level frame in the window. The SQL statement simply selects all the object names from the **Objects** table in the database, sorted into alphabetical order.

Creating a Select List Dynamically

Now it's time to fill the **<SELECT>** list with a list of the objects from the database. Our code uses the Dynamic HTML object model to create new **<OPTION>** elements for the **<SELECT>** element based on data from the RDS object. These have their text property set to the object name, and are added to the **<SELECT>** list's **options** collection using the **add** method. We've placed it in the **ondatasetcomplete()** event handler, so it will only be executed when the whole recordset is available:

```
sub adco_ondatasetcomplete()
   if window.event.reason = 0 then
      'put values into combo box
      set myList = document.all("selo")
      myadc.recordset.moveFirst
      while not myadc.recordset.EOF
        set objNewOpt = document.createElement("OPTION")
        objNewOpt.text = myadc.recordset.fields("ObjectName")
        myList.add objNewOpt
        myadc.recordset.moveNext
      wend
      myList.remove 0
   else
      msgbox "Error while reading from database", 48, "Error.."
   end if
end sub
```

Since the ADC is fully loaded, and the recordset now contains all the entries from the table, the code simply iterates through all the entries of the recordset in the ADC, and creates a new **option** object for each one, then adds it to the list. Notice that we check the reason property of the event object to make sure we got a complete recordset and there were no errors. If there were, it would return a non-zero result. Creating lists dynamically like this is a technique that's useful to add to your Dynamic HTML programming arsenal.

Reacting to the User's Selection

The final task in this page is to react to a user's selection in the list, and display the appropriate information in the left-hand Selection pane—the properties, events, methods, and collections related to the selected object. This is done using the **OnChange()** event of the **<SELECT>** list.

We retrieve the text of the selected option, and call a subroutine in the Selection frame's page called **UpdateIt()**. This expects two arguments: the actual name of the object, and the constant string **"Object"**. We'll see later how the **UpdateIt()** routine actually works:

```
Sub selo_onchange()
  strSelected = selo.options(selo.selectedindex).text
```

```
    parent.detail_sel.UpdateIt strSelected, "Object"
End Sub
```

Before we move on, notice how the technique of filling the combo box dynamically from the database not only saves coding effort, but increases maintainability. Just like any other form of programming, refined techniques like this often make all the difference in the world. The only potential disadvantage is a slight delay during the loading of the frame if there is a very large number of entries.

The Search by HTML Element Page

After seeing the implementation of the Search by Object page, the coding of the Search by HTML Element page, **search_h.htm**, will not present any surprises:

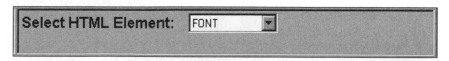

The main difference here is that we are pulling data from the **HTMLTags** table, instead of from the **Objects** table. Obviously the label text is different, but the only code lines we need to change are:

```
<script language="vbscript">
 'set parameters of ADC while page is loading
 'using values in frameset page
 dim mydac 'global reference to ADC object
 set myadc = document.all("adco")
 myadc.Server = parent.MyServerName
 myadc.Connect = "DSN=" & parent.MySystemDSN
 myadc.SQL = "select TagName from HTMLTags order by TagName"

 sub adco_ondatasetcomplete()
   if window.event.reason = 0 then
     'put values into combo box
     set myList = document.all("selo")
     myadc.recordset.moveFirst
     while not myadc.recordset.EOF
       set objNewOpt = document.createElement("OPTION")
       objNewOpt.text = myadc.recordset.fields("TagName")
       myList.add objNewOpt
       myadc.recordset.moveNext
     wend
     myList.remove 0
   else
     msgbox "Error while reading from database", 48, "Error.."
   end if
 end sub
```

And of course, we need to send the text **"Tag"** to the **UpdateIt()** routine when the user makes a selection, rather than **"Object"**:

```
sub selo_onchange()
  strSelected = selo.options(selo.selectedindex).text
  parent.detail_sel.UpdateIt strSelected, "Tag"
end sub
```

The Selection Frame Page

The Selection frame page, `proplist.htm`, is the most complex in the application. It has to deal with the linkage between the selected object or HTML element, and four different sets of items relating to that object or element. Furthermore, these elements are all stored in their own independent table, with the relationships expressed only by linkage tables within the database.

However, thanks to the work we've done preparing the Access database (back in the detailed design stage), we have available eight custom "views" of the data in the form of Access queries. These make life substantially easier when we come to script this page. First, however, we'll look at the HTML code that creates the page itself:

```html
<html>
<head>
<title>Properties, Methods, and Events List</title>
<style>
  body {background:pink; color:black; font-family:arial,sans-serif;
        font-weight:bold; font-size:10pt;}
 .rowval {font-weight:normal; font-size:10pt;}
</style>
</head>
```

Creating the Selection Tables

In this style sheet, we create the `rowval` class for a lighter (not-bold) font to use when displaying the property, event, method or collection names. This will distinguish them from the title set in bold font. Next are four data bound tables, which will hold the lists of property, event, method or collection names. Each is associated with a different RDS object–remember that there are four embedded in this page:

```html
<body leftmargin=0 topmargin=0>
   <table id="tblEvent" datasrc="#adcEvent">
     <thead><td><b>Events</b></td></thead>
     <tbody>
       <tr>
         <td>
             <span class="rowval" datafld="EventName"></span>
         </td>
       </tr>
     </tbody>
   </table>
   <table id="tblProp" datasrc="#adcProp">
     <thead><td><b>Properties</b></td></thead>
     <tbody>
       <tr>
         <td>
             <span class="rowval" datafld="PropertyName"></span>
         </td>
       </tr>
     </tbody>
   </table>
   <table id="tblMethod" datasrc="#adcMethod">
     <thead><td><b>Methods</b></td></thead>
     <tbody>
       <tr>
```

```
            <td>
                <span class="rowval" datafld="MethodName"></span>
            </td>
          </tr>
        </tbody>
      </table>
      <table id="tblColl" datasrc="#adcColl">
        <thead><td><b>Collections</b></td></thead>
        <tbody>
          <tr>
            <td>
                <span class="rowval" datafld="CollectionName"></span>
            </td>
          </tr>
        </tbody>
      </table>
```

Each table has the **datasrc** attribute set to its own RDS component, and the **<BODY>** of each one has a **<SPAN>** tag bound with the **datafld** attribute to the field in the appropriate database table that contains the item name. For example, you can see that the Collections table, **tblColl**, has the **datasrc** set to **adcColl**, and the **datafld** of the **<SPAN>** tag set to **CollectionName**.

Next come the four RDS object definitions. Note that we aren't initializing them at all with any **<PARAM>** tags, which causes the table to be blank initially:

```
<object classid="clsid:BD96C556-65A3-11D0-983A-00C04FC29E33"
        id="adcEvent" height=1 width=1>
</object>
<object classid="clsid:BD96C556-65A3-11D0-983A-00C04FC29E33"
        id="adcProp" height=1 width=1>
</object>
<object classid="clsid:BD96C556-65A3-11D0-983A-00C04FC29E33"
        id="adcMethod" height=1 width=1>
</object>
<object classid="clsid:BD96C556-65A3-11D0-983A-00C04FC29E33"
        id="adcColl" height=1 width=1>
</object>
```

Here's what the page will look like when it *has* been filled with data:

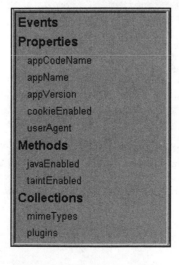

The Script in the Selection Page

You'll recall that the Search pages we looked at earlier call a routine named `UpdateIt()`, which is in our Selection page, when the user makes a selection in the combo box. They pass to it two parameters: the name of the object or HTML element that the user selected, and a discrete string—either `"Object"` if it was an object they selected, or `"Tag"` if it was an HTML element.

Our `UpdateIt()` routine uses these parameters to set up the RDS objects in the page correctly. The table here shows the names of the eight queries in the database that extract the sets of properties, events, methods and collections for each element or object:

QObjectEvent	QTagEvent
QObjectProp	QTagProp
QObjectMeth	QTagMeth
QObjectColl	QTagColl

By using code of the form:

```
outstr = "select EventName from Q" & ObjOrTag _
        &"Event where " & ObjOrTag & "Name='" & TagName & "'"
```

we create an SQL statement that takes its source data from the appropriate query. For example, the SQL queries that will be built if `window` and `Object` are passed to `UpdateIt()` would be:

```
select EventName from QObjectEvent where ObjectName='window'
```

So, here's the complete `UpdateIt()` routine. It shows the four assignments of `outstr`, the three remaining ones creating SQL strings (in this instance) of

```
select PropertyName from QObjectProp where ObjectName='window'
select MethodName from QObjectMeth where ObjectName='window'
select CollectionName from QObjectColl where ObjectName='window
```

```
Sub UpdateIt(TagName, ObjOrTag)
  dim outstr
  outstr = "select EventName from Q" & ObjOrTag _
          &"Event where " & ObjOrTag & "Name='" & TagName & "'"
  SetADC adcEvent, outstr
  outstr = "select PropertyName from Q" & ObjOrTag _
          &"Prop where " & ObjOrTag & "Name='" & TagName & "'"
  SetADC adcProp, outstr
  outstr = "select MethodName from Q" & ObjOrTag _
          &"Meth where " & ObjOrTag & "Name='" & TagName & "'"
  SetADC adcMethod, outstr
  outstr = "select CollectionName from Q" & ObjOrTag _
          &"Coll where " & ObjOrTag & "Name='" & TagName & "'"
  SetADC adcColl, outstr
End Sub
```

By design, these are exactly the four queries required for setting the SQL properties of the four RDS objects so that the four data bound tables will display all the elements associated with the selected object or HTML element. To actually set the RDS properties, we call a separate routine named `SetADC` each time. All this does is apply the properties, and call the `Refresh` method to update the bound table:

```
Sub SetADC(myadc, sql)
  myadc.Connect ="DSN=" & parent.MySystemDSN
  myadc.Server = parent.MyServerName
  myadc.SQL = sql
  myadc.Refresh
End Sub
```

Reacting to a User's Selection

The next concern is what happens when the user makes a selection from the lists of properties, events, methods and collections. We've just displayed them as plain text, inside **<SPAN>** tags that are within data bound tables. They aren't hyperlinks, so we need to find another way to detect mouse clicks. The answer is to allow the magic of event bubbling do all the work. If we react to an **onclick** event at **document** level, we'll get a notification of all user clicks on the page. Using the **srcElement** property of the event object, we can tell where the click came from.

To determine whether the user has clicked on a valid entry, we check the **window.event.srcElement.tagname** property against **"SPAN"**. As we saw, all the entries in the lists are contained within **<SPAN>** tags. This effectively filters out any unwanted clicks.

```
dim srcOfClick
set srcOfClick = window.event.srcElement
if (srcOfClick.tagname = "SPAN") then
  ...
  'process the user's selection
  ...
end if
```

Once we have determined that the event originated from a valid entry, we need to decide which list they clicked in, and extract the actual text from the HTML code for the item, as displayed on the page. The first requirement is met by comparing the **datafld** property of the **<SPAN>** element to one of **"EventName"**, **"MethodName"**, **"CollectionName"**, or **"PropertyName"**:

```
if (srcOfClick.tagname = "SPAN") then
  select case srcOfClick.datafld
    case "EventName"
      'it was a click in the Events list
      ...
    case "MethodName"
      'it was a click in the Methods list
      ...
    case "PropertyName"
      'it was a click in the Properties list
      ...
    case "CollectionName"
      'it was a click in the Colletions list
      ...
  end select
end if
```

Now we know which list they actually clicked in, and we can get the text of the item. This is easy, because we have a reference to the element in our **srcOfClick** variable. We use the **innerText** property of the element, which provides the actual name of the entry being clicked on. The beautiful thing about this technique is that it will still work even if the **<SPAN>** tag contained highly formatted text, for example:

```
<span datafld=TName><font size="-1"><i><b>window</b></i></font></span>
```

The `innerText` property of the `<SPAN>` element contains only the actual text of the entry. So now we've got everything we need to update the main Details page. The way we do it is to call a script routine written in the Details page, and pass it the name of the item we want to display. Because the format of each kind of item is different—there are differing fields in the database tables for properties, methods, events and collections, we need to call one of four different routines. These are named `SetEvent()`, `SetMethod()`, `SetProperty()` and `SetCollection()`, and we just need to pass them the appropriate item text. Here's the final code for the `document_onclick()` routine:

```
Sub document_onclick()
  dim srcOfClick
  set srcOfClick = window.event.srcElement
  if (srcOfClick.tagname = "SPAN") then
    select case srcOfClick.datafld
    case "EventName"
     parent.detail_pane.SetEvent(srcOfClick.innerText)
    case "MethodName"
     parent.detail_pane.SetMethod(srcOfClick.innerText)
    case "PropertyName"
     parent.detail_pane.SetProperty(srcOfClick.innerText)
    case "CollectionName"
     parent.detail_pane.SetCollection(srcOfClick.innerText)
    end select
  end if
end sub
```

The Details Frame Page

Finally then, we come to the Details page, `details.htm`. This is one of the most interesting pages in the application to implement. It displays detailed information of a property, method, event, or collection when selected in the left-hand Selection frame. For example, here we're displaying details of the `align` property. Notice that the title for each item also changes depending on what item is being displayed at the time, for example if we select an event, the first line in the page would read Event Name:

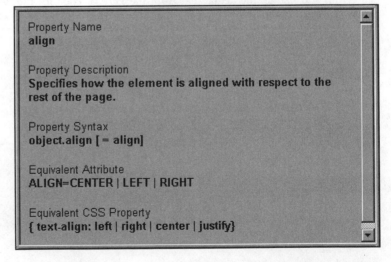

Property Name
align

Property Description
Specifies how the element is aligned with respect to the rest of the page.

Property Syntax
object.align [= align]

Equivalent Attribute
ALIGN=CENTER | LEFT | RIGHT

Equivalent CSS Property
{ text-align: left | right | center | justify}

What makes this frame tricky to implement is the requirement for it to display details from any of the four types of elements (properties, methods, events or collections) on the same display area of the page. To achieve this the Details page creates "generic" placeholders to contain the information. Let's take a look at the HTML code first. The opening section, as usual, just defines the styles for use in the page. We've got one named `rowhead` for the labels, and one named `rowval` for the actual values of the items we display:

```
<html>
<head>
<title>Element Details Screen</title>
<style>
   body     {background:pink;}
  .rowhead {color:black; font-family:arial,sans-serif;
           font-weight:normal; font-size:10pt;}
  .rowval  {margin-left:10; color:black; font-family:arial,sans-serif;
           font-weight:bold; font-size:10pt;}
</style>
</head>
```

The body section of the page is made up of five "sections". For each one there's a `<SPAN>` tag that provides the label for the section, and then another `<SPAN>` tag that provides the area for the value. These second `<SPAN>` tags are data bound, in that each has a `datasrc` and `datafld` property. We're using single-value data binding here, rather than repeated table binding like we did in the Selection page:

```
<body leftmargin=10 topmargin=10>

<span class="rowhead" id="NameLabel"></span><br>   
<span class="rowval" id="NameFld" datasrc="#adc" datafld="ID"></span><p>

<span class="rowhead" id="DescLabel"></span>
<span class="rowval" id="DescFld" datasrc="#adc" datafld="ID"></span><p>

<span class="rowhead" id="SyntaxLabel"></span><br>
<span class="rowval" id="SyntaxFld" datasrc="#adc" datafld="ID"></span><p>

<span class="rowhead" id="AttribLabel"></span><br>
<span class="rowval" id="AttribFld" datasrc="#adc" datafld="ID"></span><p>

<span class="rowhead" id="CSSLabel"></span><br>
<span class="rowval" id="CSSFld" datasrc="#adc" datafld="ID"></span><p>

<object classid="clsid:BD96C556-65A3-11D0-983A-00C04FC29E33"
        id="adc" height=1 width=1>
</object>
</body>
```

At the end of the page is the RDS object, with an ID of `adc`. Notice that each of the data bound `<SPAN>` elements has this RDS as the `datasrc`, but a "non-existent" field name for `datafld` properties. The page will be blank when opened, because the RDS cannot bind to any data.

The Details Page Script

So all we have to do now is extract the appropriate entries for the item the user selected in the left-hand Selection pane, and display them in this Details pane. You'll recall that the code in the Selection page deciphered a user's selection to find out whether it was an event, property, method or collection; and also extracted the text of the item—i.e. the event, property, method or collection name.

It then called one of four routines in our Details page, passing it the item name. The four routines are `SetEvent()`, `SetMethod()`, `SetProperty()` and `SetCollection()`. Here is the first of these:

```
Sub SetEvent(EventName)
```

```
      NameLabel.innerText = "Event Name"
      NameFld.dataFld = "EventName"
      DescLabel.innerText = "Description"
      DescFld.dataFld = "Description"
      SyntaxLabel.innerText = ""
      SyntaxFld.daFafld = ""
      AttribLabel.innerText = ""
      AttribFld.daFafld = ""
      CSSLabel.innerText = ""
      CSSFld.dataFld = ""
      SetADC "select * from Events where EventName='" & EventName & "'"
    End Sub
```

You can see from the code that all it's doing is changing the **innerText** property of each of the labels (**NameLabel**, **DescLabel**, etc), and the **dataFld** property of the corresponding **<SPAN>** tags (**NameFld**, **DescFld**, etc.). These two changes have the effect of changing the label text, in this case to Event Name, etc., and linking the RDS object named **adc** to the appropriate fields in the database tables.

Because the **Events** table only contains two fields, we remove the other labels and disconnect the corresponding fields for the other three sections by setting the **innerText** and **dataFld** properties to an empty string. When we query the other tables for a different item, as you'll see next, we have different fields to access.

The final line in the **SetEvents()** routine calls another routine named **SetADC()**, passing as a parameter a string containing an SQL query that will extract the records we want from the database. Here's the **SetADC()** routine—it's very similar to the one we used in the Selection page:

```
    Sub SetADC(sql)
      Set myadc = document.all("adc")
      myadc.Connect ="DSN=" & parent.MySystemDSN
      myadc.Server = parent.MyServerName
      myadc.SQL = sql
      myadc.Refresh
    End Sub
```

This simply sets the **Connect**, **Server** and **SQL** properties of the control, and performs a **Refresh** which updates the five bound **<SPAN>** tags in the page. This immediately causes the new values to be shown.

Displaying Property, Method or Collection Information

The other three routines, which are called if the user selected a property, method or collection, are very similar. Each one sets appropriate **innerText** property values for each of the labels, to display suitable captions, and sets the appropriate field names in the **dataFld** properties of the five **<SPAN>** tags:

```
    Sub SetProperty(PropName)
      NameLabel.innerText = "Property Name"
      NameFld.daFafld = "PropertyName"
      SyntaxLabel.innerText = "Property Syntax"
      SyntaxFld.daFafld = "PropertySyntax"
      DescLabel.innerText = "Property Description"
      DescFld.daFafld = "Description"
      AttribLabel.innerText = "Equivalent Attribute"
      AttribFld.daFafld = "AttributeValues"
      CSSLabel.innerText = "Equivalent CSS Property"
```

```
    CSSFld.dataFld = "CSSValues"
    SetADC "select * from Properties where PropertyName='" & PropName & "'"
  End Sub

  Sub SetMethod(MethName)
    NameLabel.innerText = "Method Name"
    NameFld.dataFld = "MethodName"
    SyntaxLabel.innerText = "Method Syntax"
    SyntaxFld.daFafld = "Syntax"
    DescLabel.innerText = "Method Description"
    DescFld.dataFld = "Description"
    AttribLabel.innerText = ""
    AttribFld.daFafld = ""
    CSSLabel.innerText = ""
    CSSFld.dataFld = ""
    SetADC "select * from Methods where MethodName='" & MethName & "'"
  End Sub

  Sub SetCollection(CollName)
    NameLabel.innerText = "Collection Name"
    NameFld.dataFld = "CollectionName"
    SyntaxLabel.innerText = ""
    SyntaxFld.daFafld = ""
    DescLabel.innerText = "Collection Description"
    DescFld.dataFld = "Description"
    AttribLabel.innerText = ""
    AttribFld.daFafld = ""
    CSSLabel.innerText = ""
    CSSFld.dataFld = ""
    SetADC "select * from Collections where CollectionName='" & CollName & "'"
  End Sub
```

And that's it. The information on the event, property, method or collection is displayed in the page, and the user is free to make another selection. At the same time, we've fulfilled our design brief, received a huge raise in salary, and completed our look at data binding using Microsoft's Remote Data Service techniques.

Summary

Our journey into the wonderful world of Dynamic HTML data binding ends with this case study. In these four chapters, we've built from scratch a comprehensive knowledge of how to manage data access using Dynamic HTML data binding techniques. We've seen the evolution of data access and networking architecture, which leads naturally to the universal browser-based client access to data sources that data binding provides. With the extensions to Dynamic HTML, Web page creators can now easily bind visual HTML elements to data source objects.

We worked with the two data source objects that are included with Internet Explorer 4: the Tabular Data Control (TDC), and the Remote Data Services Advanced data Control (RDS). With the TDC, we saw how easily we can create rich and interactive web-applications that take simple comma delimited text files (CSV files) as the data source. TDC can be used very effectively in situations where small, read-only data sets are involved. Not only can TDC based solution be lightweight and offer high performance, they can also have the advantage of being highly scalable, since round trips to the server are practically eliminated by the client-side caching the TDC performs. But, as we discovered, there are limitations with the TDC—including its inability to handle complex data sets with one-to many links, and the static nature of it's data set.

Our quest for a "high power" data source provider took us to the world of Microsoft's Remote Data Services: the technology umbrella and infrastructure that promises to deliver "universal data access". We worked through the layers of terminology and looked at technology's various components. We saw what ActiveX Data Objects are and how they are important, and learnt about OLE-DB and saw how it will displace ODBC extending it far beyond today's relational data access. We also examined how the three-tiered architecture of the RDC enables lightweight client access to back-end data sources through standard HTTP protocol. The "built-in" client side support in IE4, manifested through the Advanced Data Control data source object, provided us with a familiar way (through DHTML data binding) of leveraging this flexible and high-powered data access infrastructure.

Last but not least, we got hands-on working experience by designing and implementing an RDS application. The application provides "real-time" access to the comprehensive Wrox Dynamic HTML Reference Database. We coded the application using multiple instances of the Advanced Data Control (RDS client support component), accessing a back-end database through the OLE-DB provider for ODBC.

With this extensive exposure to data binding, you should now be ready to apply data binding technology in your own Internet or Intranet solutions, using the TDC for simple and quick data access, or RDS to open up a whole world of three-tiered access to proprietary or commercial data bases. Remember, if the TDC solution is too simplistic for your task, and the RDS solution is too complex, you may consider creating your own data source object. Microsoft provide the means of creating these through a set of well defined Component Object Model (COM) interfaces. You can create custom data source objects using any Windows programming language that supports COM. This is, however, a topic that's outside the scope of this book.

Advanced IE4 Programming Topics

In the previous two sections, we've learned how Dynamic HTML works, and seen the invaluable data binding extensions that Internet Explorer 4 adds to the browser. Both of these provide us with all kinds of new ways to build pages that are brighter, more exciting, more responsive, and—above all—more dynamic than ever before. However, when it comes to creating really exciting new effects, Dynamic HTML adds another set of stunning new features.

For some time, it's been possible to add fancy graphical effects to your pages by using embedded objects, such as ActiveX controls and Java applets. Both of these, (especially Java applets) were ideally suited to creating attractive and interactive moving graphics. It's also an area where the new animated GIF files performed well. However, compared to 'real' presentation applications, like Microsoft PowerPoint, the browser could never offer the same kind of experience.

With Dynamic HTML, it's possible to use a range of new techniques that can mirror the graphical effects of even the best presentation applications. This means that the browser can now take its place in the multimedia arena, as a front end for displaying slide shows and other graphical presentations. It can perform transitions between elements and pages, add filters to graphics, and create many other exciting effects.

On top of this, a new range of ActiveX controls is included with IE4. These are designed to provide even more in the way of multimedia opportunities for our Web pages. The controls provide new methods of adding video and multi-channel sound, creating a community area with its own 'chat' system, and even having animated characters (similar to Microsoft's 'Office Assistant') helping your users get to grips with our site. In this part of the book, we'll be exploring this area in depth.

With another new technology, called **Scriptlets**, we can even build our own simple components. This exciting new technique allows us to create reusable Web pages that contain HTML and script, and then embed them into other pages. Scriptlets are a whole new way of making building interactive pages much easier, and we've set aside a whole chapter in this part of the book to show you how.

Finally, we end this section with a look at how all the new features in IE4 can be integrated with server-side processing. One of the main reasons that IE4 can provide such responsive pages is that all the processing is done at the client end—in the browser. However, there are often occasions where we want to exert control over the information sent to the browser, or manage the information coming from it.

We'll look at how the browser and serve can work together, concentrating on the Active Server Pages technology that is included with Windows NT (and some other server systems). This offers that final level of interactivity that can really make your Web site stand out from the crowd.

Dialogs, Text Manipulation, and Enhanced Forms

In the first part of this book we covered a lot of Dynamic HTML fundamentals: style sheets, and the **window** object and its subsidiaries, including the very important **document** object. At that point in the text, we hadn't talked about scripting so we couldn't give very much in the way of in-depth example code. Now that we're further along in the book, we've seen a whole chapter dedicated to scripting and a number of chapters that examine data access. All of these chapters have included some example code that used parts of what we talked about in the early chapters. However, we haven't yet had a chance to focus on a few of the most important topics in isolation.

Accordingly, in this chapter we'll see example code (with detailed explanations!) that demonstrate how:

- the **showModalDialog** method can be used to display dialogs and pass information between a main form and subsidiary dialogs

- to use the **TextRange** object in an actual page to do things like finding text, selecting, and changing text

- the new text manipulation properties of HTML elements, like **innerText** and **innerHTML**, make dynamically changing the HTML page easy

- we can use the new **userProfiles** object to get information about our visitors

- the multitude of new form features that enable HTML pages and dialogs to look and act like native Window user-interface applications

We'll cover dialogs and text manipulation first with a single example, and then move onto enhanced forms.

Dialogs, Text Ranges, and Text Properties and Methods

In this section we'll cover two diverse topics that are brand new to Dynamic HTML and Internet Explorer 4.0: custom modal dialogs and truly dynamic text manipulation. In this section of the chapter we'll do a very brief review of these topics and then move onto an example that shows how all of these topics can work together to produce a page (with dialog!) that would have been unthinkable before Dynamic HTML.

Custom Dialogs

Dialogs aren't new to Internet Explorer and they certainly don't require Dynamic HTML. If you've used IE3 you've probably shown a few dialog boxes of your own. Do any of the following methods ring any bells?

`Alert`	`msgbox` (VBScript only)
`Confirm`	`inputbox` (VBScript only)
`Prompt`	

For example, with the following line of VBScript code we can create a dialog that prompts for some input and stores it in the `strReturnVal` variable:

```
strReturnVal = prompt("Enter something here:")
```

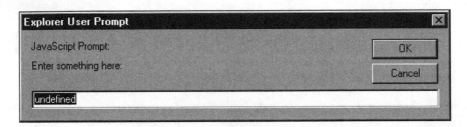

So what does IE4 give us that we didn't have before? In short, we now have the ability to create and show our own **custom** dialog boxes. These dialogs act just like the included dialogs: they're modal, they stop execution while they are displayed, and they can return information to the calling script, but what they look like (and what they do) is completely up to us. And creating dialogs isn't difficult either because they're HTML documents just like normal pages that we've been talking about for this entire book.

As an example, on the next page you can see a picture of a dialog that we've created for the example later in this chapter. We'll be talking more about the dialog itself, and how the dialog communicates with the page that shows it, later in this chapter.

The code we use to display this dialog is a bit different from the code used to display a simple dialog, but not too hard to understand. Instead of a predefined method, we use the general-purpose `showModalDialog` method of the `window` object.

```
strReturnVal = window.showModalDialog("dialog.htm", objSelRange.parentElement,
"dialogWidth=605px;dialogHeight=430px")
```

In this code, we've specified the HTML file to use for the dialog layout itself (`dialog.htm`), some information that we're passing to the dialog (`objSelRange.parentElement`), and two formatting instructions for the height and width of the dialog window (`dialogWidth=605px;dialogHeight=430px`). Like the previous example, our dialog returns a value to the `strReturnVal` variable.

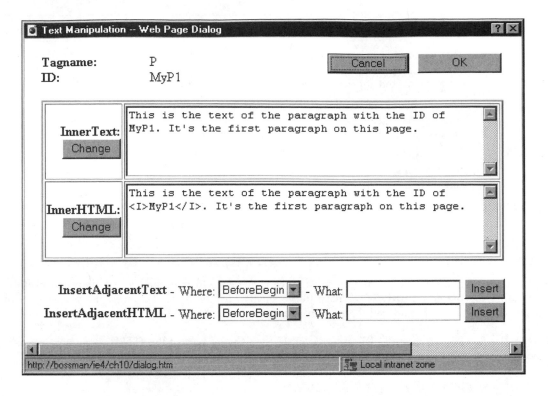

Since our dialogs are HTML pages, and they're rendered by IE4, they can include any and all of the same Dynamic HTML features we've spent this book talking about. Our example uses the `innerText` property to change the page dynamically, but dialogs can do anything: use the new enhanced form elements, display information from a data source, and so on. The sky really is the limit here.

Text Manipulation

The other important new feature of Dynamic HTML that we'll be using in our example has no corollary in previous versions of HTML. In fact, more than anything else, this is the innovation that most makes Dynamic HTML 'dynamic'–what else could it be but text manipulation after the page has loaded?

There are two main ways we can use text manipulation to make our pages dynamic: using the new HTML element properties and with the `TextRange` object.

HTML Element Properties

Almost all visible HTML elements now support at least a few of four new properties: `innerText`, `innerHTML`, `outerText`, and `outerHTML`. The following table recaps the similarities and differences between these properties.

Property	Description
innerText	The complete text content of the element, including the content of any enclosed element, but excluding any HTML tags. Assigning a new string to it replaces only the content of the element, and any new HTML tags are rendered as text, and not interpreted.
outerText	The complete text content of the element, including the content of any enclosed element, but excluding any HTML tags. It returns the same string as innerText, but assigning a new string to it replaces the entire element.
innerHTML	The complete text and HTML content of the element, including the content of any enclosed element. Assigning a new string to it replaces only the content of the element, and HTML tags within it are rendered correctly.
outerHTML	The complete text and HTML content of the element, including the start and end tags of the element and the entire text and HTML content of any enclosed element. Assigning a new string to it replaces the entire element, and the HTML content of the new string is rendered correctly.

Using these elements is relatively easy. Once we have a reference to the object we're interested in (this can be anything from the entire body of the page to the smallest list item) we can access the properties like we do all properties, with a period and the property name.

For example, this line of code displays the text of the non-header part of the HTML document by using the **body** property of the document object:

```
msgbox document.body.outerHTML
```

This line of code sets the text of a table **<TD>** element named **MyTableEl** to the string **"Hello, Dynamic HTML!"**:

```
document.body("MyTableEl").innerText = "Hello, Dynamic HTML!"
```

or alternatively, a shortened version referencing just the table name would achieve the same result:

```
MyTableEl.innerText= "Hello, Dynamic HTML!"
```

In addition to these four new properties, most elements now also support two new methods named **insertAdjacentText** and **insertAdjacentHTML**. These methods take a new string (in text or HTML, as appropriate) and a string location that can be one of **BeforeBegin**, **AfterBegin**, **BeforeEnd**, and **AfterEnd** and add the new text or HTML at the specified location.

For example, to add the HTML **<B>New bold text</B>** before a paragraph element named **MyP**, we use this line of code:

```
document.all("MyP").insertAdjacentHTML "BeforeBegin", "<B>New bold text</B>"
```

The text manipulation properties are generally simple and quick to use. They don't provide all of the features that the **TextRange** object does, but they're perfect for the quick setting and retrieving of the HTML on the page and they can be used, with other script code, to provide much Dynamic HTML functionality.

The TextRange Object

The other technique we can use to modify the text after our HTML page has loaded is the `TextRange` object.

Instead of being an inherent part of each HTML element, the `TextRange` object is something we have to explicitly create when we want to use it. A text range isn't intrinsically associated with a specific block of text. The object keeps track of what text it's currently tracking, and this can be easily changed. In fact, many of the operations that the `TextRange` object can perform on its data relate to moving the references that keep track of the beginning and end of the text.

We can create a `TextRange` object in a few different ways. By far the most common method is simply to use the `createTextRange` method of the `document.body` object.

```
set objMyRange = document.body.createTextRange
```

This method returns a `TextRange` object that includes everything between the `<BODY>` and `</BODY>` tags. Since we often want to perform some action on a smaller subset of this text, we then can use one of the many methods that `TextRange` provides to alter the text that the object points to. Here's a listing of these methods (the appendices have more information on each of these methods):

`collapse`	`expand`	`findText`
`move`	`moveEnd`	`moveStart`
`moveToBookmark`	`moveToElementText`	`moveToPoint`
`setEndPoint`		

For example, we can move the starting position of the text range named `objMyRange` one sentence forward with this code:

```
objMyRange.moveStart "sentence", 1
```

Additional `TextRange` methods offer us the ability to visibly select the current range (`select`), move the current range into view on the browser (`scrollIntoView`), get information about the range (`inRange`, `isEqual`, `parentElement`), and to paste new HTML over the top of any existing code (`pasteHTML`).

Although the `TextRange` object supports many methods, this last method is one of the most important. It's with `pasteHTML` that we can dynamically change the contents of whatever HTML our `TextRange` object is currently pointing at. Using this method is as simple as calling `pasteHTML` and passing the new HTML code. The following line of code changes whatever text `objMyRange` is pointing at to Dynamically **changed** HTML text:

```
objMyRange.pasteHTML "Dynamically <B>changed</B> HTML text"
```

Also, at any time when we have a `TextRange` object, we can query or change its text with the object's `text` and `HTMLText` properties, like this:

```
msgbox objMyRange.text
objMyRange.HTMLText = "<B>New bold text</B>"
```

The `text` property ignores all HTML tags; in contrast, `HTMLText` includes them. This approach is similar to the difference between `innerText` and `innerHTML`, and between `outerText` and `outerHTML`.

That completes our review of the most important parts of both custom dialogs and dynamic text handling. We're now ready to move on to the example that shows off these features, and this is what we'll do in the next section of the chapter.

The Dynamic Text Page with Dialog Example

Dynamic HTML allows us to accomplish a lot of things with just a bit of text manipulation code and a dialog. This next example demonstrates just that and explains the code necessary to put the new objects we've been talking about through their paces and gives the low-down on many different techniques for accomplishing common Dynamic HTML tasks.

What the Sample Does

Fire up your browser and point it to `http://rapid.wrox.co.uk/books/0707`. When you arrive, load up the text manipulation page associated with Chapter **10**.

Take a look at the page. You'll see a table listing the keystrokes this page will accept (and what they accomplish). We can change the text on the page, via the *C* and *H* commands, and also with the dialog that is displayed when we press *D*. We can also find text with *F* and reset the text, after we've modified it, with *R*.

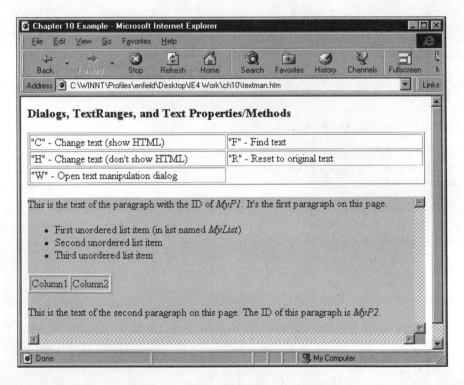

The aquamarine section below the table (light gray if you're just reading from the book) listing the possible commands is the working text area. It's here where we'll select the text we'd like to modify and where our changes (made on this page or the dialog) will appear. We've only given this section a certain amount of the page real estate; it can take as much text as we can give it, but it will scroll–inside the division–to allow all the text to be viewed. Since this part of the page is governed by the same rules of HTML as the rest of the page, we can create elements with HTML as we do elsewhere. Aside from this, and for our purposes, we'll consider this section of the page as separate from the rest.

The sample we've developed could act as a rudimentary text editor (with HTML capacity!), although our implementation might be frustrating. After all, it's not built to be a Notepad replacement! Its primary purpose is demonstrating how the text manipulation parts of Dynamic HTML work, and how a custom dialog can be integrated with an existing page to provide a different way for the user to enter and view information.

Changing Text on the Page

Before we see what our dialog can do, the page itself has a lot of functionality that we can demonstrate easily. Select a portion of the first paragraph, making sure you include the italicized *MyP1* (you'll see why in a second), and press *C* on your keyboard. In the pages that follow we've removed the table listing the command from the rest of the screen shots to save space–but don't worry, it's still the same page.

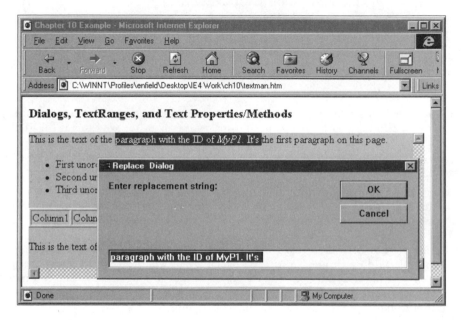

Pressing *C* after selecting some text pops up a dialog prompting us to enter new text to replace the selection. Our code has automatically filled in the entry text box with the string on the page, but notice that the word MyP1 isn't surrounded by the `<I>` and `</I>` tags as we'd expect. After all, it's displayed in italics on the page.

Since the italic tags aren't displayed, if we pressed OK, without changing a thing, we'd lose the HTML formatting. So, for now, just press Cancel. Next, with the same text selected, press *H*. The dialog that is displayed looks a lot like the one we just saw. However, now the `<I>` and `</I>` tags are present in the text box string, and the instructions say that we can enter a replacement string using 'normal text and/or HTML'.

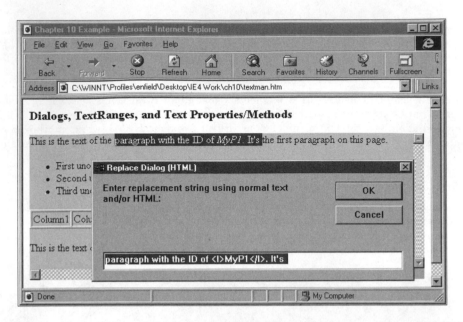

As we'll see when we look at the code, the first routine uses a part of the **TextRange** object that ignores HTML formatting tags while the second routine includes these tags.

Go ahead and type something different in the text box and press OK to see the text on the page change... without refreshing or performing any other step. This makes it easy to see why this is called 'dynamic' HTML!

Fixing Mistakes and Finding Text

Now that we've modified the page (perhaps indiscriminately) we might realize that our changes don't fit with the rest of the text. Assuming we want to get rid of the change we just made, all we have to do is press *R*. This resets the text in the working area to what it was when the page was loaded.

The one other thing we can do without using the text manipulation dialog is to find a portion of text on the page. This is simple to do: first press *F* to get a dialog asking you for the text you'd like to search for, then enter your text, and press OK. If your entry is found in the working area, you'll see it selected (which means it's all ready for you to press C or H to change it something different... and that adding search and replace functionality to the page wouldn't be that difficult at all).

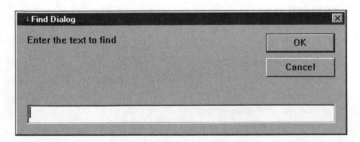

Enter some text on the page, like Column1, and press OK to begin the search and then see the first table element on the page selected.

Viewing the Dialog

Although we can already accomplish a lot with the commands we've seen so far, the one that we haven't covered–using *D* to open the text manipulation dialog–is the most powerful of all. It also involves the most code, as we'll see shortly.

Select part of the last paragraph in the working area and press *D*. After the slightest hesitation you'll see the dialog we've alluded to so often appear on your screen. We selected part of the last paragraph and now see the dialog appear with the contents of the paragraph in the two `<TEXTAREA>` fields on the page. And, in case we weren't sure what we'd selected, we can see from the two headers at the top-left part of the dialog that we're working on a block of text with the ID of MyP2 and the tagname or HTML tag of `<P>`.

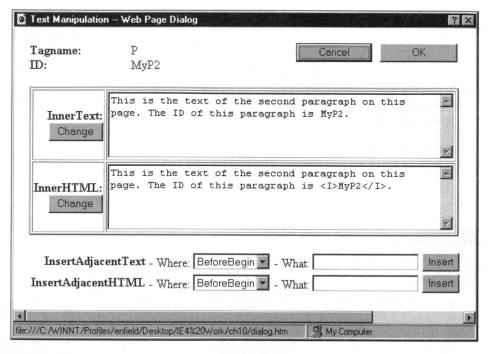

So, what's happening here? When loaded this dialog displays the contents of the element that completely encloses whatever text is currently selected on the main page. Since our only selection was part of the second paragraph, we see just the second paragraph. If we'd selected only a single letter inside of the text MyP2, we would have seen the just the text MyP2 in both of the text areas. Since *MyP2* is italicized using a set of begin and end tags (`<I>` and `</I>`) it's considered to be a separate element, and our code treats it as such.

Because we have the ability to select a variety of elements, the dialog is a great way to understand the difference between `innerText` and `innerHTML` and how the relationship of elements in a document is determined. Selecting the text 'MyP2' in isolation shows simply MyP2 for both properties. However, if we select a larger part of the second paragraph, then we can see a difference between `innerText` and `innerHTML`–the italic tags show up in the `innerHTML`.

The relationship between the **MyP2** element and the outer text division (named **TextDiv**) works the same way. If we select part of two high level elements, say, for example, part of the second paragraph and the table above it, then the element that the dialog displays will be the text division. This happens because the only element that encloses the table and the second paragraph at the same time is the text division that makes up the working area of the original page. If the dialog is displaying the text division, then we can see the outer HTML around the paragraphs (the **<P ID="MyP2">** and **</P>** tags, for example). We can't see this same HTML if we're only displaying the paragraphs themselves.

> *Using the* **outerHTML** *property of a paragraph element* **would** *allow us to see the enclosing tags, but we've neglected to do this in this example (more on this at the end of the chapter).*

Keep these relationships in mind as you play with this sample. The most important thing to remember is that the dialog displays the enclosed text for the current element and any enclosed elements, but not for the element tags themselves.

Changing Page Text

Once we have the dialog displayed and an element in the text areas, changing the page text is as easy as changing either the innerText or innerHTML text and then pressing the appropriate Change button. When we do this the text changes immediately on both the dialog and on the calling page.

To see this in action, select part of the second paragraph, open the dialog, and then move the dialog so that you can see both the second paragraph on the original page and the dialog. Add some text to one of the text boxes and press the Change button. The other text field on the dialog immediately changes to reflect the modified text, and, if you can see the calling page, you'll see that the working area now reflects the changes you made too.

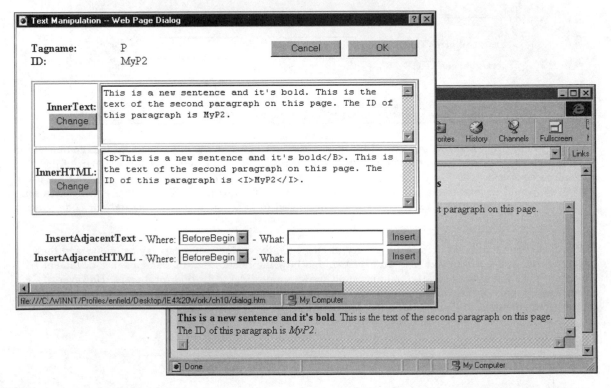

After this change, press OK to dismiss the dialog and return to the main page. Again, you can confirm that your change has taken effect. The new text is now part of the text in the document just like the text that was there when the page was loaded (you can confirm this by reselecting the second paragraph and seeing that the changes you've made are no different from the original paragraph text).

Instead of manually selecting your insertion point in the text areas, you can use the InsertAdjacentText and InsertAdjacentHTML fields at the bottom of the page. Simply select one of the four locations available, enter your text in the text box, and press the Insert button.

While you're experimenting with the list boxes and the `InsertAdjacent` methods, don't be surprised if all of your changes don't appear in the `innerText` and `innerHTML` text boxes on the dialog. If we insert text or HTML before the beginning of the current element or after the end of the current element, it will appear on the calling page itself, but won't show up in the dialog. To understand why this happens we just need to remember what our reference is really pointing at. If we're modifying a paragraph element that's set up like this:

```
<P ID="SomeID">Some text...</P>
```

And we use `InsertAdjacentText` to add the string `"Hello"` at the `BeforeBegin` location, the HTML our page will see looks like this:

```
Hello<P ID="SomeID">Some text...</P>
```

Since the new string is outside of the paragraph element, it isn't displayed in the dialog text boxes. If we exited the dialog and then selected enough top-level elements to ensure that the containing element is the text division, then we would see our new code.

Adding and Modifying New Elements

One of the coolest things we can do with this sample is add new elements to the page dynamically. Since we're modifying HTML, we have no limits except for those which HTML imposes. We can change the table or add and remove cells, add images, even add buttons and script code. Furthermore, after we've added new elements, we can use the dialog to modify them, just as if they'd always existed on the page. We'll talk about this in a second.

For example, if you display a portion of the first paragraph and add the following text somewhere in the middle of the paragraph, you'll add a graphic and the page will re-render itself to show the item correctly (be sure to use the innerHTML box, since this is a tag):

```
<IMG align=left src="wpdr.gif">
```

The `wpdr.gif` file is located on the Wrox server, and is included with the sample files for the book.

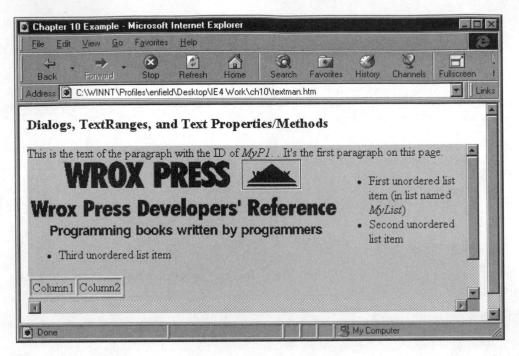

But we're not limited to adding or modifying new elements in the midst of existing paragraphs. The sample page loads with two paragraphs, named **MyP1** and **MyP2**. Adding a third paragraph, and then modifying it like it's always been on the page, is a simple thing to accomplish.

To do this, start by selecting more than one element so that when the dialog appears, the header says that we're modifying the TextDiv element of type **DIV**. With this view we can see all of the paragraph start and end tags as well as the **<UL>** and **<TABLE>** tags that create the list and the small table–since they're children of the text division they appear in the innerHTML text box. Adding a new paragraph is as easy as moving outside of an existing paragraph tag and adding something like this:

```
<P ID=MyNewParagraph>Some new text.</P>
```

Press Change with this text in the text box, and then press OK to dismiss the dialog. If you need to, scroll the window so that you can see the text you just added, select part of it, and press *D* one more time.

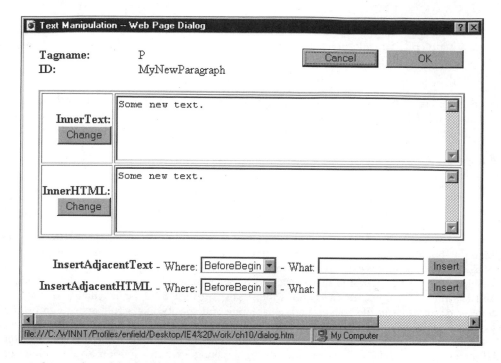

We can now select and modify the brand new paragraph we added, as if it had been in the page all along, because, as far as Internet Explorer is concerned, there's no difference between HTML we've just added and HTML that has been there since the page has been loaded.

> *However, if you view the source code, then the original HTML will still show up, not the modified version that the browser is displaying.*

This completes our discussion of what this sample can do. Before we continue and talk about the code, you might want to do some more experimentation. Add your own elements, change the existing elements, and notice the relationships between the different elements.

How the Sample Code Works

While the example does many different things and is a powerful example of what Dynamic HTML can accomplish, it isn't overly complex. The HTML and script code for this sample are contained in just two HTML files, one for the main page and one for the dialog page. The code for the main page has only two event procedures and two helping functions (although one of the event procedures is rather long!).

In this discussion we'll first talk about the main page, including how script code shows the dialog, and then we will move onto to cover the dialog and the code that actually does the text manipulation.

The Main Page

The first page we see in the browser when we start this sample is responsible for creating the working text area and then fielding user-entered keystrokes and executing the appropriate code.

The HTML of the Main Page

Most of the non-script HTML code in the `textman.htm` file isn't especially interesting. Since teaching style sheets isn't our focus in this example, we haven't used much of CSS outside of the declaration for the working text area.

However, when we create the text division the ability to define the text appearance of our page more tightly is helpful, and we've used this feature when we define the working text area. After the page header and the table listing the commands (created with a standard `<TABLE>` element), we see this bit of code:

```
<DIV ID="TextDiv" STYLE="position:relative; height:220px;
                         background-color:aquamarine;overflow:scroll">
... code removed ...

</DIV>
```

With this code we're creating the document division named `TextDiv`. The `STYLE` attribute specifies that this text division should be placed `relative` to the rest of the document's elements. This property isn't strictly necessary here because we're not using any of the other positioning properties but we've included it for completeness. We set the height of the division to be a constant 220 pixels and, since we don't specify a width, this lets the division occupy the entire width of the browser by default. Finally, we use `background-color` to paint the background aquamarine and specify that scrollbars should be provided if the text inside the division overflows the boundaries of the division. This last addition allows us to always access all of the text associated with the division, without sacrificing the knowledge that the division will remain 220 pixels high. In this page we're not showing anything after the division, so it wouldn't matter too much if we just let the division height grow indefinitely. However, this is a more robust solution that would transfer better to a real-world situation where we're sure to have more text after the part of the page we change, so we've implemented it this way.

Between the opening and closing division tags, we specify the starting HTML for our working area with:

```
<P ID=MyP1>
This is the text of the paragraph with the ID of <I>MyP1</I>.
It's the first paragraph on this page.</P>
<UL ID=MyList>
<LI>First unordered list item (in list named <I>MyList</I>)
<LI>Second unordered list item
<LI>Third unordered list item
</UL>
<TABLE ID="MyTable" BORDER="1">
<TD>Column1</TD>
<TD>Column2</TD>
</TABLE>
<P ID=MyP2>
This is the text of the second paragraph on this page. The ID of this paragraph is
<I>MyP2</I>.</P>
```

There isn't anything special about this HTML, except that it's important to note what we've named the elements (using the `ID` attribute). The text manipulation dialog helps us to identify the element we're modifying by displaying the value of the `ID` property if it exists (otherwise it will just display None).

Loading the Page

When the page is first loaded, we don't take any other action except to find and save the text the working area has to begin with. As you'll see later, we use this saved text to restore the text division when the user presses *R*.

```
Dim strOriginalText

Sub window_onLoad
  set objTempDivRange = document.body.createTextRange
  objTempDivRange.moveToElementText(TextDiv)
  strOriginalText = objTempDivRange.HTMLText
End Sub
```

Because `strOriginalText` is declared outside of a function or subroutine, it will be global to the document, and this means we can set it in one place (`window_onLoad`) and use it in another (`document_onKeyDown`). We don't usually declare variables in VBScript, but we need to in this case, otherwise `strOriginalText` would be created and then lost when any routine that used it finished.

We get the text of the division by creating a temporary `TextRange` object with `document.body.createTextRange`. This object initially includes all of the text in the body of the document. Since we're only interested in the `TextDiv` element, we use the `moveToElementText` method, passing the name of the element we're interested in, to reduce the range to encompass the appropriate text. Finally, we use the `HTMLText` property of the range and store the results in our page-level `strOriginalText` variable.

We could have accomplished the same result as the above code but in only one line. We chose to do it the first way to demonstrate how the `TextRange` object would work with this sort of task, but showing this method demonstrates the contrast between using the `TextRange` object and the HTML element properties.

In our alternative `onLoad` event we use the `document.all` collection to obtain a reference to the `TextDiv` element, and we use the `TextDiv` object's `innerHTML` property to obtain the same HTML that the `TextRange` object's `HTMLText` property provides in the above code.

```
Sub Window_onLoad
  strOriginalText = document.all("TextDiv").innerHTML
End Sub
```

In this sample we'll use both methods (we use something similar to the shorter method in the `RestoreText` subroutine). It's helpful to be familiar with both approaches because you may find situations where one method is preferable over the other.

How onKeyDown Handles the Non-Dialog Events

Most of the main page's action happens in the `document_onKeyDown` handler. This event is executed whenever a keyboard button is pressed. Its job in this page is to execute the appropriate section of code when the user presses an appropriate key. Since we don't have other individual objects handling keyboard events we can handle them all at the `document` level and not worry about canceling events with `cancelEvent`.

Before we begin to test for certain keystrokes, we save the currently selected text area in a local variable called `objSelRange` with the following code. We use `objSelRange` later in three of the keyboard handlers.

```
set objSelRange = document.selection.createRange
```

After this initialization the rest of the code consists of a large **Select Case** block that branches to handle appropriate key presses (listed by ASCII value). This block includes a section of code for each supported action.

The change text and change HTML text commands work in exactly the same way, with one small difference. We've listed the code for the non-HTML change routine here.

```
Case 67 ' "C"
change text
  If objSelRange.text <> "" Then
    strReplace = InputBox("Enter replacement string:",_
                  "Replace Dialog", objSelRange.text)
    If strReplace <> "" Then
      objSelRange.pasteHTML strReplace
    End If
  End If
```

As long as some text has been selected, we use the VBScript **InputBox** function to show a dialog and ask the user for the text they'd like to use to replace the selected text. The range's **text** property is used as the third parameter to this call so that the input box displays the currently selected text as the default value. When the **InputBox** function returns, we check to make sure that the user entered some text (a space at minimum) and, if so, we use the **pasteHTML** method to modify the **TextRange** object's current displayed text.

The only difference between this routine and the routine that handles HTML characters is in the **InputBox** line:

```
strReplace = InputBox("Enter replacement string using normal text " _
         & "and/or HTML:","Replace Dialog (HTML)", _
           objSelRange.HTMLtext)
```

When we provide the default text for the input dialog in this case, we use the range's **HTMLText** property instead of the **text** property. Since **TextRange** objects have only the **pasteHTML** method (instead of **pasteText and pasteHTML**), no other changes are necessary.

When we press *F* to start a search, the page prompts us with an input box similar to the one it uses for the change routines, except that we don't provide a default string to find.

```
Case 70 ' "F" - find text
  strFind = InputBox("Enter the text to find", "Find Dialog")
  If strFind <> "" Then
    If objFoundRange.findText(strFind) Then
      objFoundRange.select
      objFoundRange.scrollIntoView
    End If
  End If
```

The return value of the **InputBox** function is again checked to ensure that some text was entered, and then the **findText** method of the range object is used to (possibly) find the text in the current range. If this method is successful it sets **objFoundRange** to the found text, returns true, and then we use the **select** and **scrollIntoView** methods of the new range to visibly select and display the range inside the working area.

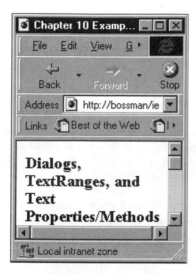
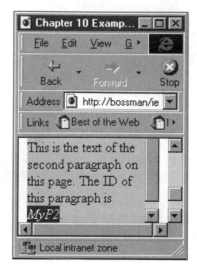

The **scrollIntoView** method will scroll any portion of the page so that the selected element is visible. This means that, if the text division is full and the scrollbars are active, IE will scroll both it and the browser window itself. Notice where the scrollbars are on the screen shots above. Pretty impressive, eh?

The last handler aside from the one that shows the dialog resets the working area's current text to the text it held when the page was loaded. It accomplishes this by calling the **RestoreText** subroutine.

```
Case 82 ' "R" - refresh text
  RestoreText(strOriginalText)
```

We've chosen to place this code in a separate routine of its own because we call it both from this handler and from the dialog handler if the user cancels their changes.

The routine itself is rather simple... so simple, in fact, that coding the routine itself into both calling procedures instead of calling this procedure would have been acceptable. However, modularizing the code this way makes it easier to upgrade later if **RestoreText** needs to perform more actions.

```
Sub RestoreText(strToRestore)
  document.all("TextDiv").innerHTML = strToRestore
End Sub
```

All this one line of code does is obtain a reference to the **TextDiv** object and set its **innerHTML** property to the string that was passed as a parameter to the procedure. When called from the reset handler, the string we pass is the original text obtained when the page loaded.

Showing the Dialog

This routine actually shows the dialog, and has a few major parts that we'll discuss in turn.

Immediately after the code enters the open dialog section, we use another function we've written (and that we'll discuss in a moment) to make sure that the selected range lies wholly inside of the text division. The **CheckAncestry** function takes a reference to a page element and the ID of another element and returns true if the first element is contained by or is the same as the second element.

```
Case 68  ' "D" - open dialog
  If Not CheckAncestry(objSelRange.parentElement, "TextDiv") Then
    msgbox "You need to select or click in the working text area."
    Exit Sub
  End If
```

The **parentElement** of the currently selected range is the smallest element that fully encloses the selected text. If this **parentElement** isn't a child of the **TextDiv** object, then we know that at least part of the selection is outside the text division working area. If this is the case we can't proceed any further so we inform the user of the reason that we're exiting and quit the procedure.

If we pass this test then we know we're dealing only with a selection inside the working area. Because we allow the dialog user to cancel any changes they make, we need to save the current text of the working area before any changes are made. We do this with the following code that works exactly like the code we already discussed in the **Window_onLoad** event.

```
Set objSaveRange = document.body.createTextRange
objSaveRange.moveToElementText(TextDiv)
strCurrentText = objSaveRange.HTMLText
```

This code could also be replaced with a single line of code similar to the one we used in **RestoreText**, although we haven't done this here.

The next line of code is the one that does all the work of loading and showing our dialog. Since we have a separate file called **dialog.htm** that implements our dialog, we just need to call the **showModalDialog** method of the window object to pause code execution and show the dialog:

```
strRetVal = window.showModalDialog("dialog.htm", _
            objSelRange.parentElement, _
            "dialogWidth=605px;dialogHeight=430px")
```

The first parameter to this method is just the filename of the page to show. The documentation calls the second parameter **Arguments**–this spot is where we put any information that we want our dialog to be able to use while it's displayed. In many cases this parameter will be empty or consist of just a string. But we're not limited to sending the dialog a number or string value. In our case, we pass a reference to the HTML element that contains our selected text (**objSelRange.parentElement**). As you've already seen, the dialog can use this reference to obtain information about the element and even to change the object on the original page. The final parameter to **showModalDialog** is a string that allows us to define the specific appearance characteristics of the displayed dialog. In our code, we use this parameter to set the height and width of the dialog.

When the user dismisses the dialog, our code continues executing. The **showModalDialog** function returns whatever the dialog set its **window.returnValue** property to before it was closed. In our example, we know that the dialog code sets this property to "save" if the user presses OK and to "restore" if the user presses Cancel or exits the dialog by pressing the close button or selecting Close from the system menu.

```
If strRetVal = "restore" Then
  RestoreText(strCurrentText)
End If
```

So, if the string is indeed **restore** we use the same **RestoreText** routine as before, but pass the text of the working area saved from immediately before we displayed the dialog.

Limiting Page Modification with CheckAncestry

In our discussion above we glossed over the way we determined whether or not the selected area was completely inside the text division. We did this with a function called **CheckAncestry**. Here's the code:

```
Function CheckAncestry(objChildEl, strParentID)
  If objChildEl.ID = strParentID Then
    CheckAncestry = True
  ElseIf objChildEl.tagName = "BODY" Then
    CheckAncestry = False
  Else
    CheckAncestry = CheckAncestry(objChildEl.parentElement, strParentID)
  End If
End Function
```

This is a recursive function, which means that it calls itself as many times as necessary to complete execution. The problem with determining if some object is contained by another object is that we don't know if the second object contains the first object to start with, and if it does, we don't know how deeply the child object is buried. We solve both of these problems by using an elegant recursive solution.

Each time **CheckAncestry** is called it checks first to see whether the **ID** of the passed element is equal to the **ID** of the supposed containing element. If this is the case, then we know that the first object is indeed contained by (or equal to) the second object and **CheckAncestry** returns **true** and exits. If we're still in the function, we then check to see that the object we're checking isn't the **body** element, because **body** is the ultimate container for all other elements. If we've checked this far without finding the parent element we know that the first object **is not** contained by the second, and so we return **false**. Finally, if neither of these cases occurs, we can continue our search by calling **CheckAncestry** again with the parent of the element we're working with now.

When **CheckAncestry** finally returns (as it has to, because even if we don't find the sought after element, we have to reach the **body** element sooner or later), then the last return value percolates back up through the individual instances of **CheckAncestry** until it's returned to the original calling code.

The VBScript documentation recommends against using recursive functions with VBScript because the VBScript engine has a relatively small stack. Since each time a recursive function calls itself new information is placed on the stack, it can be relatively easy to exhaust the stack space and cause your script to fail or Internet Explorer to crash. However, in our situation, even with an extremely complicated page, we shouldn't be calling **CheckAncestry** enough times to cause VBScript to run out of stack space.

And now that we've sufficiently discussed the main page, we're ready to move on to the code behind the dialog page.

The Dialog Page

The other half of this example is the dialog itself, created by the `dialog.htm` file. We'll break this file down into its component parts in the same way that we did the main file above, starting with the HTML we use to create the visual representation of the dialog.

Creating the Dialog with HTML

The dialog consists of three main parts:

- ▲ the header information where the **ID** and **tagname** of the element we're modifying as well as the OK and Cancel buttons are displayed
- ▲ the two **<TEXTAREA>** fields that display the **innerText** and **innerHTML** properties of the element
- ▲ the two dropdown combo boxes and text fields that allow text to be entered and inserted with the **InsertAdjacent** methods.

All of these elements are wrapped in a document division that sets the left and top margins to 20 pixels and is created with this HTML:

```
<DIV STYLE="margin-left:20px;margin-top:20px">
    ... code removed ...
</DIV>
```

The header information exists behind the scenes as two button **<INPUT>** tags and two **<SPAN>** tags. Since we want to set the ID and tagname as the page is loaded, we've created two empty **<SPAN>** tags and given them IDs so we can manipulate them in our code.

```
<b>Tagname:</b>
<SPAN STYLE="position:absolute;left:150px" ID=spnTagName></SPAN>
<INPUT TYPE=BUTTON NAME="btnCancel" VALUE="Cancel"
STYLE="position:absolute;left:365px;width:100px">
<INPUT TYPE=BUTTON NAME="btnOK" VALUE="OK"
STYLE="position:absolute;left:475px;width:100px">
<br>
<b>ID:</b>
<SPAN STYLE="position:absolute;left:150px" ID=spnIDName></SPAN>
```

Since our application only requires that the ID and tagname be set once, as the page is loaded, it would have been possible to create the same effect using `document.write` calls that would be executed as the page was loaded. However, since this is a book on Dynamic HTML we've chosen to achieve our goal using Dynamic HTML. Since we've set up the **<SPAN>** tags, they can be changed easily after the dialog loads if this ever becomes necessary.

The two text areas are created with standard **<TEXTAREA>** tags. Since both blocks are virtually the same, we've only included one here in the text; this block creates the **innerText** display.

```
<TR>
 <TD ALIGN=RIGHT>
  <B>InnerText:</B><BR>
   <INPUT ID=btnIText TYPE=BUTTON VALUE="Change" ONCLICK="UpdateProps()">
```

```
   </TD>
   <TD>
    <TEXTAREA ROWS=5 ID=txtIText STYLE="width:450px"></TEXTAREA>
   </TD>
  </TR>
```

This HTML also connects the **onClick** event of the **<TEXTAREA>** element to the **UpdateProps** routine. While the names of the button and text area are different for the **innerHTML** portion of the dialog, that event still calls the same **UpdateProps** procedure. As we'll see in a moment, the code inside of **UpdateProps** determines which button has been pressed and takes the appropriate action.

Finally, we have the HTML that creates the list box / text box combination for the **InsertAdjacent** methods. Because these two blocks are again similar, we've only listed one here.

```
  <TR>
   <TD ALIGN=RIGHT><B>InsertAdjacentText</B></TD>
   <TD> - Where:
    <SELECT ID=lstTPosn SIZE=1>
     <OPTION SELECTED>BeforeBegin
     <OPTION>AfterBegin
     <OPTION>BeforeEnd
     <OPTION>AfterEnd
    </SELECT>
   </TD>
   <TD> - What: <INPUT ID=txtInsText TYPE=TEXT SIZE=18></TD>
   <TD><INPUT TYPE=BUTTON ID=btnInsText VALUE="Insert"></TD>
  </TR>
```

The code that executes when the user presses the **btnInsText** or **btnInsHTML** buttons created in this part of the page is connected in the normal VBScript manner (using **Sub btnInsText_onClick** and **Sub btnInsHTML_onClick**). This frees us from needing to specify an **ONCLICK** attribute in our HTML as we did for the buttons above.

There's also this choice little nugget at the top of the page:

```
  <!-- Used for dialog testing
  <P ID="TestP">This is my testing <b>paragraph</b> element. OK?</P>
  -->
```

Since it's commented out, why did we leave it in the HTML at all? The answer: it's used for debugging. We'll talk about this more in a few pages.

But for now, onto the code...

Dialog Initialization

Three important events occur inside **Window_onLoad**. The first (and arguably, the most) significant thing we do is set the variable that we'll use in the rest of the code to refer to the text element that is the center of our attention.

```
Dim objTextEl

Sub window_onLoad
  Set objTextEl = window.dialogArguments 'note this property can only be used with
                                         'windows called by the showModalDialog method
  'next line used for testing
  'set objTextEl = document.all("TestP")
```

Since `objTextEl` is declared outside of any routine, it's global to the page, just like `strOriginalText`
was in the `textman.htm` source. The first line in the `onLoad` event sets this variable to the
`window.dialogArguments` variable. Remember that we passed a reference to the text element we
wanted to modify when we call `showModalDialog`? This is where we retrieve it. Whatever is passed as
the second argument to `showModalDialog` turns up in the `dialogArguments` property of the window
object in the dialog itself.

The next bit of code just reads the `tagName` and `ID` properties of the new element and uses the
`innerText` property of the empty `<SPAN>` tags we created earlier with the appropriate value. Modifying
a portion of text on the page is this easy.

```
    strTagName = objTextEl.tagName
    If strTagName = "" Then
      document.all("spnTagName").innerText = "None"
    Else
      document.all("spnTagName").innerText = strTagName
    End If

    strID = objTextEl.ID
    If strID = "" Then
      document.all("spnIDName").innerText = "None"
    Else
      document.all("spnIDName").innerText = strID
    End If
```

Finally, we call the `UpdateDisplay` routine that we'll talk about in a second to fill in the two text area
fields with the correct `innerText` and `innerHTML` values from the object that was passed to the dialog.

```
    UpdateDisplay
End Sub
```

Changing Text with innerText and innerHTML

Once the page is loaded and the text area fields are filled with the correct text, we can worry about how
we update the text element when the Change buttons are pressed. But before this, we need to talk about
how the `<TEXTAREA>` elements get the appropriate text in the first place. This is the `UpdateDisplay`
procedure's job.

```
Sub UpdateDisplay
  document.all("txtIText").value = objTextEl.innerText
  document.all("txtIHTML").value = objTextEl.innerHTML
End Sub
```

All we do in this quick two-line routine is grab the current `innerText` and `innerHTML` values from the
text element and use them to set the `value` properties of the text areas.

So, the above code executes as the last part of the page initialization, and our dialog is ready for user-input. The eager student types some new text into one of the text area fields and presses the Change button. What happens? No matter which of the two buttons were pressed, the same thing occurs: the **UpdateProps** procedure is called.

```
Sub UpdateProps
  strButtonID = window.event.srcElement.ID
  Select Case strButtonID
    Case "btnIText"
      objTextEl.innerText = document.all("txtIText").value
    Case "btnIHTML"
      objTextEl.innerHTML = document.all("txtIHTML").value
  End Select
  UpdateDisplay
End Sub
```

This procedure, although longer than a couple of lines, is still simple. We get the **ID** of the element that caused this event from the **window.event.srcElement.ID** property. Then we use a **Select Case** statement to determine which bit of code to execute. If **btnIText** caused the event, we update the **innerText** property of the element with whatever the user has typed, and we do the same (using **innerHTML**) if **btnIHTML** was pressed. These assignment statements are the code that causes a visible change in the main page.

When the element has been updated, and before exiting, we call the same **UpdateDisplay** we just talked about to make sure that both text area fields on the dialog reflect the latest HTML in the element.

Adding New Text with the InsertAdjacent Methods

In addition to the new HTML element properties, aspiring Dynamic HTML authors can also use the new **InsertAdjacentText** and **InsertAdjacentHTML** methods. In contrast to our approach with the text areas, we chose here to implement two separate procedures. We're only going to be looking at the **InsertAdjacentText** handler in the text because the two routines are so similar.

The code for this procedure is a good teaser for the section of this chapter that covers enhanced forms–here we use the intrinsic HTML list box control like we couldn't before Dynamic HTML. To execute **InsertAdjacentText** we need to obtain the text string that indicates the position (which will be something like "BeforeBegin") and the actual string to insert.

```
Sub btnInsText_onClick
  intPosn = document.all("lstTPosn").selectedIndex
  strPosn = document.all("lstTPosn").options(intPosn).text
  strText = document.all("txtInsText").value
  objTextEl.insertAdjacentText strPosn, strText
  UpdateDisplay
End Sub
```

When **btnInsText** is clicked, we obtain a reference to the **lstTPosn** list box with the **all** collection, and then retrieve the numerical index of the currently selected item. With this number, we can access the **options** collection of the same list box, and retrieve the value of the **text** property of the specified index, which is what we want for the location string. We then directly obtain the **value** property of the text box–for this we don't need to go through two steps.

After this preparation it's a simple matter to call the **InsertAdjacentText** method and then update the display as before with **UpdateDisplay**.

Unloading the Dialog

We've covered initializing the page and setting the text via the new HTML properties and methods. The only thing that leaves in our example is handling the unloading of the form so that the changes we make are only kept if we say so. If the user presses the OK button we want the calling page to save whatever we've done, but if they press Cancel, or close the dialog by any other method, the working area on the main page should revert to whatever it was before the dialog was shown.

Fortunately, because we can use the `returnValue` property of the `window` object to return anything we want to the calling page, this is easy to accomplish.

```
Sub btnOK_onClick
  window.returnValue = "save"
  window.close
End Sub

Sub btnCancel_onClick
  window.returnValue = "restore"
  window.close
End Sub
```

The code above simply returns either "save" or "restore" to the calling page and then closes the dialog using `window.close`. We could return anything at all with `window.returnValue`–in this case we return one of these two values because we've set our calling routine up to deal with them. Our main page code only responds to `restore` and assumes `save` otherwise.

This brings us to the last thing we need to worry about. Since the main page will assume we want to keep our changes unless we specify otherwise, we need to make sure that the dialog always closes with a "restore" value unless we want to save the changes we make. If the user presses the close button next to the maximize and minimize buttons, or selects Close from the system menu, the dialog will be unloaded without either of the button routines executing. So, we need to check for this in our `onUnload` event.

```
Sub Window_onUnload
  If window.returnValue = "" Then
    'assume cancel
    window.returnValue = "restore"
  End If
End Sub
```

This code sets `returnValue` to `restore` if it hasn't been set by a button routine.

When returning values from a dialog window it's important to remember to use the `window.returnValue` property and not the `window.event.returnValue` property by mistake. The `event` object's `returnValue` property is a True / False value used to cancel an event. The `returnValue` of the `window` object, on the other hand, is a string or numeric value that is passed by a dialog back to the calling `showModalDialog` function.

An alternative to this method would have been to make our main page code assume that it should discard all changes unless it was explicitly told to save them. This would have lessened the number of lines of code we needed to write, but we chose to do it this way to demonstrate an additional Dynamic HTML technique.

Additional Example Notes

In the course of developing this example, we ran into some problems and came up with a technique that can ease debugging of custom dialog boxes. We talk about these topics in this section.

Why We Omitted outerText and outerHTML

Originally this sample included the ability to modify the `outerText` and `outerHTML` properties of the text element passed to the dialog in the same way that it allows modification of `innerText` and `innerHTML`. Unfortunately, a bug in the beta versions of Internet Explorer 4.0 that we used when developing this book forced us to remove the `outerHTML` feature from the sample. For more information on the status of this problem, check out the Wrox web site.

However, the good news is that, since adding this support to the sample is relatively easy, you can add it yourself. In short, all this addition involves is adding two new text area field and Change button combinations to the dialog box, and then adding a few new lines of code to `UpdateDisplay` and `UpdateProps`. What's more, these new lines of code don't really have to be 'new'. They just mimic the existing support for `innerText` and `innerHTML`; the only change necessary is the property and the name of the text element on the dialog.

If you do add support for `outerText` and `outerHTML`, we'd recommend rereading and keeping in mind the discussion in Chapter 4 about losing object references when these properties are used incorrectly (which isn't a bug, by the way–it's supposed to work like this!).

Testing Dialogs

HTML pages shown with the `showModalDialog` method don't have a refresh button and can't be right-clicked so that Refresh can be selected from the pop-up menu. This can make testing a new dialog rather hard because there's no easy way to get the browser to reflect the changes you make to the HTML file used for the dialog.

With our experience, we found two methods of testing dialogs. The first, and easiest, way is just to test the dialog in the browser like a normal page. It is, after all, just HTML like any other page, even if it never will be shown in response to someone typing its filename into the address bar of a browser.

However, at some point you'll probably need to test your page as a dialog. You're in this boat right away if you're using features that rely on the file being shown as a dialog, like the `dialogArguments` property of the `window` object, or if you want to test that you're returning the correct value to the code that shows your dialog. In the code for this sample that you can see in the `dialog.htm` file that is downloadable from the Wrox site, we've left the testing code (commented out, of course!) in both the page itself and the `window_onLoad` event.

When you do need to test your dialog as an actual dialog instead of a normal stand-alone HTML page, you'll need to manually remove the dialog file from the `Temporary Internet Files` folder (located underneath your `Windows` folder) each time you make a change. This will ensure that IE loads the new version instead of the old.

Alternatively, you can turn off caching for your browser by selecting Internet Options... from the View menu, clicking the Settings... button in the Temporary Internet Files frame, and then changing the Check for newer versions of stored pages radio button to Every visit to the page.

Using a Browser Window Instead of a Dialog

In many cases a dialog like the one we've talked about and experimented with in this chapter would work better if it were non-modal. For example, did you ever wish you could switch back and forth between the open dialog and the main page to see exactly what affect your changes were making? If we showed the dialog non-modally, we'd be able to do this. However, there are a few possible problems we need to keep in mind if we undertake this modification.

To start, since we know that Internet Explorer doesn't have a `showNonModalDialog` method, we need a way to show the window in the first place. This isn't a problem–the `window.open` method that's been around since IE3 will do the job nicely.

Ok, but `open` doesn't have a spot in its parameter list to pass any arguments, and we need a way to use objects in the original browser from the newly opened page. Again, the object model has an answer, and in this case it's the `opener` property of the newly opened `window` object. The `opener` property provides a reference to the `window` object that created the current window.

For example, suppose this text made up part of the original page:

```
<P ID="MyP">Here's the paragraph text on the original page.</P>
```

If we used `window.open` from this page to open a page in a new browser window, we could use the following code, **in the new page**, to print the contents of the old page's paragraph element's `innerText` property in a message box.

```
MsgBox opener.document.all("MyP").innerText
```

This takes care of the basic code modifications, and ensures that we can perform the most important parts of our design independently of how the dialog page is shown. However, this isn't all we need to consider. Other design changes may (and probably will) be necessary.

In this example, we need to think about retooling the way in which the main page knows when and if to discard changes made by the dialog. We also need to consider changing the calling code because execution will no longer be stopped while the new page is displayed. We need to think about any conflicts that might arise because both the main page and dialog can access page elements at the same time (before only one form had control at a time). While these changes aren't important, they're inherent in the transition from a modal to non-modal dialog in any environment. If you're interested in pursuing this project further you can make the change using this sample as a starting point.

Working With Forms

In the second part of this chapter, we'll be extending some of the concepts you've seen so far for using dialogs in your pages. We'll also take in some of the new features in IE4 that are under review by W3C for inclusion in the new version of HTML 4.0. The two areas we'll be looking at are:

- managing User Profile information
- building 'enhanced' forms and dialogs

Collecting Visitor Information

There are numerous occasions as you travel round the Web where you come across sites that request information about you. This might be just to send you details of their products, add you to an email list, or they may in fact be collecting marketing information to sell, or for any number of other purposes. Many users are nervous about providing information to a web page, and the proposals now under discussion by W3C are designed to make it safer and easier for users and page authors to manage this situation.

Internet Explorer 4 now provides a new object within the browser object model for just this purpose. We haven't discussed this so far, because its use is quite specialized. Now is the time to put that matter right.

The Personal Information Feature

Internet Explorer 4 allows users to set up a range of information that they are prepared to share with Web sites that they visit. This is done in the Personal Information section of the Content page in the Internet Options dialog:

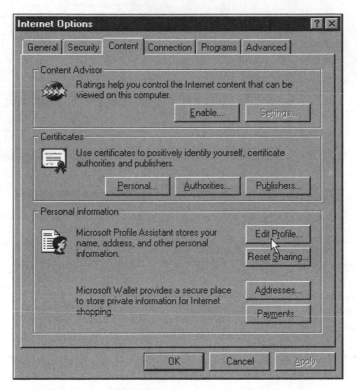

Here, they can provide a whole range of information about themselves and their company. It's a tabbed multi-page dialog, and in the next screen shot you can see the information we have entered in the Personal and Business pages:

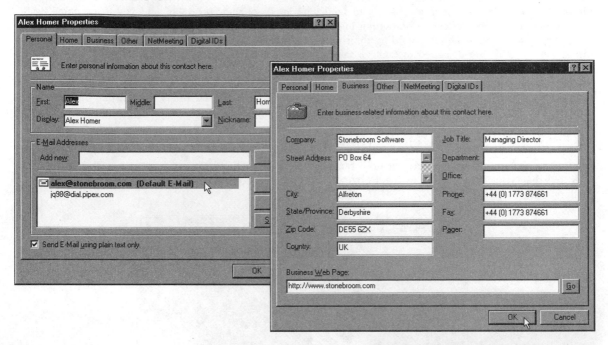

Now, when we visit a site, this information can be used in suitably coded pages, saving us from having to enter it each time. To see how, try the example page `userprof.htm` that is supplied with the samples for this book. You can run it directly from our site at `http://rapid.wrox.co.uk/ books/0707`:

Here, the page is asking for a name, address, and email address so that the requested information can be posted to the visitor. The Use my Profile Information button only appears when this page is run in Internet Explorer 4, and clicking it opens the Profile Assistant dialog. In it, the user can see the information the page is asking for, and allow or deny the use of any or all of it:

The dialog also shows who asked for the information, what they intend to do with it, and indicates in the Privacy section if the information will be sent over a secure connection. There is also a check box which enables the user to set their browser so as to always allow the checked items of information to be collected by this site:

Clicking Allow then closes the dialog, and the page can retrieve the information and fill in the text boxes on the form automatically–a real time-saver.

The userProfile Object

All this information is stored and managed by a new object within the browser hierarchy. The **navigator** object that we examined in Chapter 4 has a subsidiary object called **userProfile**. This provides methods that allow our script to read a user's profile information. It has four methods:

Method	Description
clearRequest	Clears the entire read-request queue.
addReadRequest	Adds a read request entry to the read-requests queue. Returns **True** if successful, **False** otherwise.
doReadRequest	Carries out all queued read-requests. If the site does not already have read access, the Profile Assistant dialog prompts the user to allow or deny access.
getAttribute	Returns the value of an individual request item (or 'attribute'). If access was denied, or no value available, it returns a **Null** string.

The **clearRequest** method simply clears the read-requests queue, and can be used to make sure none are pending when we come to add our own read requests:

```
navigator.userProfile.clearRequest()
```

To add a read request, we use the **addReadRequest** method any number of times. It supports the optional argument *isRequired*, which tells the Profile Assistant that this item is necessary for the entire request to be valid. This argument is not currently implemented in IE4, however:

result = navigator.userProfile.addReadRequest(*attributeName* [,*isRequired*])

attributeName is one of the standard **Vcard** sub-object property names:

Vcard.Email	Vcard.Department	Vcard.Home.Phone
Vcard.DisplayName	Vcard.Notes	Vcard.Home.Fax
Vcard.FirstName	Vcard.Office	Vcard.Business.StreetAddress
Vcard.LastName	Vcard.Homepage	Vcard.Business.City
Vcard.MiddleName	Vcard.Business.URL	Vcard.Business.State
Vcard.Cellular	Vcard.Home.StreetAddress	Vcard.Business.Country
Vcard.Gender	Vcard.Home.City	Vcard.Business.Zipcode
Vcard.JobTitle	Vcard.Home.State	Vcard.Business.Phone
Vcard.Pager	Vcard.Home.Zipcode	Vcard.Business.Fax
Vcard.Company	Vcard.Home.Country	

Vcard is a specification for a common electronic business card. It defines a format for capturing information about a person, such as their name, address, phone number, e-mail user ID, with multimedia support for photographs, sound clips, and company logos.

Executing the Read Requests

The **doReadRequest** method sends all the queued requests to the **userProfile** object, opening the Profile Assistant dialog if this site has not been granted access already. If the user has not previously set any of the items in their profile, IE4 opens the main Personal Information dialog and they can enter their profile information at this point.

The **doReadRequest** method takes a usage code which describes how the information will be used, and four other optional arguments:

```
navigator.userProfile.doReadRequest(usageCode, [friendlyName], [domain],
                                                [path], [expiration])
```

usageCode	Meaning
0	Used for system administration
1	Used for research and/or product development
2	Used for completion and support of current transaction
3	Used to customize the content and design of a site
4	Used to improve the content of site including advertisements
5	Used for notifying visitors about updates to the site
6	Used for contacting visitors for marketing of services or products
7	Used for linking other collected information
8	Used by site for other purposes
9	Disclosed to others for customization or improvement of the content and design of the site
10	Disclosed to others, who may contact you, for marketing of services and/or products
11	Disclosed to others, who may contact you, for marketing of services and/or products, but you will have the opportunity to ask a site not to do this
12	Disclosed to others for any other purpose

The *friendlyName* is the name or URL of the site requesting the information. For secure connections, this must be the URL. The *domain*, *path*, and *expiration* arguments allow the author to specify other domains that the information will be shared with (i.e. where the user will not be prompted to allow or deny the read access), and the expiry date of this sharing. It makes sense to queue all your requests before calling the **doReadRequest** method, as this prevents the Profile Assistant dialog appearing separately for each request.

Finally, we can read the values returned by the **doReadRequest** method, using multiple calls to the **getAttribute** method:

```
value = navigator.userProfile.getAttribute(attributeName)
```

How the Example Page Works

The example page we've just seen uses this technique to access the user's profile information. The first step, however, is to arrange for the button that carries out the task to only appear in IE4, and not in other browsers that don't yet support the **userProfile** object. This is relatively easy, and the section of HTML that creates the relevant part of the page looks like this:

```
<TR>
 <TD ALIGN="center">
  <SCRIPT LANGUAGE="JSCRIPT">
   <!--
    var ua = navigator.userAgent;
    if ((ua.indexOf("MSIE") != -1) & (ua.indexOf("4.") != -1))
        document.write('<INPUT TYPE="BUTTON" '
        + 'VALUE="Use my Profile Information" '
        + 'onclick="getProfile()">');
   -->
  </SCRIPT>
 </TD>
</TR>
```

The **document.write** method will only be executed if the **userAgent** property of the browser's **navigator** object includes the text **"MSIE"** and **"4."**. If it does, the HTML that creates the button is written into the page. If not, the user just gets a blank table cell.

Programming the userProfile Object

The script that does the real work is also very simple. We set a variable to refer to the **userProfile** object, and use this to add a set of **read requests** to its queue. We're not checking the return values here, though if it was important to get a particular item we could use them to tell if the read-request succeeded. Then we execute the **doReadRequest** method to actually collect the information. This is the point where the user sees the Profile Assistant dialog, and can allow or deny our request:

```
<SCRIPT LANGUAGE="JSCRIPT">
  <!--
  function getProfile()
    var blnOK;
    pr = navigator.userProfile;
    pr.clearRequest();
    blnOK = pr.addReadRequest("Vcard.FirstName");
    blnOK = pr.addReadRequest("Vcard.LastName");
    blnOK = pr.addReadRequest("Vcard.Company");
    blnOK = pr.addReadRequest("Vcard.Home.StreetAddress");
    blnOK = pr.addReadRequest("Vcard.Home.City");
    blnOK = pr.addReadRequest("Vcard.Home.State");
    blnOK = pr.addReadRequest("Vcard.Home.Zipcode");
    blnOK = pr.addReadRequest("Vcard.Home.Country");
    blnOK = pr.addReadRequest("Vcard.Email");
    pr.doReadRequest(5, "Wrox Press Limited");
    ...
```

Once we've executed **doReadRequest**, we can collect the values from the **userProfile** object's **Vcard** sub-object properties. Remember that, where information is not available or where the user has denied access, that attribute will be returned as a **null** string. We take this into account when we build up the full name from the **FirstName** and **LastName** properties:

```
   ...
   nv = pr.getAttribute("Vcard.FirstName");
   if (nv != null) nv = nv + " "
     else nv = "";
   lv = pr.getAttribute("Vcard.LastName");
   if (lv != null) nv = nv + lv;
   fm = document.forms(0);
   fm("Name").value = nv;
   fm("Company").value = pr.getAttribute("Vcard.Company");
   fm("Address").value = pr.getAttribute("Vcard.Home.StreetAddress");
   fm("Town").value = pr.getAttribute("Vcard.Home.City");
   fm("State").value = pr.getAttribute("Vcard.Home.State");
   fm("PostCode").value = pr.getAttribute("Vcard.Home.Zipcode");
   fm("Country").value = pr.getAttribute("Vcard.Home.Country");
   fm("EMail").value = pr.getAttribute("Vcard.Email");
   }
   -->
</SCRIPT>
```

That's all there is to it, although you can of course collect a lot more than just the items we've used here. However, there is one thing you may have noticed about the page we're using. It has 'hot-keys' that allow you to go straight to a text box, or set a checkbox, using the keyboard only:

Your <u>N</u>ame:	Alex Homer
C<u>o</u>mpany:	Stonebroom Software

This is just one of the new features that come under the heading of **enhanced forms**. We'll look into this topic next.

Building Client/Server Applications

One of the goals of current development trends in Web-based systems is to provide a universal client/server connection over the Internet or an Intranet, with HTTP as the basic network protocol. We've already seen one place that this is appearing, with the Remote Data Service we looked at in the previous part of the book. In fact, when it comes to a client/server application, it's usually **forms** that are the mainstay. They are used to enter information that is to be processed at the server end, and to display information back at the client where it can be edited.

True client/server applications spread the processing across both ends of the network, and possibly through business objects located at nodes within the network. The enhanced forms proposals, which are currently implemented almost in their entirety within IE4, make it easier to build client-side front-ends to server-based applications, and perform a lot of the processing on the client.

A Sample Client-Side Front-end

Here's a simple example that achieves no real purpose other than to illustrate some of the available techniques. You can run it directly from our Web site at `http://rapid.wrox.co.uk/books/0707`, or download it to run on your own system:

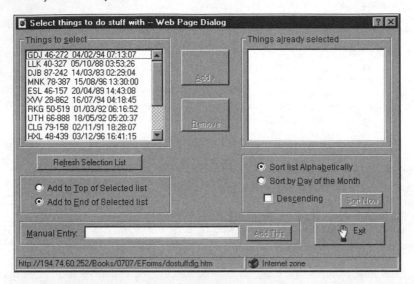

This page acts rather like some of the dialogs you see in a 'real' application, and not at all in the way you normally expect a Web page to look. The two lists allow users to select a series of items, and sort them in a range of ways. More important to us, however, is the way it illustrates the use of several new techniques. For example, when the page is first opened (as you can see in the screenshot) many of the buttons are disabled. However, clicking on the left hand list enables the Add button, and adding some entries to the right-hand list, then selecting one, enables the Remove and Sort Now buttons as well. And if we enter some text into the Manual Entry text box, the Add This button is enabled too:

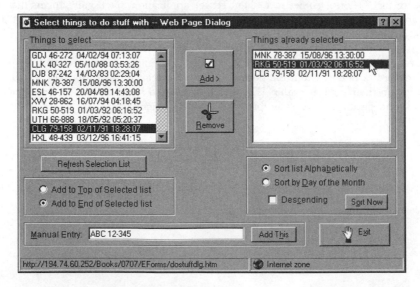

Take a look at the sample on our server, and you'll see another effect. The Add and Remove buttons have moving graphics–two simple animated GIFs. Each control also has a 'hot key', and most have pop-up tooltips as well. While you've got the page open, click the What's This? button at the top right of the window, and then click on a control on the page. A help message appears in a message box. We can get the same effect by tabbing to or clicking on a control, and then pressing the *F1* key:

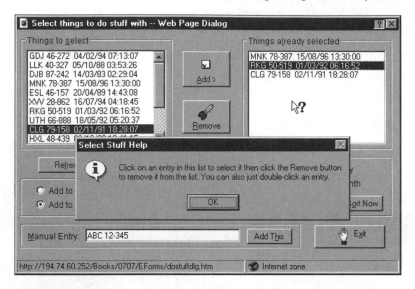

New Tags and Attributes

All this magic is courtesy of several of the proposed new tags and attributes for HTML 4.0. The new tags are `<LABEL>`, `<LEGEND>`, `<FIELDSET>`, and a variant on the `<BUTTON>` tag. New attributes include `ACCESSKEY`, `FOR`, `TITLE`, `READONLY`, `DISABLED`, and `TABINDEX`. Our sample page uses most of these, as you'll see in the next few sections of this chapter.

Using a FIELDSET to Group Controls

Most Windows applications use a frame to group together related controls, or to act as a container for several controls that set one particular value. In HTML, we group together option buttons in this way, but through the `NAME` attribute rather than the compound frame and embedded controls technique used in, for example, Microsoft Access.

The `FIELDSET` tag is designed to allow control grouping and to act as a container, but currently only does this in a graphical way in IE4. In other words, it just provides a visible frame within which the elements can be positioned in relation to the container. Our sample uses it to create the frame around the lists and the other grouped controls:

```
<! The left-hand 'select from' list >
<FIELDSET ID=fldFrom
     STYLE="position:absolute;width:215;height:165;top:5;left:5">
 <LEGEND>Things to <U>S</U>elect</LEGEND>
 <SELECT ID=lstFrom ACCESSKEY="S" TABINDEX=1 SIZE=10
     TITLE="Select a thing to do stuff with"
     STYLE="position:absolute;width:200;top:20;left:5;font-size:9pt">
 </SELECT>
</FIELDSET>
```

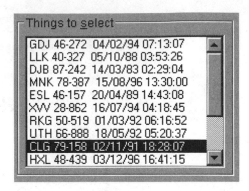

Notice the way that the **STYLE** properties for the list set it to an absolute position, but this is relative to the **FIELDSET** container. You can also see that, within the **FIELDSET**, we've used the new **LEGEND** tag. This defines the text that appears at the top of the visible frame:

Using the New BUTTON Tag Variant

The buttons on our sample page are all created with the new variant of the **BUTTON** tag, which now acts as a container for other HTML. This provides a huge number of opportunities for more exciting visual effects. In our case, we use text and an animated GIF on the Add button:

```
<BUTTON ID=btnAdd ACCESSKEY="A" TABINDEX=2 DISABLED
    TITLE="Add highlighted thing to the Selected list"
    STYLE="position:absolute;width=68;top=30;left=235;font-size:9pt">
  <IMG ID=imgbtnAdd SRC="add.gif" WIDTH=13 HEIGHT=13 VSPACE=8
    STYLE="visibility:hidden"><BR>
  <U>A</U>dd &gt;
</BUTTON>
```

Inside the opening and closing tags we define the **IMG** element for the animated GIF, plus the caption which itself contains HTML formatting tags to create the underlined letter 'A' and the '>' character. Notice also that the image is hidden (using the **visibility** style property) when the page is first loaded.

Using the New Attributes

The button we've just looked at is also disabled when the page loads, because we've included the **DISABLED** attribute. This sets the control's **disabled** property to **True**, but we can change it at will in code–as you'll see later. There is also a **READONLY** attribute that sets the **readOnly** property of appropriate controls, such as text boxes, though we don't use it in our example page.

The other new attributes that we do use include **ACCESSKEY**, which defines the 'hot-key' that will activate and set the focus to the control when pressed in conjunction with the *Alt* key (in Windows), and the **TABINDEX** attribute which defines the control's position within the tabbing order of the page. This can also be set to **-1** to omit the control from the tabbing order altogether. These attributes set the **accessKey** and **tabIndex** properties of the control, and their values can be changed at runtime by our script if required.

> *Note that the **ACCESSKEY** attribute is intended to automatically indicate the hot-key, usually by underlining it. This doesn't actually happen in IE4 at present, so we've used the **<U>** and **</U>** tags to set the underline of the appropriate letter ourselves, as you'll see if you look back at the **BUTTON** code earlier.*

The **TITLE** attribute is responsible for setting the text that is displayed in a tooltip when the mouse pauses over the control, and corresponds to the control's **title** property at runtime.

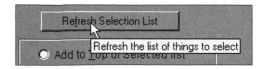

Using the New LABEL Tag

The final new tag we use in our example is the **LABEL** tag. This has a special attribute, **FOR**, which links it to a control on the page. By setting an **ACCESSKEY** for the **LABEL** tag, and specifying which element it is 'connected with', we can arrange for a 'hot-key' to switch the focus to that element.

For example, in our sample page, we use the following HTML to define the two option (or **RADIO**) buttons that control whereabouts the entry is added into the other list:

```
<! The 'Add to top or end' option buttons >
<FIELDSET ID=fldOrder
    STYLE="position:absolute;width:215;height:55; top:210; left:5">
  <INPUT TYPE=RADIO ID=optAtTop NAME=optOrder TABINDEX=6
    TITLE="Add this entry to the top of the Selected list"
    STYLE="position:absolute;top:5;left:15;background-color:silver">
  <INPUT TYPE=RADIO ID=optAtEnd NAME=optOrder TABINDEX=7 CHECKED
    TITLE="Add this entry to the end of the Selected list"
    STYLE="position:absolute;top:25;left:15;background-color:silver">
</FIELDSET>
...
<DIV STYLE="position:absolute;width:150;height:20;top:220;left:45">
  <LABEL ID=lblAtTop ACCESSKEY="T" FOR="optAtTop">
    Add to <U>T</U>op of Selected list
  </LABEL>
</DIV>
<DIV STYLE="position:absolute;width:150;height:20;top:240;left:45">
  <LABEL ID=lblAtEnd ACCESSKEY="E" FOR="optAtEnd">
    Add to <U>E</U>nd of Selected list
  </LABEL>
</DIV>
```

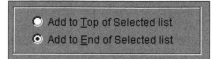

The controls themselves are defined in the **FIELDSET** section, with unique **ID**s but the same **NAME**, so that only one of them can be set at a time. However, there is no **ACCESSKEY** attribute for these controls. Instead, we've defined labels for them using the new **LABEL** tag, and set the **ACCESSKEY** and **FOR** attributes in these so that the hot-key works correctly. Again, we've used **<U>** tags to set the underline in the label text manually.

Positioning the Elements

As you'll see from the HTML source, the other feature of IE4 that makes creating a real application-like interface as a Web page possible is its absolute positioning ability. Without it, it would be almost impossible to place the controls with sufficient accuracy, and prevent them moving around as the page is resized. Of course, in our example, we use a dialog window created with the **showModalDialog** method, and prevent the user resizing it anyway–but this may not always be the case.

The Script That Makes It All Work

Many of the techniques for using HTML controls in enhanced forms are similar to existing methods, and (as you've seen in the previous section) the controls themselves are generally defined in the same way as in HTML 3.2 or earlier. The big difference is that now we can lay them out more as we would in a traditional application programming environment–and their extended features help to avoid, or at least minimize, the requirements for special ActiveX controls or Java applets.

When it comes to scripting the controls, much is again familiar. However, there is now a whole range of new events that we can react to, and many new properties that we can set–such as the **readOnly** and **disabled** properties that we mentioned earlier in this section. And of course, we can dynamically change almost all of an element's **STYLE** properties as well, in particular its position and visibility, while the page is displayed. We'll run through some of the code in our sample page, though you can always view the source to see how we've accomplished various tasks.

Setting the Input Focus and Filling the List

When the page first loads, we set the input focus to the first control using script–by default it will be on the control with a **TABINDEX** of zero. We also have to fill in the left-hand list using some random entries:

```
Sub window_onLoad()
  document.all("lstFrom").focus
  FillFromList
End Sub

Sub FillFromList()
  For j = 1 To 15
    strEntry = ""
    Randomize
    For i = 1 To 3
      strEntry = strEntry & Chr(CInt(Rnd * 25) + 65)
    Next
    strEntry = strEntry & " "
    For i = 1 To 2
      strEntry = strEntry & Chr(CInt(Rnd * 9) + 48)
    Next
    strEntry = strEntry & "-"
    For i = 1 To 3
      strEntry = strEntry & Chr(CInt(Rnd * 9) + 48)
    Next
    lngRndDate = (Rnd * 6000) + 30000
    strEntry = strEntry & "   " & FormatDateTime(lngRndDate)
    Set objNewOpt = document.createElement("OPTION")
    objNewOpt.text = strEntry
    document.all("lstFrom").options.add objNewOpt
  Next
End Sub
```

The **FillFromList** routine shown above uses the random number generator to create a string of letters and numbers, then creates a random date and adds it on the end of the string. In all, it does this 15 times to add 15 entries to the list. Notice how we add items to the **<SELECT>** list. We create a new instance of an **option** object with **document.createElement("OPTION")** then assign a value to this object's **text** property. Then we just tag it onto the end of the element's **options** collection using the **add** method.

Enabling and Disabling the Buttons

When the user selects an item in one of the lists, we need to enable either the Add or Remove button, depending on which list they clicked. We also need to enable the Sort Now button only when there are two or more items selected in the right-hand list, and the Add This button only when there is text in the Manual Entry text box. All these tasks are similar–here's the code for the 'From' list and the Sort Now and Add This buttons:

```
Sub lstFrom_onclick()
  If document.all("lstFrom").selectedIndex >= 0 Then
    document.all("btnAdd").disabled = False
    document.all("imgbtnAdd").style.visibility = "visible"
  Else
    document.all("btnAdd").disabled = True
    document.all("imgbtnAdd").style.visibility = "hidden"
  End If
End Sub

Sub SetSortButton
  If document.all("lstTo").options.length < 2 Then
    document.all("btnSort").disabled = True
  Else
    document.all("btnSort").disabled = False
  End If
End Sub

Sub txtManual_onkeyup()
  If Len(Trim(Me.value)) = 0 Then
    document.all("btnManual").disabled = True
  Else
    document.all("btnManual").disabled = False
  End If
End Sub
```

For the list, we react to the **onclick** event. The **selectedIndex** property will be **-1** if no item is selected, or the index of the selected item. All we need to do is set the **disabled** property of the button, and change the **visibility** style property of the image.

The **SetSortButton** routine is not itself an event handler, but is called when items are added to or removed from the right-hand list. It checks the number of entries by reading the **options** collection's **length** property. Only if it's two or more do we enable the button.

The third subroutine here runs when the user presses and releases a key in the Manual Entry text box. It checks the length of the string in the text box, using its **value** property, after stripping of any spaces with the **Trim** function. The button is only enabled if there is something in the text box to add.

Adding and Removing Items from the Lists

Removing items from a list is easy enough. We can get the index of the selected item from the list's **selectedIndex** property, and remove it using the **remove** method of the list's **options** collection. After we've removed an item, we run the **onclick** event code for the list to set the **disabled** property of the Remove button. We also need to run the **SetSortButton** code we saw earlier to disable the Sort Now button if there are less that two items left in the list:

```
Sub btnRemove_onclick()
  Set objFromList = document.all("lstTo")
  document.all("lstTo").options.remove objFromList.selectedIndex
  lstTo_onclick
  SetSortButton
End Sub
```

We also allow the user to remove an entry by double-clicking on it. We just run the **onclick** event code for the button:

```
Sub lstTo_ondblclick()
  btnRemove_onclick
End Sub
```

Adding an item is more complex, because we have to check out where to add it, and create the new **option** element. We get the **text** for the new option from the selected entry in our list, and look at the **checked** property of the Add To Top Of Selected List option button to see if it's to be placed at the top of the list. If so, we call the **add** method with the second optional parameter that defines the index position for the new element. In this case, the existing entries are moved down to make room for it:

```
Sub btnAdd_onclick()
  Set objFromList = document.all("lstFrom")
  Set objNewOpt = document.createElement("OPTION")
  objNewOpt.text = objFromList.options(objFromList.selectedIndex).text
  If document.all("optAtTop").checked Then
    document.all("lstTo").options.add objNewOpt, 0
  Else
    document.all("lstTo").options.add objNewOpt
  End If
  SetSortButton
End Sub
```

And again, we allow the user to double-click an entry to add it:

```
Sub lstFrom_ondblclick()
  btnAdd_onclick
End Sub
```

The other connected routine runs when the Refresh Selection List button is clicked. This needs to empty the list and then refill it with new entries. The easiest way to empty the list is to set the **length** property of the list's **options** collection to zero. Then we can set the disabled state of the Add button by running the **onclick** event code for the list, and call our **FillFromList** routine to fill it up again:

```
Sub btnRefresh_onclick()
  document.all("lstFrom").options.length = 0
  lstFrom_onclick
  FillFromList
End Sub
```

Sorting the Selected Items List

If we're programming the browser in JavaScript or JScript, we get an easy life–at least when sorting items into order is concerned. The built-in **sort** method of the **array** object does all the hard work. In VBScript, we don't have such luxuries. Mind you, we don't end up seeing double with all those curly braces scattered around in our code either!

When we come to sort the contents of a list box control using JavaScript or JScript, the easiest way is to sort the underlying **options** array. In VBScript, however, where the **options** collection doesn't have a **sort** method, we can copy the entries into our own array and sort them there, then copy them back into the **options** collection in the new order.

This is what we've done in our page, although we're a little ashamed to admit that the sorting algorithm is just a basic bubble sort. This code first creates a large array, gets the settings of the 'sort order' options from the controls on the page, then defines a reference to the list's **options** collection and the index of the last entry it contains:

```
Sub btnSort_onclick()
  Dim aList(500)
  blnByDate = document.all("optDateSort").checked
  blnReverse = document.all("chkRevSort").checked
  Set objList = document.all("lstTo").options
  intNum = objList.length - 1
  ...
```

Now we can copy the existing values for the list into our array:

```
  ...
  For i = 0 To intNum
    aList(i) = objList(i).text
  Next
  ...
```

Then comes the bubble sort. Look how we use the option settings we saved in the variables **blnByDate** and **blnReverse** to decide which of each pair of entries comes first in the list:

```
  ...
  Do
    blnDidSwap = False        'if no swaps, we're finished
    For i = 1 To intNum
      blnSwapThese = False
      If blnByDate Then
        strFirst = Mid(aList(i - 1), 12)    'use date part of string
        strSecond = Mid(aList(i), 12)
      Else
        strFirst = Left(aList(i - 1), 10)   'use first (text) part
        strSecond = Left(aList(i), 10)
      End If
      If blnReverse Then
        blnSwapThese = (strFirst < strSecond)  'sets blnSwapThese to
      Else                                     'true if they need to
        blnSwapThese = (strFirst > strSecond)  'be swapped over
      End If
      If blnSwapThese Then
        strTemp = aList(i)
        aList(i) = aList(i - 1)
        aList(i - 1) = strTemp
        blnDidSwap = True     'did a swap ...
      End If
    Next
  Loop While blnDidSwap            '... so go round again
  ...
```

Once we've sorted our array, we copy the contents back into the **options** collection of the list:

```
    ...
    For i = 0 To intNum
      objList(i).text = aList(i)
    Next
  End Sub
```

Providing Help in a Web Dialog

One thing that the extensions to Dynamic HTML make a lot easier is the way we can provide help and tips for users that work with our applications. We've done this in our example page by providing pop-up tool-tips, and context-sensitive help from the What's This? button and the *F1* Help key.

All we have to do to react to the What's This? button and the *F1* key is harness the **onhelp** event that occurs for most visible elements. By reacting to it at **document** level, and using the event object's **srcElement** property to discover the 'active' element, we can display an appropriate message.

Remember that once you've got the appropriate text, you could use a new browser window, an **IFRAME** element, or an ActiveX control to display it in a way more like a true Windows application. We actually experimented with using a pale yellow **DIV** element, but found that it didn't display correctly for list boxes and was difficult to position properly for clicks on **LABEL** elements. So, here's how it works in our application, using a message box to display the text:

```
  Sub document_onhelp()      'Window's help event occurred
    'may be with the ? button at top of the window, or by pressing F1
    'first set the default help message
    strHelpMesg = "No more information is available for this item."
    'find source element ID and remove first three letters. This means (for
    'example) that lblDateSort and optDateSort will show the same message.
    strSourceID = Mid(window.event.srcElement.id, 4)
    Select Case strSourceID
      Case "From"
        strHelpMesg = "Click on an entry in this list ... etc."
      Case "To"
        strHelpMesg = "Click on an entry in this list ... etc."
    ... code removed here ...
    End Select
    MsgBox strHelpMesg, vbInformation, "Select Stuff Help"
    window.event.cancelBubble = True
    window.event.returnValue = False
  End Sub
```

Remember to include the last line that sets the **event** object's **returnValue** property to **False**, otherwise you'll get the Internet Explorer Help window popping up as well.

Summary

We've ranged over several important Dynamic HTML programming topics in this chapter, using generally more complex scripting than you've seen in earlier parts of the book. It's the combination of script code and the almost unlimited access to the contents of the page and the browser that offers all these exciting new possibilities.

It also helps to drive the process whereby the browser can become a true programming environment, and take its rightful place as the interface for the more complex client/server applications that are starting to appear both on the Web, and on corporate Intranets and Extranets.

In this chapter we have:

- seen how to work with an example that shows Dynamic HTML's new text manipulation properties, the **TextRange** object, and the ability to create and show custom modal dialog boxes.

- discovered that that strings and even object references can be passed as a parameter to custom dialogs when the dialog is show with **showModalDialog**.

- gained more experience with the many different techniques for text manipulation that Dynamic HTML makes possible, like changing the appearance and properties of existing page elements, and adding any kind of new page element.

- seen how the new **userProfile** object, in conjunction with the browser Profile Assistant, can make collecting information from a Web page much easier from the user's point of view.

- briefly discussed the new proposals for enhanced forms in HTML 4.0, and the new tags and attributes they provide.

- seen how easy it is to create really interactive, forms based Web application front ends using Dynamic HTML, especially suited for the growing impetus toward real Web client/server programming.

We will continue the client/server theme later in Part 3, where we'll look at how Dynamic HTML, and the new features in Internet Explorer 4, can combine with server-based programming to produce really interactive applications. However, first we'll look at how the multimedia controls included with IE4 can be programmed and how we can include them within our Dynamic HTML applications.

Introduction to Multimedia

Now that you have seen how you can manipulate the HTML tags on your page using VBScript or JScript to make a page Dynamic, what other goodies has Microsoft added to IE4 to help make your web pages spring to life?

The advancement of user interfaces over the past 20 years has been set back 10 years by HTML. All of those lush, graphical interfaces you've grown accustomed to have been thrown out of the window, so that you can slowly download a page of mainly text, and maybe some animated graphics, over the Internet and view it on your computer. Proprietary solutions, such as Macromedia's Director and Flash products, have brought enhancements to the user interface of web pages. However, you're still restricted to using vendor tools, and then having to download a plug-in or ActiveX control to your browser just to be able to use it.

With the advent of IE4, you now have the ability to enhance the Dynamic HTML pages that you can create, both with some new enhancements to HTML, and with some specialized multimedia controls that Microsoft is has included with IE4. And these new controls will also be downloadable, so that users of IE3 and other ActiveX-compliant browsers will be able to take advantage of them as well.

In this chapter, we will give you a very brief introduction to the multimedia technology that IE4 offers and then take a look at the addition of filters and transitions to Cascading Style Sheets in detail. So we'll cover:

- Introduction to multimedia in IE4
- Visual Filters Effects
- Style Sheet Transitions
- Page Transitions

What's New In IE4

IE4 offers a myriad of new effects and controls to allow the users to enhance their web pages. It is the first release to actually have multimedia capabilities built into the browser. The multimedia features are all part of Microsoft's DirectX technology, which is a collection of APIs and programming tools that aim to standardize the way in which all multimedia is developed. The features in IE4 can be broken down into two types, filters/effects that can be added to Cascading Style Sheets and a set of ActiveX controls that form two components of DirectX. These are:

- **DirectAnimation**: as the name might indicate, it is a set of four controls that aid the developer with the creation of animated multimedia pages, and that are programmable in Dynamic HTML, scripting languages and Java.

- **DirectShow**: is just one control, ActiveMovie. It is used to add movies and sound to web pages. It does this by downloading audio and video files in **streams** (files which are downloaded in real time, as one continuous stream, rather than as one finite file).

There are many other DirectX components, some of which can be added to IE4 as plug-ins and such like, but these are beyond the scope of the book.

We'll cut discussion of these two components short, as in this chapter we're only going to be interested in the effects and transitions that can be added to Cascading Style Sheets. We'll take a look at them first, because they're easier to understand and add to your pages than the DirectAnimation and DirectShow controls, which we'll discuss in the next chapter.

Visual Filter Effects

In web page design until now, it has been the responsibility of the web page author to define the exact look of images and text. If a web page design called for some semi-transparent text over a graphic, then the author would have to turn to a graphical designer for such an image. The designer would use a tool such as Adobe Photoshop to create an image with the text appearing as semi-transparent over a background graphic. One of the most powerful features of Photoshop is the wide range of filters that are available, and can be used to manipulate images. So now we have an image with text over a graphic that is handed back to the web page author. Everything looks great. That is, until the author needs to change the text in the document. What can he do? Well, the text is contained in the image file. The image file was created in Photoshop, using its filters. So the only way to change the text is to go back to the graphics designer and have them change the entire image. Doesn't sound very efficient, does it?

What if you could place the background image and the text into your web page separately, and then make the text semi-transparent on the fly? Well, with the Visual Filters Effects that are part of the Cascading Style Sheets in IE4, you can do just that. There is a wide range of visual filters that you can apply to different objects on your web page.

Filters through CSS

In earlier chapters, you have seen how you can use style sheets to affect the look of your web page. By taking a plain text block and applying a style sheet to it, you can change nearly everything about that block of text. From changing its color or font, to moving it to another place on the page, to changing the text itself, cascading style sheets give you a very powerful tool to shape the look of your web page.

Now, Microsoft has added very powerful visual effects capabilities to style sheets. So what do you gain from this? Since they are a core part of IE4, there are no ActiveX controls or Java applets that need to be downloaded. Since they are part of Cascading Style Sheets, you can effectively separate the appearance of the page from the content of the page, making updates and modifications much easier. And since they are a proposed standard to the W3C as part of the HTML 4.0 specification, you will also have a solution that is portable to all browsers that support the 4.0 specification.

Adding Filters to your Page

Filters are accessed through the `filter` keyword, which is a component of style sheets. You have a number of ways that you can define filters for your objects. The `filter` keyword can be part of any normal style definition, as in this example

```
<STYLE>
DIV {height:10; width:40; "filter:flipv() Shadow(color=#00FF00)"}
</STYLE>
```

> **In order for a filter to work properly, there must also be an explicit height and width style for the object.**

Just as you have height and width styles being set for all `<DIV>` blocks on this page, you have now enabled two filters on all `<DIV>` blocks as well. Basically, anywhere you can put style sheet information throughout an HTML page, you can put visual filters. If you want to add a filter to a single element on a page, you can do this:

```
<DIV id=myFilterTest style="height:10;width:40;filter:flipv() shadow(color=#00FF00)">
Let's flip and shadow</DIV>
```

As these examples show, you can add multiple filters to a particular style. This is known as **filter chaining**. Each filter will be successively applied to the element, and the final result is what is displayed in the browser. Filters are chained together with spaces separating each individual filter. Once you have added filters to your element, you can use scripting to further control the filter and its characteristics.

Script Control of Filters

Once you have added filters to an element, you can manipulate each filter through a `filters` collection that each element with associated filters has. This `filters` collection can be accessed in the two ways that any collection can be accessed. First, you can use the ordinal position in the collection. For example, in the above example, to access the shadow filter, you can do

```
shadowFilt = myFilterTest.filters.item(1)
```

Once you have a reference to the filter, you can make changes to any of its properties

```
shadowFilt.color = &hFF00FF
```

This will change the color of the shadow from green to fuschia. If you are using VBScript, then you can use the name of the filter, instead of its ordinal value.

```
shadowFilt = myFilterTest.filters.item("shadow")
```

Or

```
shadowFilt = myFilterTest.filters("shadow")
```

Then just modify the property that you want using the new object reference that `shadowFilt` now holds.

```
shadowFilt.color = &hFF00FF
```

Or just

```
myFilterTest.filters.item("shadow").color = &hFF00FF
```

This method of accessing filter properties is the best method to use if you are working with properties that have numerical values, like color. You do not have to perform any string manipulations to set the property using the style object, as you will see now.

In addition to modifying the properties of each individual filter, you can access the entire filter set through the **style** object. The **style** object has a **filter** property that contains the string representation of the active filters. If you were to execute this code in a page containing a filter on the **myFilterTest** object, you would see:

```
dim strFilter
strFilter = myFilterTest.style.filter
```

The contents of **strFilter** variable are now "**flipv() shadow(color=#00FF00)**". Since you are able to both read and write this filter property, you now have the ability to dynamically change the filters that are applied to an element. If we want to change the current filter to a **fliph()** filter, all that we would need to do is:

```
myFilterTest.style.filter = "fliph()"
```

The two previous filters, **flipv()** and **shadow()**, would no longer operate on this element. The new filter, **fliph()**, would take effect immediately. If you wanted to access the properties of this new filter, you would use the same steps as above:

```
myFilters.filters.item("fliph").enabled = false
```

Filter Effects

Now that you have seen a bit about how to add filters to your web page, and how to manipulate their properties using script, let's take a look at what filters are you can use. Up until now, you have seen three: **fliph()**, **flipv()**, and **shadow()**

Filter effect	Description
Alpha	Sets a uniform transparency level.
Blur	Creates the impression of moving at high speed.
Chroma	Makes a specific color transparent.
Drop Shadow	Creates a solid silhouette of the object.
FlipH	Creates a horizontal mirror image.
FlipV	Creates a vertical mirror image.
Glow	Adds radiance around the outside edges of the object.
Grayscale	Drops color information from the image.
Invert	Reverses the hue, saturation, and brightness values.
Light	Projects a light source onto an object.

Filter effect	Description
Mask	Creates a transparent mask from an object.
Shadow	Creates an offset solid silhouette.
Wave	Creates a sine wave distortion along the x-axis.
Xray	Shows just the edges of the object.

Alpha

The alpha filter allows you to adjust the opacity level of your object. This filter is an **alpha channel** effect. The term alpha channel actually comes out of the graphic design world. An alpha channel is a grayscale version of the image to which it is attached. The value of each pixel in the alpha channel regulates the intensity of that pixel's color in the image. In effect, if a mask were fully transparent, a red pixel would have full intensity, in other words pure red, and if the mask is completely opaque, then this same red pixel will not appear at all.

This filter will allow you to composite two objects together and selectively allow a certain percentage of the bottom object to be shown through the top object. Or you can place an object on a page that has a background image, and use this filter to allow some of the background image to show through your object. The alpha filter can be set to a constant opacity across the whole object, or you can give it a radial or linear gradient. To add this effect:

```
Alpha(Opacity=opacity, FinishOpacity=finishopacity, Style=style, StartX=startX,
StartY=startY, FinishX=finishX, FinishY=finishY)
```

Parameter	Description	Values	
`Opacity`	Percentage of opacity	0 100	No opacity, object is invisible Completely opaque, as if no filter was applied
`FinishOpacity`	Ending level of opacity – used with gradient filters	0 100	No opacity, object is invisible Completely opaque, as if no filter was applied
`Style`	Type of gradient to be applied	0 1 2	Uniform opacity, default value Radial gradient, starting at the center of the object using the Opacity parameter Rectangular gradient
`StartX`	X coordinate for Rectangular gradient to begin	Pixels with respect to the object receiving the effect	
`StartY`	Y coordinate for Rectangular gradient to begin	Pixels with respect to the object receiving the effect	
`FinishX`	X coordinate for Rectangular gradient to end	Pixels with respect to the object receiving the effect	
`FinishY`	Y coordinate for Rectangular gradient to end	Pixels with respect to the object receiving the effect	

Here is a short example that shows what an image looks like with and without the alpha filter applied.

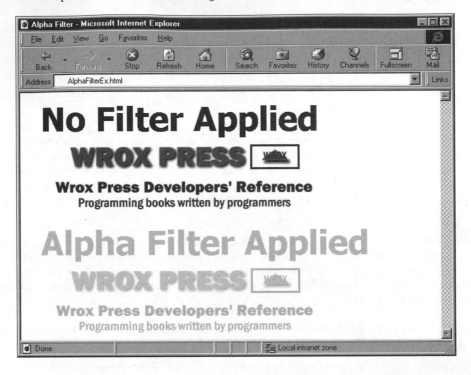

This example and code and indeed all examples in this chapter can be found on the Rapid Server at
`http://rapid.wrox.co.uk/books/0707`

Notice how both the image and the text are affected by the filter. This is because we are setting the filter to the `<DIV>` block containing both the text and the image.

```
<HTML>
<HEAD>
    <TITLE>Alpha Filter</TITLE>
</HEAD>

<BODY>

<DIV ID="divNoFIlter" STYLE="POSITION:absolute; WIDTH:430; HEIGHT:150; TOP:10;
LEFT:5%; font-size:38pt;font-family:Tahoma;font-weight:700; color:blue;">
No Filter Applied
<IMG ID="Image3" STYLE="Width:400; height:103; POSITION:RELATIVE; LEFT:20; TOP:10"
SRC="wpdr.gif">
</DIV>

<DIV ID="divAlphaFIlter" STYLE="POSITION:absolute; WIDTH:550; HEIGHT:150; TOP:200;
LEFT:5%; font-size:38pt; font-family:Tahoma; font-weight:700; color:blue;
FILTER:Alpha(Opacity=20);">
Alpha Filter Applied
```

Here is the only difference between the two `<DIV>` blocks. This block has a `Filter` style attached to it. The filter type is the Alpha filter, with an opacity of 20%, which causes 80% of the background to show through.

```
<IMG ID="Image3" STYLE="Width:400; height:103; POSITION:RELATIVE; LEFT:20; TOP:10"
SRC="wpdr.gif">
</DIV>

</BODY>
</HTML>
```

If you have ever tried to perform the same effect with tools other than IE4, then you know how difficult creating and using this effect can be. Whether you have used Photoshop to create the effect offline in a static bitmap, or have written your own alpha channel drawing method, you will agree that the IE4 is the simplest and most powerful way yet to create this eye-catching effect.

Blur

The blur effect can be used to give an object on your page the impression that it is moving at high speed, by giving the object a blurred appearance. The technique of using image blurs to enhance animation has become a new trick in an animator's repertoire. If you want to move an object across the page and give the user the impression of perceived speed, then a blur applied to the object can greatly strengthen the impression. In the TV show *Lois & Clark*, Superman's image is blurred to make it appear that he is travelling at very high speeds. Interactive CDs, such as Disney's *Toy Story*, use motion blur to add a more lifelike feel to the presentation.

Under the covers, the blur filter averages the pixels of the visible object for a specified length and direction, creating the impression that the object is moving at high speed. To add this filter to an object, you would add this to the object's style sheet:

`Blur(Add = add, Direction = direction, Strength = strength)`

Parameter	Description	Values	
`Add`	Adds the original image back to the blurred image. Especially useful with fonts.	1 0	Original image added back Only the blurred image is shown
`Direction`	Direction that the motion blur will be drawn with respect to the object.	Direction in degrees, in 45 degree increments 0 Straight Up 45 Up and to the right 90 Right 180 Straight Down etc…	
`Strength`	Number of pixels that the blur will extend	Long Integer	

Let's take a look at a comparison of two blocks that are moving across the screen. You will have to look at the page in your browser to truly see what the blur effect adds to motion of objects. Here is what it looks like as the blocks are moving.

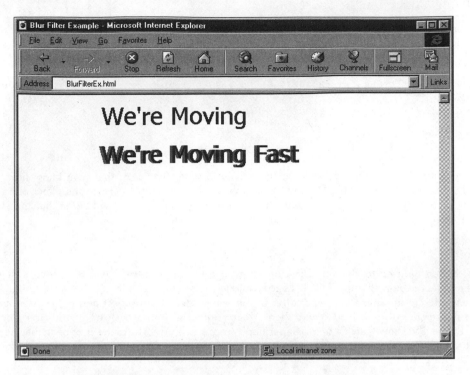

It is very simple to achieve this effect on your page.

```
<HTML>
<HEAD>
    <TITLE>Blur Filter Example</TITLE>
</HEAD>
<SCRIPT LANGUAGE="VBSCRIPT">

Sub MoveLeft
    dim leftPos
    leftPos = MoveText.Style.pixelLeft
```

There are three style properties that can give you the left position. Since we want to be able to perform mathematical operations on the value that we get, we need to use the `pixelLeft` property. This property always returns the left position in pixels, whereas the `left` property returns the distance with units as a string. Finally, the `posLeft` property returns the value of the left property in its last specified units, which we'll also use.

```
leftPos = leftPos + 3
if leftPos > 400 then
        leftPos = 0
```

Once the left position of the objects reach 400 pixels, we will move them back over to the left edge of the page. Setting their left position back to 0 does this.

```
end if
MoveText.Style.posLeft = leftPos
MoveTextFilt.Style.posLeft = leftPos
```

We will move both objects the same distance to the left. Since they are both moving together across the screen, we can use the same left position.

```
foo = Window.SetTimeOut("Call MoveLeft", 30, "VBScript")
```

By using the **SetTimeOut** method of the window object, we can repeatedly call this method. In this case, we are calling the method every 30 seconds.

```
end Sub

Sub Window_OnLoad
    call MoveLeft
```

We need to explicitly call the **MoveLeft** method the first time. Each subsequent time will be called via the **SetTimeOut** method.

```
end sub
</SCRIPT>

<BODY>

<DIV ID="divNoFilter" STYLE="POSITION:absolute; WIDTH:430; HEIGHT:50; TOP:10; LEFT:5%;
font-size:28pt;font-family:Tahoma; color:blue;">
<SPAN ID=MoveText STYLE="POSITION:relative; LEFT:1;"> We're Moving</SPAN>
</DIV>

<DIV ID="divFilter" STYLE="POSITION:absolute; WIDTH:430; HEIGHT:50; TOP:70; LEFT:5%;
font-size:28pt; font-family:Tahoma; color:blue; Filter:blur(add=1, direction=270,
strength=5)">
```

The only difference between the **divFilter** block and the **divNoFilter** block is the Filter addition to the **style** property. We have added a blur filter to this object. By selecting a direction of 270 degrees, which is opposite to the direction that we are moving the text, we will make it appear that the blur is trailing the letters as they move across the page. The **add** property causes the original text to appear on top of the blurred image. The blur is 5 pixels long, as determined by the **strength** property.

```
<SPAN ID=MoveTextFilt STYLE="POSITION:relative; LEFT:1;"> We're Moving Fast</
SPAN>
</DIV>

</BODY>
</HTML>
```

The blur filter is a very powerful filter that can be used in many situations. One place that it can be used very effectively is in doing text headlines. By adding a blur to a text headline, you can achieve a very dramatic effect, at no cost in terms of downloading a graphics file.

Chroma

The chroma effect allows you to select one color in your object and make it transparent. This is very similar to creating a transparent GIF with one exception. When using a transparent GIF, the transparency must be defined when the GIF is created and it cannot be easily changed without modifying the original file. The chroma filter will allow you to select one color, which will then be made transparent when the object is displayed.

To add this filter to an object, you would add this to the object's style sheet:

```
Chroma(Color = color)
```

Parameter	Description	Values
Color	Color that will be rendered transparent	Color expressed as #RRGGBB, where RR is the red hex value, GG is the green hex value, and BB is the blue hex value.

For example, if the filter was defined as such:

```
{STYLE="FILTER:Chroma(Color = #FF0000)"}
```

then all areas in the target object that had a color of pure red, (255,0,0), would be made transparent.

One note of caution when working with images that have been dithered or compressed. Dithering is the reduction of the color depth of an image, which is usually done to reduce file size, or to provide a common color palette. When an image is compressed, an area that was once a pure continuous color may now have multiple color artifacts in it. Since the chroma filter only makes one specific color transparent, you could end up with areas in the image that appear to be the transparent color, but really are slightly different. Your eye may not be able to tell the difference, but the chroma effects filter can, and wouldn't make those areas transparent.

So when creating images for use with the chroma filter, you need to make sure that all of the areas that you want to be transparent are the same color, and that you set that color as the transparent color when creating the filter. In general, GIF images, since their compression is lossless, are the best candidates for chroma images. The chroma filter also doesn't work well on anti-aliased images and text. In the anti-aliasing process, sharp lines are smoothed by blending the color of the line with the colors of surrounding pixels. When working with GIF images, it is also a good idea to use the 216-color browser-safe color palette. This will prevent the images from being dithered when they are displayed on a browser with 8-bit color.

Let's take a look at a quick example that shows an image with and without a chroma filter applied to it. Here is what the final page will look like when it is loaded into IE4.

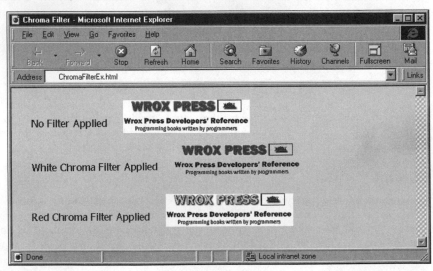

As you will see when we look at the HTML source for this example, the same GIF file is used for each of the three images. In the first image, no filter is applied. In the second, a pure white filter is applied. In the third, a red filter is applied. We've made the background yellow (sic gray) so that you can see the white chroma filter. You can also see by looking at the third image an example of what happens when anti-aliased text is affected by the chroma filter. Even though we selected the color of the text to be our chroma color, the anti-aliasing that had been performed on the text previously becomes very evident.

```
<HTML>
<HEAD>
    <TITLE>Chroma Filter</TITLE>
</HEAD>

<BODY BGCOLOR="yellow">

<DIV ID="divNoFilter" STYLE="POSITION:absolute; WIDTH:430; HEIGHT:60; TOP:10; LEFT:5%;
font-size:12pt; font-family:Tahoma; font-weight:300; color:blue;">
No Filter Applied
<IMG ID="Image1" STYLE="Width:200; height:52; POSITION:RELATIVE; LEFT:20; TOP:10"
SRC="logo_noTrans.gif">
</DIV>

<DIV ID="divChromaFilter" STYLE="POSITION:absolute; WIDTH:430; HEIGHT:70; TOP:80;
LEFT:5%; font-size:12pt; font-family:Tahoma; font-weight:300; color:blue;">
White Chroma Filter Applied
<IMG ID="Image2" STYLE="Width:200; height:52; POSITION:RELATIVE; LEFT:20; TOP:10;
FILTER:Chroma(Color=#FFFFFF);" SRC="logo_noTrans.gif">
</DIV>

<DIV ID="divRedChromaFIlter" STYLE="POSITION:absolute; WIDTH:430; HEIGHT:70; TOP:160;
LEFT:5%; font-size:12pt; font-family:Tahoma; font-weight:300; color:blue;">
Red Chroma Filter Applied
<IMG ID="Image3" STYLE="Width:200; height:52; POSITION:RELATIVE; LEFT:20; TOP:10;
FILTER:Chroma(Color=#E70000);" SRC="logo_noTrans.gif">
</DIV>

</BODY>
</HTML>
```

As you can see in the HTML source, each `<DIV>` block is identical, except for the `FILTER` style. The image in the first block, `divNoFilter`, has no filter applied to it. The image called `logo_noTrans.gif` is displayed exactly the same way it is stored. As you can see, there is no transparency information stored in the file. The second block uses a chroma filter to make all of the pure white areas transparent, allowing the background to show through. The third block makes all of the color #FF0000 transparent. Since we wanted to make the red-colored text transparent, we will need to use a 3rd party image tool, like Photoshop, to determine the exact color of the text. This was determined to be (255,0,0), which converts to a #RRGGBB value of #FF0000. If it had been even slightly different such as (254,0,0) then the filter wouldn't have worked.

There are many other possible uses of this effect. One example could be an image that looks one way, but, when you add another color to it, looks different. You could use the chroma filter, along with dynamic script control to enable and disable the filter, to create a simple animated effect. The chroma filter can also be used for making dragged images appear somewhat transparent while the mouse pointer is being held down, just like real drag and drop.

Drop Shadow

This effect will create a solid image of the object that you are applying the filter to and display it behind the object. By changing the offset of this solid image, you can create the visual impression of depth, where the object seems to be at some height above the page, and is casting a shadow on the page below it. By controlling the offset values, which can be positive or negative, you can affect what angle the perceived light is coming from as well as how high the object is off the page.

This is probably the most common and useful of all of the filters that are available in CSS. Many web sites now use graphical images for headlines and titles, just to achieve the "drop caps" or "drop shadow" effects. By using this filter, you can achieve the same effect, and gain a speed improvement in download time, as well as gaining the ability to quickly and easily change the actual text of the headline or title.

To add this filter to an object, you would add this to the object's style sheet:

```
DropShadow(Color=color, OffX=offX, OffY=offY, Positive=positive)
```

Parameter	Description	Values
Color	Color of the drop shadow. You should take care to make sure that this color, when set against the background, gives the appearance of a shadow.	Color expressed as #RRGGBB, where RR is the red hex value, GG is the green hex value, and BB is the blue hex value.
OffX	Number of pixels the drop shadow is offset from the visual object, along the X-axis.	*Pixels* – Positive move the drop shadow to the right. Negative to the left.
OffY	Number of pixels the drop shadow is offset from the visual object, along the Y-axis.	*Pixels* – Positive move the drop shadow down. Negative move the shadow up.
Positive	Determines if transparent pixels cast a drop shadow as well	*True* – All non-transparent pixels cast a shadow *False* – All pixels in object cast a shadow

Shadow

The Shadow effect can be used to create a shadow for an object on your page. The difference between the Shadow effect and the Drop Shadow effect is not very great. The Drop Shadow gives you more control over the placement of the location of the shadow. The Shadow effect can be placed in one of 8 directions from the original object, and the developer has no control over the distance that the shadow is from the object. To add this filter to an object, you would add this to the object's style sheet:

```
Shadow(Color=color, Direction=direction)
```

Parameter	Description	Values
`Color`	Color of the shadow. You should take care to make sure that this color, when set against the background, gives the appearance of a shadow.	Color expressed as #RRGGBB, where RR is the red hex value, GG is the green hex value, and BB is the blue hex value.
`Direction`	Direction that the shadow should be drawn from the object. Defaults to 225, which is down and to the left.	*Degrees* – Specified in 45-degree increments. 0 Straight up 45 Up and to the right 90 Right 135 Down and to the right 180 Straight down 225 Down and to the left 270 Left 315 Up and to the left

Let's take a look a quick example that shows an image in two states. First, the image will appear with a DropShadow filter. Next, it will have a Shadow filter applied to it. Here is what the final page will look like when it is loaded into IE4.

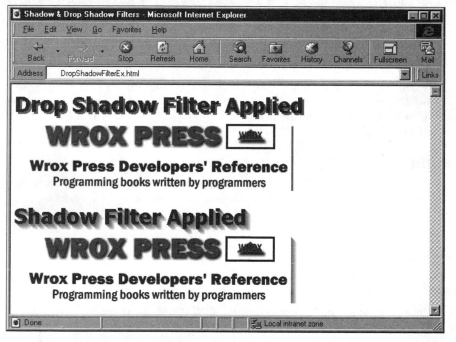

Now, let's take a look at the source code for this example

```
<HTML>
<HEAD>
    <TITLE>Shadow & Drop Shadow Filters</TITLE>
</HEAD>
```

```
<BODY>

<DIV ID="divDropShadow" STYLE="POSITION:absolute; WIDTH:500; HEIGHT:150; TOP:10;
LEFT:5; font-size:24pt;font-family:Tahoma;font-weight:700;
color:blue;FILTER:DropShadow(Color=#808080, OffX=3, OffY=3, Positive=1);">
Drop Shadow Filter Applied
<IMG ID="Image2" STYLE="Width:400; height:103; POSITION:RELATIVE; LEFT:20; TOP:10"
SRC="wpdr.gif">
</DIV>

<DIV ID="divShadow" STYLE="POSITION:absolute; WIDTH:500; HEIGHT:150; TOP:180; LEFT:5;
font-size:24pt;font-family:Tahoma;font-weight:700;
color:blue;FILTER:Shadow(Color=#909090, Direction=135);">
Shadow Filter Applied
<IMG ID="Image2" STYLE="Width:400; height:103; POSITION:RELATIVE; LEFT:20; TOP:10"
SRC="wpdr.gif">
</DIV>

</BODY>
</HTML>
```

In this example, we are creating a drop shadow on the first **<DIV>** block. By setting the **Positive** parameter to **true**, we are causing only the non-transparent pixels to cast a shadow. The shadow is being cast 3 pixels down and 3 pixels to the right of the original object. The tricky part in creating this drop shadow was determining the color that the shadow should be. Since the shadow is being cast on the background, then the color of the shadow should be a darker version of the background. The background on this page is a light gray texture. By selecting a medium gray for the drop shadow, the effect is made to look more realistic.

The second **<DIV>** block has a Shadow filter applied to it. The color of this filter is a slightly different gray to the one used by the Drop Shadow filter. As with the Drop Shadow filter, you need take care over your choice of the color that is used for the shadow. The direction parameter is set to 135, which gives a shadow down and to the right.

Flip Horizontal

This effect flips the source object in the horizontal plane, which is the same effect as looking at the object in a mirror. To add this filter to an object, you would add this to the object's style sheet:

FlipH()

This filter has no parameters.

Flip Vertical

This effect flips the source object in the vertical plane, which gives the visual effect of looking at the object upside down. To add this filter to an object, you would add this to the object's style sheet:

FlipV()

Just as the Flip Horizontal effect, this filter has no parameters. Let's take a look at an example of using the Flip Vertical and Flip Horizontal effects. This example will also show how filters can be chained together, to combine effects. Here is what the effects look like:

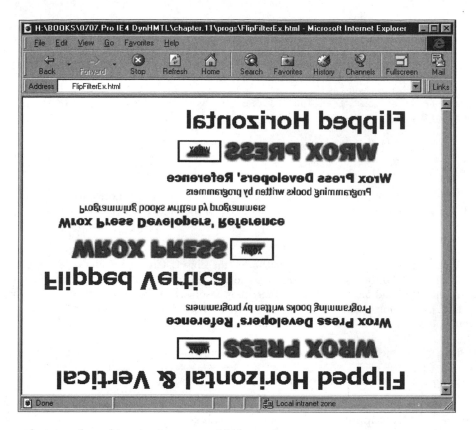

The source code to produce this page is very straightforward

```
<HTML>
<BODY>

<DIV ID="divHorizontal" STYLE="POSITION:absolute; WIDTH:550; HEIGHT:150; TOP:10;
LEFT:5%;  font-size:28pt; font-family:Tahoma; font-weight:700; color:blue;
FILTER:FlipH();">
Flipped Horizontal
<IMG ID="Image1" STYLE="Width:400; height:103; POSITION:RELATIVE; LEFT:20; TOP:10"
SRC="wpdr.gif">
</DIV>
```

This filter style will flip the image from side to side, making the object read from right to left.

```
<DIV ID="divVertical" STYLE="POSITION:absolute; WIDTH:550; HEIGHT:150; TOP:180;
LEFT:5%;  font-size:28pt; font-family:Tahoma; font-weight:700; color:blue;
FILTER:FlipV();">
Flipped Vertical
<IMG ID="Image2" STYLE="Width:400; height:103; POSITION:RELATIVE; LEFT:20; TOP:10"
SRC="wpdr.gif">
</DIV>
```

This filter style will flip the image on its horizontal axis, making the object look upside down.

```
<DIV ID="divBoth" STYLE="POSITION:absolute; WIDTH:550; HEIGHT:150; TOP:340; LEFT:5%;
font-size:28pt; font-family:Tahoma; font-weight:700; color:blue; FILTER:FlipH()
FlipV()">
Flipped Horizontal & Vertical
<IMG ID="Image2" STYLE="Width:400; height:103; POSITION:RELATIVE; LEFT:20; TOP:10"
SRC="wpdr.gif">
</DIV>

</BODY>
</HTML>
```

The last effect is an example of filter chaining. The object will have both a horizontal AND a vertical flip applied to it. If you look at the visual example, it looks as if the object as been rotated 180 degrees.

Glow

This effect adds a visual radiance around the outside of the object. This makes the object appear to glow on the page. This effect can be used in a visual way to indicate a currently selected item, such as a button or an item in a list. It would also be useful in presenting feedback to the user after an interaction. For example, instead of a button appearing depressed when the user clicks on it, you could attach a Glow filter to that button to indicate to the user that it was pressed.

To add this filter to an object, you would add this to the object's style sheet:

```
Glow(Color=color, Strength=strength)
```

Parameter	Description	Values
Color	Color of the glow effect. You should take care to make sure that this color, when set against the background, gives the appearance of radiance or glow.	Color expressed as #RRGGBB, where RR is the red hex value, GG is the green hex value, and BB is the blue hex value.
Strength	Intensity of the glow.	*0 - 100* – Integer value indicating intensity. 0 being least intense, 100 being most intense.

You can use another feature of visual filters, their scriptable properties, to animate the glow effect. This would create a visual impression that the effected item is pulsing. Here is an example that shows an effect like this. The screenshot cannot show the animation, so you will have to look at this example in your browser for the full effect.

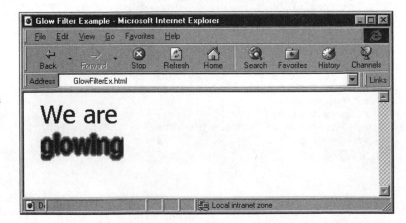

Here is the source code that produces the glow filter, and also animates its strength

```
<HTML>
<HEAD>
    <TITLE>Glow Filter Example</TITLE>
</HEAD>
<SCRIPT LANGUAGE="VBSCRIPT">
dim iDelta

Sub DoGlow
    dim glowStrength
    glowStrength = GlowText.Filters("Glow").Strength
    glowStrength = glowStrength + iDelta
    if glowStrength > 10 or glowStrength < 2 then
            iDelta = iDelta * -1
    end if
.   GlowText.Filters("Glow").Strength = glowStrength

    foo = Window.SetTimeOut("Call DoGlow",50, "VBScript")
end Sub

Sub Window_OnLoad
    iDelta = 1
    call DoGlow
end sub
</SCRIPT>

<BODY>

<DIV ID="divFIlterTest" STYLE="POSITION:absolute; WIDTH:430; HEIGHT:50; TOP:10;
LEFT:5%; font-size:28pt;font-family:Tahoma; color:blue; ">
We are<BR><SPAN ID=GlowText STYLE="POSITION:relative; WIDTH:80; HEIGHT:50;
;FILTER:Glow(Color=#8F00FF, Strength=0) ">glowing</SPAN>
</DIV>

</BODY>
</HTML>
```

Grayscale

This effect removes all of the color information from the source object, and displays it in 'black and white'. Be careful when using this effect with other effects that might rely on color information, such as the Invert effect. When multiple filters are "chained" together, as was discussed earlier, effects are applied sequentially. So if you have a Grayscale effect, which removes all color information, followed by an Invert effect, which manipulates color information, the result may not be what you want. To add this filter to an object, you would add this to the object's style sheet:

```
Gray()
```

This filter, like the **FlipH** and **FlipV** filters, takes no parameters.

XRay

This effect looks at the image and determines its grayscale value and uses a basic rounding function to determine what should be black or white. It will also locate all of the edges in an image. This filter makes the image look like a black and white negative, or like an x-ray of the object. To add this filter to an object, you would add this to the object's style sheet:

```
XRay()
```

This filter, like the GrayScale filter, takes no parameters.

Invert

The invert tag modifies the color information of the object by reversing the hue, saturation, and brightness values of each pixel in the source object. This filter doesn't "invert" the orientation of the picture. To do that, you would chain a FlipH and FlipV filter together, as we saw earlier. The values for each of these color parameters run from 0 to 255. To invert each value, the initial value is subtracted from 255. For example, if the brightness value was 100, then after applying the Invert filter, the brightness value would be 155. To add this filter to an object, you would add this to the object's style sheet:

```
Invert()
```

Let's take a look at an example of the Grayscale and Invert filters. The example page will show an image in 3 states. The first state will be normal. The second state will be with a gray filter in effect. The third will be the same image with an Invert filter in place. Here is what the page will look like:

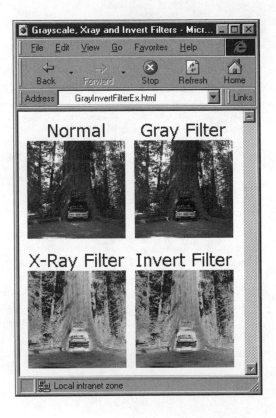

Since the book is not in color, you cannot see the differences between the Normal and Gray images. To see this, you will need to look at the page in your browser. Here is the source code that created this page.

```
<HTML>
<HEAD>
    <TITLE>Grayscale, Xray and Invert Filters</TITLE>
</HEAD>

<BODY>
<DIV ID="divNormal" STYLE="POSITION:ABSOLUTE; Left:10; WIDTH:130; TOP:10; font-
size:18pt; text-align:center; font-family:Tahoma; font-weight:300; color:blue;">
Normal<BR>
<IMG SRC="redWoodCar.gif" WIDTH=128 HEIGHT=128 BORDER=0>
</DIV>

<DIV ID="divGray" STYLE="POSITION:ABSOLUTE; TOP:10; Left:150; WIDTH:130; text-
align:center; font-size:18pt; font-family:Tahoma; font-weight:300; color:blue; ">
Gray Filter<BR>
<IMG SRC="redWoodCar.gif" WIDTH=128 HEIGHT=128 BORDER=0 STYLE="FILTER:Gray()">
</DIV>

<DIV ID="divXRay" STYLE="POSITION:ABSOLUTE; TOP:180; Left:10; WIDTH:130; text-
align:center; font-size:18pt; font-family:Tahoma; font-weight:300; color:blue; ">
X-Ray Filter<BR>
<IMG SRC="redWoodCar.gif" WIDTH=128 HEIGHT=128 BORDER=0 STYLE="FILTER:XRay()">
</DIV>

<DIV ID="divInvert" STYLE="POSITION:ABSOLUTE; TOP:180; Left:150; WIDTH:130;text-
align:center; font-size:18pt; font-family:Tahoma; font-weight:300; color:blue; ">
Invert Filter<BR>
<IMG SRC="redWoodCar.gif" WIDTH=128 HEIGHT=128 BORDER=0 STYLE="FILTER:Invert()">
</DIV>

</BODY>
</HTML>
```

As you can see, there are no parameters required for the Gray filter, XRay filter, or the Invert filter. By adding them to the Style parameter of the image tags, they are put into effect immediately. Both of these effects can be used to indicate selection of an item. For example, if you have a list of items, you could set the Gray filter to all of them except the selected one, which would appear in color.

Lights

The Lights effect is the most complicated effect that you can apply to an object. But it is also the most powerful. If you look back at the history of computer generated animations, you can see how the addition of lighting effects to a particular scene greatly enhances the realism of a scene. Blowing all of this power comes at a price. The addition of lighting effects to a scene can dramatically affect how the scene looks. Since the addition of lights to a scene will require additional processing power, it can also affect the page performance. As you can imagine, lighting effects will be much faster on a Pentium II 266 than on a 486/66, so be careful to test your effects before you deploy them.

The Lights effect component of the Visual Effects object is unique amongst visual effects in that you must accompany the style sheet entry with script calls. To add this filter to an object, you would add this to the object's style sheet:

```
Lights()
```

This statement merely adds the Lights effect to the style sheet of the object. You must then use scripting calls to control the placement and characteristics of the different types of light.

You can add up to 10 lights to a single Lights effect. If you require more lights than that, you must use additional Light styles. To add these, you would use this syntax

```
Lightsn()
```

where the value of *n* is a sequential integer starting at 1. If you want lighting effects to cover a group of objects, then you can enclose those object in a `<DIV>` element, and apply the lighting effect to the entire element.

There are three different types of light that can be added to the effect. They are:

- **Ambient light** is non-directional light that sheds parallel beams perpendicular to the surface of the page. Ambient light has color and strength values, and can be used to add more color to the page, often used in conjunction with other lights.

- **Cone light** casts a directional light on the page. The cone light fades with distance from the target position. It displays a hard edge at the distance threshold of the light.

- **Point light** is like a light bulb. You can add several to your page for great multi-point gradients.

In order to access the methods of the filter style, you will need to have a reference to the filter object. You can get this reference using the methods for script control of styles as discussed earlier in this chapter. For the examples that follow, we will assume that the following code was used to obtain the filter style reference:

```
Dim myLightFilter    'Will hold the object reference for our filter
Set myLightFilter = myFilterTestDIV.Filters("Light")
```

AddAmbient

To add an Ambient light to your page, you will use this method:

```
myLightFilter.addAmbient(R,G,B, strength)
```

You will set the color of the light by setting its *R*, *G*, & *B* values. These values range from 0 to 255. The *strength* parameter indicates the intensity of the light, and its values can range from 0 to 100

AddCone

To add a Cone light to your page, you need to use this method:

```
myLightFilter.addCone(x1,y1,z1,x2,y2,R,G,B,strength,spread)
```

The parameters *x1, y1,* and *z1* indicate the position of the light source. The x and y coordinates are in relation to the target object. The z coordinate is the height of the light above the object, and will have a direct effect on the area of the object that is affected by the light. The closer the light is to the object, then the higher the intensity will be, but the area affected will be smaller. The *x2* and *y2* parameters indicate the coordinates on the target object that the light is aimed at. This will affect the shape of the light that is cast on the target object. If the values of *x1* and *x2* are the same, and the values of *y1* and *y2* are the same, then the light cast on the target object will form a circle.

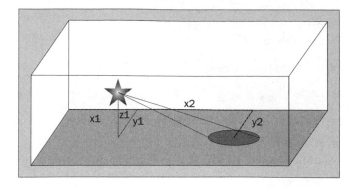

If they are different, the light will be more of an oval shape. This picture shows you how the coordinates relate to the placement of the light source and the target on the page.

The color parameters, *R, G, & B*, and the *strength* are the same as in the Ambient light. The *spread* parameter indicates the size of the cone of light. This is determined by the relationship between the vertical position of the light source and the surface of the visual object. The values can range from 0 to 90 degrees. Low spread (such as low integer values) produces a smaller shaped cone of light. High angle of spread produces an oblique oval or circle of light.

AddPoint

To add a Point light to your page, you need to use this method:

```
myLightFilter.addPoint(x,y,z,R,G,B,strength)
```

The parameters *x, y,* and *z* indicate the position of the light source. These parameters have the same effect as the *x1, y1,* and *z1* parameters of the Cone light effect. The color and strength parameters have the same affect as in the Ambient light. You should experiment with the positioning, color, and strength of the Point light to determine how it affects your page best.

ChangeColor

The ChangeColor method allows you to either set the light to a new color, or modify the color by a certain amount. To call this method you will use:

```
myLightFilter.ChangeColor(lightnumber, R,G,B, fAbsolute)
```

The *lightnumber* parameter indicates which light you are changing. The lights are numbered in sequence starting at 0 with the first light that you add to the light object. The *fAbsolute* parameter determines how to change the color based on the *R, G, & B* parameters. If *fAbsolute* is true, then the new color of the light will be determined by the values of *R, G, & B*. If *fAbsolute* is false, then the values of *R, G, & B* will be added to the existing color of the light. In this instance, negative values for *R, G,* or *B* are valid.

ChangeStrength

The ChangeStrength method allows you to adjust the strength of a light. To call this method you will use:

```
MyLightFilter.ChangeStrength(lightnumber, strength, fAbsolute)
```

As with the ChangeColor method, if *fAbsolute* is true, then the intensity of the light being modified will be changed to the value of *strength*. If *fAbsolute* is false, the value of *strength* will be added to the intensity of the light you are modifying. Again in this case, you can have negative values for the *strength* parameter.

Clear

If you wish to remove all of the lights from the Lights effect, then you can call:

```
MyLightFilter.Clear
```

This will remove all of the lights from the effect. There is no way to selectively remove lights from an effect.

MoveLight

The MoveLight method allows you to adjust the positioning of a light. To call this method you will use:

```
MyLightFilter.MoveLight(lightnumber, x, y, z, fAbsolute)
```

The values for *x, y*, and *z* will either set the new position of the light, if *fAbsolute* is true, or will adjust the existing position of the light, if *fAbsolute* is false. If you are calling the **MoveLight** method on an Ambient light, then the value of the *z* parameter will be ignored.

Light Example

Let's now look at an example of an object on a page, and selectively apply light effects to that object. You will also see how to animate the light effects. Here is an example of the page with the point light applied to it. To see the lights in motion, you will need to look at this page in IE4.

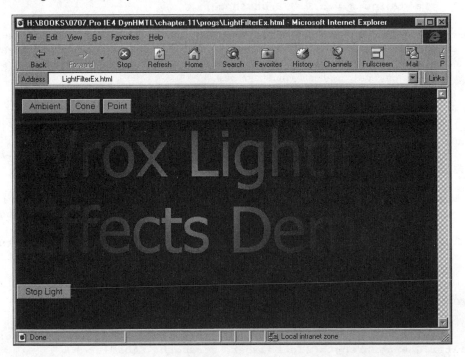

The HTML to create this page is as follows.

```
<HTML>
<HEAD>
<SCRIPT LANGUAGE="VBScript">
Dim LightFilter, bLightMoving, iMoveCount
Dim iMoveDelta
```

We will be using these global variables for the following items:

Variable	Usage
LightFilter	Holds a reference to the light effect in the style sheet.
bLightMoving	Boolean that indicates if the light should be in motion.
iMoveCount	Counter value to determine when to change the direction of the moving light.
iMoveDelta	Distance in pixels to move the light on each move iteration. Generated randomly. Can be positive or negative.

```
Sub Window_onLoad
    set LightFilter = LightTest.Filters("Light")
    bLightMoving = False
    iMoveDelta = Int(41 * rnd) - 20
End sub
```

When the page is loaded, we want to grab a reference to the Light filter in the style sheet of the LightTest element. We will store that reference in the **LightFilter** variable. The variable that indicates lights in motion is initialized to false, and the light movement delta value is initialized to a random number between –20 and + 20.

```
Sub SetAmbient
    Call LightFilter.Clear
    call LightFilter.AddAmbient(255,0,0,50)
    StopMoveLight
    MoveTheLight.style.visibility = "hidden"
End sub
```

Each of the three buttons at the top of the page calls a method to set the lighting conditions. The first step is to clear the existing lights. This is done with the **Clear** method. Then we add an ambient light source to the element. In this case, the light source is pure red with a strength of 50%. The **StopMoveLight** method is called to stop any previous light motion that is occurring. The Move The Light button is explicitly hidden, since there is no concept of moving the non-directional ambient light.

```
Sub SetCone
    StopMoveLight
    Call LightFilter.Clear
    call LightFilter.AddCone(100,100,50,10,10,0,0,255,100,40)
    call LightFilter.AddCone(300,100,50,400,100,0,255,0,100,40)
End sub
```

To set up the cone lighting effects, we first stop any light motion that may be occurring and clear any existing lights from the element. We will be adding two cone lights to the element. The first is at point (100,100) and is 50 pixels above the page. It is pointing at the point (10,10). The color of the light is pure blue, with 100% strength. The spread angle of the light is 40 degrees. The second cone light is at point (300,100) and is also 50 pixels above the page. The light is a 100% strength pure green light, with a spread angle of 40 degrees.

```
Sub SetPoint
    StopMoveLight
    Call LightFilter.Clear
    call LightFilter.AddPoint(100,40,150,0,255,0,100)
End sub
```

In this method, we are adding a point light source to the element. After stopping the motion and clearing the existing lights, a point light source is added at point (100,40) and 150 pixels above the page. The light is a 100% strength pure green light.

```
Sub MoveLight
    Call LightFilter.MoveLight(0,iMoveDelta,iMoveDelta/2,0,0)
    Call LightFilter.MoveLight(1,-iMoveDelta,-iMoveDelta,0,0)
    iMoveCount = iMoveCount + 1
    if iMoveCount Mod 20 = 0 then
            iMoveDelta = Int(41 * rnd) - 20
    end if
    if bLightMoving = True then
            foo=window.setTimeout("Call MoveLight",10,"VBSCRIPT")
    end if
End Sub
```

The **MoveLight** method moves any existing lights on the page. Since the cone light example adds two light sources, we need to call the **MoveLight** method twice. The second call, to move light source number 1, is ignored in the point light example, since there is only one light source. The light source points are moved based on the value of the **iMoveDelta** variable. The **iMoveCount** variable is incremented each time this method is called. Every 20th time that this method is called, the value of **iMoveDelta** is changed to a random value between –20 and 20.

The **bLightMoving** boolean value is checked each time this method is called. If the value is true, then the motion should continue. The **SetTimeOut** method of the window object is used to repeatedly call the **MoveLight** method every 10 milliseconds, thus providing the appearance of animation.

```
Sub StartMoveLight
    bLightMoving = True
    MoveTheLight.style.visibility = "hidden"
    StopTheLight.style.visibility = "visible"
    iMoveCount = 0
    Call MoveLight
end sub
```

This method is called when the **MoveTheLight** button is pressed. This method sets the boolean variable, **bLightMoving**, to true. This will cause the **MoveLight** method to repeat by the use of the **SetTimeOut** method. The Move The Light button is hidden and the Stop The Light button is shown in its place. The **iMoveCount** variable is reset to 0, which is controlling when the change in light movement will occur. Finally, the **MoveLight** method needs to be explicitly called the first time to begin the animation of the lights.

```
Sub StopMoveLight
    bLightMoving = False
    MoveTheLight.style.visibility = "visible"
    StopTheLight.style.visibility = "hidden"
end Sub
```

When the Stop The Light button is pressed, the **StopMoveLight** method is called. This sets the **bLightMoving** variable to false. The next time that the **MoveLight** method is called via the **SetTimeOut** method, the **bLightMoving** variable will be read as false, and the method will not call **SetTimeOut** to continue the animation.

```
</SCRIPT>
</HEAD>
<BODY BGCOLOR=Black>

<INPUT TYPE=Button VALUE="Ambient" NAME="SetAmbient" onClick="SetAmbient()">
<INPUT TYPE=Button VALUE="Cone" NAME="SetCone" onClick="SetCone()">
<INPUT TYPE=Button VALUE="Point" NAME="SetPoint" onClick="SetPoint()">
<INPUT TYPE=Button VALUE="Move Light" ID="MoveTheLight" onClick="StartMoveLight()"
STYLE="Position:absolute; Left:0; Top:310; visibility:hidden">
<INPUT TYPE=Button VALUE="Stop Light" ID="StopTheLight" onClick="StopMoveLight()"
STYLE="Position:absolute; Left:0; Top:310; visibility:hidden">
```

These 5 buttons are used to select the type of lighting to be used and to control the animation. The Move The Light and Stop The Light buttons are both initially hidden, by the use of the visibility style. They also both occupy the same position on the page through the use of the **Left** and **Top** styles.

```
<DIV ID=LightTest STYLE="Position:Relative; Width:100%; Height:100; Left:0; Top:0;
Font-family:Tahoma; Font-size:100; Color:White; FILTER:Light();">
Wrox Lighting Effects Demo
</DIV>
</BODY>
</HTML>
```

This is the `<DIV>` block that will have the lighting effects applied to it. You can see that the text color is set to white. If you look back to the Wrox Lighting Effects example image, you can see that the color of the lights greatly affect what color the image appears.

The Light filter is the most powerful filter that is included in IE4. Consequently, they are the most difficult to use as well. It's worth it, though, because the combination of lighting effects, along with animating their properties, gives you a very compelling visual display effect. Of course, with a new display effect comes the potential for overuse and misuse. Remember the `<BLINK>` tag?

Mask

The mask filter allows you to create a visual mask for any object on your page. A mask is created when you take all of the non-transparent pixels in an object and make them transparent, and then color all of the transparent pixels a specific color. This can be used to create the illusion of an image being "punched" out of its background. You could also use the mask filter in combination with the alpha filter, and transparency, to dynamically create collages of images.

To add this filter to an object, you would add this to the object's style sheet:

```
Mask(Color=color)
```

Parameter	Description	Values
Color	Color that the transparent regions in the element are painted.	Color expressed as #RRGGBB, where RR is the red hex value, GG is the green hex value, and BB is the blue hex value.

Let's take a look at the Mask effect and see how you can use it to create interesting effects. One effect that you can create is a mapping of an image onto text. An example of this is shown here.

To create this example, we have used the following HTML code.

```
<HTML>
<HEAD>
    <TITLE>Mask Filter Example</TITLE>
</HEAD>

<BODY BGCOLOR="#F8FEDE">

<DIV STYLE="POSITION:ABSOLUTE; left=10; top=10; width=128;height=128;">
<IMG SRC="redWoodCar.JPG" BORDER=0 STYLE="POSITION:absolute; HEIGHT:128;Width:128;
Left:0; Top:0;">
<CENTER>
<SPAN STYLE="POSITION:RELATIVE; Height:128; {font-size: 30pt; font-family:impact;
font-weight: bold; font-style: italic; color:white}">
On the Woods
</SPAN>
</CENTER>
</DIV>
```

```
<DIV STYLE="POSITION:ABSOLUTE; left=10; top=140; width=128;height=128;">
<IMG SRC="redWoodCar.JPG" BORDER=0 STYLE="POSITION:absolute; HEIGHT:128;Width:128;
Left:0; Top:0;">
<CENTER>
<SPAN STYLE="POSITION:RELATIVE; Height:128; Filter:Mask(COLOR=#F8FEDE); {font-size:
30pt; font-family:impact;  font-weight: bold; font-style: italic; color:black}">
In the Woods
</SPAN>
</CENTER>
</DIV>

</BODY>
</HTML>
```

We have created a `<DIV>` block that contains an image and a text `<SPAN>`. Through the use of style sheet positioning, the text is on top of the image. In the first `<DIV>` block, there is no filter applied, and the white text appears on top of image, with the transparent area around the text allowing the image to show through. In the second `<DIV>` block, there is a Mask filter applied. The critical element in that mask filter is the selection of the **Color** parameter. This is the color that all transparent pixels in the element are colored. By selecting the same color as the background color of the page, #F8FEDE, the formerly transparent areas of the text `<SPAN>` will now appear the same color as the background, thus covering those parts of the image that were visible in the first `<DIV>` block. Since the text is now transparent, the image beneath the text `<SPAN>` will now show through. This is what gives us our image mapped onto the text example.

Wave

The Wave effect distorts the target object with a sine wave distortion. This gives the object a wavy appearance, and when combined with a recurring method like **SetTimeOut** to vary some of its parameters, the effect can appear to add a wave-type motion to the object. To add this filter to an object, you would add this to the object's style sheet:

```
Wave(Add=add, Freq=freq, LightStrength=strength, Phase=phase,
Strength=strength)
```

Parameter	Description	Values	
Add	Adds the original image back to the blurred image. Especially useful with fonts.	1 0	Original image added back Only the wave image is shown
Freq	Number of waves that make up the wave distortion across the object.	*Integer*	
LightStrength	Strength of the light that is illuminating the wave effect.	Strength percentage, with 100% being full intensity.	
Phase	The starting position of the wave, as a percentage of a complete cycle.	0 25 50 100	=100% of full cycle =90 degrees =80 degrees =360 degrees
Strength	Strength of the wave effect, in percent.	0 – 100%, with 100% being full strength.	

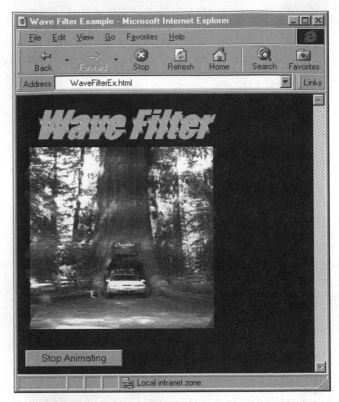

Here is an example of an image and text with a Wave effect added to it. The example also allows you to animate the Wave effect by pressing the button.

Now, let's take a look at the HTML code to create this example.

```
<HTML>
<HEAD>
    <TITLE>Wave Filter Example</TITLE>

<SCRIPT LANGUAGE="VBScript">
Dim bAnimating, wavphase
```

We will be using the **bAnimating** variable as a boolean to determine if the wave is being currently animated. The **wavphase** variable stores the current phase of the wave in degrees.

```
Sub Window_onLoad
    bAnimating = False
End sub

Sub AnimateWave
    if bAnimating then
            wavphase = (wavphase + 10) mod 100
            divNormal.filters("Wave").phase = wavphase
            foo = window.setTimeout("Call AnimateWave", 0400, "VBScript")
    end if
End Sub
```

In the `AnimateWave` method, we check to see if animation is currently enabled by checking the `bAnimating` variable. If it is false, then we fall out of this method. We then calculate a new value for the wave phase, and set the phase parameter of the Wave filter to that new value. The `SetTimeOut` method of the window object is used to schedule the execution of the `AnimateWave` method in 400 milliseconds. It is this repeated calling of the `AnimateWave` method that produces the animation effect.

```
Sub StartAnimating
    bAnimating = True
    wavPhase = 0
    StartAnimateWave.style.visibility = "hidden"
    StopAnimateWave.style.visibility = "visible"
    Call AnimateWave
end sub

Sub StopAnimating
    bAnimating = False
    StartAnimateWave.style.visibility = "visible"
    StopAnimateWave.style.visibility = "hidden"
end Sub
```

The `StartAnimating` and `StopAnimating` methods are very similar to the methods used in the Lights example to start and stop the animation of the lights.

```
</SCRIPT>
</HEAD>

<BODY BGCOLOR="#000000">

<DIV ID="divNormal" STYLE="POSITION:ABSOLUTE; Left:10; WIDTH:270; TOP:10; font-
size:40pt; text-align:center; font-family:Impact; font-style:italic; color:blue;
Filter:Wave(Add=1, Freq=3, LightStrength=25, Phase=25, Strength=12">
Wave Filter<BR>
<IMG SRC="redWoodCar.gif" WIDTH=256 HEIGHT=256 BORDER=0>
</DIV>

<INPUT TYPE=Button VALUE="Start Animating" ID="StartAnimateWave"
onClick="StartAnimating" STYLE="Position:absolute; Top:360; visibility:visible">
<INPUT TYPE=Button VALUE="Stop Animating" ID="StopAnimateWave" onClick="StopAnimating"
STYLE="Position:absolute; Top:360; visibility:hidden">

</BODY>
</HTML>
```

We have a `<DIV>` block that holds both the text and the image. There is a Wave filter that is applied to this block. The `Add` parameter is set to 1, so the original image is laid on top of the wave image. The Frequency is set to 3, which gives 3 complete wave cycles over the `<DIV>` block. The lighting is set to 25% strength. The initial position of the wave is 90 degrees, and the wave has a strength of 12%.

Filters Summary

In this section, you have seen how to apply the many different filters that are available through Cascading Style Sheets in IE4. By combining filters together through chaining, you can create complex effects that used to be only possible for graphic artists using Photoshop. But now you can easily create those effects as well. By dynamically manipulating the properties of some of the filters, you can also create very interesting and appealing animation effects.

Next, we will take a look at a special type of filter that deals with hiding and showing elements on the page: the Transitions filter.

Style Sheet Transitions

Another way to enhance the user interface of an application is to present different parts of the interface when the user needs them, and not before. This has become possible in IE4 with Dynamic HTML. You have the ability to change the **visibility** property of any object on the screen, which will make it either appear or disappear. But with plain Dynamic HTML, you have no way of controlling how that appearance or disappearance looks. When you set the **visibility** property of a hidden object to visible, the object just appears. Now, however, you can make the object appear as if it is dissolving onto the page, or building from the right. To do this, you need to use the transition filter.

Transition Filters

The transition filter basically steps in front of IE4's internal drawing functions, and allows the developer to specify how to display a particular object. Any object that has a **visibility** property can be used with the transition control. The transitions are added as a filter to the object's **style** property. This is very similar to adding a visual effect filter. You can either explicitly add the transition inside the object's **style** tag, or you can dynamically add it in script using the object's **style** property. There are two types of transitions: the **blend** transition and the **reveal** transition.

Blend Transition

The blend transition allows for a simple fade in or fade out of an object over a specified duration. The fade works by slowly dissolving away the existing object, and showing the new object gradually in its place. You have no control over the way that the fade is done, merely over how long the transition takes. To add the blend transition to an object's style, you would add this to the style sheet:

```
BlendTrans(Duration = duration)
```

Parameter	Description	Values
Duration	Length of time the transition should take	*seconds*

Reveal Transition

The reveal transition allows you to specify the visual transition that will take place. As with the blend transition, you can also specify the duration of the effect. To add the reveal transition to an object's style, you would add this to the style sheet:

```
RevealTrans(Duration = duration, TransitionType = transition)
```

Parameter	Description	Values
Duration	Length of time the transition should take	*Seconds*
TransitionType	Type of transition to use	*See the transition table following*

Reveal Transition Types

Here is a listing of the types of transitions, along with a short description of what each one looks like. The example at the end of this section will provide a visual example of each of these transitions.

Transition Name	Value	Effect
Box in	0	Draws from the outer edge inward using straight sides
Box out	1	Draws from the center outward using straight sides
Circle in	2	Draws from the outer edge inward using a circle
Circle out	3	Draws from the center outward using a circle
Wipe up	4	Draws from the bottom edge straight upward
Wipe down	5	Draws from the top edge straight downward
Wipe right	6	Draws from the left edge toward the right
Wipe left	7	Draws from the right edge toward the left
Vertical blinds	8	Divides the object being drawn into vertical narrow panels, which are drawn with a wipe right effect simultaneously.
Horizontal blinds	9	Divides the object being drawn into horizontal narrow panels, which are drawn with a wipe down effect simultaneously. Actually looks like you are opening a set of aluminum blinds and revealing the picture beneath.
Checkerboard across	10	Divides the object into a checkerboard pattern and then draws every other panel using a wipe right effect simultaneously. When that effect is complete, the other panels are then drawn using the same effect.
Checkerboard down	11	Same as the checkerboard across transition, but using a wipe down effect on each panel, rather than a wipe right.
Random dissolve	12	Randomly draws each pixel that makes up the object, so that the object appears to "sparkle" in.
Split vertical in	13	Draws from the left edge with a wipe right and from the right edge with a wipe left simultaneously, so that the object is fully drawn when the two effects meet at the middle.
Split vertical out	14	Starts a wipe left and a wipe right effect simultaneously from the center of the object.
Split horizontal in	15	Draws from the top edge with a wipe down and from the bottom edge with a wipe up simultaneously, so that the object is fully drawn when the two effects meet at the middle.
Split horizontal out	16	Starts a wipe up and a wipe down effect simultaneously from the center of the object.
Strips left down	17	Draws the object diagonally from the top right corner downward and to the left.

Table Continued on Following Page

Transition Name	Value	Effect
Strips left up	18	Draws the object diagonally from the lower right corner upward and to the left.
Strips right down	19	Draws the object diagonally from the top left corner downward and to the right.
Strips right up	20	Draws the object diagonally from the bottom left corner upward and to the right.
Random bars horizontal	21	Draws the object using single pixel wide horizontal lines that are randomly placed. If the transition has not completed in the time defined by the StartPainting method, then the whole image is immediately shown.
Random bars vertical	22	Draws the object using single pixel wide vertical lines that are randomly placed. If the transition has not completed in the time defined by the StartPainting method, then the whole image is immediately shown.
Random	23	Randomly selects from all the possible transitions.

Using the Transitions

Once you have assigned a transition style to an object, you will then need to use script methods to make the transition appear. There are three easy steps that need to be followed when working with a transition. These steps are the same for both the reveal transition, and the blend transition.

Step 1: Apply the Transition

The first step is to apply the transition. This may sound a little strange, since it sounds like when you "apply" the transition, you are making it appear. If you remember, the transition filter works by intercepting the normal IE4 redraw methods. So, by applying the transition, you are telling IE4 that you want the transition filter to handle the drawing of the object that it refers to. To apply the transition, you need to use the **Apply** method. To call this method, you need a valid reference to the filter itself. This can be obtained through the object's **filters** collection. Once you have this reference, you can call the **Apply** method by:

```
myTransObject.Filters.item(0).Apply()
```

The transition filter now has control of the redrawing of your object.

Step 2: Change the object

Since the goal of a transition is to change the appearance of an object from one look to another, you will need to identify what the final state of the object is. Since you have now taken control of the redraw process, any changes that you make to the visual appearance of the object will be held in limbo by the transition filter. For example, if you have the transition filter applied to an **<IMG>** object, you can change the Source Image property, and a new image will be drawn in its place. If you have the transition filter applied to a container object, like a **<DIV>**, then you can change any one of the **<DIV>** block's contents and have the transition filter handle the change in visual appearance.

Step 3: Play the Transition

Now that you have changed the object that the transition filter is controlling, you need to tell the filter to go ahead and begin its redraw of the object. This is called **playing the transition**. The transition filter will draw the new object using the specified transition type, in the case of the Reveal transition, or fade the new object over the old, as in the case of the Blend transition. The transition will be done over the length of time specified in the filter's `duration` property, or by an optional parameter to the `Play` method. To call the `Play` method, you would use:

```
myTransObject.Filters.item(0).Play(duration)
```

Parameter	Description	Values
duration	Option – Length of time the transition should take. Overrides the Duration property of the filter.	seconds

Once the drawing of the new object is completed, the transition filter returns control of the redraw for that object to IE4. The filter also fires an event to let you know that the transition has been completed.

Events

There is one event, **onFilterEvent**, which is fired when the transition is completed. If you have more than one object with a transition filter attached to it, you can use the **Window.Event.srcElement** property to determine which object's transition just completed.

Example

Let's take a look at an example program that shows how to use the transitions filter. This example has a displayed image with two possible sources. The user can select a type of transition and apply it to the image. By pressing a button, the image will switch to its other source, using the selected transition type. You will need to go to **http://rapid.wrox.co.uk/books/0707** to see the transitions in action. Here is what the screen looks like in mid-transition:

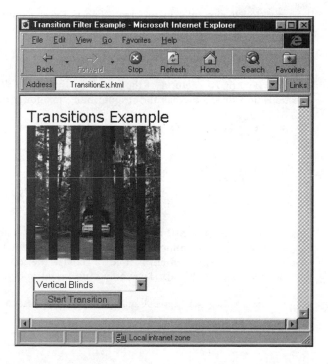

Now, let's take a look at the source code for this page.

```
<HTML>
<HEAD>
    <TITLE>Transition Filter Example</TITLE>
<SCRIPT LANGUAGE="VBScript">
dim TransDirection
dim bTransInProgress

Sub Window_onLoad()
    bTransInProgress = False
    TransDirection = 1
End Sub
```

When the page is loaded into the browser, we are initializing the two variables that are used to track the transition. The **bTransInProgress** is a boolean value that indicates if a transition is currently being played. The **TransDirection** variable is used to determine which image is currently being displayed, so that the other can be transitioned in.

```
Sub TransImage_OnFilterChange()
    bTransInProgress = False
End Sub
```

We receive the **OnFilterChange** event when the transition is complete. By resetting the value of **bTransInProgress** to false, the user is able to start another transition.

```
Sub StartTransition()
    if bTransInProgress then Exit Sub
```

If a transition is currently in progress, then the user cannot start another one. If **bTransInProgress** is true, then this method is exited, and the currently running transition can continue.

```
    call TransImage.filters.item(0).Apply()
```

By using the **Apply** method of the transition filter, we tell IE4 not to update the **TransImage** element. The transition filter now has the responsibility for doing that.

```
        if TransDirection = 1 then
            TransDirection = 2
            TransImage.src = "phantom.jpg"
        else
            TransDirection = 1
            TransImage.src = "redWoodCar.jpg"
        end if
```

This is where the **TransDirection** variable is used. The possible values for it are 1 and 2. By checking this value, we can determine which image needs to be loaded into the **TransImage** element. The **src** property of the image element is used to replace the image that is currently being displayed. Remember, since we have called the **Apply** method, no visual updates of the **TransImage** element will be done.

```
        TransImage.filters.item(0).Transition = TransChoice.selectedIndex
```

The user has selected the type of transition to be used with a **<SELECT>** control. The elements in that control correspond to the possible transition types. We set the **Transition** property of the transition filter to the selection that the user made.

```
    TransImage.filters(0).play()
    bTransInProgress = True
```

Now that we have the proper image set and the desired transition selected, we can begin the transition by calling the **Play** method. Since there is now a transition taking place, we set the **bTransInProgress** variable to true so that the user is unable to start another transition before this one completes.

```
End Sub
</SCRIPT>
</HEAD>

<BODY>
<SPAN STYLE="font-family:Tahoma; color:blue; font-size:24;">Transitions Example<BR></
SPAN>
<DIV ID=Controls STYLE="POSITION:absolute;TOP:270;LEFT:5%;Width:200;">
<SELECT ID=TransChoice>
            <OPTION>Box In</OPTION>
            <OPTION>Box Out</OPTION>
            <OPTION>Circle In</OPTION>
            <OPTION>Circle Out</OPTION>
            <OPTION>Wipe Up</OPTION>
            <OPTION>Wipe Down</OPTION>
            <OPTION>Wipe Right</OPTION>
            <OPTION>Wipe Left</OPTION>
            <OPTION>Vertical Blinds</OPTION>
            <OPTION>Horizontal Blinds</OPTION>
            <OPTION>Checker Board Across</OPTION>
            <OPTION>Checker Board Down</OPTION>
            <OPTION>Random Dissolve</OPTION>
            <OPTION>Split Vertical In</OPTION>
            <OPTION>Split Vertical Out</OPTION>
            <OPTION>Split Horizontal In</OPTION>
            <OPTION>Split Horizontal Out</OPTION>
            <OPTION>Strips Left Down</OPTION>
            <OPTION>Strips Left Up</OPTION>
            <OPTION>Strips Right Down</OPTION>
            <OPTION>Strips Right Up</OPTION>
            <OPTION>Random Bars Horizontal</OPTION>
            <OPTION>Random Bars Vertical</OPTION>
            <OPTION>Random</OPTION>
</SELECT><BR>
<INPUT TYPE="SUBMIT" NAME="startTrans" VALUE="Start Transition"
onclick=StartTransition()>
</DIV>

<IMG ID="TransImage" STYLE="Width:200;height:200;FILTER:revealTrans(Duration=3.0,
Transition=1)" SRC="redWoodCar.jpg">
```

The **TransImage** element has a style filter of type **revealTrans**. The duration is set to 3.0 seconds, and the Transition type is set to 1. The value of the Transition parameter is not important, since we are setting it dynamically each time the transition is run.

```
<IMG ID="Image3" STYLE="Position:absolute; Width:200; height:200; visibility:hidden"
SRC="phantom.jpg">
</BODY>
</HTML>
```

To speed up the processing of the transition, we load the second image into a hidden image element. This forces the browser to download the image from the server and hold it in the browser's cache. This is done so that when the **Source** property of the **TransImage** element is changed to **phantom.jpg**, the browser doesn't have to download the image from the server, allowing it to begin the transition sooner.

You will need to load this code into your web browser, as it is rather difficult to show a transition in a non-dynamic medium, such as a book. Up until this point, most web pages have been non-dynamic mediums when it comes to control of the display of objects on the screen. But now, with IE4 and the Transition filters, you can add a whole new degree of dynamic interface to your web pages.

Page Transitions

Page transitions make it possible to provide multimedia effects as a Web page is loaded or exited. Today, without page transitions, when a new page is loaded, the existing one is cleared from the browser. Then the new page is loaded element by element. The developer of a page has very little control over how the page is drawn on the screen.

What Page Transitions Do

Transitions are defined by using the **<META>** tag, in the **<HEAD>** section of a Web page. The developer can specify whether a particular transition should occur as the page is loaded or as it is exited. The transition type and duration properties are set using the variables in the special **<META>** tag. When the browser finds a transition **<META>** tag, it interprets whether the event should occur before the page is displayed or as it is exited. When that event occurs, the transition filter takes over control of the repainting in the browser, just as it does with the transition style sheet filter.

Using Page Transitions

To set a page transition, the developer must determine three items. First, they need to decide if the transition is for when the page is loaded, or when it is exited. There is no restriction on having both an entrance and an exit transition for a page. They just need to be defined separately. The developer must also determine how long the transition should take to process. Lastly, they must select the type of visual transition that they would like to see.

To add a page entrance transition to a page, you would add this to the **<HEAD>** section of the page:

```
<META http-equiv="Page-Enter"
CONTENT="RevealTrans(Duration=duration,Transition=transition)>
```

To add a page exit transition to a page, you would add this:

```
<META http-equiv="Page-Exit"
CONTENT="RevealTrans(Duration=duration,Transition=transition)>
```

The parameters for the revealTrans method are identical to the parameters for the revealTrans style sheet filter. The *duration* indicates the number of seconds that the transition should take. The maximum value for the **Duration** parameter is 30 seconds. The *transition* selects the type of visual transition that will be used to draw the screen.

Example

This example has two separate pages, with links between them to allow you to see both the page enter and page exit transitions. You will need to look at the pages in your browser to see the full effect of the page transitions. The pages again can be found at `http://rapid.wrox.co.uk/books/0707`. Here is what the browser looks like midway through a page-exit transition:

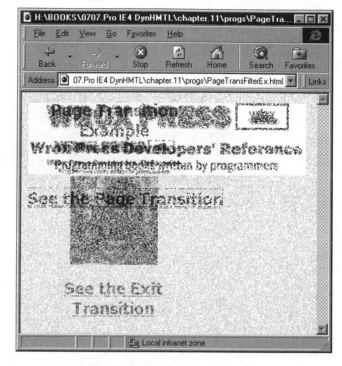

First, you will need a page that has both a page-exit and a page-exit transition. This is the HTML code for that page.

```
<HTML>
<HEAD>
    <META http-equiv="Page-Enter" CONTENT="RevealTrans(Duration=4,Transition=23)">
    <META http-equiv="Page-Exit" CONTENT="RevealTrans(Duration=4,Transition=23)">
</HEAD>
```

As you can see, we have added **<META>** tags for both a page exit transition and a page enter transition. Each has a duration of 4 seconds. We have selected transition type 23, which randomly selects from all possible transitions.

```
<BODY>

<DIV STYLE="POSITION:absolute; WIDTH:230; HEIGHT:150; TOP:10; LEFT:5%; font-
size:18pt;font-family:Tahoma;font-weight:700; color:blue; text-align:center">
Page Transition Example
    <IMG ID="Image3" STYLE="Width:200;height:52;" SRC="wpdr.gif"><BR>
```

```
        <IMG SRC="redWoodCar.JPG" WIDTH=128 HEIGHT=128 BORDER=0><P>
        <A HREF="RunPageTrans.html">See the Exit Transition</A>
    </DIV>
    </BODY>
    </HTML>
```

We just have a page that displays a background image, text, a GIF file, and a JPG file. This shows you that you can have any type of element displayed on a page that uses a page transition. Lastly, there is a link to another page. When that link is clicked, the page-exit transition is run.

Here is the short page called `RunPageTrans.html`.

```
<HTML>
<HEAD>
    <TITLE>See the Page Transitions</TITLE>
</HEAD>

<BODY BGCOLOR="#FFFF00">
<IMG SRC="wpdr.gif" WIDTH=400 HEIGHT=103 BORDER=0><P>
<A STYLE="font-size:18pt;font-family:Tahoma;font-weight:700; color:blue;"
HREF="PageTransFilterEx.html">See the Page Transition</A>
</BODY>
</HTML>
```

All that this page has is a solid background, an image, and a link back to the Page Transition example page. When this link is clicked, the other page will be loaded, and then displayed using that page's page-enter transition.

As you can see from this example, it is remarkably painless to add very dramatic page transitions to your web pages with the page transitions filter.

Summary

You have seen just how the enhancements to the cascading style sheets of IE4 can be used to create powerful visual effects. These can be used to create very compelling and rich user interfaces. You have seen how to:

- ▲ Change the way elements your page look in many different ways using the Visual Effects filters of cascading style sheets.
- ▲ Fade objects on and off your page in many different ways using Transition filters.
- ▲ And control how your page is initially displayed or exited using the Page Transitions filter with the `<META>` tag.

You can use all of these effects individually, or in many different combinations, to greatly enhance the user interface that you are presenting to the viewers of your page.

In the next chapter, we will begin to take a look at the multimedia controls that are included as part of IE4. These controls allow you to do things such as move objects along a path, and script together sequences of actions. But you'll have to read the next chapter to see what they can **really** do!

Using IE4 Multimedia ActiveX Controls

One of IE4's major advantages is the multimedia capability that Microsoft have embedded into the browser. This takes the form of five new multimedia ActiveX controls, bundled with the browser, making them readily available to everyone using it. Four of the controls provide access to the DirectAnimation layer of DirectX, while one provides access to the DirectShow layer. In this chapter, we will introduce each control to you, cover the basic methods and properties needed to effectively use the control, and then show you a small example of how to use the control.

You'll find that each control offers a lot of new features and could easily justify a chapter or more in its own right, so we can't really cover them in the detail they deserve. If you wish to know more, then perhaps the best way is to take a look at what other people are doing. If you see something interesting on a web page, take a look at the source and see what new techniques the author of the page has come up with. A good starting place is the Microsoft web site for the Multimedia Technology demos, which can be found at **http://www.microsoft.com/ie/ie40/demos/**

These new controls will allow you to:

- ▲ Download and play audio and video files live using the Active Movie control
- ▲ Move an object on a web page in a predetermined path using the Path control
- ▲ Script actions of different objects on the page over time using the Sequencer control
- ▲ Create and control sprite-based images on your web page using the Sprite control
- ▲ And quickly render vector graphics on your web page from a few lines of script code using the Structured Graphics Control

First let's take a look at the features of the ActiveMovie control, and how it can be used to embed video and audio files in your web pages.

DirectShow

The Active Movie ActiveX control is the primary means of displaying sound and video within IE4. It provides access to the Direct Show component of the DirectX foundation layer. This means that it provides support for rich audio and video within your web page – including all current and future codecs (audio compression standards) supported by Direct Show. As you will see it is easy to use, and allows much more complex sound interactions on your web page than have previously been possible.

The Active Movie multimedia control

The Active Movie control has quite a list of properties, methods, and events. However, we need only concern ourselves with a subset of these to provide rich content to our readers. Here is a complete listing of the control properties.

Property	Description
allowChangeDisplayMode	Indicates whether or not the end-user can change the display mode at run time between seconds and frames.
allowHideControls	Indicates whether or not the end-user can hide the control panel at run time.
allowHideDisplay	Indicates whether or not the end-user can hide the display panel at run time.
appearance	Specifies the appearance of the display panel's border.
autoRewind	Indicates whether or not the multimedia stream should automatically return to the selection's starting point when it reaches the end of the selection.
autoStart	Indicates whether or not to automatically start playing the multimedia stream.
balance	Specifies the stereo balance.
borderStyle	Specifies the control's border style.
currentPosition	Specifies the current position within the playback file, in seconds.
currentState	Specifies the playback file's current state: stopped, paused, or running.
displayBackColor	Specifies the display panel's background color.
displayForeColor	Specifies the display panel's foreground color.
displayMode	Indicates whether or not the display panel shows the current position in seconds or frames.
enableContextMenu	Indicates whether or not to enable the shortcut menu.
enabled	Specifies whether or not the control is enabled.
enablePositionControls	Indicates whether or not to show the position buttons in the controls panel.
enableSelectionControls	Indicates whether or not to show the selection buttons in the controls panel.
enableTracker	Indicates whether or not to show the trackbar control in the controls panel.
fileName	Specifies the name of the source data file.
filterGraph	Contains the interface pointer to the current filter graph object.
filterGraphDispatch	Contains the interface pointer to the current filter graph object.
fullScreenMode	Expands the area of the playback panel to fill the entire screen.

Property	Description
movieWindowSize	Specifies the size of the playback panel.
playCount	Specifies the number of times to play the multimedia stream.
rate	Specifies the playback rate for the stream.
readyState	Specifies the state of readiness for this ActiveMovie Control, based on how completely the source file has loaded.
selectionEnd	Specifies the ending position in this multimedia stream, in seconds, relative to the stream's beginning.
selectionStart	Specifies the starting position in this multimedia stream, in seconds, relative to the stream's beginning.
showControls	Indicates whether or not the controls panel is visible.
showDisplay	Indicates whether or not the display panel is visible.
showPositionControls	Indicates whether or not the position controls are visible.
showSelectionControls	Indicates whether or not the selection controls are visible.
showTracker	Indicates whether or not the trackbar is visible.
volume	Specifies the volume, in hundredths of decibels.

The methods of the Active Movie control are much smaller in scope; all except the **aboutbox** are useful in typical coding of web pages. The most useful, as you will see in the code examples, is the **isSoundCardEnabled** property.

Method	Description
aboutBox	Displays version and copyright information about the ActiveMovie Control.
isSoundCardEnabled	Determines whether the computer's sound card is enabled.
pause	Suspends a play operation without changing the current position.
run	Starts a multimedia stream from the specified starting position or continues playing a paused stream.
stop	Stops playback and resets the position as indicated by the **autoRewind** and **selectionStart** properties.

The events for the Active Movie control provide means to handle more complex sound and video manipulation on your web page.

Event	Description
displayModeChange	Indicates changes to the **displayMode** property.
error	Indicates that an error occurred.
openComplete	Indicates changes to the control's state of readiness.

Table Continued on Following Page

Event	Description
positionChange	Indicates changes to the current media position.
readyStateChange	Indicates changes to the control's state of readiness.
stateChange	Indicates player state changes.
timer	Handles timer events.

There are quite a lot of properties, methods, and events in the active movie control. They do provide for flexible and complex handling of media, and allow authors to customize their UI. Fortunately for less complicated web pages we will only need to be concerned with a few of these, the most important being: **readyStateChange**, **stateChange**, and **isSoundCardEnabled**. We'll take a look at how they're used.

ReadyStateChange Event

This event will fire, as one would expect, whenever the **readyState** property changes.

```
Sub myAMControl_ReadyStateChange(State)
if myAMControl.ReadyState = 4 then
    myAMControl.Run()
end if
End Sub
```

Authors should check the control's state of readiness before attempting to call the **run()** method. Authors should call the **run()** method only if the **State** parameter, or the controls **readyState** property, equals 4 or 3. Note that unlike other events the **on** prefix is not used, hence it is not **onReadyStateChange**. This can cause confusion.

Settings

The possible settings for the **readyState** parameter are

Value	Description
1	The **fileName** property has not been initialized.
0	The ActiveMovie Control is asynchronously loading a file.
3	The control has downloaded enough data to start playing the file, but has not yet received all data.
4	All data has been downloaded.

StateChange Event

The ActiveMovie Control raises the **stateChange** event when the control's state changes.

```
Sub myAMControl _StateChange(oldState, newState)
    if newState = 0 and oldState = 2 then 'loop sound only if previously playing
    myAMControl.Run()
    end if
End sub
```

The `currentState` property of the control, as well as the second parameter to the event, contains the active state of the media stream.

Settings

Following are possible settings for the `oldState` or `newState` parameters.

Value	Description
0	The playback is stopped.
1	The playback is paused.
2	The playback is playing.

IsSoundCardEnabled Method

While it may seem like a property at first, `isSoundCardEnabled` is actually a method.

```
var g_useSound = myAMControl.IsSoundCardEnabled();
```

When invoked it queries the system for available sound cards and returns a boolean to indicate success. This simple method allows us, as web authors, to write pages that know if the user can hear us. This lets us write conditional pages that do more than 'gracefully degrade' without sound, and can have states explicitly written without sound.

Settings

Setting	Description
True	Sound card is enabled.
False	No sound cards are enabled.

Control implementation

The Active Movie control can be instanced in two main ways; 'above' the page via an **HREF**, or within the page as an object. The first method allows for extremely easy scripting, but limited control of appearance or playback.

```
<A HREF="/relative/path/to/sound.mp3">play me</A>
```

Obviously this is similar to the functionality that can be obtained via the **<BGSOUND>** tag or with existing plug-ins; as such it is of little interest here. The real fun starts with the second option, embedding the control within the web page. When embedding the active movie control on the page an author can declare explicitly in the **<PARAM>** tags, or later in script, both the media resources and the appearance of the control. Let's take a look:

```
<OBJECT ID="mixer" CLASSID="CLSID:05589FA1-C356-11CE-BF01-00AA0055595A"
STYLE="TOP:1;LEFT:0;WIDTH:1;HEIGHT:1;visibility:hidden;">
<PARAM NAME="ShowControls" VALUE="-1">
```

```
<PARAM NAME="AutoStart" VALUE="0">
<PARAM NAME="AutoRewind" VALUE="-1">
<PARAM NAME="FileName" VALUE="SOUND.WAV">
</OBJECT>
```

In this instance we've opted not to have the control panel display at all. This is the most common mode, as it allows for custom UIs to be implemented by the web designer. For video playback it would be common to display only the video window for the same reasons; it allows the author to define the UI of the page and use the active movie control only for playback. Here we can see a simple example of scripting the control.

Progressive downloads

The Active Movie control uses **progressive downloading** by default; what this means is that as soon as enough data is available the control will allow either user input or scripts to start playback. The sufficiency of the downloaded data can be determined by the `readyState` property. Once enough data is available the `readyState` property will be 3, when all data is downloaded it will be 4. Due to the nature of the Quicktime and AVI video formats however this setting will never occur; these formats keep their indexes at the end of the file and as such cannot be played until all the data is present. If the control is being used with the UI displayed, the play button will be inaccessible until downloading is complete. If a script attempts to play the stream before download is complete an error will result. Obviously, under these circumstances, the utility of progressive downloading is rather limited. However, as new video compression formats become available, this functionality will become much more compelling.

Control manipulation

The Active Movie control supports the methods one would expect of a well-behaved control: `Run()`, `Pause()`, and `Stop()`. For support of sound playback it has balance, volume, and rate properties. By combining these methods an author can present video or audio in a way which fits their web page stylistically; creating truly background sounds with low volume, or panning the sound to the left to match a speaker gif.

With some scripting the playback can respond to the user dynamically. The volume can be based off a slider, or you can take the mouse move event and alter the pan property to match the x coordinate of the mouse. Many possibilities present themselves, all of which allow for a more dynamic user experience to be created. Now let's look at a simple example.

Simple Movie Player Example

If you run the Simple Movie Player example from `http://rapid.wrox.co.uk/books/0707` then you're presented with these three buttons after a short pause:

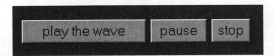

You can play and pause the sample and restart it from the point you paused it. The code needed to do this is relatively simple.

```
<HTML>
<HEAD>
    <TITLE>Active Movie simple intro</TITLE>
</HEAD>
```

```
<BODY BGCOLOR=Black>
<OBJECT ID="mixer" CLASSID="CLSID:05589FA1-C356-11CE-BF01-00AA0055595A"
    STYLE="TOP:1;LEFT:0;WIDTH:1;HEIGHT:1;visibility:hidden;">
    <PARAM NAME="ShowControls" VALUE="-1">
    <PARAM NAME="AutoStart" VALUE="0">
    <PARAM NAME="AutoRewind" VALUE="-1">
    <PARAM NAME="PlayCount" VALUE="1">
    <PARAM NAME="FileName" VALUE="SND.WAV">
</OBJECT>
```

The object is instanced on the page with no user interface (UI) presented to user. The default start and end actions have been preset.

```
<INPUT TYPE=button id=btn1 VALUE="loading waves" onClick="playsound('snd.wav')">
<INPUT TYPE=button id=btn2 VALUE="pause" onClick="mixer.Pause();">
<INPUT TYPE=button id=btn2 VALUE="stop" onClick="mixer.Stop();">
```

This code just sets up the events and ids for the three buttons.

```
<SCRIPT LANGUAGE="JScript">
g_SoundCard = mixer.IsSoundCardEnabled();
```

In the first script block, we use the global variable **g_soundCard** for the sound card to see if it's safe to use the controls methods without multiple calls to the function.

```
function playsound(soundtoplay){
    if(mixer.readystate == 4 && g_SoundCard){
            mixer.Run();
            btn1.value = "playing";
    }else{
            btn1.value = "wave not loaded yet";
    }
}
</SCRIPT>
```

The function checks to see if the wave has finished loading and if the soundcard is present. Next we set handlers for two very important events.

```
<SCRIPT LANGUAGE="VBScript">
sub mixer_readystatechange(a)
    btn1.value = "play the wave"
end sub
sub mixer_statechange(a,b)
    if b = 1 then
            btn1.value = "wave paused"
    else
            btn1.value = "wave stopped"
    end if
end sub
</SCRIPT>
</BODY>
</HTML>
```

In the `readystatechange` event we can set global states to indicate that we are still loading the files; both visually to the user, and programmatically via globals. The `statechange` event can be used to drive sample loops or signal that the media stream has changed behaviors. Notice that `btn1`'s text changed when we stop or pause the playback, and also when the wave finishes playing normally.

The only changes needed to play video rather than just the audio are in the object declaration; let's look at a simple AVI example:

```
<OBJECT ID="mixer" WIDTH=180 HEIGHT=80
    CLASSID="CLSID:05589FA1-C356-11CE-BF01-00AA0055595A">
    <PARAM NAME="ShowDisplay" VALUE="0">
    <PARAM NAME="ShowControls" VALUE="0">
    <PARAM NAME="MovieWindowWidth" VALUE="184">
    <PARAM NAME="MovieWindowHeight" VALUE="85">
    <PARAM NAME="AutoStart" VALUE="0">
    <PARAM NAME="AutoRewind" VALUE="-1">
    <PARAM NAME="FileName" VALUE="RockClmb.avi">
</OBJECT>
```

Note that the height and width are specified both in the `<PARAM>` tags, and in the object's style declaration. This allows greater control over the UI, and you should also note a few extra pixels are used in the MovieWindow metrics. This prevents unwanted UI artifacts where the playback window and the underlying `<DIV>` meet.

It is quite important also to set the `ShowDisplay` value to 0; though this may seem counter intuitive at first. This prevents the time counter and other display elements from appearing, not the display of the movie itself.

Dynamic Properties Example

In this example we've used immediate script to alter a looping waveform based on user input. We play a short looped sound wave and the user can press the << button on the left to decrease the rate at which the sample is played (effectively making it lower in pitch). The user can also press the >> button on the right to play the sample at a higher rate (making the sample higher).

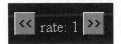

> *This example can be downloaded or run from http://rapid.wrox.co.uk/books/0707 as can all of the examples in the chapter.*

Once again, the code required to do this is very simple.

```
<HTML>
<HEAD>
    <TITLE>Active Movie dynamic properties example</TITLE>
</HEAD>

<BODY BGCOLOR=Black text=yellow>
<OBJECT ID="looping" CLASSID="CLSID:05589FA1-C356-11CE-BF01-00AA0055595A"
    STYLE="TOP:1;LEFT:0;WIDTH:1;HEIGHT:1;visibility:hidden;">
    <PARAM NAME="ShowControls" VALUE="-1">
    <PARAM NAME="AutoStart" VALUE="-1">
    <PARAM NAME="AutoRewind" VALUE="-1">
```

```
        <PARAM NAME="PlayCount" VALUE="0">
        <PARAM NAME="FileName" VALUE="loop.WAV">
    </OBJECT>
```

We start by setting the **AutoStart** and **AutoRewind** properties to true, and set the number of iterations with the **PlayCount** property, 0 being infinite. With the Active Movie control you must set both **AutoStart** and **AutoRewind** to true (-1) in order for the looping to work. Then we alter the playback of the waveform by adjusting its rate property.

```
<input type=button id=btn1 value="<<" onClick="looping.rate-=0.3; btn2.innerText =
'rate: ' + looping.rate;">
<span id=btn2>rate: 1</span>
<input type=button id=btn3 value=">>" onClick="looping.rate+=0.3; btn2.innerText =
'rate: ' + looping.rate;">

</BODY>
</HTML>
```

This allows the user to change the playback rate of the wave. The rate property cannot be set below zero or the control will throw a script error. You can see that if one were to adjust the rate of a stream it could be used for more than one application on a page. Of course this would work just as well for the AVI example with one caveat; movies tend to respond poorly to high rates of playback. It is easy to extrapolate this simple case to useful UI purposes, such as basing the rate of a pure sine wave on the mouse location to create a 'homing' tone directed at a desired UI element.

UI Implementation Example

Our next example shows how to implement a basic UI for the active movie control.

393

We have favored simplicity over functionality in order to keep the code readable. In this page we illustrate two things: dynamic parameter handling, and UI maintenance. This example builds on the first example. We add the movie control as before:

```
<HTML>
<HEAD>
    <TITLE>Active Movie UI Sample</TITLE>
</HEAD>

<BODY Background=bg2.png>
<OBJECT ID="mixer" CLASSID="CLSID:05589FA1-C356-11CE-BF01-00AA0055595A"
style="WIDTH:445;HEIGHT:155;position:absolute;top:55;left:90">
    <PARAM NAME="ShowDisplay" VALUE="0">
    <PARAM NAME="ShowControls" VALUE="0">
    <PARAM NAME="MovieWindowWidth" VALUE="445">
    <PARAM NAME="MovieWindowHeight" VALUE="162">
    <PARAM NAME="AutoStart" VALUE="0">
    <PARAM NAME="AutoRewind" VALUE="-1">
    <param name="Volume" value="-5000">
    <PARAM NAME="FileName" VALUE="RockClmb.avi">
</OBJECT>
```

We then add a second active movie control for incidental sounds, together with the buttons on the UI.

```
<OBJECT ID="btnsnd" CLASSID="CLSID:05589FA1-C356-11CE-BF01-00AA0055595A"
style="WIDTH:0;HEIGHT:0">
    <PARAM NAME="ShowDisplay" VALUE="0">
    <PARAM NAME="ShowControls" VALUE="0">
    <PARAM NAME="AutoStart" VALUE="0">
    <PARAM NAME="AutoRewind" VALUE="-1">
    <PARAM NAME="FileName" VALUE="click.wav">
</OBJECT>
<img id=btn1 src="playup.gif" onClick="am('play'); btnsnd.Run();"
style="position:absolute;top:250;left:80;filter:alpha(opacity=60)">
<img id=btn2 src="pauseup.gif" onClick="am('pause'); btnsnd.Run();"
style="position:absolute;top:250;left:260">
<img id=btn3 src="stopup.gif" onClick="am('stop'); btnsnd.Run();"
style="position:absolute;top:250;left:400">
```

In the immediate script on the image tags we first call a function to implement the appropriate method of the mixer control (the movie), then call the run method of the **btnsnd** control (the **click** wave).

```
<SCRIPT LANGUAGE="VBScript">
sub mixer_readystatechange(a)
```

Once media is ready remove the opacity fade from the play button, and set the volume to -3000 (essentially silent).

```
    btn1.style.filter = ""
    mixer.volume = -3000
end sub

sub mixer_statechange(a,b)
```

If playback stops, reset the play and stop buttons to the up state, and reset volume to silent.

```
        if b = 0 then
                btn1.src = "playup.gif"
                btn3.src = "stopup.gif"
                mixer.volume = -3000
        end if
end sub
```

This function is called from the play buttons handler. It recursively raises the volume to 0 (full volume)

```
sub ramp()
    mixer.volume = mixer.volume + 100
    if mixer.volume < 0 and mixer.currentstate = 2 then
            call window.setTimeout("call ramp()", 0075, "vbscript")
```

Note that we insert a delay before the next call to the ramp function. This allows the Active Movie control sufficient time to work. If this delay were not here no sound or playback would occur until the recursive loop was done.

```
        end if
end sub
</SCRIPT>

<SCRIPT LANGUAGE="JScript">
g_SoundCard = mixer.IsSoundCardEnabled();

function am(todo){
    if(todo == "play"){
            if(mixer.readystate == 4 && g_SoundCard){
                    btn1.src = "playdn.gif";
                    btn2.src = "pauseup.gif";
                    btn3.src = "stopup.gif";
                    mixer.Run();
                    ramp();
            }
    }
    if(todo == "pause"){
            if(mixer.readystate == 4 && g_SoundCard){
                    btn2.src = "pausedn.gif";
                    btn3.src = "stopup.gif";
                    mixer.Pause();
            }
    }
    if(todo == "stop"){
            if(mixer.readystate == 4 && g_SoundCard){
                    btn2.src = "pauseup.gif";
                    btn3.src = "stopdn.gif";
                    mixer.Stop();
                    mixer.volume = -3000;
            }
    }
}
</SCRIPT>
</BODY>
</HTML>
```

The final part of the script determines which button has been pressed and displays the correct button graphics to indicate which button has been pressed, and which haven't.

Active Movie Issues

As can be seen from the UI example there are limitations to the Active Movie control:

▲ The performance of the page will degrade with multiple controls – this is true of all controls.

▲ When mixing sounds from two or more active movie controls the user will experience delays in the sound playback.

▲ Additionally, on WindowsNT, mixing of sounds via the active movie control doesn't work in this release of the control.

Though there are ways around some of these issues, it becomes clear that the active movie control is best suited for simple uses where ease of implementation is an issue, and complexity is not required.

Direct Animation

For pages which require the kind of complexity that active movie cannot support Microsoft provides Direct Animation (DA) as part of the minimum configuration of IE4. DA is a library of multimedia effects. It contains several hundred functions within its API, and as such it includes a heavy learning curve for intrepid authors who wish to master it. The DA library may be accessed via the DAExpress ActiveX control, or through the multimedia controls which encapsulate it such as the structured graphics control.

DA provides some very powerful tools for multimedia. For example, its sound capabilities include mixing, synthesis, and 3D spatialization. This control differs conceptually from others in its utilization; it has no play or stop methods. Rather, in DA, one describes the world/model desired and then sets the control in motion.

To play a sound it must first be described in terms of its duration. This can be a literal value of the length of the wave file, or it can be a description of edge action such as 'loop'. For interactions with events outside of the DA control's display region, e.g. with page elements, there is a third and very useful description involving 'behaviors'.

Behaviors are central to understanding DA. Everything in DA is a behavior. What this means is that a sound isn't an object with methods, like `play()`; rather the sound, its duration, and any actions it may have such as looping are collectively understood as a single behavior object.

To create a sound that we can play in response to external events we declare the sound behavior property of the DA control to be a modifiable behavior of silence. This causes the control to playback silence until that behavior is modified to be another behavior, such as a wave file, and resumes the silence behavior when the new (modified) behavior is completed.

Overcoming the Limitations of the Active Movie Control

This example is an alteration of the UI example, using DA to overcome the mixing limitations of the active movie control. Try running the two examples together, pressing the play and pause buttons continuously, to see the differences. The first change is that the immediate script now calls the **playsound** function.

```
...
<IMG id=btn1 src="playup.gif" onClick="am('play'); playsound();"
style="position:absolute;top:250;left:80;filter:alpha(opacity=60)">
<IMG id=btn2 src="pauseup.gif" onClick="am('pause'); playsound();"
style="position:absolute;top:250;left:260">
<IMG id=btn3 src="stopup.gif" onClick="am('stop'); playsound();"
style="position:absolute;top:250;left:400">
```

The DA control must be instanced on the page before references to it in script.

```
<OBJECT ID="DAControl" STYLE="position:absolute; left:10; width:1; height:1;"
CLASSID="CLSID:B6FFC24C-7E13-11D0-9B47-00C04FC2F51D"></OBJECT>
<SCRIPT LANGUAGE="JScript">
```

We then get a pointer to the library from the control and create a global variable containing the sound behavior.

```
        m = DAControl.MeterLibrary;
```

This is done by assigning the sound property of the importation result, which is returned by the **importSound** function in the DA library, to the **mysnd** variable. This is done to pre-load the sound behavior into memory, if multiple sounds will be used then pre-loading sounds in this manner may not be efficacious.

```
        mysnd = m.ImportSound("click.wav").Sound;
```

Then we set the DA controls sound property to be a modifiable behavior, in this case silence – which is returned by the Silence function in the DA library.

```
        DAControl.Sound = m.ModifiableBehavior(m.Silence);
```

Now that the world has been described we can start the control. Once started the DA control will keep doing what was described until it is destroyed by closing the page. You can think of the DA control like a lemming; it keeps running on the course it was given. As an author you can give it new courses to run dynamically, but you cannot stop it.

```
        DAControl.Start();
```

The next part is the dark heart of the DA implementation: we call the **SwitchTo** method of the (modifiable) sound property of the DA control. This method takes a behavior as an argument, here we pass the global **mysnd** which contains the sound behavior we imported earlier. This changes the behavior to the sound contained in **mysnd**, and the DA control will dutifully play that sound then return to playing silence upon completion of the **mysnd** behavior.

```
      function playsound(){
              DAControl.Sound.SwitchTo(mysnd);
}
</SCRIPT>
</BODY>
</HTML>
```

As mentioned earlier if sounds are not preloaded, the **playsound** function could be written to take a file reference as a **<PARAM>** and the sound importation could be done in the **SwitchTo** method call itself:

DAControl.Sound.SwitchTo(m.ImportSound(soundParamOfPlaysoundFunction).Sound);

This would incur a slight performance loss while it retrieves the file, which is why we used pre-loading in this example; users are very sensitive to delays for things like button click sounds. Now we'll take a look at other controls that form part of DA.

Path Control

The Path control allows you to move objects on a web page dynamically over time. There are two simple steps to using the path control. First, specify the path that the object should follow. Then, set how long it should take to complete the path. The Path control will take care of moving your object. This is a big advantage over scripting the movement directly in code. You can select a simple path, such as a rectangle or oval, or a more complex path, using lines or splines.

Properties

The control has the following properties:

Property	Description	Values
autoStart	This property determines if the playback of the Path control should begin as soon as the page has finished loading. The default value is false, in which case the Path must be explicitly played.	True(1) or False(0)
bounce	This property determines what happens when the object reaches the end of the path. If **bounce** is set to True, then the object will follow the path in reverse until it reaches the starting point. If **bounce** is set to False, then playback is stopped.	True(1) or False(0)
direction	This property determines if the path is followed from beginning to end (forward) or end to beginning (reverse).	Forward = 0 (default) Reverse = 1
duration	The time that it will take for the object to fully traverse the path.	Seconds and milliseconds, using the 0.000 format.
playState	This read-only property returns the current status of the control.	Stopped = 0 Playing = 1 Paused = 2

Property	Description	Values
repeat	The property determines the number of times that the path is repeated once it reaches the end. For controls where the **bounce** property is True, a full cycle of beginning-end-beginning is needed before the repeat value is considered.	> 0 – Number of times to repeat 0 – Disabled -1 – Repeats infinitely
target	This determines the object that will be moved by the path control.	Any valid page object that has **top** and **left** properties
time	This is the elapsed time since playback started. When the playback is paused, this timer is paused as well. For controls with a Repeat value greater than 1, the time is kept from the initial play. It isn't reset when the path is repeated	Milliseconds

The methods of the Path object fall into two categories: path and control.

Path Methods

The Path methods are used to determine the path the object will follow when the Path control is played. The parameters for each method will be called out in detail later in the chapter.

Method	Description
rect	Specifies a rectangular path for the Target object to follow. The path will begin at the top-left corner, with the forward direction set to clockwise.
oval	Specifies an oval-shaped path for the Target object to follow. The path will begin at the top center position, or 12 o'clock. The forward direction is set to clockwise.
polygon	Specifies a closed path made up of straight lines for the Target object to follow. The lines are determined by a series of points. The first point in the series is the starting point of the path. The last line in the path is from the last point in the series to the first point.
polyLine	Specifies an open path made up of straight lines for the Target object to follow. The difference between the **polyLine** and the **polygon** is that the starting and ending point for the **polyLine** path can be different, while they must be the same for the **polygon** path.
spline	Specifies a path made up of spline curves for the Target object to follow.
keyFrame	Specifies a path made up of a series of points along the path, and the time that the Target object should reach that point. The object will travel in a straight line between each point in the series.
addTimeMarker	This method is used to set a marker at a specific time during playback. When that marker is reached, an event is fired, which can be handled by the Path control's container.

Control Methods

The control methods are used to control the playback of the Path control.

Method	Description
play	Begins the playback of the Path control at the current elapsed time
pause	Stops the playback of the Path control. Freezes the elapsed time of the control. Invoking the **play** method will restart playback at the position the control was paused.
stop	Stops the playback of the Path control and sets the elapsed time to 0
seek	Sets the **Time** parameter to a specific value.

You can use the path control to move any type of object on an HTML page. The only requirement for the object is that it must have **top** and **left** style properties. For example, if you wished to move an image around a path, you would need to declare the image in the web page as follows:

```
<IMG ID=imgMyImage SRC="images\myImg.jpg" STYLE="position:absolute;LEFT: 20; TOP:
80;WIDTH:75;HEIGHT:75">
```

To insert the Path control into your page, you would use an **<OBJECT>** tag containing the **CLASSID** of the Path control. If your Dynamic HTML editor supports the insertion of ActiveX controls, then you should be able to select the Path control from a list, and the editor will add the **CLASSID** to the **<OBJECT>** tag. If you are like most of us and are still using Notepad to develop your sites, just type in the **CLASSID** exactly as it is shown here.

```
<OBJECT ID="myPath" CLASSID="CLSID:D7A7D7C3-D47F-11D0-89D3-00A0C90833E6">
```

The properties and methods of the path can be set in two ways: using **<PARAM>** tags inside of the object definition, or by using Object reference in script. Let's take a look at a short example that will move an object over a number of different paths. We will look at how to set the properties of the Path using both methods.

```
<IMG ID=imgMyImage SRC="images\myImg.jpg" STYLE="position:absolute;LEFT: 20; TOP:
80;WIDTH:75;HEIGHT:75">
```

We first insert an image and set its ID to **imgMyImage**. Then we set its position to a point at (20,80).

```
<OBJECT ID="myPath" CLASSID="CLSID:D7A7D7C3-D47F-11D0-89D3-00A0C90833E6">
```

Next, we define an object called **myPath**. If we were using scripting to configure the properties and methods of this control, then we would also include a **</OBJECT>** tag to terminate the object definition.

Now, we will set the parameters for our path control.

```
<PARAM NAME=Bounce VALUE=1>
```

By setting the **Bounce** parameter to 1 (True), the object will follow the path to the endpoint, then reverse its direction and play back to the beginning.

```
<PARAM NAME=Direction VALUE=0>
```

The value of 0 for the **Direction** parameter will play the path from beginning to end. This is the default value, and it is not explicitly necessary to set it here.

```
<PARAM NAME=Duration VALUE="2.575">
```

The **Duration** parameter determines the time that it will take for the object to traverse its path. This is the time it takes for the object to move from the beginning to the end of the path. In this example, it will take the object 2 seconds and 575 milliseconds to move from the beginning to the end. Since the **Bounce** parameter is set to True, it will take another 2.575 seconds to move back to the beginning, which will complete its path.

```
<PARAM NAME=Repeat VALUE="3">
```

This tag sets the **Repeat** parameter to 3. This will cause the path to be repeated 3 times. Since the **Bounce** parameter has already been set to True, this means that the object will follow the path from start to finish and back to start three times.

```
<PARAM NAME=Target VALUE=imgMyImage>
```

To tell the Path control which object to move, we need to set the **Target** parameter. This tag tells the Path control that it will be moving the object with an ID of **imgMyImage**. The other method for setting the parameters of the Path control is through the use of script. This example will show the method for setting these same parameters using script.

```
Sub SetParams()
    myPath.Bounce = True
    myPath.Direction = 0
    myPath.Duration = 2.575
    myPath.Repeat = 3
    myPath.Target = imgMyImage
End Sub
```

Now that we have defined the parameters for our Path control, we need to set the path itself.

Rectangle Path

As stated earlier, there are 6 ways to define the path that an object can follow. The simplest of these paths is the Rectangle. A point, a height value, and a width value define a rectangular path. The Target object will move along the path in the following manner:

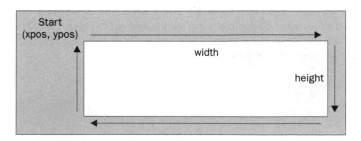

As with the Parameters, there are two ways of defining the path in the web page. You can use the `<PARAM>` tag to define the path:

```
<PARAM NAME="Shape" VALUE="Rect(xpos,ypos,width,height)">
```

The values for the parameters are in pixels. The **xpos** and **ypos** values are absolute positions within the document. To define this same path in script would be as follows:

```
myPath.Rect(xpos,ypos,width,height)
```

Oval Path

The next path is the Oval path. The oval shape that the object will follow is defined by top-center point of the oval, its width, and its height.

> *The usual way of defining an oval's position, based on the position of its center, is not used here. The position that is set is a point on the oval itself, at the 12 o'clock position.*

The Target object will move along the path in the following manner:

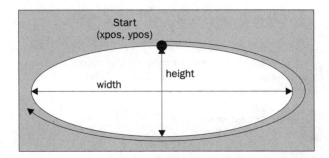

The oval path is defined by:

```
<PARAM NAME="Shape" VALUE="Oval(xpos,ypos,width,height)">
```

if you are using the tag method. To define the oval path using scripting, you need:

```
myPath.Oval(xpos,ypos,width,height)
```

Polygon Path

The next type of path, in order of increasing complexity, is the Polygon path. This path allows you to define a set of points on the web page, and have the Target object move between them. The object will start at the first point that you define and move towards the second. When it reaches the second point, it will move towards the third point. It will proceed in this manner until it reaches the final point that you define. Once it reaches that point, the object will move towards the first point in the series, effectively closing the Polygon.

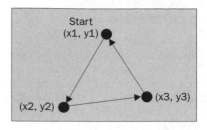

Here is an example using 3 points:

To define this path using tags, you will do the following:

```
<PARAM NAME="Polygon" VALUE="3,x1,y1,x2,y2,x3,y3">
```

The first parameter, 3, defines the total number of points in the series. The remaining parameters define each of the points in the path, in the order that they are to be followed. To define this path in script, you will need to perform two steps. You will first need to create an array that contains all of the points in the path. Then, you will pass that array as a parameter to the **polygon** method of the Path object.

```
pointArray = Array(x1,y1,x2,y2,x3,y3)
myPath.Polygon(3, pointArray)
```

Again, the first parameter to the **polygon** method is the total number of points in the path.

PolyLine Path

A variation to the Polygon path is the PolyLine path. Whereas the Polygon path creates a closed path by moving the object from the last point in the series back to the first point, the PolyLine path will end when the object reaches the last point in the series of points. Using the same three points as the previous example, the Target object will move in this path:

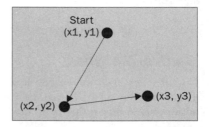

As you can see, the Target object will move to the third point and then stop. The implementation of this type of path is nearly identical to that of the Polygon path. To define this path using tags, you will do the following:

```
<PARAM NAME="PolyLine" VALUE="3,x1,y1,x2,y2,x3,y3">
```

The first parameter, 3, defines the total number of points in the series. The remaining parameters define each of the points in the path, in the order that they are to be followed. To define this path in script, you will need to perform two steps. You will first need to create an array that contains all of the points in the path. Then, you will pass that array as a parameter to the **polyLine** method of the Path object.

```
pointArray = Array(x1,y1,x2,y2,x3,y3)
myPath.polyLine(3, pointArray)
```

Again, the first parameter to the **PolyLine** method is the total number of points in the path.

Spline Path

You can create complex curvilinear paths by using the Spline type of path. A spline is a curve that is defined by a set of four points. One point defines the beginning of the curve, another defines the end of the curve. The other two points are known as control points. They affect the shape of the curve. A spline is a very good way to represent complex curves. However, this power comes at a price. It is very difficult to create a desired curve by picking the four points of the spline out of thin air. Tools such as Adobe Illustrator or Corel Draw are much more adept at creating and manipulating splines. So, for the sake of this example, we will assume that you already have the four points that you need to make up the spline.

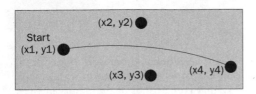

As you can see, the Target object will move from the Start point to the End point, but its path will be affected by the position of the other two points. To define this path using tags, you will do the following:

```
<PARAM NAME="Spline" VALUE="n,x1,y1,x2,y2,x3,y3,x4,y4">
```

The first parameter, *n*, defines the total number of points in the series. Remember that there are 4 points to define each curve in a spline, so the value for *n* should be a multiple of 4. To define this path in script, you can either use the array method, as used for the Polygon and PolyLine. Otherwise you can simply pass a comma-delimited string of numbers, as is shown below.

```
myPath.spline(n,x1,y1,x2,y2,x3,y3,x4,y4)
```

Again, the first parameter to the **Spline** method is the total number of points in the path.

Control Methods

Now that we have shown you how to define a path, you will need to be able to control its playback. There are four methods that can be used to control the playback of a Path. Each control method also has an associated event, that is fired when the control method is called.

Play Method

This method begins playback of the path at the current elapsed time. The current elapsed time is held by the **time** property. When the Path is first played, the current elapsed time is 0. When the Path is played the **onPlay()** event is also fired, which allows the programmer a chance to perform some actions when the playback is started.

The **play** method is called by

```
myPath.play()
```

Pause Method

This method pauses the playback of the path. The current elapsed time, as held in the **time** property, is maintained at whatever value it held when the playback is paused. Issuing a **play()** method subsequent to a **pause()** method will restart the playback of the path at the point at which it was paused. When the Path is paused the **onPause()** event is also fired.

The **pause** method is called by

```
myPath.pause()
```

Stop Method

This method stops the playback of the path. The current elapsed time, as held in the **time** property, is reset to zero when the playback is stopped. Issuing a **play()** method subsequent to a **stop()** method will cause the playback of the path to start from the beginning. When the Path is stopped the **onStop()** event is also fired.

The **stop** method is called by

```
myPath.stop()
```

Seek Method

This method changes the current elapsed time of the path. The current elapsed time represents the current playback position in the Path. By changing the current elapsed time, the Target object of the Path will assume whatever position on the page is called for at the specific elapsed time position. This command allows you to precisely position your playback positions. The **seek** method does not affect the playback status of the path. If the Path is paused, it will remain paused. If it is playing, then it will continue playing. When the **seek** method is called, the **onSeek()** event is also fired.

The **seek** method is called by

```
myPath.seek(s.mss)
```

The parameter **s.mss** represents the desired elapsed time to position the Path to. The format of the parameter is in **seconds.milliseconds**.

Bookmarks

In addition to directly positioning the playback position of a Path control, you can set bookmarks along the timeline of the Path. When the Path control encounters one of these bookmarks during playback, an event is fired, which can then be handled by the web page.

To create a bookmark in a Path, you will use the **addTimeMarker** method. Bookmarks can either be added in the **<PARAM>** tags of the Path control definition, or added using script. The syntax for adding a bookmark using the **<PARAM>** tag is

```
<PARAM NAME="addTimeMarkerN" VALUE="time, markername, [fAbsolute]">
```

Since you can add multiple bookmarks to a single path, you will need to uniquely identify each one. This is done by adding a sequential integer suffix to the **NAME** value, represented by the **N** in the above syntax. For example, to add three bookmarks you would have

```
<PARAM NAME="AddTimeMarker1" …
<PARAM NAME="AddTimeMarker2" …
<PARAM NAME="AddTimeMarker3" …
```

To add a bookmark to a Path control using script, you would add the following code

```
myPath.addTimeMarker(time,markername,[fAbsolute])
```

The value for the **time** parameter indicates the elapsed time position that you wish to set the bookmark. Its value is represented in the format *seconds.milliseconds*. The *markername* parameter is used to identify a particular bookmark. You will see in a few seconds where this value is used. The *fAbsolute* flag is an optional parameter. If set to True, then the bookmark will be encountered only once during playback, regardless of any looping that the Path may do. This is the default setting, so if you omit the *fAbsolute* flag, then the bookmark will be encountered a maximum of one time. If this flag is false, then the bookmark will be encountered every time it is passed, even during looping.

When a bookmark is encountered, it will fire one or more events, depending on the current playback state. A bookmark can be encountered by the execution of a **seek** method to an elapsed time concurrent with a bookmark's position. When this occurs, the **onMarker()** event is fired. This event includes one parameter, *markername*, which is the name that the particular bookmark was given in its declaration. The parameter can help the event handling code determine which bookmark was encountered, and then take appropriate actions. A bookmark can also be encountered during normal playback. When this occurs, the **onMarker()** event is still fired, but a second event, **onPlayMarker()** is also fired. This event also includes the *markername* parameter. Between them, these two events provide a high degree of control and information when a bookmark is encountered.

Path Example

Now, let's take a look at a simple example of how the Path control can be used to move objects around a web page. In this example, we will make two buttons move around the page, controlled by different Path controls.

```
<HTML>
<BODY>
<SCRIPT LANGUAGE="VBScript">
```

We would like one of the buttons to be able to control its own movement. This event handler for the **btnStartStop** object will first check the **playstate** of the Path control. If the Path is currently playing, then the Path will be paused, and the caption on the button will be changed.

```
Sub btnStartStop_onClick
    if pthPolyline.Playstate = 1 then ' Playing
            pthPolyline.Pause()
            btnStartStop.Value = "Click Me to Go"
```

If the Path is either stopped or paused, then the code will call the **play()** method of the Path. This will either restart the control from where it was paused, or, if the Path reached its end, it will be restarted from the beginning.

```
    else ' Stopped or Paused
            pthPolyline.Play()
            btnStartStop.Value = "Click Me to Stop"
    end if
end sub

</SCRIPT>
```

The first Path is an Oval shaped path that the `btnCircle` object will be following. The Path will repeat indefinitely, and will begin immediately upon the page being loaded. It will take 10 seconds for the control to complete one revolution of the oval.

```
<OBJECT ID="pthOval" CLASSID = "CLSID:D7A7D7C3-D47F-11D0-89D3-00A0C90833E6">
    <PARAM NAME="AutoStart" VALUE="1">
    <PARAM NAME="Repeat" VALUE="-1">
    <PARAM NAME="Bounce" VALUE="0">
    <PARAM NAME="Duration" VALUE="10">
    <PARAM NAME="Shape" VALUE="Oval(50,75,400,200)">
    <PARAM NAME="Target" VALUE="btnCircle">
</OBJECT>
```

This path is an 8 segment PolyLine, defined by the 9 points listed as parameters. This path will also repeat indefinitely, and the `btnStartStop` object will traverse the path from coordinates (0,0), along the PolyLine to coordinates (0,150), and then backwards along the PolyLine back to coordinates (0,0).

```
<OBJECT ID="pthPolyline" CLASSID = "CLSID:D7A7D7C3-D47F-11d0-89D3-00A0C90833E6">
    <PARAM NAME="Repeat" VALUE="-1">
    <PARAM NAME="Bounce" VALUE="1">
    <PARAM NAME="Duration" VALUE="10">
    <PARAM NAME="Shape" VALUE="PolyLine(9, 0,0,250,10, 50,150, 250,200, 10,250,
150,250, 50,275, 205,150, 0,150)">
    <PARAM NAME="Target" VALUE="btnStartStop">
</OBJECT>
```

The two objects that will be moved have to have a `top` and `left` parameter defined. The Path control can only manipulate objects that have both of these parameters.

```
<INPUT ID=btnStartStop TYPE=BUTTON VALUE="Click Me to Go"
STYLE="POSITION: absolute; LEFT: 0; TOP: 0">
<INPUT ID=btnCircle TYPE=BUTTON VALUE="Circling..."
STYLE="POSITION: absolute; LEFT: 300; TOP: 300">
</BODY>
</HTML>
```

Since it is somewhat difficult to see motion on a printed page, the best way to see Path control in action in to view the page in your IE4 browser. After the page is loaded, it will look something like this.

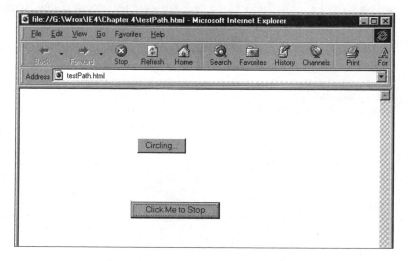

As you can see, this can be a very powerful control for scripting the movement of elements on a web page. One of the strengths of Macromedia Director has always been its ability to move objects on the screen, and to alleviate the developer from plotting every position that the object must take in each and every frame. Now, with IE4 and the Path control, you can accomplish the same thing in your web pages.

Sequencer Control

You have just seen how the path control gives you a Macromedia Director-like control over the position of objects on you web pages. Now we will take a look at the Sequencer control which adds an order of magnitude of control to what the Path control already gives you. The Sequencer control provides sequence control and timing control over other controls, built-in functions, and scripts on the page. The sequencer can manage:

- Manipulating HTML controls
- Calling VBScript or other scripts
- Calling the methods of ActiveX Controls
- Setting and reading the properties of ActiveX Controls.

The sequencer can either perform its sequence of functions once, or loop the sequence as many times as is needed. The Sequencer object is inserted into a web page with the following `<OBJECT>` tag.

```
<OBJECT ID=mySeq CLASSID="CLSID:37992B41-F5E3-11CF-97DF-00A0C90FEE54">
</OBJECT>
```

Where *mySeq* is replaced by the name that you wish to assign to the object. Once you have added the control to your page, then you will use scripting to set the parameters that you need to use the control.

Action Sets

Sequences are grouped together into what are know as **Action Sets**. A single Sequencer object can have multiple Action Sets, each operating independently. The advantage of multiple Action Sets is that their playback can be individually controlled. For example, stopping one Action Set while allowing the other to continue running.

For performance optimizations, it is best to have one sequencer object controlling one Action Set with all of the sequenced actions on the page in that Action Set. If your page design warrants multiple Action Sets, then it is more advantageous from a performance standpoint to have multiple Action Sets in one sequencer object than multiple sequencer objects, each with one Action Set. This is due to the overhead in having multiple instances of an ActiveX control loaded as opposed to one control instance handling multiple tasks.

At Method

The **At** Method is used to inform the sequencer object of the actions that it needs to take. It is defined as follows:

```
mySeq("ActionSet").At(time, "script", [loop, interval, tiebreak, drop
threshold])
```

The value of *ActionSet* indicates the Action Set that this sequencer event is a part of. From a more technical standpoint, you can think of an Action Set as a collection of sequencer events, each one added by the **At** method.

The value of *time* indicates when this event should occur during the Action Set. The format is **seconds.milliseconds**. This is the elapsed time since the Action Set started playing. The timing of the sequencer is based on absolute time. This will allow for consistent playback timings, regardless of the speed of the computer that is viewing the sequence.

The value of *script* is the procedure that should be called when this event in the Action Set is reached. You can pass parameters to the procedure if you want to. The syntax for passing parameters is

```
script(param1,...).
```

The value of *loop* indicates the number of times the action should be repeated. This parameter is optional. If it is omitted, then the default value of 1 is used. This will cause this event to only be executed one time. If the value is <0 then the action will be repeated indefinitely. If the value is 0, then the action will never occur. This is a convenient way of dynamically removing actions from a sequence during playback.

The value of *interval* indicates how often the action should be repeated. This is an optional parameter. If the *loop* parameter is set to 1, then this value is ignored. The syntax for this parameter is **seconds.milliseconds**. The default value is 33 milliseconds, with is written as 0.033. This value happens to correspond to a frequency of 30 actions per second. The minimum value is 0.020, or 20 milliseconds. This is fastest that the sequencer could possibly repeat an action.

The value of *tiebreak* sets the priority for this action in the Action Set. The priority determines which action is executed first when multiple actions occur at the same time. This parameter is also optional. A *tiebreak* value of 0 is the highest possible priority. The priority decreases as the value of *tiebreak* increases. To give an action the lowest possible priority, set its *tiebreak* value to -1, which is also the default value.

The value of *drop threshold* is used to set the latest possible time that an action can be executed. This is an optional parameter. This parameter uses the same time syntax as the *interval* and *time* parameters, **seconds.milliseconds**. The default value is -1.00, which indicates that this action should always be executed, no matter how much time has elapsed since it was supposed to be executed. This parameter comes into play when there are multiple events occurring at one time, or if a particular event takes a long time to execute. It is conceivable that the elapsed time of the Action Set could have passed the *time* value for this action. In some time-critical sequences, you may choose not to perform an action, rather than perform it late. In these cases, the *drop threshold* parameter can determine how late is acceptable for the action to take place.

The remaining methods of the Sequencer control are used to control the playback of the Action Set. These methods are:

Method	Description	Parameter
play	Begins the playback of the Action Set at the current elapsed time.	
pause	Stops the playback of the Action Set. Freezes the playback time position of the Action Set. Invoking the Play method will restart playback at the time position the Action Set was paused.	
stop	Stops the playback of the Action Set and sets the playback time position to 0.000.	
seek	Sets the Time parameter to a specific value.	Time – seconds.milliseconds

Play Method

This method begins playback of the Action Set at the current elapsed time. The current elapsed time is held by the **time** property. When the Action Set is first played, the elapsed time is 0. When the Action Set is played the **onPlay()** event is also fired, which allows the programmer a chance to perform some actions when the playback is started.

The **play** method is called by

```
mySeq("ActionSet").play()
```

Pause Method

This method pauses the playback of the Action Set. The elapsed time, as held in the **time** property, is maintained at whatever value it held when the playback is paused. Issuing a **play()** method subsequent to a **pause()** method will restart the playback of the Action Set at the point at which it was paused. When the Action Set is paused the **onPause()** event is also fired.

The **pause** method is called by

```
mySeq("ActionSet").pause()
```

Stop Method

This method stops the playback of the Action Set. The current elapsed time, as held in the **time** property, is reset to zero when the playback is stopped. Issuing a **play()** method following a **stop()** method will cause the playback of the Action Set to restart from the beginning. When the Action Set is stopped the **onStop()** event is also fired.

The **stop** method is called by:

```
mySeq("ActionSet").stop()
```

Seek Method

This method changes the elapsed time value of the Action Set. The elapsed time value represents the current playback position of the Action Set. This command allows you to precisely position your playback positions. The **seek** method does not affect the playback status of the Action Set. If the Action Set is paused, it will remain paused. If it is playing, then it will remain playing. When the **seek** method is called, the **onSeek()** event is also fired.

The **seek** method is called by:

```
mySeq("ActionSet").seek(s.mss)
```

The parameter **s.mss** represents the desired elapsed time to position the Action Set to. The format of the parameter is in **seconds.milliseconds**.

Events

There are several events that occur when using the Sequencer control. These are:

Event	Description	Parameters
onInit	Fired when the sequencer control has finished loading. When this event occurs, the control is ready to begin playback	*none*
onPlay	Fired when the Action Set changes from a paused or stopped state to a playing state.	*ActionSetName*
onPause	Fired when the Action Set is paused.	*ActionSetName*
onStop	Fired when the Action Set is stopped.	*ActionSetName*
onSeek	Fired when the **seek** method is called.	*ActionSetName, newTime*

Properties

There are two properties of each Action Set that is created in the Sequencer control

Property	Description	Values
playState	Returns the current playback state of the Action Set. This is a read-only property.	Stopped = 0 Playing = 1 Paused = 2
time	This is the elapsed time since playback of the Action Set was started. While this value is read-write, you should use the Seek method to change it.	Seconds and milliseconds, using the 0.000 format.

Sequencer Example

In this Sequencer control example, we will be demonstrating how to make "dynamic" Dynamic HTML. This example uses one Sequencer object, with two Action Sets. These action sets control the visibility, placement, and color of various elements on the page. The example displays several layers of text which move around the screen and change color at set times. Because this is a "dynamic" example, it is difficult to show what the screen will always look like. Here is what the page looks like at some point after it is loaded:

The key elements to the example, which can be found on the Wrox web site at `http://rapid.wrox.co.uk/books/0707`, are the document division, or `<DIV>` elements. These hold the various sections of text, the initialization of the sequencer Action Sets, and the scripts that perform the manipulation of the elements.

The first two procedures **Play** and **Bkg** handle the "dynamic" portion of this application. The **play** and **bkg** methods are called by the Sequencer control to perform various operations on the elements. These operations include changing the visibility parameter from "visible" to "hidden" to make the element disappear. These operations also move elements on the page, which gives us the drop shadow effect that you see in the preceding screen shot.

```
<HTML>
<BODY>
<SCRIPT LANGUAGE="VBScript">
Sub Play(A)
    Select Case A
            Case "W"
                    LtrW.style.visibility="visible"
            Case "R"
                    ltrW.style.color = "coral"
                    LtrR.style.visibility="visible"
```

```
                Case "O"
                        ltrR.style.color = "coral"
                        LtrO.style.visibility="visible"
                Case "X"
                        ltrO.style.color = "coral"
                        LtrX.style.visibility="visible"
                case "Finish"
                        ltrX.style.color = "coral"
                case "Reset"
                        LtrW.style.visibility="hidden"
                        LtrR.style.visibility="hidden"
                        LtrO.style.visibility="hidden"
                        LtrX.style.visibility="hidden"
                        ltrW.style.color = "blue"
                        ltrR.style.color = "blue"
                        ltrO.style.color = "blue"
                        ltrX.style.color = "blue"
        End Select

End Sub

Sub Bkg(i)
    Select case i
            case 1
                    LettersAlt.style.visibility = "hidden"
                    Letters.style.visibility = "visible"
            case 2
                    Letters.style.top=10
                    Letters.style.left=10
            case 3
                    LettersAlt.style.top=-5
                    LettersAlt.style.left=-5
                    LettersAlt.style.visibility = "visible"
            case 4
                    Letters.style.visibility = "hidden"
                    Letters.style.top=0
                    Letters.style.left=0
                    LettersAlt.style.top=0
                    LettersAlt.style.left=0
    end select
end sub
```

This next procedure is used to program the Action Sets of the sequencer control. There are two Action Sets in this example. The first one, **Letters** controls the animation of the WROX letters. It accomplishes this by calling the **Play** procedure with a different parameter every second starting 500 milliseconds after the playback starts. These events will be repeated every 10 seconds until the Action Set is stopped.

```
Sub seqSpell_OnInit
    Call seqSpell("Letters").at(0.500,"Play(""W"")", -1, 10.0)
    Call seqSpell("Letters").at(1.500,"Play(""R"")", -1, 10.0)
    Call seqSpell("Letters").at(2.500,"Play(""O"")", -1, 10.0)
    Call seqSpell("Letters").at(3.500,"Play(""X"")", -1, 10.0)
    Call seqSpell("Letters").at(4.500,"Play(""Finish"")", -1, 10.0)
    Call seqSpell("Letters").at(8.500,"Play(""Reset"")", -1, 10.0)
```

The animation of the background text is accomplished by the **Bkg** Action Set. This action set calls the **Bkg** procedure with a different parameter to perform the animation effect.

```
    Call seqSpell("Bkg").at(1.00,"Bkg(1)",-1,4.0)
    Call seqSpell("Bkg").at(2.00,"Bkg(2)",-1,4.0)
    Call seqSpell("Bkg").at(3.00,"Bkg(3)",-1,4.0)
    Call seqSpell("Bkg").at(4.00,"Bkg(4)",-1,4.0)
```

Once we have initialized both Action Sets, they are ready for playback. This playback is started by issuing the **play** method for both Action Sets.

```
    Call seqSpell("Letters").play()
    call seqSpell("Bkg").play()
End Sub
</SCRIPT>
```

The Sequencer object is inserted into the page and given the identifier **seqSpell**. As you can see, there are no parameters necessary for the Sequencer object.

```
<OBJECT ID="seqSpell"
    CLASSID="CLSID:B0A6BAE2-AAF0-11d0-A152-00A0C908DB96">
</OBJECT>
```

The background text is added to the page in these two **<DIV>** blocks. They are given the exact same position and style parameters, except for two. The color of one is Yellow and the color of the other is Blue. Likewise, one is initially visible and the other invisible.

```
<DIV id=LettersAlt Style="position: absolute; TOP:0; LEFT:0; HEIGHT: 200; WIDTH: 550;
visibility:visible">
<FONT FACE="'Verdana'" Color="#EEEE00" SIZE="+4"><B><CENTER>Who Publishes the top
computer books?</CENTER></B></FONT>
</DIV>

<DIV id=Letters Style="position: absolute; TOP:0; LEFT:0; HEIGHT: 200; WIDTH: 550;
visibility:hidden">
<FONT FACE="'Verdana'" Color="#1111FF" SIZE="+4"><B><CENTER>Who Publishes the top
computer books?</CENTER></B></FONT>
</DIV>
```

This next **<DIV>** block holds the four **<DIV>** blocks that each hold one letter in the word WROX. The **<DIV>**s for the letters are placed inside another **<DIV>** so that they can be repositioned as a unit. Each individual letter **<DIV>** is initially made invisible.

```
<DIV ID=Wrox STYLE="position: absolute; TOP:50;LEFT:150;">
<!--Spell out Wrox using 4 letters each stored in its own DIV block-->
<DIV ID="ltrW" STYLE="position: relative; TOP:0;LEFT:0;font:48pt Verdana;font-
weight:bold;color:blue;visibility:hidden">W</DIV>
<DIV ID="ltrR" STYLE="position: absolute; TOP:0;LEFT:70;font:48pt Verdana;font-
weight:bold;color:blue;visibility:hidden">R</DIV>
<DIV ID="ltrO" STYLE="position: absolute; TOP:0;LEFT:120;font:48pt Verdana;font-
weight:bold;color:blue;visibility:hidden">O</DIV>
<DIV ID="ltrX" STYLE="position: absolute; TOP:0;LEFT:170;font:48pt Verdana;font-
weight:bold;color:blue;visibility:hidden">X</DIV>
```

```
    </DIV>
    </BODY>
    </HTML>
```

As you can see, it is very easy to add a sequencer control to your web page. All that you need to do is

- ▲ Add the Object to your page
- ▲ Wait for the `onInit` event to tell you the control is ready
- ▲ Create an Action Set with calls to your dynamic control procedures
- ▲ Call the `play` method, then sit back and enjoy

Next, we will take a look at a new way to present animated images on your web page: the Sprite Control.

Sprite Control

Until the release of IE4, animation of a web page meant one of a few things. You could have an animated GIF, which looped through a series of frames, all of which were the same size and in the same position on the page. You could have created an animation using a tool such as Shockwave or Flash from Macromedia, but that would have meant using a new tool, and also downloading a large playback engine to the client. Alternatively, you could have created a custom Java applet which showed your animation, but as you are an IE programmer, you probably don't want to mess with Java. Well, the answer is now at hand.

One of the most powerful features of most animation packages is the ability to create and manipulate sprites. A sprite is an animated graphical control. One of the advantages of a sprite is that it can be moved over a background, and the sprite itself takes care of restoring the background to its original state after the sprite has moved.

The IE4 Sprite control gives you a very powerful tool to create animated images. With GIF animation, you have to set your playback speed at the time you create the animation. There is no way to control its playback from within your web page. The Sprite control gives you the flexibility to control the playback at a very fine level of detail. By combining the sprite control with the path control that we talked about before, you can move animated images around on the screen. By tying in script control, you can let the user's interactions determine the motion and actions of your sprite. We will take a look at the sprite control, how to use it, and then show a small example of what it can do.

Object Tag

The sprite control is inserted into a web page using the following object tag:

```
<OBJECT ID=mySprite CLASSID="clsid:FD179533-D86E-11d0-89D6-00A0C90833E6">
</OBJECT>
```

This version of the tag will set the placement of the sprite image according to the way the HTML is laid out on the page. If you wish to specify the location of the sprite precisely, then you will need to include a `STYLE` parameter in the `<OBJECT>` tag, and put your positioning parameters there.

```
<OBJECT ID=mySprite STYLE="LEFT: 150; TOP: 150; WIDTH: 200; HEIGHT: 200"
CLASSID="clsid:FD179533-D86E-11d0-89D6-00A0C90833E6">
</OBJECT>
```

The **HEIGHT** and **WIDTH** control the size of the area that the sprite will occupy. It will not affect the size of the images that the sprite displays. The style parameter is also important if you wish to use the path control. If you remember from the discussion of the path control, you need to have an object with a **TOP** and **LEFT** property in order to move that object with the path control.

Source Images

There are a series of images that make up each of the frames in your sprite. Each frame can be in a separate file, or can be stored in what is called an image strip file, where multiple frames are stored in a larger file.

The image strip file is created by creating each of the frames of animation as a separate graphic, then combining all of the frames into one image file. The file can be laid out in the square grid format that you prefer. The frames are numbered from left to right, beginning at the top left, and moving to the leftmost frame on the following line when the rightmost image is reached.

There are two key issues when creating your individual frames. First, make sure that items in the image that you don't want to move, like the red triangle in the above image strip, remain in exactly the same place. Any change in their location from frame to frame will be noticeable in the animation. Second, make sure that when you are combining the individual frames into the final image strip file that each frame is exactly the same size, and that the edge of one frame just touches, but does not overlap, the following frame. You can use any graphics file format that your browser supports, such as GIF, JPG, WMF and PNG (Portable Network Graphic format).

The documentation states that you can use separate image files for each frame in your sprite. However, there is no documented facility for doing so.

Once you have created your image strip file, you will need to tell the sprite control where to find this image. This is done through the **sourceURL** property. You will also need to set three properties that define the layout of your image strip file. These properties are

Property	Description	Values
numFrames	Total number of frames in the image strip	In the above image - 6
numFramesAcross	Number of columns in the image strip	In the above image - 1
numFramesDown	Number of rows in the image strip	In the above image - 6

SourceURL Property

The **sourceURL** property tells the sprite control where to load the image strip file from. The value for this property can either be a full URL, or a location relative to the page that contains the Sprite control. As with nearly all of the properties and methods of the Sprite control, you can set the value using either a **<PARAM>** tag enclosed in the **<OBJECT>** definition, or by using a scripting language. In either case, you can always use script to change the property during run-time.

To set the `SourceURL` property with a `<PARAM>` tag, you would add

```
<PARAM NAME="SourceURL" VALUE="image\WROXanim.gif">
```

To set or modify this parameter using script, you would

```
mySprite.SourceURL="image\WROXanim.gif"
```

Either of these entries would cause the image file name `WROXanim.gif`, located in the **images** directory relative to the location of the web page, to be loaded into the Sprite control.

Simple Playback

There are two methods for determining the playback characteristics of a Sprite. The simplest playback method is to cycle through the frames of the image strip file in the order they are stored. Each frame would be displayed for the same amount of time. To accomplish this, you simply set the `TimerInterval` property to the length of time that you want each frame to be displayed.

To set this property using the `<PARAM>` tag, you would add:

```
<PARAM NAME="TimerInterval" VALUE="200">
```

To set or modify this parameter using script, you would use:

```
mySprite.TimerInterval = 200
```

These entries would cause the sprite to display each frame for 200 milliseconds. This would present an animation frame rate of 5 frames per second. To start the playback of this sprite, you would simply issue the `Play()` method.

Later in this section, we will cover all of the other properties and methods that you can use to control the playback of the Sprite.

Advanced Playback

If playing the sprite frames in order, at a fixed frame rate, was simple playback, then advanced playback will allow you to set the order that frames are played, and how long each frame is displayed individually. To define how the frames are displayed, you will need to create a frame map for your sprite. The frame map is similar in structure to the script for the sequence control. You define the order in which frames are displayed when the sprite is run, and how long each image is visible on the screen. The frame map is a series of image numbers and durations that define the playback. Each entry in the series contains a frame number, then the duration in milliseconds. A semicolon separates each entry.

For example, in this `FrameMap` parameter:

```
<PARAM NAME="FrameMap" VALUE="5,500;4,1000;2,500;1,250;3,1000;0,500">
```

the following image sequence will be displayed:

▲ Image 5 (6th in the series) will be displayed for 0.5 seconds,

▲ Image 4 will be displayed for 1 second,

▲ Image 2 will be displayed for 0.5 seconds,

▲ Image 1 will be displayed for 0.25 seconds,

▲ Image 3 will be displayed for 1 second,

▲ and Image 0 (1st in the series) will be displayed for 0.5 seconds.

You can define this same Frame Map using script as follows:

```
MySprite.FrameMap="5,500;4,1000;2,500;1,250;3,1000;0,500"
```

You can use script to change the frame map at runtime, as long as the sprite is not playing back. You can use the same methods for controlling playback of the sprite that were used for the simple playback method. Simply call the `play()` method, and the sprite will begin playing, this time following the instructions in the frame map. When using a frame map to control sprite playback, the `TimerInterval` parameter is not used, and its value is ignored.

Properties

These properties are used to set the configuration parameters for the Sprite control

Property	Description	Values
autoStart	If set to True, the Sprite will automatically start playback once the entire image strip file has been loaded.	*True* or *False*
colorKey	Sets the transparency color for a source image.	*R, G, B* – representing the color values 0-255 for the three color components
useColorKey	If a transparency color is set using the `ColorKey` parameter, then this parameter determines whether or not to make those colors transparent	*True* or *False*
frame	Frame number of the currently displayed image. For example, if the 3rd image in the image strip is currently displayed, then the value of this property would be 3.	*1 – number of frames* For a FrameMap, returns the position in the frame map, not the images position in the image strip
initialFrame	Frame that sprite should start playback at. Does not change the current frame of the sprite.	*1 – number of frames* For a FrameMap, returns the position in the frame map, not the images position in the image strip
maximumRate	Sets or returns the maximum number of frames the control will render per second.	*fps* – Frames per second

Property	Description	Values
`mouseEventsEnabled`	By default, the control will respond to mouse events, such as `click` and `mouse_over`. By setting this to False, the control will not respond to mouse events.	*True* or *False*
`playRate`	Sets or returns the playback speed of the sprite. Can be used to speed up or slow down sprite playback. To play the sprite backwards, use negative values.	*1.0* – plays at normal speed $>$ *1.0* – plays faster than normal $<$ *1.0* and $>$ *0.0* – plays slower than normal *0* – Does not play.
`playState`	Returns the playback state of the sprite.	*0* – stopped *1* – playing *2* – paused
`repeat`	Sets or returns the number of times the sprite is to loop during playback	*1* – default. Plays once *-1* – Plays forever *n* $>$ 1 – Plays *n* times *0* – Disabled. Plays once
`time`	Returns the elapsed playback time for the sprite, including looping.	Milliseconds since the initial playback point

Bookmark and Playback Control Methods

The Sprite control has a number of methods that allow you to set bookmarks so you can be notified during sprite playback.

AddFrameMarker

This method allows you to set bookmark at a particular frame, or frame marker, in the sprite series. If you are using a frame map, then the frame number corresponds to frame's position in the frame map, not in the image strip. When the frame containing the bookmark is reached by the sprite, either through playback or a `seek` method, an event will be fired.

You can add bookmarks using either script or `<PARAM>` tags. To add a frame marker using the `<PARAM>` tag, you would add

```
<PARAM NAME="addFrameMarkerx" VALUE="frame, markername, [fRelative]">
```

If you are adding more than one frame marker using the `<PARAM>` tag then you will need to use different values for *x* at the end of the Name value. This value should start at 1 and increase sequentially for each successive tag.

To add a frame marker using script, you would add

```
mySprite.addFrameMarker(frame, markername, [fRelative])
```

The *frame* parameter is used to set the frame number at which to set the bookmark. The *markername* parameter is a string that identifies this bookmark. It is passed to the event handler function that is fired when the particular bookmark is encountered. The *fRelative* parameter is an optional parameter. The default value, True, will fire the notification events every time the bookmark is encountered during playback, even during looping. By setting this value to False, the notification will happen only the first time the bookmark is reached.

AddTimeMarker

This method allows you to set bookmark at a particular elapsed time during playback of the sprite. When the **Time** parameter, which indicates the elapsed playback time, reaches the value associated with the bookmark, either through playback or the **Seek** method, an event will be fired.

You can add bookmarks using either script or **<PARAM>** tags. To add a time marker using the **<PARAM>** tag, you would add

```
<PARAM NAME="AddTimeMarkerx" VALUE="time, markername, [fRelative]">
```

If you are adding more than one time marker using the **<PARAM>** tag then you will need to use different values for **x** at the end of the **Name** value. This value should start at 1 and increase sequentially for each successive tag.

To add a time marker using script, you would add

```
mySprite.AddTimeMarker(time, markername, [fRelative])
```

The *time* parameter is used to set the elapsed time at which to set the bookmark. This parameter is in the form **seconds.milliseconds**. The *markername* parameter is a string that identifies this bookmark. It is passed to the event handler function that is fired when the particular bookmark is encountered. The *fRelative* parameter is an optional parameter. The default value, True, will fire the notification events every time the bookmark is encountered during playback, even during looping. By setting this value to False, the notification will happen only the first time the bookmark is reached.

Playback Control Methods

The Sprite control also has a number of methods that are used to control the playback of the sprite.

Play

This method is used to start playback at the current position of the sprite. The first time a sprite is played, the starting position is determined by the **InitialFrame** parameter. When this method is called, it does not reset the current position of the sprite. The **onPlay** event is fired when this method is called.

The **play** method is called by

```
mySprite.play()
```

Pause

This method is used to pause playback of the sprite. The current position of the sprite is maintained. A subsequent call of the **play** method will restart the playback of the sprite from the point at which it was paused. The **onPause** event is fired when this method is called.

The **pause** method is called by

```
mySprite.pause()
```

Stop

This method is used to stop playback of the sprite. The current position of the sprite is reset to the position determined by the **InitialFrame** parameter. The **onStop** event is fired when this method is called.

The **stop** method is called by

```
mySprite.stop()
```

Seek

This method is used to change the current elapsed time of the sprite. When this method is called, the sprite will display the frame that corresponds to this elapsed time value. This method will also cause the **onSeek** event to be fired.

The **seek** method is called by

```
mySprite.seek(s.mss)
```

The parameter indicates the time position to seek to. The value is in the form *seconds.milliseconds*.

FrameSeek

This method is used to change the current frame of the sprite. When this method is called, the sprite will update its display to show the image that corresponds to the new frame. This method will also cause the **onFrameSeek** event to be fired.

The **frameSeek** method is called by

```
mySprite.frameSeek(frame)
```

The **Frame** parameter indicates the frame number to seek to. If you are using a Frame Map, then the frame number is actually the position in the Frame Map, not the frame in the image strip file.

Events

The sprite object has a number of events that can notify the script when certain things happen.

Event	Description	Parameter
onClick	Fired when the user clicks the sprite once.	*none*
onDblClick	Fired when the user double-clicks the sprite.	*none*
onFrameSeek	Fired after the **frameSeek** method has been called.	New frame number as the result of the seek

Event	Description	Parameter
onMediaLoaded	Fired when a piece of sprite media is completely downloaded.	URL of the media being downloaded
onMouseDown	Fired when the user depresses the mouse button over a sprite.	*button* – Bit field indicating which button(s) was pressed *shift* – Bit field indicating key modifiers *x,y* – mouse position in the page
onMouseMove	Fired every time the user moves the mouse across the non-transparent area of the sprite.	*button* – Bit field indicating which button(s) was pressed, if any *shift* – Bit field indicating key modifiers *x,y* – mouse position in the page
onMouseOut	Fired when the cursor leaves the non-transparent area of the sprite.	*none*
onMouseUp	Fired when the user releases the mouse button over a sprite.	*button* – Bit field indicating which button(s) was pressed *shift* – Bit field indicating key modifiers *x,y* – mouse position in the page
onMouseOver	Fired when the cursor enters a non-transparent area of the sprite.	*none*
onPause	Fired when sprite playback is paused.	*none*
onPlay	Fired when the sprite begins playback.	*none*
onSeek	Fired after the **seek** method is called.	New elapsed time as the result of the seek
onStop	Fired when the sprite stops playback.	*none*

Sprite Example

Now, let's take a look at a simple example of a Sprite control and how it can be used. We will create a sprite that will animate in place until it is clicked. Every time the sprite is clicked, it will reverse the direction of the animation.

We will use the **<OBJECT>** tag to insert the Sprite control into the page. The **<OBJECT>** tag can accept a **STYLE** parameter, which allows us to place the control where we want it on the page.

```
<HTML>
<BODY>
<OBJECT ID="WroxLogo"
    STYLE="position:absolute; LEFT: 50; TOP: 50; WIDTH: 100; HEIGHT: 50"
    CLASSID ="clsid:FD179533-D86E-11d0-89D6-00A0C90833E6">
    <PARAM NAME="Repeat" VALUE="-1">
    <PARAM NAME="PlayRate" VALUE="1">
    <PARAM NAME="MouseEventsEnabled" VALUE="True">
    <PARAM NAME="AutoStart" VALUE="True">
```

We have set up this sprite to loop repeatedly, by setting the **Repeat** parameter to -1. The **PlayRate** has been set to 1, which will play the sprite animation at normal speed. Since we have not set a value for the **timerInterval** property, the animation will take place at the default speed. The default value for the **timerInterval** property is 100 milliseconds, giving a playback speed of 10 frames per second.

Since we will use the mouse to reverse the direction of the sprite, we will set the **MouseEventsEnabled** parameter to True. While this is the default value, and doesn't need to be explicitly set, it increases the readability of the code. The **AutoStart** parameter is set to True, which will cause the sprite to begin animating once it has completed loading.

```
    <PARAM NAME="SourceURL" VALUE="wroxanim.gif">
    <PARAM NAME="NumFrames" VALUE="6">
    <PARAM NAME="NumFramesAcross" VALUE="1">
    <PARAM NAME="NumFramesDown" VALUE="6">
```

The name of the image strip file that we will be using is called **wroxanim.gif**, and is assigned to the **sourceURL** property. This is the same image that was shown earlier in the section. It has a total of 6 frames, arranged in one column and six rows.

```
</OBJECT>

<DIV STYLE="position:absolute; top: 10; left:10; font-size:18pt; font-family: Verdana;
color:blue;">Click the logo to Reverse!</DIV>

<SCRIPT LANGUAGE="VBScript">

Sub WroxLogo_OnClick
    WroxLogo.Pause()
    WroxLogo.PlayRate = WroxLogo.PlayRate * -1
    WroxLogo.Play()
end sub
</SCRIPT>

</BODY>
</HTML>
```

By handling the **onClick** event of the sprite control, we can reverse the playback direction of the sprite. This is done by changing the sign on the **PlayRate** parameter. Initially, the **PlayRate** parameter was +1.0, indicating normal playback speed in the forward direction. By changing the **PlayRate** parameter to a -1.0, the sprite will play back at the same speed, but in the opposite direction.

When you view this example in your browser, you will see:

You have now seen how easy it is to add an animated sprite control to you web page. All that you need to do is:

▲ Add the Object to your page

▲ Identify the characteristics of the sprite, including the image source file and the layout of the image source file.

▲ Call the **Play** method, then sit back and enjoy

Next, we will take a look at a way of providing complex graphics on your web page that do not take a long time to download by using the Structured Graphics Control.

Structured Graphic Control

As we have added all sorts of graphical functionality to web pages, users have begun to notice one disturbing fact: the more graphical a page, then the longer it takes to download. While all of these nice graphically rich interfaces are pleasant to look at, at today's prevalent download speeds, they are taking too long to download. The net effect is an interface that few people actually see, since they give up and move on to some other page.

Why is it that images are so big? Even image file formats such as JPG or GIF, which compress the data that makes up the image, still store the bits that comprise the image. But why not make the computer do some thinking when it displays an image rather that just telling it: put a blue dot here, then a red dot, then a blue dot, which is in effect what most traditional graphic files do.

If you could tell the computer to draw a box at the required coordinates and fill it with green, you would have to send 5 pieces of information to the computer: Left Position, Top Position, Height, Width, and Color. That would seem to be much more efficient than a whole series of green dot here, green dot here, green dot here...

What you want are **vector graphics**. Vector graphics store the commands needed to reproduce the image rather than the bits that make up the image. Granted, you can't translate every image file to a vector file. If you had a scanned high-resolution photograph, you would not want to describe how to reproduce that image using vector commands. On the other hand, if you have a simple graphic, such as a pie chart or a schematic, then you can easily convert that image to a vector, and therefore greatly reduce its size, which makes it load faster, which in turn makes everybody happy! You also get the added benefits of being able to scale and rotate that image to your heart's content at design time, and dynamically at run time.

The vector graphic control that has been added with IE4 is called the Structured Graphic control. It allows you to build vector graphics by scripting each of the drawing commands that is required to build your image.

Adding the Structured Graphic Object

To add the control to your webpage, use this `<OBJECT>` tag:

```
<OBJECT ID=mySGraphic
CLASSID="CLSID:369303C2-D7AC-11d0-89D5-00A0C90833E6">
</OBJECT>
```

There is one parameter type for this object. Its use is very similar to the parameter for the Sequencer control. Then `<PARAM>` is defined as:

`<PARAM NAME=LINEnnnn VALUE=property | method>`

The value of `LINEnnnn` identifies the order in which the graphic is built. The value of *nnnn* must start at `0001`, and must be sequential. For example, the first tag would be `NAME=LINE0001`, the next would be `LINE0002`, then `LINE0003`, and so on. If you skip a number, then the construction of the graphic will not continue past that point. The entry for the `VALUE` part of the parameter consists of a method of the object, such as draw a rectangle or fill an object, and the parameters that are required by that method. All of the drawing methods can also be included in a separate file, then loaded automatically when the Structured Graphic control is initialized.

Coordinate System

The Structured Graphic object can use two different coordinate systems. The coordinate system is used by the drawing methods to place each of the drawing primitives that make up the final structured graphic object. In both coordinate systems, the X values start at 0 at the center point, and increase towards the right.

In the Windows coordinate system, the 0 value of Y is at the center of the structured graphic object. Increasing values of Y move further down in the object. It is called the Windows coordinate system since this is the way that coordinates are laid out on the Windows screen. This also happens to be the way the Dynamic HTML lays out the coordinate system on the browser's window.

The Cartesian coordinate system is exactly opposite to the Windows system. In the Cartesian system, which is derived from traditional geometry, the 0 value for Y is at the center of the object. Increasing values of Y move you towards the top of the object.

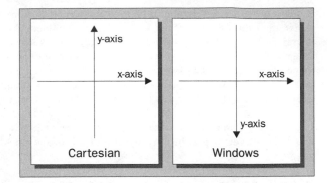

This diagram shows both coordinate systems side-by-side.

Drawing Methods

These methods are used to generate the image that the structured graphic object will display.

Arc

This method allows you to draw a single circular or elliptical arc inside the control. The arc is defined by setting the center point for the arc, a bounding rectangle, and its rotation parameters. To add an arc to the Structured Graphics control, use this **<PARAM>** tag:

```
<PARAM NAME = "Linennnn" VALUE="Arc(x, y, width, height, startAngle,
arcAngle, rotation)">
```

The *x* and *y* parameters are used to define the location of the center point of the arc. The *width* and *height* parameters define the height and width of a bounding rectangle that encompasses the entire arc. All four of these parameters are pixel values. The *startAngle* parameter sets the starting angle of the arc. The *arcAngle* parameter sets the angle that the arc sweeps from the starting angle. The **rotation** parameter sets the rotation of the entire arc. All three angle parameters are in degrees, with 360 degrees making up a complete revolution. The *start Angle* and *arcAngle* values start at 0 degrees along the positive x-axis, and increase counterclockwise. The *rotation* parameter starts at 0 degrees along the positive x-axis, and increases clockwise.

Oval

This method is used to draw an ellipse. It can also be used to draw a circle, which is a special form of an ellipse. To add an oval to the Structured Graphics control, use this **<PARAM>** tag:

```
<PARAM NAME="Linennnn" VALUE="Oval(x, y, width, height, rotation)">
```

The *x* and *y* parameters are used to define the location of the center point of the arc. The *width* and *height* parameters define the height and width of a bounding rectangle that encompasses the entire oval. All four of these parameters are pixel values. The *rotation* parameter sets the rotation of the oval. To create a circle, you would use a square bounding rectangle, which would have the same value for the *width* parameter as it does for the *height* parameter.

Pie

To create a pie shaped image in a Structured Graphics control, you need to use the **pie** method. This method is an extension of the .**arc** method. The **arc** method simply draws an arc based on the parameters provided. The **pie** method uses the same parameter list as an **arc** method, but in addition to drawing the arc, the ends of the arc are connected to the center point of the arc. To add a pie image to the Structured Graphics control, use this **<PARAM>** tag:

```
<PARAM NAME = "Linennnn" VALUE="Pie(x, y, width, height, startAngle,
arcAngle, rotation)">
```

The parameters used by the **pie** method are identical to the parameters of the **arc** method. Most people are used to having pie pieces that are cut from a circular object. To create a pie piece from a circular object, you will need to ensure that the *width* and *height* parameters are of the same value. Since the **Pie** method creates a closed shape, it will be affected by whatever fill pattern and color is in effect. These modifiers will be introduced shortly.

Polygon

This method is used to draw a polygon image on the Structured Graphics control. The polygon is composed of at least 3 line segments which are connected to create a closed figure. The method for defining the polygon is nearly identical to the definition of the polygon path for the Path control. To add a polygon to the Structured Graphics control, use this **<PARAM>** tag:

```
<PARAM NAME="Linennnn" VALUE="Polygon(nPoints, x1, y1, x2, y2, x3, y3 [,
x4, y4 ...], rotation)">
```

The *nPoints* parameter defines the total number of points that will make up the vertices of the polygon. Since a polygon must have at least 3 vertices, then this parameter must be 3 or greater. The next series of parameters define the points that make up the vertices of the polygon. Again, there must be at least 3 sets of points to make up the polygon. The final parameter, *rotation*, sets the rotation of the polygon. This parameter's values are in degrees, with positive values indicating a clockwise rotation. The value for the rotation can be larger than 360 degrees. For example, a rotation of 450 degrees would be identical to a rotation of 90 degrees.

PolyLine

This method is used to draw a multi-segmented line on the Structured Graphics control. The **polyline** method is similar to the **polygon** method, in that it is defined as a series of points. In **polygon**, a line is drawn connecting the final point in the series with the first point in the series, which effectively closes the object. The **polyline** does not automatically connect the final point with the first point, leaving you with just a line segment. As with the **polygon**, this **polyLine** is very similar to the PolyLine path of the Path control. To add a polyline segment to the Structured Graphics control, use this **<PARAM>** tag:

```
<PARAM NAME="Linennnn" VALUE="PolyLine(nPoints, x1, y1, x2, y2, x3, y3 [,
x4, y4 ...], rotation)">
```

The parameters are the same as the parameters of the **polygon** method.

Rect

The **Rect** method is used to create a special form of polygon. The four-sided polygon, or rectangle, is defined by the location of the upper left corner, along with its height and width. As you can probably guess by now, the **rect** method is very similar to the Rect path of the Path control. To add a rectangular object to the Structured Graphics control, you will use this **<PARAM>** tag:

```
<PARAM NAME="Linennnn" VALUE="Rect(x, y, width, height, rotation)">
```

The x and y parameters are used to define the location of the top-left corner of the rectangle. The *width* and *height* parameters define the height and width of the rectangle. All four of these parameters are pixel values. The *rotation* parameter sets the rotation of the rectangle. To create a square, you would use the same value for the *width* parameter as you do for the *height* parameter.

RoundRect

The `RoundRect` method is used to create a rectangular object on the Structured Graphics control. The difference between this object and the one created by the Rect method is the shape of the corners. In a `Rect` object, the corners are formed by two straight lines meeting at a 90 degree angle. In the `RoundRect`, the corners are formed by an arc, giving the corners a rounded look. To add a rounded rectangular object to the Structured Graphics control, you will use this `<PARAM>` tag:

```
<PARAM NAME="Linennnn" VALUE="RoundRect(x, y, width, height, arcWidth, arcHeight, rotation)">
```

The *x, y, width, height,* and *rotation* parameters are identical to the parameters of the `Rect` method. One difference is that since the corners are now rounded, the point defined by *(x,y)* no longer falls on the rectangle. The *arcWidth* parameter defines the horizontal diameter of the arc at each corner. The *arcHeight* parameter defines the vertical diameter of each arc. By having separate values for *arcWidth* and *arcHeight*, you can have rounded corners that are oval shaped, rather than only circular shaped.

SetFillColor

This method is used to set both the foreground and background fill colors for the Structured Graphics control. By setting the fill color, it will be used by all subsequent closed objects, like the oval and rectangle. These objects will be filled with the specified color. The colors will remain in effect until another `SetFillColor` method is encountered. To set the fill color, you will use this `<PARAM>` tag:

```
<PARAM NAME="Linennnn" VALUE="SetFillColor(rForeColor, gForeColor, bForeColor [, rBackColor, gBackColor, bBackColor ])">
```

An RGB triplet defines the color. The RGB triplet is made up of the intensity of the three component colors, red, green, and blue, on a scale of 0 to 255. For example, a pure brown is made up of 255 red component, 0 green component, and 255 blue component. To set this as a fill color, you would use

```
<PARAM NAME="Line0001" VALUE="SetFillColor(255,0,255)">
```

The background color is defined in the same way, with an RGB triplet. The background color is used when displaying a gradient fill, which will be discussed shortly.

SetFillStyle

In addition to filling closed objects with a solid color, there are a number of different fill patterns that can be applied. These are applied using the `SetFillStyle` method. To add this method to the Structured Graphics control, you would use

```
<PARAM NAME="Linennnn" VALUE="SetFillStyle(type)">
```

Value	Description
1	Solid
3	Hatch horizontal
4	Hatch vertical
5	Hatch forward diagonal
6	Hatch backward diagonal
7	Hatch cross
8	Hatch diagonal cross
9	Horizontal gradient
10	Vertical gradient
11	Radial gradient
12	Line gradient
13	Rectangular gradient
14	Shaped gradient

The *type* parameter is used to determine the fill type that will be used. The fill types that are available are

SetGradientFill

One of the fill methods that can be selected using the **SetFillStyle** method is the gradient fill. This fill is a transition from foreground color to background color. In order to define the direction that the transition takes, some additional parameters need to be set. These are set with the **SetGradientFill** method. This method is only valid when used with a fill style of 11. To use this method, use this **<PARAM>** tag:

```
<PARAM NAME="Linennnn" VALUE="SetGradientFill(startX, startY, finishX,
finishY, strength)">
```

The *startX* and *startY* parameters indicate the starting position of the gradient. The *finishX* and *finishY* parameters indicate the ending position of the gradient. The *strength* parameter indicates the intensity of the color at the starting position. A value of 1 indicates that the starting color will be the pure foreground color. Decimal values less than one indicate a starting color that is a percentage of the foreground color.

SetGradientShape

If you select a fill style of 14, then you can define the shape of the gradient that you want to use. This shape is a polygon that is defined in same way as a polygon drawing object. To add this method, use

```
<PARAM NAME="Linennnn" VALUE="Polygon(nPoints, x1, y1, x2, y2, x3, y3 [,
x4, y4 ...])">
```

The *nPoints* parameter defines the total number of points that will make up the vertices of the gradient polygon. Since a polygon must have at least 3 vertices, then this parameter must be 3 or greater. The next series of parameters define the points that make up the vertices of the gradient polygon. Again, there must be at least 3 sets of points to make up the gradient polygon.

SetHatchFill

This method is used to specify whether the hatch fill, as selected by the `SetFillStyle` method, is transparent or not. If the hatch fill is not transparent, then the background color will be used in the non-colored areas of the hatch. If it is transparent, then the Structured Graphics control will be transparent. To add this method to the Structured Graphics control, you will use

```
<PARAM NAME="Linennnn" VALUE="SetHatchFill(isTransparent)">
```

The *isTransparent* parameter is a boolean value that indicates the transparency of the hatch fill. A value of True indicates a transparent fill. A value of False indicates a non-transparent fill. This method is used for fill types 3 through 8, as defined by the `SetFillStyle` method.

SetLineColor

This method sets the line color for drawing graphics. The line color determines the color of line segment objects, like the arc and polyline. It is also used to determine the color of the outline of closed objects, like the oval and rectangle. For a closed object, the fill color can be different from the line color. As with the `SetFillColor` method, once this method is applied, it is used for a succeeding drawing operations. To set the line color, use this `<PARAM>` tag

```
<PARAM NAME="Linennnn" VALUE="SetLineColor(r, g, b)">
```

The *r, g,* and *b* parameters indicate the color as defined by an RGB color triplet. Their possible values range from 0 to 255.

SetLineStyle

In addition to setting the color of the line used when drawing graphics, you can also change the style of the line. The line can either be solid or dashed. To set the line style, you can use this `<PARAM>` tag

```
<PARAM NAME="Linennnn" VALUE="SetLineStyle(style)">
```

The possible values of the *style* are 0 for no outline, 1 for solid, and 2 for dashed. The default line style is a solid line. Once a line style is set, it will be used for all subsequent drawing operations.

SetFont

This method is used to set the font that will be used by the Structured Graphics control for all Text drawing. The font and its characteristics, once set, will be used for all subsequent text operations. To set the font characteristics, use this `<PARAM>` tag

```
<PARAM NAME="Linennnn" VALUE="SetFont(name, height, weight, isItalic,
isUnderline, isStrikethrough)">
```

The *name* parameter indicates the font name, such as Verdana or Tahoma. The *height* parameter sets the size of the font in points. The *weight* of the font is used to set the "boldness" of the font. The possible values are integers ranging from 0 to 700. A value of 300 is a normal weighting. A value of 700 would be a heavy bold. The last three parameters, *isItalic, isUnderline,* and *isStrikethrough,* are boolean values that specify if the font has italic, underlined, or strikethrough characteristics. The default values for each parameter are False (0), which produces normal text.

Text

This method is used to draw text onto the Structured Graphics control. The font characteristics of the text are set by the **SetFont** method. The color of the text is set using the **SetFillColor** and **SetLineColor** methods. To draw text onto the Structured Graphics control, use this **<PARAM>** tag

```
<PARAM NAME="Linennnn" VALUE="Text('str', x, y, rotation)">
```

The **str** parameter is the string of text that will be rendered onto the Structured Graphics control. The **x** and **y** parameters indicate the starting point for the text. This point represents the baseline of the left edge of the first character. The text is drawn upward and to the right from this point. This is different from the other drawing elements, which are specified by their top-left point. The **rotation** parameter is used to indicate the rotation of the text around the point defined by (**x, y**). The rotation is in degrees, with positive values indicating a clockwise rotation.

Control Methods

Once you have defined the Structured Graphics control using **<PARAM>** tags, you can make some modifications to the image from script as well. These methods can not be used to draw any additional shapes, but can be used to modify the appearance by rotation, scaling and translating.

Clear

This method is used to clear the contents of the control from the display. This will make the graphics disappear from the control. To call this method from script, you would use

```
mySGraphic.clear
```

SetIdentity

The **SetIdentity** method is used to reset the control to its original drawn position. This method can be used to counteract the effects of any rotation, scaling, or translation that has been done to the control. To call this method, you would use:

```
mySGraphic.setIdentity
```

For example, if you have some script code that rotates and scales your Structured Graphic object while the user is viewing the page, and you want to reset the appearance of the object to its original state, you would call the **setIdentity** to do that.

Rotate

This method allows you to rotate the control along all three axes. You can select the rotation amounts for each axis individually. This method can be combined with the **setTimeout** function or the sequencer control to add dynamic motion to the Structured Graphics control. To call this method, you would use

```
mySGraphic.rotate(x-rotation, y-rotation, z-rotation [, fRelative])
```

The **x-rotation, y-rotation**, and **z-rotation** parameters indicate the degrees of rotation of each axis of the control. The **fRelative** parameter determines if the rotation is absolute or relative. If this parameter is true, then the rotation parameters are added to the existing rotation position. If false, then the rotation is explicitly set to the rotation given by the rotation parameters.

Scale

This method allows you to scale the Structured Graphics object along each of its three axes. This method can be used dynamically, to show an object that is growing or shrinking. To call this method, you would use:

```
mySGraphic.scale(x-scale, y-scale, z-scale [,fRelative])
```

The *x-scale, y-scale*, and *z-scale* parameters indicate the scaling of each axis of the object. The scaling value of 1.0 indicates the original scale of the object. Values less than 1.0 will shrink the size of the axis. Values greater than 1.0 will increase the scale. If the *fRelative* parameter is true, this indicates that the scaling parameters are relative, and will be applied to whatever the current scaling is. If this parameter is false, then the scaling parameters will be absolutely applied to the Structured Graphics object.

Translate

This method is used to adjust the origin of the control in the three-dimensional space that the image objects are drawn onto. This method can be used to make the image appear to move left or right, or move into or out of the page. To use this method, you would use:

```
mySGraphic.translate(x-coordinate, y-coordinate, z-coordinate, [fRelative])
```

The *x-coordinate, y-coordinate*, and *z-coordinate* indicate the translation values of the origin in pixels. If the *fRelative* parameter is true, which is its default value, then the coordinate parameters will be added to the existing origin position. If *fRelative* is false, then the origin will be set to the values specified by the coordinate parameters.

Control Properties

There are a number of properties that you can set to control the display and functionality of the Structured Graphics control.

Property	Description	Values
coordinateSystem	Sets the coordinate system to use for the world.	0 – Windows 1 – Cartesian
drawSurface	Sets or returns the drawing surface, the visible rendering of the control's contents for use in script.	*DrawingSurface* object
extentHeight, extentWidth, extentLeft, extentTop	Sets the height, width, left and top values of the structured graphic.	*Pixels*
mouseEventsEnabled	Sets or returns whether mouse events are to be processed against the Structured Graphics object.	*True or False*
sourceURL	Enables the Structured Graphic control to use an external file as the structured graphic primitive description.	Valid URL reference

Events

The sprite object has a number of events that can notify the script when certain things happen.

Event	Description	Parameter
onClick	Fired when the user clicks the structured graphic once.	*none*
onDblClick	Fired when the user double-clicks the structured graphic.	*none*
onMouseDown	Fired when the user depresses the mouse button over a structured graphic.	*button* – Bit field indicating which button(s) was pressed *shift* – Bit field indicating key modifiers *x,y* – mouse position in the page
onMouseMove	Fired when the user moves the mouse across the structured graphic.	*button* – Bit field indicating which button(s) was pressed *shift* – Bit field indicating key modifiers *x,y* – mouse position in the page
onMouseOut	Fired when the cursor leaves the structured graphic.	*none*
onMouseUp	Fired when the user releases the mouse button over a structured graphic.	*button* – Bit field indicating which button(s) was pressed *shift* – Bit field indicating key modifiers *x,y* – mouse position in the page
onMouseOver	Fired when the cursor enters a non-transparent area of the structured graphic.	*none*

Metafile Converter

By using these methods, you should be able to create very detailed, yet lightweight graphics for your web page. But unless you are a LOGO or OpenGL programmer, then it's probably quite difficult to draw graphics by using these methods. If you are doing something simple, like some circles or boxes, then it isn't too tough, but if you want to make a complex object using the structured graphic control, then you have a tough task on your hands.

Fortunately, Microsoft has included a tool with the Internet Client Software Developer's Toolkit (found at **http://www.microsoft.com/msdn/sdk/inetsdk/asetup/default.asp**) that will allow you to convert Windows Metafiles to the lines of code needed to create a structured graphic object. This will allow you to use a drawing tool, such as Microsoft PowerPoint or Adobe Illustrator, to save your creation as a metafile, and then using the tool called **WMFCNV.EXE** to convert that metafile to a structured graphics object. The output of this tool will create the **<OBJECT>** tag and all of the **<PARAM>** tags for your image. This will be saved to a file, which can then by loaded in the Structured Graphics control by use of the **sourceURL** property. You could create an effective animation by saving the frames of your animation as files, then use the **sourceURL** property to load different frames at different times.

Structured Graphics Example

Now we will take a look at a simple example that will show you some of the different methods of the Structured Graphics Object, and how you can perform simple animation using just script.

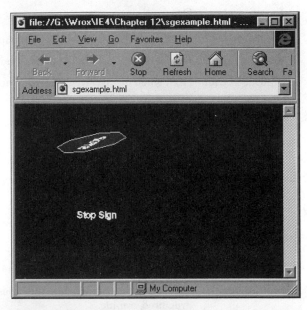

This example will consist of a Stop Sign image that rotates along its three axes, and some text that scales dynamically. Here is what the screen will look like during the animation.

The code starts by calling the **AnimateAll** method:

```
<HTML>
<HEAD>
<SCRIPT LANGUAGE="VBScript">

' Set up a variable to control the direction of the scaling
dim iCount

Sub Window_OnLoad()
    iCount = 0
    AnimateAll
end sub
```

The **AnimateAll** method will perform two manipulations on the Structured Graphics controls on this page. It will rotate the **sgStopSign** control by 3 degrees in the X direction, 2 degrees in the Y direction, and 1 degree in the Z direction. This will give the appearance of the stop sign tumbling.

```
Sub AnimateAll
    Call sgStopSign.rotate(3,2,1)
    if iCount > 5 then
```

The **iCount** variable that was declared earlier is used to control the direction of the scaling of the **sgText** control. Each time through the animation loop, **iCount** will be incremented.

```
            if iCount > 10 then
                iCount = 0
                call sgText.setIdentity
```

When **iCount** is greater than 10, it will be reset to 0. The **setIdentity** method of the **sgText** control will be called as well. This will reset the text in the control to its original size.

```
        else
                call sgText.scale(1.2,1.2,1.2)
                iCount = iCount + 1
        end if
```

If the value of **iCount** is between 6 and 10, then the **scale** method will be called on the **sgText** control. This call will increase the scale on each of the three axes by 20%, causing the text to grow larger.

```
      else
              call sgText.scale(0.9, 0.9, 0.9)
              iCount = iCount + 1
```

If the value of **iCount** is between 0 and 5, then the **scale** method will be called, but this time it will decrease the scale of each axis by 10%.

```
      end if
      foo = Window.setTimeOut("Call AnimateAll", 10, "VBScript")
End Sub
</SCRIPT>
</HEAD>
```

The **setTimeOut** method of the window object will be called to trigger another call to the **AnimateAll** method in 10 milliseconds. This has the effect of animating both Structured Graphics controls, by either scaling or rotating the object frequently. Next, the stop sign is defined by the **<OBJECT>** tag as an octagon.

```
<BODY BGCOLOR="#0000FF">
<OBJECT ID=sgStopSign
STYLE="POSITION:ABSOLUTE;HEIGHT:100;WIDTH:100;TOP:0;LEFT:50;ZINDEX: 0"
CLASSID="CLSID:369303C2-D7AC-11D0-89D5-00A0C90833E6">
<PARAM NAME="Line0001" VALUE="SetLineColor(255,255,255)">
<PARAM NAME="Line0002" VALUE="SetFillColor(255,0,0,0,0,255)">
<PARAM NAME="Line0003" VALUE="SetFillSTYLE(1)">
<PARAM NAME="Line0004" VALUE="SetLineSTYLE(1)">
<PARAM NAME="Line0005" VALUE="Polygon(8, -45,15, -15,45, 15,45, 45,15, 45,-15, 15,-45,
-15,-45, -45,-15, 0)">
```

A stop sign is red, so the fill color is set to pure red, or (255, 0, 0). The outline of a stop sign is white, so the line color is set to pure white, or (255, 255, 255). The polygon is drawn such that the center of the stop sign is at the origin of the control. Since the control is 100 pixels high and 100 pixels wide, and is 50 pixels from the left edge, then the center of the stop sign will be at 50 pixels from the top of the page, and 100 pixels from the left edge. The letters 'STOP' are drawn into the control in white, and are placed so that they are centered within the polygon.

```
<PARAM NAME="Line0006" VALUE="SetFont('Arial', 24,500,0,0,0)">
<PARAM NAME="Line0007" VALUE="SetLineColor(255,255,255)">
<PARAM NAME="Line0008" VALUE="SetFillColor(255,255,255,255,0,0)">
<PARAM NAME="Line0009" VALUE="Text('STOP',-30,5,0)">
</OBJECT>
```

Another Structured Graphics object is added that presents the text 'Stop Sign' on the page. This text is initially 24 point Arial in white. This is the text that will be dynamically scaled up and down while the sign is rotated.

```
<OBJECT id=sgText
STYLE="POSITION:ABSOLUTE; HEIGHT: 100; LEFT: 0; TOP: 100; WIDTH: 220; ZINDEX: 0"
CLASSID = "CLSID:369303C2-D7AC-11D0-89D5-00A0C90833E6">
<PARAM NAME="Line0001" VALUE="SetLineStyle(1)">
<PARAM NAME="Line0002" VALUE="SetLineColor(255,255,255)">
<PARAM NAME="Line0003" VALUE="SetFillColor(255, 255, 255)">
<PARAM NAME="Line0004" VALUE="SetFillStyle(1)">
<PARAM NAME="Line0005" VALUE="SetFont('Arial', 24, 300, 0, 0, 0)">
<PARAM NAME="Line0006" VALUE="Text('Stop Sign',-50, 0)">
</OBJECT>
</BODY>
</HTML>
```

That's all there is to creating a simple example of the Structured Graphics control, complete with animation. You will need to view the page at `http://rapid.wrox.co.uk/books/0707` in order to actually see the animation take place.

Structured Graphics – The Drawing Surface

However the Structured Graphics control doesn't just stop there. We skipped very briefly over the properties of the control, but there is one property in particular that can be used to access a large set of library functions to aid the drawing of vector graphics. This is the `drawSurface` property which provides access to the `DrawingSurface` object.

The **drawing surface** maintains the graphics state for two-dimensional viewspace of the Structured Graphics control. This state includes attributes such as line style, fill style, border style, font style, and any transformations which have been applied to the graph. The drawing surface may be extracted from the structured graphics object at runtime and manipulated via the DA library.

```
set DALib = sgSign.Library
set DAsur = sgSign.DrawSurface
```

These assignments may be made in any order. Once the drawing surface has been extracted there are many library functions at your disposal to manipulate it.

DA library function	Purpose
ArcDegrees	Draws an arc segment in degrees
ArcRadians	Draws an arc segment in radians
AutoSizeFillScale	Scales fill pattern to bounding box
BorderColor	Sets border color
BorderDashStyle	Sets border as dashed
BorderJoinStyle	Sets border join style

DA library function	Purpose
BorderWidth	Sets border width
Clear	Clears surface
Crop	Sets a clipping region for future drawing
CropPoints	Same as crop but takes DAPoints
DrawPath	Takes DAPath as argument and displays it
FillColor	Sets fillcolor for polygon
FillImage	Sets texture fill for polygon
FillPath	Same as polygon but takes DAPath
FillStyle	Sets the style for the fill
FillTexture	Sets a tiling fill image
FixedFillScale	Prevents fill from scaling
Font	Sets font
GradientExtent	Sets gradient fill rolloff
GradientExtentPoints	Sets fill rolloff in points
GradientRolloffPower	Sets the rolloff sharpness
GradientRolloffPowerAnim	Sets the rolloff sharpness in DANumbers
GradientShape	Sets a polygon shape for the gradient fill
HorizontalFillScale	Scales the fill to fit the bounding box horizontally
Line	Draws a single line segment
LineColor	Sets line color
LineDashStyle	Sets as dashed
LineEndStyle	Sets end style for line
LineJoinStyle	Sets join style for line
LinePoints	Same as line but takes DAPoints
LineWidth	Sets line width
Opacity	Sets opacity
OpacityAnim	Sets opacity as a DANumber
Oval	Draws an oval
OverlayImage	Creates an overlay image from a DAImage
PieDegrees	Draws a filled arc segment
PieRadians	Draws a filled arc segment in radians
Polygon	Draws a closed polygon

Table Continued on Following Page

DA library function	Purpose
Polyline	Draws an open polygon
Rect	Draws a rectangle
Reset	Resets transformational state for further renders
RestoreGraphicsState	Restores graphics state from saved state from stack
RoundRect	Draws a round rectangle
SaveGraphicsState	Saves the graphics state to a stack
SecondaryFillColor	Sets secondary color for gradients and fills
Text	Draws text
TextPoint	Draws text but takes DAPoints for coords
Transform	Alters the current graphics state of the drawing surface
VerticalFillScale	Scales the fill to fit the bounding box vertically

Of this rather copious list most will seem reminiscent of the parametric structured graphics options. These methods will be used in scripting just as they would in the initial declaration of the object to create the vector surfaces which will be rendered on the page.

Simple Scripting of Primitives Example

The most basic use of the drawing surface is to add to or replace the existing vector image with new components declared in script. This can be used to animate existing images or to dynamically change the rendered image of the control.

This is a simple example, which displays a static red stop sign. It is only intended to illustrate the extraction of the drawing surface, and manipulations thereof.

```
<HTML>
<HEAD><title>Drawing Surface Example</title></HEAD>

<BODY BGCOLOR="#0000FF">
<OBJECT ID=sgSign STYLE="HEIGHT:200;WIDTH:200" CLASSID="CLSID:369303C2-D7AC-11D0-89D5-
00A0C90833E6"></OBJECT>
```

Note that the structured graphics control does not need to have any vector primitives declared before scripting. First we **dim** the library and surface variables.

```
<SCRIPT LANGUAGE="VBScript">
dim DALib, Dasur
```

Next we set these to the appropriate properties from the structured graphics control. Unlike typical object properties these are both interface pointers.

```
set DALib = sgSign.Library
Set DAsur = sgSign.DrawSurface
```

Now we can use the methods of the drawing surface to create some vector primitives.

```
call DAsur.fillcolor(DALib.ColorRgb255(0,255,0))
call DAsur.oval(-60,-50,90,90)
call DASur.Text("GO",-30,0)
```

Finally we return the modified surface to the structured graphics control.

```
sgSign.DrawSurface = Dasur
</SCRIPT>
</BODY>
</HTML>
```

One caveat is if the drawing surface isn't modified before it is returned to the control it will error, this isn't recommended.

Drawing Surface Methods

The drawing surface provides much greater control over gradients and fills than is possible from parameters alone. Through the drawing surface one can specify the scaling of both texture fills and gradient fills. The rolloff or 'attack' value of the gradient fill can be set from scripting as well. Marked improvement in the declaration of polygons comes from the added ability to use DA behaviors as the basis for polygons and polylines. By using DA behaviors non-static shapes can be declared; that is shapes that are declared based on dynamic points, and deform over time without further scripting. While this is very useful functionality to have available, it is also very complex to code. An analysis of this type of coding is best suited to a book on DA itself. For authors requiring more complexity in their pages than that which will be discussed here, we would recommend further reading on DA itself.

What will be discussed here, what we feel to be compelling about the drawing surface, are two things; **transformations**, and the **graphics 'stack'**. The drawing surface provides access to much more complex transformations than the simple calls to rotate available to the control itself. The range of transformations is broader, and by concatenating transformations an author can produce complex deformations on the vector objects. The other main piece of functionality that the drawing surface provides is the graphics 'stack'. An author may 'push' the current graphics state onto a 'stack' before making changes or deformations, then 'pop' the graphics state back off before returning the drawing surface to the structured graphics control. This allows an author to have multiple sections of the structured graphic transforming differently.

Transformations

Transformations are a collection of methods available through the **transform** method of the drawing surface object. The **transform** method takes a parameter of a DA library call, and returns a DA behavior.

Transformation	Effect
`lib.Compose2(xf1, xf2)`	Combines two transforms as one
`lib.Compose2Array(xforms)`	Combines an array of transforms as one
`lib.FollowPath(path, duration)`	Converts a vector drawing into a path

Table Continued on Following Page

Transformation	Effect
`lib.FollowPathEval(path, evaluator)`	Same as path but using a DANumber for duration
`lib.FollowPathAngle(path, duration)`	Creates a path behavior, the target of which will be oriented tangentially to the path itself
`lib.FollowPathAngleEval(path,evaluator)`	Same as path angle but duration is a DANumber
`lib.FollowPathAngleUpright(path, duration)`	Same as path angle but orientation will always be in a positive x direction
`lib.FollowPathAngleUprightEval(path, evaluator)`	DANumber
`lib.Rotate2(radians)`	Rotates the surface counter clockwise in radians
`lib.Rotate2Anim(radians)`	Rotates the surface based on a DANumber
`lib.Rotate2-Degrees(degrees)`	Rotates the surface counter clockwise in degrees
`lib.Rotate2Rate(radians)`	Rotation is repeated over time
`lib.Rotate2RateDegrees(degrees)`	Rotation is repeated over time
`lib.Scale2(sx, sy)`	Independent scaling in X and Y
`lib.Scale2Anim(sx, sy)`	Independent scaling in X and Y based on a DANumber
`lib.Scale2Rate(x, y)`	Independent scaling in X and Y over time
`lib.Scale2Uniform(uniformFactor)`	Scales both X and Y
`lib.Scale2UniformAnim(uniformFactor)`	Scales both X and Y based on a DANumber
`lib.Scale2UniformRate(rate)`	Scales both X and Y over time
`lib.Scale2Vector(v)`	Scales vector behaviors
`lib.Transform3x2Anim(matrix)`	Implements a matrix transform based on DANumbers
`lib.Translate2(tx, ty)`	Translates by the X and Y given
`lib.Translate2Anim(tx, ty)`	Translates by the X and Y given in DANumbers
`lib.Translate2Point(loc)`	Translates a point to the point given
`lib.Translate2Rate(x, y)`	Translates by the X and Y given over time
`lib.Translate2Vector(v)`	Translates vector behaviors
`lib.XShear2(a)`	Shears a vector object in X
`lib.XShear2Anim(a)`	Shears a vector object in X based on a DANumber
`lib.XShear2Rate(rate)`	Shears a vector object in X over time
`lib.YShear2(a)`	Shears a vector object in Y

Transformation	Effect
`lib.YShear2Anim(a)`	Shears a vector object in Y based on a DANumber
`lib.YShear2Rate(rate)`	Shears a vector object in Y over time

The `compose2` method is of particular interest as it allows us to create transformations built up of component parts. With this, and the graphics stack, an author can create animations with multiple axes of rotation, with different motions and timelines for the scenes disparate elements.

DANumbers

Transformations in DA need not be static, they can be based on **DANumbers**. A DANumber is a numeric behavior. DANumbers are created with the library `DANumber()` method with takes an integer, or any method which evaluates to an integer, as an argument. To create a dynamic number we can use other DA library calls as the argument to the method e.g.

```
Set m = SGControl.library
MyDANumber = m.DANumber(m.Sin(m.LocalTime))
```

This would create a DANumber whose value was between –1 and 1 varying sinusoidal to time. DANumbers allow us to create highly complex animations by setting a few of the parameters of the animation to be dynamic values. The interaction of even a few number behaviors will create seemingly asynchronous deformations in the animation.

Transformations Example

Let's look at an example of transformations using dynamic numbers. We'll create a smoothly animated swinging pendulum, which follows the normal laws of physics, in that it swings from side to side, slowing down as it approaches the highest point of the arc, then changing direction and speeding up again.

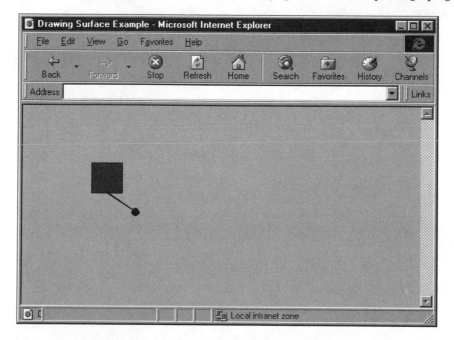

Firstly in the code, we need to set the rotation of a rectangle in radians to be equal to the sign of time, producing a 1/6th or 60 degree arc.

```
<HTML>
<HEAD><title>Drawing Surface Transform Example</title></HEAD>

<BODY BGCOLOR="#0000FF">
<OBJECT ID=sgSign STYLE="HEIGHT:200;WIDTH:200" CLASSID="CLSID:369303C2-D7AC-11D0-89D5-
00A0C90833E6"></OBJECT>

<SCRIPT LANGUAGE="VBScript">
dim DALib, DAsur, DAN1, DAN2

set DALib = sgSign.Library
set DAsur = sgSign.DrawSurface
```

Next we must create a DANumber behavior, before we can use the **sin** method from the library to produce a number behavior from the integer return of the **localTime** method.

```
set DAN1 = DALib.Sin(DALib.localTime)

call DAsur.fillcolor(DALib.red)
call DAsur.rect(-20,-40,40,40)
```

The **transform** method of the drawing surface is invoked. We use the number behavior we created as the animated rate for the transformation. This creates the pendulum motion.

```
call DAsur.transform(DALib.rotate2Anim(DAN1))
call DAsur.fillcolor(DALib.ColorRgb255(0,0,155))
call DAsur.rect(0, 0, 1,40)
call DAsur.oval(-5, 40, 10, 10)

sgSign.DrawSurface = DAsur
</SCRIPT>
</BODY>
</HTML>
```

Run the example for yourself to see how it works.

Composite Transformations

We have seen how to rotate an element about the drawing surface center, but what if we want to rotate around a different point within the drawing surface. Via the **compose2** methods of the library we can combine the offset and rotational transformations into a single behavior.

```
call DAsur.transform(DALib.compose2(DALib.translate2(0,-20),DALib.rotate2rate(1)))
```

Any combination of transform behaviors may be aggregated with the **compose2** and **compose2array** methods. These methods apply to the **transform2** class, 3 dimensional transforms need to use the **compose3** methods.

The graphics stack

The drawing surface can maintain multiple graphics states on a stack. This stack is accessed via the save and restore graphics state methods. By pushing a graphics state onto the stack an author can make changes which will only affect the new elements. That is changes and transformations will only effect the elements in the current state. An example of why this is useful is a standard clock.

Clock Hands – Graphic Stack Example

There are three hands on the clock, each moving at a different pace.

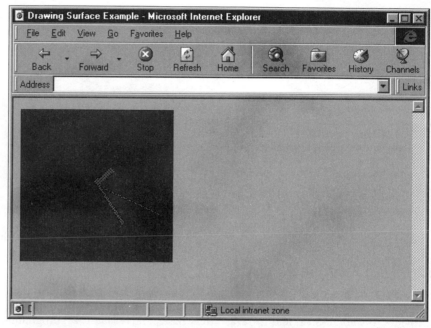

Without the graphics stack we could only implement one rotational rate, with it we have a functional clock.

```
<HTML>
<HEAD><title>Drawing Surface Example</title></HEAD>

<BODY BGCOLOR="#0000FF">
<OBJECT ID=sgSign STYLE="HEIGHT:200;WIDTH:200" CLASSID="CLSID:369303C2-D7AC-11D0-89D5-
00A0C90833E6"></OBJECT>

<SCRIPT LANGUAGE="VBScript">
dim DALib, DAsur
set DALib = sgSign.Library
Set DAsur = sgSign.DrawSurface
```

Draw the face of the clock, here simplified to a square.

```
call DAsur.fillcolor(DALib.red)
call DAsur.rect(-100,-100,200,200)
```

Then push the graphics context onto the stack to isolate the rotational transforms for the hands.

```
DAsur.SaveGraphicsState()
call DAsur.transform(DALib.rotate2Ratedegrees(30))
call DAsur.fillcolor(DALib.ColorRgb255(0,0,155))
call DAsur.rect(0, 0, 2,90)
DAsur.RestoreGraphicsState()
```

Pop back off of the stack to the original context, then push again before adding more elements. This isolates the rotations from each other.

```
DAsur.SaveGraphicsState()
call DAsur.transform(DALib.rotate2Ratedegrees(15))
call DAsur.fillcolor(DALib.ColorRgb255(0,0,155))
call DAsur.rect(0, 0, 4,60)
DAsur.RestoreGraphicsState()

DAsur.SaveGraphicsState()
call DAsur.transform(DALib.rotate2Ratedegrees(5))
call DAsur.fillcolor(DALib.ColorRgb255(0,0,155))
call DAsur.rect(0, 0, 8,30)
DAsur.RestoreGraphicsState()

sgSign.DrawSurface = DAsur
</SCRIPT>
</BODY>
</HTML>
```

It is easy to see how this example could be extended to produce a simple particle system in 2 dimensions.

Drawing Surface summary

We have seen how to draw vector graphics from script, how to transform the graphics, and how to create disparate transformations within a single graphic. This is only the beginning of the capabilities that DA provides to web authors, and to Java, Visual Basic, and Visual C++ programmers as well. Looking through the API that is exposed just in the context of the drawing surface it is evident that this is a complex and powerful multimedia runtime engine.

Although we have only covered the drawing surface here, the entire DA runtime API library is accessible through the structured graphics controls library. The controls library is in fact a pointer to the DA library itself. This is a result of the structured graphics control being on top of DA, more precisely the structured graphics control is a wrapper for the DA runtime.

Summary

You have just seen how the capabilities of IE4 to create varying and powerful multimedia effects can be used to create very compelling and rich user interfaces. The range of multimedia controls allow you to provide very media rich interfaces without a great deal of programming, and without having to download a bunch of extra controls and plug-ins. In this chapter you have seen how to:

- Download and play audio and video files with the Active Movie Control

- Move objects around on the page with the Path control

- Control objects over time using the Sequencer control

- Animate images on your page, yet retain scripted control, with the Sprite control

- Create lightweight yet powerful graphics using the Structured Graphics control

- And combine the Structured Graphics control with the power of Direct Animation to create great effects on your page.

You can use all of these controls individually, or in many different combinations, to greatly enhance the user interface that you are presenting to the viewers of your page. The best way to do it is to just try different things out and see what new and different ways you can combine these multimedia controls together, and with the other features of Dynamic HTML.

NetShow, Chat and the Agent Control

We've already looked at the new core technologies that form IE4's implementation of Dynamic HTML, and seen several of the components that are provided with the full installation of IE4—such as new Active Movie multimedia control. In this chapter, we're going to cover some of the various other technologies and controls that Microsoft makes available to developers—in what it refers to as the Component Library. Not all of these controls in the Component Library come with the full installation of IE4, but some, such as the Chat Control, are available separately with the Internet Client SDK. The SDK is downloadable from
`http://www.microsoft.com/msdn/sdk/inetsdk/asetup/default.asp`

The controls within the Component Library allow you to create very rich user experiences, either by providing streaming media within the web page, or an interactive chat feature, or an interactive agent character that guides the user through difficult tasks. We'll provide you with a reference of each controls' properties, methods and events—in addition to a set of example pages—so that you can quickly integrate these controls into your current project.

In this chapter, you'll see:

▲ The **NetShow** control and how to use it to provide video in the page

▲ The **Chat** control and how to use it to offer visitors extra features

▲ The **Agent** control, and how to use the characters it provides to create rich pages

First we'll take a look at what you need to do to install these components.

Installation of Controls

Notice that even if you did opt for a 'full' installation of IE4, you won't have the Agent and Chat controls, as they only come with the Internet Client SDK. If you don't wish to download the full SDK (at 80 MB, it can take quite a while), or if you didn't install the full version of IE4, then you can get the different components from the following URLs:

▲ NetShow 2.0 is available from:
`http://www.microsoft.com/netshow/download.htm`

▲ The Chat Control (1.1) is available from:
`http://www.microsoft.com/ie/download/?/msdownload/ieplatform/chat/chat.htm`

▲ The Agent Control (1.5) is available from:
`http://www.microsoft.com/workshop/prog/agent/agentdl.htm`

However to run the samples, you don't need actually download the controls beforehand, as the samples should download the necessary controls automatically, the first time you run them. If, however, for any reason, the controls don't automatically download, then we do recommend downloading the controls manually from the above URLs and then trying again.

First off, then, we'll take a look at the NetShow control.

The Microsoft NetShow Control

NetShow is a platform for streaming multimedia over networks that range from low-bandwidth dial-up Internet connections to high-bandwidth switched local area networks. From simple audio to sophisticated interactive Web-based applications, companies use NetShow to offer new streaming content for applications such as training, corporate communications, entertainment, and advertising to users all over the world.

About the NetShow Control

The NetShow control allows pages to receive and playback streaming media in the **Active Streaming Format** (ASF). Streaming media formats have been available on the Internet for more than a year, however, up until now they have required the user to have a plugin or a special player installed, and the Web site itself to have special server software to broadcast the file. A year ago, Internet users didn't have the 28.8 kbps connections needed to reliably deliver streaming media, and so the technology never really took off. Today, however, most users have at least a 28.8 kbps connection, with a lot of users sporting 33.6 kbps or even 56 kbps modems. It's this increase in bandwidth that has contributed towards the rise in the use of streaming media formats.

The NetShow control and server differ from other competing formats in that both the player and the server are free (but only available for use on Windows NT and Windows 95). This allows a site administrator to easily add support for streaming media without purchasing an expensive server, although it does require A/V SCSI Drives and a fast 'Net connection—all of which may cost extra money. Microsoft has also announced recently that the next version of NetShow (as of writing the current version was 2.0) will support other streaming media formats such as Real Audio and Real Video.

Beyond simply delivering audio and video information in a streaming format, NetShow also allows the server to **multicast** an ASF file. Normally servers have to create a separate connection to every client that requests a document, so if ten clients are requesting the same document the server must create ten separate connections. If the server could send the same document over the network once, and have those clients which are interested in the document receive it and those that are not just ignore it, the server's load would be greatly reduced.

This is essentially the concept behind multicasting. Like a television or radio station, the NetShow server can send out an ASF file over the network, thus allowing ten, hundreds, thousands or millions of clients to receive the ASF without any additional performance hit to the server. More importantly, it does this without a greater requirement of bandwidth on the connecting infrastructure.

Note that changes to the standard Internet infrastructure are required to support multi-casting—namely, IP Multicast must be enabled on all routers between the server and the client. So while we'll be looking at webcasting in more detail later in this book, we won't be looking at multicasting, for this reason.

Basic Implementation

The NetShow control is simply an ActiveX control that contains a comprehensive set of properties, methods and events. It's very simple to insert into a web page—all we have to do is use the correct `<OBJECT>` tag:

```
<OBJECT ID="nsplay1" WIDTH=160 HEIGHT=120
  CLASSID="CLSID:2179C5D3-EBFF-11cf-B6FD-00AA00B4E220"
  CODEBASE="http://www.microsoft.com/netshow/download/en/
            nsasfinf.cab#Version=2,0,0,888">
```

This code will instantiate the NetShow control within the page. However, so far we haven't specified where the ASF file is located. To do that we must supply the URL by setting the `FileName` property:

```
<PARAM NAME="FileName"VALUE="mmst://ns1.npr.org/newscast/news.auto.asf">
</OBJECT>
```

> *Notice the special protocol* `mmst:`*, rather than* `http:`*, to be used for the ASF file.*

Since any properties of the control can also be set using `<PARAM>` tags within the `<OBJECT>` tag, we can load and control the NetShow player without using client-side scripting. This is an ideal solution if you are only interested in playing a file in a fixed way, and do not want to give the user any control of it.

> *You can run or download this example from our Web site at* `http://rapid.wrox.co.uk/`
> `books/0707/`*. Please not that this example might not work correctly for you, and indeed may cause errors, if you are running it via a proxy server.*

This simple page plays the National Public Radio News ASF as soon as the page loads, and it looks like this:

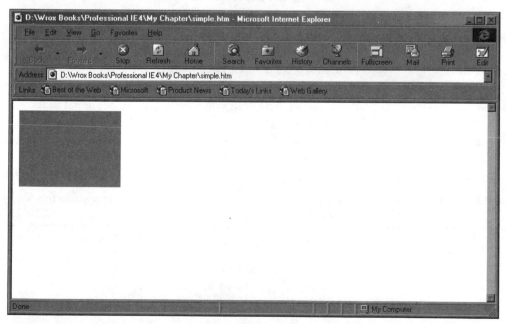

Since we did not specify that the NetShow control should display any user controls, and the ASF we specified is audio-only, the control is displayed as a simple gray object at the default size.

Properties, Methods and Events

You are already familiar with the **FileName** property which specifies the URL for the ASF file you want to play, however NetShow exposes a myriad of properties, methods and events that we can take advantage of in our client-side code. Considering the sheer number of these, we can't provide an example that uses all of them—however, we will create a couple of pages that will take advantage of a lot of them to give the user a very rich experience.

Properties of the NetShow Control

This section lists all the properties of the NetShow control. We've sorted them into sections to make it easier to find the one you need, and included a brief description. In general we are most interested in the ASF playback and quality properties, less interested in the ASF information properties, and we are rarely interested in how the control is actually getting the information, etc. As you've already seen, the NetShow control only requires that the **FileName** property be set to a value, the remaining properties allow you to customize how the control behaves.

ASF Playback Property	Description
allowChangeControlType	Returns or sets a Boolean value specifying whether the user can change the way controls are displayed.
allowChangeDisplaySize	Returns or sets a Boolean value specifying whether or not the display size can be set at run time.
allowScan	Returns or sets a Boolean value specifying whether or not file scanning is enabled for files that support scanning (fast forwarding and rewinding).
animationAtStart	Returns or sets a Boolean value specifying whether or not the title animation is displayed during initial file buffering.
autoRewind	Returns or sets a Boolean value specifying whether or not the file position is automatically set to zero after a file has played to the end.
autoStart	Returns or sets a Boolean value specifying whether or not a file automatically begins playing when the control is loaded.
clickToPlay	Returns or sets a Boolean value specifying whether or not file playback is toggled by a mouse click.
controlType	Returns or sets a long value specifying the way the control is displayed.
currentMarker	Returns or sets a long value specifying the current position in a file by marker number.

ASF Playback Property	Description
displaySize	Returns or sets a long value specifying the size of the image display window.
invokeURLs	Returns or sets a Boolean value specifying whether or not the NetShow Player automatically invokes URLs in an Internet or intranet browser.
openState	Returns the open state of the control.
playCount	Returns or sets a long value specifying how many times a file plays.
playState	Returns the play state of the control.
rate	Returns or sets a double value specifying the rate at which a file plays.
transparentAtStart	Returns or sets a Boolean value specifying whether the image window is transparent when an ASF file begins playing.

ASF Quality Property	Description
bandwidth	Returns a long value specifying the bandwidth of the current file in bits per second.
bufferingCount	Returns a long value specifying the number of times buffering occurred during file playback.
bufferingTime	Returns a double value specifying the control's buffering time.
lostPackets	Returns a long value specifying the number of packets lost.
receivedPackets	Returns a long value specifying the number of packets received.
receptionQuality	Returns a long value specifying the percentage of packets received in the last 30 seconds.
recoveredPackets	Returns a long value specifying the number of packets recovered.

ASF Information Property when compiled within file	Description
author	Returns a string containing the author of the current file.
baseURL	Returns or sets a string specifying the base HTTP URL.
canScan	Returns or sets a Boolean value specifying whether the current file can fast forward or fast reverse.
canSeek	Returns or sets a Boolean value specifying whether the current file can seek to a specific time.
canSeekToMarkers	Returns or sets a Boolean value specifying whether the current file can seek to a marker.
channelDescription	Returns a string containing the description of the channel.

Table Continued on Following Page

ASF Information Property when compiled within file	Description
channelName	Returns a string containing the name of the channel.
channelURL	Returns a string containing the location of the channel metafile.
contactAddress	Returns a string containing the contact address of the channel.
contactEmail	Returns a string containing the contact e-mail address of the channel.
contactPhone	Returns a string containing the contact phone number of the channel.
copyright	Returns a string containing the copyright information from the current file.
creationDate	Returns a date value containing the creation date of the current file.
currentPosition	Returns or sets a double value specifying the current position in a file by time.
description	Returns a string specifying the description field from the current file.
duration	Returns a double value specifying the play duration of the current file in seconds.
fileName	Returns or sets a string value specifying the name of the current file or opens a new file.
imageSourceHeight	Returns a long value specifying the original image height in pixels for the current file.
imageSourceWidth	Returns a long value specifying the original image width in pixels for the current file.
isBroadcast	Returns or sets a Boolean value specifying whether or not the source is a broadcast.
isDurationValid	Returns or sets a Boolean value specifying whether or not the source is live.
markerCount	Returns a long value specifying the number of markers in the current file.
rating	Returns a string containing the rating of the current file.
sourceLink	Returns a string containing the path to the ASF file.
sourceProtocol	Returns a string containing the protocol used to receive data.
title	Returns a string containing the title of the current file.

Netshow Control Property	Description
codecCount	Returns an integer specifying the number of installable codecs used by the file.
cursorType	Returns or sets a long value specifying the cursor type.
enableAutoProxy	Returns or sets a Boolean value specifying whether or not HTTP proxy information is automatically set.

Netshow Control Property	Description
enableContextMenu	Returns or sets a Boolean value specifying whether or not a menu appears when the right mouse button is clicked.
enableHTTP	Returns or sets a Boolean value specifying whether or not the control attempts to receive data using HTTP.
enableMulticast	Returns or sets a Boolean value specifying whether or not the control attempts to receive multicast data.
enableTCP	Returns or sets a Boolean value specifying whether or not the control attempts to receive data using TCP.
enableUDP	Returns or sets a Boolean value specifying whether or not the control attempts to receive data using UDP.
errorCode	Returns a double value specifying the current error code.
errorCorrection	Returns a string containing the error correction type of the current file.
errorDescription	Returns the description of the current error state.
fixedUDPPort	Returns the UDP port number.
hasError	Returns whether or not the control currently has an error.
HTTPProxyHost	Returns the control's HTTP proxy server.
HTTPProxyPort	Returns the control's HTTP proxy port number.
mainWindow	Returns a long value specifying the window handle of the Player control's main window.
sendErrorEvents	Returns or sets a Boolean value specifying whether the control sends error events.
sendKeyboardEvents	Returns or sets a Boolean value specifying whether keyboard events are sent by the control.
sendMouseClickEvents	Returns or sets a Boolean value specifying whether mouse click events are sent by the control.
sendMouseMoveEvents	Returns or sets a Boolean value specifying whether mouse move events are sent by the control.
sendOpenStateChangeEvents	Returns or sets a Boolean value specifying whether the control sends **openStateChange** events.
sendPlayStateChangeEvents	Returns or sets a Boolean value specifying whether the control sends **playStateChange** events.
sendStateChangeEvents	Returns or sets a Boolean value specifying whether state change events are sent by the control.
sendWarningEvents	Returns or sets a Boolean value specifying whether or not the control sends **warning** events.
useFixedUDPPort	Returns or sets a Boolean value specifying whether or not the control uses a fixed UDP port number.
useHTTPProxy	Returns or sets a Boolean value specifying whether or not the control uses a proxy server for HTTP streaming.

Methods of the NetShow Control

This section lists all the methods of the NetShow control sorted alphabetically. We've included a brief description that includes the type of value that is returned, and the parameters that the method supports including what the variable type is for each parameter.

Method	Description	Parameters
aboutBox	Displays the NetShow client about box.	none
cancel	Cancels the current open operation.	none
getCodecInstalled	Returns a Boolean value specifying whether the codec is installed.	*CodecNumber* as long
getCodecDescription	Returns a string containing the name of the installed codecs.	*CodecNumber* as long
getCodecURL	Returns a string containing the URL for the installed codec.	*CodecNumber* as long
getMarkerName	Returns a string containing the name for a marker.	*MarkerNumber* as long
getMarkerTime	Returns a double value specifying the time for the marker.	*MarkerNumber* as long
open	Opens a specified ASF.	*FileNameURL* as string
pause	Pauses the playback of the open ASF.	none
play	Starts the playback of the open ASF.	none
stop	Stops the playback of the open ASF.	none

Events of the NetShow Control

This section lists all the events of the NetShow control sorted alphabetically. We've included a brief description of the event and the parameters.

Event	Description	Parameters
autoStartFailure	Fired when a file failed to start automatically.	*Result* as long indicating reason
buffering	Fired when the control is beginning or ending buffering.	*Start* as Boolean (**TRUE** means that buffering has just started)
click	Fired when a mouse click occurred in the image window.	*Button* as long indicating the mouse button clicked (left **0**, right **1**, middle **2**), *Shift-State* as Boolean, *x* as single relative to image window, *y* as single relative to image window
dblClick	Fired when a mouse double-click occurred in the image window.	*Button* as long indicating the mouse button clicked (left **0**, right 1, middle **2**), *Shift-State* as boolean, *x* as single relative to image window, *y* as single relative to image window

Event	Description	Parameters
disconnect	Fired when the connection to the NetShow server was broken.	*Reason* as a long value
endOfStream	Fired when file playback has ended.	*Result* as a long value representing the final status when the ASF playback is done
error	Fired when an error occurs.	None
keyDown	Fired when a key was pressed.	*KeyCode* as integer, *Shift-State* as long
keyPress	Fired when a key was pressed and released.	*KeyASCII* as integer
keyUp	Fired when a key was released.	*KeyCode* as integer, *Shift-State* as long
markerHit	Fired when a marker was reached.	*MarkerNumber* as long
mouseDown	Fired when a mouse button was pressed.	*Button* as long indicating the mouse button clicked (left 0, right 1, middle 2), *Shift-State* as boolean, *x* as single relative to image window, *y* as single relative to image window
mouseMove	Fired when the mouse pointer was moved.	*Button* as long indicating the mouse button clicked (left 0, right 1, middle 2), *Shift-State* as boolean, *x* as single relative to image window, *y* as single relative to image window
mouseUp	Fired when a mouse button was released.	*Button* as long indicating the mouse button clicked (left 0, right 1, middle 2), *Shift-State* as Boolean, *x* as single relative to image window, *y* as single relative to image window
newStream	Fired when a new stream is started in a channel.	none
openStateChange	Fired when the control changes OpenState.	*WarningType* as long, *Param* as long, *Description* as string
playStateChange	Fired when the control changes PlayState.	*OldState* as long, *NewState* as long
scriptCommand	Fired when a command (or URL) was received from the current file.	none
stateChange	Fired when the state of file playback changed.	none
warning	Fired when the control encounters a problem.	*Type* as string, *Param* as string

A NetShow Television Page

The following sample page gives the user an option of five different NetShow broadcasts, with the option to customize the controls, while displaying information about the ASF file being played:

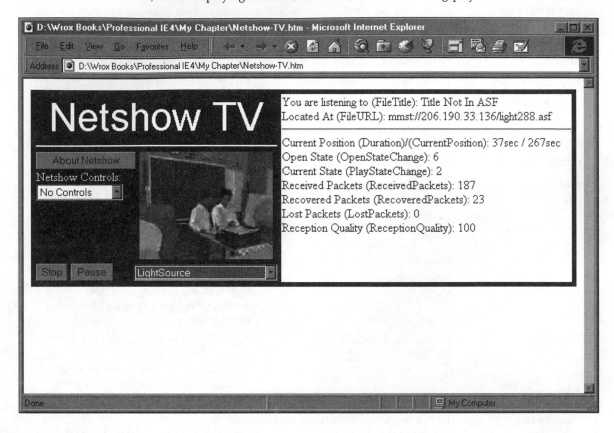

You can run or download this example from our Web site at **http://rapid.wrox.co.uk/ books/0707/**. *Please note that this example might not work correctly for you, and indeed may cause errors, if you are running it via a proxy server.*

As you can see from the screen shot, we have a simple two-cell table that defines the layout. On the left-hand side we provide the user with the option of stopping and pausing the playback of the ASF file, changing the display of controls within the NetShow window, and the choice of which ASF file to play. On the right-hand side we are displaying a selection of information about the file, such as the URL and the reception quality, which are updated dynamically.

The <OBJECT> Tag

The actual **<OBJECT>** tag for this page is the same as in our previous example. All we really want to do is to load the control onto the page and instruct it to start playing an ASF file:

```
<OBJECT ID="nsplay1" WIDTH=176 HEIGHT=144
  CLASSID="CLSID:2179C5D3-EBFF-11cf-B6FD-00AA00B4E220"
  CODEBASE="http://www.microsoft.com/netshow/download/en/
           nsasfinf.cab#Version=2,0,0,888">
  <PARAM NAME="FileName" VALUE="mmst://ns1.npr.org/newscast/news.auto.asf">
</OBJECT>
```

The Control Buttons

We're using standard HTML buttons for the Play, Stop, Pause and About NetShow buttons, and
`<SELECT>` tags to create the combo boxes for the types of controls to display and the ASF file itself. The
only difference is that we've specified an `ID` for each of these elements, so that we can respond to their
`onclick` and `onchange` events:

```
<SELECT ID=cboNsState>
  <OPTION VALUE="0">No Controls</OPTION>
  <OPTION VALUE="1">Simple Controls</OPTION>
  <OPTION VALUE="2">Full Controls</OPTION>
</SELECT>
```

The Status Information

Finally we're using `<SPAN>` tags to specify where the dynamically generated text in the right-hand table
column is placed. This allows us to update a section of a single line, without disturbing the rest of the text.
We could use `<DIV>` tags instead, however IE4 places a line break before and after a `<DIV>`, whereas it
doesn't with `<SPAN>` tags. We have to give a unique `ID` to each `<SPAN>` so that we can easily reference
the tag:

```
Open State (OpenStateChange): <SPAN ID=OpenStateChange></SPAN><BR>
```

Responding to Button Clicks

When the page initially loads it starts playing the National Public Radio News. In order to control the
ASF file playback, we need to respond to the `onClick` events of the form buttons:

```
Sub btnPlay_onclick()
  nsplay1.Play
  document.all.StopButtons.Style.Display = ""
  document.all.PlayButtons.Style.Display = "none"
End Sub

Sub btnStop_onclick()
  nsplay1.Stop
  document.all.StopButtons.Style.Display = "none"
  document.all.PlayButtons.Style.Display = ""
End Sub

Sub btnPause_onclick()
  nsplay1.Pause
  document.all.StopButtons.Style.Display = "none"
  document.all.PlayButtons.Style.Display = ""
End Sub
```

As you can see, we are calling the appropriate method of the NetShow control (`nsplay1`)–such as `Play`, `Stop` or `Pause`. Since we don't want to give the user an option to play an ASF file that is already being played, we change the CSS display value to `"none"` to hide those playback options that are unavailable to the user.

Responding to Selection List Changes

Next we want to provide the user with an easy method to change the control display and the ASF file. We used the `<SELECT>` tag to create the combo boxes, so now we need to figure out which event to respond to. The `onclick` event will be fired every time the mouse button is clicked on the control and, since a user can click several times before actually changing the value, it isn't a good idea to respond to this event. Instead we respond to the `onchange` event, which is fired only after the selection has changed. We also make sure that the values we used in the `<SELECT>` tag were the same values that the NetShow control needs. This way we can very easily pass the value of the `<SELECT>` box direct to the NetShow control:

```
Sub cboNsState_onchange ()
  nsplay1.ControlType = cboNsState.value
End Sub

Sub Station_onchange()
  nsplay1.FileName = Station.value
End Sub
```

Displaying the Status Information

Now comes the hard part. We want to display information to the user about the file being played. Some of the information needs to be updated constantly (like the reception quality) while other items only need to be updated once (like the URL). We can very easily respond to the `Buffering` event to determine when we should write the information that needs to be updated once. This event is fired whenever NetShow starts and stops buffering the ASF feed:

```
Sub NSPlay1_Buffering(Start)
  if Start = True then
    document.all("Buffer").InnerText = "Buffering..."
    foo = window.setTimeOut("Call ShowPos", 1000, "VBScript")
    call DisplayInformation
  else
    document.all("Buffer").InnerText = ""
  end if
End Sub
```

As you can see, if the buffering process is starting we change the value of the `Buffer <SPAN>` tag to `"Buffering…"` by changing the `InnerText` of the appropriate `<SPAN>` tag. Then we set up the browser to call the `ShowPos` subroutine after one second by calling the `SetTimeOut` method of the `window` object. Finally we call a sub-routine named `DisplayInformation`, which updates the information that only needs to be updated once. If the buffering process is ending, on the other hand, we simply place an empty string into the `Buffer <SPAN>` tag to clear the text currently displayed.

The DisplayInformation Subroutine

The `DisplayInformation` subroutine writes the File Name, URL and the total number of seconds into the appropriate `<SPAN>` tag. We are simply using the `InnerText` method to set the text of the `<SPAN>` tag to the strings returned from the NetShow control's properties. The only special case is the `FileTitle` property. Since this is optional for the ASF file, and we don't want it left blank if the file does not contain a title, a simple check if it is null is made—and, if so, we substitute some text:

```
Sub DisplayInformation
  document.all("FileTitle").InnerText = NSPlay1.Title
  If NSPlay1.Title = "" then
    document.all("FileTitle").InnerText = "Title Not In ASF"
  End If
  document.all("FileURL").InnerText = NSPlay1.FileName
  document.all("Duration").InnerText = CInt(NSPlay1.Duration)
End Sub
```

After one second into the playback of the ASF file, IE4 will run the `ShowPos` sub-routine. This sub-routine simply updates the information in several `<SPAN>` tags to reflect the current position into the ASF, and information about the reception quality:

```
Sub ShowPos
  document.all("CurrentPosition").InnerText = CInt(NSPlay1.CurrentPosition)
  document.all("ReceivedPackets").InnerText = NSPlay1.ReceivedPackets
  document.all("RecoveredPackets").InnerText = NSPlay1.RecoveredPackets
  document.all("LostPackets").InnerText = NSPlay1.LostPackets
  document.all("ReceptionQuality").InnerText = NSPlay1.ReceptionQuality
  foo = window.setTimeOut("Call ShowPos", 1000, "VBScript")
End Sub
```

After we have updated the information, we call the `setTimeOut` method of the `window` object so that this routine is called again one second later. This allows us to easily update our information every second without having to have a timer control on the page. Alternatively, we could have used the `setInterval` method instead, which would mean that we didn't have to keep resetting the timeout. However, then we'd have to clear it once the file had finished playing.

Handling Errors While Playing a File

Finally in the unfortunate event of an error in the NetShow control, we want to handle that error condition gracefully. To do this we can respond to the `Error` event of the NetShow control. In this case, we are simply displaying a message box with information about the error:

```
Sub NSPlay1_Error()
  strError = "The following error occured:" & chr(10) _
           & "Error Code: " & NSPlay1.ErrorCode & chr(10) _
           & "Description: " & NSPlay1.ErrorDescription
  x = msgbox(strError,16,"NetShow Error")
End Sub
```

Creating Active Streaming Files

Active Streaming Files can be created in several ways. Typically an ASF is created as a `.mov`, `.wav` or `.avi` file, then converted to the ASF format using Microsoft's conversion tools, but ASFs can also be created from live video feeds or from Microsoft PowerPoint 97 presentations.

Unfortunately since the Active Streaming Format is relatively new, the editing tools leave much to be desired. Microsoft currently offers a set of seven tools that will convert and edit ASFs, however most of these tools are clunky command-line applications. If you want to create an ASF, you will probably build the bulk of the file using either PowerPoint (if it is a presentation) or standard `.avi` editing tools if it is a video. Once this file is created, you run the appropriate conversation tool to create the raw ASF.

With the raw ASF, you can move to the ASF Editor and make final edits and synchronize the playback with the audio and script commands. Script commands allow you to specify commands for the NetShow player to perform during playback. Typically these commands are used to create "page flips" where the Netshow control causes the browser to navigate to an HTML page. This allows you to provide the user with additional information (like slides) during the playback of the audio. The most important feature of the ASF Editor is its ability to optimize the playback bandwidth to correspond with the bandwidth of the network that will be deploying the files. As a general rule-of-thumb, if the ASF will be deployed over the Internet you should select a 28.8 kbs bandwidth. If you are deploying the ASF over an Intranet then you can increase the bandwidth, which will improve the playback quality.

NetShow Control Summary

As you can see, the NetShow control allows us to create a very rich user experience for the playback of streaming media files. Instead of having the file playback inside of the standalone player, you can integrate the playback into the graphical layout of the HTML page. This allows you to control the way in which the user experiences the information, and this makes the difference between a web site and a great web site.

The Microsoft Chat Control

The Microsoft Chat control allows you to connect to a Chat server, running either the Microsoft Internet Chat (MIC) or the Internet Relay Chat (IRC) protocols. Until recently Internet Chat clients were either very proprietary, or were very difficult to use. Most Internet users either downloaded several chat clients, one for each separate system they wanted to chat on, or invested a lot of time learning clients like mIRC.

About the Chat Control

The Microsoft Chat control allows user to go to a URL and get automatically logged into a chat room. This simplifies both the user's experience, as they only have to navigate to a simple URL, and problems with users not being able to connect with their own chat software. The only problem with Chat control 1.1 is that it does not support all types of chat servers.

Basic Implementation

The Chat control comes with a standard user interface, although you can build your own and use the chat control only to connect to the server. The following diagram shows what the default user interface looks like, and what the various panes are:

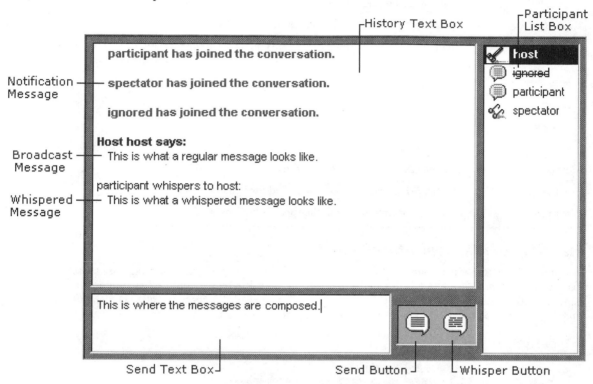

In order to take advantage of the features of the Microsoft Chat control, you really need to be familiar with the Microsoft Internet Chat Client or the standard IRC commands. If you already understand how chat commands work, then you will be able to easily customize how the chat control works. Typically you need to be a host (or operator) on the chat room in order to issue any of the chat commands. Below is a table of the most common chat (IRC) command and their descriptions.

Chat Command	Description
ban	Marks a username or an IP address as banned from the server and/or chat room. Banned users are not allowed to connect to the chat server or chat room that they are banned from.
help	Displays a general help screen or gives help for the specified command.
ignore	Does not show the messages from a specified user.
invite	Invites a specified username to the specified chat room.
leave	Disconnects from a chat room. (Same as part)

Table Continued on Following Page

Chat Command	Description
list	Lists all of the channels on the chat server.
join	Connects to a chat room.
kick	Disconnects another user from a chat room or the chat server.
part	Disconnects from a chat room. (Same as leave)
mode	Changes the user parameters for a specified user. These parameters include ban status, host/participant/spectator status, as well as flags about the current chat room.
msg	Sends a private message to a specified user. (Same as whisper)
nick	Changes your username on the chat server.
query	Starts a private conversation with a specified user.
quit	Disconnects from the chat server.
topic	Changes the topic of the chat room.
whisper	Sends a private message to a specified user. (Same as msg)
whois	Displays information about the specified username.

Inserting the Control into a Page

In order to insert the Chat control into a page we use the `<OBJECT>` tag. In the tag we can set the `UIOption` parameter to `2047` which gives us all of the default features, and the general appearance is set using the `Appearance` property. A value of `3` makes the control display using all 3-D elements. The background color is specified in the `BackColor` parameter—here we're using red:

```
<OBJECT
  STANDBY="Dowloading the Microsoft MSChat ActiveX Control"
  CODETYPE="application/x-oleobject"
  CLASSID="clsid:D6526FE0-E651-11CF-99CB-00C04FD64497"
  CODEBASE="MSChatOCX.Cab#Version=4,71,413,0"
  WIDTH=600
  HEIGHT=350
  ID=Chat>
  <PARAM NAME="UIOption"    VALUE="2047">
  <PARAM NAME="Appearance"  VALUE="3">
  <PARAM NAME="BackColor"   VALUE="255">
</OBJECT>
```

The Properties, Methods and Events

There are many other properties that can be set in `<PARAM>` tags, or dynamically from scripting code. This sections lists all these, plus the methods and events that the control supports.

Properties of the Chat Control

This section lists all the properties of the Chat control, sorted into categories depending on the type of information that the property returns. We've included a brief description of the property value.

Chat Room Property	Description
history	Returns a string containing the contents of the history text pane.
lastMessageReceived	Returns a string containing the last message received from the chat server.
lastMessageSent	Returns a string containing that last message sent to the chat server.
maxMembers	Returns or sets a long value specifying the maximum number of users that can join the current chat room.
memberCount	Returns a long value specifying the number of users that are in the current chat room.
rating	Returns a string containing the chat room's rating using the Platform for Internet Content Selection.
roomPath	Returns a string containing the URL for the current chat room.
roomTopic	Returns or sets a string containing the current chat room's topic.

Chat User Property	Description
thisParticipantAlias	Returns a string containing the current user's alias.
thisParticipantID	Returns a string containing the current user's ID number.
thisParticipantName	Returns a string containing the current user's MS Windows user name.

Chat Control Property	Description
appearance	Returns or sets a long value specifying the control's UI appearance.
backColor	Returns or sets the background color for the text panes of the UI.
borderStyle	Returns or sets a long value specifying the how the borders between the panes of the UI are drawn.
height	Returns or sets the height of the control in HiMetrics. 1 HiMetric = 0.01 millimeters.
maxHistoryLength	Returns or sets a long value specifying the maximum length of the history pane in characters.
maxMessageLength	Returns or sets a long value specifying the maximum number of characters that are allowed in the Send text pane of the UI.
state	Returns a long value specifying the control's current state.
UIOption	Returns or sets a long value specifying the user interface options. Note: This property is a bitmask.
width	Returns or sets a long value specifying the width of the control in HiMetrics.

Methods of the Chat Control

This section lists all the methods of the Chat control sorted alphabetically. We've included a brief description and a list of the parameters that each method supports.

Method	Description	Parameters
aboutBox	Displays the chat client about box.	None
banParticipant	Bans or unbans a specified user from the current chat room.	*Name* as string that specifies the username to be banned, *State* as Boolean that specifies whether to ban or unban the username.
cancelEntering	Cancels the entering of a chat room.	None
clearHistory	Empties the contents of the History pane.	None
enterRoom	Connects the chat client to a specified chat room.	*RoomPath* as string with the chat room path, *RoomPassword* as string (use a null value if there is no password), *ThisParticipantAlias* as string specifying the user's alias, *SecurityPackage* as string set to null, *Flags* as string set to 1 to join a standard chat room, *Type* as string sets the parameters of the chat room if the room is being created.
exitRoom	Disconnects a user from a chat room.	None
getParticipantRealName	Gets the real names of chat users from the server.	*ParticipantID* as long indicating the userID (specify -1 to use the user selected in the participant list) *Alias* as string specifying the alias of the user (use either PartcipantID or Alias), *Synchronous* as Boolean (specify FALSE for web purposes) *RealName* as string– specify null for web purposes
inviteParticipant	Invites another chat user to the user's current chat room.	*Alias* as string specifying the user alias to be invited to the chat room.
kickParticipant	Kicks a member from the current chat room.	*ParticipantID* as long indicating the userID specify -1 to use the user selected in the participant list, *KickMessage* as string that specifies the text message the user will see when they are banned.
moveSplitBar	Changes the cursor to a cross hair so that the chat control can be resized.	None

Method	Description	Parameters
selectParticipants	Selects, deselects or inverts the current selection in the Participant pane.	*Value* as short indicating what to select (deselect highlighted member 0, select all 1, or reverse selection 2).
sendMessage	Sends a message to the server or chat users.	*DestinationList* as long indication what userID to send the message to -1 sends to the whole room, *Count* as integer determines the number of people who will receive the message 0 sends to the whole room, *Message* as string.
setParticipantStatus	Changes the status of a member in a chat room.	*ParticipantID* as long, *Mask* as long indicating what type of status will be changed, *Status* as long indicating the new status.

Events of the Chat Control

This section lists all the events of the Chat control sorted alphabetically. We've included a brief description of the event and its parameters.

Event	Description	Parameters
onBeginEnumeration	Fired when the control first joins a chat room, but before the Participants pane is populated with usernames.	None
onEndEnumeration	Fired when the Participants pane is fully populated with the list of users currently connected to the chat room.	None
onEnterParticipant	Fired when a new user joins the current chat room.	*ParticipantID* as long, *Alias* as string, *Status* as integer specifying whether they are host 1, participant 2, spectator 4.
onError	Fired when an error occurs in the control.	*ErrorCode* as long, *Description* as string
onExitParticipant	Fired when a user leaves the current chat room.	*ParticipantID* as long
onHistoryFull	Fired when the History pane is 90% of its maximum number of characters.	*Percent* as integer specifying the exact percentage of the history box
onMessage	Fired when the user receives a messages from another chat user.	*SenderID* as long, *Message* as string, *MessageType* as integer indicating whether it was whispered, etc.

Table Continued on Following Page

Event	Description	Parameters
onParticipantAliasChanged	Fired when a chat user changes his alias.	*ParticipantID* as long, *OldAlias* as string, *NewAlias* as string
onParticipantInvited	Fired when a chat user invites somebody to the current chat room.	*RoomName* as string specifying the chat room you are invited to, *Alias* as string specifying the user that invited you.
onParticipantKicked	Fired when a user is kicked from the current chat room.	*ParticipantID* as long, *Reason* as string specifying the kick message.
onParticipantRealName	Fired when the **GetParticipantRealName** method completes successfully and the Synchronous parameter is set to **false**.	*Alias* as string, *RealName* as string
onParticipantStatusChanged	Fired when a member changes status.	*ParticipantID* as long, *Status* as long specifying the new status
onRoomTopicChanged	Fired when the chat room topic has been changed.	*NewRoomTopic* as string
onRoomTypeChanged	Fired when the chat room type has been changed.	*NewRoomType* as integer
onStateChanged	Fired when the current user's status has changed.	*NewState* as integer (disconnected 0, connecting 1, connected 2).
onTextMessageSent	Fired when the user sends a message to the server.	*TextMessage* as string, *MessageType* as short

A Chat Control Demonstration

We've built a simple page demonstrating the use of the Chat control. This page loads the control and then allows the user to connect to a chat room, as well as setting their chat alias and using some of the chat commands.

> *You can run or download this example from our Web site at* **http://rapid.wrox.co.uk/ books/0707/**. *Please note that this example might not work correctly for you, and indeed may cause errors, if you are running it via a proxy server.*

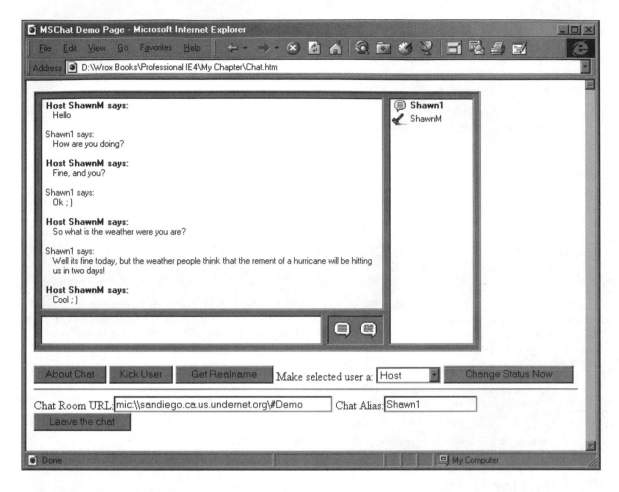

Inserting the Chat Control

As you can see, we have inserted the Chat control, and then placed a row of chat command buttons, followed by the chat room and chat alias boxes. Since the chat control itself is very complicated, we opted not to use Dynamic HTML to hide the chat commands unless they became an option. The `<OBJECT>` tag looks like this:

```
<OBJECT
  STANDBY="Dowloading the Microsoft MSChat ActiveX Control"
  CODETYPE="application/x-oleobject"
  CLASSID="clsid:D6526FE0-E651-11CF-99CB-00C04FD64497"
  CODEBASE="MSChatOCX.Cab#Version=4,71,413,0"
  WIDTH=600
  HEIGHT=350
  ID=Chat>
  <PARAM NAME="UIOption"   VALUE="2047">
  <PARAM NAME="Appearance" VALUE="3">
  <PARAM NAME="BackColor"  VALUE="255">
</OBJECT>
```

Adding the Control Buttons

After we've inserted the control, we then specify all of the buttons and text boxes that we will be using to control the chat control. Again we are using the standard `<INPUT>` controls, and placing an `ID` or a `NAME` so that we can easily control them via scripting:

```
...
<INPUT TYPE = "BUTTON" NAME="btnKick" VALUE="Kick User">
...
```

Joining a Chat Room

When the user enters the URL for the chat room that they would like to connect to, and their user name, they click the Join the Chat button. Actually this button is also used to cancel the connection process and to leave a chat room. When the user clicks on the Join the Chat button, we run the following sub-routine:

```
Sub FluxBtn_OnClick
  Select Case Chat.State
  Case 1
```

The first thing we do is to find out what the button should be doing since that same button does different things depending on what state the Chat control is in. If the control is not connected to a chat server, then its `State` is `1` and we want to connect. We determine if the user has entered an alias, and if not we display an error message and exit the sub-routine. If they did enter an alias, we connect to the URL they specified:

```
    If Alias.Value = "" then
      msgbox "You need to specify an alias!"
      Exit Sub
    Else
      Chat.EnterRoom Room.Value, "", Alias.Value, "", 1, 1
    End If
```

Canceling the Joining

If the control is in the process of connecting to the chat server and the button is clicked, then we simply clear the History pane of the Chat control, and cancel the connection process:

```
    Case 2
      Chat.CancelEntering
      Chat.ClearHistory
```

Leaving a Chat Room

Finally, if the control is already connected to a chat room, we simply exit that room—which also disconnects us from the server—and we clear the History pane:

```
    Case 3
      Chat.ExitRoom
      Chat.ClearHistory
  End Select
End Sub
```

The onStateChanged() Event

Whenever the Chat control changes its state, it fires the **onStateChanged** event. We are using this to change the caption (**value**) of the **FluxBtn** (so that the user always sees exactly what the button will do) and the background color of the control, to provide some feedback as to the current state. If the control has just disconnected from the chat server, we change the caption of the button to Join the chat, and set the background color to red:

```
Sub Chat_onStateChanged(ByVal NewState)
  Select Case NewState
  Case 1
    FluxBtn.Value = "Join the chat"
    Chat.BackColor = 255
```

If the control is currently trying to connect to the server, we change the caption of the button to Cancel Entering and set the color of the background to yellow:

```
  Case 2
    FluxBtn.Value = "Cancel Entering"
    Chat.BackColor = 33023
```

Finally after the control has successfully connected to the chat server, we set the caption of the button to Leave the chat and the background color to green:

```
  Case 3
    FluxBtn.Value = "Leave the chat"
    Chat.BackColor = 49152
  End Select
End Sub
```

Using Chat Commands

Once a user is connected, the chat commands become available. In order to use chat commands like **kick**, **ban** and **change user status**, you need to be a host in the chat room you are currently connected to. For our purposes we have created a new chat room on the server called #Demo. By using several instances of this page, we can get several 'users' to connect to the chat room.

Kicking a User

The first command available to a host is the **kick** command. Kicking a user forces them to leave the chat room. Typically users are kicked from a chat room for creating some sort of disturbance. To kick a user in our demonstration all we have to do is select the user from the Participants pane and click the Kick User button.

The Chat control handles most of the error conditions for us, and displays intelligent dialog boxes; however IE4 will bubble the error up through the web pages, thus causing another error dialog to be generated. While we could trap the error, it is easier to put in the **On Error Resume Next** command. This will cause the script interpreter to continue running the script if an error occurs:

```
Sub btnKick_onClick()
  On Error Resume Next
```

When we **kick** a user, the chat client allows us to send a message to them indicating why they were kicked from the chat room. We are asking the user to enter in the text that they want the kicked user to see:

```
strMessage = InputBox ("What do you want the kick message to say?", _
              "Kick User","You have been kicked from this chat room.")
```

Finally we use the **KickParticipant** method of the Chat control to actually kick the user. In order to use this method, we need to specify the **Participant ID** and the string that describes why they were kicked. If we specify **-1** the chat control will find the **Participant ID** for the user that is currently selected in the Participants pane:

```
   Chat.KickParticipant -1, strMessage
End Sub
```

Changing a User's Status

The other host-only command that we have provided on our demonstration page is **user status**. On an MIC server there are three types of users: **hosts**, **participants** and **spectators**. On an IRC server there are only **hosts** and **participants**.

Hosts are in charge of the chat room and can manage both the room and the users in the room. **Participants** can only read and type in messages, and **spectators** can only read messages in the chat room and send messages to hosts.

The **setParticipantStatus** method allows a host to change the status of any user connected to the chat room. In this case we have the three options placed into a **<SELECT>** box, and are having the user click the Change Status Now button. Here is the code for that button:

```
Sub btnStatGo_onClick()
   On Error Resume Next
   Chat.SetParticipantStatus -1, 1, cboUserStat.Value
End Sub
```

The **setParticipantStatus** method requires three parameters: the **Participant ID**, a **mask** value, and a **data** value. We are again using **-1** for the **Participant ID**, so the Chat control will use the **Participant ID** of the user selected in the Participants pane.

setParticipantStatus can change not only the **type** of user, but also the **whisper** status and the **ignore** status. The masks are **1**, **2** and **3** respectively. The next value we have stored in the **cboUserStat <SELECT>** box. The values for the three types of users are hosts (**1**), participants (**2**) and spectators (**4**).

Getting a User's Real Name

Finally there is the **getParticipantRealName** method. This method will get the real name of a chat user, and requires four parameters. The first two are the **Participant ID** and the participant **Alias**. Like the two previous methods, this one also uses the **Participant ID** to track the real name down, however it can also accept the **Alias** for a user. In our example we are using **-1** to indicate that we want the Chat control to use the currently selected user from the Participants list. Only one of these two parameters needs to be specified, and the unused parameter must be **null** or an empty string.

The third, `Section`, parameter determines how the response will be sent to our code. If this were a C++ application, we could have the Chat control place the string containing the real name into memory address that we would specify as the fourth parameter. However since VBScript does not allow us to use pointers we have to specify `false` and `null` for the third and fourth parameters respectively. This setting forces the chat control to fire the `onParticipantRealName` event which will return the real name to us:

```
Sub btnName_onClick()
  Chat.GetParticipantRealName -1, "", FALSE , ""
End Sub
```

The `onParticipantRealName` event code provides two parameters, the alias of the user we wanted the real name for and the real name of that user. In our example we are simply displaying that information in the form of a dialog box.

```
Sub Chat_OnParticipantRealName (Alias, RealName)
  strMessage = Alias & " is really " & RealName
  Call msgbox(strMessage)
End Sub
```

Chat Control Summary

As you can see the Chat control offers a large degree of customization and allows us the opportunity to easily create chat sections for our sites without having to write our own chat clients. While the example we showed just had the chat control plopped onto the page, it can be fully integrated into the layout of a site to create a very rich user experience. For example, while a user is reading an article, the Chat control can be placed on the page so that they are logged into a chat room full of other users reading and discussing the same article. Similarly you could have a technical support technician in a chat room with the chat control on the pages of a sites tech support, so that users could easily get technical support or referrals to where the information was kept on the site. By integrating the control into the layout, you can take advantage of the social interaction of users, which will start to create a sense of community within your site.

The Microsoft Agent Control

When it comes to providing help and guidance to new users, or even just spicing up our web pages, nothing attracts the attention better than the new animated character technologies that are now beginning to appear.

If the user's system is equipped with a soundcard, Microsoft Agent can produce synthesized speech—and if there's a microphone, it can react to spoken commands. This means that it's also useful where we're providing applications for users who are visually challenged or who have difficulty working with the written word.

About the Agent Control

Microsoft Agent is a new technology that combines spoken text output and speech recognition with an interactive graphical screen display, and can provide an alternative programmable interface for our applications. It uses a software server application running on the user's machine to control the animated character, and to hold the commands and actions for that character in a queue. They are played asynchronously with (i.e. at the same time as) the application's code itself.

Installing and programming Agent in a web page is simplicity itself. All we have to do is create the page—the browser looks after the background work of installing the Agent server and character automatically. This will become apparent next, as we look at what the Agent can do.

What Can Microsoft Agent Do?

Microsoft Agent can produce an animated character on screen, and add a speech balloon to it where the text specified by the programmer is displayed. The character also speaks the text through the soundcard, provided that a text-to-speech engine is installed, with the text scrolling simultaneously in the speech balloon.

Below the character is a small tooltip-like status window, which shows whether the character is listening—i.e. can accept speech input—or what the character has heard. The user can then give the character commands through a microphone if they have one connected to their machine.

The character can also react to events that occur in the web page. For example, it can intervene if the user selects a control on a form, or clicks on a hyperlink. It can also intervene automatically to give the user advice or help if it detects that they are carrying out a task 'the hard way'.

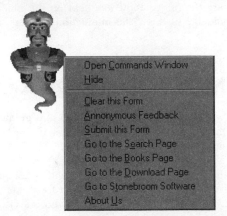

Right-clicking the character displays the usual short-cut menu. Here, the user can dismiss or suspend the character, open the Commands window, or close the agent altogether.

When the character is suspended or hidden, an icon appears in the taskbar notification area, and clicking this brings it back to life. The character's appearance and disappearance are accompanied by an appropriate animation.

Lastly, Microsoft Agent has a properties dialog box that allows users to customize how the various agents behave. It is accessed as usual by right-clicking the character and selecting Properties:

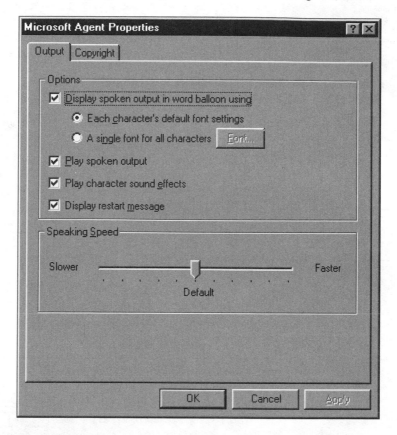

The first page controls how the output should appear, and the other pages define the character's behavior—for example to enable or disable speech recognition, and set a whole range of parameters and other attributes.

The Agent in Action

So, enough background—let's see Agent in action. The default character we've already seen is called Genie. We've used it to add interactivity to a simple web-based form. You can run or download this example with the rest of the samples for this book from our Web site at **http://rapid.wrox.co.uk/books/0707/**

Opening the page starts up the Agent control and the Genie character welcomes you to our site:

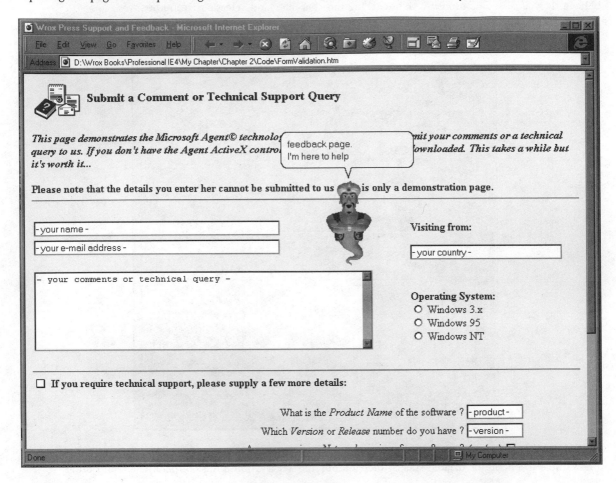

Now scroll down to the bottom of the page. Here you'll find the normal Submit and Clear buttons; try submitting the page without filling in any details. You get a message box warning that you haven't supplied enough information:

At the same time, the Genie tells you what information you must supply. It lists the fields that require a value, and let's you know how you can supply your comments anonymously if you want to:

Now type in your name, and click in the **e-mail** text box. Don't type anything yet, but watch the Genie. He prompts you for the information this field requires:

So type in your email address, then click in another text box. As the cursor leaves the **e-mail** text box, the Genie confirms the email address that you entered:

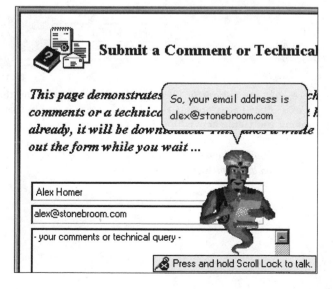

The page also reacts to other events. Click on the 'Was there a specific Error Message?' checkbox to set it, and the Genie leaps into life—waving his arms about and telling you to be sure to respond to the error message by filling in the boxes with the relevant details.

You'll find other events that the Genie reacts to in the page. However, before we leave it, just left-click on the Genie to open the Commands window—you can see he's getting bored with waiting for us to do something. This window contains a list of commands that we've defined and implemented in this web page:

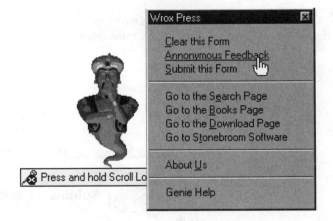

Here, you can submit or clear the form without clicking the buttons on the page itself, or you can go to several other pages on our site. There's also an option that plays several animations in turn, including moving the Genie across the screen to a new position. Click About Us, sit back, watch and listen.

You can stop the current animation and clear the agent's animation queue at any time, by simply clicking on the character.

Learning How Agent Works

Before we can do anything at all to program the agent, we have to insert it into our web page or application. In this book, we're mainly concerned with applications created for use in a web browser, so we'll be discussing the agent in this context. However, we use almost exactly the same techniques to program it in a compiled application written in a traditional programming language. The only real difference lies in how we install it and insert it into our applications.

Installing and Inserting the Agent

The Microsoft Agent developer's kit is downloadable for free from Microsoft's web site. Point your browser at **http://www.microsoft.com/workshop/prog/agent/** and follow the links. It includes the agent itself, and supporting code. You can also download the documentation for it; this includes details of how third parties can create new Agent characters.

Installation is as simple as running the executable download file for each of the engines you want to have available, which registers the controls on your machine and makes them available in the References dialog of Visual Basic, or the equivalent in other languages. You can then add the Agent control to an application's form just like any other ActiveX control. In a Web page, we can insert it using the ActiveX Control Pad, Visual InterDev, etc.

However, the code required for inserting the control into a Web page is so simple that you may prefer to keep a copy in a text file, and just add it as required to each page. Here's all we need:

```
<OBJECT ID="MyAgent" width=0 height=0
  CLASSID="CLSID:F5BE8BD2-7DE6-11D0-91FE-00C04FD701A5"
  CODEBASE="http://activex.microsoft.com/controls/agent/msagent.exe#VERSION=1,5,0,0">
</OBJECT>
```

This inserts the Agent object into the page. However, if you want speech then you'll have to insert speech synthesis capabilities for the Agent control separately. This will automatically download the speech engine. Here's the code you'll need for that:

```
<OBJECT width=0 height=0
  CLASSID="CLSID:B8F2846E-CE36-11D0-AC83-00C04FD97575"
  CODEBASE="http://activex.microsoft.com/controls/agent/cgram.exe#VERSION=1,5,0,0">
</OBJECT>
```

You do not have to assign this object an ID because you will not be referencing it. Before we can start using the Agent, we'll take a look at the Agent's overall structure.

The Microsoft Agent Characters

Because the Agent control is based on an open architecture, it is possible to create our own custom agents using a set of tools provided by Microsoft. However, creating an agent is a very complex and time intensive task, as we have to create all of the animations frame by frame to produce the character's personality. Instead, Microsoft has provided three different Agent characters for us to use. Each character has a complete set of animations, and its personality and speech characteristics have been fully tested:

Genie
`http://agent.microsoft.com/characters/genie/genie.acf`

Robby
`http://agent.microsoft.com/characters/robby/robby.acf`

Merlin
`http://agent.microsoft.com/characters/merlin/merlin.acf`

Each of the three characters has a different voice and set of animations.

The Agent Object Model

The Agent has, like most new technologies, a defined object model that controls the relationships between each object it exposes to the outside world. The Agent object model consists of 11 objects and is relatively simple. However we usually don't think of the Agent control simply as an object model—the 'control' is itself composed of four separate controls, the Agent server, the character object, the text-to-speech engine, and the command and control engine, The following diagram makes the conceptual layout clearer. Notice that at the heart of it is the Agent, and *not* the Character object.

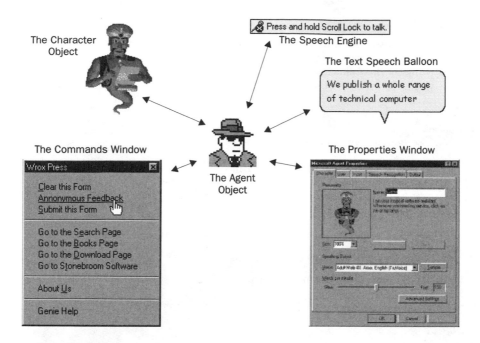

The Character Object

The Speech Engine

The Text Speech Balloon

We publish a whole range of technical computer

The Commands Window

The Properties Window

The Agent Object

The first thing that we need to make clear is that the Agent object is never visible to the user. What they see on screen is the **Character** object which is created by the agent. The agent is a software **server** that collects information and instructions and queues them up ready to pass them on to the **Character** object at the appropriate time. We can (to some extent) control when the agent passes the instructions to the character, and we can react to various events that happen to the character. These events are passed back to the agent, which notifies our code.

Despite the complexity of the agent, its object model is quite simple. For our purposes we only need to be concerned with the **Agent** object, the sub-objects of the **Agent**, and the **Request** object. The remaining objects, **SpeechInput**, **AudioOutput**, **CommandsWindow**, and **PropertySheet** are not critical to using the control.

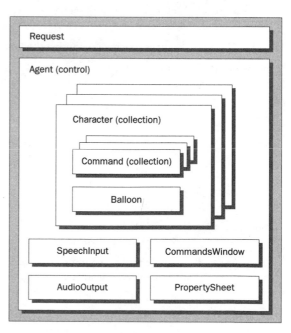

The Request Object

Since the Agent server processes some of the methods (like **Load**, **Get**, **Play**, and **Speak**) asynchronously, the **Request** object is provided to allow us to check on the status of a command in the queue—providing it is one of the following methods: **Get**, **Hide**, **Interrupt**, **Load**, **MoveTo**, **Play**, **Show**, **Speak**, and **Wait**. In order to check on the status of a method we first set a variable equal to the method:

```
Dim TheRequest
Set TheRequest = Genie.Get "Animation", "Sad"
```

The **Request** object has only three methods we can call.

Method	Description
status	Returns a long value specifying the current status of the command in the queue.
number	Returns a long value specifying the error code if an error has occurred.
description	Returns a string containing a description of the error that has occurred if an error occurred.

The Agent Object

The Agent Object is the parent object for most of the control's other objects. In itself, it doesn't contain many properties or events, as it represents the Agent server—and as a programmer we are more interested in controlling the characters:

Property	Description
connected	Returns or sets a Boolean value specifying if the current agent object is connected to the agent server.
name	Returns a string containing the name used by code for the current control.
suspended	Returns a Boolean value specifying whether the agent server is in a suspended state.

Event	Description
activateInput	Fired only to the application owning the character that has just been given focus by the user or a line of code. It returns the ID of the character that is currently active.
balloonHide	Fired when a character's text balloon is currently hidden. Returns the ID of the character whose balloon was just hidden.
balloonShow	Fired when a character's text balloon is currently visible. Returns the ID of the character whose balloon was just displayed.
bookmark	Fired when the server has encountered a bookmark tag placed into the text that the character is speaking. Returns the bookmark ID.

Event	Description
click	Fired when the user has single-clicked an agent character. Returns: the character ID, the button the user clicked on the mouse, the status of the shift key, and the x-y location of the cursor.
command	Fired when a character's command is selected from the commands window or spoken.
dblClick	Same as the click event, but fired when then user double-clicks a character.
deactivateInput	Fired when a character loses focus.
dragComplete	Fired when the user finishes dragging a character on the screen. Returns: the character ID, the button the user clicked on the mouse, the status of the shift key, and the x-y location of the cursor.
dragStart	Fired when a user starts dragging a character across the screen. Returns: the character ID, the button the user clicked on the mouse, the status of the shift key, and the x-y location of the cursor.
hide	Fired when a character is hidden. Returns the character ID and a long value specifying the reason the character was hidden.
idleComplete	Fired when the server stops the idling state of a character. Returns the character ID.
idleStart	Fired when the server starts the idling state of a character. Returns the character ID.
move	Fired when a character is moved on the screen. Returns the character ID, the x-y position of the character, and a long value specifying the cause for the move.
requestComplete	Fired when the server completes a queued command. Returns the **Request** object.
requestStart	Fired when the server starts a queued command. Returns the **Request** object.
restart	Fired when the agent server restarts from a suspended state.
show	Fired when a character is displayed. Returns the ID of the character that has just displayed and a long value specifying why the character was displayed.
shutdown	Fired when the user manually shuts down the agent server.
size	Fired when a character's size has changed. Returns the character ID, and its current width and height.

The Characters Object

In terms of controlling the actions of an individual agent on the screen, the character object is the most important object to understand, as it contains all of the methods and events related to the direct control of any of the currently active agents. Since the Agent control allows us to have multiple characters running at the same time, the character object is a collection. If we are using a scripting language that does not support collections, i.e. JScript or JavaScript, then we can use the **character** sub-object of the **characters** object.

Whenever we use a method of the **characters** object, we must specify the character ID for the Agent character we want the property or method to be applied to. Since frequently we will be referring to that character, it's a good idea to create a variable that refers to it:

```
Set Genie = Agent.Characters("Genie")
```

If we are using JavaScript or JScript, we would need:

```
genie = agent.characters.character("Genie");
```

Now that we know how to refer to our characters, here are the properties and methods for the **characters** object:

Property	Description
description	Returns a string containing the description of the referring character.
extraData	Returns a string containing extra data for the character that was compiled by the Agent Character Editor.
hasOtherClients	Returns whether the currently specified character is being used by other applications.
idleOn	Returns a Boolean value specifying whether the agent server is controlling the referring characters *Idling* animations.
left	Returns a long value specifying the number of pixels from the screen origin to the left edge of the agent character.
moveCause	Returns a long value specifying what caused the characters last move.
name	Returns a value that contains the default name for the agent character.
pitch	Returns a long value specifying the pitch that the character sends to the text-to-speech engine to generate its speech.
soundEffectsOn	Returns a value specifying whether sound effects have been enabled for the referring character.
speed	Returns a long value specifying the speed of the referring character's speech.
top	Returns a long value specifying the number of pixels from the screen origin to the top of the referring character.
visibilityCase	Returns a value specifying what caused the character to become visible.
visible	Returns a Boolean value specifying whether or not a character is visible.
width	Returns a long value containing the current width of the referring character.

Method	Description
activate	Gives the referring character focus for speech and mouse input.
gestureAt	Plays one of the gesturing animations towards the specified x-y coordinates.
get	Downloads the specified animation state or audio file for the character from an HTTP server.

Method	Description
hide	Hides the referring character.
interrupt	Allows one character to stop another characters current animation task and move to the next task in the queue.
moveTo	Moves the referring character to the specified x-y coordinates.
play	Plays the specified animation or state.
show	Displays the character if the character is in a hidden state, and plays the *Showing* animation sequence.
speak	Speaks the specified text through the text-to-speech engine and displays it in the text-balloon.
stop	Stops the current animation and clears the queue for the referring animation.
stopAll	Stops all animation requests for the referring character.
wait	Forces the referring character to pause its queue until the specified command/object has completed. This is used to synchronize animations with multiple characters.

The Commands Object

One of the most interesting features of the Agent control is its ability to allow interaction with the user, via the Commands window or the speech recognition engine. The **Commands** object allows us to define what commands are available to the user, and how those commands are available.

Since we might be referring to a command several times, it's a good idea to create a variable that refers to the specific **command** object. Like the **characters** object the **commands** object is also a collection, so for languages that do not support collections we have to use the **command** sub-object:

```
Set cmdEmail = Agent.Characters("Genie").Commands("CheckEmail")
```

If we use JavaScript, then the following is required:

```
cmdEmail = agent.characters.character("Genie").Commands.Command("CheckEmail");
```

Now that we know how to refer to commands, here are the properties and methods for the **commands** object:

Property	Description
caption	Returns or sets a string containing the caption for your application in the Commands Window
confidence	Returns or sets a long value specifying whether the string set with the ConfidenceText property is shown when the character is listening for commands.
confidenceText	Returns or sets a string containing the text that is displayed when the character is listening for commands.
count	Returns a long value specifying the current number of command objects in the Commands collection.

Table Continued on Following Page

Property	Description
enabled	Returns or sets a Boolean value determining whether or not the command is enabled in the character's popup menu.
visible	Returns or sets a Boolean value that determines whether the Commands collection for this application is visible in the current character's pop-up menu.
voice	Returns or sets a string containing the text that is used by the speech recognition engine for the current character's command.

Method	Description
add	Adds the specified command. Requires the following coma-delineated list: ID of the command, name that appears in the popup menu, string for speech recognition of the command, enabled flag, visible flag.
command	Returns the command object for the specified command. Used by languages that do not support collections.
insert	Inserts a command before a specified command. Requires the following coma-delineated list: ID of the command, ID of the command that is the reference, a flag indicating whether it should be before or after the reference command, name that appears in the popup menu, string for speech recognition of the command, enabled flag, visible flag.
remove	Removes the specified command from the commands collection.
removeAll	Removes all of the command from the collection.

The Balloon Object

The **Balloon** object describes the display attributes for the text balloon. Unless you have a specific artistic reason for adjusting the appearance of this window, then don't. The user of your web-page will expect items such as tool tips, which is what the text balloon really is, to have a certain appearance on their systems. If you arbitrarily modify those settings, you can quickly annoy and confuse your users.

Property	Description
backColor	Returns or sets the background color of the text balloon as a decimal RGB number.
borderColor	Returns or sets the border color of the text balloon as a decimal RGB number.
charSet	Returns or sets a long value specifying the character set to use for the text displayed in the balloon.
charsPerLine	Returns or sets the number of characters that can be displayed in the text-balloon.
enabled	Returns or sets a Boolean value indicating whether the text balloon is enabled.
fontName	Returns or sets the font used in the text balloon for the specified character.
fontBold	Returns or sets a Boolean value indicating whether the text is bold.
fontItalic	Returns or sets a Boolean value indicating whether the text is in italics.
fontSize	Returns or sets a long value specifying the font's size in points.

Property	Description
fontUnderline	Returns or sets a Boolean value indicating whether or not a font is underlined.
foreColor	Returns or sets the foreground color for the text balloon.
numberOfLines	Returns or sets the number of lines that can be displayed in the text balloon.
visible	Returns or sets a Boolean value indicating the number of lines that can be displayed in the text balloon

Using the Microsoft Agent Control

The Agent control was created to give programmers a tool to interact with users on a social level. As such, as the programmer, you have to be very careful how you use the characters. Whether you create your own characters using the tools provided by Microsoft or use one of the three supplied Agent characters, you have to be careful not to offend or upset your users.

Due to its complexity, and its vast potential, we are only going to cover a limited number of the control's capabilities. We have prepared two examples. The first is yet another variation on a Hello World example, and the second (which you saw earlier in the chapter) uses the Agent to provide feedback when validating a form.

The Hello World Example

Our first example is the traditional hello world. As you can see we have constructed a simple page that hosts Merlin. Merlin loads into the cache and then talks to the user, playing a couple of animations as he talks. You can run or download this example from our Web site at `http://rapid.wrox.co.uk/books/0707/`:

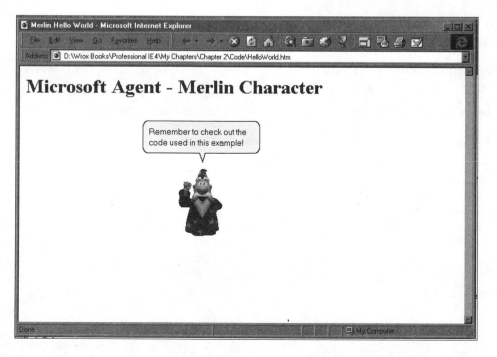

Inserting and Connecting the Agent Control

In order to use the Agent control we have to place the `<OBJECT>` tag into the body of the HTML page:

```
<OBJECT ID="MyAgent" width=0 height=0
  CLASSID="CLSID:F5BE8BD2-7DE6-11D0-91FE-00C04FD701A5"
  CODEBASE="http://activex.microsoft.com/controls/agent/msagent.exe#VERSION=1,5,0,0">
</OBJECT>
```

We also need to insert speech synthesis capabilities for the Agent control separately. Here's the code needed for that:

```
<OBJECT width=0 height=0
  CLASSID="CLSID:B8F2846E-CE36-11D0-AC83-00C04FD97575"
  CODEBASE="http://activex.microsoft.com/controls/agent/cgram.exe#VERSION=1,5,0,0">
</OBJECT>
```

Once we've inserted our Agent control into a page (or application) we need to make sure that it has connected to the Agent server by setting the **Agent** object's **Connected** property to **True**. We'll generally do this in the **window_onLoad** event, so that it appears as soon as we load the page:

```
Sub Window_onLoad()
  On Error Resume Next
  MyAgent.Connected = True
```

This means that our application is now connected to the **Agent** server. Usually Internet Explorer will automatically connect the instantiated agent object to the server, however this insures that the connection is established (and is required when you are trying to use the agent control in a VB or a VC++ application).

Specifying the Character

Next we need to specify what character to load, and assign that character to an object reference. We use the **Load** method of the **characters** object and specify the URL for the agent characters definition file. Since we want that standard Microsoft **Merlin** character, we are using the appropriate URL:

```
MyAgent.Characters.Load "Merlin", _
  "http://agent.microsoft.com/characters/merlin/merlin.acf"
```

Now we create an object reference to the character so that we can easily refer to it:

```
Set Merlin = MyAgent.Characters("Merlin")
```

To reduce the delay and preserve bandwidth, the Agent control does not download all of the animations or the animation states. Rather, the programmer has to specify which animations and states need to be downloaded for their page. We plan on using the **speaking** and **showing** states in addition to the following animations: **Greet, GreetReturn, Pleased, PleasedReturn, GetAttention, GetAttentionReturn**. We use the **Get** method of the **characters** object to specify which animations and states to download:

```
Merlin.Get "State", "Showing, Speaking"
```

Playing and Speaking Animations

As the downloading of the remaining animations might take some time, we wanted to provide the user with some feedback as to what is happening. Since we have the `Showing` and `Speaking` states, the Merlin character now has everything it needs to begin talking. We can display Merlin, move him to screen position 300-300, and have him tell the user that additional stuff is downloading:

```
Merlin.Show
Merlin.MoveTo 300,300
Merlin.Speak "I am still downloading. Please wait."
Merlin.Get "Animation", "Greet, GreetReturn, Pleased, " _
           & "PleasedReturn, GetAttention, GetAttentionReturn"
```

Finally, when all of the animations have downloaded, we can begin with our Hello World example. Since we want to be polite to our users, the first thing we do is have Merlin play the `Greet` animation using the `Play` method:

```
Merlin.Play "Greet"
Merlin.Play "GreetReturn"
...
```

Hiding the Character

The rest of the script uses `Play` and `Speak` methods to make Merlin move and talk to the user. When he has finished his short presentation, we hide him using the `Hide` method:

```
   ...
   Merlin.Hide
End Sub
```

As you can see, it is rather easy to create web pages that take advantage of the Agent control. However, this example does not really show how the control can be used to create an interactive experience. The following example shows how to use an Agent character to provide feedback to a user filling out a form.

Using Genie to Validate a Form

In the previous example, you saw how to use an agent character's animation and speech services to create a rich multimedia experience for the user. While you can use Agent characters to lecture your users, a better use is to assist them in complex or difficult tasks.

Why Use Form Validation?

Form validation has always been a major issue with Internet developers. Traditionally the form had to be submitted to the server, validated there, and then sent back if there was an error or missing information. Recently developers have used client-side script to pre-validate the form before submission; if an error is found then they can display a dialog box and cancel the submission. The only problem with these methods is that they are reactive, not proactive. Instead of guiding the user to the correct solution, they scold the user for making an error.

By using an Agent character, you can easily guide the user into inputting the information you are looking for. When our hypothetical form is loaded into the browser, we display the Genie character and run through an introduction script:

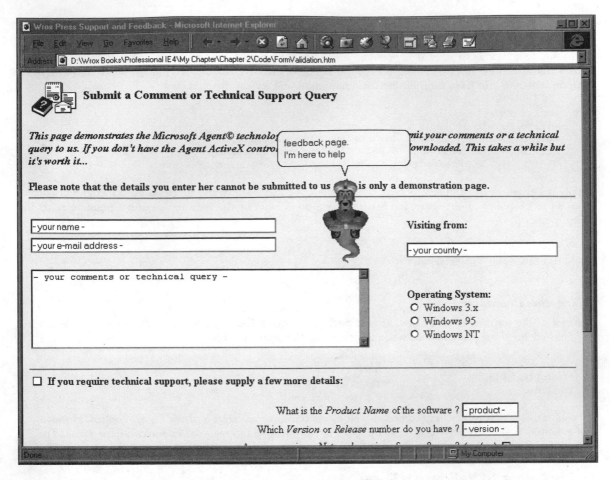

As the user changes the information in the fields, or moves the focus to a particular control, our Genie provides information and guidance. In addition to validating the form, the Genie also provides a set of commands that the user can use to submit the form anonymously, or to navigate to a different page.

Responding to Form Elements

In responding to the input of the user, we need to decide when we want to display information. Typically, we want to validate the field after the user leaves the element, i.e. when the `blur` event is fired; and we want to inform the user of the type of information we need when the `focus` event is fired.

For our example we will use the Are you running a Network version of our software ? (yes/no) checkbox. Since a checkbox always changes its state whenever it is clicked, we will respond to the `onclick` event instead of the focus or blur events. The first thing we need to do is to determine the state of the checkbox. Since this event is fired after the state of the checkbox has changed, we only want to inform the user what we mean by Network if they have checked it:

```
Sub Network_onclick
  On Error Resume Next
  If frmThis.Elements("Network").Checked Then
    Genie.Get "Animation", "Think"
    Genie.Play "Think", True
    Genie.Speak "By a \Pau=200\Network \Pau=100\version, we mean ..."
    Genie.Play "RestPose"
  End If
End Sub
```

As you can see, all we are doing is having the Genie play a series of animations and then tell the user what we mean by a Network Version. Notice that `\Pau=200\` is actually a tag that the Agent control uses to give a slight pause in the speaking of the text. The control offers a series of in-line speech tags to slightly modify how the text-to-speech engine converts the text into speech. These tags are case-insensitive.

Speech Tag	Description
`\Chr=`*string*`\`	Defines the character of the voice where *string* is either `"Normal"` (default) for a normal voice, `"Monotone"` for a monotone voice, or `"Whisper"` for a whispered voice.
`\Ctx=`*string*`\`	Sets of context of the speech and how special symbols are spoken. Values for *string* are `"Address"` for a street address or phone number, `"Email"` for an email address or `"Unknown"` (default) for an unknown context.
`\Emp\`	Emphasizes the next word spoken. The tag must be before the next word, and contain no spaces between it and the next word.
`\Lst\`	Repeats the last spoken statement in the previous `Speak` method.
`\Map="`*spokentext*`"` `="`*balloontext*`"\`	Specifies that the *spokentext* should be sent to the text-to-speech engine while the *balloontext* should be displayed in the text balloon.
`\Mrk=`*number*`\`	Specifies a bookmark in the text. The *number* is a long value specifying the number of the bookmark.
`\Pau=`*number*`\`	Pauses the speaking for the specified *number* of milliseconds.
`\Pit=`*number*`\`	Sets the base pitch for the spoken text in hertz.
`\Rst\`	Resets all of the speech tags to their default values.
`\Spd=`*number*`\`	Sets the base speed in *number* of words per minute at which the text is spoken and typed to the balloon window.
`\Vol=`*number*`\`	Sets the base volume for playback. 0 is muted, and 65535 is the maximum volume.

Providing Commands

Agent characters can do many things besides just talk to the user. We can also provide a series of commands that they can perform, and if the command-and-control engine is installed the characters can even respond to voice commands.

By providing commands for our Agent characters, we increase the social interaction users will have with the characters. While the commands that appear on the popup menu will be easy to use, it is critical that you take into account human nature when you specify the words to use for voice commands. The command-and-control engine provides the capability to specify multiple phrases and optional words that can execute a command. If your commands are too difficult or too strict, your users will soon become annoyed.

In our form validation example, we have given Genie a set of commands that allow the user to submit the form anonymously, clear the form, navigate to a series of pages, and describe who they are. To establish these commands we have to use the **Commands** object. Since we want these commands to be available as soon as the page loads, we have placed this code in the **window_onLoad()** routine.

The first thing that we do is establish what text will be displayed in the Command window for our application:

```
Genie.Commands.Caption = "Wrox Press"
```

The next thing we want to do is to start adding commands. For that, we use the **Add** method of the **Commands** object. This requires an **ID** string for the command, the text that will appear in the popup menu and Commands window, and the text the will be used for speech recognition. When specifying the text for speech recognition, items in square brackets **[]** are considered optional, while multiple optional phrases are separated by a pipe **|** character:

```
Genie.Commands.Add "ClearForm", "&Clear this Form", "Clear [Form]"
```

Finally, we want to enable the Genie to accept commands, so we set the **Enabled** property to true.

```
Genie.Commands.Enabled = True
```

Now that we have created the available commands, Genie can offer these to our user. However, we still need to respond to those commands. The agent object provides the **Command** event to notify our code that the user has selected one of our commands. This event includes the **ID** string of the command that was selected. We can take this value and use a **Select..Case** statement to determine what to do:

```
Sub MyAgent_Command(ByVal strCommand)
  On Error Resume Next
  Select Case strCommand.Name
    Case "ClearForm"
      Call ClearThisForm
    Case ...
      ...
  End Select
End Sub
```

The neatest way, as we've shown in our example, is to code each command as a separate sub-routine that performs the task. Providing the user with a set of commands is therefore simple, as the agent control handles the most difficult tasks automatically.

Agent Control Summary

As you have seen from our examples, the Agent control offers the capability to create a rich and interactive experience for our users. If used properly, the Agent can quickly develop a social relationship with users, which results in an increase in productivity and a lasting impression. This, of course, can have the direct result of an increase in traffic for our site.

Of course, when you are coding any agent character you need to keep in mind that you must be polite and considerate to the user. You can use an agent to explain in detail why an error dialog has been displayed, or to guide a user though the steps to recover from the error.

Summary

In this chapter we've seen how to take some of the components of the IE4 **Component Library** and use them to create a rich user experience in our pages. We've seen how the NetShow control can be integrated into a Web page to allow streaming media playback, and how to place the Chat control to allow an interactive chat feature designed to bring a sense of community to our site. We have also seen how the Agent control and its characters can be used to assist users in a difficult task, or introduce them to new material.

If used creatively, these technologies could be combined to create a Web site that will entertain, educate and inspire users without requiring huge amounts of development time.

So, in this chapter, we've seen:

- ▲ The **NetShow** control and how to use it
- ▲ The **Chat** control and how to use it
- ▲ The **Agent** control, and how to use agents to create helpful, pro-active pages

In the next chapter, we'll look into how we can create our own components for use in a Web page, using a new technology called **Scriptlets**.

Dynamic HTML Scriptlets

Scriptlets are one of the latest innovations in IE4. They are the missing link that further enriches the Dynamic HTML object model, and makes it interesting not only to Web developers, but also to VB and VC++ developers. The integration between IE4 and the upcoming Windows 98 shell pushes Dynamic HTML as a real development platform. However, any real-world application development platform must provide a way (and if possible an efficient and safe way) to reuse code. Scriptlets are just this: self-contained and programmable Dynamic HTML pages that can be hosted inside other HTML pages as components.

In this chapter, we'll introduce the concept of Scriptlets, and show you how to get started using them in your own pages. While the underlying technology that makes them work is quite complex, as a Web author we can ignore most of this complexity and let Internet Explorer handle it in the background for us automatically. As you'll see, Scriptlets offer an exciting mix of easy construction, with quite amazing abilities. In effect, they allow us to create our own ActiveX controls, without resorting to a 'real' programming language like Visual Basic, C++, Delphi, etc.

So, we'll be covering:

- What Scriptlets are, and what they can do

- When you should and shouldn't use them in your pages

- How we define the various parts of a Scriptlet, including the interface code, the visible and the script sections

- Some examples of Scriptlets in use, showing you how they work

- How Scriptlets can be used in other applications, such as Visual Basic or Office 97

To start with, we'll take an overview of what Scriptlets are, and see a couple of simple examples.

What are Scriptlets?

Until the release of IE4, the only way to create a custom ActiveX control was to use a 'real' programming language like C++. While this is still the case for large and complex controls, often we (as Web developers) would like to create smaller, simple controls that encapsulate code we reuse many times on our site. Since the development time to create real ActiveX controls is greater than the time it takes to copy and paste that reusable code onto every page, or into a linked client-side code file, we are often tempted to take the easy way out.

With the availability of Scriptlet technology, we have an easy way to encapsulate client-side code as an ActiveX control component. This allows us to quickly create platform independent (with the upcoming release of IE4 for the UNIX and Macintosh platforms) components that we can deploy onto the Web.

Scriptlet Architecture

Scriptlets are simply HTML pages that contain client-side script, which conforms to a standard scripting architecture. This architecture, similar to VC++ and VB, defines what routines and variables are **public** (that is exposed to the control's container on the page) and **private** (hidden from the control's container).

When a scriptlet is loaded into memory, it is loaded into an instance of the HTML parsing engine that is itself wrapped inside a COM container. This container is placed inside the HTML parsing engine of the original HTML page that contains the reference to the Scriptlet. This implementation means that the Scriptlet can let Internet Explorer handle all of the housekeeping tasks of the component, so that all we have to worry about is creating the HTML page that contains the internal logic of our Scriptlet. Once it is inserted into the original HTML page, it effectively becomes an ActiveX control.

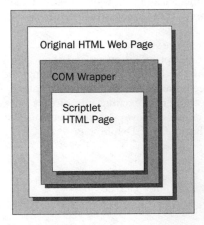

It's important to realize that our Scriptlet control has the option of providing a user interface. Since it is parsed by the HTML parsing engine, we can use standard HTML and Dynamic HTML within our Scriptlet to provide information to the user. In the remainder of this first section of the chapter, we'll show you very briefly two simple examples of Scriptlets in use, and see the basics of their implementation.

The Simple 'Typing' Scriptlet

Our first example is a Scriptlet with a user interface. All it does is appear to 'type' a message onto the screen. The main page contains a text box and buttons that can be used to control the Scriptlet:

You can run or download this page, `typetext.htm`, *from our Web site at* `http://rapid.wrox.co.uk/books/0707`.

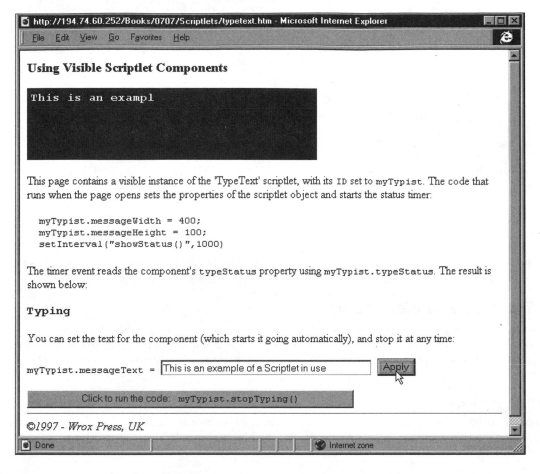

The Scriptlet itself is a Dynamic HTML page, which produces white mono-spaced text on a black background:

```
<html>
<head>
<script language=jscript>
...
... script goes here
...
</script>
<style>
  BODY {background-color:black; color:white; font-family:"Courier New",Monospace;
      font-size:12pt; font-weight:bold}
</style>
</head>
<body>
  <div id=objDiv style="position:absolute; top:5; left:5; width:100; height:100">
    <p id=objPara></p>
  </div>
</body>
</html>
```

The main page, **typecomp.htm,** that uses this Scriptlet contains all the descriptive text, instructions, text box, and buttons. It also contains an **<OBJECT>** tag that inserts the Scriptlet page **typetext.htm:**

```html
<html>
<head>
  <title>Using Visible Scriptlet Components</title>
</head>
<body onload="startCode()">
<h3>Using Visible Scriptlet Components</h3>
<object id=myTypist width=400 height=100 type="text/x-scriptlet"
        data="typetext.htm" style="position:relative;">
</object>
...
... rest of page goes here
...
</body>
</html>
```

As you can see, the Scriptlet simply contains standard HTML that the IE4 parsing engine can display within the window defined by the **<OBJECT>** tag in the main (original) page.

Defining The Scriptlet's Interface

Of course, to be able to manipulate the Scriptlet, the original page has to have a way of accessing it. Scriptlets define an **interface**, which the page that contains them can use to reference the public properties, methods and events supported by the Scriptlet – in the same way as it would with any other ActiveX control.

Defining Properties

A **property** is simply a variable within the control. Any variable that has **public_** prefixing the variable name will be exposed as a property that can be accessed by the Scriptlet's container. This is the easiest way to declare a property and set the default value of it:

```jscript
<script language=jscript>
//public property variables
public_property1 = "Hello"
```

If you have any experience programming controls for Windows, then you know that COM also allows us to define a function that behaves like a property. This is especially useful if we need to perform input validation or other calculations before we set the value inside the control. The Scriptlet architecture allows us to declare a function for the **put** and **get** operations of a property. When the code in the container tries to place a value into a property, it calls the function that has **public_put_** prefixing the property name – for example, here is the definition for a property named **roomSize:**

```
//private internal 'member' variable
var m_roomSize = 0

function public_put_roomSize(newvalue)
  {
  if ((newvalue > 0) & (newvalue < 99)) m_roomSize = newvalue
  }
```

The variable **m_roomSize** is a private internal variable that will be used inside the Scriptlet's code sections. It cannot be accessed from outside the Scriptlet, and so can only be set using the **public_put_roomSize** function (i.e. the **roomSize** property). This allows us to validate the new value proposed by the user and reject any unsuitable ones, as we've done in the code above.

Likewise, when the code in the container tries to **get** the value of a property, it calls the function that has **public_get_** prefixing the property name. In this case, we can just return the value of the internal variable **m_roomSize**:

```
function public_get_roomSize()
  {
   return m_roomSize
  }
```

By providing both the **put** and **get** functions, we produce a property that is read/write to the outside world. If we want our property to be read-only or write-only, we define just the **put** or the **get** function, as appropriate.

> *Keep in mind also that we can only define a property using one of the two outline methods we've discussed here. If we use the* **put** *and* **get** *functions method then we cannot have a variable in our Scriptlet which has* **public_** *prefixing a property name that we are also using for the* **put** *and* **get** *functions.*

Defining Methods

A **method** is declared simply by adding the prefix **public_** to the name of the function or subroutine that carries out the method:

```
function public_rollsOfWallpaper(intLengthEach)
  {
    ... some code to calculate the result ...
    intNumberOfRolls = ...
    return intNumberOfRolls
  }
```

Any functions or variables within our Scriptlet not named with the **public_** prefix will only be accessible to code within the Scriptlet, and not from the containing page. Like all routines, we can pass values into the routine as parameters (such as **intLengthEach** above), and we return the value, if there is one, just as we would from any other function. Of course, the function does not have to return a value if it's only required to carry out some direct action within the Scriptlet.

> *The interface of a Scriptlet can also be defined in another way, using the JavaScript* **public_declaration** *object. We'll see how this is done later in the chapter. We'll also see how events are declared and implemented.*

Setting Properties and Calling Methods

In the main (container) page, we can use the properties and methods of the Scriptlet just as we would with any other ActiveX control or integral HTML object:

```
MyScriptlet.roomSize = 42;                'set the roomSize property
alert(MyScriptlet.roomSize);              'retrieve the roomSize property
alert(MyScriptlet.rollsOfWallpaper(33));  'call the rollsOfWallpaper method
```

The 'Typing' Scriptlet Code

Our Typing Scriptlet, `typetext.htm`, provides four properties and one method:

▲ The property **messageText** (write only) is used to set the text of the message to be 'typed'.

▲ The property **typeStatus** (read only) returns the current status of the 'typing' process.

▲ The properties **height** and **width** (write only) are used to set the size of the typing area.

▲ The method **stopTyping()** stops the current 'typing' process.

You can see how these properties and methods are defined by the interface in the code section below. This is the entire script section of the **typetext.htm** Scriptlet:

```
<script language=jscript>
//private internal 'member' variables
var m_messageText = " ";
var m_typeStatus = "Idle";

//other internal variables
var timer = null;
var nPosition = 0;
var nLength = 0;


//---------------------------------------------
//put routine for text (write only)

function public_put_messageText(newString)
{
  nPosition = 0;
  if (newString.length > 0)
  {
    m_messageText = newString;
    nLength = m_messageText.length;
    timer = setInterval("typeText()", 200);
    m_typeStatus = "Typing";
  }
  else
  {
    nLength = 0;
    m_messageText = "";
    clearInterval(timer);
    document.all("objPara").innerHTML = "";
    m_typeStatus = "Idle";
  }
}


//---------------------------------------------
//get routine for typeStatus (read only)

function public_get_typeStatus()
{ return m_typeStatus }
```

```
//--------------------------------------------
//put routine for height (write only)

function public_put_messageHeight(newValue)
{
  if ((newValue > 9) & (newValue < 1000))
    document.all("objDiv").style.pixelHeight = newValue
  else
    alert("messageHeight must be between 10 and 999");
}

//--------------------------------------------
//put routine for width (write only)

function public_put_messageWidth(newValue)
{
  if ((newValue > 9) & (newValue < 1000))
    document.all("objDiv").style.pixelWidth = newValue
  else
    alert("messageWidth must be between 10 and 999");
}

//--------------------------------------------
// public method for the component

function public_stopTyping()
{
  clearInterval(timer);
  m_typeStatus = "Stopped";
}

//--------------------------------------------
//private internal routines

function typeText()
{
  if (nPosition < nLength)
  {
    nPosition++;
    document.all("objPara").innerHTML = m_messageText.substr(0, nPosition);
  }
  else
  {
    clearInterval(timer);
    m_typeStatus = "Complete";
  }
}
```

```
</script>
```

As you will be able to see from the code, the Scriptlet works by using the **setInterval** method of its own **window** object, and simply changing the text that is displayed in the **<DIV>** tag **objDiv** each time the interval occurs. At the same time, it sets appropriate values for the internal **m_typeStatus** variable, which provides the read-only **typeStatus** property. This simple example should prove that the architecture of Scriptlets is relatively simple, and indicate how they allow us to create custom client-side controls quickly and easily.

It's As Easy As That!

So, using Scriptlets is as simple as using an ActiveX control. All we have to do is place an `<OBJECT>` tag within our HTML page that will contain the Scriptlet, and then we can use the Scriptlet just as we would use any other ActiveX control:

```
<object id=myTypist width=400 height=100 type="text/x-scriptlet"
        data="typetext.htm" style="position:relative;">
</object>
```

The only differences between a Scriptlet `<OBJECT>` tag, and an `<OBJECT>` tag that defines an ActiveX control, are the values of the `type` and `data` attributes, and the lack of a `ClassID` (or GUID). The `type` attribute defines the MIME type that Internet Explorer should use when parsing the Scriptlet code; the MIME type for Scriptlets is `"text/x-scriptlet"`. The `data` attribute defines the location of the Scriptlet code, as a standard URL. This is similar to the `codebase` attribute used for ActiveX controls.

> *Notice that there are no parameters declared using `<PARAM>` tags. This is because Scriptlets do not currently support parameters, however Microsoft is working on adding support for parameter tags for a future release of Internet Explorer.*

The Simple 'Decorator' Scriptlet

Our second simple example shows how we can create a Scriptlet that does *not* have a user-interface. This page contains a Scriptlet that calculates the amount and cost for paint, wallpaper, and carpet to completely decorate a room. The Decorator Scriptlet simply encapsulates a series of functions that could easily be re-used several times in our pages. As you can see, all we have is a simple page that contains a few buttons to access the various properties and methods of the Scriptlet:

> *You can run or download this page, `decorate.htm`, from our Web site at `http://rapid.wrox.co.uk/books/0707`.*

In order to use the Decorator Scriptlet, we place the appropriate `<OBJECT>` tag in the main page. In this case since we do not want the control to be visible, we've set the CSS `visibility` property to `hidden`:

```
<object id=myDecObj width=1 height=1 type="text/x-scriptlet"
        data="decocalc.htm" style="visibility:hidden">
</object>
```

As you can see from the following screenshot, the Rolls of Wallpaper button simply calls the `rollsofWallpaper` method of the `myDecObj` control (our Scriptlet), passing it a value which is the price of each roll:

```
<BUTTON ONCLICK="myDecObj.rollsOfWallpaper(6.49)" STYLE="width:500">
  Click here to run the code: <CODE>myDecObj.rollsOfWallpaper(6.49)</CODE>
</BUTTON>
```

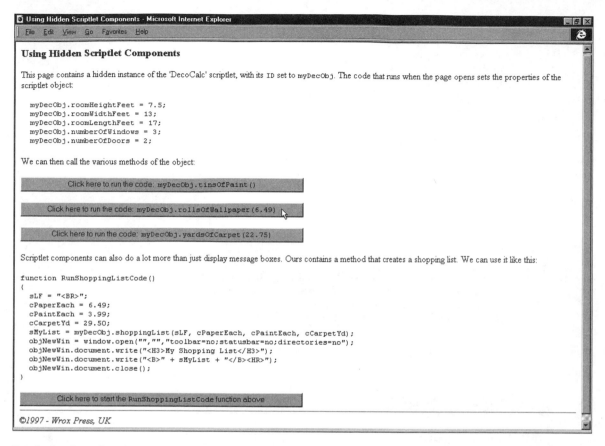

Inside the Scriptlet, the **rollsOfWallpaper** function calls another internal sub-routine (named **getRollsWallpaper**) which does the calculation and returns the result.

```
function public_rollsOfWallpaper(cPriceEach)
{
  alert("You'll need " + getRollsWallpaper(cPriceEach))
}
```

The **rollsOfWallpaper** function then displays this as an **alert** dialog, as you can see here:

This is just one example – the Decorator Scriptlet contains several other properties and methods, and you can experiment with it yourself using the sample page available from our Web site at **http://rapid.wrox.co.uk/books/0707**. The code within the Scriptlet is fully commented so that you can see what's going on. For example, this Scriptlet also provides a **shoppingList** method which returns a string value, instead of displaying the result in an **alert** dialog:

```
function public_shoppingList(sBreak, cWallpaper, cPaint, cCarpet)
{
  if (sBreak == null) sBreak = "";
  sList = getRollsWallpaper(cWallpaper) + sBreak
        + getPintsPaint(cPaint) + sBreak
        + getYardsCarpet(cCarpet);
  return sList
}
```

In the main page, we can use the method to create a shopping list of materials in a new browser window. The **sBreak** parameter of the method is the string or character used to delimit each item in the list, and the other three parameters are the individual prices of each item:

```
function RunShoppingListCode()
{
  sLF = "<BR>";
  cPaperEach = 6.49;
  cPaintEach = 3.99;
  cCarpetYd = 29.50;
  sMyList = myDecObj.shoppingList(sLF, cPaperEach, cPaintEach, cCarpetYd);
  objNewWin = window.open("","","toolbar=no;statusbar=no;directories=no");
  objNewWin.document.write("<H3>My Shopping List</H3>");
  objNewWin.document.write("<B>" + sMyList + "</B><HR>");
  objNewWin.document.close();
}
```

And here's the result:

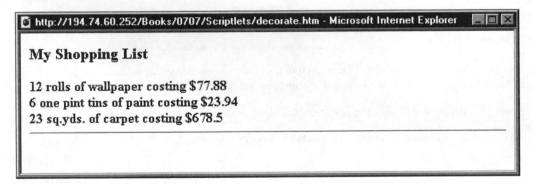

Using Scriptlets in HTML Pages

Having seen an overview of some simple uses of Scriptlets, we'll consider in more detail where and why we might use them. It is also important to realize that, because they behave in many ways like ActiveX controls, our viewers can control whether they actually appear in our pages through the options available in their browser. Firstly, however, let's look at when we should and shouldn't consider using Scriptlets.

Why Should You Use Scriptlets?

Scriptlets are simple and powerful, provided that you really need them. If you are a C/C++ developer writing image-processing or data-warehousing applications, it's unlikely that you'll need to learn about Scriptlets. But if the Web and HTML are part of your everyday work, Scriptlets can be incredibly useful. Here's a brief top-ten list of reasons why you – as a Web developer – should consider using Scriptlets:

- You can write them in any (repeat, *any*) scripting language. You don't need to know C/C++ or any other programming language.

- You can prototype them in a matter of minutes, and things will certainly be even easier once updated development tools become available.

- You can create your own HTML objects, and describe them in terms of properties, methods and events.

- Your entire edit-compile-debug cycle is reduced to hitting Save and *F5* in the IE4 main window.

- For the very first time you have the opportunity of writing reusable HTML code, which is a primary requirement in any large-scale Web-oriented project.

- You can exploit all the power of the Dynamic HTML object model and implement cool effects such as text or image drag-and-drop, mouse over and out object manipulation, and style changes.

- You can also use your Scriptlets in desktop applications, through a dedicated ActiveX control.

- You can use them to customize and enhance your Windows Active Desktop and your disk folders.

- You can always convert your samples to ordinary ActiveX controls once you've fully tested their public interface.

When Shouldn't You Use Scriptlets?

Scriptlets contain ordinary script code, which can be a disadvantage since the browser must interpret it before producing output. This is not a problem for small and simple components, but might be an issue when the size of the Scriptlet increases. A complex component such as a calendar, composed of a table and some ActiveX Form controls (i.e. combo boxes and text boxes) may take a while to load and respond. The corresponding Office 97 Calendar ActiveX control appears to load and run much faster. Here are some possible snags you should consider carefully before writing and distributing Scriptlets:

- A Scriptlet may run slower than a corresponding ActiveX control.

- Scriptlets don't support any kind of code protection, and are open to inspection and alteration by others.

- A user can modify Scriptlets, inadvertently or not, and this might result in run-time errors.

- Scriptlets aren't subject to licensing, and may be copied without permission.

- Scriptlets don't get downloaded if your security level is set to High for the Internet zone they come from.

- At present, there are no authoring tools that fully support Scriptlets, though these will surely appear in the near future.

▲ A Scriptlet may include a collection of files (video, images, sounds, controls, other Scriptlets or HTML pages), but no utility for gathering all these together in a `CAB` or `ZIP` file is available.

▲ Scriptlets are supported only by IE4. Netscape Navigator 4 and other browsers simply ignore them.

▲ To host Scriptlets in desktop applications you need the Microsoft Scriptlet Control.

When using Scriptlets with the Microsoft Scriptlet Control, you need to specify an absolute path to the source code. This works well if the path is a real URL, but forces you to indicate a specific installation directory if you are using it locally.

The lack of dedicated authoring tools is a drawback that should disappear over time. Topics such as licensing and protection might become a central issue if Scriptlets succeed in populating the Windows 98 desktop and folders. Reusable components must be safely and easily distributable, and this issue will need careful consideration when you choose your development strategy.

Internet Zones and Scriptlet Security

IE4 introduces **security zones,** and allows users to associate them with any files that can open or download. They choose the level of security depending on where the page comes from, and how much they trust its source. Many Web sites adopt secure protocols to prevent unauthorized people from spying on the data sent and received. IE4 recognizes these sites, and displays a lock icon on the status bar while viewing documents from them. IE4 lets users divide the Internet into four different zones, so that they can assign each Web site to a zone with a suitable security level. The zones are: Local Intranet, Trusted Sites, Restricted Sites, Internet. Local Intranet and Internet have a default security level of Medium. The default safety level is high in Trusted Sites and low in Restricted Sites, so consequently the security settings are Low and High, respectively.

All the files that IE4 finds locally on your computer are assumed to be completely safe, and no security settings are applied to them. This allows you to open and run documents and programs on your computer without prompting or interruption. The security levels for each of the various zones is completely up to you.

Web sites in the Restricted Sites zone may be those from which you want to avoid running or opening any scripts or active content. Scriptlets are portions of Web information subject to security restrictions. IE4 will only download a remote Scriptlet to your machine if you include the source Web site in a zone with a security level of Medium or Low. The Internet Options dialog box (available from the View menu) allows you to change the security settings, choosing from the general values (Low, Medium, High) or by defining your own settings.

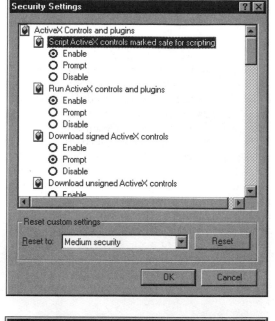

In this case, to avoid problems when loading remote Scriptlets, make sure that your have enabled the Script ActiveX controls marked safe for scripting option in your Security Settings, as illustrated here:

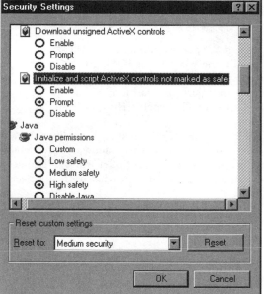

In addition, check that you haven't disabled the Controls not marked safe for scripting and initialization option. This should be Prompt or Enable, as shown:

The Structure of a Scriptlet

A Scriptlet is a regular HTML page that has two main parts: **body** and **script** code. However, a Scriptlet is also a very peculiar HTML page, whose scripting code makes it programmable from external callers, such as a host HTML page or a Visual Basic form. There is a strict relationship between the body and script. The body includes the objects on which script code will work in order to produce the desired effect. Since both code and body are contained in the same file, we have a self-contained component ready to be used as an object. In addition, the script code uses a conventional syntax to make public some of its own variables and routines. In this way we can automate the behavior and the appearance of the page:

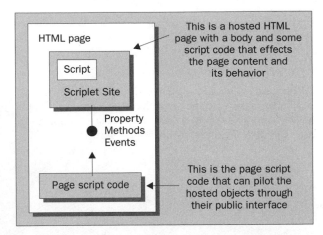

As we mentioned earlier, a Scriptlet's automation interface is expressed in terms of properties, methods and events.

The Body of a Scriptlet

Since a Scriptlet is ultimately an HTML page, we can view it through any browser – though what we actually see won't be interesting in most cases. In other words, not all the Scriptlets are self-initialized and display something useful without being scripted. If we have a component that displays a user-specified text string in a particular fashion, we need to provide that text string before using the Scriptlet. Thus, outside its host site, it will probably show a default string which might be empty or contain copyright information.

The body can include images, links, lines, text, and even ActiveX controls, applets, sounds, and anything else. It represents the user interface of the module, and includes the constituent elements on which the script code within the Scriptlet will act. The actual body may be defined at design-time, or created dynamically depending on what we really need to do.

For example, if we want a dynamic text string to become a Scriptlet, we might want to have a body like this:

```
<body>
  <span id="text"> Change this text at runtime through a property. </span>
</body>
```

We change the actual text using an exposed attribute that ends up setting the **outerText** property of the given element. The following VBScript code that does just that:

```
Sub DoSetText( sText )
  Set coll = document.all.tags("SPAN")
  coll.item(0).outerText = sText
End Sub
```

Alternately, we could also have an empty body which will be filled when needed with an HTML string:

```
<body>
</body>
```

```
Sub DoSetText(sText)
  sPrefix = "<span id=text>"
  sSuffix = </span>
  sHtmlText = sPrefix + sText + sSuffix
  Set coll = document.all.tags("SPAN")
  if coll.length > 0 then
    coll.item(0).outerHtml = sHtmlText
  else
    document.body.insertAdjacentHTML "AfterBegin", sHtmlText
  end if
End Sub
```

In the above sample, we insert a new **SPAN** element if one does not exist, or change the existing one if it is already there.

The Script Section of a Scriptlet

The script portion of a Scriptlet has a conventional structure. We must expose the public interface of the object, as well as include some internal 'helper' routines. The script procedures we write will provide the Scriptlet behavior, and take care of responding to all the Dynamic HTML events that are supported by the Scriptlet itself. Using special naming conventions, we declare some of these routines as **public** and allow the container script code to access them. Scripting may use a mix of VBScript, JavaScript, JScript, and any other scripting language supported in the browser.

Defining the Public Interface

At the start of this chapter, we saw one way to define the interface of a Scriptlet – with VBScript and the implicit declarations which use the **public_** prefix. JavaScript offers a **public_description** object that works as a class definition module. In a certain sense, using this object is similar to writing a header file for a C++ class. We can use it to assign properties and methods to the Scriptlet by name. For each attribute, we specify the name of the 'helper' script routine that implements it. A container's element will refer to that attribute using an external name, which is determined following a special naming convention.

First of all, we have to initialize the **public_description** object like this:

```
<script language="Javascript">
public_description = new CreateThisScriptlet();
</script>
```

CreateThisScriptlet is not a system routine, but just the name we give to the actual function we want to use to create the interface. This is a typical body for it:

```
function CreateThisScriptlet () {
  this.put_color = put_color;
  this.get_color = get_color;
  this.title = window.document.title;
  this.paint = doPaint;
  this.event_onPainting = "";
}
```

`CreateThisScriptlet` defines properties, methods and events for the new object, assigning them dynamically to the `this` pointer. As we saw earlier in the chapter, to fully expose a **property** called `color` we need to write two script procedures called `get_color` and `put_color`. They must be assigned to the corresponding elements in the `public_description` object, and take care of reading and writing the property value. In the `get` function we usually only need to return the current setting. The `put` function, however, saves the new value and often applies the changes to the Scriptlet output. Notice that we must use the `put` and `get` prefix to qualify it as a read/write property. If we want a read-only or write-only property, we just omit the declaration we don't need.

Defining Methods and Events in JavaScript

Methods don't follow any convention, and the name we assign to the public descriptor is the same one we invoke outside the Scriptlet. In the above sample, the `doPaint` procedure will execute after any external caller invokes the `paint` method. There is absolutely no need to implement the `paint` function with a script procedure called `doPaint`—though it is preferable for the sake of clarity. Feel free to give it the same name as your dog if you prefer!

Events have no actual code implementation. In an ActiveX control, for instance, you need to declare events just to let the development tool build the proper type library, so that the container knows about these events. This is also true for Scriptlets. A component fires events, but the actual code that runs in response is decided and executed in the container page. In other words, the host and object swap their respective roles. When raising an event, any object (Scriptlets, ActiveX controls) ends up invoking a dynamic method on the host, allowing the host to provide the code that is executed in response to the event.

At first sight, the line

```
this.event_onPainting = "";
```

seems to be necessary to make sure that event is properly notified and received. If you want a Visual Basic 5 ActiveX control to raise a given event, you absolutely need to declare it. This ensures that the container will get a pointer to a connection-point interface that includes an entry-point with the name `onPainting`:

```
Event onPainting(ByVal data As Long)
```

This is certainly true for ActiveX controls, but not for Scriptlets. If we want our Scriptlet to raise an event called `onPainting`, we don't need to declare it explicitly, because the Scriptlet custom events are all routed through the same entry-point: `onScriptletEvent`. More on this later. For now, just keep in mind that we aren't strictly required to declare events, but it is nice if we do so simply for documentation's sake.

Javascript vs VBScript

In the previous section, we discussed how to define the Scriptlet's public interface using JavaScript . As we saw at the beginning of this chapter, this is not the only approach we can take. By using a special naming convention for all the properties and methods you want to expose, you can make them **public** by design.

If you're an expert Windows programmer, this should sound familiar, and remind you of the two options you have for exporting functions from within a DLL. You can list all of them in a **DEF** file, or you can make them public using the special keyword `declspec(dllexport)` in the prototype.

Look at how to convert the previous sample using the **public** keyword:

```
Function public_get_color
Sub public_put_color
Sub public_paint
' note that there are no declarations for events
```

This approach, called **default interface description**, allows us to use VBScript instead of JavaScript. However, bear in mind that the JavaScript approach creates a single niche in our code where the whole of the object's public interface is described. Furthermore, it allows us to have different public and private names for all the methods and properties.

> *Note that the JavaScript approach always takes priority over the default interface description approach if both exist in the same Scriptlet.*

Ambient Properties

A Scriptlet runs inside a special container object that offers the following ambient properties.

Property	Type	Description
scrollbar	*Boolean*	If **true** enables the use of scrollbars. If the Scriptlet content is too large for its actual size, both vertical and horizontal scrollbars will appear automatically. Default is **false**.
selectableContent	*Boolean*	If **true** allows users to select the Scriptlet's content and drag it or copy it to the clipboard. Otherwise the user can't select anything in the Scriptlet's area. Default is **false**.
version	*String*	Identifies the current version of the Scriptlet container object. At present it is **"4.0 Win32"**.
frozen	*Boolean*	Read-only property. If **false**, indicates that the page hosting the Scriptlet is ready to handle events.

These **stock** attributes are accessible through an object called **external**, which is a new property of the Dynamic HTML **window** object. We can use them to control the environment of our Scriptlet to some extent, for example we can enable the use of scrollbars from within a Scriptlet with a line like this:

```
window.external.scrollbar = true
```

Accessing the External Object

The **external** object is available only when the Scriptlet page is actually viewed as a Scriptlet within another page. If we load and view the Scriptlet as an ordinary HTML page (for example, select it from the File | Open menu) the **external** object doesn't get initialized. Attempting to use it will then result in a runtime error. Curiously, this situation seems to be handled differently by the two scripting engines that come with IE4. Consider the following HTML code:

```
<HTML>
<BODY>
```

```
<SCRIPT language="Javascript" for="window" event="onload">
  alert("External.version is: " + window.external.version);
</SCRIPT>

<SCRIPT language="VBScript" for="window" event="onload">
  MsgBox "External.version is: " & window.external.version
</SCRIPT>

</BODY>
</HTML>
```

Both the scripts catch the **onLoad** event of the **window** object, and try to display a message box with the current value of the **window.external.version** property. The JavaScript procedure traps the exception and returns the string **"undefined"**, while the VBScript procedure produces the error like the one shown here:

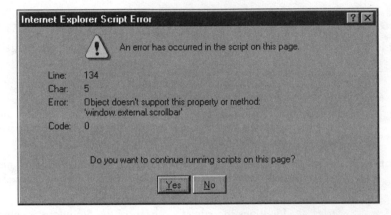

Detecting When a Scriptlet is Running – Our Custom InScriplet Variable

A Scriptlet is nothing more than a Web page viewed through a special container. Though it may not always make sense, we might also want it to display properly if viewed directly with a browser, rather than embedded into another page. Unfortunately, this produces a runtime script error if we refer to the **window.external** object in our code. It would be nice to be able to detect whether the page is being viewed directly in a browser, or as a Scriptlet. In this way, we could only access the ambient properties when appropriate.

To do this, we introduce a custom JavaScript variable named **InScriptlet** into our Scriptlet code, and set it to **true** if we are running the page as a Scriptlet, or **false** if not. This is done using the JavaScript **typeOf** method, which tells us what kind of value a variable or property is holding:

```
InScriptlet = (typeOf (window.external.version)=="string");
if( InScriptlet ) {
  window.external.scrollbar = true;
}
```

JavaScript will never prompt us with a script error. In the above situation, the **window.external.version** property will be of type **string** if it actually exists (i.e. we are running a Scriptlet), or **undefined** if the **external** object doesn't exist because we are running the page directly.

The Container Object

All Scriptlets runs in an HTML page by the means of an embedded container. This container recreates for the Scriptlet the same habitat as IE4, and makes available the **ambient** properties listed earlier. In addition, it provides the following methods:

Method	Description
`bubbleEvent`	Passes the current event down to the host environment, whether an HTML page or a Visual Basic form.
`raiseEvent`	Fires a custom event for the Scriptlet. Each event is identified by name but routed through the single `onScriptletEvent` of the container.
`setContextMenu`	Allows us to associate a pop-up menu with the Scriptlet. The menu will appear after a right-click on the Scriptlet's area of the page.

A Scriptlet receives notification of all the standard Dynamic HTML events for the **window** and **document** objects, and any other elements it contains. **bubbleEvent** is the method we use to pass (or bubble) any events we trap in the Scriptlet back up to the container. If we don't pass these events explicitly, event bubbling stops at the container and the host HTML page (or VB form, etc.) will never know that an event occurred.

If we want to handle an **onclick** event, for example, then bubble it back up to the container page, we could use the following code within our Scriptlet:

```
<script language="VBscript"
  for="document" event="onclick">
  if (InScriptlet) And Not (window.external.frozen) Then
    window.external.bubbleEvent
  end if
</script>
```

Aside from just checking to see if the Scriplet page is being run as a Scriptlet (indicated by the **InScriptlet** variable) we also have to check to make sure that the hosting container is ready to receive events. This is done by making sure that the **window.external.frozen** property is **false**.

Once the event gets back up to the container page, we can handle it there. We do this using the container window's **event** object, and examine it to get information about the event. So code to handle a bubbled event might look like this:

```
<script language="jscript" for="Scriptlet1" event="onclick">
// inspect event object to see which button was clicked
if (window.event.button = 2)
  alert ("Right-Button Clicked");
</script>
```

*If the Scriptlet is hosted in a non-Web browser environment, such as a C++, Visual Basic, or Office97 application, we have to use the **event** object that hangs off the Scriptlet control, rather than the integral **window** object's **event** object. We'll look at hosting Scriptlets in these kinds of applications towards the end of this chapter.*

Handling Custom Events

The `raiseEvent` method fires custom events, such as the `onPainting` event we discussed earlier. Its prototype is

```
RaiseEvent(name, data)
```

The following is a typical call to the `raiseEvent` method:

```
window.external.raiseEvent "onPainting", window.document
```

The first argument of `raiseEvent` is the name of the event we want to raise. The second is the data we want to associate with the event, and notify to the receiver. Whatever name we assign to the event, it will always be detected and handled in the container through the `onScriptletEvent` – which is the counterpart of `raiseEvent`. Because of this, there is no need to declare our events in a Scriptlet, as they all arrive through the built-in `onScriptletEvent` event.

When the client is notified of a custom event (i.e. one that is not a standard DHTML event), it can distinguish which of the Scriptlet's event this is with multiple `if..then` statements, or with a `select..case` or `switch` statement—based on the `name` argument. For example:

```
<script language="jscript" for="Scriptlet1" event="onscriptletevent(eventname,
eventdata)">
if(eventname == "onPainting") {
    alert("Start painting");
}
else {
  if(eventname == "onEndPainting") {
    alert("End painting");
  }
}
</script>
```

The Scriptlet would raise these events to the container using:

```
window.external.raiseEvent "onPainting", window.document
window.external.raiseEvent "onEndPainting", window.document
```

The `window.document` parameter simply represents the data we want to pass to the container's event code. This, of course, will change according to the actual requirements of your code. As previously discussed, the `window.external.frozen` property should be checked before firing events.

All the events a Scriptlet raises are perceived by the container as occurrences of the same event, `onScriptletEvent`, with different parameters. This also means that we can define events at any time, and qualify them with a string.

Adding a Context Menu

The Scriptlet container object also allows us to create and assign a pop-up **context menu** to a Scriptlet. To do this we must use either VBScript or JavaScript, as these are the only script languages guaranteed to create arrays compatible with the expectations of the `setContextMenu` method.

To create a context menu that shows *n* items, we define an array of *2*n* elements. For each pair of elements in the array, the first item is the caption that will be shown on the menu, while the second is the name of the function that will executed when the user selects that item on the menu (notice that these procedures cannot take parameters). If we want an item separator, just add a couple of empty items. Finally, we pass the array to the `setContextMenu` method of the `window.external` object:

```
<SCRIPT language="VBScript" for="window" event="onload">
   dim menuItems(6)

   menuItems(0) = "&One"
   menuItems(1) = "One"

   menuItems(2) = "&Two"
   menuItems(3) = "Two"

   menuItems(4) = "&Three"
   menuItems(5) = "Three"

   window.external.setContextMenu(menuItems)
</SCRIPT>
```

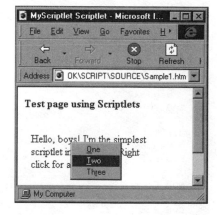

Once we have assigned the context menu to the `external` object, we're done. We have to do nothing more to set up the menu, and have no need to investigate which button the user presses. The container takes care of handling the right-click event, and running the appropriate code, automatically. Here's the result:

Creating Dynamic Context Menus

The best place to create the context menu is the `window.onLoad` event, as we did in the previous example. If we use a different event, we have to wait for that event to occur before the context menu is initialized and displayed. The context menu can be changed in code during Scriptlet execution, but all the items displayed at any moment in time must occupy consecutive locations in the menu items array. The following example produces the same menu as in the previous example the first time it is clicked. From the second time onwards, the menu changes to include a separator and a fourth menu item:

```
<script language="VBscript">
dim menuItems(10)
dim bFirstTime

Sub InitMyScriptlet
  if InScriptlet then
    window.external.selectableContent = mSelectable
    menuItems(0) = "&One"
```

```
      menuItems(1) = "One"
      menuItems(2) = "&Two"
      menuItems(3) = "Two"
      menuItems(4) = "&Three"
      menuItems(5) = "Three"
      menuItems(6) = "xxx"        ' stub the next items
      menuItems(7) = ""           ' stub the next items
    window.external.setContextMenu(menuItems)
    bFirstTime = 1
  end if
End Sub

Sub document_onmousedown
  if bFirstTime = 0 then
    menuItems(6) = ""          ' separator
    menuItems(7) = ""          ' separator
    menuItems(8) = "&Four"
    menuItems(9) = "Four"
    window.external.setContextMenu(menuItems)
  else
    bFirstTime = 0
  end if
End Sub

Sub One
  MsgBox "One"
End Sub

Sub Two
  MsgBox "Two"
End Sub

Sub Three
  MsgBox "Three"
End Sub

Sub Four
  MsgBox "Four"
End Sub
</script>
```

The context menu gets initialized first in `window.onload` event, then is updated in the `document_onmousedown` event. In any case, before the menu is displayed, our Scriptlet will receive an `onmousedown` event, so we have the opportunity to initialize it, or make changes to it, there. Here's the result—you can run or download this page, `MenuDemo.htm`, from our Web site at `http://rapid.wrox.co.uk/books/0707`:

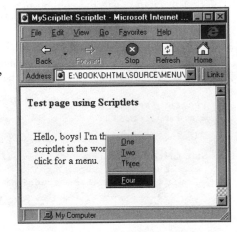

If you aren't using different arrays for different menus, you probably declared an oversized array to make room for new items. In this case, we recommend you use:

```
menuItems(6) = "xxx"    ' stub the next items
menuItems(7) = ""       ' stub the next items
```

to suppress the unnecessary items, by assigning a non-empty caption and an empty or non-existing procedure. Otherwise you risk being flooded with item separators from the multiple empty strings.

Writing Our First Scriptlet

Images are widely used on Web pages, but you rarely see them in scrollable areas. Writing a Scriptlet that is able to scroll images is really a matter of a few minutes work. What we have to do is create and set up an **IMG** tag in the Scriptlet, and then enable the container's scrollbars. The body of the Scriptlet contains only an empty image element. Here is the entire source code for the Scriptlet:

```
<html id=MyPage>
<head>
<title>ScrollImage Scriptlet</title>
</head>
<body>

<script language="VBscript" for="window" event="onload">
  InitMyScriptlet
</script>

<script language="VBscript">

' Initialize the control
' ----------------------------------------------
Sub InitMyScriptlet
  if InScriptlet then
    window.external.scrollbar = True
  end if
End Sub

' Set the image to show
' ----------------------------------------------
Sub DoSetImage(sImage)
  document.images(0).src = sImage
End Sub
</script>


<script language="JavaScript">

// declare the object interface
public_description = new CreateMyScriptlet();
var InScriptlet = (typeOf(window.external.version) == "string");

function CreateMyScriptlet() {
  this.put_Image = put_Image;
}
```

```
function put_Image (sImage) {
  DoSetImage(sImage)
  return 1;
}
</script>
<img id="image" src="" alt="">
</body>
</html>
```

And here's the result, showing a couple of intrepid *Wrox* programmers on the trail of another exciting new technology:

You can run or download this page, `Scroller.htm`, *from our Web site at* `http://rapid.wrox.co.uk/books/0707`.

How It Works

The public interface is made up of a single property that is declared write-only for simplicity. It is defined inside the JavaScript **CreateMyScriptlet** function. Most Scriptlets also need a one-time initialization that is usually performed in response to the **window.onload** event:

```
<script language="VBscript" for="window" event="onload">
    InitMyScriptlet
</script>

Sub InitMyScriptlet
  if InScriptlet then
    window.external.scrollbar = True
  end if
End Sub
```

In this case, the event handler calls `InitMyScriptlet`, which simply enables the scrollbars. We don't have to worry about setting horizontal and vertical scrolling individually—all the magic is accomplished inside the Scriptlet container object automatically.

Initially, the Scriptlet has no image to display. This screenshot shows how it appears if we view it as a standard HTML document. This is an example of a Scriptlet that absolutely requires scripting to do something meaningful.

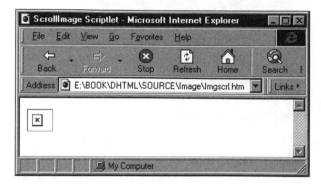

The property `image` is implemented via the `put_Image` function. Note that `put_Image` is a JavaScript routine that ends up calling `DoSetImage`, which is VBScript, instead:

```
Sub DoSetImage(sImage)
  document.images(0).src = sImage
End Sub
```

`DoSetImage` just assigns the given image file name to the only `IMG` element found in the Scriptlet body.

Extending Our First Sample

The first improvement for this example that comes to mind is adding programmable tool-tip text. Suppose we want to make available a new read/write property called `Text`:

```
function CreateMyScriptlet() {
  this.put_Image = put_Image;
  this.put_Text = put_Text;
  this.get_Text = get_Text;
}
```

By adding the two lines highlighted above, we declare the property as an attribute of our Scriptlet. The `put_Text` and `get_Text` could have the following implementation

```
m_Text = ""

function put_Text(sText) {
  DoSetText(sText);
  m_Text = sText;
  return 1;
}

function get_Text() {
  return m_Text;
}
```

When implementing a readable property, we should always consider maintaining an internal 'member' variable to make it persistent. In this example we're using the variable m_Text. When an external caller sets a new value to the **Text** property, the VBScript's **DoSetText** routine is called. Because an **IMG** element has an **alt** attribute (which stores the alternative text representation of the image), we just need to assign our **Text** property to it to get the tool-tip we want. The **Text** property may be set via scripting in the container's page at any moment, according to runtime conditions:

```
Sub DoSetText(sText)
  document.images(0).alt = sText
End Sub
```

Hosting a Scriptlet in a Web page

You'll recall that we insert Scriptlets into an HTML page using the **<OBJECT>** tag. As a reminder, here's how:

```
<object id="ImgScrl1"
  data="ImgScrl.htm" width="450" height="300"
  type="text/x-scriptlet">
</object>
```

The **data** attribute specifies the file name or URL where the Scriptlet may be found, while **type** attribute tells IE4 that it is attempting to load a Scriptlet. Once it has done so, everything works as if we are dealing with ordinary ActiveX controls. This means, for instance, that we can access the Scriptlet properties via the usual object-based syntax. The following is the source code that creates the scrolling image page you saw in the previous screenshot:

```
<html>
<title>Test page using ScrollImage</title>

<b>Test page using ScrollImage</b>
<script language="VBScript" for="window" event="onload">
ImgScrl1.Image = "image.gif"
ImgScrl1.Text = "Hassie and Jerry Lee"
</script>

<p>
<object id="ImgScrl1" data="ImgScrl.htm"
width="450" height="300" type="text/x-scriptlet">
</object>
</p>

<p> </p>
</body>
</html>
```

How Scriptlets Work Under the Hood

Whenever IE4 shows an HTML page, it creates a container window that covers the entire client area. The window class name is Shell DocObject View. It has a child window called Internet Explorer_Server which is identical in size. This window represents the surface where **MSHTML** (the IE4 module providing the Dynamic HTML functionality) draws its output. In short, Internet Explorer_Server windows are the real HTML view objects.

The illustration below shows the pile of IE4 windows that are created when it displays a standard HTML file:

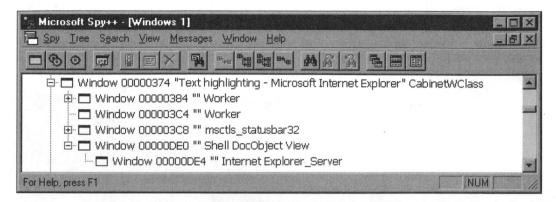

Now, look at what happens when IE4 is hosting a Scriptlet:

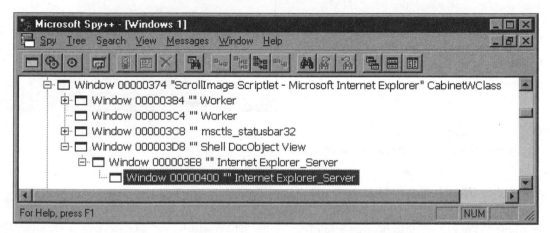

Behind the scenes, IE4 uses another instance of its Internet Explorer_Server view object for handling Scriptlets. This allows the Scriptlets to inherit the Dynamic HTML object model and scrolling capabilities. Conceptually, running a Scriptlet is just like running a nested copy of IE4 itself.

Writing Our Second Scriptlet

By now, you should have grasped the idea of what Scriptlets are, and how to write them. It's time to design and code a sample which is a little more complex. What we have in mind is a Clock object that you can put in all your pages as a reminder of time passing. A digital clock is made up of three components: hours, minutes and seconds. We can render it using a simple text string that needs formatting each time it is updated, or we can use a small table that keeps the various logical parts of the time separate. A very simple HTML table can be defined like this:

```
<TABLE>
  <TR>
    <TD VALIGN="TOP" ALIGN="CENTER">0</TD>
```

```
      <TD VALIGN="TOP" ALIGN="CENTER">0</TD>
      <TD VALIGN="TOP" ALIGN="CENTER">0</TD>
    </TR>
  </TABLE>
```

All the tags (**TABLE**, **TR**, **TD**) expose lots of attributes that set the formatting and layout of the table, but for our purposes they can all be ignored. However, a better approach would be to make them properties of the Clock Scriptlet. This sounds reasonable—especially for **BORDER** and **CELLSPACING** attributes.

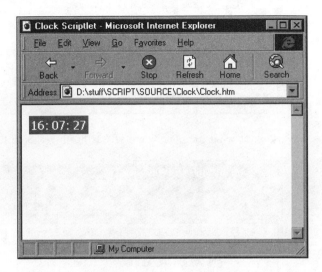

A clock is a self-initialized component, so it doesn't need specific initialization code to work properly. If you open this Scriptlet in a browser you're able to use it straight away. Once more, this demonstrates that a Scriptlet is an HTML page that runs inside another HTML page:

The final 'extended' version of this page, which you'll meet later in the chapter, can be run or download from our Web site at **http://rapid.wrox.co.uk/books/0707.**

Coding the Clock Scriptlet

Our HTML clock component will exploit the **setInterval** and **clearInterval** methods of the **window** object. We just need to provide a function to stop and restart it, and some events. Here's the complete source code:

```
<HTML id=MyPage>
<TITLE>Clock Scriptlet</TITLE>

<script language="VBscript" for="window" event="onload">
  InitClock
</script>

<script language="VBscript">

Sub InitClock
  DoSetColor mBgColor, mFgColor
  DoUpdateClock
  if InScriptlet then
    window.external.selectableContent = True
  end if
```

```
    if mEnabled then
      mTimer = window.setInterval("DoUpdateClock", 1000)
      mStartedAt = Time
    end if
End Sub

Sub DoSetColor(b, f)
  Set coll = document.all.tags("TABLE")
  coll.item(0).style.backgroundColor = b
  coll.item(0).style.Color = f
  coll.item(0).style.fontFamily = "Tahoma"
End Sub

Sub DoUpdateClock
  t = Time
  mHour = Hour(t)
  mMins = Minute(t)
  mSecs = Second(t)
  set coll = document.all.tags("TD")
  coll.item(0).innerHTML = Right("00"+CStr(mHour),2) + ":"
  coll.item(1).innerHTML = Right("00"+CStr(mMins),2) + ":"
  coll.item(2).innerHTML = Right("00"+CStr(mSecs),2)
End Sub

Function DoFormatTime
  s = FormatDateTime(Time(), vbLongTime)
  DoFormatTime = s
End Function

Function DoGetTime
  DoGetTime = Time
End Function

Function DoAlarm
  if (InScriptlet And (Not window.external.frozen)) then
    window.external.raiseEvent "OnAlarm", window.document
  end if
End Function
</script>

<script language="JavaScript">
public_description = New CreateClock();  // declare the interface
var InScriptlet = (typeOf (window.external.version) == "string");

mBgColor = "gray";
mFgColor = "white";
mEnabled = 1;
mTimer = 0;
mStartedAt = 0;
mAlarm = 0;

function CreateClock() {
  this.put_Text = put_Text;
  this.get_Time = get_Time;
  this.get_StartedAt = get_StartedAt;
  this.put_ClockBgColor = put_ClockBgColor;
```

```
    this.put_FgColor = put_FgColor;
    this.get_FgColor = get_FgColor;
    this.put_BgColor = put_BgColor;
    this.get_BgColor = get_BgColor;
    this.Enable = Enable;
    this.Alarm = Alarm;
    this.event_OnStart = "";
    this.event_OnStop = "";
    this.event_OnAlarm = "";
}

function put_ClockBgColor(color) {
    document.bgColor = color;
    return 1;
}

function put_Text(sText) {
    document.all("Text1").innerHTML = sText;
    return 1;
}

function get_Time() {
    return DoFormatTime();
}

function get_StartedAt() {
    return mStartedAt;
}

function put_ForeColor( color ) {
    mFgColor = color;
    DoSetColor(mBgColor, mFgColor);
    return 1;
}

function get_ForeColor() {
    return mFgColor;
}

function put_BackColor(color) {
    mBgColor = color;
    DoSetColor(mBgColor, mFgColor);
    return 1;
}
function get_BackColor() {
    return mBgColor;
}

function Enable(b) {
    mEnabled = b;
    if (b) {
        mTimer = window.setInterval("DoUpdateClock", 1000);
        if (InScriptlet) and (not window.external.frozen)) {
            window.external.raiseEvent("OnStart", 0);
            mStartedAt = DoGetTime();
        }
    }
```

```
    else {
      window.clearInterval(mTimer);
      Alarm(0);
      if (InScriptlet and (not window.external.frozen)) {
        window.external.raiseEvent("OnStop", 0);
      }
    }
    return 1;
}

function Alarm(secs) {
  if (secs) {
    mSnooze = window.setInterval("DoAlarm", secs);
  }
  else {
    window.clearInterval(mAlarm);
  }
  return 1;
}
</script>

<BODY>
<TABLE>
<TR>
    <TD VALIGN="TOP" ALIGN="CENTER">0</TD>
    <TD VALIGN="TOP" ALIGN="CENTER">0</TD>
    <TD VALIGN="TOP" ALIGN="CENTER">0</TD>
</TR>
</TABLE>
</BODY>
</HTML>
```

The Clock Interface Definition

The public interface of the Scriptlet exposes the following properties, methods and events:

Name	Description
FgColor	Sets and gets the foreground color of the clock, i.e. color of the digits.
BgColor	Sets and gets the background color of the clock area.
ClockBgColor	Sets the background color of the Scriptlet area.
Time	Returns the current time formatted accordingly to the user settings.
StartedAt	Returns the last time when the clock Scriptlet was started.
Text	Sets the text to be displayed below the clock.
Enable(state)	A method that disables and enables the clock causing it to stop and go.
Alarm(secs)	A method that sets up an alarm to raise an onAlarm event every given number of milliseconds.
onStop	This event is fired each time the clock gets disabled.
onStart	This event is fired each time the clock is started.
onAlarm	This event signals that the given period is expired.

The `Time` property is read-only, and returns the current time. It makes use of the current user's format settings for the date and time with VBScript's `FormatDateTime` function. `FgColor` and `BgColor` define the color of the text and the clock background–by default, we have white text on a gray background. `StartedAt` has a secondary role, and its only purpose is to enrich the Scriptlet's interface. `ClockBgColor` is a write-only property assigned to the background color of the entire site area, which is usually darker than the clock itself.

`Text` is another write-only property that contains the text string we might want to associate with the clock. This text is the body of a `SPAN` tag with an `ID` of `Text1`. Since this is implemented via the element's `innerHTML` property, we can assign it text containing HTML tags as well, and be sure it will be correctly handled. This provides us with the opportunity to format the text, be it in italic or bold font, or to include images, links, etc. For instance:

```
Clock1.Text = "Current Time offered by <i>WROX Press</i>"
```

The final property, `Enable`, is at the core of the component. It accepts a Boolean value, and starts or stops the clock.

Updating the Time

All the updates of the clock are controlled by the `setInterval` method of the `window` object:

```
mTimer = window.setInterval("DoUpdateClock", 1000);
```

The `setInterval` method takes a string denoting the script code to be executed each time the given interval expires, and an interval period expressed in milliseconds. The code above causes the `DoUpdateClock` procedure to be called once every second. As you might guess, `DoUpdateClock` just refreshes the table representing the digital clock. First it obtains the current time in terms of hours, minutes and seconds. Then it sets the `innerHTML` properties of the three `TD` elements:

```
Sub DoUpdateClock
  t = Time
  mHour = Hour(t)
  mMins = Minute(t)
  mSecs = Second(t)
  set coll = document.all.tags("TD")
  coll.item(0).innerHTML = Right("00"+CStr(mHour),2) + ":"
  coll.item(1).innerHTML = Right("00"+CStr(mMins),2) + ":"
  coll.item(2).innerHTML = Right("00"+CStr(mSecs),2)
End Sub
```

Stopping the Clock

The `setInterval` method returns a unique identifier for the timer it starts running, and we save this in a variable `mTimer`. To stop the clock, we just pass this variable to the `window` object's `clearInterval` method:

```
window.clearInterval(mTimer);
```

The `onStop` and `onStart` events are fired after the clock has been stopped and restarted. The `onStart` event isn't raised when the Scriptlet is loading for the first time. As you have seen in our earlier discussions, the event declarations are not really required for the Scriptlet to work. The host page will always receive `onScriptletEvent` events, whatever the actual event the component raises with the `raiseEvent` method. However, we've included the event declarations simply to document the Scriptlet's interface.

Hosting the Clock Component

A sample page that hosts our Clock component might look like this:

Here's the code for the complete page, including the **<OBJECT>** tags that insert the Clock Scriptlet:

```
<html>
<title>Test page using Clock</title>
<b>Test page using Clock</b>

<SCRIPT LANGUAGE="VBScript" FOR="window" EVENT="onload">
  Clock1.BgColor = "lightblue"
  Clock1.FgColor = "blue"
  Clock1.Alarm 5000
</SCRIPT>

<SCRIPT LANGUAGE="VBScript" FOR="Clock1" EVENT="onscriptletevent(n,o)">
  if n = "onStart" then
    MsgBox "Current time is " + Clock1.Time
  end if
  if n = "onStop" then
    MsgBox  "Started at " + CStr(Clock1.StartedAt)
  end if
  if n = "onAlarm" then
    CRLF = Chr(13) + Chr(10)
    sMsg = "Alarm " + Clock1.Time + CRLF + "Continue?"
    i = MsgBox(sMsg, vbYesNo, "Clock")
    if i = vbNo then Clock1.Alarm 0
  end if
</SCRIPT>

<SCRIPT LANGUAGE="VBScript">
Sub Button1_Click()
  if Button1.Caption = "Stop" Then
    Clock1.Enable(0)
    Button1.Caption = "Start"
  else
    Clock1.Enable(1)
    Button1.Caption = "Stop"
```

```
      end if
   End Sub
   </SCRIPT>

   <p>
   <OBJECT ID="Clock1" WIDTH=100 HEIGHT=70 align="bottom"
     type="text/x-scriptlet" DATA="clock.htm">
   </OBJECT>
   </p>

   <OBJECT ID="Button1" WIDTH=96 HEIGHT=32
       CLASSID="CLSID:D7053240-CE69-11CD-A777-00DD01143C57">
       <PARAM NAME="Caption" VALUE="Stop">
   </OBJECT>
   </body>
   </html>
```

During the `onload` event it assigns the clock colors. By clicking on the button you can stop or restart the clock.

Adding an Alarm to the Clock Container Page

Our clock page as it stands doesn't do very much, so we've added a function that simulates an alarm-clock. We can use several of the other methods and events that our Clock component has built into it. By assigning an interval in milliseconds using the `Alarm` method, like this:

```
   Clock1.Alarm 5000
```

we are notified of a specific `onAlarm` event after that period expires (in this case, 5 seconds). Our Clock component provides this custom event via the `onScriptletEvent` in the container page. The `Alarm` method works by setting an interval:

```
   function Alarm(secs) {
     if (secs)
       mAlarm = window.setInterval("DoAlarm", secs);
     else
       window.clearInterval(mAlarm);
     return 1;
   }
```

To cancel the alarm, we simply pass zero to the Alarm method, which clears the interval timer. When that interval is up, the `DoAlarm` routine in our component is executed. This routine raises an event that can be detected in our page:

```
   Function DoAlarm
     if (InScriptlet And (Not window.external.frozen)) then
         window.external.raiseEvent "onAlarm", window.document
     end if
   End Function
```

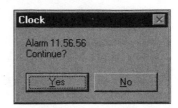

Notice that our code checks both that we are actually running the component as a Scriptlet, and that the container page is ready to receive events, first.

A Few Gotchas

Before we go on to discuss how we can host Scriptlets inside desktop applications rather than Web pages, there are a few 'gotchas' to be aware of when developing Scriptlets. Some that almost drove us crazy are:

- ▲ How to resize the Scriptlet area (or site).
- ▲ How to cancel a Scriptlet event.
- ▲ How to use hidden Scriptlets.
- ▲ How to match in with the host page's environment.

Resizing the Scriptlet's Site

The HTML code in our Clock component begins with:

```
<HTML ID=MyPage>
```

Why would we want an HTML page to have an **ID**, you might ask? It's because we can then access the frame window of the Scriptlet. This window (as you'll recall from the earlier section "How Scriptlets Work Under the Hood") is the second Internet Explorer_Server window. Once we can get a reference to it, we can change its size:

```
Set s = MyPage.style
s.pixelHeight = s.pixelHeight + mVertOffset
s.pixelWidth = s.pixelWidth + mHorzOffset
```

To change the height and width of a Scriptlet site, we need to access the **style** object of the HTML page itself, as shown above. Once we've got a reference to this **style** object (remember that the page represents the Scriptlet as a whole), it's easy to access and modify the **pixelHeight** and **pixelWidth** properties. If we don't define an explicit ID for the page, we're unable to do this.

Canceling Scriptlet Events

Custom Scriptlet events are a wonderful invention, but they don't return a value that can be examined to cancel the event–so you have to do your best to work around it. (For standard bubbled events, however, we can return a value via the **event** object).

A simple trick is to define a write-only property, say **CancelEvent**, then set it to **true** from the host page's script code if we need the Scriptlet to stop executing the rest of its code. Suppose that in the Scriptlet we raise an event before accomplishing a given task:

```
function put_CancelEvent(b) {
  mCancelEvent = b;
  return 1;
}
...
window.external.raiseEvent "onBeforeSomething", 0
if Not mCancelEvent then
  ...
  ... do something
  ...
end if
...
```

The member variable **mCancelEvent** is the internal buffer that represents the **CancelEvent** property. The **onBeforeSomething** event reaches the host environment before the Scriptlet performs the "do something" actions. Here, the host page can cancel the event by just setting the **CancelEvent** property to **true**:

```
<script language="VBScript" for="Scriptlet1" event="onscriptletevent(n,o)">
  If n = "onBeforeSomething" Then
    Scriptlet1.CancelEvent = True
  End If
</script>
```

Hidden Scriptlets

Scriptlets are code components that resemble ActiveX controls. Consequently, there might be situations where we would use a Scriptlet as a silent and invisible 'server'. For instance, think of the Clock sample we discussed earlier. In some situations, we might want to hide it and just exploit its alarm function. We don't want the Scriptlet to have a user interface, but we still need to use it as a regular object. The easy way out is to set the **visibility** property of its **style** object to **hidden**:

```
<object id=Scriptlet1 width=1 height=1 type="text/x-scriptlet"
  data="scriptlet.htm" style="visibility:hidden">
</object>
```

This technique can be used to add an invisible Scriptlet to any HTML page. If you just need a hidden component, that's all you need to do. However, sometimes things get a bit more complicated. For instance, we might want the object to appear and disappear on command. Look at the screenshot below:

> *You can run or download this page,* **RunClock.htm,** *from our Web site at* **http://rapid.wrox.co.uk/books/0707.**

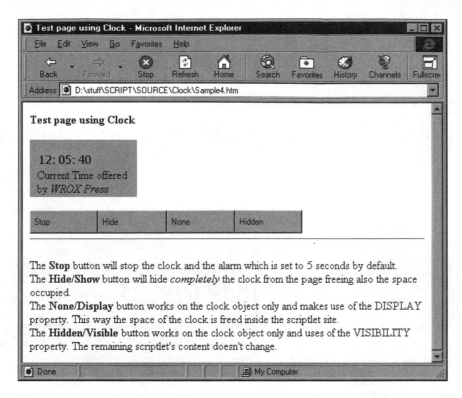

The page shows the existing Stop button, plus three new buttons related to the visibility of the clock. The Hide button removes and inserts the entire Scriptlet in the page, while the other two act to show or hide parts of the clock component in different ways, without affecting the container. We can take one of three possible approaches to hiding a Scriptlet dynamically:

- Using the **style.visibility** property for the various objects.
- Using the **style.display** property for the various objects.
- Resizing its site.

Changing the style.visibility Property

visibility is a property of the **style** object, and applies to every element that can appear in an HTML page. To make an element visible we assign "**visible**" to the property, otherwise we hide it using "**Hidden**". We don't necessarily need to do it in the host page, as shown earlier. We can teach our Scriptlet to change the flag itself. To demonstrate this, we added a new **SetVisibility** method to the Clock sample, which runs when the Hidden button is clicked:

```
function SetVisibility(b) {
  if(b)
    document.all("Table1").style.setAttribute("visibility", "visible");
  else
    document.all("Table1").style.setAttribute("visibility", "hidden");
  return 1;
}
```

It works on the table element that actually implements the clock. The table has been assigned an ID of **Table1**:

```
<TABLE id="Table1">
...
</TABLE>
```

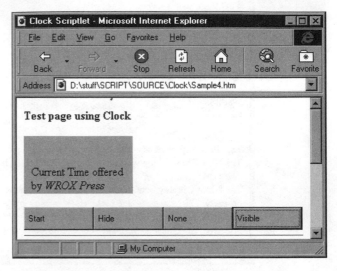

The function retrieves the **style** object of the element and changes the value of the **visibility** attribute according to the Boolean parameter passed to the routine. The effect of hiding it is shown here:

As you can see, only the table with the clock in it has disappeared. The text label and the rest of the Scriptlet's page remain unchanged. This happens by design, because **visibility** doesn't free the space occupied by the element it actually hides.

Changing the style.display Property

The **display** property, on the other hand, does just this. Except for the arguments it accepts, **display** works the same as **visibility**. The only difference is that it physically removes the element from the Scriptlet document:

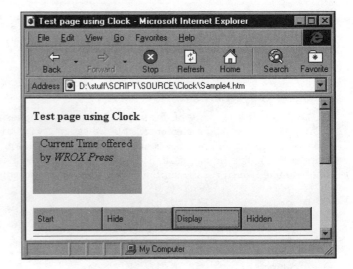

Notice in this screenshot that the label shifts upwards when we remove the clock. The `display` property tells IE4 whether the element should be rendered or not–it expects the value `"None"` for removing the element, and an empty string (the default) for rendering it. We've implemented this capability in the `SetDisplay` routine that runs when the Display button is clicked:

```
function SetDisplay(b) {
  if (b)
    document.all("Table1").style.setAttribute("display", "");
  else
    document.all("Table1").style.setAttribute("display", "none");
  return 1;
}
```

At this point, you might think that hiding the entire Scriptlet from the host page is an insignificant task. You're wrong. Yes, you can access the `display` property of the whole Scriptlet like this:

```
document.body.style.setAttribute("display", "none");
```

or get the host page to change the Scriptlet's display property, like this:

```
Scriptlet1.style.setAttribute("display", "none");
```

Resizing the Scriptlet

Both the methods we saw above make the Scriptlet completely invisible. However, the Scriptlet's area of the host page is not always properly cleared–particularly in the case of the first method. And if we want to do the job from code within the Scriptlet component, this is the method we have to use. If we want the clock to disappear leaving no footprints, we may need to resize its window as well. This causes the container page to redraw itself properly, as if we had instantiated an invisible object:

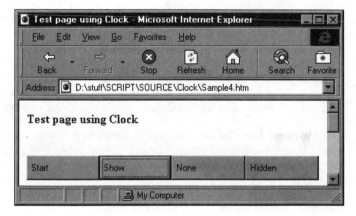

Here's the code for the Hide button, that implements this technique.:

```
function Show(b) {
 if (b) {
   MyPage.style.pixelHeight = mHeight;
   MyPage.style.pixelWidth = mWidth;
   document.body.style.setAttribute("display", "");
 }
 else {
   document.body.style.setAttribute("display", "none");
   mHeight = MyPage.style.pixelHeight;
   mWidth = MyPage.style.pixelWidth;
   MyPage.style.pixelHeight = 1;
```

```
      MyPage.style.pixelWidth = 1;
    }
    return 1;
  }
```

To access the **style** object for resizing the Scriptlet, we need to specify the **ID** of the Scriptlet page (**MyPage**) as we saw earlier. This code assigns the current height and width to global member variables, then resizes the site to 1 x 1 pixels (using zero causes the Scriptlet object to be invalidated). It can be resized back to the original size using these stored values.

Matching in with the Host Page's Environment

A Scriptlet can access its parent (host page) environment, and read–say–the background color of the page in order to insert itself neatly in the host frame. The parent window object is available from the **window.parent** property. So, in order to adopt the parent's background color, the Scriptlet can just use the following code, probably in the **window_onload** event:

```
document.bgColor = window.Parent.document.bgColor
```

In fact, this technique can also be employed to inherit stylesheet information from the parent, or any other exposed properties of the host document.

Hosting Scriptlets in Desktop Applications

Scriptlets behave in a very similar way to ActiveX controls in a Web page, because–as we saw earlier–they are wrapped up in another software layer that exposes a COM interface. This wrapper is Internet Explorer_Server, otherwise known as the Microsoft Scriptlet Control. This also holds true when we start to consider the use we can make of Scriptlets in ordinary desktop applications. A Scriptlet can be hosted in a Visual Basic form or in an MFC-based application, just as easily as it can in an HTML page.

The Microsoft Scriptlet Control, which comes with IE4, is responsible for this language-independence. It means that, outside a Web page, we can use Scriptlets everywhere that ActiveX controls are accepted. The Scriptlet Control is wrapped around the Scriptlet in the same way as in a Web page, and its ActiveX (COM) interface works just the same in VB, C++, Office 97, Delphi, and many other languages. The proof is in the screenshot below, which demonstrates that even from a VB Form, we find the Internet Explorer_Server window in the middle again!

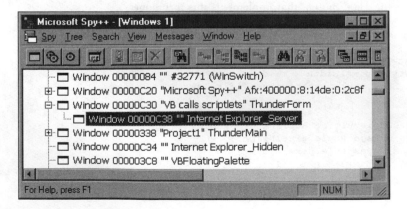

Using the Scriptlet Control

In Visual Basic or MFC applications, you use the same Clock and the ScrollImage Scriptlets we saw earlier, as ActiveX controls. The only real difference is that in MFC applications—like JavaScript and JScript—the property and method names are case sensitive. Let's see what the control has to offer to programmers.

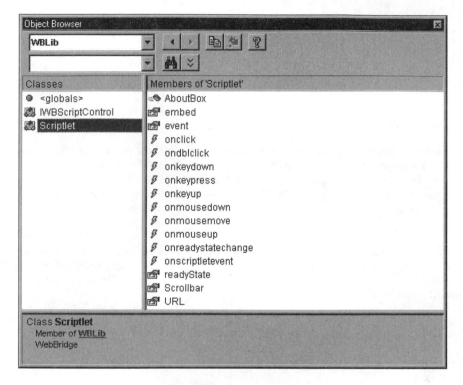

The illustration above shows how the Scriptlet Control presents itself from within the Visual Basic 5 Object Browser. The **embed** property isn't implemented yet, and **event** points to an object that hangs off the scriptlet control, and describes the events that occur in much the same way as IE4's **window.event** object. The **scrollbar** property plays the role we discussed earlier, when talking about the ambient properties that a Scriptlet document can inherit from its container. A few words, however, must be said about the **readyState** property.

Managing 'State Readiness' in Scriptlets

Making calls from an application into an object before it is declared to be ready is dangerously unsafe. If we're unlucky, it's easy to get a system error due to un-handled page faults. In other cases, our commands are simply ignored. The Scriplet container's read-only **readyState** property indicates the state of the Scriplet HTML page. While IE4 traps all exceptions, checking for the correct **readyState** becomes a must when using Scriptlets (and all Dynamic HTML-based code) from within a desktop environment.

An object passes through different states: **uninitialized, loading, complete**. Each time the property **readyState** changes, the container is notified with an **onReadyStateChange** event. Usually this event is fired multiple times while the Scriptlet is loading. The final time it denotes that the Scriptlet HTML page is fully loaded and we can start invoking script code safely:

```
Sub Scriptlet1_onreadystatechange()
  If Scriptlet1.readyState = 4 Then
    Scriptlet1.BgColor = "black"
    Scriptlet1.FgColor = "lightgreen"
  End If
End Sub
```

When the loading has completed, **readyState** contains a value of **4**. At this point, for example, we can set the colors.

Specifying the URL

Inserting Scriptlets into desktop application poses another problem: how do we specify the source path of the component? The Microsoft Scriptlet Control doesn't seem to offer a way to specify a relative path to the Scriptlet code. For example, we can't just indicate the file name, and leave the system to search in the current directory or in the common paths. Absolute paths work well if we're using Scriptlets from the Internet (when the paths are real URLs), but force us to indicate a specific installation directory in the case of local Scriptlets.

All this wouldn't be a problem if the **URL** property could be set at runtime. Unfortunately, we need to assign the URL at design-time, and if we leave the URL field blank, the Scriptlet Control doesn't load. If we specify a string that IE4 isn't able to convert into a valid file name, we get a runtime exception and– again–the control won't load.

A possible partial workaround is to assign a semi-relative path that refers to the current drive, but specifies a fixed directory. It might be a common path where you store all the local Scriptlets. For example:

```
URL = file:///Script\Clock.htm
```

points to the file **Clock.htm** that must reside in the **\Script** directory on the current drive.

If your goal is to use Scriptlets as ordinary ActiveX controls within a desktop Windows application, then consider that a Scriptlet still remains a separate file that you have to distribute together with the application executables. A revolutionary approach may be saving the HTML file (and all the files *it* requires) in the resource file of the module. When the application is initializing, extract the resources and create temporary files. At this point specifying a fixed directory is no longer an issue, since you can create it dynamically and copy the Scriptlet files in.

An Example in Visual Basic

This example uses the Clock Scriptlet component we created earlier in the chapter, within a normal Visual Basic application–and proves that our Scriptlets can behave just like ordinary ActiveX controls. In Design view, the VB window looks like this. You can see the Scriptlets control in the Toolbox, and the Clock component on the Form:

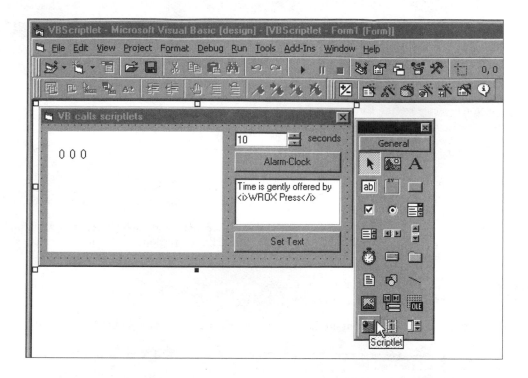

The source code for this project is in the **Scriptlets/Vbslet** *folder of the samples that you can download from our Web site at* **http://rapid.wrox.co.uk/books/0707**.

What we need to do is

- Insert the Scriptlet ActiveX control
- Assign it an area (or site) on the form
- Set the **URL** name in the Properties dialog
- Type in some code to handle the **onReadyStateChange** event
- Initialize the Scriptlet as required
- Add the various controls to the Form, such as buttons, list boxes, textboxes, etc
- Write the rest of the code to link the Form controls and the Scriptlet together

If the Scriptlet requires code to be run when it loads, we do this in the **onReadyStateChange** event rather than in the **Form_Load** event. Until the control's **readyState** property is equal to **4** (i.e. loading is complete), it's unsafe to execute code within the Scriptlet because is in an inconsistent state.

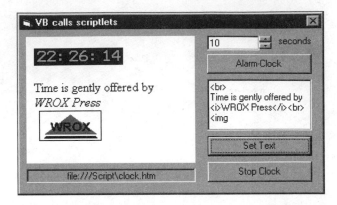

This screenshot shows the final application running, and you'll recognize the Clock component:

The application behaves like the Clock HTML page we saw earlier. In particular, it contains a button that sets an alarm in seconds, and changes the background color of the corresponding textbox to emphasize this. We multiply by 1000 since the Clock component's method expects its input in milliseconds:

```
Scriptlet1.Alarm (Val(Text1.Text) * 1000)
Text1.BackColor = &HC0C0C0
```

The alarm originates regular events that are handled in **onScriptletEvent** within the VB code:

```
Sub Scriptlet1_onscriptletevent(ByVal name As String, ByVal eventData As Variant)
   If name = "OnAlarm" Then
      Scriptlet1.FgColor = "red"
      Beep
      res = MsgBox("Would you stop the alarm?", _
            vbExclamation Or vbYesNo, "Clock Alarm!")
      If res = vbYes Then
         Scriptlet1.Alarm 0
         Text1.BackColor = &HFFFFFF
      End If
      Scriptlet1.FgColor = "lightgreen"
   End If
End Sub
```

In addition, the application shows the current location of the Scriptlet, and allows you to stop the clock and set a label.

Summary

Most seasoned HTML authors have been looking for a more versatile and flexible scripting language for some time. ActiveX controls and Java applets were fine, but often required long downloads and sometimes local installation. There could often be a delay while support files for components written in C++ or VB were installed. Scriptlets provide a way round all this, with small files that download quickly and perform relatively fast.

Many people are also coming to prefer the HTML metaphor to something like Microsoft PowerPoint, or other presentation software. In particular, Dynamic HTML provides lots of new ways of producing animated and exciting presentations. Scriptlets offer that extra something that finally makes the process of creating all kinds of pages so much easier where special custom effects are required. We just create a Scriptlet component to provide the effect we want, and can use it in a Web page, a PowerPoint presentation, a custom application, or even drop it into a Microsoft Word document. Scriptlets are HTML components that can fully exploit the power of Dynamic HTML, and offer an excellent way to put script reusability into practice.

It's difficult to say now if Scriptlets will be widely accepted by the programming community in the months to come. We've consciously used the word "programming" instead of "Web developing", because there is a good chance that Scriptlets will soon populate and animate the Windows 98 desktops and folders as well as appear in some new applications. As for the Internet, don't forget that today Microsoft's implementation of Dynamic HTML–on which Scriptlets are based–is supported only by IE4, and only under Win32. This will change soon, maybe by the time you read this, but it's unlikely that Dynamic HTML will be supported by Netscape or other browsers in its present form. Like it or not, this will delay the acceptance of Scriptlets. On the other hand, we have the Active Desktop and Windows 98, which offer an integrated environment and put the Web browsing objects (and hence the browser metaphor) everywhere. It's likely that this, more than the Web side, will determine the success of Dynamic HTML and Scriptlets.

In any case, in this chapter, we've shown you what Scriptlets are, and what they can do. There's no doubt you'll agree that they are a compelling new technology, and one that can only make IE4 developer's lives that bit easier.

Client Server and ASP Programming

You have seen in this book the new and exciting way to make pages dynamic. But Dynamic HTML wasn't the first technique to achieve this. In the past, dynamic web pages meant those that had different content based on various inputs to the page. In some cases, you could select several choices from a form, and then that information would be passed onto a server that modified the content of the page it sent back based on your choices. Or if you executed a query against a database, then the results of that query could be output as a web page. There have been many tools that you could use on a web server to support this type of dynamic web pages. Programming languages such as Perl and C++ made the creation of dynamic web pages possible, but not accessible to the masses. With the advent of Microsoft's Active Server Pages, the creation of dynamic web pages became much easier. Active Server Pages provided a robust object model that allowed the web page developer to do things such as query the browser type of the client, access data from a SQL database, and even use their own custom objects.

IE 4 has introduced the second type of dynamic web page. This time, the "dynamics" take place at the browser, after the page has been downloaded from the web server. In this chapter we will take a look at combining the two technologies. Through the use of three examples, we will show you how to use Active Server Pages on the server, combined with Dynamic HTML at the client, to make your web pages even more dynamic.

This chapters covers:

- An overview of Active Server Pages
- The Browser Capabilities Component example
- The Tabular Data Control example
- The Structured Graphics Control example

Let's first take a quick look at what Active Server Pages are.

An Overview of Active Server Pages

In a nutshell, Active Server Pages (ASP) allows the developer to write scripting code that is executed on the server, and which can affect the HTML that is eventually downloaded to the client. ASP script can be written in any Active Scripting-compatible scripting language, such as VBScript or JScript. The examples here will use VBScript as the ASP scripting language.

Let's look at a simple ASP Example. Here is an HTML file that outputs a series of numbers to the screen:

```
<!DOCTYPE HTML PUBLIC "-//W3C//DTD HTML 3.2//EN">
<HTML>
<HEAD>
    <TITLE>Count from 1 to 10</TITLE>
</HEAD>

<BODY>
1<BR>
2<BR>
3<BR>
4<BR>
5<BR>
6<BR>
7<BR>
8<BR>
9<BR>
10<BR>

</BODY>
</HTML>
```

So as you can see, this is very straightforward for building a series of numbers. But what if you wanted to have, for some strange reason, a web page that listed a series of numbers from 1 to 500. It really is not very efficient to write the HTML by hand. That would be rather tedious.

> *Though a cunning programmer, when faced with this dilemma, and without the availability of ASP, would have dutifully written a macro for their favorite editor that would have automated numbering from 1 to 500 in the HTML source code. But us programmers would rather be smart than cunning.*

We will take advantage of the latest tools available. In this case, to solve this problem, the best tool is Active Server Pages. An Active Server Page web page that produces the same result, but with many fewer lines of code, would look like this:

```
<!DOCTYPE HTML PUBLIC "-//W3C//DTD HTML 3.2//EN">
<HTML>
<HEAD>
    <TITLE>Count from 1 to 10</TITLE>
</HEAD>

<BODY>
<% for i = 1 to 10 %>
<%= i %>
<BR>
<% next %>

</BODY>
</HTML>
```

You can see from this example that we have removed 6 lines of code from the application. This economy will be even greater if now we needed to count to 100. The straight HTML method would have required the addition of 90 lines to the source. The ASP version can be changed to count to 100 simply by modifying the upper bound in the **for** loop.

How Active Server Pages Works

In short, what Active Server Pages does is act as a filter running on the web server. Microsoft's Internet Information Server 3.0 was the first web server to support Active Server Pages. When a request comes into the web server for a page with the extension .ASP, the web server passes that page to the Active Server Page process for handling. The ASP processor will scan through the source file looking for text that is offset with the `<%...%>` tags. The server's script processor processes the text contained in these tags. Looking back at the previous example, you can see a `for...next` loop that counts from 1 to 100. Inside the body of the loop, there is a command `<%= i %>`, which will output the value of the loop counter to the outgoing HTML stream. Then, the server will output a `<BR>` tag, to cause a line break in the outgoing HTML stream. If the script language looks familiar to you, then it should, it's the very same VBScript that we've been using throughout the book. In fact, since Active Server Pages uses the same Active Scripting engine that IE4 uses, you can use any scripting language you want. The only difference is that the default language with IE4 is JScript, or JavaScript, and the default language for Active Server Pages is VBScript.

Another strength of ASP is its ability to hide the programming logic that creates a page. If you load the ASP code above into your browser and view the HTML source, you will find that it strangely looks exactly like the straight HTML code. Why is this? ASP is running the script code in the source file on the server. The script code is itself generating HTML, which ASP inserts into the proper place in the output stream. What does this mean for the developer? With ASP, you have the opportunity to hide computations, database structures, and login information from the browsing public. With ASP, only the final HTML is returned to the user. This also means that the dynamic web page that ASP creates can be dynamic on *any* browser. Because the dynamics are added at the server, the final HTML can be designed to support any target platform, no matter how limited its capabilities.

There is no way possible to cover all the aspects of ASP in this chapter. And that is not the point of this chapter either. We will be looking at ways to extend Dynamic HTML to use Active Server Pages. For a background on Active Server Pages, check out the book from Wrox Press, entitled *Professional Active Server Pages ISBN 1-861000-72-3*. Even if you are not familiar with ASP, as long as you understand VB Script, you should have little trouble following the examples in this chapter.

Example 1 – To DHTML or not to DHTML?

So now you have learned how to do all these fancy things with Dynamic HTML. You have redesigned your sites to use these new tricks. You have told all of your friends to go and download IE4. But now we have to come back to the real world. The real world tells us that even with all the great features that IE 4 brings, it will probably be some time before it becomes everyone's everyday browser. So what should you do? Should you exclude everyone who does not yet use IE4? Or should you put all of those great features on the shelf until more people are using browsers that support Dynamic HTML? Well, there is an answer that makes everybody happy - by using Active Server Pages, your web server can identify the capabilities of the browser that is making the request. Then, through the use of Active Server Scripting, you can change the makeup of the page on the fly. This will allow you to provide Dynamic HTML-enhanced content to those that support it. And, you can provide static HTML to everyone else.

Browser Capabilities Component

The heart of this dynamic changing of content is the Browser Capabilities component. This Active Server Component examines the **HTTP_USER_AGENT** field that is sent by every browser when it requests a page from the web server. This value is then compared against a table that is held in a file on the web server called **BROWSCAP.INI**. You can find the latest version of this file at: `http://www.microsoft.com/iis/usingiis/developing/downloads/browscap.ini`.

Here is what the IE4 entry looks like in **BROWSCAP.INI**:

```
;;ie 4
[IE 4.0]
browser=IE
Version=4.0
majorver=#4
minorver=#0
frames=TRUE
tables=TRUE
cookies=TRUE
backgroundsounds=TRUE
vbscript=TRUE
javascript=TRUE
javaapplets=TRUE
ActiveXControls=TRUE
Win16=False
beta=False
AK=False
SK=False
AOL=False
crawler=False

;;ie 4 final release
[Mozilla/4.0 (compatible; MSIE 4.0; Windows 95)]
parent=IE 4.0
platform=Win95
beta=False

[Mozilla/4.0 (compatible; MSIE 4.0; Windows NT)]
parent=IE 4.0
platform=WinNT
beta=False

[Mozilla/4.0 (compatible; MSIE 4.0 Crawler; Windows 95)]
parent=IE 4.0
platform=Win95
beta=False
crawler=True

[Mozilla/4.0 (compatible; MSIE 4.0 Crawler; Windows NT)]
parent=IE 4.0
platform=WinNT
beta=False
crawler=True
```

The file is laid out such that there is a parent entry that is denoted by the [IE 4.0] entry. The values under this entry are those that are common to all versions of IE4. Each of the other sections include an entry **parent=IE 4.0**. This serves as an include statement, so that all entries from the IE 4.0 section are included here. The heading title, such as [Mozilla/4.0 (compatible; MSIE 4.0b1; Windows NT)] corresponds to the **HTTP_USER_AGENT** value passed by the client to the server.

The Browser Capabilities component exposes a method for each entry in the **BROWSCAP.INI** file section that matches the **HTTP_USER_AGENT** value. The method will return the value, which is usually either true or false, to the ASP script that is accessing the method. If the entry does not exist in the **BROWSCAP.INI** file, rather than return an error, the method will just return false.

Using the Browser Capabilities Component

Let's look at how you would use this component in an Active Server Page.

```
Set BCap = Server.CreateObject("MSWC.BrowserType")
If BCap.tables Then Response.Write "<TABLE><TR><TD>"
Response.Write "Let's put some text here."
If BCap.tables Then
  Response.Write "</TD><TD>"
Else
  Response.Write "   "
End If
Response.Write "Are we inside a table or not?"
If BCap.tables Then
  Response.Write "</TD></TR></TABLE>"
Else
  Response.Write "<P>"
End If
```

This will create a table if the browser supports them, or just place the two items of text next to each other, separated by non-breaking spaces, if not. Modern browsers will receive:

```
<TABLE><TR><TD>
Let's put some text here.
</TD><TD>
Are we inside a table or not?"
</TD></TR></TABLE>
```

While non-tables browsers will receive:

```
Let's put some text here.
   
Are we inside a table or not?"
<P>
```

So you can see that it is very easy to change the output from the web server based on the browser that is making the request. Now, let's take a look at a way to dynamically create a Dynamic HTML page.

Providing Different Content to Different Browsers

One of the multimedia controls that were introduced in Chapter 12 was the Sprite control. This control allows you to finely control the playback of animated images. This provides for a much more powerful animated effect than GIF animation. But what about those who don't have the latest and greatest browser?

Using the Browser Capabilities component and Active Server Pages, you can give the IE4 users the more advanced animation with the Sprite control, and then provide a different page, using GIF animation as a fallback, to those with other browsers.

The code to make this decision is very simple, and only takes up a small part of the entire page. The rest of the page is devoted to supporting both the IE4 version and the non-IE4 version, with a simple if-then-else separating them.

```
<%
    Set BCap = Server.CreateObject("MSWC.BrowserType")
    if BCap.browser = "IE" and BCap.majorver >=4 then
%>
```

By checking the browser property, it can be determined if the request is coming from an Internet Explorer browser. The **BROWSCAP.INI** file does not contain an indication as to the support of specific controls, like the Sprite control. Since we know that the Sprite control was first introduced with IE4, and is not available on Netscape or any other browser, then we can use this check to see if the browser making the request meets that criteria. The **USER_AGENT** value that is passed to the server from an IE4 client running on Windows NT is:

```
Mozilla/4.0 (compatible; MSIE 4.0; Windows NT)
```

If we look at the section in the **BROWSCAP.INI** file that matches the **USER_AGENT** value, there is the following entry:

```
[Mozilla/4.0 (compatible; MSIE 4.0; Windows NT)]
parent=IE 4.0
platform=WinNT
beta=False
```

Since there is an entry for parent, we need to look at the **[IE 4.0]** entry. The first few lines from this entry are:

```
[IE 4.0]
browser=IE
Version=4.0
majorver=4
minorver=0
```

So when the value of **Bcap.browser** is queried, the value **IE** is returned. Now that the browser has been identified as a version of Internet Explorer, we can check the value for the major version. We check the **majorver** entry rather than the **Version** entry to allow for this code to continue working with subsequent versions of Internet Explorer. The returned value is 4, so we know that the client that made the request supports the Sprite control. Therefore, the server can include that control in its response to the client. This is the code that will produce an animated image using the Sprite control:

```
<OBJECT ID="WroxLogo"
    STYLE="position:absolute; LEFT: 50; TOP: 50; WIDTH: 100; HEIGHT: 50"
    CLASSID ="clsid:FD179533-D86E-11d0-89D6-00A0C90833E6">
    <PARAM NAME="Repeat" VALUE="-1">
    <PARAM NAME="PlayRate" VALUE="1">
    <PARAM NAME="MouseEventsEnabled" VALUE="True">
    <PARAM NAME="AutoStart" VALUE="True">
    <PARAM NAME="SourceURL" VALUE="wroxanim.gif">
    <PARAM NAME="NumFrames" VALUE="6">
    <PARAM NAME="NumFramesAcross" VALUE="1">
    <PARAM NAME="NumFramesDown" VALUE="6">
</OBJECT>

<BODY>
<DIV id=divPlayingNotification>
    <H2>You do have IE4! - You are looking at the Sprite Control.  Enjoy!</H2>
</DIV>

</BODY>
```

This is what you'll see if you're running IE4:

You can run this page from our web site at **http://rapid.wrox.co.uk/books/0707**.

Now that the IE4 version of the page has been generated, the server needs to generate a page for all other versions. At this point, you could make additional checks to ensure that the client supports GIF Animation. But, for the sake of this example, we will just let the browser handle the tag if it doesn't support it:

```
<% else %>
<BODY>
    <IMG SRC="WroxGifAnim.gif" WIDTH=77 HEIGHT=39 BORDER=0>
    <H2>You do not have IE4 - You are looking at an Animated GIF.  Time to upgrade!</H2>
</BODY>

<% end if %>
```

This is what you'll see when running the same example, if you're not running Internet Explorer 4, but an earlier version of Internet Explorer:

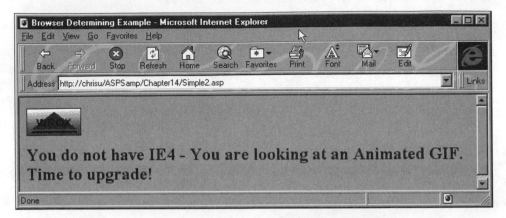

You have seen from this simple example how easy it is at the server to determine the capabilities of the client that is requesting the information from the server. Based on this information, browser-specific and browser version-specific code can be added or removed dynamically. This allows the page to always be tailored as closely as possible to the client making the request.

Example 2 – ASP and the Tabular Data Control

As you saw back in Chapter 7, the Tabular Data control could be used to dynamically populate a table in your web page. In the examples in that chapter, the data source file for the TDC was a text file that was stored on the web server. This was an interesting example, but in the real world, it is very rare that databases exist in text files. Usually, they will exist in a relational database that is accessible via SQL and ODBC.

But you still want to be able to use the power of the Tabular Data Control. By combining the TDC control of IE 4, with the database access capabilities of Internet Information Server's Active Server Pages, you can successfully meld these two technologies into a very effective and efficient database retrieval platform.

The first thing that we will need to do is examine the format of the data file that is delivering that data to the Tabular Data control. This data file is stored as a text file on the web server, which the control retrieves to populate the table. Here is a short sample of data from that file:

```
Author,Title,ISBN,Subject,Series,Url
Bruce Hartwell,Instant PowerBuilder Objects,1861000065,Powerbuilder,Instant,h123.htm
Ivor Horton,Beginning Visual C++ 5,1861000081,Visual C++,Beginning,h124.htm
Oleg Yaroshenko,Beginner's Guide to C++ 2nd Edition,186100012X,C++,Beginning,h125.htm
Mike Blaszczak,Professional MFC Programming with Visual C++ 5,1861000146,Visual
C++,Professional,h126.htm
Stephen Jakab,Instant Visual Basic 5 ActiveX Control Creation,1861000235,Visual
Basic,Instant,h127.htm
Ivor Horton,Beginning Java,1861000278,Java,Beginning,h128.htm
Sing Li,Professional Visual C++ 5: ActiveX/COM Control Programming,1861000375,Visual
C++,Professional,h129.htm
```

The first line of the file identifies the fields that will be in each record. In this case, there are 6 fields per record: `Author`, `Title`, `ISBN`, `Subject`, `Series`, and `URL`. The subsequent lines in the file each represent a record of data, with each field separated by a comma. The first record in the file is:

Author	Title	ISBN	Subject	Series	URL
Bruce Hartwell	Instant PowerBuilder Objects	1861000065	Powerbuilder	Instant	h123.htm

Active Server Pages and Databases

To begin the migration to an Active Server version, we need to convert the text data file to a database that you can access from an Active Server Page. For this, we can use any ODBC accessible database. To keep things simple, we will choose Microsoft Access. Access will provide us a very easy mechanism to create the database. You can directly import a delimited text file into an Access database and a new table will be created for you. The Access text import Wizard will take care of all the steps for you. The only change that you need to make when running the wizard is to tell Access that the first line in the file contains the field names.

If you let the wizard complete its wizardry, you will have a table in your database called `Bookinfo`.

Creating an ODBC System Data Source

The next step that you need to do is make this database available to the Active Server. This is done by creating an ODBC Data Source that points to the database that contains this new table. In order for an Active Server page to access a database, the ODBC Data Source must be a System DSN. This can be created using the ODBC control panel applet. You will need to create a DSN with the name `707BookInfo`.

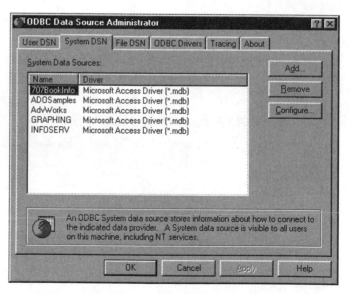

Now that we have the mechanism in place to access the database through ODBC, we can move to providing the information that the TDC needs.

Integrating with the Tabular Data Control

A Tabular Data Control can take as input a text file, with the first line identifying the fields, and then each record following on its own line terminated by a carriage return and line feed. The Active Server page generally turns out HTML pages for display in a web browser. You can also write an Active Server page that produces a text file as output. This will work well for us.

If you remember from Chapter 6, the <OBJECT> definition for the Tabular Data control looks like this:

```
<!-- This is a Tabular Data control. It can be used to feed text-based data into -->
<!-- HTML fields that are set up with datasrc/datafld attributes                  -->

<OBJECT ID="books" WIDTH=100 HEIGHT=51
    CLASSID="CLSID:333C7BC4-460F-11D0-BC04-0080C7055A83">
<PARAM NAME="FieldDelim" VALUE=",">
<PARAM NAME="DataURL" VALUE="bookinfo.txt">
<PARAM NAME="UseHeader" VALUE=True>
</OBJECT>
```

The <PARAM> that sets the DataURL is actually a pointer to the URL that the control should access to obtain the data to be used by the control. If we replace this line with a reference to an Active Server page, then when the control access the data, the Active Server page will be processed by the server and the correct data will be returned to the control. However, as you may well remember from chapter 6, just embedding this control in the page, won't display any results. You need to return the results from the control, in the form of a table.

To access the database from an Active Server page, you will use the Active Data Objects library that comes with the Active Server Page server. This control allows you to access the database through ODBC and manipulate tables through recordsets. Since a detailed explanation of how to use the ADO database access is too big a topic to cover here, we would suggest looking at a copy of Wrox's book, *Professional Active Server Pages*.

Creating an ASP-based Book Info file

Here is the Active Server Pages source file that will substitute for the `bookinfo.txt` file in the original control:

```
<%
    ' Create the Database Connection Object
    Set DBConn = Server.CreateObject("ADODB.Connection")
```

There are 4 top-level objects in the Active Server Pages object model. One of these objects is the Server object. This object allows for the creation of other object through the use of the **CreateObject** method. The **ADODB.Connection** object is a member of the **ADODB** collection of objects. The responsibility of this object is to manage the communication between the ADO objects and a physical database.

```
    ' Open the ODBC datasource entitled BOOKINFO
    DBConn.Open("707BOOKINFO")
```

Once you have instantiated the **Connection** object, you can use its **Open** method to create the connection with the ODBC System DSN that you created previously.

```
' Define the SQL Query - this will retrieve all records from the
' BookInfo Table
sql = "SELECT * FROM BookInfo;"
```

To retrieve the records that we want from the **BookInfo** table, we will use the SQL statement to select all of the fields from all of the rows in the table named **BookInfo**.

```
' Execute the SQL Query and return the results in the RS Recordset
' Object
set RS = DBConn.Execute(sql)
```

Now that we have defined the SQL query that will retrieve the information that we want, we will use the **Execute** method of the **Connection** object. The **Execute** method will take as input a SQL statement and pass that to the ODBC Data source. The database will execute the query and return the information to the object in the form of a Recordset object. The **Recordset** object encapsulates the methods and properties needed to access the individual rows and fields of a result from a database query.

```
' Write the header line to the output file and terminate with a
  Carriage Return and LineFeed
Response.Write ("Author,Title,ISBN,Subject,Series,Url")
Response.Write(vbCrLf)
```

The **Response** object in an Active Server page allows the developer to modify the response that will be returned to the browser. The **Write** method outputs the string information passed in its parameter to the requesting browser. We will use this method to output the information contained in the database to the data stream that will be read by the Tabular Data Control.

```
' Now loop through the recordset and write out the information to the
  file
Do While not RS.EOF
        Response.Write(RS("Author"))
        Response.Write(",")
```

The recordset that we have created to contain the results of the SQL query allows us to access each of the fields in each row. We write the contents of each field, in order, to the output stream, and separate them with a comma.

```
        Response.Write(RS("Title"))
        Response.Write(",")

        Response.Write(RS("ISBN"))
        Response.Write(",")

        Response.Write(RS("Subject"))
        Response.Write(",")

        Response.Write(RS("Series"))
        Response.Write(",")

        Response.Write(RS("Url"))

        ' Terminate with a Carriage Return and LineFeed
        Response.Write(vbCrLf)
```

As per the definition of the input file for the Tabular Data control, a new line character should terminate each record. In other words, a carriage return and linefeed.

```
            ' Move to the next record in the RecordSet
            RS.MoveNext
    Loop
%>
```

The **recordset** object contains all of the rows in the result. After the data from each record is written to the response file, you need to move to the next record. This is done with the **MoveNext** method of the **recordset** object.

Using the New Book Info file

If you save this file and view it locally in your web browser, you will find that IE4 is unable to view the file. It will ask you if you want to Open or Download the **bookInfo.asp** file. Obviously, this is not going to be very helpful to the Tabular Data Control.

Because of the way that Active Server Pages work, you need to access them through a web server. The web server, which can be any of a number that support Active Server Pages, including IIS, PWS, and O'Reilly WebSite, is required to execute the scripting calls inside the ASP file. This execution is done on the server when the HTTP request for an ASP file is received. The script is executed, and the data is returned to the calling application in the same way that a static web page would have been returned. So, when you access the **BookInfo.asp** file through a web server, you will see this:

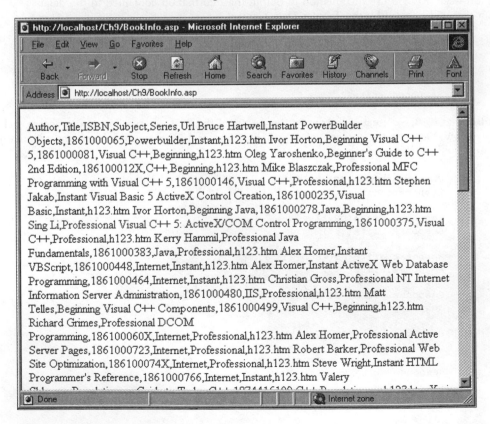

Well, it looks like the data that you need is there, but the formatting seems to be a bit messed up. Each record is supposed to be on a separate line, not separated by what appears to be a space. But, our data really is correct. If you remember back to your HTML parsing and display standards, you will find that carriage return and line feed characters are not interpreted when displaying an HTML file.

> *Yes, I could have used a command in the ASP file to change the response header from HTML to TXT, but why do that when the TDC control doesn't care?*

If you view the source file that is producing this web browser content, you will see a file that looks exactly the same as your original `BookInfo.TXT` file. Exactly the same formatting of data, so that it can be used for the Tabular Data Control. Here is the HTML source from the `BookInfo.asp` file when it is displayed in the browser.

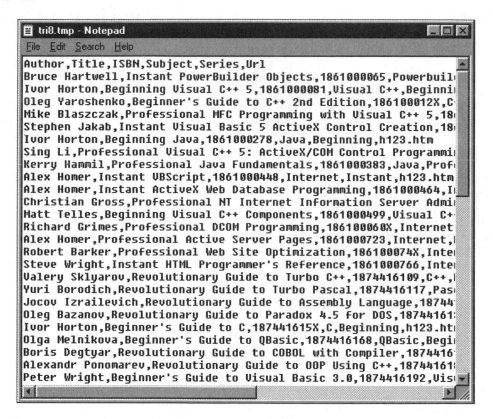

```
tri8.tmp - Notepad
File  Edit  Search  Help

Author,Title,ISBN,Subject,Series,Url
Bruce Hartwell,Instant PowerBuilder Objects,1861000065,Powerbuil
Ivor Horton,Beginning Visual C++ 5,1861000081,Visual C++,Beginni
Oleg Yaroshenko,Beginner's Guide to C++ 2nd Edition,186100012X,C
Mike Blaszczak,Professional MFC Programming with Visual C++ 5,18
Stephen Jakab,Instant Visual Basic 5 ActiveX Control Creation,18
Ivor Horton,Beginning Java,1861000278,Java,Beginning,h123.htm
Sing Li,Professional Visual C++ 5: ActiveX/COM Control Programmi
Kerry Hammil,Professional Java Fundamentals,1861000383,Java,Prof
Alex Homer,Instant VBScript,1861000448,Internet,Instant,h123.htm
Alex Homer,Instant ActiveX Web Database Programming,1861000464,I
Christian Gross,Professional NT Internet Information Server Admi
Matt Telles,Beginning Visual C++ Components,1861000499,Visual C+
Richard Grimes,Professional DCOM Programming,186100060X,Internet
Alex Homer,Professional Active Server Pages,1861000723,Internet,
Robert Barker,Professional Web Site Optimization,186100074X,Inte
Steve Wright,Instant HTML Programmer's Reference,1861000766,Inte
Valery Sklyarov,Revolutionary Guide to Turbo C++,1874416109,C++,
Yuri Borodich,Revolutionary Guide to Turbo Pascal,1874416117,Pas
Jocov Izrailevich,Revolutionary Guide to Assembly Language,18744
Oleg Bazanov,Revolutionary Guide to Paradox 4.5 for DOS,18744161
Ivor Horton,Beginner's Guide to C,187441615X,C,Beginning,h123.ht
Olga Melnikova,Beginner's Guide to QBasic,1874416168,QBasic,Begi
Boris Degtyar,Revolutionary Guide to COBOL with Compiler,1874416
Alexandr Ponomarev,Revolutionary Guide to OOP Using C++,18744161
Peter Wright,Beginner's Guide to Visual Basic 3.0,1874416192,Visi
```

Lastly, all that we need to do is modify the `<PARAM>` of the Tabular Data control so that it draws the data from the `ASP` file instead of the `TXT` file. To do this properly, we need to reference the `ASP` file through a server.

```
<OBJECT ID="books" WIDTH=100 HEIGHT=51
    CLASSID="CLSID:333C7BC4-460F-11D0-BC04-0080C7055A83">
<PARAM NAME="FieldDelim" VALUE=",">
<PARAM NAME="DataURL" VALUE="BookInfo.asp">
<PARAM NAME="UseHeader" VALUE=True>
</OBJECT>
```

Now you can view the TDC example again, this time it will draw the information from a database on the web server rather than from text file.

> *We will only get a blank page if we just embed the control into the page as it stands currently. To get the TDC to display data, the results have to be returned in the form of a table using the **DATASRC** attribute of table. Refer back to chapter 6 if you're unsure of how to do this.*

This short example has showed another way that you can meld the database access capabilities of Active Server Pages with the Tabular Data control of IE4. Once you have loaded the recordset into the TDC, you can use the sorting and filtering capabilities of the TDC to look at different views of the data.

Example 3 – Creating Simple Graphs with Structured Graphics and Active Server Pages

Now that you have seen how to access databases with Active Server pages, let's take a look at another way of using ASP with some of the new features of IE4. One of the most powerful new tools that is included with IE4 is the Structured Graphics control. This control allows for the creation of very lightweight vector-based graphics. The example in Chapter 11 showed how you could combine the different elements available in the Structured Graphics control to create a simple image like a stop sign. You can just as easily use this powerful control to create other types of graphics.

When you think about ways to combine databases with graphics, what comes to mind? One of the best ways to represents lists of data is to present them in the form of a graph. If you can take a list of numbers and display them as a graph, it becomes much easier for you to describe the information to someone looking at the graph than if you present them with a list of numbers. There have been ActiveX controls that allow you to create graphs from a list of data. But these were accompanied with the problems that come with ActiveX controls. Namely, if the user didn't have the control installed on their computer, then they would have to wait while the control is downloaded before viewing any of the information. But what if you could guarantee that they would already have the control installed on their machine?

The Structured Graphics control is available on every system that has IE4 installed on it. While it may not have all of the bells and whistles that graphing-specific ActiveX controls have, it still provides plenty of power to produce simple graphs. The key to using the Structured Graphics control for graphing is to couple it with Active Server Pages. Not only can Active Server pages access a database, the server-side scripting capabilities perform the calculations needed to help you format the graph.

Retrieving the Data from the Database

To begin our example we need to build an Active Server page that queries the database for the information that we require, and returns that to the user in a table. Once we are sure that our code to retrieve the information is correct, then we return the information to the Structured Graphic Control instead.

Our example will use a simple fictitious sales database. The database has one table, called BookSales. The data contained in this table represents the sales for a book by region. The data looks like:

Region	Sales
Asia	$18,250.00
Canada	$11,550.00
Europe	$26,500.00
Other	$18,000.00
United States	$65,000.00
	$0.00

BookSales : Table — Record: 6 of 6

If you remember back to the previous example, we showed you how to create an ODBC System DSN. You will need to create a System DSN called `707GRAPHING` that points to the database that contains the BookSales table. Once you create this DSN, you will be able to access the data using Active Server Pages.

To complete the next step, we will use this Active Server page to generate a table that displays the data stored in the table and also computes the percentage that each entry is of the total. This percentage value will be used to determine the size of each pie piece when we get around to displaying the graph.

```
<%
    ' Create the Database Connection Object
    Set DBConn = Server.CreateObject("ADODB.Connection")

    ' Open the ODBC datasource entitled GRAPHING
    DBConn.Open("707GRAPHING")

    'Define the SQL Query - this will calculate the total sales across all regions
    sql = "SELECT Sum([Sales]) AS Total FROM BookSales;"

    ' Execute the SQL Query and return the results in the RS Recordset Object
    set    RS = DBConn.Execute(sql)

    dim TotalSales
    TotalSales = RS("Total")

    'Define the SQL Query - this will retrieve all of the regional sales
    sql = "SELECT * FROM BookSales;"

    ' Execute the SQL Query and return the results in the RS Recordset Object
    set RS = DBConn.Execute(sql)
%>
<HTML>
<BODY>
<TABLE Border=1>
<TR>
    <TH>Region</TH>
    <TH>Sales</TH>
    <TH>Percentage</TH>
</TR>
<%
    'Now loop through the recordset and write out the information to the table
    Do While not RS.EOF
            Response.Write("<TR><TD>")
            Response.Write(RS("Region"))
```

```
                Response.Write("</TD><TD align=center>")
                Response.Write(FormatCurrency(RS("Sales")))
                Response.Write("</TD><TD align=center>")
                Response.Write(FormatPercent(RS("Sales")/TotalSales,2))
                Response.Write("</TD></TR>")

                ' Move to the next record in the RecordSet
                RS.MoveNext

        Loop
%>
</TABLE>

</BODY>
</HTML>
```

When you view this page through your ASP server, you will see:

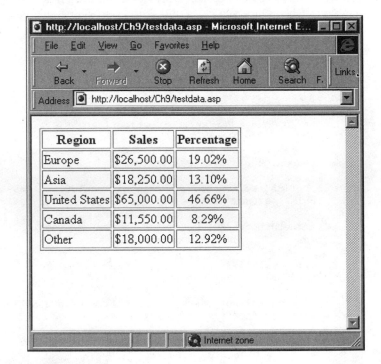

Creating a Pie Chart using Structured Graphics

Next we'll define the **<OBJECT>** and **<PARAM>** tags that will create a Pie Chart similar to what we want our final control to look like. First, we will just hardcode data into the control. Once we have the control the way we like it, we can change from the hardcoded data to data that is generated by Active Server page scripting. If you remember back to Chapter 11, and the introduction of the Structured Graphics Control, then here is a Dynamic HTML file that will create a pie chart:

```
<HTML>
<BODY BGCOLOR="Silver">
<OBJECT ID=sgPie STYLE="HEIGHT:220;WIDTH:520;TOP:0;LEFT:0;ZINDEX: 0"
CLASSID="CLSID:369303C2-D7AC-11D0-89D5-00A0C90833E6">
<PARAM NAME="Line0001" VALUE="SetLineColor(255, 0, 0)">
<PARAM NAME="Line0002" VALUE="SetLineStyle(1)">
<PARAM NAME="Line0003" VALUE="SetFillColor(64,128,64)">
<PARAM NAME="Line0004" VALUE="Pie(-250, -100, 200, 200,0,45,0)">
<PARAM NAME="Line0005" VALUE="Rect(0,-40,10,10,0)">
<PARAM NAME="Line0006" VALUE="SetFillColor(64,0,64)">
<PARAM NAME="Line0007" VALUE="Pie(-250, -100, 200, 200,45,80,0)">
<PARAM NAME="Line0008" VALUE="Rect(0,-10,10,10,0)">
<PARAM NAME="Line0009" VALUE="SetFillColor(255,255,0)">
<PARAM NAME="Line0010" VALUE="Pie(-250, -100, 200, 200,125,165,0)">
<PARAM NAME="Line0011" VALUE="Rect(0,20,10,10,0)">
<PARAM NAME="Line0012" VALUE="SetFillColor(0,255,255)">
<PARAM NAME="Line0013" VALUE="Pie(-250, -100, 200, 200,290,20,0)">
<PARAM NAME="Line0014" VALUE="Rect(0,50,10,10,0)">
<PARAM NAME="Line0015" VALUE="SetFillColor(128,0,255)">
<PARAM NAME="Line0016" VALUE="Pie(-250, -100, 200, 200,310,50,0)">
<PARAM NAME="Line0017" VALUE="Rect(0,80,10,10,0)">
<PARAM NAME="Line0018" VALUE="SetFont('Arial', 24,300,0,0,0)">
<PARAM NAME="Line0019" VALUE="SetLineColor(0,0,0)">
<PARAM NAME="Line0020" VALUE="SetFillColor(0,0,0,192,192,192)">
<PARAM NAME="Line0021" VALUE="SetFillSTYLE(1)">
<PARAM NAME="Line0022" VALUE="SetLineSTYLE(1)">
<PARAM NAME="Line0023" VALUE="Text('Legend',30,-70,0)">
<PARAM NAME="Line0024" VALUE="SetFont('Arial', 18,300,0,0,0)">
<PARAM NAME="Line0025" VALUE="SetFillColor(10,10,10,0,0,0)">
<PARAM NAME="Line0026" VALUE="Text('Value 1',20,-30,0)">
<PARAM NAME="Line0027" VALUE="Text('Value 2',20,0,0)">
<PARAM NAME="Line0028" VALUE="Text('Value 3',20,30,0)">
<PARAM NAME="Line0029" VALUE="Text('Value 4',20,60,0)">
<PARAM NAME="Line0030" VALUE="Text('Value 5',20,90,0)">

</OBJECT>

</BODY>
</HTML>
```

Basically, we are performing 3 main drawing tasks in this Dynamic HTML file:

▲   We are drawing the pie chart, with each piece in a different color

▲   We are drawing the text for the legend to the right of the chart

▲   We are drawing a rectangle in the color of the pie piece that matches the entry in the legend.

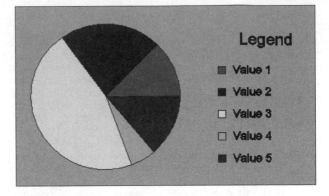

When you view this page in your IE4 browser, you will see:

As you can see from the screen shot, you now have a rudimentary pie chart that is showing some data. The next step is to use the results returned by the Tabular Data control to build the pie chart.

Integrating the Data with the Chart

So now that we have a way of retrieving and displaying the contents of the database table in the browser, we can move on to drawing the pie chart using live data.

```
<%
dim iRectTop
dim giLineCnt
```

In this step, you are creating two variables that will be used during the creation of the Structured Graphics control. The `iRectTop` variable will be used to identify the top position of the rectangle that defines the area of the text for the legend, and also for the square that links the text in the legend to the color in the pie chart.

Numbering the PARAM Line tags

The `giLineCnt` variable is used to maintain the current line count for the `<PARAM>` tags. This function should be added after the existing ASP code that loops through the recordset

```
Function GetLine()
        if giLineCnt < 10 then
                GetLine = "LINE000" & CStr(giLineCnt)
        else
                if giLineCnt >= 10 and giLineCnt < 100 then
                        GetLine = "LINE00"+Cstr(giLineCnt)
                end if
        end if
        giLineCnt = iLineCnt + 1
End Function
```

One of the issues in dynamically creating the `<PARAM>` entries for the Structured graphics control is that the `LINExxxx` values must be sequential. In order to do this, we have created a function that will perform two functions. First, it will maintain the current line count. This will be held in the `iLineCnt` variable, and will be incremented every time the function is called. Second, this function will correctly format the `LINE` value, and will return that to the caller. Since there is no generic Format function in VBScript, we have had to use some trickery to properly format the string that represents the line number. The requirement for the `<PARAM>` tag is that the number needs to be 4 digits, with the leading zeros kept intact.

Adding the Structured Graphics Control

```
%>
</TABLE>
<P>

<OBJECT ID=sgPie STYLE="HEIGHT:220;WIDTH:520;TOP:0;LEFT:0;ZINDEX: 0"
CLASSID="CLSID:369303C2-D7AC-11D0-89D5-00A0C90833E6">
<PARAM NAME="Line0001" VALUE="SetLineColor(255, 0, 0)">
<PARAM NAME="Line0002" VALUE="SetLineStyle(1)">
```

The first thing we will do to create the Pie chart is to instantiate the Structured Graphics object. This is the same code that is used in the pie chart that we created earlier from static data. The first two `<PARAM>` entries set the line color to pure red and the line style to solid.

```
Randomize
```

This VBScript procedure will seed the random number generator. We will be using randomly generated colors for each of the sections of the pie chart.

```
iLineCnt = 3
```

We will initialize the `iLineCnt` variable to 3 since we have already added two `<PARAM>` entries. This means that the next time that the `GetLine()` function is called, `LINE0003` will be returned to the caller.

```
dim iDegPos
iDegPos = 0
```

The `iDegPos` variable is used to define the starting position of the current pie piece, in degrees. We will increment this value after each piece is drawn, so that the next piece will be drawn where the first piece ends.

```
iRectTop = -40
```

The value of `iRectTop` identifies the vertical position of the top of the rectangle that will be drawn in the legend. This rectangle will be drawn in the same color as the pie piece for each specific entry.

Moving through the database

Since we have already looped through the database once in this ASP file, we need to reset the current record pointer to the first record in the recordset. The `MoveFirst` method will change the current record to the first record. We will then begin our loop through all of the records in the recordset.

```
dim szParam
dim iTmpColor
RS.MoveFirst
    do while not RS.EOF
            szParam = "<PARAM NAME="""
```

We will be using the **szParam** variable to build each of the **<PARAM>** entries before writing it to the output stream. Since the **<PARAM>** tag includes embedded quotes, we need to use a double quote so that VBScript does not interpret the quote to mean the end of the string. In this instance, with the three quotes at the end of the line, the last quote is used to terminate the string. The previous two will be interpreted by VBScript and will produce a quote character as part of the string. The variable **szParam** will have the value **<PARAM NAME = "** after this line has been executed:

```
szParam = szParam + GetLine()
```

We will now call the **GetLine()** function and append its output to the current value of **szParam**. If you recall earlier, we initialized the value of **iLineCnt** to 3, so the value that this function will return is **LINE0003**.

Coloring the Pie Chart

We will be generating a random color for each pie in the pie chart. To produce this random color, we will generate a random value for each of the R, G, and B parts of the color. This random value should be between 0 and 255.

```
szParam = szParam + """ VALUE=""SetFillColor("
dim iCnt
for iCnt = 1 to 3
        iTmpColor = Int(256 * Rnd)
        szParam = szParam + CStr(iTmpColor)
        if iCnt <> 3 then
                szParam = szParam + ","
        end if
next
```

To generate this random number, we use the **Rnd** function, which returns a decimal value between 0 and 1. We then multiply this by 256, to return a number between 0 and 255. Then we take the integer portion of the result, which can be used as a color value.

```
szParam = szParam & ")"">"
Response.Write (szParam + vbCrLf)
```

Once we have created the text of the **<PARAM>** entry, we will use the **Write** method of the **Response** object to output the string we created to the client. By appending the **vbCrLf** variable, which is the VBScript constant for carriage return and line feed, the source code displayed by the browser will break the line after the tag. The HTML parser doesn't care, it just treats it as white space.

```
szParam = "<PARAM NAME="""
szParam = szParam + GetLine()
szParam = szParam + """ VALUE=""Pie(-250, -100, 200, 200,"
```

Now that we have set the color, we will draw the piece of the pie chart for this record.

Drawing the Pieces of the Pie

The first four parameters of the **Pie** method set the top, left, height, and width of the bounding box that contains the pie element. The bounding box is described as the smallest box that will contain a full circle pie element. The center of the pie element will be at the center of the bounding box. For this example, we have placed the top of the box 250 pixels above the centerline of the Structured Graphics object, and the left of the box 100 pixels to the left. The box will be 200 pixels high, and 200 pixels wide. This will give us a pie element with a radius of 100 pixels.

```
szParam = szParam + CStr(iDegPos) + ","
```

Next, we set the starting position, in degrees, of the pie piece. This starting position, which was initialized to 0, is the point at which the previous piece ended.

```
szParam = szParam + CStr(Cint(RS("Sales")\TotalSales*360))
```

Now we will calculate the size of the piece in degrees. We have calculated the total sales and stored that value in the **TotalSales** variable. By dividing the sales for the current record into the total, we arrive at the percentage of total sales. Then, multiplying by 360 degrees will produce the angle of the arc that should be swept by the pie piece.

```
iDegPos = iDegPos + CInt(RS("Sales")\TotalSales*360)
```

The angle of the piece is also added to the **iDegPos** variable. This variable will now hold the ending point of the element being added, so that the next one can be added directly adjacent to it.

```
szParam = szParam + ",0)"">"
Response.Write (szParam + vbCrLf)
```

The last parameter, rotation, is set to 0. Since these elements will make up a complete circle, there is no need to rotate any of the pieces. As long as this value was the same for every Pie **<PARAM>** tag, any value between 0 and 360 could be used here.

Drawing the Legend Color References

Next, we will draw a rectangle in the legend that will show the color used for the current piece.

```
szParam = "<PARAM NAME="""
szParam = szParam + GetLine()
szParam = szParam + """ VALUE=""Rect(0,"
szParam = szParam + CStr(iRectTop)
iRectTop = iRectTop + 30
```

This rectangle will be drawn with its top position specified by the **iRectTop** variable. The value of **iRectTop** will then be incremented to space the rectangles vertically in the legend. By adding 30 pixels to **iRectTop**, and having a rectangle height of 10 pixels, the next rectangle in the legend will be 20 pixels below the previous rectangle.

> *We will not be drawing the text for the legend here as it would require setting the fill color and line colors to black each time.*

```
szParam = szParam + ",10,10,0)"">"
Response.Write (szParam + VBCrlf)

RS.MoveNext
Loop
```

Drawing the Legend Text

After completing all of the pieces in the pie, we will move on to the text for the legend. The legend caption will be in a 24 point Arial typeface with normal weighting.

```
szParam = "<PARAM NAME=""" + GetLine() + """ "
szParam = szParam + "VALUE=""""SetFont('Arial', 24,300,0,0,0)"">"
Response.Write (szParam + VBCrlf)

szParam = "<PARAM NAME=""" + GetLine() + """ "
szParam = szParam + "VALUE=""""SetLineColor(0,0,0)"">"
Response.Write (szParam + VBCrlf)

szParam = "<PARAM NAME=""" + GetLine() + """ "
szParam = szParam + "VALUE=""""SetFillColor(0,0,0,192,192,192)"">"
Response.Write (szParam + VBCrlf)

szParam = "<PARAM NAME=""" + GetLine() + """ "
szParam = szParam + "VALUE=""""SetFillSTYLE(1)"">"
Response.Write (szParam + VBCrlf)

szParam = "<PARAM NAME=""" + GetLine() + """ "
szParam = szParam + "VALUE=""""SetLineSTYLE(1)"">"
Response.Write (szParam + VBCrlf)
```

These `<PARAM>` entries are used to set the color for the fill and line to black, and styles for the fill and line to solid. This will produce the most legible text. Because the background for the page is gray, the background color in the `SetFillColor` method is set to gray as well.

```
szParam = "<PARAM NAME=""" + GetLine() + """ "
szParam = szParam + "VALUE=""""Text('Legend',30,-70,0)"">"
Response.Write (szParam + VBCrlf)
```

The `Text` entry is used to output the title for the legend. In this case, the title simply reads *Legend*. This title is centered above the colored rectangles and labels in the legend.

```
szParam = "<PARAM NAME=""" + GetLine() + """ "
szParam = szParam + "VALUE=""""SetFont('Arial', 18,300,0,0,0)"">"
Response.Write (szParam + VBCrlf)

szParam = "<PARAM NAME=""" + GetLine() + """ "
szParam = szParam + "VALUE=""""SetFillColor(10,10,10,0,0,0)"">"
Response.Write (szParam + VBCrlf)
```

The font for the labels inside the legend is set to 18 point Arial with normal weighting. The color is lightened slightly from pure black to make it stand out slightly from the title above the legend.

```
iRectTop = -30
```

The `iRectTop` variable will be used to position the bottom of each line of text. Since the colored rectangles are 10 pixels high, and we would like the bottom of the rectangle to line up with the bottom of the text, the first line of text should be placed 30 pixels above the centerline of the control.

```
RS.MoveFirst
```

The current record pointer should be reset to the first record so that we can loop through the records to retrieve the names to put into the legend.

```
Do While not RS.EOF
        szParam = "<PARAM NAME=""" + GetLine() + """ "
        szParam = szParam + "VALUE=""Text('"
        szParam = szParam + RS("Region")
        szParam = szParam + "',20," + CStr(iRectTop)
        iRectTop = iRectTop + 30
```

The value contained in the Region field of each record is drawn onto the Structured Graphics control using the text method. The vertical position is then incremented by 30 pixels, which is the same spacing that was used when the colored rectangles were drawn. This will ensure that the text will remain aligned with the rectangles.

```
        szParam = szParam + ",0)"">"
        Response.Write (szParam + VBCrlf)

        RS.MoveNext
    Loop
%>
</OBJECT>

</BODY>
</HTML>
```

We have now successfully created an Active Server page that will generate both a table and a graph from data stored in a database. When is page is viewed through the IE4 browser, you will see:

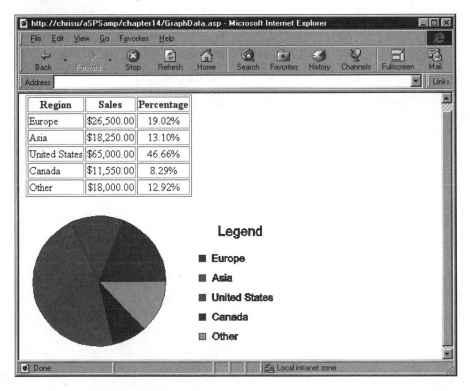

You might notice that the colors on your graph are different from the shading in this example. This is due to the random selection of colors that was implemented above.

There are many other ways that structured graphics controls can be used through Active Server pages. Since all of the data necessary to create the graph has already been retrieved, you could ask the user if they would prefer a line or bar chart, instead of a pie chart. The Active Server page code would remain almost exactly the same. The only difference would be in the type of graphics that were created with the Segmented Graphics control.

Summary

You have just seen three examples on how the integration of the features of IE4 with Active Server pages can be used to create more "dynamic" web pages. The most important parts of the chapter we have discussed are:

▲ Using the incoming request to determine if the requesting browser supports the features of IE4. Once this is known by the server, it can return a page that takes full advantage of the features of IE4 to a client that can support it. If the client does not support it, it can return the information in a less effective, yet still complete manner.

▲ How to combine the IE4 Tabular Data control to provide client-side filtering and sorting capabilities, with the database access power of Active Server pages. By using the Database object of the Active Server, the information that populates the Tabular Data control can come from any ODBC-accessible data source.

▲ And how to use the database capabilities of Active Server Pages and the Segmented Graphics control of IE4 to build graphs of live data. This technique can produce graphs can be displayed on any IE4 client without the need for downloading a special ActiveX Graphing control.

In the first three parts of our journey through the world of IE4, we have seen the many new and exciting features that it adds the world of web page design. And by combining the power of this new client platform, with the versatility and accessibility of Active Server Pages, you now have access to a very powerful, and complete, application development environment. Next, we will take a look at the ways in which IE 4 is changing the way you interact with your computer at every level. The new features that will reshape the face of Windows are Channels and the Active Desktop.

Working with the Active Desktop

PART

4

By now, we've covered all the major new features in Internet Explorer 4 and Dynamic HTML—with the exception of one topic. In fact, depending on the options you selected when you installed IE4, this may be the thing that struck you first as being something really new and exciting. The browser is now very closely integrated with the entire Windows operating system. If you installed it in full 'Desktop Integration Mode', you'll already have seen how it changes the entire Windows desktop.

This is what Microsoft refer to as the Active Desktop, and it blends with the topics we met at the end of the previous chapter where we considered the Active Server environment. Together, they provide a single-application, all-encompassing view of the Web and your own computer. Now, you aren't using just a desktop machine, but a part of the global network that is the Internet.

As developers, the Active Desktop provides a whole raft of new opportunities. Perhaps the most exciting of these is webcasting. By this we can arrange for our Web sites to appear as Channels or Subscriptions on the user's system, and be available any time, at the click of a button, even when the user is offline. Also we don't require the user to actively browse pages any more for regular updates to the pages, they can just tell IE4 to go and get them on its own at specified times during the week. We can even place our Web pages or custom components directly on the user's desktop, permanently visible and updated over the 'Net on a regular basis.

The Active Desktop paradigm even extends to application installation. Using a system called Open Software Distribution, we can even install and upgrade software on the user's system automatically, when and as required, from our Web site on the other side of the world. Without a doubt, the Active Desktop provides many new and exciting ways to develop your site, so as to take full advantage of it. In this part of the book, you'll see how to get started.

Webcasting, Active Channels and Application Channels

With an overwhelming amount of information now available online, how much time do you spend surfing the globe to your favorite Web sites only to find that there have been no changes since your previous visit? If we scale up this time by the Internet population we can see that the world wastes a huge amount of time and bandwidth achieving absolutely nothing but frustration.

Wouldn't it be nice if you could be automatically notified when such sites have been updated with new information? Furthermore, wouldn't it be good if such updated content could be automatically downloaded so that the complete set was readily available for perusal at a more convenient time. This could be when your link to the Internet is no longer available thus enabling the online communications costs to be reduced. As an example, consider a mobile user who could have the latest news and sports articles downloaded to a laptop during the day–this information could then be available for reading offline, perhaps on the evening train ride home.

IE4 has implemented a powerful set of features which work in conjunction with Dynamic HTML and ActiveX (scripting and software components) to provide the automated delivery of compelling, personalized and up-to-date information. Dynamic HTML enables rich content without the user having to invoke redundant or time-consuming trips to the web server. This is known as **webcasting**, and, as much as anything else in IE4, fulfills Bill Gate's vision of *Information at Your Fingertips*, (see Appendix A for further details).

So in this chapter we are going to see:

- ▲ How webcasting effectively turns the Web surfer into a Web subscriber
- ▲ The benefits webcasting brings, and the method used to subscribe to channels
- ▲ How the basic process can be improved if the content provider creates **Active Channels** by means of specifying suitable webcasting options using **Channel Definition Format (CDF)** files
- ▲ Extensions to CDF to create **Application Channels** which ensure the desktop has downloaded and installed the latest versions of the operating system, device drivers and applications software.

Webcasting

Previous to the introduction of webcasting, a web user had to actively browse Web sites and request or 'pull' information from the Web server down to the client machine. Fortunately many vendors (including PointCast, BackWeb and Marimba) recognized this as a problem and implemented products with useful features to address these issues. These features are known as **webcasting** or **'push technologies'**.

In the webcasting model, the web user first indicates some interest in a site or information theme – for example this could be a site that produces a daily news bulletin addressing the latest changes and announcements in software and hardware technologies. Any detected changes to this information are highlighted to the user and, optionally, the information will be downloaded automatically into the users' cache.

Smart Pull vs True Push

As the amount of information on the Internet and corporate Intranets grow, the previous model for data retrieval is becoming both time consuming and inefficient. Furthermore the current Internet infrastructure and network traffic implications severely restricts opportunities for rich end-user experiences. Webcasting enables key information and compelling content to reach an intended audience in a personalized and timely manner, without overloading either the networks, or a reader's tolerance for irrelevant information.

Webcasting is designed to meet the needs of two kinds of Web users:

- **Dial-up users who spend the majority of time offline** (for example, home and mobile users). Webcasting enables users to quickly obtain a set of pages that they are interested in without having to navigate them one-by-one to ensure they are available in the cache. This means that less time is necessary on-line, although this situation may reverse as users end up subscribing to more and more channels.

- **LAN-based corporate users who have a constant Internet connection.** Webcasting will inform these users when the site content changes. Automatic download to the users' cache is not so critical but, depending on the complexity of the Web content and the type of Internet connection, it can improve performance and ultimately the users' experience.

IE4 provides three different types of webcasting:

- **Basic Webcasting** – IE4 performs a scheduled **webcrawl** of the site content looking for updated items and optionally downloads the content. Webcrawl is the term given to exploring all referenced hyperlinks and embedded content down to a predefined depth.

- **Managed Webcasting** – IE4 allows a content provider to fully control how information is webcast by authoring a CDF file–this provides an index of Web resources and a recommended schedule for when the local cached copy should be updated.

- **True Webcasting** – IE4 interfaces with other software components using ActiveX technologies to receive information transmitted using various IP communications protocols.

IE4 basic and managed webcasting works with any server, any HTTP proxy, any HTML Web site, and any Web authoring tool. While these are regarded as a 'push' technologies, they are in fact just IE4 automating the initiation of standard HTTP requests – so really, a more accurate description for these mechanisms would be **smart pull technologies**.

With true webcasting, **true-push** is possible where information is actually broadcast using special communication protocols and appropriately configured networks. These avoid having to establish direct connections with each user and enables the efficient use of bandwidth by the server only having to transmit the information once, rather than repetitively for each target desktop. In the future, we can expect satellites to push large volumes of information in this way, and someday we will no doubt be able to tune into our favorite Internet Channel! True webcasting is supported by Microsoft NetShow, which we looked at in Chapter 13, but its webcasting capabilities are beyond the scope of this book.

Subscriptions

IE4 automatically allows basic webcasting of any Web site without requiring any changes to the structure or content of the site. It does this by performing a webcrawl of the site content checking for any updated content and optionally downloading the changed items for off-line use. IE4 looks at the **robots.txt** file contained in the root directory of the HTTP server to determine which files it should crawl. Care has to be taken when specifying the depth of files for the webcrawl, since if you set a value too large then a huge quantity of information could be retrieved.

To prevent IE4 from crawling your site, simply insert the following line into the **<HEAD>** of any page, **<META NAME="ROBOTS" CONTENT="NOFOLLOW">**. If you wish to protect a set of pages against IE4 webcrawling, then you can put the following information in the **robots.txt** file:

> *User-Agent:MSIECrawler*
>
> *Disallow:/**pathname**/*
>
> ***pathname*** *being the path that IE4 should not crawl.*

The process of configuring IE4 to periodically check for updated content and download it is known as **subscribing** to the site. Subscriptions build on the concept of **favorites**, found in previous versions of Internet Explorer, which are simply shortcuts to frequently visited sites. With IE4, these become **smart favorites** and have the ability to schedule the webcrawl, notify the user of any changes, and deliver the content to the desktop. If any changed content is detected then the user can be notified by a red (black in the screenshot) **gleam** icon on the Favorites menu, on the list of subscriptions or alternatively by the receipt of an email message.

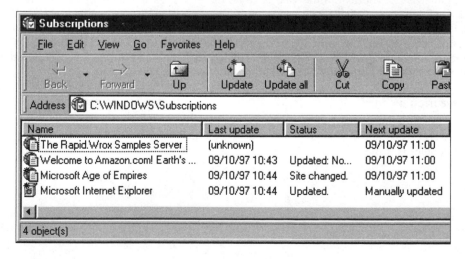

Such subscriptions work with any existing Web site and with minimal effort they can provide the following benefits:

- ▲ Users can easily stay up-to-date with changing Web sites without having to manually monitor the content

- ▲ Home users can download their favorite sites to work offline thus reducing phone bills and obtaining better performance

- ▲ Mobile users can take the Web anywhere

Subscribing to a Web Site

In order to subscribe to a Web site, we first need to navigate to the location from which we begin our webcrawl. It is important that the URL shown in the address bar is the address of the area for subscription – take care because there are some scenarios using frames when the web browser's address bar does not get updated with the name of your displayed document. The actual URL of a document within a frameset can be examined by right clicking on the page and selecting Properties.

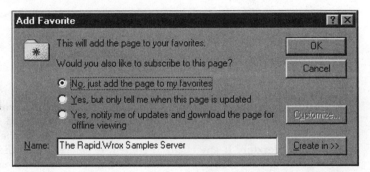

Once we have successfully navigated to the Web page to which we wish to subscribe, choose the Add to Favorites menu option from the Favorites menu. Following this selection, we are presented with the Add Favorite dialog.

Here, we can either add a shortcut to the Web page on the Favorites menu, as in IE3, or subscribe to the Web page. Two options are available with subscriptions: in both cases we are notified when a Web page is updated but the second option requests that the changed content is automatically downloaded to the desktop. We can either accept the subscription based on the default values or, if we want to do more than just add the item to our favorites, we can press the Customize button. This runs the customization wizard, which allows you to specify additional information to fine tune your subscription.

The Customization Wizard

To access the Customization Wizard, click on the Customize button. This wizard guides us in turn through several dialog screens that allow us to configure the various subscription options. If we specify that the changed Web content is to be downloaded, the wizard asks us if we wish to webcrawl any referenced pages.

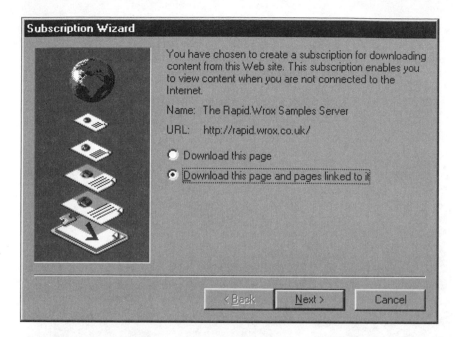

If the webcrawl mode is requested, the next screen in the wizard's sequence allows the webcrawl depth (i.e. number of levels of linked pages) to be specified. But we must take care with our choice of depth value as some Web documents have a large number of hyperlinks embedded into them, and selecting this option could cause an avalanche of requests for documents consuming both online time and disk space.

You can also determine within the Wizard whether you wish to be notified of content changes via e-mail.

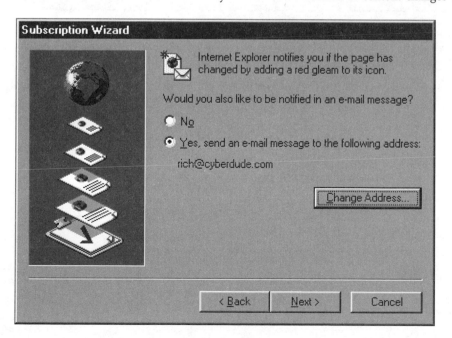

If we have selected the content to be downloaded, the next screen in the Wizard's sequence allows us to choose whether the downloaded should occur automatically, by means of a configured schedule, or by the user manually requesting the option to be invoked. If we choose to design our own schedule then we can get to the Custom Schedule dialog by pressing the Edit button.

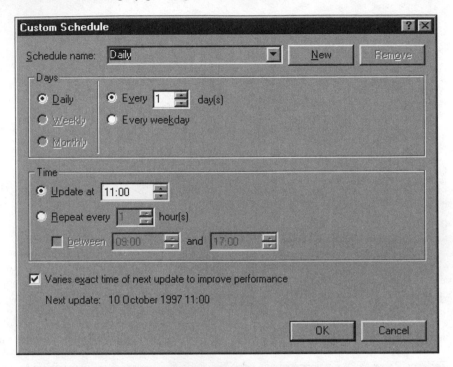

Finally, we can specify the login details if the Web site we are subscribing to forces user authentication. Most Web sites are enabled for anonymous access but you will be told of any logon requirements when you first navigate to a restricted site.

Configuring a subscription

Even though the Customization Wizard is useful, it does not give us access to all the options we can set for our subscription. To modify the other parameters and maintain the values that we have already set, we first have to view the list of our subscriptions. This is achieved via the Manage Subscriptions menu item from the Favorites menu. By right clicking on an item in the list, we can view the subscription content via the Open menu item, instigate a manual update, copy and delete the subscription, and access the further options via the Properties command. Selecting the Properties option provides the following tabbed dialog. The Subscription tab provides mostly information, plus an option to unsubscribe to the Web site.

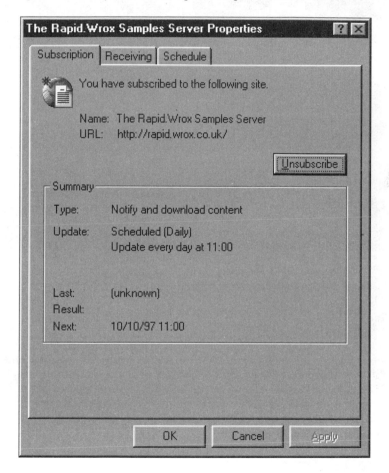

The Receiving tab allows us to specify whether we are only notified of content changes, or if the content should be downloaded. We can be either notified through e-mail, or through a gleam on the subscription icon in the icon tray. It also provides access to a login screen similar to the one we saw in the Customization Wizard. This Receiving tab also provides us with a route to a very useful screen via the Advanced button. When this button is invoked, the Advanced Download Options dialog is displayed.

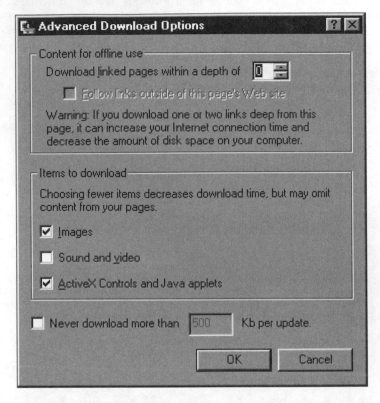

This page can save us a lot of time by instructing IE4 to only download the type of content that we are interested in. It enables us to specify the maximum download size per update and the type of content we wish to download. HTML documents are automatically part of the subscription and are usually not too heavy on our Internet connection. However, we are given the option of whether we want to download images, sound and video, ActiveX controls and Java applets.

Finally, the Schedule tab provides us with the following options for retrieving any updated Web content that belong to our subscription:

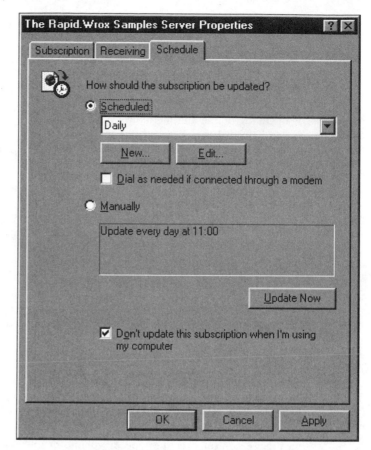

- ▲ **Schedule** – this option allows us to choose a default schedule, a publisher's recommended schedule or create one of our own. Custom schedules allow us to specify reoccurring updates based on months, weeks, days, hours and minutes.

- ▲ **Manual** – this option provides us with a mechanism to update the subscription contents immediately when we click the Update Now button. (However, rather than navigating to this button, a more convenient alternative is to update all our subscriptions, by selecting the Update All Subscriptions menu item from Favorites menu).

Once you've customized a schedule, you can then download content to browse at any time, even when you're not actually connected to the Internet.

Working Offline

After subscribing to a Web site, IE4 automatically visits the pages at a frequency based on the selected schedule. Any pages that are downloaded as part of the subscription's webcrawling or during online browsing are cached on the desktop's hard drive.

The user can direct IE4 to operate in Offline mode by selecting the File|Work Offline menu item–this is indicated by an 'offline icon' in the status bar and by the addition of the text [Working Offline] to the title bar of the window.

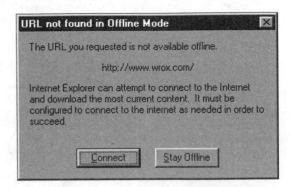

If the user is operating offline and the mouse pointer is hovering over an item that is not cached, the mouse pointer will adopt a no-entry sign. If the user then clicks on such an item, a dialog will be displayed giving the user the option of either connecting to the network to proceed or staying offline.

Disadvantages of Basic Webcasting

While basic webcasting is easy to for the average Web user to setup, the technique of webcrawling has several disadvantages that highlight the need for a better managed approach.

Some of the problems are:

- Setting up a subscription for Web content is the responsibility of the Web user and, as we have seen, numerous options need to be set in order to make the webcrawling fruitful – some inexperienced users might find the range of options bewildering.

- When a user subscribes to a site and requests a webcrawl to several levels of depth, there is no precise control over the type or volume of information received. Often large quantities of unwanted information will be downloaded to the desktop, and consume both bandwidth and hard disk.

- Unless the times of Web content changes are made available to the user and an appropriate schedule is configured, it is unlikely that the user will receive well-timed update notifications. It is possible that IE4 could update the subscription contents just before the newest content is made available on the site.

- Some Web site administrators do not like external systems webcrawling their sites since this can produce a high load on the server to the detriment of any clients currently accessing their systems. IE4 will conform to the HTML <META> tags that request (but cannot force) webcrawlers to ignore the site.

While Microsoft has provided a useful webcrawling facility within IE4, basic webcasting does not provide the complete solution for a really productive 'push' service. In order to overcome the problems associated with Basic webcasting, Microsoft has introduced within IE4 the next level of webcasting, known as **managed webcasting**. We mentioned earlier that managed webcasting enables content providers to write a CDF file that will fully control how information is webcast, so let's now see this in action.

Active Channels

An **Active Channel** is a Web site that has been designed for managed webcasting by sending timely and appropriate information to a Channel Definition Format (CDF) compatible Web Browser such as IE4. Channels are created by referencing all appropriate resources, relevant to a theme, within a single item – the CDF file. The actual contents may be taken from all over the web site or any web site, and indeed, different channels may even overlap and take the same content from a web site. With managed webcasting the Web site author is in control of both the channel content and the scheduling, and so the information delivery system is no longer the hit-and-miss as it was with basic webcasting.

The information can be delivered to the user using one or more of the following mechanisms:

- Web browser – the traditional approach
- Theatre/Kiosk/Full Screen mode – giving the largest window in which to present the information
- Screen Savers – which are cycled through when no user activity is occurring
- Active Desktop Items – mini windows placed on the Active Desktop
- HTML mail – delivering content direct to the users' inbox.

And as we have already discussed, once the information has arrived at the desktop, the user no longer needs to be online to inspect its content.

Active Channel User Interface

The Active Channel user interface is similar to the concept of a television – where a series of buttons allow the user to view and switch between the channel providers. Channel providers will typically provide icons and logos representing their Active Channel. The channel buttons can be accessed several ways. One method of accessing the channels is through the channel bar. The channel bar contains buttons for all of the channels to which the user has subscribed, plus the channel guide, which contains a list, maintained by Microsoft, of all the known Active Channels.

Alternatively, the channels can be accessed via the Favorites menu, either from the IE4 menu bar or, if the Active Desktop is enabled, using the Windows shell Start button.

The Channel Pane and Channel Links

You can also access channels using the View Channels icon in the Quick Launch band of the task bar. This invokes IE4 in full screen mode with a **channel pane** on the left-hand side of the screen.

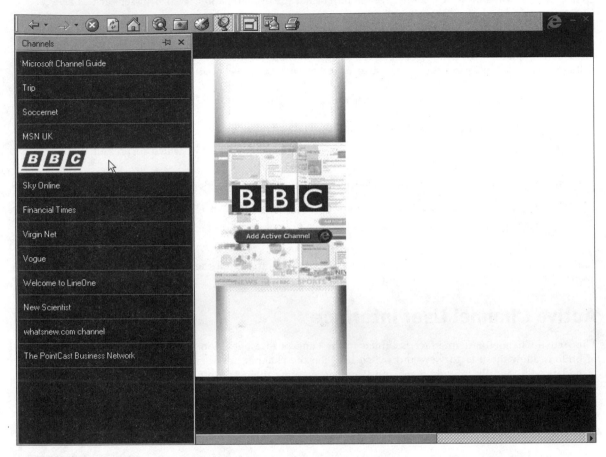

The web site author provides access to a channel by including a hyperlink to a CDF file on one of their Web pages. We'll look at how you can create a link yourself in Chapter 17. Typically this link will be an image highlighting that a subscription to a channel is available such as the Add Active Channel link in the previous screenshot.

Once the Web user clicks the hyperlink, the channel subscription confirmation box is displayed showing the channel name and associated URL of the CDF file. This is similar to the Subscription dialog that we obtained earlier when we subscribed using basic webcasting. As before, we can invoke the Customization Wizard to override the default CDF subscription properties, for example, we can adjust the notification method or change the amount and type of content that is downloaded to the desktop cache. On acceptance of the channel subscription dialog, the channel is displayed full screen giving the channel author a large canvas on which to deliver their compelling content.

The channel pane within IE4 can also show **sub-items** with the channel, and clicking a parent item can further expand the channel hierarchy to show its contents. The channel provider must specify such information in the CDF file. The user can select such items to navigate directly to the associated item within the channel.

A channel provider can tag certain pages for screen saver contents. All screen savers from subscribed sites will be rotated through when no machine usage has been detected for a configured period of time. All of these channels are created using one language, namely CDF.

The Channel Definition Format Language

CDF is an easily authored language that allows site authors to optimize, personalize and have complete control of how a site is webcast. The CDF standard for creating channels provides the following benefits:

- Any conventional Web site can easily become an Active Channel by providing one or more CDF files.

- Scheduling information can be centrally defined by the content provider and thus will be set to the schedule that reflects the author's intentions for updating the site

▲ The channel content indexing is independent of the site structure, so tightly defined channel contents can be defined.

▲ Content can be personalized using ASP.

▲ The CDF structure is an open standard supported by many vendors and is freely available to all Web site authors.

XML and SGML: The Parent Languages

Before we look any further at CDF, we need to look very briefly at the language from which it was derived, XML or eXtensible Markup Language. XML is emerging as a standard language for describing and interchanging information. It is supported by many of the major Internet software vendors and will be used in many of their technologies and future proposals. If XML sounds similar to HTML, that's because it is. Indeed, HTML and XML are both derived from the same parent, known as SGML or Standard Generalized Markup Language. SGML is a theoretical language (one that you can't program in or compile – it only exists in paper format) for describing other languages. Its most popular application is HTML. However, HTML is just one application of SGML, and it lacks many of SGML's intended benefits, such as adaptability.

HTML isn't adaptable, because the set of tags you're given are the ones that you're stuck with. Say you wanted something other than an `<OBJECT>` tag to place objects with; unfortunately, that's too bad, you're stuck with just this tag. HTML is just one fixed and unchangeable application of SGML. XML, however, isn't just a single application of SGML: it's a programmable version of SGML, albeit a very simplified one. Therefore, XML isn't limited by a fixed set of tags, since you can define them yourself. If you were a car dealer, setting up a car database, you could invent your own `<CADILLAC>` and `<CHEVROLET>` tags. Think of it like this: XML is like the rules of grammar, an overall structure for defining language; meanwhile, HTML is the vocabulary, the actual words that you use.

Further information on XML can be found at `http://www.w3.org/xml`.

CDF's Relationship to HTML

So, CDF is an application of XML, in the same way that HTML is an application of SGML. CDF is an HTML-like language itself. You can use tags, you can set attributes: it's all very familiar. In fact, unless you look closely at CDF and you already know some HTML, you probably wouldn't be able to tell the two apart. So why do you even need CDF? Well, CDF is like a mini-HTML language that has been created to serve a very specific purpose. HTML has one very wide-ranging purpose, which is defining documents - generally for display on an intranet or the web. This can make HTML inflexible, at times, since it can be used by anybody from a graphic designer, developing a new hi-tech multimedia site, to a university lecturer publishing a white paper. How can HTML possibly meet the diverse needs of everyone?

CDF, on the other hand, has a simple set of purposes: organize the structure of an IE4 channel, and lay down a recommended schedule for updating the channel. CDF is basically used to outline the URLs of graphics on the channel, position the channel graphics on the screen, and set an automatic schedule for downloading. This is all it needs to do, and so consequently is very simple to learn.

A complete reference guide to CDF is available in Appendix F – please refer to this as you proceed through our remaining discussions on channels.

Microsoft CDF Generator – Creating the CDF

However, we'll start by creating a CDF file, using a simple wizard type tool – called the Microsoft CDF Generator (also known as Liburnia during development) – that can be used by inexperienced channel developers to quickly provide a channel for their Web site. We'll then look at what each of the CDF tags does in our example CDF file, before we can go on to utilize our CDF file in an example web site. The CDF Generator is provided in the Microsoft Internet Client SDK that is freely downloadable from the Microsoft Web site at `http://www.microsoft.com/msdn/sdk/inetsdk/asetup/default.asp`.

The Structure of our Example Channel Site

Before we can begin, we need to define an arbitrary structure for our example web site. This example will have seven Dynamic HTML pages and one CDF file. These are:

- `default.htm` – the home page which has the Add Active Channel graphic and hyperlinks to the following subsidiary pages that make up the content of the channel.

- `first.htm` – First Topic

- `first-a.htm` – First Topic Part A

- `first-b.htm` – First Topic Part B

- `second.htm` – Second Topic

- `third.htm` – Third Topic

- `scrnsave.htm` – a screen saver

- `channel.cdf` – the example CDF which we met earlier. This contains a definition of the channel and hierarchical organization of the main and sub-pages, the URLs of the graphics, and a few automatic download scheduling options.

We can now get down to the business of creating `channel.cdf`.

Starting the CDF Generator

Once the SDK is installed you find the Generator located in the `BIN` directory of the SDK, which goes by the file name of `CDFGEN.EXE`. If you run this file to invoke the generator, you will see displayed a window containing two panes to provide the following:

- CDF Structure – an 'explorer' type view illustrating the hierarchical representation of the file contents. Each entry in the tree represents a CDF element tag; the tag type is indicated by an appropriate icon and text entry. In large complex CDF files it is possible, via the menu options, to hide tags of a certain type in order to clarify the structure and contents.

- CDF Contents – the complete file in text format. You are unable to edit within this window directly, any editing must be done via the CDF generator's wizard.

CDF Structure   CDF Contents

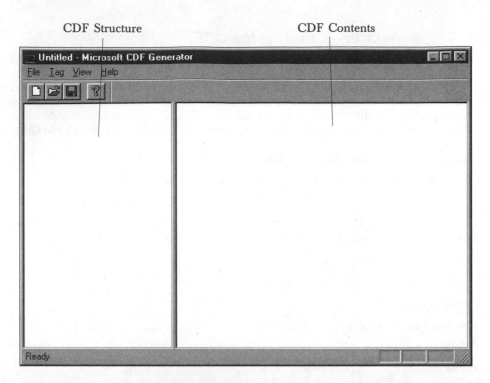

To create our CDF file, we first select the New menu item from the File menu, which then invokes the CDF Creation Wizard to help us generate the element tags in our channel. You are greeted by a set of dialogs.

General Channel Information Dialog

The first dialog allows us to specify the general channel information:

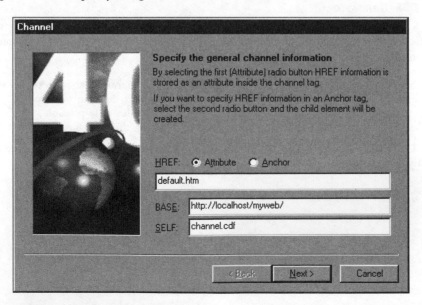

Enter the following values:

- ▲ **HREF** – default.htm – this is the URL of the top page of the channel (this can be resolved using **BASE**)

- ▲ **BASE** – http://*your_web_address*/ – this is the default address of the channel site and used to resolve file names – this value should be set to an appropriate address for the Web server from which you are running the example. In this example, our web server is called **localhost** and the directory the files are placed in is **myweb**.

- ▲ **SELF** – channel.cdf – this is the URL of the CDF file (the full name can be resolved using BASE)

When you select the **HREF**, you also have a choice of whether to enter the URL of the top page as either an Attribute or Anchor. It doesn't matter whether you insert the **HREF** value as an attribute of the **<CHANNEL>** element or if you include it as an attribute of the **<A>** element, as they both provide the same function. The Anchor choice was probably included for compatibility with Netscape pages. For the sake of our example, just click on Attribute, if it isn't already selected, then click on Next to go onto the next dialog.

Additional Information Dialog

This dialog provides data for the **<TITLE>** and **<ABSTRACT>** elements. Enter the following:

- ▲ **Title** – Example Channel – this is the title of the channel and appears as a tool-tip on the channel button.

- ▲ **Abstract** – This is an example channel – this describes the content of the channel and is in channel guides.

- ▲ **Log** – *uncheck*– this is used to log events; we shall not be using this.

Click Next to go onto the next dialog.

Logos Dialog

This dialog is for the images and icons. Enter the following:

- ▲ **Icon** – icon.gif – this is the image filename (**.ICO**) used on the Favorites menus

- ▲ **Image** – logo.gif – this is the image filename (**.GIF** or **.JPG**) used on the channel bar and channel pane. You need to check this option as it's unchecked by default.

- ▲ **Wide** – *leave unchecked*, as we won't be using it.

Click on Next.

Scheduling Dialog

The scheduling dialog is used to define when the site will be polled for updates and can be used to control when the traffic peaks will occur. We shall enter:

- **Start Date** – 1997.09.16T22:14+0000 – this is date from which the schedule will apply

- **End Date** – 1999.09.16T22:14+0000 – this is the date on which the schedule will expire

- **Timings**: The timings are entered by spin button controls. Click on the three check boxes, to enable the spin button controls:

> **Interval time** – this specifies the period of time in which the schedule is repeated
>
> **Earliest time** – this specifies the start of the time period in which a download may occur
>
> **Lastest time** – this specifies the end of the time period in which a download may occur

> Enter **Day** – 1, **Hour** – 4 and **Minutes** – 7

The **Start Date** and **End Date** values must take this format *yyyy.mm.ddThh:mm+TimeZoneOffset*. So, the start date 1997.09.16T22:14+0000 actually translates to 16th September 1997, the time is 10:14 in the evening, and there is no timezone offset. Click on Next.

Log Destination and Login Information Dialogs

The final two dialogs are used to specify a log destination for client activity and to specify a username and password to enable the server to authenticate the user.

> *The logging feature provided by Active Channels enables a user to collect page-hit information from both offline and online users. The logs are stored client-side in a location, specified in the CDF generator and placed in the* **<LOGTARGET>** *element. This element is used in conjunction with the* **<LOG>** *element, which indicates which items are to be logged. Web publishers receive the page-hit logging files in something known as* **Extended Log File Format***. Every page hit that is logged has two types of records associated with it. The first record is a header and records following the header give details of the page hits.*

Uncheck both the Log Target and the Login boxes as we won't be entering anything in either of them. Then click on Next once more. This leads you to a final confirmation dialog which displays the CDF you have just generated and asks you to confirm that the contents are fine, before continuing. Click on Finish and the values you have entered are then used to generate the CDF file.

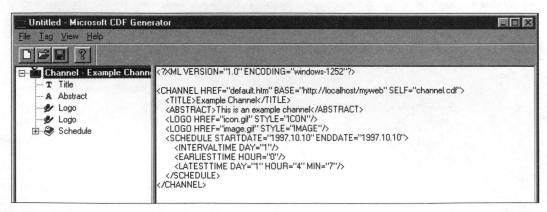

Having created the channel outline, we now need to add the channel contents to the CDF.

Adding and Modifying Channel Items

All <CHANNEL> elements contained within the top-level channel definition of a CDF file represent folders or **sub-channels**. Sub-channels are used to create a hierarchy of channel items. An **item**, in this context, corresponds to a web page. We can add an item to our channel by selecting the channel icon, right clicking and selecting New followed by the tag type required. Likewise, by selecting an icon, right clicking and selecting Properties we can amend the properties of an element tag. This will display a dialog allowing the values to be modified. Finally, by selecting the Delete menu option we can permanently remove the element tag from the CDF file.

If we go back to our initial structure of our example site we can see that `first.htm`, `first-a.htm` and `first-b.htm` are grouped together, in that order, in the channel hierarchy. So, we'll need to create the page `first.htm` first, as this must be added as a sub-channel. To do this, we need to right click on the channel icon, but this time select Channel from the New submenu and then follow the CDF Creation Wizard dialog screens as described previously. This time only add the following details and be sure to uncheck all other boxes, throughout the wizard.

- ▲ **HREF** – first.htm – this is the URL of the top page of the channel (this can be resolved using **BASE**)

- ▲ **BASE** – http://*your_web_address/*

- ▲ **SELF** – channel.cdf

- ▲ **ABSTRACT** – The first topic

The confirmation dialog should then look like this:

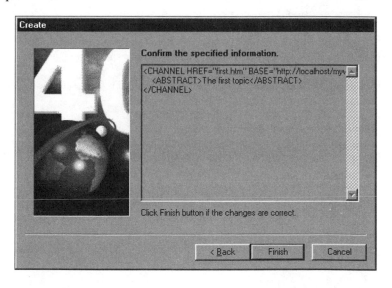

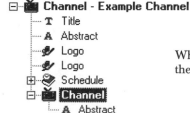

When we add `first-a.htm` and `first-b.htm` as items, we need to add them to the 'first' sub-channel icon as highlighted.

However, when we add the other remaining items, we must add them to the main channel icon. To add an item, we must right click on the appropriate channel icon, select the Item menu item from the New item and then follow the CDF Creation Wizard dialog screens. If you later decide that an item needs a child or two, then you will have to go back and delete the item and recreate it as a channel.

When adding items you'll see that this is slightly different to the general information dialog we saw earlier for adding a channel. The first dialog allows us to specify the general item information. For example, we would enter the following values for `first-a.htm`:

- ▲ **HREF** – first-a.htm – this is the URL of the top page of the sub-channel, add it as an Attribute once more.

- ▲ **Last modified date** – *leave date* – this is used by the channel client to decide whether the content has changed from the version in its cache

- ▲ **The Level** – 0 – this is the number of levels the channel client should webcrawl

- ▲ **Item is pre-cached** – *leave checked* – this indicates whether the channel client should download the content. If **PRECACHE** is checked, then content is downloaded, but only when the user has specified if channel content should be downloaded. If **PRECACHE** is unchecked, content is not downloaded and the **LEVEL** attribute is ignored.

- ▲ **Usage** – *leave unchecked* – indicates how an item should be used. When we add the screen saver this should be set to ScreenSaver

The remaining dialogs allow us to specify additional information and the images. These are the same as for specifying the channel attributes that we saw earlier. You should enter items for `first-a.htm`, `first-b.htm`, `second.htm`, `third.htm` and `scrnsave.htm`. You must make use of the final confirmation dialog to check the contents of the CDF files, as once you've confirmed that the file is OK, you can't then directly edit the CDF file in CDF contents panel of the generator. Once all of the items have been added, the CDF Generator clearly shows the contents and structure of our CDF file.

All the code from this chapter can be run on-line from our rapid server at:
`http://rapid.wrox.co.uk/books/0707`

Before we move on to examine our CDF file, we need to note one very small bug in CDF generator. That is in the **BASE** attribute of the **CHANNEL** element, the path name has not been closed properly. It should have an extra / symbol, attached to the end. Open up the CDF file in Notepad and amend the URLs accordingly.

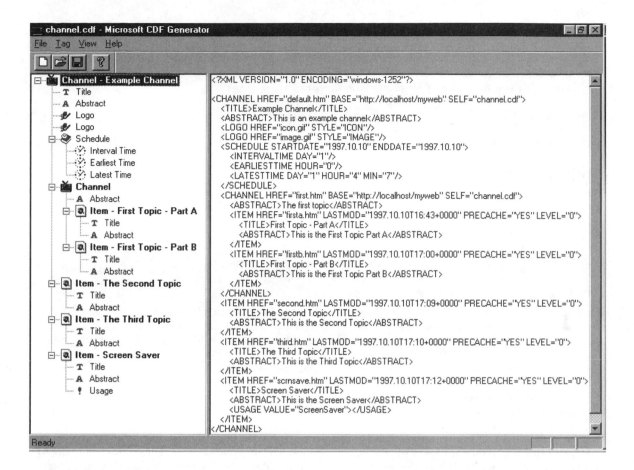

How the CDF file works – Step by Step

We shall now dissect the CDF code that we generated for our channel.

Document Header

The CDF file begins with a line that identifies the XML. XML enables document types to be defined, authored and shared across networks. This is used as a header in the same way a **<HTML>** element defines the beginning of a **<HTML>** document.

```
<?XML VERSION="1.0" ENCODING="UTF-8"?>
```

The Main Channel

At the top of the code listing, just after the document header, you'll find the topmost channel definition. Here's what it looks like:

```
<CHANNEL HREF="default.htm" BASE="http://localhost/myweb/"
         SELF="channel.cdf">
```

The `HREF` attribute refers to our channel home – the page that will be the first shown when a subscription to the channel is undertaken, or when the channel is clicked within the channel pane. Like many HTML tags, the `<CHANNEL>` tag can house other tags within it. Because of this, it needs to be closed using the `</CHANNEL>` tag at the end of the file. The `BASE` address must be amended to the address of the virtual root from which you are running for example in this case.

```
</CHANNEL>
```

Indentation of code helps us to see match the opening tags with the closing tags.

Providing a Title for the Top-Level Channel

We can provide a Title and an Abstract for the channel. The Title appears on the channel pane and the Abstract is shown as a tool tip if we leave the mouse pointer over the channel button within the channel pane. Typically, the Abstract will be much more descriptive than the Title.

```
<TITLE>Example Channel</TITLE>
    <ABSTRACT>This is an example channel</ABSTRACT>
```

Providing the Custom Images

If we don't specify any custom images for our channel, then IE4 will provide default images for the channel button and the small icon image in the Channels submenu off the Favorites menu. It's a good idea to provide these images because it makes each channel instantly more distinguishable from the others.

The `HREF` attributes dictates where the appropriate image can be found.

```
<LOGO HREF="icon.gif" STYLE="ICON"/>
<LOGO HREF="logo.gif" STYLE="IMAGE"/>
```

One interesting thing to notice is that `<LOGO>` doesn't provide a closing `</LOGO>` tag as you might expect in HTML. Instead, the tag is closed by a simple `/` symbol. This is because some tags are always going to be **empty**, because they can't house other tags or text, so they don't need a separate closing element tag to mark where the tag finishes. Instead the `/` symbol is used to denote where the definition of attributes ends.

Providing the Schedule

We can specify the time schedule for the client to update its channel content. By specifying a time range, we can ensure that the server is not hit simultaneously by all subscribers. We also specify the date from which the schedule will start to apply and the date when it ceases to apply.

In our case we state that the content should be retrieved between 4am and 7am, thereby avoiding using up the precious bandwidth during the periods when we expect most web surfers to be hitting our site.

```
<SCHEDULE STARTDATE="1997.09.16T22:14+0000"
                ENDDATE="1999.09.16T22:14+0000">
        <INTERVALTIME DAY="1"/>
        <EARLIESTTIME HOUR="4"/>
        <LATESTTIME HOUR="7"/>
</SCHEDULE>
```

Creating our Sub-Channel

We create the equivalent of folders in our channel definition by providing sub-channels. Simply, these are created when we declare **<CHANNEL>** tags within other outer channels.

```
<CHANNEL HREF="first.htm" BASE="http://localhost/myweb/">
```

As with the top-level channel, we provided a title and abstract for it.

```
<TITLE>First Topic</TITLE>
<ABSTRACT>This is the first topic</ABSTRACT>
```

If we do not supply a title, then the **HREF** we specified in the channel definition will be used instead. We must not forget to close off sub-channels with a **</CHANNEL>** tag.

Of course, as well as channels and sub-channels, we should also provide references to specific items of information rather than just homepages to different areas of our Web site.

Creating our Items

Our example uses three items defined below the main channel and two items below the sub-channel. They are defined using **<ITEM>** tags. Here's the first one:

```
<ITEM HREF="scrnsave.htm" LASTMOD="1997.09.17T22:08+0000"
            PRECACHE="YES" LEVEL="0">
    <TITLE>Screen Saver</TITLE>
    <ABSTRACT>This is the Screen Saver</ABSTRACT>
    <USAGE VALUE="ScreenSaver"></USAGE>
</ITEM>
```

Just like with our channels, **<ITEM>** tags provide the **HREF** attribute that displays the associated page when the item is clicked. Note that in many ways item and channel definitions are similar. Items too can have a title and abstract like channels, and also need to be closed. In the case of items, this is done using the **</ ITEM>** tag.

The **<USAGE>** tag indicates how an item should be used. If the tag is omitted or the value attribute set to Channel then the item is a standard entry in the channel pane. For our screen saver page we must set the **value** attribute to **ScreenSaver**. Other values are listed in Appendix F.

The main difference between sub-channels and items is that items are **end-of-the-road** nodes – that is they can't be expanded to show more items or sub-channels. As such, we can't define items and sub-channels within an **<ITEM>** tag.

This completes our explanation of our CDF file, but leaves us with an important unanswered question, namely how do we run the CDF file that we've just created? Well unfortunately you can't see any results unless you first incorporate it into a full web site, which we'll look at doing now.

Creating a Simple Web Channel

In this section, we'll develop a simple web site and webcast the content using our newly created CDF file. We'll start by creating the page, the user will first see, **default.htm**.

The Default Page

This page does all of the work. It provides an Add Active Channel link – the connection to the `channel.cdf` file – and three hyperlinks to our three main pages on this site.

```
<HTML>
<HEAD>
<TITLE>Home Page</TITLE>
<SCRIPT language="JavaScript">

function isMsie4orGreater() {
var ua = window.navigator.userAgent;
var msie = ua.indexOf ( "MSIE " );

if  (msie > 0)
  {return (parseInt ( ua.substring ( msie+5, ua.indexOf ( ".", msie ) ) )
             >=4) && (ua.indexOf("MSIE 4.0b") <0) ;}
else {return false;}}

</SCRIPT>
</HEAD>
<BODY bgcolor="#FFFF00">
<HR>
<CENTER>
<H1><FONT FACE="Arial">Channel Home Page</FONT></H1>
<A NAME="AddChannel"
HREF="http://www.microsoft.com/ie/ie40/download/?/ie/ie40/download/redirect.htm">
<IMG SRC="ieaddchannel.gif" border=0 width=136 height=20></a>
<SCRIPT language="JavaScript">

if ( isMsie4orGreater()) { AddChannel.href
            ="http://localhost/myweb/channel.cdf"; }

</SCRIPT>
</CENTER>
<HR>
<P ALIGN="center"><A HREF="first.htm">
    <FONT FACE="Arial">First Topic</FONT></A></P>
<P ALIGN="center"><A HREF="second.htm">
    <FONT FACE="Arial">Second Topic</FONT></A></P>
<P ALIGN="center"><A HREF="third.htm">
    <FONT FACE="Arial">Third Topic</FONT></A></p>
</BODY>
</HTML>
```

This is what our default page will look like:

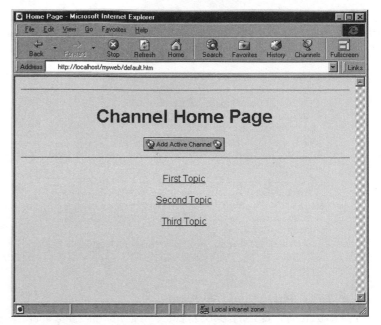

The main items of interest in this page are the two bits of JavaScript that are included. We'll take a look at them now. The first part is added as specified by the licensing agreement for the use of the Microsoft **Add Active Channel** icon – and the use of this icon is a prerequisite if you want your channel published in the Microsoft Channel Guide.

```
function isMsie4orGreater() {
var ua = window.navigator.userAgent;
var msie = ua.indexOf ( "MSIE " );
if  (msie > 0)
  {return (parseInt ( ua.substring ( msie+5, ua.indexOf ( ".", msie ) ) )
        >=4) && (ua.indexOf("MSIE 4.0b") <0) ;}
else {return false;}}
```

The function **isMsie4orGreater()** checks if the Web Browser accessing the page is the final released version of IE4. If IE4 isn't detected, then the hyperlink of the **Add Active Channels** hyperlink remains pointing to the IE4 download page. The second part only comes into play if the client is IE4, in which case the hyperlink is amended to the URL of our channels' CDF file.

```
if ( isMsie4orGreater()) { AddChannel.href
        ="http://localhost/myweb/channel.cdf"; }
```

Apart from that this page only needs to provide three links to the other three main **Topic** pages on our example site.

```
<P ALIGN="center"><A HREF="first.htm">
   <FONT FACE="Arial">First Topic</FONT></A></P>
<P ALIGN="center"><A HREF="second.htm">
   <FONT FACE="Arial">Second Topic</FONT></A></P>
<P ALIGN="center"><A HREF="third.htm">
   <FONT FACE="Arial">Third Topic</FONT></A></p>
```

The First Topic Page

The page `first.htm` is the most interesting of the remaining pages. It needs to define two smaller subsections, part A and part B, and also supply a link back to the main `default.htm`.

```
<HTML>
<HEAD>
<TITLE>First Topic</TITLE>
</HEAD>
<BODY BGCOLOR="#FFFF00">
<HR>
<H1 ALIGN="center"><FONT FACE="Arial">First Topic</FONT></H1>
<HR>
<P ALIGN="center"><A HREF="first-a.htm">
<FONT FACE="Arial">Part A</FONT></A></P>
<P ALIGN="center"><a href="first-b.htm">
<FONT FACE="Arial">Part B</FONT></A></P>
<P> </P>
<P><A HREF="default.htm">Back</A></P>
</BODY>
</HTML>
```

First Topic Part A and B Pages

`first-a.htm` and `first-b.htm` are basically the same apart from the title and heading:

```
<HTML>
<HEAD>
<TITLE>First Topic - Part A</TITLE>
</HEAD>
<BODY BGCOLOR="#FFFF00">
<HR>
<H1 ALIGN="center"><FONT FACE="Arial">First Topic - Part A</FONT></H1>
<HR>
<P> </P>
<P><A HREF="default.htm">Home</A> 
<A HREF="first.htm">Back</A></P>
</BODY>
</HTML>
```

The Second and Third Topic Pages

`second.htm` and `third.htm` just need to provide links back to `default.htm`. Apart from different titles, and headings, they are identical.

```
<HTML>
<HEAD>
<TITLE>Second Topic</TITLE>
</HEAD>
<BODY BGCOLOR="#FFFF00">
<HR>
<H1 ALIGN="center"><FONT FACE="Arial">Second Topic</FONT></H1>
<HR>
<P><A HREF="default.htm">Back</A></P>
</BODY>
</HTML>
```

The ScreenSaver

The screensaver is where you can provide a reminder of what your channel does. We've just put a simple scrolling marquee across the top bar:

```
<HTML>
<HEAD>
<TITLE>Screen Saver</TITLE>
</HEAD>
<BODY BGCOLOR="#FFFF00">
<HR>
<MARQUEE DIRECTION="left" BGCOLOR="red" BEHAVIOR="scroll" SCROLLAMOUNT=10
SCROLLDELAY=200>This is a scrolling Channel Screen Saver</MARQUEE>
<HR>
<P><A HREF="default.htm">Back</A></P>
</BODY>
</HTML>
```

> *If you're having problems getting the screensaver to appear, then you might want to change the* **HREF**
> *value in* **channel.cdf**, *from just a filename to a full URL e.g.* **http://localhost/myweb/**
> **scrnsave.htm**. *Otherwise, if your program doesn't find your screensaver file, your screensaver might
> be replaced by the default Microsoft one.*

Other Requirements

Finally we need three graphics, one for use within our channel and the other to provide icons for the structure that is displayed in the channel pane.

- 80x32-pixel logo, named **LOGO.GIF** (it could be **.GIF** or **.JPG** file, although animated GIFs not supported). This is reference in the **channel.cdf** file and appears in the channel bar and the channel pane, which displays all the subscribed channels.

- 16x16-pixel icon, named **ICON.GIF** file. This appears in the Channels submenu of the Favorites menu.

- 140x24-pixel logo named **IEADDCHANNEL.GIF** file. We've created our own rather than copy the Microsoft one.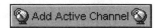

> *All of the graphics needed to run this example are available from:*
> **http://rapid.wrox.co.uk/books/0707**

Installing the Channel

Place the files in your chosen directory on your web server and then go to the default page. You will see that it has a channel subscription link plus three hyperlinks to the three main topic pages. The first topic page has links to two other pages. If we click on the Add Active Channel image, IE4 will bring up the Subscription dialog that we have seen earlier in this chapter. Unless we want to make some modifications, we can just click on the OK to set up the subscription to the channel with the default settings.

When we have done this, IE4 will open in full-screen mode with the channel pane displayed on the left hand side of the window.

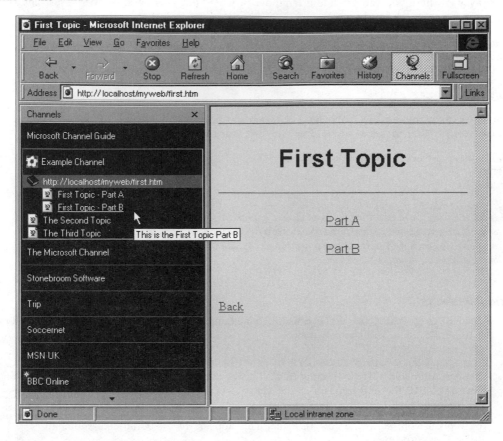

All the code from this chapter can be run on-line from our rapid server at:
`http://rapid.wrox.co.uk/books/0707`

For best results the channel should be used over HTTP. It is possible to subscribe to a channel on the hard disk, but not all of the channel features will be available. If you are running Windows 95 or NT Workstation, you can use the Microsoft Personal Web Server. This can be used as a local server so you can access it using HTTP in a similar manner to it being on a remote Internet server.

You will notice that we have now displayed our new channel with its special logo in the channel pane. The name of the channel, the hierarchical structure and the links are all defined in the CDF file. Clicking on the channel button will ensure the default channel page is displayed and expand the channel content list below the button to show all the first level items. Subsequent clicking on the channel button will either contract or expand this list. Clicking on item causes the associated URL to be displayed.

The name that is displayed for each entry is called an **item title**. If we allow our mouse pointer to hover over a title, we will notice that a small tool tip like box appears with a further description. This is called the **abstract** of the sub-channel. The closed book icon indicates a sub-channel item that can contain further items and sub-channels. Clicking on the sub-channel icon will expand it to show the lower level content associated and the icon converts an open book icon.

So that's CDF – a simple method for a site author to present an existing site as a channel – and you should now be able to implement a channel for the key pages in your web site. In a later case study in the next chapter, we shall see how we can get the best out of Active Channels by mixing server-side scripting via ASP, a channel database, and clever server code to allow us to create personalized channels.

Advantages of Active Channels

By now you should appreciate that the combination of CDF and Dynamic HTML provides Web authors with a powerful arsenal of Web tools. CDF provides an automated information delivery system and Dynamic HTML enables the delivery of rich and compelling content far exceeding the capabilities of the previous HTML standards.

The great thing about creating channels using CDF is that it is a simple process that needs no amendments to the existing Web content. As site developers, all we have to do is identify the content that we want to webcast, organize this information into a hierarchical set of related pages, create the CDF file and finally provide a hyperlink on our site to the CDF file.

The desktop user now has a mechanism for managing the overwhelming amount of information that is continually being generated and published on the Internet. The webcrawling mechanism used by basic webcasting can mean opening the floodgates and resulting in huge volumes of irrelevant information flowing on to the desktop. CDF now enables the webcast content to be precisely defined and can control the flow of information in a timely and personalized manner.

Application Channels

One of the great advantages of Web computing is the fact that applications are centrally controlled and deployed dynamically as and when needed. This centrally managed architecture greatly lowers the cost of client administration. If part of a Web application is enhanced or a bug is fixed, the next time the user accesses this part of the system they will automatically be using the latest logic. This contrasts to, for example, a Visual Basic application that is installed using a setup utility from disks or a CD-ROM. If a new version is made available, the application has to be reinstalled – and if there are a large number of desktops, perhaps distributed over the corporate enterprise, this can be a long and costly exercise.

One of the fundamental concepts from the Java world is network computing – the notion that ALL client executable logic can be dynamically deployed over the network. While this certainly provides zero cost client administration, it is very questionable whether the infrastructure of today's can deliver the rich, but complex and large, applications that we demand today, within the brief period of time that the user is willing to wait. For example, if you were performing a word processing operation and was unsure of a spelling, would you be willing to wait for a length of time whilst the spell checker was downloaded? Certainly not if your network was the Internet!

The alternative to the Java network computer concepts is the Active Desktop – which is currently available on the Windows platform, and later targeted for implementation on the Macintosh and Unix systems. Recently, Microsoft have publicly acknowledged that the **total cost of ownership** is one of the most important topics in enterprise computing today and have created a "Zero Administration" initiative. This includes the ability for remote and automatic management of the desktop, irrespective of how 'thick' or 'thin' the client applications and configuration is.

Most organizations release PCs into the corporate enterprise with a known standard configuration. However, over time, as users request new applications and device drivers/software components are updated, it becomes difficult for the IT support personnel to know exactly which components are installed on each machine. Unfortunately, installing and configuring applications, and solving software conflicts requires considerable technical expertise, and thus usually involves high labor costs.

Under the 'Zero Administration' initiative for the Active Desktop, the software updating process becomes simple and automated. For example, with respect to the operating system, when a system component, device driver, or even a new version of the operating system is available, the system management subsystem will be able to automatically update itself with the new components without any user intervention.

Could we imagine the time when we arrive at work in the morning to see a message in your mail inbox saying something like "Good Morning Richard – I noticed that Microsoft have released some bug fixes to Visual C++ … so I have installed them for you!" Well, with IE4's **Applications Channels**, that time has now arrived. Using this type of channel, IE4 can automatically download and install application updates that are released over the Internet. This is made possible by the support within IE4 of the **Open Software Description**.

Open Software Description

The Open Software Description (OSD) is another application of XML endorsed by many of the major Internet software vendors. It uses XML tags to provide an interoperability standard for the description of software components including their versions, dependencies and relationships to other components. OSD is not constrained by the languages and tools used to generate the software or the type of target platform.

The combination of OSD and the Internet 'push' mechanisms provide systems with the ability to automatically retrieve and install updates to crucial software. These automation technologies are likely to be a significant step in reducing the cost of ownership by avoiding the management and installation issues that we have already discussed. The user benefits by getting a punctual software upgrade and a timely advantage of the new features and bug fixes.

Application Channels use CDF and OSD to deliver appropriate software components (including applications, ActiveX Controls and Java class libraries) to the desktop. The *Internet Explorer 4.0 Updates Channel* is an example of an application channel and ensures that the IE4 is always running the latest and optimum version. Applications Channels are very similar to the Active Channels that we discussed earlier; the only difference being that Application Channels push data to be *executed* and Active Channels push data to be *read*.

It is important to appreciate that OSD is not related to the distribution, management or installation of software and relies on other mechanisms to provide these features. The OSD instructions can be place in several places including:

- ▲ located within the software's archive / distribution file (e.g. a `.CAB`, `.ZIP` or `.JAR` file) – this file contains all resources required for the installation and is compressed, and optionally digitally signed for accountability
- ▲ located within the CDF file and identified as a OSD resource by means of an `<SOFTPKG>` tag
- ▲ located within the HTML file and identified as a OSD resource by means of an `<OBJECT>` tag

We have included a reference guide for the OSD syntax in Appendix F.

Application Channels in Action

We shall now look at an example of an Application Channel whereby we want to push the latest version of an application to the desktops as soon as an updated version is available. However, in this scenario, our users want complete control over the program installation – they just want to be notified via the Inbox when a copy of the updated software has been downloaded and is resident in the cache, ready for installation.

As it would be a very time consuming and non-trivial task to actually implement an application channel, we'll just a look at a dummy example file which could be used to implement an application channel instead. The following CDF file uses the `<SOFTPKG>` section to specify the software distribution and thus define the channel as an Application Channel. The user subscribes to an Application Channel in the same fashion as subscribing to an Active Channel that we discussed earlier, i.e. the user navigates to the CDF file and then follows the subscription dialogs.

```
<CHANNEL href="http://localhost/myweb/theappl.htm">
<SELF href="http://localhost/myweb/TheAppl.cdf" />
<TITLE>Wrox - TheAppl app-channel</title>
<ABSTRACT>This is my first app-channel.
</ABSTRACT>
<LOGO HREF="http://localhost/myweb/logo-app.gif" style="IMAGE" />

<SOFTPKG NAME="Wrox - TheAppl"
    HREF="http://localhost/myweb/TheAppl-dist.htm"
        VERSION="1,4,0,0"
    PRECACHE="Yes"  >
    <TITLE>App Channel Software Distribution</title>
    <USAGE VALUE="EMAIL"></USAGE>
     <IMPLEMENTATION>
        <CODEBASE HREF="http://localhost/myweb/vb1/theappl.exe" />
     </IMPLEMENTATION>
</SOFTPKG>

</CHANNEL>
```

Let's look at the contents in detail.

Channel Information

The CDF file defines a channel called *Wrox - TheAppl app-channel* and specifies the title, abstract and logo. This information is used in the channel bar and channel pane.

```
<CHANNEL HREF="http://localhost/myweb/theappl.htm">
<SELF HREF="http://localhost/myweb/TheAppl.cdf" />
<TITLE>Wrox - TheAppl app-channel</TITLE>
<ABSTRACT>This is my first app-channel.
</ABSTRACT>
<LOGO href="http://localhost/myweb/logo-app.gif" style="IMAGE" />
```

It's important to remember to complete the channel specification with a `</CHANNEL>` tag.

The Software Distribution Channel

The software distribution channel is called *Wrox – The Appl*. Once the channel has been installed, we can inspect the status of the distribution in the Windows Registry by inspecting the key:

```
HKEY_LOCAL_MACHINE\SOFTWARE\Microsoft\Code Store Database\Distribution
Units\Wrox - TheAppl
```

Since the name of the distribution is part of the registry key, it must be unique. Thus many people will use globally unique identifiers (GUIDs) to ensure this, however we aren't in this example. The installed version is stored in the registry and compared with that in the `<SOFTPKG>` to decide if the software has been updated and installation is required. The `precache="yes"` attribute tells the channel not to install the software but just to download it and store it in the Internet cache. The alternative is using `autoinstall="yes"` which, as it suggests, will automatically install the updated software.

```
<SOFTPKG NAME="Wrox - TheAppl"
         HREF="http://localhost/myweb/TheAppl-dist.htm"
         VERSION="1,4,0,0"
         PRECACHE="Yes"  >
```

As usual, we must remember to complete the software distribution specification with a `</SOFTPKG>` tag.

Title

This specifies the title of the distribution. This is used in the email message that indicates and update version has been downloaded.

```
<TITLE>App Channel Software Distribution</TITLE>
```

Usage

This specifies that the user will be notified via an email message

```
<USAGE VALUE="EMAIL"></USAGE>
```

Implementation

This specifies the software distribution unit i.e. the software files and the installation instructions (possibly another OSD specification).

```
<IMPLEMENTATION>
    <CODEBASE HREF="http://localhost/myweb/vb1/theappl.exe" />
</IMPLEMENTATION>
```

That's it – the brevity of this example shows how easy it to implement an Application Channel. Once the channel has detected the updated software, the system send an email to notify the user that the upgrade is waiting in the cache for them.

Summary

In this chapter we have seen how webcasting provides the automated delivery of Internet resources. The type of items that can be 'pushed' to the desktop are:

- Information – users can stay up to date with their frequently used sites and use the content off-line to reduce costs or provide mobility.
- Executables – users' machines can be optimally configured with the latest versions

We have also seen two standards that provide the high levels of interoperability needed in Internet distributed computing. These are:

- Channel Definition Format (CDF) – describes the delivery of information
- Open Software Distribution (OSD) – describes software components and their dependencies

We shall now take a look at an example of how you can implement your own customized channel and integrate it with Active Server Pages.

The Wrox Custom Channel Example

In Chapter 16, we talked about webcasting in its basic and managed forms, and saw a simple example showing how managed webcasting uses a CDF file to allow IE4 to create a subscription to a channel hosted from a site. While this provided good introductory reading, we're now going to show you how these techniques can be expanded upon to create your own customized channel, which we'll put together over the course of this chapter.

This chapter covers

- ▲ Installation of the Wrox Custom Channel Example
- ▲ Creating an active channel
- ▲ Providing channel links
- ▲ The Wrox Channel Database
- ▲ The ASP file that creates the Content Preview page and drives the whole application

An Overview of the Wrox Custom Channel Example

You may have noticed that, even though the job of creating CDF files in Liburnia (the Microsoft CDF Generator) was relatively simple, it still required some degree of user interaction. Even though a site may have many channels covering different areas of content, it would be great to have the CDF files created dynamically from a database. This certainly makes channel maintenance easier, but also provides us greater flexibility. For instance, we can provide a custom channel content selection screen to our site visitors, who can then *choose* what they want to be in their own personal channel. This means that when they update the channel content via the subscription, they download exactly what they've specified.

In this section, we're going to build an example that shows how all of this is possible. We're going to use a database to store all the possible channel and item links to our site, and present a custom channel selection screen to our visitors which will allow them to determine what's in their particular custom channel. We're also going to present a 'preview' of the channel contents, and dynamically generate the CDF file based on their selections. We're then going to link in this channel file from a hyperlink that will provide a mechanism to subscribe to their custom channel. This diagram shows the process involved in subscribing to predefined channels, negotiating the custom channel content selection page, creation of the custom CDF file, and finally subscription to that CDF file from the content preview page.

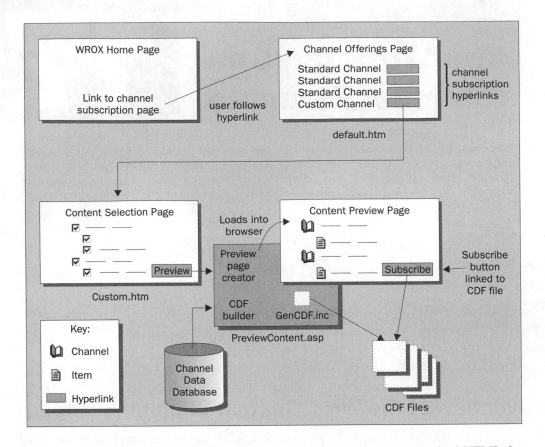

We haven't shown all the pages used in the example as many of them are just standard HTML documents. What we've in fact done is focused on the heart of the example. You'll notice how we've specifically tailored the site to provide a revolutionary channel webcasting experience by asking the visitor to specify what should go into their custom channel. A lot of the hard work is done in just one main file (`PreviewContent.asp`). This script actually determines the selected options in the previous screen, ties in with the database, creates a preview of the CDF channel information that will be included in the subscription, generates the CDF file in a more readable indented format, and finally provides the hyperlink to the custom CDF file. For each concurrent user, the link will point to a particular file, so one user won't subscribe to another user's custom channel. We'll show you how all of this is possible a little later. For now, you may want to familiarise yourself with the application, so follow these installation instructions carefully.

Installing the Wrox Custom Channel Example

We've made the installation process of the example as simple as we can, by using the MS Access system DSN without a specific file location, and by creating a CDF file based on a *virtual* directory instead of a physical one. Here are the steps you'll need to follow to install the example:

▲ Download the source code from our site: **rapid.wrox.co.uk/books/0707** onto your machine, which must be running either Personal Web Server or IIS with ASP.

▲ Create a single directory called **Download** somewhere on one of the server's disks, and extract the source code from the zip file into **Download** preserving the directory information so that the code is extracted into a hierarchical structure.

▲ Create a virtual root, or alias, using Personal Web Server or IIS, called **/ChannelExamples** and be sure to give it **Executable** as well as **Read** access. This root should point to **Download** directory–not at the **Wrox** directory directly.

▲ Create an ODBC data source for the **WroxChannel.mdb** database in the **database** directory, with the System Data Source Name of WroxChannel. If you need help with this, consult Chapter 15.

> *We've used Access 97 to create the database. If you're using a previous version of MS Access, then load in the fixed width file (Unit.txt) provided with the source code and use the results of this import operation as your database.*

Many parts of the system (including the CDF file itself) need a fully specified hostname. The name of the server that was used in development is **TheTranquil**. You can modify the database so that all the HREF values point to your server, but an easier alternative, depending which server you are running, is to do the following.

Personal Web Server and Windows 95

For Personal Web Server and Active Server Pages on Windows 95, create a **hosts** file in the **Windows** directory, if a file of that name doesn't already exist. Next copy the contents of **hosts.sam** file, which is also located in your **Windows** directory, into the **hosts** file. Add a new line to the file, as shown below. It doesn't matter if your IP address is not 127.0.0.1 as the example should still work. Stop and restart the Personal Web Server to make the changes come into effect.

```
# For example:
#
#      102.54.94.97      rhino.acme.com        # source server
#       38.25.63.10      x.acme.com            # x client host

127.0.0.1        localhost
127.0.0.1        thetranquil
```

IIS and NT Server

For NT and IIS with Active Server Pages installed, create a new virtual domain called **TheTranquil**. To do this, load up the **WinNT\System32\Drivers\etc\hosts** file in a text editor (where WinNT is the base installation directory of your Windows NT installation). You should have this file installed automatically, if you have already installed IIS.

Add a line (just like with the Win95 version) under this line:

```
...
127.0.0.1   localhost
127.0.0.1   thetranquil
```

Save the file to put the changes into effect with the next request. You don't need to restart the IIS service.

This example presumes that the default document is default.htm. *If this is not the case with your server then either resolve any partial references, or enable the default document and specify it as* default.htm. *Alternatively, you can create an* .asp *file in each directory where a* default.htm *file can be found, and enter the following code:*

```
<%@ LANGUAGE="VBSCRIPT" %>
<% Response.Redirect "default.htm" %>
```

Once this is done, the application is set up and should run without problems on your server. The next step is to see what it does, and how to use it.

The Aim of the Example

Please read this section carefully, as we'll write it only once! The purpose of this example is demonstrate how some of the restrictions of channels can be overcome with the use of other technologies, such as Active Server Pages (ASP).

We've included many pages directly from Wrox's web site in this example. We've incorporated HTML versions of a small set of the pages which will be used to demonstrate how CDF files can be used to host channels from the content. All the pages you really need to see the example working are provided in the downloadable source code .zip file, however, you will need to have an active Internet connection to see all of them working. You will have to a have a web server to view any of the pages.

The emphasis of the example is not so much on the Wrox site itself, but how we host standard and custom channels from it. The following has been changed to work for this example:

In the main Wrox home page:

▲ The dropdown list box just above the View Title button now contains only 4 book titles (the names of the new and existing titles that will be hosted in the *WroxBooks* channel you'll see later).

▲ A link to the Channel Offerings Page has been provided in the Announce section of the page.

In the Books directory:

▲ 6 directories, one per book, have been created to hold HTML documents that relate to the appropriate book. The Links section in the default.htm file within each directory has been amended to point to the other associated pages in that directory.

▲ Files have been created to show the previously published, forthcoming and new book titles available. This was specifically done for demonstrating channels.

Of course, extra pages have been created which do the real work. We'll talk about this later, after we've shown you around the example.

Using the Example

When you load up the **default.htm** file in the browser (via HTTP from the **/channelExamples/ Wrox** subdirectory), you'll notice that the screen looks remarkably similar to the Wrox home page, but a link is provided that lets you subscribe to channels. Follow this link by clicking on it.

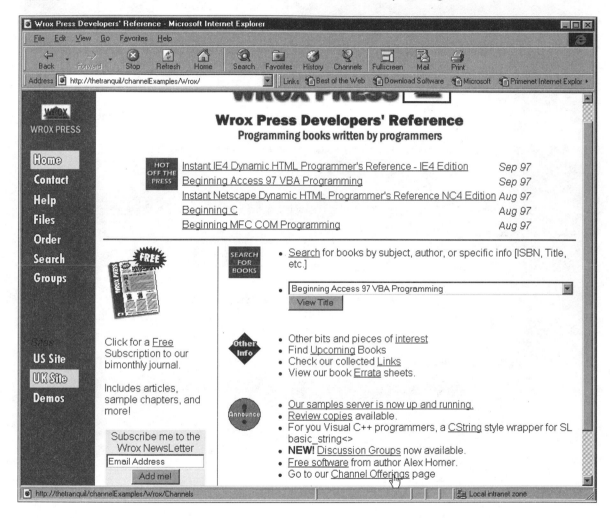

This will take you to the Channel Offerings page. From here, you can select one of the default channels for subscription, or create your own.

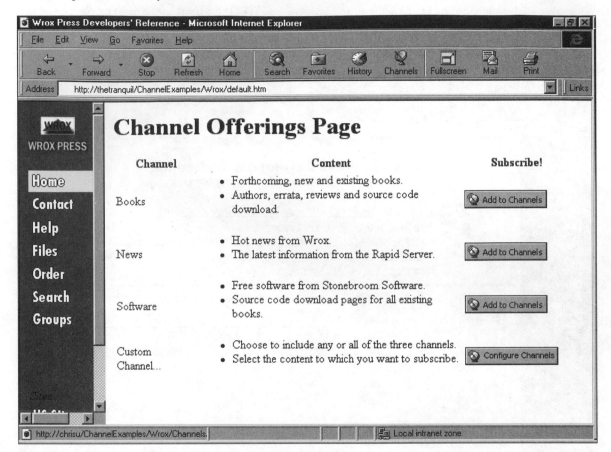

Click on the Custom Channel item to navigate to the Content Selection page. Here, you can select various categories that should be included in your custom channel subscription. If you select a top-level item, all the sub-level items become selected. If you deselect a top-level item, then the appropriate sub-items become deselected. If you deselect all sub-items of a selected top-level item, then it too becomes deselected and so on.

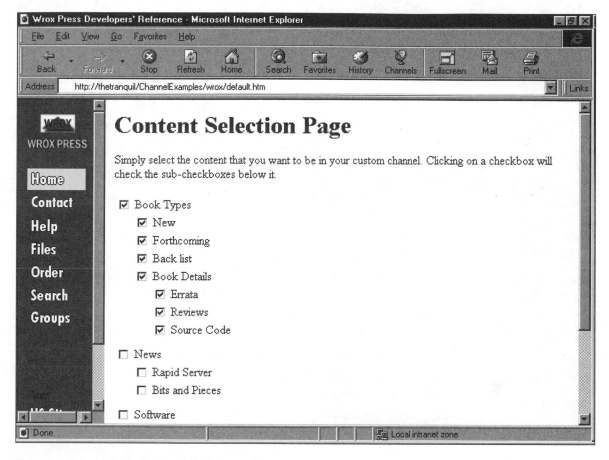

When you're happy with your selection, you can preview the content of the channel by clicking on the Preview button. Alternatively, if you wish to go back and subscribe to a standard channel, then click on the Back standard navigation button.

Clicking on the Preview button displays the Content Preview Page that gives a representation of the content of the CDF file to which you can now subscribe.

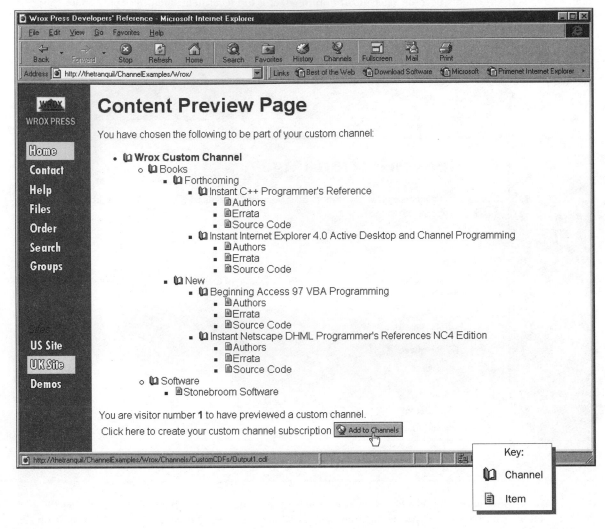

You can now go ahead with the subscription to your custom channel by clicking on the Add to Channels button, or go back to modify your selection by clicking on the Back button.

Clicking on the Add to Channels button follows a hyperlink to your generated custom CDF file, and will launch the Add Active Channel Content dialog.

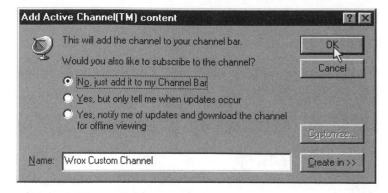

From here, you can choose how you want to subscribe to the channel. For the moment, just select the first option and add the channel to the channel bar. When you click on OK, IE4 will fire up and display the channel bar and channel content associated with the channel or item you click on from the channel bar.

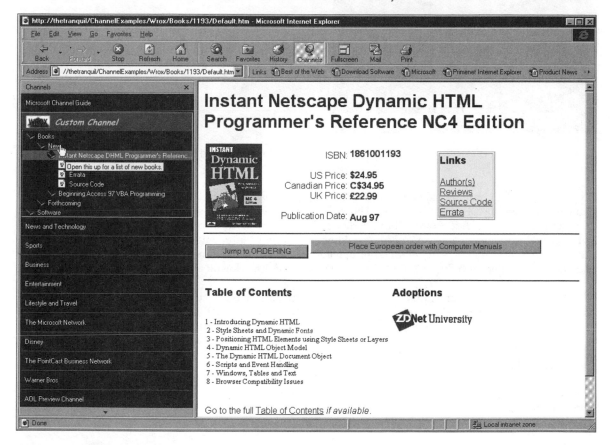

Click on the New channel, and the associated content will be shown as above (provided you selected this as part of your channel content).

If you're running the Active Desktop, and have your channel pane Active Desktop Item shown, you'll also notice that the channel has been added to the bottom of the list of your existing channels.

In the same way, you can subscribe to the standard (static) channels provided from the Channel Offerings Page.

If you recreate the Custom channel with different content, your existing channel will not reflect the changes automatically. This is because we chose the first option (which is just to add the channel to our Channel Bar) from the Add Active Channel dialog. If we had chosen to be informed whenever an update had occurred then the channel's CDF file would already have been updated. If we went the whole hog and chose the third option, to be notified of updates, *and* download channel content, then any Wrox pages changed and pointed to by the CDF file's contents would also be downloaded.

To update any changes, you can then right click on the channel and select Refresh from the popup menu. This will cause the CDF code to refresh with your newly generated CDF file.

Building the Wrox Custom Channel Example

Now we've seen how to use the example and what it can do, we'll take a look at how we went about putting it together.

Creating an Active Channel

There are three main steps in creating an Active Channel. They are:

- Designing the Active Channel
- Creating the CDF file
- Posting the CDF file

In the following three subsections, we'll take a brief look at the design decisions of each of these stages in turn. Let's first turn our attention to what content each of the channels is going to include.

Designing the Active Channels

Our example provides three default channels, and the ability to create a custom channel that incorporates all the content for selection from our example. The three standard channels have been chosen to cover a different category of information from the example site content.

Channel Name	Description
WroxBooks	This channel will cover the *new* books that have just come out, *forthcoming* books, the *backlist* of existing books, errata, reviews and source code. (The book details and the list of authors are automatically included with any type of book subscription).
WroxNews	Rapid server and other information.
WroxSoftware	Source code and free software.

You'll notice that the Books and Software channels slightly overlap because they both contain source code pages (pages that have links to source code). This is an accurate scenario because you'll often find that in a large web site, certain pages will be cross-referenced by several channels.

The custom channel encompasses all of these areas and news items, but lets visitors choose which items will be part of their custom channel subscription.

Creating the CDF Files

Because all of the channel and item information will reside in the database, it won't be too difficult to build up each CDF file dynamically based on a subset of selected options available for the custom channel subscription. Once the routines are in place to dynamically create CDF files from the Content Preview Page, we can just select each main category in turn and request a custom CDF file to be built. We can then rename each file based on the category selected, and link it to the standard channel hyperlinks. We'll also need to modify the logos which are referenced in the CDF file, so that each channel is instantly distinguishable from the others.

The custom channel CDF file is generated automatically on the fly. We'll have a detailed look how this is done a little later.

Posting the CDF Files

Once the standard CDF files are created using the process given above, we can *move* them from the `ChannelExamples\Wrox\Channels\CustomCDFs` directory to the `ChannelExamples\Wrox\Channels\` directory. We've called the book, news and software CDF files `WroxBook.cdf`, `WroxNews.cdf` and `WroxSoftware.cdf` respectively. The custom CDF file is automatically created using the FileSystemObject in Active Server Pages. The generated file is of the form `Outputn.cdf` where *n* is the current session number of the user, and is stored in the `ChannelExamples\Wrox\Channels\CustomCDFs` directory. Each user may overwrite their own custom CDF file, but otherwise the files won't get deleted. In a more complicated example, we may require the user to login, and we could automatically provide a user ID number that would be used in combination with a password for identification in the future. We could store all custom channel settings so that the last settings could be easily retrieved and modified. This is particularly important, as the list of content selection options may be big for a large site. However, for this example, we'll assume the subscriber either chooses to subscribe, or reselects the custom subscription options before their session is terminated.

Enabling Subscriptions to the Active Channels

In order to get from the home page to the Channel Offerings Page, we simply follow a hyperlink. The standard channel subscription links to the CDF files are **static**, that is they always point to the same CDF files. However, in the case of a dynamically generated CDF file, a static hyperlink will not do because there may be several users all creating a custom CDF file concurrently. To resolve this problem, we use the session number as part of the CDF output filename. This ensures it is unique amongst the current users. In addition, if a user creates a CDF file, but then recreates it with different options, their old file will be overwritten with the new one because their session number would remain the same, unless they use a different instance of the browser or have restarted their computer between instances. Also, because we create the custom CDF file before we draw the whole page, we can dynamically adjust the hyperlink at the bottom of Content Preview Page to point to their newly generated CDF file. Following the hyperlink then instigates Add Active Channel Content dialog, as you saw earlier.

Providing the Channel Links

Next we have to provide links to all our channels within our pages.

Linking to the Channel Offerings Page

Within the other HTML on Channel Offerings page, we've defined a hyperlink that points to our `Channels` directory. Following the link loads up the `default.htm` file within it. The hyperlink is simply defined as:

In the details.htm file in the Wrox directory:

```
Go to our <A HREF="Channels">Channel Offerings</A> page
```

Linking to the Standard Channels

The Channel Offerings Page provides hyperlinks to the WroxBook, WroxNews and WroxSoftware channels. We've provided the channel name, content and subscription button in a table. In order to instigate the subscription wizards, our hyperlinks point to the appropriate CDF files.

In the default.htm file in the Channels directory:

```
<HTML>
<!-- HTML cut for clarity -->
<H1>Channel Offerings Page</H1>

<TABLE>
<TH>
    Channel
<TH>
    Content
<TH>
    Subscribe!

<TR>
<TD>
    Books
<TD>
    <UL>
        <LI>
            Forthcoming, new and existing books.
        <LI>
            Authors, errata, reviews and source code download.
    </UL>
<TD>
    <A HREF="WroxBooks.cdf">
    <IMG SRC="../Images/AddToChannels.gif" BORDER=0 ALT="Click here to subscribe to
the Books channel.">

<!-- Same type of thing for the WroxNews and WroxSoftware channels. -->
<!-- Also provide a link to the Custom Channel Content Selection Page. -->
</TR>
</TABLE>

</BODY>
</HTML>
```

In addition to links to the standard channels provided, we also wish to go to the custom channel Content Selection Page when we navigate the Custom Channel hyperlink.

Linking to the Custom Channel Subscription Page

The link to the Content Selection Page is different from the links to the other channels that you've just seen. Instead of linking straight to a CDF file, we link to an HTML document. This document presents a form to any visitor who wishes to create their own custom channel. The link takes the form of a standard graphical hyperlink to the page.

In the default.htm file in the Channels directory:

```
<HTML>
<!-- HTML cut for clarity -->

<TR>
<TD>
    Software
<TD>
    <UL>
        <LI>
                Free software from Stonebroom Software.
        <LI>
                Source code download pages for all existing books.
    </UL>

<TD>
    <A HREF="WroxSoftware.cdf">
    <IMG SRC="../Images/AddToChannels.gif" BORDER=0 ALT="Click here to subscribe to
the Software channel.">

<TR>
<TD>
    Custom Channel...
<TD>
    <UL>
        <LI>
                Choose to include any or all of the three channels.
        <LI>
                Select the content to which you want to subscribe.
    </UL>
<TD>
    <A HREF="Custom.htm">
    <IMG SRC="../Images/AddToChannels.gif" BORDER=0 ALT="Click here to initialize the
Custom Channel Wizard">
</TR>
</TABLE>

</BODY>
</HTML>
```

Following the hyperlink takes us to the custom channel Content Selection Page.

The Content Selection Page

This page provides named checkboxes that show a three-level hierarchy of the main categories, (the standard channel names) and the sub-categories at the second and third levels (the channel content that can be specified by the user). The page has two distinct parts to it: the page display, which shows the checkboxes and the titles within a table; and the client-side script code. This code makes the page more interactive. If the user checks a main category checkbox then all sub-category checkboxes are automatically checked. The reverse happens when it is unchecked. Additionally, the main category checkboxes are automatically checked when at least one sub-category checkbox is checked, and automatically unchecked when all child category checkboxes are unchecked.

Defining the Form

The whole set of checkboxes is wrapped up in a standard HTML form so that the results are available at the server end. We provide a submit type button to send the form to **PreviewContent.asp**–the file that will produce the CDF file based on the selected options. We're not going to show all the code from this selection page here, but we will provide a selection of the more interesting parts.

First, we use the **<FORM>** tag to specify that the checkbox values will be sent to the server when the form is submitted.

In the Custom.htm file within the Channels directory:

```
<HTML>
<HEAD>
<META NAME="GENERATOR" Content="Microsoft Visual InterDev 1.0">
<META HTTP-EQUIV="Content-Type" content="text/html; charset=iso-8859-1">
<TITLE>Content Selection Page</TITLE>
</HEAD>
<BODY>

<H1>Content Selection Page</H1>

Simply select the content that you want to be in your custom channel.
Clicking on a checkbox will check the sub-checkboxes below it.

<FORM ACTION="PreviewContent.asp" METHOD="POST" NAME="Me">
```

Next, we display the named checkboxes and titles in a table. Here, we're showing the HTML just for the WroxBook channel. Notice that we've defined a checkbox as **CHECKED**, which means it's checked by default, rather than unchecked.

Custom.htm file continued:

```
<TABLE>
    <TR>
            <TD>
                    <INPUT TYPE="CHECKBOX" NAME="chkBookTypes" CHECKED>
            <TD COLSPAN=3>
                    Books Types

    <TR>
            <TD>
                    <TD>
                            <INPUT TYPE="CHECKBOX" NAME="chkNew">
                    <TD COLSPAN=2>
                            New

    <TR>
            <TD>
                    <TD>
                            <INPUT TYPE="CHECKBOX" NAME="chkForthcoming">
                    <TD COLSPAN=2>
                            Forthcoming
```

615

```
        <TR>
            <TD>
                    <TD>
                            <INPUT TYPE="CHECKBOX" NAME="chkBackList">
                    <TD COLSPAN=2>
                            Back list

        <TR>
            <TD>
                    <TD>
                            <INPUT TYPE="CHECKBOX" NAME="chkBookDetails">
                    <TD COLSPAN=2>
                            Book Details

        <TR>
            <TD>
                    <TD>
                            <TD>
                                    <INPUT TYPE="CHECKBOX" NAME="chkErrata">
                            <TD>
                                    Errata

        <TR>
            <TD>
                    <TD>
                            <TD>
                                    <INPUT TYPE="CHECKBOX" NAME="chkReviews">
                            <TD>
                                    Reviews

        <TR>
            <TD>
                    <TD>
                            <TD>
                                    <INPUT TYPE="CHECKBOX" NAME="chkSourceCode">
                            <TD>
                                    Source Code
<!-- Some checkboxes cut out for clarity -->

        </TR>
</TABLE>
```

To get the nice indenting effect, we've used the **COLSPAN** parameter of the **<TD>** tag. This simply states that we want the data in that table cell to span over a number of columns, and that the table should not be formatted so that the width of the cell becomes the width of the longest text item. In fact, we just want our table cells to be the width of the checkboxes, because we wish to provide the indentation based on the checkboxes alone. The accompanying text is there for descriptive purposes only.

You'll also notice that each checkbox has a unique name. For instance, the checkbox for the Errata item is defined as:

```
<INPUT TYPE="CHECKBOX" NAME="chkErrata">Errata
```

Finally, we provide the Submit button which will send this information to the **PreviewContent.asp** file on the server. The ASP file isn't referenced in the code below because it was set in the **ACTION** attribute at the top of the form.

Custom.htm file continued:

```
<P>
Once you're happy with your selection, click on the preview button below.
You'll then be shown the channel contents, and have the opportunity to subscribe to
the channel.
<P>

<CENTER>
    <INPUT TYPE="SUBMIT" NAME= "cmdCreateChannel" VALUE="Preview Content">
</CENTER>

</FORM>
</BODY>
</HTML>
```

Writing the Code

Now we've seen the HTML page that is shown to the user, we're going to look at an extract of the code that brings this page to life. Once again, the extract just encompasses the code behind the WroxBooks categories. From the Content Selection Page, you'll see that the categories are:

- **BookTypes**

    New

    Forthcoming

    Back list

- **BookDetails**

    Errata

    Reviews

    Source code

We've provided code for the **onClick** event for each of the associated checkboxes. The top-level **chkBooks** checkbox is responsible for checking or unchecking its children. Here's the code that does this:

Custom.htm file continued:

```
<SCRIPT LANGUAGE="VBScript">

Dim frmMe 'Declare a global form variable
Set frmMe = Document.Forms("Me") 'and set it to the form.

chkBookTypes_onClick()     '4 Test calls ensure sub checkboxes are in sync.
chkBookDetails_onClick()
chkNews_onClick()
chkSoftware_onClick
```

```
Sub chkBookTypes_onClick()
    Dim blnCheck
    blnCheck = frmMe.chkBookTypes.Checked

    frmMe.chkNew.Checked = blnCheck
    frmMe.chkForthcoming.Checked = blnCheck
    frmMe.chkBackList.Checked = blnCheck
    frmMe.chkBookDetails.Checked = blnCheck
    'Update Book Details sub checkboxes.
    chkBookDetails_onClick()
End Sub

Sub chkBookDetails_onClick()
    Dim blnCheck
    blnCheck = frmMe.chkBookDetails.Checked

    frmMe.chkErrata.Checked = blnCheck
    frmMe.chkReviews.Checked = blnCheck
    frmMe.chkSourceCode.Checked = blnCheck
End Sub
```

We define a global variable that references the form from the object hierarchy. This saves us some typing later, and makes our code more readable.

```
Dim frmMe 'Declare a global form variable
Set frmMe = Document.Forms("Me") 'and set it to the form.
```

To recap on the object hierarchy of the browser, take a look at chapter 3.

We've defined the Book Types check box to be checked by default.

Custom.htm file:

```
<TR>
        <TD>
                <INPUT TYPE="CHECKBOX" NAME="chkBookTypes" CHECKED>
        <TD COLSPAN=3>
                Books Types
```

However, this doesn't automatically check the sub-checkboxes. To do this, we can call the `onClick` events for the 3 top-level checkboxes. This doesn't check them, but executes code that ensures the sub-checkboxes are in synchronization.

Still in the Custom.htm file:

```
chkBookTypes_onClick()       '4 Test calls ensure sub checkboxes are in sync.
chkNews_onClick()
chkSoftware_onClick
```

Now, each checkbox is responsible for the checked state of the parent also. Because each child checkbox has the same functionality in this respect, we can call a separate subroutine. Here's how it's called:

Custom.htm file continued:

```
Sub chkNew_onClick()
    BookTypes
End Sub

Sub chkForthcoming_onClick()
    BookTypes
End Sub

Sub chkBackList_onClick()
    BookTypes
End Sub

Sub chkErrata_onClick()
    BookDetails
End Sub

Sub chkReviews_onClick()
    BookDetails
End Sub

Sub chkSourceCode_onClick()
    BookDetails
End Sub
```

The subroutine ensures that the parent checkbox is checked if at least one of its child checkboxes are checked, and ensures it's unchecked if none of the child checkboxes are checked. There are two such subroutines for the WroxBooks channel content selection.

```
Sub BookTypes
    If frmMe.chkNew.Checked Or frmMe.chkForthcoming.Checked Or
frmMe.chkBackList.Checked Then
            frmMe.chkBookTypes.Checked = True
    Else
            frmMe.chkBookTypes.Checked = False
    End If
End Sub

Sub BookDetails
    If frmMe.chkErrata.Checked Or frmMe.chkReviews.Checked Or
frmMe.chkSourceCode.Checked Then
            frmMe.chkBookDetails.Checked = True
    Else
            frmMe.chkBookDetails.Checked = False
    End If
End Sub

<!-- Items cut out for clarity -->

</SCRIPT>
```

OK, that's all there is to this custom channel Content Selection Page. Before we move on to the real meaty ASP script of the whole example, let's have a look at the database. You'll need to understand it to see how it's used in creating the custom CDF file.

The Wrox Channel Database

The database only has one table in it–the Unit table. Channels and items have many similarities, with the main difference being that channels can have sub-channels and items, whereas items are the **node** terminators (the leaves on the tree, if you like). Once again, we've grouped the channels and items under the umbrella term **units**.

This table holds the channel and item information. To appreciate the data structure we'll need to capture the hierarchy necessary for the CDF file, and therefore the channel, consider the following diagram:

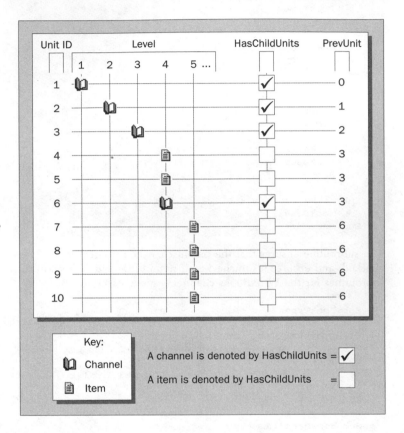

The data we've shown here has not been taken straight from the database, but is a simpler set to demonstrate how we use it to capture the information necessary to create the CDF file.

You'll notice that the UnitID is unique and would be created as an `AutoNumber` field. In this example, the values increment from 1 to the number of records. In reality, it doesn't matter what these are as long as they're unique and tie up with the PrevUnit value. Next comes the channel depth. This is used to reconstruct the hierarchy.

Here's how we're going to reconstruct the intended hierarchy from the values stored in our Unit table.

First, we get a recordset sorted alphabetically by the Unit title (the titles of the channel and item elements). Really, this sorting is only done to make the channel hierarchy more readable. You may be wondering why we don't sort by level, and then alphabetically by title. Well, this is unnecessary because the **table walking** routine you'll see later navigates the table appropriately. What we do is look at all the top-level units in turn. The unit can either be an item, or a channel. If it's an item, then we output the item details but we don't need to do any more with it because we know we don't have to expand any levels below it. This is denoted by the **HasChildUnits** field containing **False** for that record. If we've found a channel, then we output its details, and look for the first record (from the top of the recordset) with a level one more than the current channel, and a **PrevUnit** value equal to the **UnitID** of the current record. This may lead to us outputting and expanding further channels until there are none left to expand, while outputting any details relating to items we come across on the way. We perform these steps for each top-level item or channel from the recordset.

> *You may be wondering what exactly we output, and where it goes. We actually output channel preview information, and construct the CDF file at the same time based on extra information stored in the records. You'll see how this is done a little later.*

Now you've got a feel for how the database stores the unit information, let's move on to have a look at the crux page of the whole example—the custom channel Content Preview Page.

The Content Preview Page

This page is the real heart of the application. It may not look as if it does much when you saw the page created in your test run of the application, but in fact it performs the following steps:

- Opens a unique file that will grow to become the custom CDF file
- Inspects the input form values from the previous screen
- Opens the Unit table in the database
- Copies the recordset's contents to an array
- Provides and uses special CDF generating routines
- Navigates the array, following the chain, producing a preview of the channel content on screen while writing the CDF tags into the file in an indented format using the CDF generating routines
- Dynamically creates a hyperlink that points to the new CDF file.

Let's have a step by step look at how it achieves these objectives.

Setting up the Script

Before we've used the database in the script, we've included the **Adovbs.inc** file that defines various Active Data Objects (ADO) constants. This simply improves the readability of the code where we'd otherwise have to use meaningless numbers instead. The file is located in the **Channels** directory.

In the file PreviewContent.asp:

```
<%@ LANGUAGE="VBSCRIPT" %>

<!-- #include file="Adovbs.inc" -->
<HTML>
<HEAD>
<META NAME="GENERATOR" Content="Microsoft Visual InterDev 1.0">
<META HTTP-EQUIV="Content-Type" content="text/html; charset=iso-8859-1">
<TITLE>Content Preview Page</TITLE>
</HEAD>
<BODY>

<H1>Content Preview Page</H1>

You have chosen the following to be part of your custom channel:
```

Our next step is to use the `FileSystemObject`'s features to write the custom CDF file to the server's hard disk. But how do we go about getting the unique file name?

Generating a Unique CDF File Name

In this example, we keep a running count of the number of sessions created since the application was started. We do this by setting up an application level variable (`lngSessionNumber`) within the `Application` object:

In the global.asa file:

```
Sub Application_OnStart
    Application.Lock
    Application("lngNewCustomChannelNumber") = 0
    Application("lngSessionNumber") = 0
    Application.Unlock
End Sub
```

We've also defined a value in the `Application` object called `lngNewCustomChannelNumber`. This will keep track of the total number of visitors who have created a custom channel.

Then, whenever a new session is started, we simply increment the application-wide value `lngSessionNumber`. We've placed code that modifies the value in between `Application.Lock` and `Application.UnLock` statements. This is because the `Application` object provides shared memory between all our active sessions, and so it's very important that only one session should be able to update it at any one given time. Notice that we've also taken out the specific file name reference in the data connection. We don't need this, as the DSN name is sufficient. This makes setting up the example on another machine much easier. The first few lines of the sub procedure are generated automatically by Visual InterDev, which we've used as our tool of choice, instead of NotePad, to help generate this example. While not really necessary, it has helped us to cut a few corners.

```
Sub Session_OnStart
    '==Visual InterDev Generated - DataConnection startspan==
    '--Project Data Connection
            Session("WroxChannelDB_ConnectionString") =
```

```
        "DSN=WroxChannel;DriverId=25;FIL=MS Access;MaxBufferSize=512;PageTimeout=5;"
                Session("WroxChannelDB_ConnectionTimeout") = 15
                Session("WroxChannelDB_CommandTimeout") = 30
                Session("WroxChannelDB_RuntimeUserName") = ""
                Session("WroxChannelDB_RuntimePassword") = ""
        '==Visual InterDev Generated - DataConnection endspan==
        Application.Lock
        Application("lngSessionNumber") = Application("lngSessionNumber") + 1
        Application.Unlock
        Session("HasCreatedCustomChannel") = False
    End Sub
```

In addition to keeping track of the session number, we've also initialized a session value called **HasCreatedCustomChannel**. This will be used to determine whether the visitor has created a custom channel before in that session (so we don't increment **lngSessionNumber** unless they haven't created one before). It's also important to decrement **lngSessionNumber** so that we have an accurate number of sessions that are active. This is done in the **Session_OnEnd** event.

```
    Sub Session_OnEnd
        Application.Lock
        Application("lngSessionNumber") = Application("lngSessionNumber") - 1
        Application.Unlock
        Set Session("HasCreatedCustomChannel") = Nothing
    End Sub
```

Thus, we can now use the value depicted by **lngSessionNumber** to generate a unique CDF file, with the number being part of the file name. We need to decrement the number so our application won't create new CDF files *ad infinitum* for the same session, but rather any existing CDF file created by that session user will be overwritten with a new version.

Before we construct the file name, we test to see if the user in their session has created a custom CDF file before. If they haven't, then the **lngNewCustomChannelNumber** value of the Application object is incremented, and the **HasCreatedCustomChannel** value of the **Session** object is set to **True**, so any new custom channels created by the user will not be counted as being created by another visitor.

In the file PreviewContent.asp:

```
    If Session("HasCreatedCustomChannel") = False Then
            Application.Lock
            Application("lngNewCustomChannelNumber") =
  Application("lngNewCustomChannelNumber") + 1
            Application.Unlock
            Session("HasCreatedCustomChannel") = True
    End If
```

Back in our main ASP script, we create the **FileSystemObject** so we can write the CDF file to the hard disk. We've stored the file name in a variable that's available in the entire page. We've done this so we can use the file name when fixing the hyperlink at the end of the page so it points to the new file. Notice especially that we've used the **MapPath** method of the Server object. This allows us to get a physical file path (such as **C:\WebShare\WWWRoot\ChannelExamples\Wrox\Channels**) for our virtual directory (that we created during setup). This, like the step to remove the physical file location in the data connection, is a step which makes installation on new systems a much easier process.

```
    Set objFSO = CreateObject("Scripting.FileSystemObject")
    strFileName = "Output" & Application("lngSessionNumber") & ".cdf"
    Set objNewFile = objFSO.CreateTextFile(Server.MapPath("/ChannelExamples") &
"\Wrox\Channels\CustomCDFs\" & strFileName)
```

Bringing in the Database

As the script runs, we initialize a variable called **gintLastLevel**. This is a global variable to the script that we use to keep track of the current unit level from the database. This is especially important when we come on to a recursive routine (one that calls itself) later which builds up the view presented to the user, and also calls routines to produce the CDF file.

In the file PreviewContent.asp:

```
    gintLastLevel = 0
```

In the next step, we create a connection to the database using the **Connection** object. We open the data source called **WroxChannel**, which was configured during the example setup procedure.

```
    Set dbWrox = Server.CreateObject("ADODB.Connection")
    dbWrox.Open("WroxChannel")
```

To get at the data, we create a recordset on the fly. We now instruct the connection object (called **dbWrox**) to retrieve all the records from the **Unit** table, based on an SQL query, and return them in the **rsUnit** recordset. We've specified explicitly that the query we're executing is provided as an SQL statement (rather than a table, or stored procedure). This, together with the fact that by default the recordset is opened as forward only, speeds up the record retrieval process.

```
    Set rsUnit = dbWrox.Execute("SELECT Unit.* FROM Unit ORDER BY Unit.Title", ,
    adCmdText)
```

But what does the recordset contain afterwards? Well, we'll discuss the fields, and what function they serve next.

The Unit Table Fields

Although we've talked about a few of the fields our Unit table must contain in order to capture the CDF structure in essence, we also need some other fields which will be used to give the CDF file *flesh*. Here's a list of all the fields in the Unit table, and their associated functions.

Field Name	Description
UnitID	An autonumber field which provides a unique identifier of each row.
HasChildUnits	A Yes/No value which indicates if the unit is a channel (and therefore has sub-channels or items).
PrevUnit	A long integer value that links in with the UnitID to establish hierarchy and dependency.
Level	Used in conjunction with PrevUnit to contruct the hierarchy.
Identifier	A text value with the name of the checkbox from the Content Selection Page.

Field Name	Description
Title	The title text to be used in the **TITLE** element of the **CHANNEL** or **ITEM** items.
Abstract	A more verbose description of the unit.
Base	The base URL for the channel.
HREF	The full URL of the page to be referenced (if Base isn't given), or the name of the document to be retrieved from the provided Base virtual directory.
ImageREF	The location from where the Channel Bar Active Desktop Item channel logo should be obtained.
ImageWideHREF	The location from where the Internet Explorer 4.0 Channel Bar channel logo should be obtained.

The Identifier field is an interesting one. This field is necessary to tie the units defined in the records to a selection made from the Content Selection Page. For example, in a vain attempt to be famous, we may instruct the **Authors.htm** file (depicting us–the authors of the books) to be included whenever a book type (such as new, forthcoming or backlist) is selected. In this case, we enter the name of that checkbox, and not the name of the checkbox directly representing the item. This provides us with great flexibility in determining what will be included in the channel automatically, as long as the parent category is chosen.

Now we've had a look at the fields we'll be retrieving into our recordset, we'll see how access speed to the records can be improved considerably using the recordset's **GetRows** method.

Getting the Results into an Array using GetRows

In addition, to speed up access even more, we're going to store the records contained in our recordset in an array structure. This will greatly speed up any data retrieval operations, because we'll be scanning through the data several times. If the recordset isn't empty, then we define some meaningful identifiers that we'll use to effectively refer to the fields in our array. We transform the recordset into an array using the **GetRows** method of the recordset.

> One thing we should mention about GetRows is the way it organizes the array. The array becomes a transposed version of the recordset where the records and fields have been swapped over. This means that arUnit(x, y) refers to the x'th field, and the y'th row. For more information on the getrows method, see the documentation installed with ASP.

In the file PreviewContent.asp:

```
If Not rsUnit.EOF Then
        arUnit = rsUnit.GetRows()
        rsUnit.Close
        Set rsUnit = Nothing
        intUnitID = 0
        intHasChildUnits = 1
        intPrevID = 2
        intLevel = 3
        intIdentifier = 4
```

```
            intTitle = 5
            intAbstract = 6
            intBase = 7
            intHREF = 8
            intImageHREF = 9
            intImageWideHREF = 10
    Else
            Dim arUnit
            arUnit = Empty
    End If
```

Since we know we'll have at least one record in the Unit table, the **Else** part of the code should never execute. However, we've still put it in for safety. Now we've effectively got our array of records, we'll need to set about using the information stored there to construct our Channel and Item hierarchy.

Retrieving the Channels and Items

Before we consider how we write the HTML that creates our channel preview, or how the CDF element tags are written to the file we opened earlier, let's consider the algorithm we're going to use for the 'tree walking' task. This is going tackle the problem of displaying and writing the CDF structure.

Using Recursion to Expand and Output the CDF Structure

The tree-walking algorithm is best demonstrated as a high-level pseudo-code algorithm. It is essentially called to expand one channel, but it expands sub-channels and items as it executes.

```
Loop through all the rows in the Unit table
    If we find a unit that leads off from the unit we've just encountered And the
    level of the current unit is one more than that of the unit we just encountered And
    we selected the unit to be included in the previous content selection page Then
    If the unit has a child unit Then
            Output the channel information
            Expand any units from this channel
    Else
            Output the item
    End If
End Loop
```

In reading this, you may notice that there's a statement within the code that seems to require the operation that is being performed by the entire algorithm! This is **recursion**, that is, where the subroutine calls itself. Without going into a full lesson in recursion here, we must be careful that the recursion eventually stops, otherwise we go on calling the same subroutine forever. This is known as the **base case** for our recursion, and all recursive algorithms must contain at least one base case.

We are now in a position to explain the coded algorithm. Recall how the loop iterates through all records looking for a unit that leads off a previous unit. We can start the process off by calling our recursive subroutine–**ExpandFrom**–with the previous unit ID, and the current unit level using:

In the file PreviewContent.asp:

```
If Not IsEmpty(arUnit) Then
        XML
        ExpandFrom 0,1
        GenList(0)
End If
```

Don't worry about the **XML** and **GenList** calls. We'll deal with those a little later.

Let's have a look how the Books subchannel would be expanded. These are the records that will be used to build the structure.

UnitID	HasChildUnits	PrevUnit	Level	Identifier	Title
1	Yes	0	1	Wrox	Wrox Custom Channel
2	Yes	1	2	chkBooks	Books
3	Yes	2	3	chkBacklist	Back list
4	No	2	3	chkForthcoming	Forthcoming
5	No	2	3	chkNew	New
6	Yes	3	4	chkNew	Instant HTML Reference
7	No	6	5	chkNew	Authors
8	No	6	5	chkCode	Code
9	No	6	5	chkErrata	Errata
10	No	6	5	chkReviews	Reviews

Based on the data above, the routine would be called like this:

```
ExpandFrom 0,1
```

This means that we should expand from the Unit table row that has a **PrevUnit** value of 0, and a **Level** value of 1.

> *Our table above is not sorted alphabetically on Title, because this is done in the query. This makes data entry an easier process as we don't impose any ordering of records. As long as the data is correct, the algorithm will construct the CDF file as required.*

Tracing the Recursion

So, we want to expand the unit structure starting with **UnitID=1**, and we're looking for the first unit leading from it.

Note that our algorithm expands one unit. The easiest way to expand all the channels is achieved if we provide a top-level channel that encompasses all the other sub-channels and items. Our CDF file needs this anyway, so we might as well make life easy for ourselves and include it as the first record in the table.

For simplicity in this example, assume all units are selected from the Content Selection Page.

Our pseudo-code would then look like this:

```
Call: ExpandFrom (UnitID=)1, (Level=)1
Is there a unit with PrevUnit=1, Level=1+1? Yes, record with UnitID=2
    Is it a channel? Yes, so output the channel and expand it
            Output CHANNEL info
            ExpandFrom (UnitID=)2, (Level=)2
    Otherwise
            Output the ITEM information
```

Note that because **ExpandFrom 2, 2** is called first, **ExpandFrom 3, 3** won't be called until the previous call returns. This is the basis for recursion. Here's what happens with **ExpandFrom 2, 2**:

```
Call: ExpandFrom (UnitID=)2, (Level=)2
Is there a unit with PrevUnit=2, Level=2+1? Yes, record with UnitID=3
    Is it a channel? Yes, so output the channel and expand it
            Output CHANNEL info
            ExpandFrom (UnitID=)3, (Level=)3
    Otherwise
            Output the ITEM information

Call: ExpandFrom (UnitID=)3, (Level=)3
Is there a unit with PrevUnit=3, Level=3+1? Yes, record with UnitID=6
    Is it a channel? Yes, so output the channel and expand it
            Output CHANNEL info
            ExpandFrom (UnitID=)6, (Level=)4
    Otherwise
            Output the ITEM information

Call: ExpandFrom (UnitID=)6, (Level=)4
Is there a unit with PrevUnit=6, Level=4+1? Yes, record with UnitID=7
    Is it a channel? No, so just output the item
            Output CHANNEL info
            ExpandFrom (UnitID=)6, (Level=)4
    Otherwise
            Output the ITEM information
```

Here, no **ExpandFrom** call is made, so the algorithm *backtracks* (or unwinds) to the previous call. **ExpandFrom** expands *all* units with the required **PrevUnit** and **Level** values, so the next call is still:

```
Call: ExpandFrom (UnitID=)6, (Level=)4
Is there another unit with PrevUnit=6, Level=4+1? Yes, record with UnitID=8
    Is it a channel? No, so just output the item
            Output the ITEM information
```

And so on, until no further units fulfill these criteria. Eventually we get back to:

```
Call: ExpandFrom (UnitID=)2, (Level=)2
```

but we've expanded the Backlist record (UnitID=3), and so the only other records that match these criteria are the ones with UnitID of 4 and 5. Since neither of these have any child units, we just output the **ITEM** information for them, and our algorithm has run to completion.

Make sure you don't enter any records that refer to themselves, otherwise the algorithm will recurse infinitely.

Converting this algorithm into code gives us the complete **ExpandFrom** subroutine:

In the file PreviewContent.asp:

```
Sub ExpandFrom(intPrevUnitID, intLevelin)
    Dim intRow

    For intRow = 0 To UBound(arUnit, 2)
            strIdentifier = arUnit(intIdentifier, intRow)
            If Len(strIdentifier) Then
                    blnOK = (Request.Form(strIdentifier) = "on")
            Else
                    blnOK = False
            End If
            If arUnit(intPrevID, intRow) = intPrevUnitID And arUnit(intLevel, intRow)
= intLevelin And blnOK Then
                    'We've got the next unit.
                    If arUnit(intHasChildUnits, intRow) Then
                            'Expand channel.
                            GenChannel(intRow)
                            ExpandFrom arUnit(intUnitID, intRow), arUnit(intLevel,
intRow) + 1

                            WriteSpace(intLevelin - 1) :EndChannel
                    Else
                            'Output item.
                            GenItem(intRow)
                            WriteSpace(gintLastLevel - 1) : EndItem
                    End If
            End If
    Next
End Sub
```

The first thing to note is that we've explicitly dimensioned a variable called **intRow**. Although we've used implicit declarations before, we've made sure this was explicit and that the scope of the variable is obviously local to the **ExpandFrom** routine, which is absolutely necessary. The reason that this is so important is because we're relying on different instantiations (different nested calls) of the subroutine to have their own values of **intRow**. If ASP scans the routines, and finds a global variable called **intRow** (which it does later), then without this explicit declaration, a global variable would be used and our code would not work correctly.

In the next section, we iterate through all of the records, and check to see whether the appropriate checkbox matching that table row was selected in the Content Selection Page. All checkboxes checked in that page would provide a value of 'on' when the value is requested using **Request.Form**(*checkbox name*). If it wasn't checked, then no value is returned, and the comparison fails.

```
strIdentifier = arUnit(intIdentifier, intRow)
If Len(strIdentifier) Then
    blnOK = (Request.Form(strIdentifier) = "on")
Else
    blnOK = False
End If
```

Remember how we defined a top-level channel in our Unit table? You may be wondering which checkbox matches up with that record. Well, none of them do. What we've in fact done to ensure this record will always be matched is included a hidden type in our Content Selection Page code:

In the Custom.htm file:

```
<HTML>
<HEAD>

<!-- Lines missed out for clarity -->

<FORM ACTION="PreviewContent.asp" METHOD="POST" NAME="Me">

<INPUT TYPE="HIDDEN" NAME="Wrox" VALUE="on">

<TABLE>
<!-- …etc…-->
```

Note how we've defined the value as 'on'. In this way, it looks just like a checkbox, and we don't need to code around this one case. The next part is very interesting. It performs the check to see if the current table (or array, if you like) row fulfills the criteria.

```
          If arUnit(intPrevID, intRow) = intPrevUnitID And arUnit(intLevel, intRow)
  = intLevelin And blnOK Then
                    'We've got the next unit.
```

If this is the case, then we check to see if the unit is a channel or an item. If it's a channel, then we generate the channel preview and CDF file content from one master routine called **GenChannel**. We pass it the row number so it knows the source record to use. Then, you can see that our **ExpandFrom** routine calls itself recursively with the **UnitID** and the **Level** +1 values of the **intRow**th record as parameters. However, if the unit is an item, then we generate the preview and CDF elements for it using **GenItem**, and once again we give it the table row number, which effectively stops the recursion.

```
                 If arUnit(intHasChildUnits, intRow) Then
                      'Expand channel.
                      GenChannel(intRow)
                      ExpandFrom arUnit(intUnitID, intRow), arUnit(intLevel,
  intRow) + 1
                      WriteSpace(intLevelin - 1) : EndChannel
                 Else
                      'Output item.
                      GenItem(intRow)
                      WriteSpace(gintLastLevel - 1) : EndItem
                 End If
          End If
```

In addition to this, there's also a call to a routine called **WriteSpace** that generates spaces in the CDF file. The **GenChannel** and **GenItem** routines do most of the work of creating the preview, and building the CDF file. However, after we've output the channel or item details to the CDF file and screen, we need to close the channel or item and ensure that we indent the tags to make our CDF file more humanly readable. The **EndChannel** and **EndItem** routines are responsible for code generation to close the channel or item tag respectively.

The next step is to see how the preview and CDF files are generated.

Generating the Preview and CDF File

Before we look at how the channel and item code is generated, let's first think back to some code we've already seen, that we originally glossed over:

In the file PreviewContent.asp:

```
If Not IsEmpty(arUnit) Then
        XML
        ExpandFrom 0,1
        GenList(0)
End If
```

The **XML** routine generates code that inserts the **XML** CDF element in the CDF file. Because nothing has been inserted into this file, it's inserted at the current writing position, which happens to be at the start of the file:

In the CDF file being built:

```
<?XML VERSION="1.0"?>
```

We're going to cover the CDF code generation routines to a little later. Before we do that though, let's take a look at how the channels and items preview is created.

The CDF file is mainly composed of **CHANNEL** and **ITEM** CDF elements. It's natural that we should therefore split up the work of generating the file into the two routines–**GenChannel** and **GenItem**. We'll look first at how channels are generated in the file, as well as the preview that the user will see.

Generating the Channel Preview

In this section, we're going to concentrate on how the preview is generated, rather than the CDF file tags even though the routines to do both are called in the same parent routines. Don't worry because we will cover the CDF element generating routines a little later.

The **GenChannel** subroutine is concerned with creating the indented channel CDF elements in the CDF file, and the indented list preview on screen. Let's now have a look at the definition of this routine.

In the file PreviewContent.asp:

```
Sub GenChannel(intRow)
    intNewLevel = arUnit(intLevel, intRow)
    GenList(intNewLevel)
    If intNewLevel = 1 Then Response.Write "<STRONG>"
    Response.Write "<LI><IMG SRC=""../Images/Channel.gif"" WIDTH=19 HEIGHT=16
ALIGN=ABSMIDDLE>" & arUnit(intTitle, intRow) & vbCrlf
    If intNewLevel = 1 Then Response.Write "</STRONG>"
    gintLastLevel = intNewLevel
    WriteSpace(intNewLevel - 1) : Channel arUnit(intBase, intRow), arUnit(intHREF,
intRow)
    LogoBar arUnit(intImageHREF, intRow), intNewLevel
    LogoWide arUnit(intImageWideHREF, intRow), intNewLevel
    WriteSpace(intNewLevel) : Title arUnit(intTitle, intRow)
    WriteSpace(intNewLevel) : Abstract arUnit(intAbstract, intRow)

End Sub
```

Before we start the explanation, recall that we set a global variable earlier in the code:

```
gintLastLevel = 0
```

This variable represents the last level of the channel or item that we are looking at in the array. We've set the value equal to 0 initially, but it will vary as we follow the hierarchy from the **ExpandFrom** routine.

The first step is to get the level defined by the row **intRow**. We then generate list items that will indent our preview so that the structure is representative of the actual CDF file structure. This is done with:

```
GenList(intNewLevel)
```

The idea behind the **GenList** routine is to generate HTML for the unordered lists, ready to accept details of the channel or item that is to be output. Imagine we wanted to output two lists of items, the second being a sublist of the first. This is what the HTML would look like:

```
<UL>
    <LI> Level 1
    <LI> Level 1
    <UL>
            <LI> Level 2
            <LI> Level 2
    </UL>
</UL>
```

This is the purpose of the **GenList** routine. We need to remember the level of the last unit that was output, and generate HTML to output another **<UL>** tag to start an unordered list if the current unit level is greater. But if the level of the current unit is less than that of the previous unit, then we need to output the appropriate number of **</UL>** tags instead. Within the **<UL>** and **</UL>** tags, the list of units is generated and output. You'll recall in our **GenChannel** routine that we update the value of **gintLastLevel** to the value of the current unit level, so that we always know the level of the last unit output.

```
Sub GenList(intNewLevel)
        For intIndex = gintLastLevel To intNewLevel - 1
                Response.Write "<UL>" & vbCrlf
        Next
        For intIndex = intNewLevel To gintLastLevel - 1
                Response.Write "</UL>" & vbCrlf
        Next
End Sub
```

OK, now we know how we generate the unordered lists (and therefore get the hierarchy of the CDF file in the preview), we need to see what HTML we output that will become the items of the list.

```
Sub GenChannel(intRow)
    intNewLevel = arUnit(intLevel, intRow)
    GenList(intNewLevel)
    If intNewLevel = 1 Then Response.Write "<STRONG>"
    Response.Write "<LI><IMG SRC=""../Images/Channel.gif""  WIDTH=19 HEIGHT=16
ALIGN=ABSMIDDLE>" & arUnit(intTitle, intRow) & vbCrlf
    If intNewLevel = 1 Then Response.Write "</STRONG>"
```

Well, if the unit has a level of 1 (the first, and only, top level unit), then we make it stand out by making it bold by encompassing the title of the unit between the `<STRONG>` and `</STRONG>` tags in HTML. In addition, we output an open book graphic that shows that the unit is a channel. Now, we update the global variable `gintLastLevel` so we know how many lists to open or close the next time around.

```
    gintLastLevel = intNewLevel
    WriteSpace(intNewLevel - 1) : Channel arUnit(intBase, intRow), arUnit(intHREF, intRow)
    LogoBar arUnit(intImageHREF, intRow), intNewLevel
    LogoWide arUnit(intImageWideHREF, intRow), intNewLevel
    WriteSpace(intNewLevel) : Title arUnit(intTitle, intRow)
    WriteSpace(intNewLevel) : Abstract arUnit(intAbstract, intRow)
End Sub
```

> *You may be wondering why we didn't specify system folder icons and sub-channel and item images. IE4's default icons of books for the sub-channels, and pages for the items happen to be quite convenient. However, there's nothing to stop you adding them in your CDF generating routines.*

After we've done that, we indent the CDF file with a number of spaces, which is achieved by the `WriteSpace` routine. Notice that we're providing the `intNewLevel` - 1 as a parameter, because we want it to be indented one step less than the channel body we have yet to generate. Next we generate the channel CDF tag in the file. This is done with the `Channel` routine, which accepts the `Base` and `HREF` field values. We then generate the logo tag that will furnish our Channel Bar Active Desktop Item with an appropriate image as specified by the parameter to the `LogoBar` routine, and then generate a CDF element that will provide us with a wider version for our channel bar within IE4 itself. We add indentation spaces and generate the `TITLE` CDF element, and then the `ABSTRACT` tag.

Before we move on to see how the `ITEM` element preview is created, let's just have a quick look at the `WriteSpace` routine we've talked about on numerous occasions. It's quite simple, but it makes a world of difference to the readability of the CDF files we generate.

```
Sub WriteSpace(intNewLevel)
    For intIndex = 1 To intNewLevel
            objNewFile.Write "  "
    Next
End Sub
```

Generating the Item Preview

The code to generate and output the item preview (and CDF file elements) is remarkably similar to the `GenChannel` routine, and we're not going to restate the principles behind how it works.

```
Sub GenItem(intRow)
    intNewLevel = arUnit(intLevel, intRow)
    GenList(intNewLevel)
    Response.Write "<LI><IMG SRC=""../Images/Item.gif"" WIDTH=15 HEIGHT=16
ALIGN=ABSMIDDLE>" & arUnit(intTitle, intRow) & vbCrlf
    gintLastLevel = intNewLevel
    WriteSpace(intNewLevel - 1) : Item arUnit(intHREF, intRow)
    WriteSpace(intNewLevel) : Title arUnit(intTitle, intRow)
    WriteSpace(intNewLevel) : Abstract arUnit(intAbstract, intRow)
End Sub
```

Finish off the Preview

Apart from the CDF file element generating routines, there isn't much left to do. It's customary to close any open objects, and set them equal to **Nothing** to explicitly free the resources they're consuming.

```
        objNewFile.Close
        Set objNewFile = Nothing
        dbWrox.Close
        Set dbWrox = Nothing
    %>
```

Here's a good point to include our CDF file element generating routines that we called earlier. We've defined them in a separate file called **GenCDF.inc**, which we've just included into our script. In this way, we separate this code out of the main script, and hide it neatly in another file.

```
    <!-- #include file="GenCDF.inc" -->
```

We then output the tail part of the Content Preview Page by showing the user how many custom channels have been created.

```
    You are visitor number <STRONG><%= Application("lngNewCustomChannelNumber") %></
    STRONG> to have previewed a custom channel.
```

We then make our hyperlink at the bottom of the page point to our newly generated CDF file, by fixing up the HREF attribute dynamically.

```
    <TABLE>
    <TR>
    <TD>
        Click here to create your custom channel subscription
    <TD>
        <A HREF=" <%= "CustomCDFs/" & strFileName %> ">
        <IMG BORDER=0 SRC="../Images/AddToChannels.gif">
    </TR>
    </TABLE>

    </BODY>
    </HTML>
```

The last step is to see how the CDF elements are written to the file.

The CDF Generation Routines

Although this part may sound one of the most complicated, you'll probably be glad to hear that we've in fact already done all the real hard work earlier. We've defined several routines that simply write some CDF tags to a file depicted by our object **objNewFile** and insert in the appropriate places the parameters that we obtained from our Unit table. You can use these routines easily in their own code simply by using an **include** statement, just like we did.

The file system object supports both the **Write** and **WriteLine** methods that output text to the file. Because we want our CDF file code to be easily readable, we've decided to use the **WriteLine** version, which simply means that a new line character is added at the end of each line output to the file. Here's the entire list of CDF file element generating routines:

In the file GenCDF.inc:

```
<%
    Sub XML()
            objNewFile.WriteLine "<?XML VERSION=""1.0""?>"
    End Sub

    Sub Channel(strBase, strHREF)
            objNewFile.WriteLine "<CHANNEL BASE=""" & strBase & """ HREF=""" & strHREF
& """>"
    End Sub

    Sub LogoBar(strImageHREF, intNewLevel)
            If strImageHREF <> "" Then
                    WriteSpace(intNewLevel)
                    objNewFile.WriteLine "<LOGO HREF=""" & strImageHREF &  """
STYLE=""IMAGE""/>"
            End If
    End Sub

    Sub LogoWide(strImageWideHREF, intNewLevel)
            If strImageWideHREF <> "" Then
                    WriteSpace(intNewLevel)
                    objNewFile.WriteLine "<LOGO HREF=""" & strImageWideHREF & """
STYLE=""IMAGE-WIDE""/>"
            End If
    End Sub

    Sub Title(strTitle)
            objNewFile.WriteLine "<TITLE>" & strTitle & "</TITLE>"
    End Sub

    Sub Abstract(strAbstract)
            objNewFile.WriteLine "<ABSTRACT>" & strAbstract & "</ABSTRACT>"
    End Sub

    Sub Log(strValue)
            objNewFile.WriteLine "<LOG VALUE=""" & strValue & """/>"
    End Sub

    Sub Item(strHREF)
            objNewFile.WriteLine "<ITEM HREF=""" & strHREF & """>"
    End Sub

    Sub EndItem
            objNewFile.WriteLine "</ITEM>"
    End Sub

    Sub EndChannel
            objNewFile.WriteLine "</CHANNEL>"
    End Sub
%>
```

You'll notice that we haven't provided any routines to generate the **<USAGE>** *CDF element. This is what happens in the news channels, and so we saved ourselves work using this to our advantage.*

This brings us to the end of our tour of the Wrox Custom Channel example.

Summary

In this chapter, we've shown you how to host channels from a Web site. We've provided three channels that showcase the reference parts of the sample Wrox web site. We've shown you how the structure of the Web site is independent of the structure of the CDF file, and how users can subscribe to them. However, the main purpose of this case study was to show you how you can use several technologies together, such as Active Server Pages, client-side scripting, and of course, news channels, to create custom channels. When used wisely, it ensures that subscribers are getting the content they're after, and can save on download time and telephone bills as well.

The most important points in this chapter are:

- It is easy to host your own channels from your own Web page. In the simplest form, all you'll need to do is provide a hyperlink to a CDF file.

- We can get extra flexibility by allowing users to determine what they want to have as part of their custom channel, using Active Server Pages.

- We can link in a database and generate a preview of the channel's contents, as well as generating the formatted CDF file. Using a database in this manner means that our site can be more easily maintained.

- Channel technology is still in its infancy. You can expect many more bells and whistles to be added to the Webcasting experience.

We've looked at Webcasting and Channels in some detail. The final chapter in this section deals with the Active Desktop.

True Web Integration and the Active Desktop

With the introduction of the Web and specialized Web browsers, the Internet became far more widely accessible. For the first time, the Internet was something that everyday people could use effectively, as users didn't need to know any special transfer commands to access its content: they just used the browser interface provided, and the functionality provided by HTML documents. That was a revolution in information exchange. Now, with the advent of IE4, and the shell integration mode, we're seeing another revolution.

As you already know, the Dynamic HTML aspects of IE4 have brought about new possibilities that could not be fulfilled quite so easily using previous technology. It's the mixture of Dynamic HTML functionality, and the fact that the desktop now becomes a big browser that has paved the way for a whole new genre of information collection and seamless Internet/Intranet connectivity. This is collectively known as **True Web Integration**, and a very important aspect of it that we'll be considering is the **Active Desktop**.

The next wave of information blasters and desktop utilities will be **Active Desktop Items**. These can be anything from standard HTML pages, to Dynamic HTML documents with embedded controls and Java applets, to ActiveX Documents. These desktop items can sit on the Active Desktop, which provides us with the ability to customize our working desktop in a manner not previously available.

So, in this chapter, we'll be considering:

- What True Web Integration is, what it provides, and its component parts.
- What the Active Desktop is, and how it differs from the standard Windows 95 'shell'.
- What Active Desktop Items are, what they do, and how we use them.
- Ways of creating our own Desktop Items using Dynamic HTML, and how to install them across the Web.

First, then, let's take a look at the facilities provided by True Web Integration.

True Web Integration

The shell integration mode replaces a subset of the Windows 95 operating system, and it's this which allows the browser to be the central proponent for true web integration. We can turn this feature on and off, as well as get to the many customization dialogs from menu items off the Start menu.

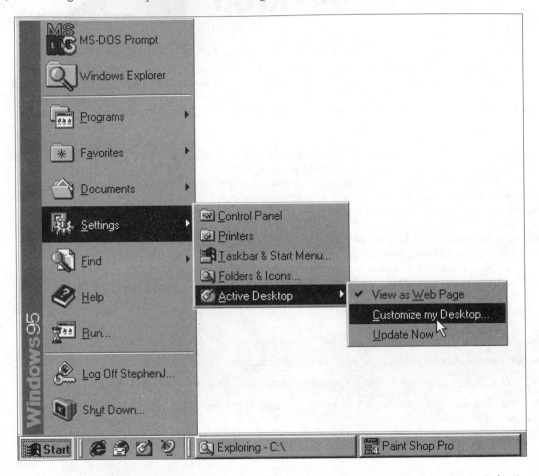

The quickest way to disable the active desktop and re-enable the standard Windows 95 look (and vice-versa) is by selecting the View as Web Page menu item. In addition to simply turning the Active Desktop on and off, we can also customize more settings to make the desktop behave how we'd want. Selecting the Folders & Icons menu item brings up the Folder Options dialog.

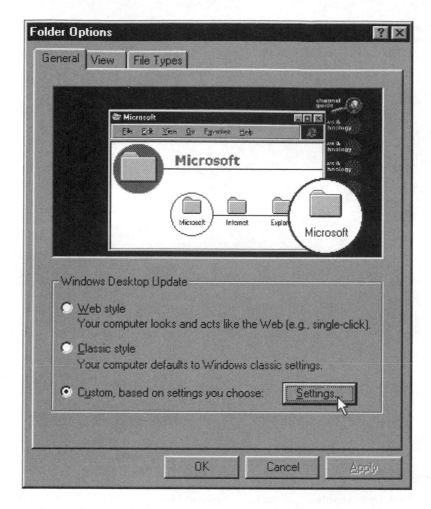

From here, we can click on the Settings button to bring up the Custom Settings dialog.

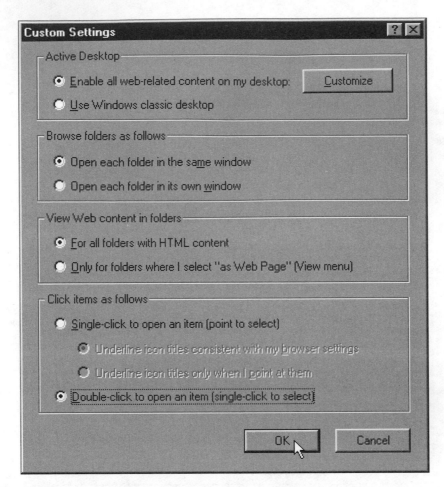

When the Active Desktop is enabled, the Customize button brings up a new version of the Display Properties dialog. It now also allows us to keep tabs on our Active Desktop Items. We'll have a look at this dialog in the next section, which deals explicitly with the Active Desktop.

With true web integration, we also have the option of creating our own HTML documents, which can act as a background in folder windows. If we only want this to happen for certain folder windows, then we can select the second option in the View Web content in folders section of the dialog.

Furthermore, everything, from our desktop icons right through to file lists in folders, becomes hyperlinks. This means that one-click can be used to launch the application behind an icon, or load a file from a list. While this is intended as an effort saving measure, it can become annoying when selecting multiple files for instance, because we have to *hover* our mouse pointer over each item to select it.

These set-up changes can seem rather cosmetic. However, the real benefits of the active Desktop lie in the centralized browser. Using this, the Windows 95 operating system can smoothly access information held almost anywhere – on the local machine, on a network machine, on a company Intranet or even on the

Internet itself. This true web integration helps us not to be so concerned with *where* the information is and what *type* of application we should load to accept the information. We've seen a limited form of the latter with file associations. In any case, it does provide us with mechanisms that allow us to get at the information we want more easily.

Many of the views IE4 presents us with are in fact HTML pages, or applications that are embedded within the browser. For example, the screenshot shows that it's possible to use the browser to navigate through folders on a local machine, and even set up the display just as we want it. The browser has integrated the various parts of the operating system (in this case Windows Explorer), and it still gives us all the functionality that we're accustomed to.

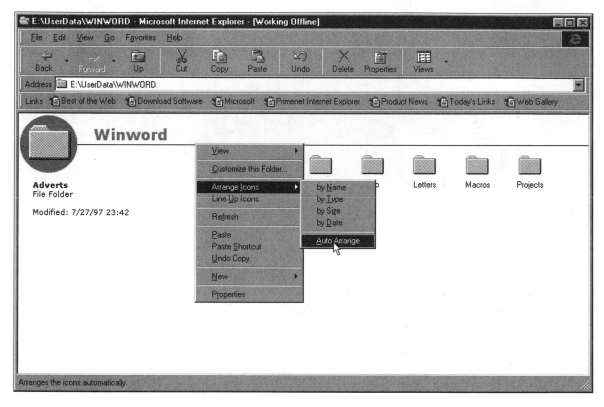

As you can see, when the browser is used in this manner, the toolbar buttons and menus change to represent the viable actions in the current context. So, since we're browsing the disk contents, we can use actions appropriate to finding our documents.

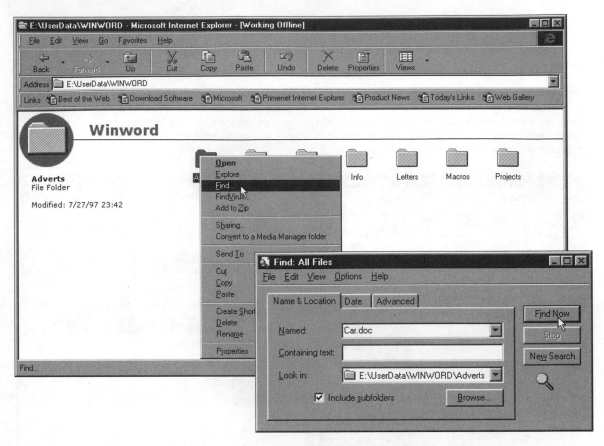

It's also possible to take this further, and load up a Word or Excel document into the browser window. However, you can still resort to the conventional ways of viewing your disk contents, either through the Windows Explorer, or the Editing Documents directory from your Office applications.

The differences are also more widespread. For instance, opening up the My Computer view from the Desktop produces this:

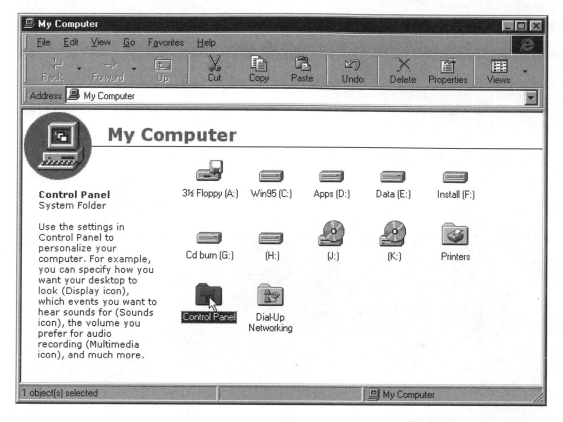

The appearance of this window has changed dramatically. In fact, it's only the customary icons that still look similar. The whole window is actually an HTML document, which is generated on the fly.

If you wish, you can make the window's content look more like the standard My Computer window by deselecting the View as Web Page item from the menu.

The Control Panel is similar in that it, too, is a Web page linked to various parts of Windows. These views are now inherent in the operating system.

Let's now move on to have a brief look at Active Desktop.

The Active Desktop

With the Active Desktop, we're given a new way to customize our working environment. We can add Active Desktop Items to our desktop and position and size them as we want.

We can also specify a background HTML file to be displayed, or just opt out and use standard Windows desktop. Those facilities can be altered through a tab on the Display Properties dialog.

The Active Desktop Settings Tab

With the Active Desktop enabled, we get an extra tab–Web–in the Display Properties window. It can be displayed by selecting the Customize my Desktop menu item off the Start|Active Desktop menu or by selecting the Customize button on the Custom Settings dialog we've just explained. However, the quickest way to display the Display Properties dialog is by right-clicking on the desktop, and selecting the Active Desktop|Customize my Desktop menu item. The importance of the new Web tab is that it lets us add and delete Active Desktop Items directly. Clicking on the tab brings it to the fore.

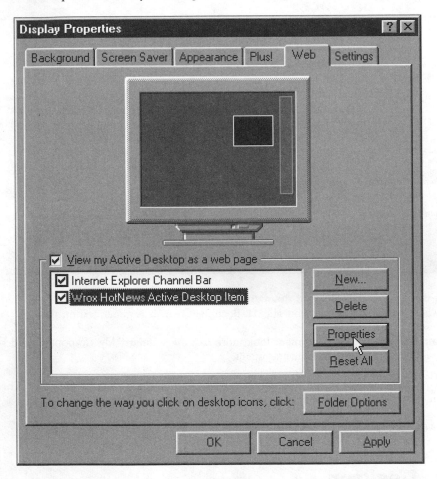

From this we can see that IE4 comes with one desktop item already installed–the Channel Bar. If we have several desktop items installed, clicking on one in the list will highlight the shape representing the desktop item to which it refers. Clicking on the Properties button displays the Active Desktop Item Properties dialog for the selected Desktop Item. The button isn't available when the Internet Explorer Channel Bar item is selected, because this is a special desktop item unlike others that you can download across the Web. We can also go to the Folder Options dialog from here, and (once again) enable or disable the Active Desktop.

If you now flip across to the Background tab, you'll notice that this dialog has subtly changed. From here, we can now select an Internet document (HTML page) to display on the desktop, or alternatively we can just stick with an ordinary format for our wallpaper, a bitmap (BMP) graphic file.

Companies may wish to provide some sort of site map, and displaying it on the desktop provides the most accessible place for employees. On the other hand, you might just wish to create your own personalized background screen, with some of your favorite pictures, links and utilities running within it.

Here's an example Active Desktop:

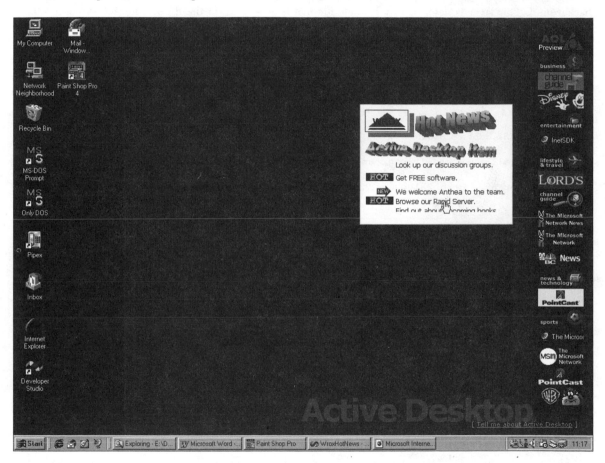

You'll notice that in addition to the Channel Bar, we've installed another desktop item - the Wrox Hot News Active Desktop Item. You'll see how it's created and installed later in the chapter, but now it's time to look at the mechanics of the Active desktop.

Active Desktop Structure

With shell integration mode enabled, the Active Desktop is built in two layers:

▲ A transparent **icon layer** that displays all of the user's existing desktop shortcuts

▲ A background **HTML layer** that hosts all Desktop Items

It's the HTML layer that provides us with the facility of displaying an HTML document as the desktop background. This layer is described by a single file that is generated on the fly by Internet Explorer 4.0. This file is named **DESKTOP.HTT** can be found on your machine at **C:\WINDOWS\APPLICATION DATA\MICROSOFT\INTERNET EXPLORER** and the file contains the following, when there are no Active Desktop Items (apart from the default ones) installed:

```
<!-- The following file is an HTML Wallpaper for use with Microsoft      -->
<!-- Internet Explorer 4.0.                                              -->

<HTML>
<HEAD><BASE HREF="C:\WINDOWS\Web\Wallpaper\Wallpapr.htm">
</HEAD>
<BODY scroll=no style="background: black; margin: 0; font: 8pt Verdana">

<TABLE border=0 height=100% width=100% cellpadding=0 cellspacing=0 style="font: 8pt
Verdana">
<TR valign=bottom>
    <TD align=right>
        <SPAN style="
            position:               relative;
                left:                   -75pt;
            letter-spacing: -4px;
            font:                   41pt verdana;
            font-weight:    bold;
            color:                  #424242"
        >Active Desktop<SPAN style="
            font:                   4pt Verdana;
            letter-spacing:         0;
            color:                  #424242"
        >TM</SPAN>
        </SPAN>
    <BR>
        <SPAN style="
            position:       relative;
                top:            -10pt;
                left:           -20pt;
            font:           8pt verdana;
            color:      #FF9C31;"
        >[ <a  href="res://ie4tour.dll/adinfo.htm"
            style="
            color:      #FF9C31;
            text-decoration: underline"
    >Tell me about Active Desktop</a> ]</span>
    <BR>
    </TD></TR></TABLE>        <OBJECT id=1 name="DeskMovrW" style="position:absolute;
            Background=orange; HEIGHT: 525; LEFT: 558; TOP: 16; WIDTH: 99; Z-INDEX:
                1002"
```

```
            resizeable="XY"
            classid="clsid:131A6951-7F78-11D0-A979-00C04FD705A2">
   </OBJECT>


<OBJECT
   classid="clsid:72267F6A-A6F9-11D0-BC94-00C04FB67863"
   id=ActiveDesktopMover
   STYLE="position:absolute; container:positioned; LEFT: 0;TOP: 0; WIDTH: 0; HEIGHT:
0;zIndex: 5"
>
<PARAM name="Interval" value=500>
<PARAM name="SizerID" value="ActiveDesktopMover">
<PARAM name="Enabled" value="True">
<PARAM name="TargetName" value="DeskMovr">
<PARAM name="WindowOnly" value="False">
</OBJECT>

<OBJECT
   classid="clsid:72267F6A-A6F9-11D0-BC94-00C04FB67863"
   id=ActiveDesktopMoverW
   STYLE="position:absolute; container:positioned; LEFT: 0;TOP: 0; WIDTH: 0; HEIGHT:
0;zIndex 19"
>
<PARAM name="Interval" value=500>
<PARAM name="SizerID" value="ActiveDesktopMoverW">
<PARAM name="Enabled" value="True">
<PARAM name="TargetName" value="DeskMovrW">
<PARAM name="WindowOnly" value="True">
</OBJECT>

</BODY></HTML>
```

It's within this automatically generated file that all your selected Active Desktop Items are made available for viewing. If you go to change your background from the wallpaper to the Waves picture that comes as standard with Windows 95, then the content of the file changes to reflect this:

```
<!----
***** This file is automatically generated by Microsoft Internet Explorer 4.0
(deskhtml.dll) *****
-------->
<HTML>
<BODY background="file:///C:/WINDOWS/Waves.bmp" style="border:none;" bgcolor=#008080
topmargin=0 leftmargin=0 rightmargin=0 bottommargin=0>
    <OBJECT id=0 name="DeskMovrW" style="position:absolute;
         Background=orange; HEIGHT: 525; LEFT: 616; TOP: 16; WIDTH: 99; Z-INDEX:
1000"
         resizeable="XY"
         classid="clsid:131A6951-7F78-11D0-A979-00C04FD705A2">
    </OBJECT>
<OBJECT
   classid="clsid:72267F6A-A6F9-11D0-BC94-00C04FB67863"
   id=ActiveDesktopMover
   STYLE="position:absolute; container:positioned; LEFT: 0;TOP: 0; WIDTH: 0; HEIGHT:
0;zIndex: 5"
>
```

```
<param name="Interval" value=500>
<param name="SizerID" value="ActiveDesktopMover">
<param name="Enabled" value="True">
<param name="TargetName" value="DeskMovr">
<param name="WindowOnly" value="False">
</OBJECT>

<OBJECT
    classid="clsid:72267F6A-A6F9-11D0-BC94-00C04FB67863"
    id=ActiveDesktopMoverW
    STYLE="position:absolute; container:positioned; LEFT: 0;TOP: 0; WIDTH: 0; HEIGHT:
0;zIndex 19"
>
<param name="Interval" value=500>
<param name="SizerID" value="ActiveDesktopMoverW">
<param name="Enabled" value="True">
<param name="TargetName" value="DeskMovrW">
<param name="WindowOnly" value="True">
</OBJECT>

 </BODY> </HTML>
```

However you can't change the contents of the file manually as any changes you make will be overwritten. You can only change it indirectly, as the result of your actions – such as adding a desktop item to the desktop.

The two layers are arranged like this:

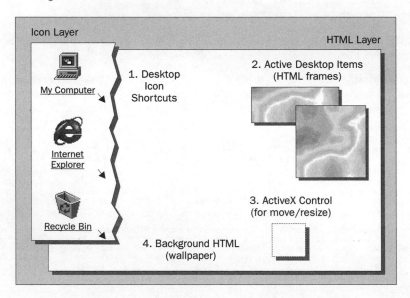

Now we've had a look at the Active Desktop structure, let's now turn our attention to desktop items that sit on it.

Active Desktop Items

So far, we've mentioned Active Desktop Items quite a few times without really looking too deeply at what they are, and how they can be used. They are one of the most interesting aspects of the Active Desktop, and so we're going to devote a large portion of this chapter to their use and construction.

Active Desktop Items are primarily intended to bring live Web content straight to your desktop. Some typical examples of the Desktop Items available today are:

- Tickers for sports scores, stock quotes, or weather

- Headline lists for news stories or announcements

- Pop-up broadcast messages for internal corporate announcements

- Notifications of new mail, chat, or public discussion forums

- Pictures of sports highlights or breaking news stories. A picture can be configured for daily update; clicking the picture could launch a browser window to preview the related story

You can have a look at some examples from Microsoft's site at `http://www.microsoft.com/ie/ie40/gallery`. You'll get the option to navigate here the first time you click on the New button in the Web tab of the Display Properties dialog.

One of the major advantages of the Desktop Item is that content can be refreshed automatically. This is actually achieved via WebCasting and subscriptions, which were covered in the last chapter. An Active Desktop Item is basically a small, borderless frame, which is embedded in the Active Desktop. As we've shown earlier, you can add and remove them using the Web tab on the Display Properties window. You can also alter their size and position using the mouse.

Building Active Desktop Items

When creating Active Desktop Items, there are several things to consider. To start with, we have to build the desktop item itself. Very simple Desktop Items may just consist of an HTML document that you want to have displayed on the desktop. For instance, companies might provide different Active Desktop Items that the employees can anchor in their working environment. In this case, each item could be particular to a department, or a project, while others might provide links to company information in their Intranet. At the simplest level, these HTML Active Desktop Item documents can be updated by hand, with the effects being propagated throughout the rest of the company.

However, to get the best from Active Desktop Items, they have to be designed *as* Active Desktop Items. What this means is that we should create items that give us the functionality we would like them to provide, without being 'too heavy'. Typically for this, we'll have to move away from traditional HTML and bring in other elements to our pages. So we may write dynamic HTML and script code to give our desktop items a bit of versatility – which is especially important when an Internet connection is not constantly available. Of course, there's nothing to stop us bringing in ActiveX controls and Java applets as well.

When we've built our Active Desktop Item, we need to think about making it available for others to use. In an Intranet scenario, this is very easy to achieve, as usually we'd just reference the document on a local file server. However, this approach is impractical when distributing items across the Internet. For this, we need to create a **host document**, which shows our item working, and provides a mechanism whereby users can install it remotely across the web at a click of a mouse button.

Steps in Developing an Active Desktop Item

There are four main steps to creating an Active Desktop Item and host document. We need to:

- ▲ Design and code the Active Desktop Item
- ▲ Create the CDF file which is used for installing the item over the Web
- ▲ Post the CDF file to onto the Web server
- ▲ Enable subscriptions to the new Active Desktop Item

We can write and test our Active Desktop Item without having it installed on our Desktop. In this case, we code it and test it just as if we were creating any other HTML document—we simply load it up in IE4 to make sure it works OK.

> *Of course, we could manually add it to our desktop after this stage using the Web tab from the Display Properties dialog, if we'd so wish.*

Next, we must write the CDF file that will be used to install the item over the Web. The CDF structure is covered in depth in Chapter 16.

Once we've created our CDF file, we must copy it to a place on our Web server that's accessible by the outside world. This is what is meant by *posting* the CDF file. The last stage is where we provide an elegant host document that can be used to install our Active Desktop Item onto users' desktops.

In the next section, we'll take you through this process, using the Wrox Hot News Active Desktop Item as an example.

The Wrox Hot News Active Desktop Item

People always like to know what's going on around them, and in the computing world, it's difficult to find out about the new developments and important topics as they occur. In this section, we're going to develop the Wrox Hot News Active Desktop Item. This item will allow whoever installs it to know what's happening at Wrox: any new book releases, pertinent technology (such as the introduction of the Rapid server-the server used to host live examples) and so on. Of course, this is just a simple example, but it serves to demonstrate the principles of distributable Desktop Item creation.

> *You can install this desktop item from our Web site at* `http://rapid.wrox.co.uk/books/0707/`

Simply click on the Add to Desktop button from the page to install the desktop item. Once installed, this is how the item appears on your desktop.

Wrox's site is complicated and uses many server-side technologies and frames. Following the upcoming books and discussion groups links will cause a message box to display stating that the VBScript code can't access the parent frame (because we didn't go in from the root of Wrox's site). Simply click on OK to dismiss the dialog. The content we were seeking will still be displayed correctly.

Downloading and Installing the Example

In addition to installing the example over the Web, you can also download the source code from `http://rapid.wrox.co.uk/books/0707/` and install it on your own machine as long as you're running a web server (such as the Personal Web Server or the Microsoft Internet Information Server). You'll need to modify the following files and update them with the name of your own server:

> `InstallHotNews.htm`
>
> `HotNews.cdf`

You'll also need to create a virtual directory that points to a directory holding the extracted files. Once you've done that, you can add the item to your desktop by loading up the `InstallHotNews.htm` file **over HTTP** and clicking on the Add to Desktop button from the page. Click Yes on the first dialog, and OK on the second. You'll then see the Downloading Subscriptions progress indicator dialog. After a short while, the desktop item should appear on your desktop.

The Item Structure

If you've installed the desktop item, you'll notice that the five lines are information continuously scroll upwards. If you put your mouse pointer over any item of news, then they all stop scrolling, and your mouse pointer metamorphs into a hand. Each item that's shown is actually a hyperlink – with many of them pointing at the relevant parts of our Wrox Web site. If you move the mouse pointer out off the items, then the list starts scrolling again.

Let's have a look at the structure of our item in more detail.

The Item Divisions

The item itself consists of seven divisions. Five of them are used for the five news item lines, and one is used for the title picture, and one for the footer. The news items are displayed one under another. All of the news divisions scroll up slowly. When an item becomes totally obscured by the title division, it is moved to behind the footer division. It them slowly scrolls into view, and then eventually disappears behind the title division again.

The divisions are laid out like this.

```
Title Division
───────────────────────────
News Item
───────────────────────────
News Item
───────────────────────────
News Item
───────────────────────────
News Item
───────────────────────────
News Item
Footer Division
```

The News Link Divisions

At the start of the desktop item, we've defined five news line divisions. These are called `divLink0` through `divLink4` and each will hold precisely one item of news. We've defined each division to be 20 pixels high, and they're all set be located at the same point. We'll actually move them into more useful positions a little later by using some script code.

In the file `WroxHotNews.htm`:

```html
<HTML>
<HEAD>
    <TITLE>Wrox Hot News Active Desktop Item</TITLE>
</HEAD>

<BODY>

<!-- Title division code goes here -->

<DIV ID=divLink0 STYLE="Position:Absolute; Width:253; Height:20; Top:0; Left:10; z-
index:-1">
    <A HREF="mailto:feedback@wrox.co.uk">
            <FONT STYLE="Position:Relative; Left:16;
                                  Font:10pt/10pt verdana; Font-weight:normal; Letter-
spacing:-1; Text-decoration:none; Color:Black">
                    <IMG STYLE="Position:Relative; Top:0; Left:0" SRC="new.gif"
BORDER=0 ALIGN="ABSMIDDLE">
                We welcome Anthea to the team.
            </FONT>
    </A>
</DIV>
```

```
<!-- divLink1, divLink2 and divLink3 cut for clarity. -->

<DIV ID=divLink4 STYLE="Position:Absolute; Width:253; Height:20; Top:80; Left:10; z-
index:-1">
     <A HREF="http://www.wrox.co.uk/Stonebroom/Stonebroom.htm" TARGET="Free Software">
          <FONT STYLE="Position:Relative;
                                   Font:10pt/10pt verdana; Font-weight:normal; Letter-
spacing:-1; Text-decoration:none; Color:Black">
                    <IMG SRC="hot.gif" BORDER=0 ALIGN="ABSMIDDLE">
                    Get FREE software.
          </FONT>
     </A>
</DIV>

<!-- Footer division code goes here -->

</BODY>

<SCRIPT LANGUAGE="VBSCRIPT">
<!--
  Script code to manipulate news items and create respond to events.

-->
</SCRIPT>
</HEAD>
</HTML>

<!-- ActiveX timer control reference -->
```

Let's have a closer look at one of these divisions. In the **STYLE** parameter for the **<DIV>** tag, we've given the division a **z-index** of -1. This ensures that it's displayed below any divisions that have a higher **z-index**.

```
<DIV ID=divLink4
STYLE="Position:Absolute; Width:253; Height:20; Top:0; Left:10; z-index:-1">
```

It's also worth noticing how we've packaged together the components for a news item:

```
     <A HREF="http://www.wrox.co.uk/Stonebroom/Stonebroom.htm" TARGET="Free Software">
          <FONT STYLE="Position:Relative;
                                   Font:10pt/10pt verdana; Font-weight:normal; Letter-
spacing:-1; Text-decoration:none; Color:Black">
                    <IMG SRC="hot.gif" BORDER=0 ALIGN="ABSMIDDLE">
                    Get FREE software.
          </FONT>
     </A>
</DIV>
```

What we've done is put a **<FONT>** tag within the hyperlink definition. This allows us to control how the news text should appear, and not have to resort to using the default underlined hyperlink font style. Also notice how the **<FONT>** tag encloses the image as well as the text. This stops spaces between the graphics and the following text being underlined.

The Title and Footer Divisions

In order for the news link items to gradually *disappear* off the top of the page, and then *reappear* from the bottom, we use another two divisions – one at the top of our desktop item, and another at the bottom. The top division is the title division and we've given it the dimensions of our logo image. Because we haven't specified a `z-index` value, then the default of zero is used. This means that it will always appear in front of any news items that it overlaps.

```
<DIV ID=divTitle STYLE="Position:Absolute; Width:253; Height:100; Top:0; Left:0;">
    <IMG ID=Image1 WIDTH=253 HEIGHT=100 SRC="Title.gif" STYLE="Position:Absolute;
Top:0; Left:0">
</DIV>
```

The footer division is also straightforward.

```
<DIV ID=divFooter STYLE="Background:White; Position:Absolute; Width:255; Height:20;
Top:0;Left:0">
</DIV>
```

Notice how we've set the background to be white. Unlike the title division, we're not displaying any images in the footer section. By specifying the background as white, we hide any news divisions underneath it.

Working with the Divisions

Originally, we created 5 divisions to hold the news topics, and positioned them all in the same place. We're now going to look at their positioning, and how we've increased the flexibility of the desktop item by using dynamically generated event handlers. Here's an overview of how this works:

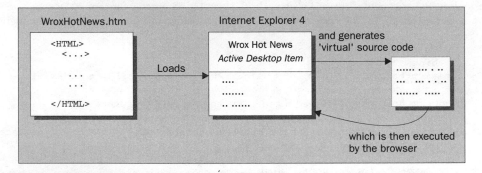

This means that it's possible to edit the source code and add or remove news item divisions. The rest of the code will then look at how many divisions you've defined, and position them accordingly, finishing up by positioning the footer division.

However, in order to provide this increased flexibility, we need to store references to the `<DIV>` objects from the browser object hierarchy. This makes it practical to update the positions of each news item division as they scroll. You'll recall that the scrolling stops when the mouse pointer is placed over *any* news item, and scrolling resumes when the mouse pointer is moved off *all* news item divisions. Furthermore, because we don't know the number of news items that will be defined *when the program script is written*, we also need to dynamically generate the event routines for each news item division. This has only become possible with the introduction of DHTML.

Getting a Handle on the News Divisions

The only restriction that we place on the news divisions is that their names must start with **divLink**, followed by a consecutive integer number. So, our topic divisions would have the names **divLink0**, **divLink1, divLink2, ..., divLinkn-1, divLinkn**. This stricture is simply to identify the **div** as a news division, and to determine their relative order.

Our first step is to iterate through all the objects within the document, and just pick out the appropriate news item **DIV** objects. These objects are then stored in a (re-dimensional) array in order to facilitate flexible processing on them at a later stage.

The iteration starts at **divLink0** and continues until **divLinkn+1** ,which is not a valid news division. Once we've reached found **divLinkn +1** , we now know how many news divisions were provided, and we've kept a reference to each one in the array.

```
intIndex = 0
While Not IsEmpty(GetObject("divLink" & intIndex))
  ReDim Preserve LinkArray(intIndex)
  Set LinkArray(intIndex) = GetObject("divLink" & intIndex)
  CreateLinkMouseOverEvent("divLink" & intIndex)
  CreateLinkMouseOutEvent("divLink" & intIndex)
  intIndex = intIndex + 1
Wend
```

We've written an auxiliary function called **GetObject** to return a reference to an object based on the name of the object we're after.

```
Function GetObject(strName)
  For Each objItem In Document.All
    If objItem.ID = strName Then
      Set GetObject = objItem
      Exit Function
    End If
  Next
  'If we get to here, then GetObject is empty, since we haven't set it to anything.
End Function
```

All that this function does is iterate through the **Document.All** collection trying to find an object that has the same name as the parameter we specified. If one is found, then the function returns the reference to the object. If no such object is found, then the function returns the value **empty**. We can't just obtain the reference to the object using:

```
objRequired = Document.All(requiredName)
```

If we do use that method, and an object of that name doesn't exist, then we'll get an assignment error. Also, we always get the result of **false** when we try and inspect if the returned value is **empty**:

```
If Not IsEmpty(Document.All(requiredName)) Then
  'Continue processing.
End If
```

Now that we can determine whether the object we're looking for exists, we can re-dimension our array, making room for the new object reference to be stored. We have used the **Preserve** keyword, which just informs the VBScript interpreter to keep any previous values that are already defined in the array.

```
While Not IsEmpty(GetObject("divLink" & intIndex))
   ReDim Preserve LinkArray(intIndex)
   Set LinkArray(intIndex) = GetObject("divLink" & intIndex)
```

Next, we dynamically create the event handlers for each news division. This might seem a complicated concept to grasp, but it's absolutely necessary to do this in order to get the flexibility we require. We need to create two events for each item – the **MouseOver** event to stop the scrolling, and the **MouseOut** event to initiate the scrolling again.

```
CreateLinkMouseOverEvent("divLink" & intIndex)
CreateLinkMouseOutEvent("divLink" & intIndex)
   intIndex = intIndex + 1
Wend
```

What we do is pass the names of the news divisions to our two routines, and these create the dynamic event handlers for each news division.

Dynamically Creating Event Handlers

Writing code, which then writes more code, might not seem advantageous. Yet it is this that makes Active Server Pages such a desirable system for back end servers. Different HTML documents are returned to the client as an outcome of computation or based on information submitted to the page.

The dynamically generated event handlers that we're going to cover work in a similar way. We've already seen how the news **<DIV>** tags in the same source document are queried, and in response to that, we can generate the appropriate event handlers for those tags. What we essentially do is construct a couple of subroutines that differ in their name and functionality. This is done once for each news **<DIV>** tag, and the result is that the browser reads the generated routines as if they were a part of the document. However, the subroutines are *virtual* in nature, which means that they don't reside in a file on the server. Because they're generated on-the-fly, it's impossible to view the underlying source code.

The **CreateLinkMouseOverEvent** subroutine accepts the name of the current news division, and incorporates that as part of the event name.

```
Sub CreateLinkMouseOverEvent(strElement)
   Document.WriteLn "<SCRIPT LANGUAGE=""VBSCRIPT"">"
   Document.WriteLn "Sub " & strElement  & "_onMouseOver()"
   Document.WriteLn "IeTimer1.Enabled = False"
   Document.WriteLn "End Sub"
   Document.WriteLn "</SCRIPT>"
End Sub
```

On calling the routine with **strElement** having the value **divLink0**, we'll get the appropriate **divLink0_onMouseOver** event handler.

```
<SCRIPT LANGUAGE="VBSCRIPT">
Sub divLink0_onMouseOver()
IeTimer1.Enabled = False
```

```
End Sub
</SCRIPT>
```

We've made a reference to a timer Active control that we use to update the positions of the news items which will be used to move the scroll the news divisions, and we'll talk more about it a little later.

The **CreateLinkMouseOutEvent** subroutine, which is responsible for generating the **onMouseOut** events for the news divisions, works in much the same way as the last routine:

```
Sub CreateLinkMouseOutEvent(strElement)
  Document.WriteLn "<SCRIPT LANGUAGE=""VBSCRIPT"">"
  Document.WriteLn "Sub " & strElement & "_onMouseOut()"
  Document.WriteLn "IeTimer1.Enabled = True"
  Document.WriteLn "End Sub"
  Document.WriteLn "</SCRIPT>"
End Sub
```

Setting up the Default News Division Positions

So far, all of our divisions are sitting at the top of the page and, clearly, this is far from useful. We're accepting an arbitrary number of news divisions, and we don't want to impose any positioning calculations on anyone that adds extra news items. Also, we wouldn't know at program design time where the footer division should go as it depends on knowing the number of news divisions. What we've chosen to do is calculate the positions where the divisions should go, and then move them there.

```
  intIndex = 0
  For Each objItem In LinkArray
    objItem.Style.PosTop = 100 + (intIndex * 20)
    intIndex = intIndex + 1
  Next
  divFooter.Style.PosTop = LinkArray(UBound(LinkArray)).Style.PosTop + 10
```

Because our array holds references to objects, it effectively becomes a collection. This means that we can use the **For Each** iterator to easily get at our objects. We end up by moving the footer so it half covers the last news item division. This last news item scrolls into full view as the top news item disappears behind the logo graphic.

Scrolling the News Items

Now we're at the stage where the news topics have their appropriate starting positions, and clicking on one would initiated the related hyperlink action. However, they don't move anywhere yet. We achieve the scrolling effect by making use of the timer ActiveX control, which we've called **IeTimer1**.

```
<OBJECT ID="IeTimer1" WIDTH=0 HEIGHT=0
 CLASSID="CLSID:59CCB4A0-727D-11CF-AC36-00AA00A47DD2"
    CODEBASE="http://activex.microsoft.com/controls/iexplorer/
timer.ocx#Version=4,70,0,1161"
    TYPE="application/x-oleobject">
    <PARAM NAME="_ExtentX" VALUE="1032">
    <PARAM NAME="_ExtentY" VALUE="1032">
    <PARAM NAME="Interval" VALUE="100">
</OBJECT>
```

The timer has been set up so that it fires every tenth of a second. When it does, it calls the `IeTimer1` subroutine. The code to move the news topic divisions is held within this subroutine.

```
Sub IeTimer1_Timer()
  For Each objItem In LinkArray
    If objItem.Style.PosTop + objItem.Style.PosHeight -10 < divTitle.Style.PosTop +
divTitle.Style.PosHeight Then
      objItem.Style.PosTop = divFooter.Style.PosTop
    Else
      objItem.Style.PosTop = objItem.Style.PosTop - 1
    End If
  Next
End Sub
```

We iterate through all of the news divisions in our array, item by item. If the item is totally obscured by the title division, then we move it back down to be exactly behind the footer division. However, if the item is (at least partially) visible, then we just move it up by one pixel. This gives us our scrolling wraparound effect.

Installing Our Item over the Internet

Now that we've created our Wrox Hot News desktop item, we now need to make it available for installation. It's customary to show the desktop item functioning in the page, and provide a link that will allow the desktop item to be downloaded and installed on the user's machines.

Here's how our finished download and install screen appears:

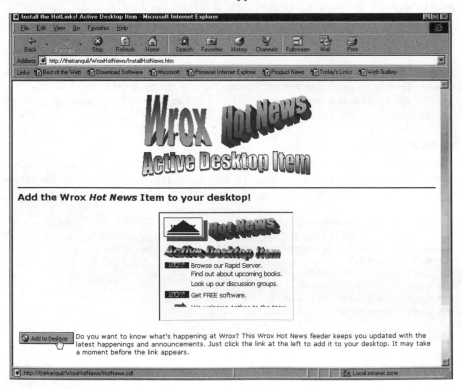

You can try out this sample from our Web site at `http://rapid.wrox.co.uk/books/0707/`

If you click on the Add to Desktop button image, then you'll get the option of installing the item.

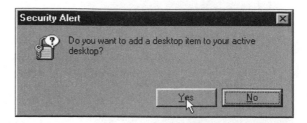

If you then click on Yes, you'll then be presented with options regarding the update schedule.

For now, just click on Yes, and wait for the subscription progress indicator to disappear. Now flip back to the desktop. You'll notice that our Wrox Hot News Desktop Item has been added to your desktop. You can hide the item by clicking on its close gadget, or you can remove it entirely using Web tab in the Display Properties window.

Now we've seen how simple it is to install an Active Desktop Item over the Internet, let's have a look at the underlying CDF file that achieves this.

Creating a CDF File

Creating a CDF file for an Active Desktop Item is very similar to the process of creating a CDF file for a channel. This is because Active Desktop Items are similar to cut-down channels. The CDF we use in the example uses four elements that are used just like HTML tags. These are:

- CHANNEL
- LOGO
- USAGE
- ITEM

We provide a full reference of CDF elements in Appendix F.

Creating the Wrox HotNews CDF File

We're only going to create a bare-bones CDF file here that can be used to install the Wrox Hot News Active Desktop Item across the Web. A new CDF file should be created for each Active Desktop Item you wish to host, since only one desktop item can be hosted by a CDF file. Here's the entire CDF file:

In the HotNews.cdf file:

```
<?XML version="1.0"?>
<CHANNEL>
    <ITEM HREF="http://YourServerName/WroxHotNews/Install/WroxHotNews.htm">

            <TITLE>Wrox HotNews Active Desktop Item</TITLE>

            <USAGE VALUE="DesktopComponent">
                    <OPENAS VALUE="HTML"/>
                    <WIDTH VALUE="310"/>
                    <HEIGHT VALUE="234"/>
                    <CANRESIZE VALUE="YES"/>
            </USAGE>

    </ITEM>
</CHANNEL>
```

How It Works

The first line simply defines the CDF file be an Extensible Markup Language (XML) document. However, we don't need a closing tag as we do with HTML.

```
<?XML version="1.0"?>
```

Next, we define a channel. This is not to be confused with an Active Channel of the type that can be accessed via the Channel Bar. When we subscribe to an Active Desktop Item via a CDF file, no entries appear in the Channel Bar.

```
<CHANNEL>
    <!-- Item information goes here -->
</CHANNEL>
```

The `<ITEM>` tag defines where our active desktop item is located on the Web server. It also encloses the title, usage and various options that we can provide to specify how our item is to be set up on the desktop.

```
<ITEM HREF="http://YourServerName/WroxHotNews/Install/WroxHotNews.htm">
    <!-- Title, usage and options go here -->
</ITEM>
```

To give our Active Desktop Item a name (that is used in the list of the Web tab from the Display Properties dialog), we need to provide a `<TITLE>` element.

```
<TITLE>Wrox HotNews Active Desktop Item</TITLE>
```

Because CDF files can be used to host Active Desktop Items, Active Screensavers, Active Channels etc, we need to specify that the intended use is indeed to host an Active Desktop Item. This is done with the `<USAGE>` element.

```
<USAGE VALUE="DesktopComponent">
    <!-- Desktop Item options go here -->
</USAGE>
```

Finally, we specify the setup attributes which determines how the Active Desktop Item should be incorporated into the HTML layer, and the parameters we'll need to supply to the ActiveX control that deals with the moving and resizing of the item.

```
<OPENAS VALUE="HTML"/>
<WIDTH VALUE="310"/>
<HEIGHT VALUE="234"/>
<CANRESIZE VALUE="YES"/>
```

We've set ours up so that it's an HTML document (rather than a GIF image), and we've given it a default width and height, and we've specified explicitly that it can be resized in both dimensions.

Attributes of the USAGE element

You may have noticed that all of the definitions within the **<USAGE>** open and closing tags took this form:

<Name VALUE=*"Value"* />

These were all **child elements** of the **<USAGE>** element and they all take this syntax. These child elements can only be used during the definition of an Active Desktop Item. In many ways, they closely resemble HTML attributes of elements, i.e. you can only use **SRC** within another tag such as **<IMG>**. Here's a list of all of the valid child elements that can be used with **<USAGE>** and all of their possible values.

Name	Value	Description
CANRESIZE	**"No" | "Yes"**	Specifies whether the Active Desktop item can be resized in both x and y directions. The default value is "Yes".
CANRESIZEX	**"No" | "Yes"**	Specifies whether the width of the Active Desktop item can be changed. The default value is "Yes".
CANRESIZEY	**"No" | "Yes"**	Specifies whether the height of the Active Desktop item can be changed. The default value is "Yes".
HEIGHT	***"pixels"***	Specifies the height, in pixels, of the Active Desktop denoted by the parent **<ITEM>** tag.
OPENAS	**"HTML" | "Image"**	Indicates the content type of the Active Desktop Item specified in the parent **<ITEM>** tag. HTML documents are hosted as a floating frame (HTML **<IFRAME>** tag), and images are hosted using the HTML **<IMG>** tag.
WIDTH	***"pixels"***	Specifies the width, in pixels, of the Active Desktop denoted by the parent **<ITEM>** tag.

Now that our CDF file has been written, we can copy it across to the Web server into an area that's accessible by the outside world. Once this is done, the final step is to create the host document that is the friendly interface which links to the CDF file we just created.

Creating the Host Document

The host document can be thought of as an attractive link to the CDF file. It should provide information about the desktop item, and possibly show the desktop item within the page so that users can see what they'd get on their desktop, should they decide to subscribe to the desktop item. Of course, we also need to provide the hyperlink to the CDF file so that users know where to click to install the desktop item.

Starting the HTML Host Document

We start writing the HTML document in the usual way. One thing to note is that we've given our page a rating, so that it will show up on browsers that have content rating enabled.

```
<HTML>
  <HEAD>
    <TITLE>Install the HotLinks! Active Desktop Item</TITLE>
    <META http-equiv="PICS-Label" content='(PICS-1.0 "http://www.rsac.org/
ratingsv01.html" l gen true comment "RSACi North America Server" for "http://
www.wrox.co.uk" on "1997.05.01T08:15-0500" exp "1998.05.01T08:15-0500" r (n 0 s 0 v 0
l 0))'>
  </HEAD>
  <BODY>
```

Next, we add the logo for the page.

```
    <CENTER><IMG SRC="InstallLogo.gif" WIDTH=397 HEIGHT=193 ALT="Wrox Hot News Active
Desktop Item"></CENTER>
```

Now we can add a little text to make the purpose of the page obvious.

```
    <HR NOSHARE SIZE=2 COLOR="#000000">
    <FONT FACE="Verdana, Arial, Helvetica" SIZE=4>
      <STRONG>Add the Wrox <EM>Hot News</EM> Item to your desktop!</STRONG>
    </FONT>
    <P>
```

To introduce immediate interest, and show the users what they'd be missing if they didn't subscribe to the desktop item, we can show it in the host document.

Showing the Item in the Host Document

It's a good idea to show our desktop item in the download page so that people browsing our site could get a taste of what is does, without having to install it first. Obviously, we don't want to re-code our desktop object once again for the host document. It's possible to display the desktop item in its own separate floating frame – just as it will be displayed from the HTML layer – within the host document.

```
    <CENTER>
      <IFRAME SCROLLING=NO WIDTH=270 HEIGHT=220 FRAMEBORDER=1 SRC="InstallDirectory/
WroxHotNews.htm">
      </IFRAME>
    </CENTER>
```

Notice how we've set the floating frame to display a border. This makes it easier for users to see the desktop item as a separate part of the host document.

Now we've included the item in the host document, we can move onto the hyperlink that will be used to initiate the installation process.

Providing the Install Hyperlink

The last step is to create the hyperlink to the CDF file (in our case `HotNews.cdf`).

```
    <P>
    <TABLE>
      <TR VALIGN=TOP>
        <TD>
          <A HREF="HotNews.cdf">
            <IMG SRC="btn_addadi.gif" WIDTH=110 HEIGHT=24 ALT="Click here to add a new
desktop item to your Active Desktop" BORDER=0></A>
          <TD>
        <FONT FACE="Verdana, Arial, Helvetica" SIZE=2>
              Do you want to know what's happening at Wrox?
              This Wrox Hot News feeder keeps you updated with the latest happenings
and announcements.
              Just click the link at the left to add it to your desktop. It may take a
moment before the link appears.
          </FONT>
      </TR>
    </TABLE>

  </BODY>
</HTML>
```

When the hyperlink is followed, the browser doesn't navigate to a new URL, but instigates the process that creates the subscription to the Active Desktop item.

Providing Current News Topics

In this example, we've concentrated mainly on designing and implementing an Active Desktop Item using Dynamic HTML, and the host document which is used to install the item remotely on the desktop. However, we haven't discussed in any great length the topic of using current data – the data that we used in the example was hardcoded.

This isn't as restrictive as you may imagine. For example, using this approach, it's possible for anyone to publish Active Desktop items in their own Web space. They can simply just modify the document, and the cached copy at the client could be updated automatically the next time an Internet connection is established, using the subscription generated.

Another alternative is to use the **Tabular Data Control**, as discussed in Chapter 6. This control allows us to bind fields to a text file containing the up-to-date data. It's only the data file that needs updating in such a case, and the item could be changed to display an arbitrary number of news items using only a small set of topic divisions.

Alternatively, using Active Server Pages, it's also possible to dynamically create the desktop item code. In this case, we'd create the news divisions in the ASP script, and this would be interpreted when the client browser receives the desktop item source code. As a result, the news information can be based in a text file, or even a database on the server.

No matter which approach is adopted, each desktop item downloaded as described has its own automatic subscription. This means that even if the desktop item source resides on a distant Web server, we can still use the latest state of the cached desktop item without a live Internet connection. This approach works fine as long as we don't use any ActiveX controls or Java applets that explicitly try and establish a connection when no connection exists.

One final thing to remember: files referenced by your Active Desktop Item will be downloaded to the browser's cache when the item is first installed. If extra files are needed, then they must be referenced in the CDF file via the `<ITEM>` element. This will ensure the file is downloaded to the cache for when it is needed.

Summary

Through the Active Desktop and the shell integration mode, Windows is really becoming a Web based platform. More and more applications are accessible through the browser, and some parts of the operating system are now Web pages, using special ActiveX controls and Java applets.

With the event of the Active Desktop came Active Desktop Items, which have made it possible to keep up-to-date with the latest news and information. We've covered the design aspects of such desktop items, and have built the Wrox Hot News Active Desktop item with its associated CDF file and host document.

The most important points covered are:

- The Active Desktop is a result of True Web Integration. With the event of the integrated shell mode, we can now host documents directly on the desktop.

- Active Desktop Items can be written using a variety of means, using HTML, Dynamic HTML, ActiveX controls, ActiveX documents and Java applets.

- IE 4.0 uses subscriptions to keep the data content of the installed components current. A subscription is automatically created for each component installed across the Web, and is really just a scheduled update of Web content.

This brings us to the end of the book. We hope that you agree with us that IE4 represents a giant leap forward, and can no longer be considered as simply a browser, but a complete Web application development system. It's been impossible to give more than a quick overview of how to program some of the new technologies, but we hope that we've given you more than just a taste of what you can do, and, ideally, a springboard for you to develop your own IE4 sites and applications. We aim to devote some future titles to covering specific aspects of IE4, to give them the in-depth coverage they deserve. We already provide a Dynamic HTML IE4 reference, which goes into more depth on what you can achieve with Dynamic HTML, as well as offering a comprehensive reference section on all the tags, properties, methods and events. It's called *Instant IE4 Dynamic HTML Programmer's Reference- ISBN 1-861000-68-5*. We also provide a sister title for Netscape Communicator 4, *Instant Netscape Dynamic HTML Programmer's Reference, ISBN 1-861001-193*. Keep your eyes on the Wrox web site `http://www.wrox.com` for more details of future titles.

The Background to IE4 and the Active Desktop

While Microsoft and many other companies have only recently recognized the importance of the Internet, this collection of interconnected networks has actually been around for a number of years, after starting off as a US Department of Defense project in the late 1960s. The DOD was concerned that their communications infrastructure could be wiped out by a single nuclear strike on their central systems. They decided to conduct research into the development of a decentralized computer network such that multiple data routes would exist. If one route malfunctioned, or was destroyed, data could still traverse an alternative route.

This network later became available for use to research / education establishments and commercial organizations, and became known first as Bitnet and later as the Internet. It adopted a suite of communications protocols called **TCP/IP** (Transmission Control Protocol/Internet Protocol) that enabled a number of services to simultaneously operate on the network–common examples include File Transfer, Bulletin Boards and Electronic Mail. Since these early days, the growth of the Internet has been exponential.

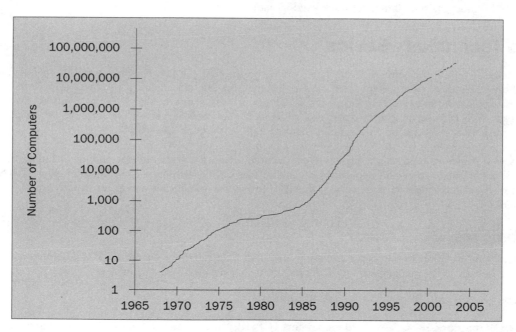

No one is sure of the user base, but recent estimates indicate that there are probably around 60 million Internet users worldwide. Aside from Email, the most popular Internet service used today is the **World Wide Web** (WWW). The WWW is a subset of the Internet technologies previously mentioned, where the information is presented through a graphical rather then a text base interface.

Web Origins

By 1990 the largest Internet site in Europe was CERN (Conseil European pour la Recherche Nucleaire) in Geneva, Switzerland (`http://www.cern.ch/`). One of their researchers, a Tim Berners-Lee, proposed a hypertext project that was a system to link and help access the numerous items of information located on the Internet.

> *The term hypertext was first used in 1965 by Ted Nelson. He defined hypertext as being a mechanism for augmenting items of text by linking to other items of text to form a web of relationships.*

By late 1990, a pilot implementation of the WWW was operating on a NeXT computer and by January 1992, a version was publicly available from CERN. During 1993, interest in Web technology grew rapidly. In February 1993, a point & click graphical version of a web browser called Mosaic was demonstrated by the National Center for Supercomputing Applications (NCSA) (`http://www.ncsa.uiuc.edu`).

This was later followed by similar offerings from other organizations. In March 1994, several Mosaic developers left NCSA to form Netscape Communications Corporation and continued to work on Web and Internet products. Netscape soon became recognized as a leading company in this arena.

By mid 1994 interest in the Web was huge and the originators at CERN decided that standards should be devised and controlled by an independent organization. In July 1994, the World Wide Web Consortium (W³C) `http://www.w3.org/` was formed to guide the development of Web technology standards. By the end of 1995, most major Internet software vendors had joined the W³C.

Web Technology Basics

Many people confuse the terms Internet and WWW, or consider the two as equivalent but, in fact, the two are entirely distinct. It is important to recognize that the Web isn't a network itself, but an application that operates over networks using TCP/IP protocols. The Web architecture is based on the client/server model and uses a Web Browser (client) to retrieve documents from a Web Server on the Internet, which may be located on a local network, or on a remote network half way around the world.

Today's web browsers support the display of multimedia within the retrieved documents–including text, graphics, sound, and video–and hyperlinks in which items on the document are linked to other Web resources. By clicking on such a hyperlink, the Web Browser automatically navigates to the target document.

Uniform Resource Locator

All Internet information resources are uniquely identified by a reference called a **URL** (Uniformed Resource Locator). The naming scheme involves three concatenated items as follows:

```
<protocol>://<machine id>/<local name>
```

▲	`<protocol>`	identifies the TCP/IP protocol used to retrieve the resource
▲	`<machine id>`	identifies the server on which the resource is located–this is either an **IP address** (a unique sequence of four 8 bit numbers e.g. 194.1.23.12) or a **domain name** (e.g. www.wrox.com)
▲	`<local name>`	identifies the resource on the server and can include a directory structure

For example:

`http://www.microsoft.com/sitebuilder/whatsnew.htm`

A URL can be referenced from the address line of a Web Browser or the HTML text associated with a hyperlink.

HyperText Transfer Protocol

To retrieve a document, the Web Browser first analyses the URL to determine the protocol, the server and the local name. If the machine ID is a logical (domain) name, the Web browser communicates first with another predefined server called a DNS (Domain Name Server). This server returns the associated IP address by means of a lookup table that maps logical domain names to IP addresses, or by routing the request to other DNS machines that may contain the required information. The Web Browser then uses this address and the TCP/IP communications protocol to communicate with the server holding the required document–this can involve routing packets of information over several network machines to eventually reach the target server.

The first part of the URL specifies the message protocol (i.e. the communications layer above TCP/IP that defines the message content) that is used to retrieve this information, for Web access this is typically **HTTP** (HyperText Transfer Protocol). Other protocols supported by most browsers include **NEWS** (newsgroups), **MAIL** (Electronic Mail), **FTP** (File Transfer Protocol) and **Gopher** (a file transfer/navigation application that was a forerunner to the Web).

The Web Browser requests the required document in an HTTP request message. The Web Server receives this request and after processing it completes the operation by either returning the document in the response or by returning an error response. If the document was sent, the Web Browser will determine if there are any other embedded resources within the document, such as images, and fires off additional requests for the additional information.

HyperText Markup Language

HyperText Markup Language (HTML) is a page description language for defining the content of hypertext documents that are displayed in a format established by the Web Browsers rendering scheme. HTML is actually a classification of SGML (Standard Generalized Markup Language) that has been adapted for use in electronic communications, such as the World Wide Web. HTML files are typically suffixed with either **htm** or **html**.

> *The* **.htm** *extension is particular to NT machines (8.3 naming convention) and* **.html** *is usually associated with UNIX systems (LFN).*

An HTML document contains a series of **tags** and text that define the structure and content of the document. A tag is a reserved keyword that is delimited by the '<' and '>' characters. Some tags (but not all) can appear in both start and end formats with the latter preceded by a forward slash. For example, **<I>** and **</I>** are used to start and end italic formatting. Some tags also include **attributes** that further qualify the meaning of a tag e.g. **<FONT FACE="Comic Sans MS">** to specify the typeface of subsequent text.

Several elements must always be included in HTML documents and the inclusion of some elements is recommended as standard practice. Both sets of elements are shown in the basic HTML document skeleton following code:

```
<!DOCTYPE HTML PUBLIC "-//IETF//DTD HTML//EN">    'recommended only
<HTML>
<HEAD>
    <TITLE>Document title                         'recommended only
    </TITLE>                                         'recommended only
</HEAD>
<BODY>
Document content
</BODY>
</HTML>
```

When the Web was first established, the type of HTML documents that circulated on the Internet were those originating from research and academic circles. Such documents were typically textual, and could be nicely formatted using just a minimal number of tags. Then with the introduction of commercial sites, there became a need for visual effects, compelling images and fancy fonts, and not just plain document content.

This led to the evolution of aesthetic tags and one company, Netscape, led the way with a number of their own tags. Unfortunately, this proprietary approach meant that the original concept of platform independence for HTML across all browsers was lost. There were also the commercial risks of using proprietary tags which could, potentially, restrict the user base (Microsoft's ActiveX controls present the same problems in a slightly different form). Furthermore, in some cases, such as the <DIV> document division tag, the two main browsers don't even display standard tags in the same way. This forces web masters (or designers) to experiment with tags, generating more complex, expensive and unwieldy pages, until a compromise can be reached wherein the desired look-and-feel exists in each browser.

As a tool for creating rich interactive and addictive applications, standard HTML lacks the capabilities to compete with the development products that create today's top multimedia CD-ROM titles. There have been several application languages developed to help address this such as Java, but IE4 has its own solution in the form of the next generation of HTML called Dynamic HTML. This has been developed by Microsoft in collaboration with the W³C and is available for other vendors to support. The Microsoft version of Dynamic HTML has a number of differences from Netscape's implementation of Dynamic HTML.

Cascading Style Sheets

With the advances in technology, web designers want the power to create more impressive web sites and be able to implement these features by making changes to only one document that will, in turn, affect their whole site—in other words, they need templates. The solution to this is **Cascading Style Sheets** (CSS) which were developed by W³C to provide a standard for the effective markup of pages, the layering of text and images, and the exact positioning of items. IE4 and Dynamic HTML builds on the W³C CSS specification to enable faster updating and more interactive Web pages as well as data binding.

The four reasons for using style sheets are:

▲ Many web pages can refer to the same style sheet file—this reduces files sizes and thus speeds up Web access

▲ Presentation and content are separated—this makes the content sections less cumbersome and provides simpler maintenance of pages.

▲ It enables consistency throughout a Web site–a single change can be made to a style sheet and all associated pages will adopt the new appearance

▲ They provide a greater typographic control over a web page than can be achieved with just standard HTML tags and attributes

A style sheet contains a series of style rules that can be linked to elements in an HTML document. We looked at how style sheets work in detail in Chapter 2.

Web Directions

The first generation of web browsers was only capable of handling text and simple multimedia such as images and sound. These early pages are now called static pages since they lacked the facilities for user interaction that we are accustomed to from typical PC software.

The next generation addressed these limitations by providing facilities for active pages enabling dynamic content, user interaction and an architecture for distributed client / server processing. This was achieved by the web browser's support for downloaded software components, scripting languages and mechanisms for the integration to existing applications.

IE4 is the latest generation of Web Browsers that provides facilities for users to be more productive and capabilities to match the compelling content of television, video and CD-ROM software. Whereas the previous Web Browsers have only 'pulled' information down to the desktop, the new variants also include **Channel** facilities that allow content to be transmitted or 'pushed' from the Web Server to the user.

Intranets

Once the Internet was firmly established in many developers' terminology, the expression Intranet quickly followed. Whereas the Internet is public and open to all, an Intranet is closed and has user access controls enforced. Intranets take advantage of the open Internet standards and the familiar Web browser software to provide employees, close partners and suppliers with access to corporate information and processes.

Because an Intranet provides applications that are server-based, the corporate IT department does not have to deploy client-side software or configure user's machines (apart from browsers). With an Intranet, users can navigate to an internal Web site and have seamless access to the application without any setup or configuration necessary. If any application is changed, perhaps due to a bug fix or enhancement, the IT department can just make updates on the server, instantly upgrading all desktops with the new functionality. This dynamic application distribution can produce considerable savings to organizations which have many hundreds of desktops distributed throughout the enterprise.

Organisations are using Intranets to make it easier for their staff and partners to collaborate and locate and process information. To most companies information is key and many have huge amounts of investment in existing data systems and electronic documents–mechanisms enabling the reuse of such existing information can have considerable impact on performance.

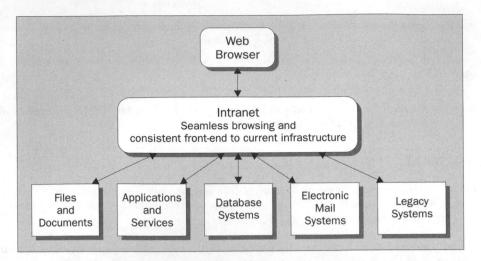

Since Internets and Intranets use the same Web technology, the techniques used in this book will be applicable to the development of both. However, with Intranet implementations you have an advantage in that you have more control over the system components. For example, you can enforce that all Web Browsers will be IE4, and you can monitor the network, and tune and upgrade to provide a suitable levels of service.

Point to Point Tunnelling

Many corporations have multiple offices, often located throughout the world. The cost of linking the offices together has traditionally been very expensive and often prohibited the installation of interoffice networks or Intranets. Fortunately, Microsoft has collaborated with manufacturers to develop a **Point-to-Point Tunnelling** (PPTP) protocol that encapsulates TCP/IP, NetBEUI and IPX protocols and provides an encrypted channel through public networks. This can be used to securely deploy Intranets using the Internet as the transport. The cost of local calls to ISPs makes this a much more cost-effective solution than installing expensive leased lines.

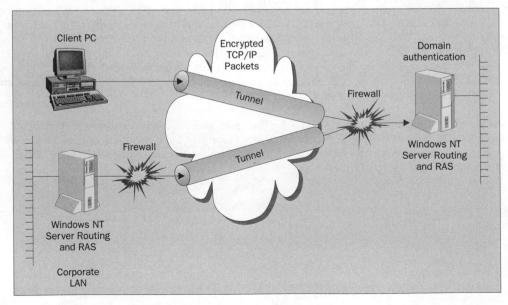

PPTP is supported on both Windows NT and Windows 95. For interconnecting multiple LANs over the Tunnel, additional protocol routing logic is required to ensure that packets destined for the local machines are not sent over the network, which would of course waste the valuable bandwidth. This functionality can be achieved using Microsoft's **Router and Remote Access Service**–at the time of writing this was in beta and known by its code name **Steelhead**.

Challenges & Risks

One of the biggest challenges of implementing Web solutions must be keeping track of the volatile Internet standards and technologies that are available. Visits to major software vendors' Web sites regularly reveal updated information on new releases of software, or press releases detailing new software technology that's on its way. Furthermore, the technology wars between many of the big names do not help organizations gain any confidence that any investment in a Web solution can form the basis of a long-term solution.

Whilst we cannot define a foolproof strategy, experience over recent years has demonstrated that the investment in software technology from vendors that support industry standards has always proven a successful route.

Other major causes for concern are: performance, security, and protection against viruses. We shall now discuss these issues.

Web Performance

The principle factors that affect the response times of a Web application are: the network performance / bandwidth, the speed of the Web Server and the size of the files transmitted.

> *For a more comprehensive discussion of Web performance issues, the reader is referred to Professional Web Site Optimization, ISBN 1-861000-74-X, published by Wrox Press.*

Network Bandwidth

As discussed earlier, the Internet is the interconnection of a conglomeration of autonomous computer networks. Each individual network administrator is responsible for their own network and can specify any rules and regulations for ensuring the correct use of their network services. However, because nobody really owns the Internet as a whole, there is no organization responsible for guaranteeing the quality of service. When we send packets of information over the Internet, they can be routed over a number of networks–if they get lost on route or take excessive delivery times, there is no one who you can complain to. Fortunately, thanks to standards, the Internet currently seems to be hanging together well.

Access to the Internet is made by linking to one of the networks–the providers of such facilities are called **Internet Service Providers** (ISP). There are several different communication technologies that can be used for the connection, and the charges made by the ISP are usually proportional to the speed of access.

To help perceived performance we need to avoid excessive communications. IE4 caches HTML, multimedia and other files locally and should the user navigate to page that references the same resource, the HTTP protocol will ensure that the content downloading is not repeated unless the file has been updated. The move towards scripting and objects enables client-side intelligence and helps to preserve bandwidth. This book has focused in detail on some techniques that are available with Dynamic HTML that enable a great deal of activity to occur on the client without any need to communicate with the Web Server.

For example:

▲ Special graphic effects can be achieved without downloading high bandwidth images

▲ Data can be sorted and filtered without contacting the original database

▲ Page content can change due to events such as the user pointing or clicking the mouse

In addition, the IE4 channel facilities avoid the waste of bandwidth that often occurs when we check for updates to our favorite pages, only to find there have been no changes.

Web Server Performance

The performance of the Web Server is dependent on a number of factors including:

▲ Speed of the processor

▲ Amount of memory and cache sizes

▲ Speed of the disk drives

▲ Type of operating system

▲ Complexity of any scripting or applications that the server may interface with

▲ Amount of dynamic page generation as opposed to using static pages

▲ Amount of audit logs that are being generated

Ideally the machine should be dedicated to the Web role and not have other applications consuming the resources. Once the capacity of a Web Server is exceeded, it should be replicated with a multi-server configuration. The DNS server which maps domain names onto IP addresses can be adjusted to work in a round robin fashion such that HTTP requests are evenly distributed over the available machines in the Web Server cluster.

Resource Size

When developing Internet Web applications, it is important to remember that most users will be connecting with slow 28.8Kbps modems. It is therefore important to consider the size of files, since the download time is proportional their size. The sizes of HTML files are usually insignificant when compared to the size of multimedia files. Whilst users expect high impact sites, the Web page author must be selective in the use of images.

The two popular image formats are `.GIF` and `.JPG` and both use compression algorithms to reduce the file size. Such algorithms are effected by the complexity of image (such as number of colors) and not just the image size–it is possible that a large simple image can have a smaller file size than a small complex image. Files created with the `.JPG` format can also store an image in a format such that it is rendered by first displaying a low resolution version of the image and then gradually improving the resolution in a series of scans until the final sharp image is shown. This mechanism gives the user the impression of a fast page since they can quickly gauge the content of the page and possibly decide to interrupt the rendering by selecting a hyperlink and navigating elsewhere.

Web Security

In today's world of electronic commerce, the need for secure communications has obviously become crucial. However, there is a lot of unfortunate and ignorant hype over Internet security. While it is common to come across headlines in the computer press about security breaches, we should take comfort from the relative rarity of such events. Remember, the journalists are out to alarm and exaggerate to attract you attention–nobody is interested in reading "ABC Inc. still have a secure system". People who start the scare stories are often the same people who are quite happy to risk handing over a credit card to complete strangers in a shop, and allow them to swipe, and potentially copy, their credit card. In fact, there now exists a comprehensive set of technologies enabling companies to build secure business applications for deployment over the Internet. The biggest security threat is often in your own organization – most of the security breaches are due to the Web administrator not fully understanding the available security measures and so implementing them wrongly.

There are five main requirements for the security of a Web application:

- Protection against the infiltration of any private sub-systems and networks
- Privacy of confidential information
- Confidence of the identity of the end users (both server and client)
- Guarantee against message tampering.
- Protection against viruses

We shall now see how these issues are addressed.

Firewall Technology

The security needs of Internet systems are very different to traditional networking. For example, there is no centralized infrastructure providing responsibility for network security and it is on a global scale, with connected systems being open to a user base of potentially millions. In order for a business to access the full potential of the Internet and the huge user base, it must open its network and provide a shop window to promote its affairs. While most visitors will be happy to look through this window, there will always be a few inquisitive people that will attempt to view items that were not intended for public scrutiny. Worse still, a small number of resourceful people will go one step further and attempt to break the window, climb through and, doubtless, cause severe havoc. As the Internet popularity expands, there is a rapidly increasing number of people who are finding new and ingenious mechanisms for their attacks. Unfortunately, the severe damage caused by these people is often not found until it is too late.

Of course, the failsafe method is to physically isolate your corporate networks from your Internet servers. However, this imposes severe restrictions: for example, your desktop users cannot have Internet access and your Internet servers cannot share corporate information. **Firewalls** are the accepted mechanism for protecting your private corporate systems from users on the Internet and can range in complexity depending on the security requirements of an organization. They work by intelligently analyzing and routing the packets of information passing between two networks, typically the internal network and the public Internet–the Firewall rejects the transmission of packets that conflict with any rules that have been specified.

The Windows NT TCP/IP protocol stack and Steelhead provide some packet filter features which involve monitoring the IP ports and addresses, and enforce rules to which a system's external users can connect.

However, to provide additional security, most organizations implement an additional perimeter network, which is protected by a dedicated firewall, with the Internet servers being multi-homed and connected to both perimeter and corporate networks.

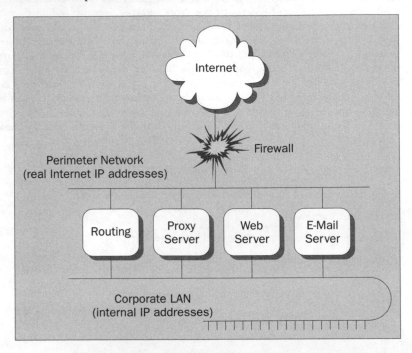

Access Controls

The process of determining the user's identity and having confidence that it really is that person is known as **authentication**. A Web Site administrator must use the server configuration tools to assign file system permissions to the Web resources and indicate those files that require a user to be authenticated before any access is allowed.

IE4 supports the following three types of authentication and the processing is handled by the HTTP protocol:

- **Anonymous** – mechanism to allow access by a guest account user
- **Basic Authentication** – mechanism to provide simple authentication as defined by the W³C
- **Windows NT Challenge / Response** – mechanism developed by Microsoft to securely authenticate users

Web Browsers from outside of the Microsoft camp typically only support the first two authentication types.

As soon as the user navigates to a resource that is protected from anonymous users, the request is rejected and the Web Browser and the Web Server start a negotiation process, using the HTTP, in an attempt to identify the user. This involves the Web Browser prompting the user for a user name and password that is then submitted with another request for the resource. Providing the Web Server identifies the user and confirms that access is allowed, the request for the resource will be completed and the required information returned to the Web Browser.

The difference between Basic Authentication and Windows NT Challenge / Response is the latter provides encryption of the user name and password whereas Basic Authentication sends this information undisguised (although this can be overcome using Secure Channel encryption). Another advantage with NT Challenge / Response and IE4 in an Intranet environment is that should the user be currently logged onto a NT domain, then that user account / password will automatically be used and so avoid the user having to duplicate any logon process. However, NT Challenge / Response is currently only supported by Microsoft Windows NT Web Servers (i.e. Internet Information Server (IIS) and Peer Web Services (PWS)).

Secure Channels Services

Secure Channels Services is a software technology that provides a higher level of security by enabling additional endpoint authentication, message encryption and message authentication. Secure Channels transparently slots into the TCP/IP Protocol Stack as shown:

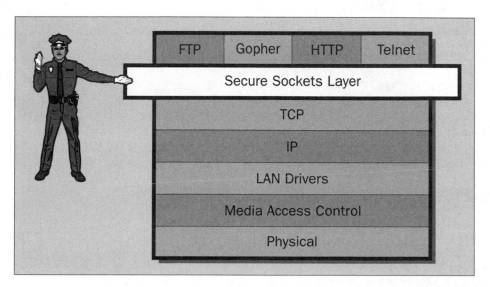

These technologies rely on **cryptography**-the ancient mathematical science that was originally used for military communications and was designed to conceal the contents of a message should it fall into the hands of the enemy. Recent developments have created further uses of cryptography, including mechanisms for authenticating users on a network, ensuring the integrity of transmitted information, and preventing users from repudiating their transmitted messages.

Secure Channels is shipped with IE4 and provides the following features:

- Privacy – packets cannot be examined
- Integrity – packets cannot be tampered with
- Authentication – enables either the client or server to request identification of the other

It actually provides support for several standard security protocols:

- SSL 2.0 / SSL 3.0 – Secure Socket Layer developed by Netscape

▲ PCT 1.0-Private Communications Technology developed by Microsoft

▲ TLS (future release)-Transport Layer Security which is intended to provide a simpler and more robust solution by using the best parts of SSL and PCT

IE4 automatically enables a Secure Channel when it navigates to a resource that a Web Server has protected with a supported security protocol. As a user, we can easily recognize that such security is in place by the lock icon appearing in the middle of the status bar.

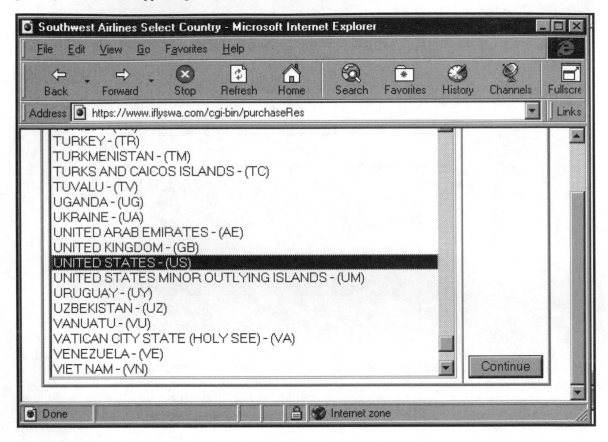

Encryption

Encryption technologies provide enterprises with the best mechanisms of protecting their information without putting the business at risk. Encryption is the process of applying an algorithm to scramble the data in the message in such a way that makes it very difficult and time consuming, if not practically impossible, to deduce the original, given only the encoded data. Inputs to the algorithm typically involve an additional secret item called a **key** that prevents the message from being decoded even if the algorithm is publicly known.

The safekeeping of keys–their generation, storage and exchange–is of paramount importance to ensure the security of data. There is no point applying the strongest levels of cryptographic algorithms if the keys are stored on a scrap of paper, hidden in a desk draw, which could be easily unearthed.

The strength of the encryption is dependent on two basic items: the characteristics of the mathematical algorithm and the length of the keys involved. Under U.S. arms regulations, the export of mass-market software with greater than 40-bit level encryption is restricted–although there is no limitation on the level of encryption sold within the US or Canada.

Unfortunately, 40-bit encryption has been proven to provide little security from attack. Today's powerful processors, costing just several hundred dollars, can crack such a message in few hours by using brute calculation-that is, trying every possible key until the decrypted message has been found. Supercomputers can crack such messages in under a second! Each extra bit of key doubles the time needed for the brute force attack and so most experts now claim that 128-bit keys are required to ensure complete confidence and vital for markets such as electronic commerce.

Many non-U.S. companies have now developed add-on cryptographic products–using 128-bit key technology – to fill the vacuum left by the US software industry's inability to compete in this market. Naturally, there is frequent discussions between concerned parties and the future of these export restrictions are unclear.

There are, in fact, two methods of encryption based on these principles-**symmetric** and **asymmetric**.

In symmetric encryption, the encryption algorithm requires the same secret key to be used for both encryption and decryption. However, the problem is that of **key exchange** i.e. the mechanism for safely ensuring both parties – the sender and the receiver – are aware of the secret key. This is one of the weakest areas of such cryptography. How do we send the key to our partners? We cannot just send it in an email message because it could be intercepted and, possibly unknowingly, compromise our security. Furthermore, how can we be sure that our partners will keep our key secure? A practical solution to this problem is asymmetric cryptography.

Asymmetric cryptography uses two keys that are mathematically related. One key is called the **private key** and is never revealed, and the other key is called the **public key** and is freely given out to all. The complexity of the relationship between the public key and the private key means that, provided the keys are long enough, it is practically impossible to determine one from the other. The algorithm named RSA after Ron Rivest, Adi Shamir, and Len Adleman made it into a useful system following its development at Stanford University in 1977. This public key system is patented by RSA Data Security Inc. `http://www.rsa.com/`.

A sender uses the receiver's public key to encrypt the message. Only the receiver has the related key to decrypt the message.

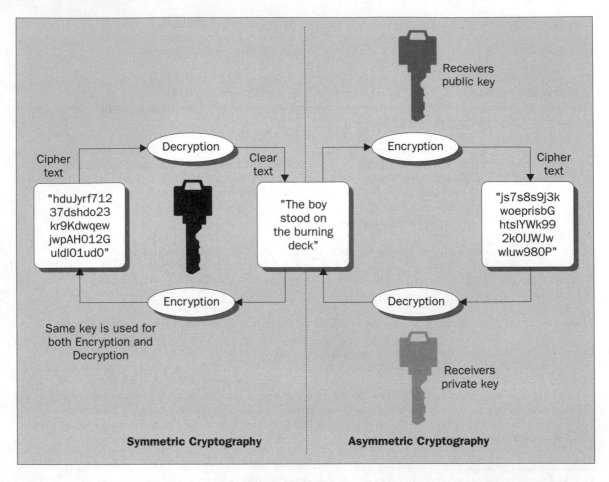

A further use of public/private keys is as **digital signatures**, which involves swapping the role of the private and public keys. If a sender encrypts a message using their private key, everyone can decrypt the message using the sender's public key. A successful decryption implies that the sender, who is the only person in possession of their private key, must have sent the message. This stops repudiation, since the sender cannot claim that they did not actually send the message.

One severe problem with asymmetric cryptography is that the processing required is CPU intensive, whereas the algorithms used by symmetric cryptography are fast and efficient. Because of this, Secure Channels and many other implementations of this idea work in the following manner:

- As part of the initial session establishment a random secret key is generated; this secret key is encrypted with the partner's public key and transmitted to the partner who can decrypt the secret key using their private key

- All subsequent messages are encrypted using the secret key and the efficient symmetric algorithms

Digital Certificates & Certificate Authorities

A **digital certificate** is an item of information that binds the details of an individual or organization to their public key. The most widely accepted format for digital certificates is the X.509 standard and is relevant to both Web Browsers and Web Servers. If we can obtain access to someone's certificate, we will then have, amongst other things, their public key and can handle the security techniques that we have already discussed.

But stringent procedures are required to prevent imposters just generating a false certificate and pretending that they are someone else. The solution is **Certificate Authorities** (CAs) who are responsible for the issuing of digital certificates. A CA is a commonly trusted third party who is responsible for verifying both the contents and ownership of a certificate.

There is an ever-increasing number of CAs. Different CAs will employ different amounts of effort in their verification processes and they must publicly divulge what checks they perform. Then users can apply the appropriate levels of trust for each CA they encounter. Also, different classes of certificates are available which reflect the level of assurance given by the CA–a certificate for users who just surf the web requires less verification than a certificate for a business server. If two entities trust the same CA, they can swap digital certificates to obtain access to each other's public key and from then onwards they can undertake secure transmissions.

Digital certificates include the CA's digital signature (i.e. information encrypted with the CA's private key). This guarantees that no one can create a false certificate. The public keys of trusted CA's are stored for use by the Secure Channel Services in applications like IE4. When we navigate to a Web resource that is protected by a Secure Channel–we can inspect the digital certificate by clicking on the Certificates button on the Page Properties dialog.

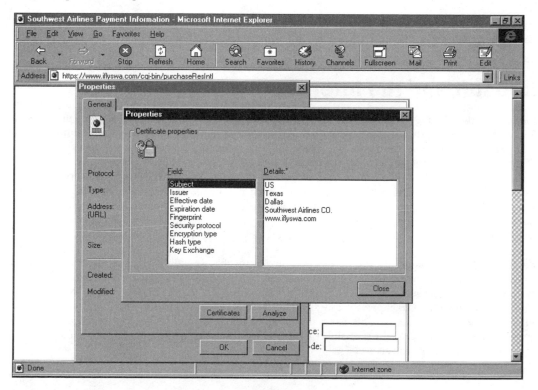

Virus Protection

AuthentiCode

The software products that can be purchase in a shop typically have the software author's name printed on the box and are shrink-wrapped. While there are no guarantees that such items are virus free, we buy the software on the basis that we trust the author and are confident that has not been tampered with since it was released.

We discussed earlier that the recent generation of browsers provides support for the dynamic deployment of software executables onto the client. With the possibility of such components containing some nasty logic, it is a major requirement that an electronic type of shrink-wrapping is used to identify the author and confirm that is identical to its original published form. The solution to these concerns is Microsoft's Authenticode that uses digital signature technology to verify software downloaded. Authenticode is supported by IE4.

It is important to understand that Authenticode only provides 'Accountability'–it doesn't guarantee that the code is 100% bug and virus free.

Sandboxing

Authenticode is complementary to an earlier method of web security known as **sandboxing**. Sandbox code is prevented from accessing critical parts of a computer or network (e.g. a disk drive). Whilst these restrictions enhance the protection of the system it has a severe impact on what the code can actually achieve.

The current script languages supported by Web browsers are safe. The most recent versions of the scripting languages don't allow any direct access to the disk, devices or underlying operating system.

Microsoft and the Internet

Microsoft's Internet strategy is to use Internet standards to deliver a comprehensive set of products and services that can seamlessly integrate desktops, LANs, legacy systems, GroupWare applications and the public Internet to provide a more effective computing environment for the corporate enterprise.

This strategy is to be Microsoft's trump card as they address their two recent major concerns. Firstly, Microsoft's Windows domination of the desktop has been threatened by the concept of a low cost Network Computer (NC) in which any required executable logic is automatically downloaded as required in small chunks from a central file server. It is suggested that by minimizing the complexity of both the NC hardware and the installed software will result in much lower administration costs.

In addition, it has been generally recognized that for Microsoft to continue its impressive growth curve, it must now conquer the server market. Until recent times, organizations had taken the traditional best of breed approach for their server solutions-Novell NetWare for a file & printer server, UNIX machines for communication gateways, Oracle or Sybase for relational databases, Lotus for Email and GroupWare, Netscape for Internet, and so on. This has typically left a hotchpotch of technologies within an organization that greatly increases the range of staff skills needed to support the enterprise, and thus increases the running costs of the IT infrastructure.

Windows NT Server

The Microsoft answer for enterprise infrastructures is Windows NT, a single robust and high performance multipurpose network operating system that can act as any of:

- File server
- Print server
- Application server
- Communication server
- Database server

Windows NT was first conceived by Bill Gates in 1988 when he decided that Microsoft would develop an operating system that was portable, secure, scalable, extensible, compatible and internationally applicable.

These goals meant that Windows NT can be converted to run on a number of different hardware platforms and operate in a number of languages and character sets, all with minimal changes to the core code. In addition, it can provide support for symmetric multiprocessing (SMP), enabling it to run on machines with multiple CPUs.

Windows NT extensions can be developed by writing applications that conform to a well-defined application programming interface (API) called **WIN32**. In addition, support was provided for DOS, OS/2 and POSIX applications.

Strong levels of security were built into the core of Windows NT in order to meet and exceed a certifiable security standard, the **C2** security guidelines required by the U.S. Department of Defense's security evaluation criteria. Windows NT security contrasts sharply with the thin and weak security layers that are often bolted on to the top of other operating systems. Compliance with the C2 security standard was originally only required for government organizations, but many commercial organizations have demanding corporate security needs and recognize the value of the enhanced security that such systems offer.

To design Windows NT, Microsoft hired David Cutler, who had worked on a number of operating systems, including the PDP-11 and VAX, at Digital Equipment Corporation. After five years of development, Windows NT was released. It was delivered in two versions: NT 3.1 and NT Advanced Server 3.1. The 3.1 indicates the roots of its user interface in Windows 3.x, but that is where the similarities
.

In late 1994, Microsoft clarified the roles of the two versions by changing their names to give a clear indication of their purpose. Windows NT 3.1 became Windows NT Workstation 3.51 and Windows NT Advanced Server 3.1 became Windows NT Server 3.51. While being based on the same core code, the internal scheduling of tasks was optimized so that one functions best as a desktop operating system and the other as a robust enterprise level multi-purpose network operating system. In 1996, NT version 4.0 (Workstation and Server) was released and adopted the same acclaimed user interface from Window95.

The operating system initially dreamt up by Bill Gates and David Cutler was code-named Cairo. This ideal has proven very elusive, and Cairo has recently changed from being an actual product release to an encompassing philosophy.

Windows NT Roadmap

▲   1988 - conception

▲   1992 - Windows NT 3.1

▲   1994 - Windows NT 3.5 & 3.51

                   Products renamed Server and Workstation

                   Extensive bug fixes and optimisation

▲   1996 - Windows NT 4.0

                   Windows 95 user interface

                   Network OLE / Distributed COM

▲   1998 - Windows NT 5.0

                   Next generation Directory Services

                   Clustering technology

                   Plug and play device support

                   Powerful distributed computing facilities

▲   21st Century - Cairo

Active Server Products / BackOffice 97

Providing additional value to Windows NT is a number of dynamic products and components which work together to provide a comprehensive Active Server solution. Some of these servers are grouped under the **BackOffice** portfolio of products.

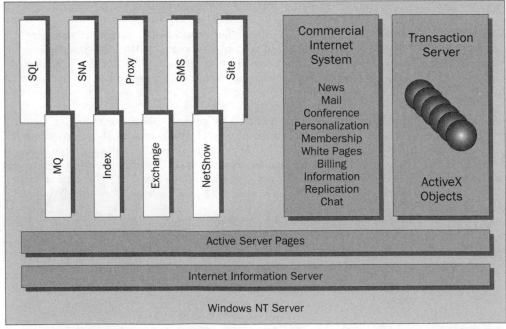

The range of technologies available to allow this comprehensiveness are shown in the diagram above, and itemized below.

Transaction Server	Provides facilities to share resources, manage transactions and administrate component deployment. Provides the infrastructure needed for multi-tier client server solutions.
Message Queue Server	Provides assured delivery message switching. Handles network outages and heterogeneous networking architectures.
Internet Information Server (IIS)	Provides Internet services include WWW (Web-based information publishing and application delivery), FTP and Gopher.
Active Server Pages (ASP)	Provides extensions to the IIS Web services for server side scripting.
Index Server	Provides search engine facilities.
Exchange	Provides integrated system for email, personal and group scheduling, Server electronic forms, and groupware applications
SQL Server	Provides large-scale relational database management system designed specifically for distributed client-server computing.
Systems Management Server	Provides centralized management tool for software distribution, hardware/ software inventory and diagnostic facilities.
SNA Server	Provides facilities for interfacing with legacy IBM and other host systems using SNA protocols.
Proxy Server	Provides Internet access to the corporate desktop in a secure manner. Provides caching of popular Web pages.
Commercial Internet System	Provides facilities for Internet communities, includes servers for membership, personalization, billing, white pages, chat, mail, newsgroups, user locator, content replication, information retrieval
Site Server	Provides web site environment and support for electronic commerce facilities.
NetShow Server	Provides streaming media services for Video and Audio broadcasting
'Wolfpack' (code name)	Provides clustering facilities allowing multiple NT nodes to combine to provide high availability and scalability.

The single infrastructure and the consistent approach found throughout Windows NT and these products considerably reduces training and support costs.

To tie this general information back to IE4.0, it's worth looking at which of these server functions the browser is likely to communicate with in a Web application.

Internet Information Server

The foundation of Microsoft's NT Web strategy is **Internet Information Server** (IIS) which has been designed for easy of use, scalability, portability, security, and extensibility, and is recognized by many to be superior to any of the alternatives.

Today's Web sites have moved well beyond the delivery of static HTML files and need to dynamically generated pages with content based on the user and any previously entered fields. To enable such functionality a Web servers must provide extensions allowing integration to software components, databases and legacy system. The most common method is called the **Common Gateway Interface** (CGI), which is an industry standard and supported by nearly every Web server implementations. A CGI application is a program and is invoked when an HTTP request references the executable file name, for example:

```
http://www.wrox.com/_vti_bin/search.exe?info=Internet
```

The CGI specification details how such a program accesses any input information and generates the output HTML file. The problem with CGI is that each invocation of a process is very resource intensive and a busy Web server could have severe performance problems.

An alternative open approach is the **Internet Server Applications Programming Interface** (ISAPI), which is supported by Microsoft's IIS. An ISAPI extension is Dynamic Link Library (DLL) which means it is loaded only once, on first demand, and then stays resident in the same process as the Web Server. In addition to server extensions, the ISAPI specification also provides for server filters. These are used to intercept and optionally process every HTTP request.

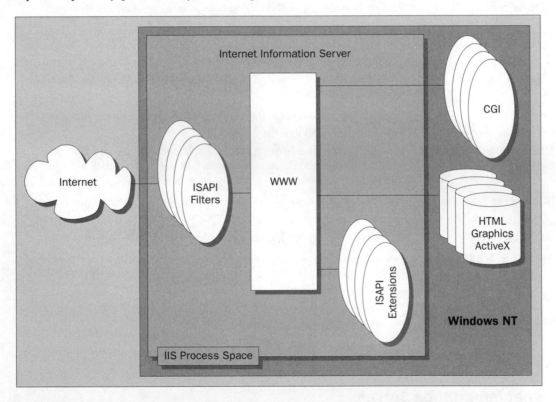

Although the development and internals of ISAPI extension is different to that of a CGI program, the way they are referenced is similar. For example:

```
http://www.wrox.com/_vti_bin/search.exe?info=Internet
```

Filters can be used for such tasks as additional security measures, auditing, redirecting requests, etc. The simplest method the development of ISAPI extensions and filters is to use the ISAPI Wizard supplied with Microsoft's Visual C++. This Wizard takes the developer through a number of dialogs to inquire on the options required and then generates the skeleton of an appropriate ISAPI application with inserted comments where the developer's code needs to be added.

Active Server Pages

Active Server Pages (ASP) builds on top of the ISAPI technology and provides a server-side application framework making it even easier than using high level languages like Visual C++ to build dynamic Web applications. ASP allows executable script logic to be embedded within an HTML page. When an HTTP request references an ASP document, the output HTML file is generated using a combination of static information and information generated by the scripting. The URL reference for an ASP page is similar to those for ISAPI and CGI:

```
http://www.wrox.com/_vti_bin/search.exe?info=Internet
```

ASP enables the scripting to interface to a number of internal objects, which automatically handle many of the menial tasks, and so simplifies the script logic. These objects provide ASP with the concept of a user session and allow variables to persist across Web pages, until either the session is programmatically abandoned or the Web browser is closed. Prior to ASP, the handling of user context across multiple HTTP requests was a complex process.

In addition, ASP scripting can interface with external software components, including those supplied with ASP, those provided by Windows NT and other BackOffice products, and those developed by ourselves and other independent software vendors. For example, ASP is supplied with **Active Data Objects** (ADO) that provides a high performance interface to databases that are **Open Database Connectivity** (ODBC) or **OLE DB** compliant.

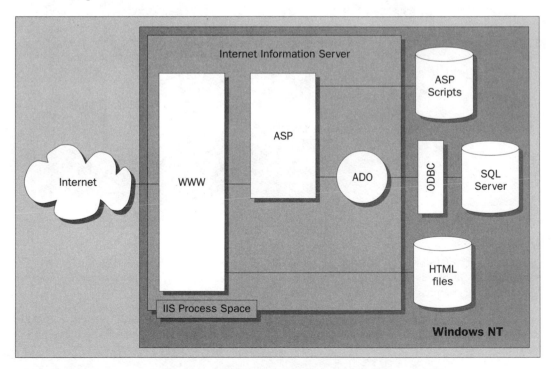

Transaction Server

Microsoft Transaction Server (MTS) is designed to simplify the development of multi-tier applications by supplying much of the infrastructure to provide a robust, scaleable, high performance and distributable architecture. Future versions of MTS will work with the Wolfpack clustering technologies to provide dynamic load balancing, scalability and high availability.

MTS also insulates the developer from many of the traditional complexities by automatically handling all threading issues, object re-pooling, the sharing of resources and the handling of transaction context across objects. This means that a developer just needs to concentrate on developing the 'business logic', as the underlying plumbing is handled for them.

ASP can integrate with software components running in MTS and can combine to deliver mission critical Web applications for the enterprise.

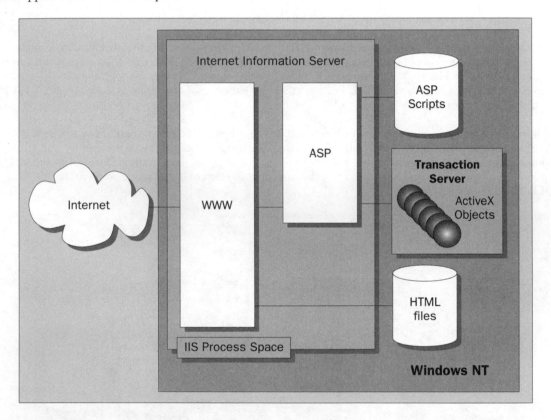

Index Server

An important aspect of Internet technology is the means to quickly search through large quantities of information and identify relevant resources. Index Server provides high performance search facilities using a sophisticated query language.

Index Server provides facilities to perform full text searches on HTML and Microsoft Office (MS Word, MS Excel, and MS PowerPoint) documents–extensions also allow software vendors to provide search support for their own proprietary file formats. This means that an organization does not have to convert existing office documents to HTML in order to provide search facilities.

NetShow Server

NetShow provides broadcasting facilities for live and prerecorded audio, illustrated audio and video over the Internet or corporate enterprise. It integrates with IIS to provide an efficient, reliable and scalable solution.

It uses the new **Multicasting** and **Streaming** technologies to reduce bandwidth. Multicasting is a new open mechanism for the transmission of identical information, such as live events, to multiple users simultaneously. It contrasts with the traditional TCP/IP unicasting where the server must transmit a separate copy to each user. Streaming allows users to see or hear the broadcast as soon as it arrives, as opposed to the traditional multimedia mechanisms where the entire file has to be transferred before the information can be used.

NetShow comes with a number of authoring and production tools to create high impact broadcast content.

SQL Server

A major requirement for today's Internet is a secure, reliable, and scaleable place to store information. SQL Server provides a high-performance relational database management system specifically designed for distributed client-server computing.

A Web application can easily retrieve and store information in a SQL Server database by using ASP scripting to interface with the ADO component. Alternatively, SQL server provides a Web Assistant Wizard which allows a database administrator to define a query that is automatically merged into an HTML document either on a scheduled basis or when the contents of the database changes.

ActiveX

ActiveX (or third generation OLE technology) is a framework that allows software components to co-operate even if they have been written by different vendors, at different times, using different tools and different languages, and regardless of whether the objects are located in the same process, same machine or distributed over multiple machines. Put simply, ActiveX provides the *software plumbing* between software objects and insulates the component developer from such complexities.

ActiveX encompasses an ever-growing series of technologies, each of which defines the interfaces between the objects to implement the particular technology. For the Internet, examples include:

- ActiveX Scripting – enables script logic to included in the downloaded Web page or a server-side ASP page
- ActiveX Controls – enables client components to be dynamically downloaded as needed and used within a web page
- ActiveX Documents – enables the browser to support non HTML documents
- ActiveX Server Components – enables the Web Server (IIS and ASP) to interface to server software components

Component Object Model (COM)

Underneath ActiveX is the generic **Component Object Model** (COM) which defines the binary interface between objects. The original specification of COM always allowed for co-operating objects to be located on different machines but this was not implemented until Windows NT 4.0 and was then called **Distributed COM** (DCOM). Because of this, in reality DCOM and COM are now the same animals. DCOM is layered on top of the DCE (Distributed Computing Environment) RPC (**Remote Procedure Call**) specifications. The following diagram illustrates how objects use COM/DCOM to co-operate even across process and machine boundaries.

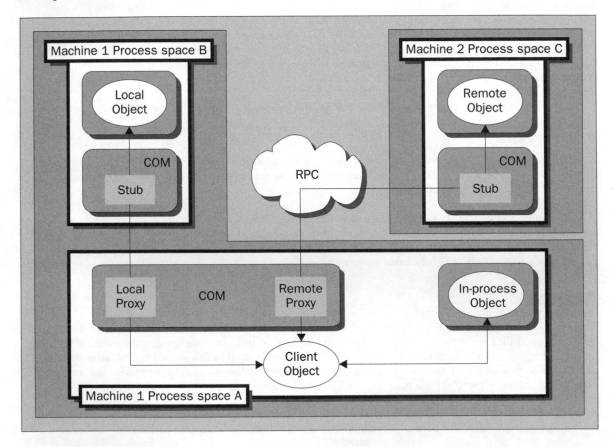

Whilst ActiveX and DCOM were not originally committee-driven standards, they have since become market-driven technologies that are fully published from the lowest level communications protocols to the highest level API functions. In addition, Microsoft has donated ownership of the technology's specifications to an open industry association–**The Active Group**, `http://www.activex.org/`, working under the auspices of The Open Group–to promote the common adoption of the ActiveX core technologies. At the time of writing, it was not clear whether this independent stewardship would come to fruition or be blighted by the differing aims of the committee members.

The Active Platform

Microsoft has given the architecture that addresses their seamless integration strategy, as well as the dynamic delivery of applications, the name **Active Platform**. This encompasses both the client (**Active Client/Desktop**) and server (**Active Server**) technologies to achieve their goal. Its complete support for the ActiveX and Internet standards enables developers to integrate HTML, scripting, components, and transactions to build powerful, scaleable and highly available applications that run across the enterprise. This architecture frees developers from the complexity of programming infrastructures to allow them to concentrate on delivering business solutions.

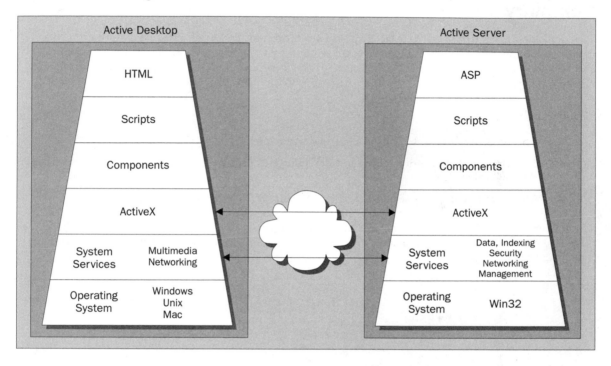

The foundation of the Active Server is Windows NT Server plus ActiveX and the BackOffice, security, network, and data components. This provides a great set of tools for the creation of distributed applications where different parts of a solution can reside on different machines—a multi-tier client server architecture. Such architectures allow systems to be broken down into the following three loosely coupled logical areas or services:

- The first area—**presentation services**—relates to the user interface or the user's interaction with the system.

- The second area—**business services**—relates to the business rules or the logic that controls the behaviour of the system.

- The third area—**data services**—relates to the actual storage and retrieval of data.

Structuring the services into individual components means the system is well organised, and easy to maintain and enhance. The use of Distributed COM allows the components to be deployed over multiple clients and servers.

The Active Client

It is, of course, the active client and its possibilities that has been the focus of much of this book. Strictly speaking, the Active Client is not IE4.0 itself but rather a set of components that allow client-side support for HTML and ActiveX technologies. It is intended to be cross-platform and to extend the functionality of the desktop–offering not just a greater range of input (multi-media, sound, databases) but a greater flexibility of response. Furthermore, by allowing the client to take as much responsibility as possible for the management of information, the client/server division of tasks becomes more reasonable.

Summary

This appendix has aimed to put Internet Explorer 4.0 in context, and to examine some of the broader development concerns it raises. Furthermore, it has explored the design philosophy that lies behind IE4, and looked at the suite of Microsoft technologies–existing, imminent and emerging–for which IE4 is the client-side flagship.

Specifically, we looked at:

- The origins of the web, and its most basic structure
- Performance and security issues, and the emergent technologies–some demonstrated by IE4–to deal with them
- Microsoft's plans for a seamless and transferable web environment

The following appendices return to the nuts and bolts of programming with and for IE4, but we hope that this more discursive approach will enable you, as a developer, to make more informed decisions about your long-term strategy.

JavaScript Reference

General Information

JavaScript is included in an HTML document with the **`<SCRIPT>`** tag. Here's an example:

```
<HTML>
<HEAD>

<!-- wrap script in comments
<SCRIPT LANGUAGE = "JavaScript">
    script code goes here
</SCRIPT>
-->

</HEAD>
<BODY>
    HTML goes here
</BODY>
</HTML>
```

The following points should be kept in mind:

- The main core of your JavaScript code should be put in the **`<HEAD>`** section of the document. This ensures that all the code has been loaded before an attempt is made to execute it. "On-the-fly" scripts that generate HTML at specific parts of the document can be placed exactly as required.

- The script code should be wrapped in a comment tag, as this stops older (non-JavaScript) browsers from trying to read the code.

- JavaScript is case-sensitive.

- In Javascript, semicolons (;) are used to separate statements when they are on the same line. If the statements are not on the same line, semicolons are optional.

Values

JavaScript recognizes the following data types:

- **strings**–"Hello World"

- **numbers**–both integers (86) and decimal values (86.235)

- **boolean**–true or false

A null (*no value*) value is assigned with the keyword **null**.

JavaScript also makes use of 'special characters' in a similar way to the C++ programming language:

Character	Function
\n	newline
\t	tab
\f	form feed
\b	backspace
\r	carriage return

You may 'escape' other characters by preceding them with a backslash (\), to prevent the browser from trying to interpret them. This is most commonly used for quotes and backslashes, or to include a character by using its octal (base 8) value:

```
document.write("This shows a \"quote\" in a string.");
document.write("This is a backslash: \\");
document.write("This is a space character: \040.");
```

Variables

JavaScript is a **loosely typed** language. This means that variables do not have an explicitly defined variable type. Instead, every variable can hold values of various types. Conversions between types are done automatically when needed, as this example demonstrates:

```
x = 55;      // x is assigned to be the integer 55
y = "55";    // y is assigned to be the string "55"
y = '55';    // an alternative using single quotes

z = 1 + y;
<!-- even though y is a string, it will be automatically
 converted to the appropriate integer value so that 1 may
 be added to it. -->

document.write(x);
<!-- the number 55 will be written to the screen. Even
 though x is an integer and not a string, Javascript will
 make the  necessary conversion for you. -->

n = 3.14159;  // assigning a real (fractional) number
n = 0546;     // numbers starting 0 assumed to be octal
n = 0xFFEC;   // numbers starting 0x assumed to be hex
n = 2.145E-5; // using exponential notation
```

Variable names must start with either a letter or an underscore. Beyond the first letter, variables may contain any combination of letters, underscores, and digits. JavaScript is case sensitive, so `this_variable` is not the same as `This_Variable`.

Variables do not need to be declared before they are used. However, you may use the `var` keyword to explicitly define a variable. This is especially useful when there is the possibility of conflicting variable names. When in doubt, use `var`.

```
var x = "55";
```

Assignment Operators

The following operators are used to make assignments in JavaScript:

Operator	Example	Result
=	x = y	x equals y
+=	x += y	x equals x plus y
-=	x -= y	x equals x minus y
*=	x *= y	x equals x multiplied by y
/=	x /= y	x equals x divided by y
%=	x %= y	x equals x modulus y

Each operator assigns the value on the right to the variable on the left.

```
x = 100;
y = 10;
x += y;  // x now is equal to 110
```

Equality Operators

Operator	Meaning
==	is equal to
!=	is not equal to
>	is greater than
>=	is greater than or equal to
<	is less than
<=	is less than or equal to

Other Operators

Operator	Meaning
+	Addition
-	Subtraction
*	Multiplication
/	Division
%	Modulus
++	Increment
--	Decrement
-	Unary Negation
& or AND	Bitwise AND
| or OR	Bitwise OR
^ or XOR	Bitwise XOR
<<	Bitwise left shift
>>	Bitwise right shift
>>>	Zero-fill right shift
&&	Logical AND
||	Logical OR
!	Not

String Operators

Operator	Meaning
+	Concatenates strings, so `"abc"` + `"def"` is `"abcdef"`
> >= < <=	Compare strings in a case-sensitive way. A string is 'greater' than another based on the Latin ASCII code values of the characters, starting from the left of the string. So `"DEF"` is greater than `"ABC"` and `"DEE"`, but less than `"abc"`.

Comments

Operator	Meaning
`// a comment`	A single line comment
`/* this text is a multi-line comment */`	A multi-line comment

Input/Output

In JavaScript, there are three different methods of providing information to the user, and getting a response back.

Alert

This displays a message with an OK button.

```
alert("Hello World!");
```

Confirm

Displays a message with both an OK and a Cancel button. True is returned if the OK button is pressed, and false is returned if the Cancel button is pressed.

```
confirm("Are you sure you want to quit?");
```

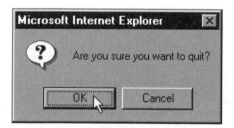

Prompt

Displays a message and a text box for user input. The first string argument forms the text that is to be displayed above the text box. The second argument is a string, integer, or property of an existing object, which represents the default value to display inside the box. If the second argument is not specified, "<undefined>" is displayed inside the text box.

The string typed into the box is returned if the OK button is pressed. False is returned if the Cancel button is pressed

```
prompt("What is your name?", "");
```

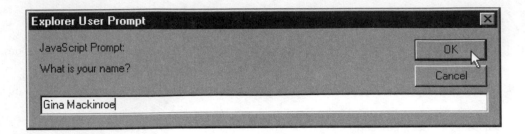

Control Flow

There are two ways of controlling the flow of a program in JavaScript. The first involves **conditional** statements, which follow either one branch of the program or another. The second way is to use a **repeated iteration** of a set of statements.

Conditional Statements

JavaScript has one conditional statement:

if....else, which is used to run various blocks of code, depending on conditions. These statements have the following general form in JavaScript:

```
if (condition)
{
 code to be executed if condition is true
}
else
{
 code to be executed if condition is false
};
```

In addition:

- ▲ The **else** portion is optional.
- ▲ **if** statements may be nested.
- ▲ Multiple statements must be enclosed by braces.

Here is an example:

```
person_type = prompt("What are you ?", "");
if (person_type == "cat")
  alert("Here, have some cat food.")
else
{
  if (person_type == "dog")
    alert("Here, have some dog food.")
  else
  {
    if (person_type == "human")
```

```
        alert("Here have some, er, human food!");
    };
};
```

Notice that the curly brackets are only actually required where there is more than one statement within the block. Like many other constructs, they can be omitted where single statements are used. The final semicolon is mandatory:

```
if (condition)
    code to be executed if condition is true
else
    code to be executed if condition is false;
```

Loop Statements

for– executes a block of code a specified number of times.

```
for (i = 0; i = 10; i++)
{
    document.write(i);
}
```

while– executes a block of code while a condition is true.

```
while (condition)
{
    statements to execute ...
}
```

break– will cause an exit from a loop regardless of the condition statement.

```
x = 0;
while (x != 10)
{
    n = prompt("Enter a number or 'q' to quit", "");
    if (n == "q")
    {
        alert("See ya");
        break;
    }
}
```

continue– will cause the loop to jump immediately back to the condition statement.

```
x = 0;
while (x != 1)
{
    if (!(confirm("Should I add 1 to n ?")))
    {
        continue;
        // the following x++ is never executed because if follows continue
        x++;
    }
}
```

```
x++;
}
alert("Bye");
```

Built-in Functions

JavaScript provides a number of built-in functions that can be accessed within code.

Function	Description
escape(*char*)	Returns a string of the form %*XX* where *XX* is the ASCII encoded value of *char*.
eval(*expression*)	Returns the result of evaluating the numeric expression *expression*
isNaN(*value*)	Returns a Boolean value of **true** if *value* is not a legal number.
parseFloat(*string*)	Converts *string* to a floating-point number.
ParseInt(*string, base*)	Converts *string* to an integer number with the base of *base*.
typeOf(*object*)	Returns the data type of *object* as a string, such as **"boolean"**, **"function"**, etc.

Built-in Objects

JavaScript provides a set of built-in data-type objects, which have their own set of properties and methods, and which can be accessed with JavaScript code.

Array Object

The **Array** object specifies a method of creating arrays and working with them. To create a new array, use:

```
cats = new Array();      // create an empty array
cats = new Array(10);    // create an array of 10 items

// or create and fill an array with values in one go:
cats = new Array("Boo Boo", "Purrcila", "Sam", "Lucky");
```

Properties	Description
length	A read/write Integer value specifying the number of elements in the array.

Methods	Description
join([*string*])	Returns a string containing each element of the array, optionally separated with *string*.

Methods	Description
`reverse()`	Reverses the order of the array.
`sort([function])`	Sorts the array, optionally based upon the results of a function specified by *function*.

Early versions of JavaScript had no explicit array structure. However, JavaScript's object mechanisms allow for easy creation of arrays:

```
function MakeArray(n)
{
  this.length = n;
  for (var i = 1; i <= n; i++)
    this[i] = 0;
  return this
}
```

With this function included in your script, you can create arrays with:

```
cats = new MakeArray(20);
```

You can then populate the array like this:

```
cats[1] = "Boo Boo";
cats[2] = "Purrcila";
cats[3] = "Sam";
cats[4] = "Lucky";
```

The following code creates a two dimensional array and displays the results;

```
a = new Array(4)
for (i=0; i < 4; i++) {
  a[i] = new Array(4)
  for (j=0; j < 4; j++) {
    a[i][j] = "["+i+","+j+"]"
  }
}
```

Boolean Object

The `Boolean` object is used to store simple yes/no, true/false values. To create a new Boolean object, use the syntax:

```
MyAnswer = new Boolean([value])
```

If *value* is `0`, `null`, omitted, or an empty string the new Boolean object will have the value `false`. All other values, *including the string* `"false"`, create an object with the value `true`.

Methods	Description
toString()	Returns the value of the Boolean as the string **true** or **false**.
valueOf()	Returns the primitive numeric value of the object for conversion in calculations.

Date Object

The **Date** object provides a method for working with dates and times inside of JavaScript. New instances of the **Date** object are invoked with:

```
newDateObject = new Date([dateInfo])
```

dateInfo is an optional specification for the date to set in the new object. If it is not specified, the current date and time are used. *dateInfo* can use any of the following formats:

```
milliseconds (since midnight GMT on January 1st 1970)
year, month, day (e.g. 1997, 0, 27 is 27th Jan 1997)
year, month, day, hours, minutes, seconds
month day, year hours:minutes:seconds (e.g. September 23, 1997 08:25:30)
```

Methods	Description
getDate()	Returns the day of the month as an Integer between 1 and 31.
getDay()	Returns the day of the week as an Integer between 0 (Sunday) and 6 (Saturday).
getHours()	Returns the hours as an Integer between 0 and 23.
getMinutes()	Returns the minutes as an Integer between 0 and 59.
getMonth()	Returns the month as an Integer between 0 (January) and 11 (December).
getSeconds()	Returns the seconds as an Integer between 0 and 59.
getTime()	Returns the number of milliseconds between Jan. 1, 1970 at 00:00:00 GMT and the current **Date** object as an Integer.
getTimeZoneOffset()	Returns the number of minutes difference between local time and GMT as an Integer.
getYear()	Returns the year (generally minus 1900 - i.e. only two digits) as an Integer.
parse(*dateString*)	Returns the number of milliseconds in a date string, since Jan. 1, 1970 00:00:00 GMT.
setDate(*dayValue*)	Sets the day of the month where *dayValue* is an Integer between 1 and 31.
setHours(*hoursValue*)	Sets the hours where *hoursValue* is an Integer between 0 and 59.

Methods	Description
setMinutes (*minutesValue*)	Sets the minutes where *minutesValue* is an Integer between 0 and 59.
setMonth (*monthValue*)	Sets the month where *monthValue* is an Integer between 0 and 11.
setSeconds (*secondsValue*)	Sets the seconds where *secondsValue* is an Integer between 0 and 59.
setTime (*timeValue*)	Sets the value of a **Date** object where *timeValue* is and integer representing the number of milliseconds in a date string, since Jan. 1, 1970 00:00:00 GMT.
setYear (*yearValue*)	Sets the year where *yearValue* is an Integer (generally) greater than 1900.
toGMTString ()	Converts a date from local time to GMT, and returns it as a string.
toLocaleString ()	Converts a date from GMT to local time, and returns it as a string.
UTC (*year, month, day* [*, hrs*] [*, min*] [*, sec*])	Returns the number of milliseconds in a date object, since Jan. 1, 1970 00:00:00 Universal Coordinated Time (GMT).

Function Object

The **Function** object provides a mechanism for compiling JavaScript code as a function. A new function is invoked with the syntax:

```
functionName = new Function(arg1, arg2, ..., functionCode)
```

where **arg1**, **arg2**, etc. are the arguments for the function object being created, and **functionCode** is a string containing the body of the function. This can be a series of JavaScript statements separated by semi-colons.

Properties	Description
arguments []	A reference to the **Arguments** array that holds the arguments that were provided when the function was called.
caller	Specifies the function that called the **Function** object.
prototype	Provides a way for adding properties to a **Function** object.

Arguments Object

The **Arguments** object is list (array) of arguments in a **Function** object.

Properties	Description
length	An Integer specifying the number of arguments provided to the function when it was called.

Math Object

Provides a set of properties and methods for working with mathematical constants and functions. Simply reference the **Math** object, then the method or property required:

```
MyArea = Math.PI * MyRadius * MyRadius;
MyResult = Math.floor(MyNumber);
```

Properties	Description
E	Euler's Constant *e* (the base of natural logarithms).
LN10	The value of the natural logarithm of 10.
LN2	The value of the natural logarithm of 2.
LOG10E	The value of the natural logarithm of E.
LOG2E	The value of the base 2 logarithm of E.
PI	The value of the constant π (pi).
SQRT1_2	The value of the square root of a half.
SQRT	The value of the square root of two.

Methods	Description
abs(*number*)	Returns the absolute value of *number*.
acos(*number*)	Returns the arc cosine of *number*.
asin(*number*)	Returns the arc sine of *number*.
atan(*number*)	Returns the arc tangent of *number*.
atan2(*x, y*)	Returns the angle of the polar coordinate of a point *x, y* from the *x*-axis.
ceil(*number*)	Returns the next largest Integer greater than *number*, i.e. rounds up.
cos(*number*)	Returns the cosine of *number*.
exp(*number*)	Returns the value of *number* as the exponent of *e*, as in e^{number}.
floor(*number*)	Returns the next smallest Integer less that *number*, i.e. rounds down.
log(*number*)	Returns the natural logarithm of *number*.
max(*num1, num2*)	Returns the greater of the two values *num1* and num2.
min(*num1, num2*)	Returns the smaller of the two values *num1* and *num2*.
pow(*num1, num2*)	Returns the value of *num1* to the power of *num2*.
random()	Returns a random number between 0 and 1.
round(*number*)	Returns the closest Integer to *number* i.e. rounds up *or* down to the nearest whole number.

Methods	Description
sin(*number*)	Returns the sin of *number*.
sqrt(*number*)	Returns the square root of *number*.
tan(*number*)	Returns the tangent of *number*.

Number Object

The Number Object provides a set of properties that are useful when working with numbers:

```
MyArea = Math.PI * MyRadius * MyRadius;
MyResult = Math.floor(MyNumber);
```

Properties	Description
MAX_VALUE	The maximum numeric value represented in JavaScript (~1.79E+308).
MIN_VALUE	The minimum numeric value represented in JavaScript (~2.22E-308).
NaN	A value meaning 'Not A Number'.
NEGATIVE_INFINITY	A special value for negative infinity ("-Infinity").
POSITIVE_INFINITY	A special value for infinity ("Infinity").

Methods	Description
toString([*radix_base*])	Returns the value of the number as a string to a radix (base) of 10, unless specified otherwise in *radix_base*.
valueOf()	Returns the primitive numeric value of the object.

String Object

The **String** object provides a set of methods for text manipulation. To create a new string object, the syntax is:

```
MyString = new String([value])
```

where **value** is the optional text to place in the string when it is created. If this is a number, it is converted into a string first.

Properties	Description
length	An Integer representing the number of characters in the string.

Methods	Description
anchor ("*nameAttribute*")	Returns the original string surrounded by `<A>` and `</A>` anchor tags, with the `NAME` attribute set to "*nameAttribute*".
big()	Returns the original string enclosed in `<BIG>` and `</BIG>` tags.
blink()	Returns the original string enclosed in `<BLINK>` and `</BLINK>` tags.
bold()	Returns the original string enclosed in `<B>` and `</B>` tags.
charAt (*index*)	Returns the single character at position *index* within the `String` object.
fixed()	Returns the original string enclosed in `<TT>` and `</TT>` tags.
fontcolor("*color*")	Returns the original string surrounded by `<FONT>` and `</FONT>` tags, with the `COLOR` attribute set to "*color*".
fontsize("*size*")	Returns the original string surrounded by `<FONT>` and `</FONT>` anchor tags, with the `SIZE` attribute set to "*size*".
indexOf (*searchValue* [, *fromIndex*])	Returns first occurrence of the string *searchValue* starting at index *fromIndex*.
italics()	Returns the original string enclosed in `<I>` and `</I>` tags.
lastIndexOf (*searchValue* [, *fromIndex*])	Returns the index of the last occurrence of the string *searchValue*, searching backwards from index *fromIndex*.
link("*hrefAttribute*")	Returns the original string surrounded by `<A>` and `</A>` link tags, with the `HREF` attribute set to "*hrefAttribute*".
small()	Returns the original string enclosed in `<SMALL>` and `</SMALL>` tags.
split (*separator*)	Returns an array of strings created by separating the `String` object at every occurrence of *separator*.
strike()	Returns the original string enclosed in `<STRIKE>` and `</STRIKE>` tags.
sub()	Returns the original string enclosed in `<SUB>` and `</SUB>` tags.
substring (*indexA, indexB*)	Returns the sub-string of the original `String` object from the character at *indexA* up to and including the one **before** the character at *indexB*.
sup()	Returns the original string enclosed in `<SUP>` and `</SUP>` tags.
toLowerCase()	Returns the original string with all the characters converted to lowercase.
toUpperCase()	Returns the original string with all the characters converted to uppercase.

Reserved Words

The following are reserved words that can't be used for function, method, variable, or object names. Note that while some words in this list are not currently used as JavaScript keywords, they have been reserved for future use.

abstract	else	int	super
boolean	extends	interface	switch
break	false	long	synchronized
byte	final	native	this
case	finally	new	throw
catch	float	null	throws
char	for	package	transient
class	function	private	true
const	goto	protected	try
continue	if	public	typeof
default	implements	reset	var
delete	import	return	void
do	in	short	while
double	instanceof	static	with

The VBScript Language

Array Handling

Dim—declares an array variable. This can be static with a defined number of elements or dynamic and can have up to 60 dimensions.

ReDim—used to change the size of an array variable which has been declared as dynamic.

Preserve—keyword used to preserve the contents of an array being resized. If you need to use this then you can only re–dimension the rightmost index of the array.

```
Dim strEmployees ()
ReDim strEmployees (9,1)

strEmployees (9,1) = "Phil"

ReDim strEmployees (9,2)            'loses the contents of element (9,1)
strEmployees (9,2) = "Paul"

ReDim Preserve strEmployees (9,3)   'preserves the contents of (9,2)
strEmployees (9,3) = "Smith"
```

LBound– returns the smallest subscript for the dimension of an array. Note that arrays always start from the subscript zero so this function will always return the value zero.

UBound—used to determine the size of an array.

```
Dim strCustomers (10, 5)
intSizeFirst = UBound (strCustomers, 1)     'returns SizeFirst = 10
intSizeSecond = UBound (strCustomers, 2)    'returns SizeSecond = 5
```

> The actual number of elements is always one greater than the value returned by **UBound** because the array starts from zero.

Assignments

Let—used to assign values to variables (optional).
Set—used to assign an object reference to a variable.

```
Let intNumberOfDays = 365

Set txtMyTextBox = txtcontrol
txtMyTextBox.Value = "Hello World"
```

Constants

Empty—an empty variable is one that has been created but not yet assigned a value.
Nothing—used to remove an object reference.

```
Set txtMyTextBox = txtATextBox        'assigns object reference
Set txtMyTextBox = Nothing            'removes object reference
```

Null—indicates that a variable is not valid. Note that this isn't the same as **Empty**.
True—indicates that an expression is true. Has numerical value −1.
False—indicates that an expression is false. Has numerical value 0.

Error constant:

Constant	Value
vbObjectError	&h80040000

System Color constants:

Constant	Value	Description
vbBlack	&h00	Black
vbRed	&hFF	Red
vbGreen	&hFF00	Green
vbYellow	&hFFFF	Yellow
vbBlue	&hFF0000	Blue
vbMagenta	&hFF00FF	Magenta
vbCyan	&hFFFF00	Cyan
vbWhite	&hFFFFFF	White

Comparison constants:

Constant	Value	Description
vbBinaryCompare	0	Perform a binary comparison.
vbTextCompare	1	Perform a textual comparison.
vbDatabaseCompare	2	Perform a comparison based upon information in the database where the comparison is to be performed.

Date and Time constants:

Constant	Value	Description
VbSunday	1	Sunday
vbMonday	2	Monday
vbTuesday	3	Tuesday
vbWednesday	4	Wednesday
vbThursday	5	Thursday
vbFriday	6	Friday
vbSaturday	7	Saturday
vbFirstJan1	1	Use the week in which January 1 occurs (default).
vbFirstFourDays	2	Use the first week that has at least four days in the new year.
vbFirstFullWeek	3	Use the first full week of the year.
vbUseSystem	0	Use the format in the regional settings for the computer.
vbUseSystemDayOfWeek	0	Use the day in the system settings for the first weekday.

Date Format constants:

Constant	Value	Description
vbGeneralDate	0	Display a date and/or time in the format set in the system settings. For real numbers display a date and time. For integer numbers display only a date. For numbers less than 1, display time only.
vbLongDate	1	Display a date using the long date format specified in the computers regional settings.
vbShortDate	2	Display a date using the short date format specified in the computers regional settings.

Table Continued on Following Page

Constant	Value	Description
vbLongTime	3	Display a time using the long time format specified in the computers regional settings.
vbShortTime	4	Display a time using the short time format specified in the computers regional settings.

File Input/Output constants:

Constant	Value	Description
ForReading	1	Open a file for reading only.
ForWriting	2	Open a file for writing. If a file with the same name exists, its previous one is overwritten.
ForAppending	8	Open a file and write at the end of the file.

String constants:

Constant	Value	Description
vbCr	Chr(13)	Carriage return only
vbCrLf	Chr(13) & Chr(10)	Carriage return and linefeed (Newline)
vbLf	Chr(10)	Line feed only
vbNewLine	–	Newline character as appropriate to a specific platform
vbNullChar	Chr(0)	Character having the value 0
vbNullString	–	String having the value zero (not just an empty string)
vbTab	Chr(9)	Horizontal tab

Tristate constants:

Constant	Value	Description
TristateTrue	−1	True
TristateFalse	0	False
TristateUseDefault	−2	Use default setting

VarType constants:

Constant	Value	Description
vbEmpty	0	Un–initialized (default)
vbNull	1	Contains no valid data
vbInteger	2	Integer subtype
vbLong	3	Long subtype
vbSingle	4	Single subtype
vbDouble	5	Double subtype
vbCurrency	6	Currency subtype
vbDate	7	Date subtype
vbString	8	String subtype
vbObject	9	Object
vbError	10	Error subtype
vbBoolean	11	Boolean subtype
vbVariant	12	Variant (used only for arrays of variants)
vbDataObject	13	Data access object
vbDecimal	14	Decimal subtype
vbByte	17	Byte subtype
vbArray	8192	Array

Control Flow

For...Next—executes a block of code a specified number of times.

```
Dim intSalary (10)
For intCounter = 0 to 10
   intSalary (intCounter) = 20000
Next
```

For Each...Next Statement—repeats a block of code for each element in an array or collection.

```
For Each Item In Request.QueryString("MyControl")
  Response.Write Item & "<BR>"
Next
```

Do...Loop—executes a block of code while a condition is true or until a condition becomes true.

```
Do While strDayOfWeek <> "Saturday" And strDayOfWeek <> "Sunday"
   MsgBox ("Get Up! Time for work")
   ...
Loop

Do
   MsgBox ("Get Up! Time for work")
   ...
Loop Until strDayOfWeek = "Saturday" Or strDayOfWeek = "Sunday"
```

If...Then...Else—used to run various blocks of code depending on conditions.

```
If intAge < 20 Then
   MsgBox ("You're just a slip of a thing!")
ElseIf intAge < 40 Then
   MsgBox ("You're in your prime!")
Else
   MsgBox ("You're older and wiser")
End If
```

Select Case—used to replace **If...Then...Else** statements where there are many conditions.

```
Select Case intAge
Case 21,22,23,24,25,26
   MsgBox ("You're in your prime")
Case 40
   MsgBox ("You're fulfilling your dreams")
Case 65
   MsgBox ("Time for a new challenge")
End Select
```

Note that **Select Case** can only be used with precise conditions and not with a range of conditions.

While...Wend—executes a block of code while a condition is true.

```
While strDayOfWeek <> "Saturday" AND strDayOfWeek <> "Sunday"
   MsgBox ("Get Up! Time for work")
   ...
Wend
```

Functions

VBScript contains several functions that can be used to manipulate and examine variables. These have been subdivided into the general categories of:

- ▲ Conversion Functions
- ▲ Date/Time Functions
- ▲ Math Functions

▲ Object Management Functions

▲ Script Engine Identification Functions

▲ String Functions

▲ Variable Testing Functions

For a full description of each function, and the parameters it requires, see the VBScript Help file. This is installed by default in your **Docs/ASPDocs/VBS/VBScript** subfolder of your IIS installation directory.

Conversion Functions

These functions are used to convert values in variables between different types:

Function	Description
Asc	Returns the numeric ANSI code number of the first character in a string.
AscB	As above, but provided for use with byte data contained in a string. Returns result from the first byte only.
AscW	As above, but provided for Unicode characters. Returns the **Wide** character code, avoiding the conversion from Unicode to ANSI.
Chr	Returns a string made up of the ANSI character matching the number supplied.
ChrB	As above, but provided for use with byte data contained in a string. Always returns a single byte.
ChrW	As above, but provided for Unicode characters. Its argument is a **Wide** character code, thereby avoiding the conversion from ANSI to Unicode.
CBool	Returns the argument value converted to a **Variant** of subtype **Boolean**.
CByte	Returns the argument value converted to a **Variant** of subtype **Byte**.
CDate	Returns the argument value converted to a **Variant** of subtype **Date**.
CDbl	Returns the argument value converted to a **Variant** of subtype **Double**.
CInt	Returns the argument value converted to a **Variant** of subtype **Integer**.
CLng	Returns the argument value converted to a **Variant** of subtype **Long**.
CSng	Returns the argument value converted to a **Variant** of subtype **Single**.
CStr	Returns the argument value converted to a **Variant** of subtype **String**.
Fix	Returns the integer (whole) part of a number.
Hex	Returns a string representing the hexadecimal value of a number.
Int	Returns the integer (whole) portion of a number.
Oct	Returns a string representing the octal value of a number.
Round	Returns a number rounded to a specified number of decimal places.
Sgn	Returns an integer indicating the sign of a number.

Date/Time Functions

These functions return date or time values from the computer's system clock, or manipulate existing values:

Function	Description
Date	Returns the current system date.
DateAdd	Returns a date to which a specified time interval has been added.
DateDiff	Returns the number of days, weeks, or years between two dates.
DatePart	Returns just the day, month or year of a given date.
DateSerial	Returns a **Variant** of subtype **Date** for a specified year, month, and day.
DateValue	Returns a **Variant** of subtype **Date**.
Day	Returns a number between **1** and **31** representing the day of the month.
Hour	Returns a number between **0** and **23** representing the hour of the day.
Minute	Returns a number between **0** and **59** representing the minute of the hour.
Month	Returns a number between **1** and **12** representing the month of the year.
MonthName	Returns the name of the specified month as a string.
Now	Returns the current date and time.
Second	Returns a number between **0** and **59** representing the second of the minute.
Time	Returns a **Variant** of subtype **Date** indicating the current system time.
TimeSerial	Returns a **Variant** of subtype **Date** for a specific hour, minute, and second.
TimeValue	Returns a **Variant** of subtype **Date** containing the time.
Weekday	Returns a number representing the day of the week.
WeekdayName	Returns the name of the specified day of the week as a string.
Year	Returns a number representing the year.

Math Functions

These functions perform mathematical operations on variables containing numerical values:

Function	Description
Atn	Returns the arctangent of a number.
Cos	Returns the cosine of an angle.
Exp	Returns **e** (the base of natural logarithms) raised to a power.
Log	Returns the natural logarithm of a number.

Function	Description
Randomize	Initializes the random–number generator.
Rnd	Returns a random number.
Sin	Returns the sine of an angle.
Sqr	Returns the square root of a number.
Tan	Returns the tangent of an angle.

Object Management Functions

These functions are used to manipulate objects, where applicable:

Function	Description
CreateObject	Creates and returns a reference to an ActiveX or OLE Automation object.
GetObject	Returns a reference to an ActiveX or OLE Automation object.
LoadPicture	Returns a picture object.

Script Engine Identification

These functions return the version of the scripting engine:

Function	Description
ScriptEngine	A string containing the major, minor, and build version numbers of the scripting engine.
ScriptEngineMajorVersion	The major version of the scripting engine, as a number.
ScriptEngineMinorVersion	The minor version of the scripting engine, as a number.
ScriptEngineBuildVersion	The build version of the scripting engine, as a number.

String Functions

These functions are used to manipulate string values in variables:

Function	Description
Filter	Returns an array from a string array, based on specified filter criteria.
FormatCurrency	Returns a string formatted as currency value.
FormatDateTime	Returns a string formatted as a date or time.

Table Continued on Following Page

721

Function	Description
FormatNumber	Returns a string formatted as a number.
FormatPercent	Returns a string formatted as a percentage.
InStr	Returns the position of the first occurrence of one string within another.
InStrB	As above, but provided for use with byte data contained in a string. Returns the byte position instead of the character position.
InstrRev	As InStr, but starts from the end of the string.
Join	Returns a string created by joining the strings contained in an array.
LCase	Returns a string that has been converted to lowercase.
Left	Returns a specified number of characters from the left end of a string.
LeftB	As above, but provided for use with byte data contained in a string. Uses that number of bytes instead of that number of characters.
Len	Returns the length of a string or the number of bytes needed for a variable.
LenB	As above, but is provided for use with byte data contained in a string. Returns the number of bytes in the string instead of characters.
LTrim	Returns a copy of a string without leading spaces.
Mid	Returns a specified number of characters from a string.
MidB	As above, but provided for use with byte data contained in a string. Uses that numbers of bytes instead of that number of characters.
Replace	Returns a string in which a specified substring has been replaced with another substring a specified number of times.
Right	Returns a specified number of characters from the right end of a string.
RightB	As above, but provided for use with byte data contained in a string. Uses that number of bytes instead of that number of characters.
RTrim	Returns a copy of a string without trailing spaces.
Space	Returns a string consisting of the specified number of spaces.
Split	Returns a one–dimensional array of a specified number of substrings.
StrComp	Returns a value indicating the result of a string comparison.
String	Returns a string of the length specified made up of a repeating character.
StrReverse	Returns a string in which the character order of a string is reversed.
Trim	Returns a copy of a string without leading or trailing spaces.
UCase	Returns a string that has been converted to uppercase.

Variable Testing Functions

These functions are used to determine the type of information stored in a variable:

Function	Description
IsArray	Returns a **Boolean** value indicating whether a variable is an array.
IsDate	Returns a **Boolean** value indicating whether an expression can be converted to a date.
IsEmpty	Returns a **Boolean** value indicating whether a variable has been initialized.
IsNull	Returns a **Boolean** value indicating whether an expression contains no valid data.
IsNumeric	Returns a **Boolean** value indicating whether an expression can be evaluated as a number.
IsObject	Returns a **Boolean** value indicating whether an expression references a valid ActiveX or OLE Automation object.
VarType	Returns a number indicating the subtype of a variable.

Variable Declarations

Dim—declares a variable.

Error Handling

On Error Resume Next—indicates that if an error occurs, control should continue at the next statement. **Err**—this is the error object that provides information about run–time errors.

Error handling is very limited in VBScript and the **Err** object must be tested explicitly to determine if an error has occurred.

Input/Output

This consists of **Msgbox** for output and **InputBox** for input:

MsgBox

This displays a message, and can return a value indicating which button was clicked.

```
MsgBox "Hello There",20,"Hello Message","c:\windows\MyHelp.hlp",123
```

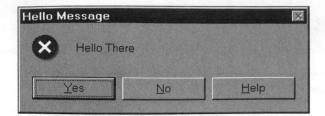

The parameters are:

`"Hello There"`–this contains the text of the message and is obligatory.

`20`– this determines which icon and buttons appear on the message box.

`"Hello Message"`–this contains the text that will appear as the title of the message box.

`"c:\windows\MyHelp.hlp"`–this adds a Help button to the message box and determines the help file that is opened if the button is clicked.

`123`–this is a reference to the particular help topic that will be displayed if the Help button is clicked.

The value of the icon and buttons parameter is determined using the following tables:

Constant	Value	Buttons
vbOKOnly	0	OK
vbOKCancel	1	OK Cancel
vbAbortRetryIngnore	2	Abort Retry Ignore
vbYesNoCancel	3	Yes No Cancel
vbYesNo	4	Yes No
vbRetryCancel	5	Retry Cancel
vbDefaultButton1	0	The first button from the left is the default.
vbDefaultButton2	256	The second button from the left is the default.
vbDefaultButton3	512	The third button from the left is the default.
vbDefaultButton4	768	The fourth button from the left is the default.

Constant	Value	Description	Icon
`vbCritical`	16	Critical Message	
`vbQuestion`	32	Questioning Message	
`vbExclamation`	48	Warning Message	
`vbInformation`	64	Informational Message	

Constant	Value	Description
`vbApplicationModal`	0	Just the application stops until user clicks a button.
`vbSystemModal`	4096	Whole system stops until user clicks a button.

To specify which buttons and icon are displayed you simply add the relevant values. So, in our example we add together **4 + 256 + 16 + 4096** to display the Yes and No buttons, with No as the default, with the **Critical** icon, and the user being unable to use any application, besides this one, when the message box is displayed.

You can determine which button the user clicked by assigning the return code of the **MsgBox** function to a variable:

```
intButtonClicked = MsgBox ("Hello There",35,"Hello Message")
```

Notice that brackets enclose the **MsgBox** parameters when used in this format. The following table determines the value assigned to the variable **intButtonClicked**:

Constant	Value	Button Clicked
`vbOK`	1	OK
`vbCancel`	2	Cancel
`vbAbort`	3	Abort
`vbRetry`	4	Retry
`vbIgnore`	5	Ignore
`vbYes`	6	Yes
`vbNo`	7	No

725

InputBox

This accepts text entry from the user and returns it as a string.

```
strTextEntered = InputBox ("Please enter your name","Login","John Smith",500,500)
```

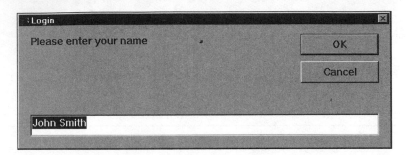

`"Please enter your name"`—this is the prompt displayed in the input box.
`"Login"`— this is the text displayed as the title of the input box.
`"John Smith"`— this is the default value displayed in the input box.
`500`—specifies the x position of the input box.
`500`—specifies the y position of the input box.

As with the `MsgBox` function, you can also specify a help file and topic to add a Help button to the input box.

Procedures

`Call`—optional method of calling a subroutine.
`Function`—used to declare a function.
`Sub`—used to declare a subroutine.

Other Keywords

`Rem`—old style method of adding comments to code.
`Option Explicit`—forces you to declare a variable before it can be used.

Visual Basic Run—time Error Codes

The following error codes also apply to VBA code and many will not be appropriate to an application built completely around VBScript. However, if you have built your own components then these error codes may well be brought up when such components are used.

Code	Description	Code	Description
3	Return without GoSub	71	Disk not ready
5	Invalid procedure call	74	Can't rename with different drive
6	Overflow	75	Path/File access error
7	Out of memory	76	Path not found
9	Subscript out of range	322	Can't create necessary temporary file
10	This array is fixed or temporarily locked	325	Invalid format in resource file
11	Division by zero	380	Invalid property value
13	Type mismatch	423	Property or method not found
14	Out of string space	424	Object required
16	Expression too complex	429	OLE Automation server can't create object
17	Can't perform requested operation	430	Class doesn't support OLE Automation
18	User interrupt occurred	432	File name or class name not found during OLE Automation operation
20	Resume without error		
28	Out of stack space	438	Object doesn't support this property or method
35	Sub or Function not defined		
47	Too many DLL application clients	440	OLE Automation error
48	Error in loading DLL	442	Connection to type library or object library for remote process has been lost. Press OK for dialog to remove reference.
49	Bad DLL calling convention		
51	Internal error		
52	Bad file name or number	443	OLE Automation object does not have a default value
53	File not found		
54	Bad file mode	445	Object doesn't support this action
55	File already open	446	Object doesn't support named arguments
57	Device I/O error		
58	File already exists	447	Object doesn't support current locale setting
59	Bad record length		
61	Disk full	448	Named argument not found
62	Input past end of file	449	Argument not optional
63	Bad record number	450	Wrong number of arguments or invalid property assignment
67	Too many files		
68	Device unavailable	451	Object not a collection
		452	Invalid ordinal
70	Permission denied	453	Specified DLL function not found

Table Continued on Following Page

Code	Description	Code	Description
454	Code resource not found	1025	Expected end of statement
455	Code resource lock error	1026	Expected integer constant
457	This key is already associated with an element of this collection	1027	Expected 'While' or 'Until'
		1028	Expected 'While', 'Until' or end of statement
458	Variable uses an OLE Automation type not supported in Visual Basic	1029	Too many locals or arguments
481	Invalid picture	1030	Identifier too long
500	Variable is undefined	1031	Invalid number
501	Cannot assign to variable	1032	Invalid character
1001	Out of memory	1033	Un–terminated string constant
1002	Syntax error	1034	Un–terminated comment
1003	Expected ':'	1035	Nested comment
1004	Expected ';'	1036	'Me' cannot be used outside of a procedure
1005	Expected '('		
1006	Expected ')'	1037	Invalid use of 'Me' keyword
1007	Expected ']'	1038	'loop' without 'do'
1008	Expected '{'	1039	Invalid 'exit' statement
1009	Expected '}'	1040	Invalid 'for' loop control variable
1010	Expected identifier	1041	Variable redefinition
1011	Expected '='	1042	Must be first statement on the line
1012	Expected 'If'	1043	Cannot assign to non–ByVal argument
1013	Expected 'To'		
1014	Expected 'End'		
1015	Expected 'Function'		
1016	Expected 'Sub'		
1017	Expected 'Then'		
1018	Expected 'Wend'		
1019	Expected 'Loop'		
1020	Expected 'Next'		
1021	Expected 'Case'		
1022	Expected 'Select'		
1023	Expected expression		
1024	Expected statement		

For more information about VBScript, visit Microsoft's VBScript site at:

```
http://www.microsoft.com/vbscript/us/techinfo/vbsdocs.htm
```

The Browser Object Model

The Dynamic HTML Object Model contains 12 **objects** and 15 **collections**. Most of these are organized into a strict hierarchy that allows HTML authors to access all the parts of the browser, and the pages that are loaded, from a scripting language like JavaScript or VBScript.

The Object Model In Outline

The diagram shows the object hierarchy in graphical form. It is followed by a list of the objects and collection, with a brief description. Then, each object is documented in detail, showing the properties, methods, and events it supports.

Note that not all the objects and collections are included in the diagram. Some are not part of the overall object model, but are used to access other items such as dialogs or HTML elements.

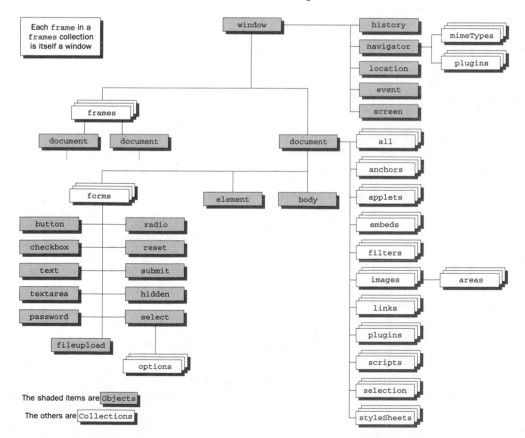

Object Name	Description
Document	An object that exposes the contents of the HTML document through a number of collections and properties.
Event	A global object that exposes properties that represent the parameters of all events as they occur.
History	Exposes information about the URLs that the client has previously visited.
Location	Exposes information about the currently displayed document's URL.
MimeType	An object that provides information about a MIME type.
Navigator	Exposes properties that provide information about the browser, or user agent.
Selection	Represents the currently active selection on the screen in the document.
Style	Represents an individual style element within a style sheet.
TextRange	Represents sections of the text stream making up the HTML document.
Screen	Exposes information about the client's monitor screen and system rendering abilities.
Window	Exposes properties, methods and events connected to the browser window or a frame.
StyleSheet	Exposes all the styles within a single style sheet in the styleSheets collection.

Collection Name	Description
all	Collection of all the tags and elements in the body of the document.
anchors	Collection of all the anchors in the document.
applets	Collection of all the objects in the document, including intrinsic controls, images, applets, embeds, and other objects.
areas	Collection of all the areas that make up the image map.
cells	Collection of all the <TH> and <TD> cells in the row of a table.
elements	Collection of all controls and elements in the form.
embeds	Collection of all the embed tags in the document.
forms	Collection of all the forms in the page.
frames	Collection of all the frames defined within a <FRAMESET> tag.
images	Collection of all the images in the page.
links	Collection of all the links and <AREA> blocks in the page.
options	Collection of all the items in a <SELECT> element.
plugins	An alias for collection of all the embeds in the page.
rows	Collection of all the rows in the table, including <THEAD>, <TBODY>, and <TFOOT>.
scripts	Collection of all the <SCRIPT> sections in the page.

Collection Name	Description
`filters`	Collection of all the filter objects for an element.
`imports`	Collection of all the imported style sheets defined for a stylesheet object.
`styleSheets`	Collection of all the individual style property objects defined for a document.
`mimeTypes`	Collection of all the document and file types supported by the browser.

The Objects in Detail

This section documents all the properties, methods and events available for each object in the browser hierarchy.

The Document Object

Exposes the entire HTML content through its own collections and properties, and provides a range of events and methods to work with documents.

Property Name	Attribute Name	CSS Name	Description
`activeElement`			Identifies the element that has the focus.
`alinkColor`	`ALINK`		The color for active links in the page i.e. while the mouse button is held down.
`bgColor`	`BGCOLOR`	`background-color`	Specifies the background color to be used for an element.
`body`			Read-only reference to the document's implicit body object, as defined by the `<BODY>` tag.
`cookie`			The string value of a cookie stored by the browser.
`domain`			Sets or returns the domain of the document for use in cookies and security.
`fgColor`	`TEXT`		Sets the color of the document foreground text.
`lastModified`			The date that the source file for the page was last modified, as a string, where available.
`linkColor`	`LINK`		The color for unvisited links in the page.

Table Continued on Following Page

Property Name	Attribute Name	CSS Name	Description
location			The full URL of the document.
parentWindow			Returns the parent window that contains the document.
readyState			Specifies the current state of an object being downloaded.
referrer			The URL of the page that referenced (loaded) the current page.
selection			Read-only reference to the document's selection object.
title	TITLE		Provides advisory information about the element, such as when loading or as a tooltip.
url	URL		Uniform Resource Locator (address) for the current document or in a `<META>` tag.
vlinkColor	VLINK		The color for visited links in the page.

Collections	Description
all	Collection of all the tags and elements in the body of the document.
anchors	Collection of all the anchors in the document.
applets	Collection of all the objects in the document, including intrinsic controls, images, applets, embeds, and other objects.
embeds	Collection of all the embed tags in the document.
forms	Collection of all the forms in the page.
frames	Collection of all the frames defined within a `<FRAMESET>` tag.
images	Collection of all the images in the page.
links	Collection of all the links and `<AREA>` blocks in the page.
plugins	An alias for collection of all the embeds in the page.
scripts	Collection of all the `<SCRIPT>` sections in the page.
styleSheets	Collection of all the individual style property objects defined for a document.

Method Name	Description
clear	Clears the contents of a selection or document object.
close	Closes a document forcing written data to be displayed, or closes the browser window.
createElement	Creates an instance of an image or option element object.
createStyleSheet	Creates a Style sheet
elementFromPoint	Returns the element at the specified x and y coordinates with respect to the window.
execCommand	Executes a command over the document selection or range.
open	Opens the document as a stream to collect output of **write** or **writeln** methods.
queryCommandEnabled	Denotes if the specified command is available for a document or TextRange.
queryCommandIndeterm	Denotes if the specified command is in the indeterminate state.
queryCommandState	Returns the current state of the command for a document or TextRange object.
queryCommandSupported	Denotes if the specified command is supported for a document or TextRange object.
queryCommandValue	Returns the value of the command specified for a document or TextRange object.
write	Writes text and HTML to a document in the specified window.
writeln	Writes text and HTML to a document in the specified window, followed by a carriage return.

Event Name	Description
onclick	Occurs when the user clicks the mouse button on an element, or when the value of a control is changed.
ondblclick	Occurs when the user double-clicks on an element.
ondragstart	Occurs when the user first starts to drag an element or selection.
onerror	Occurs when an error loading a document or image arises.
onhelp	Occurs when the user presses the *F1* or *Help* key.
onkeydown	Occurs when the user presses a key.

Table Continued on Following Page

Event Name	Description
onkeypress	Occurs when the user presses a key and a character is available.
onkeyup	Occurs when the user releases a key.
onload	Occurs when the element has completed loading.
onmousedown	Occurs when the user presses a mouse button.
onmousemove	Occurs when the user moves the mouse.
onmouseout	Occurs when the mouse pointer leaves the element.
onmouseover	Occurs when the mouse pointer first enters the element.
onmouseup	Occurs when the user releases a mouse button.
onreadystatechange	Occurs when the readyState for an object has changed.

The Event Object

The global object provided to allow the scripting language to access an event's parameters. It provides the following properties:

Property Name	Description
altKey	Returns the state of the *Alt* key when an event occurs.
button	The mouse button, if any, that was pressed to fire the event.
cancelBubble	Set to prevent the current event from bubbling up the hierarchy.
clientX	Returns the *x* coordinate of the element, excluding borders, margins, padding, scrollbars, etc.
clientY	Returns the *y* coordinate of the element, excluding borders, margins, padding, scrollbars, etc.
ctrlKey	Returns the state of the *Ctrl* key when an event occurs.
fromElement	Returns the element being moved from for an **onmouseover** or **onmouseout** event.
keyCode	ASCII code of the key being pressed. Changing it sends a different character to the object.
offsetX	Returns the *x* coordinate of the mouse pointer when an event occurs, relative to the containing element.
offsetY	Returns the *y* coordinate position of the mouse pointer when an event occurs, relative to the containing element.
reason	Indicates whether data transfer to an element was successful, or why it failed.
returnValue	Allows a return value to be specified for the event or a dialog window.
screenX	Returns the *x* coordinate of the mouse pointer when an event occurs, in relation to the screen.

Property Name	Description
screenY	Returns the *y* coordinate of the mouse pointer when an event occurs, in relation to the screen.
shiftKey	Returns the state of the *Shift* key when an event occurs.
srcElement	Returns the element deepest in the object hierarchy that a specified event occurred over.
srcFilter	Returns the filter that caused the element to produce an **onfilterchange** event.
toElement	Returns the element being moved to for an **onmouseover** or **onmouseout** event.
type	Returns the name of the event as a string, without the 'on' prefix, such as 'click' instead of 'onclick'.
x	Returns the *x* coordinate of the mouse pointer relative to a positioned parent, or otherwise to the window.
y	Returns the *y* coordinate of the mouse pointer relative to a positioned parent, or otherwise to the window.

The History Object

Contains information about the URLs that the client has visited, as stored in the browser's History list, and allows the script to move through the list.

Properties	Description
length	Returns the number of elements in a collection.

Methods	Description
back	Loads the previous URL in the browser's History list.
forward	Loads the next URL in the browser's History list.
go	Loads a specified URL from the browser's History list.

The Location Object

Contains information on the current URL. It also provides methods that will reload a page.

PropertyName	AttributeName	Description
hash		The string following the # symbol in the URL.
host		The hostname:port part of the location or URL.
hostname		The hostname part of the location or URL.
href	HREF	The entire URL as a string.

Table Continued on Following Page

737

PropertyName	AttributeName	Description
pathname		The file or object path name following the third slash in a URL.
port		The port number in a URL.
protocol		The initial substring up to and including the first colon, indicating the URL's access method.
search		The contents of the query string or form data following the ? (question mark) in the complete URL.

MethodName	Description
assign	Loads another page. Equivalent to changing the `window.location.href` property.
reload	Reloads the current page.
replace	Loads a document, replacing the current document's session history entry with its URL.

The MimeType Object

Provides information about the page's **MIME** data type.

Properties	Attribute	Description
description		Returns a description of the **MimeType**.
enabledPlugin		Returns the plug-in that can handle the specified **MimeType**.
name	NAME	Specifies the name of the element, control, bookmark, or applet.
suffixes		A list of filename suffixes suitable for use with the specified **MimeType**.

The Navigator Object

This object represents the browser application itself, providing information about its manufacturer, version, and capabilities.

Property Name	Description
appCodeName	The code name of the browser.
appName	The product name of the browser.
appVersion	The version of the browser.

Property Name	Description
`cookieEnabled`	Indicates if client-side cookies are enabled in the browser.
`userAgent`	The user-agent (browser name) header sent in the HTTP protocol from the client to the server.

Collection	Description
`mimeTypes`	Collection of all the document and file types supported by the browser.
`plugins`	An alias for collection of all the embeds in the page.

Method Name	Description
`javaEnabled`	Returns True or False, depending on whether a Java VM is installed and enabled.
`taintEnabled`	Returns False, included for compatibility with Netscape Navigator

The Screen Object

The **screen** object provides information to the scripting language about the client's screen resolution and rendering abilities.

Property Name	Description
`bufferDepth`	Specifies if and how an off-screen bitmap buffer should be used.
`colorDepth`	Returns the number of bits per pixel of the user's display device or screen buffer.
`height`	Returns the height of the user's display screen in pixels.
`updateInterval`	Sets or returns the interval between screen updates on the client.
`width`	Returns the width of the user's display screen in pixels.

The Selection Object

Returns the active selection on the screen, allowing access to all the selected elements including the plain text in the page.

Properties	Attribute	Description
`type`	`TYPE`	The type of the selection, i.e. a control, text, a table, or none.

Methods	Description
clear	Clears the contents of the selection.
createRange	Returns a copy of the currently selected range.
empty	Deselects the current selection and sets selection type to none.

The Style Object

This provides access to the individual style properties for an element. These could have been previously set by a style sheet, or by an inline style tag within the page.

Property Name	Attribute Name	CSS Name	Description
background	BACKGROUND	background	Specifies a background picture that is tiled behind text and graphics.
backgroundAttachment		background-attachment	Defines if a background image should be fixed on the page or scroll with the content.
backgroundColor		background-color	Specifies the background color of the page or element.
backgroundImage		background-image	Specifies a URL for the background image for the page or element.
backgroundPosition		background-position	The initial position of a background image on the page.
backgroundPositionX			The x coordinate of the background image in relation to the containing window.
backgroundPositionY			The y coordinate of the background image in relation to the containing window.
BackgroundRepeat		background-repeat	Defines if and how a background image is repeated on the page.
border	BORDER	border	Specifies the border to be drawn around the element.
borderBottom		border-bottom	Used to specify several attributes of the bottom border of an element.
borderBottomColor			The color of the bottom border for an element.
borderBottomStyle			The style of the bottom border for an element.
borderBottomWidth		border-bottom-width	The width of the bottom border for an element.

Property Name	Attribute Name	CSS Name	Description
borderColor	BORDERCOLOR	border-color	The color of all or some of the borders for an element.
borderLeft		border-left	Used to specify several attributes of the left border of an element.
borderLeftColor			The color of the left border for an element.
borderLeftStyle			The style of the left border for an element.
borderLeftWidth		border-left-width	The width of the left border for an element.
borderRight		border-right	Used to specify several attributes of the right border of an element.
BorderRightColor			The color of the right border for an element.
BorderRightStyle			The style of the right border for an element.
BorderRightWidth		border-right-width	The width of the right border for an element.
borderStyle		border-style	Used to specify the style of one or more borders of an element.
borderTop		border-top	Used to specify several attributes of the top border of an element.
borderTopColor			The color of the top border for an element.
borderTopStyle			The style of the top border for an element.
borderTopWidth		border-top-width	The width of the top border for an element.
borderWidth		border-width	Used to specify the width of one or more borders of an element.
clear	CLEAR	clear	Causes the next element or text to be displayed below left-aligned or right-aligned images.
clip		clip	Specifies how an element's contents should be displayed if larger that the available client area.
color	COLOR	color	The text or foreground color of an element.
cssText			The text value of the element's entire **STYLE** attribute.

Table Continued on Following Page

Property Name	Attribute Name	CSS Name	Description
cursor		cursor	Specifies the type of cursor to display when the mouse pointer is over the element.
display		display	Specifies if the element will be visible (displayed) in the page.
filter		filter	Sets or returns an array of all the filters specified in the element's style property.
font		font, @font-face	Defines various attributes of the font for an element, or imports a font.
fontFamily		font-family	Specifies the name of the typeface, or 'font family'.
fontSize		font-size	Specifies the font size.
fontStyle		font-style	Specifies the style of the font, i.e. normal or italic.
fontVariant		font-variant	Specifies the use of small capitals for the text.
fontWeight		font-weight	Specifies the weight (boldness) of the text.
height	HEIGHT	height	Specifies the height at which the element is to be drawn, and sets the **posHeight** property.
left		left	Specifies the position of the left of the element, and sets the **posLeft** property.
letterSpacing		letter-spacing	Indicates the additional space to be placed between characters in the text.
lineHeight		line-height	The distance between the baselines of two adjacent lines of text.
listStyle		list-style	Allows several style properties of a list element to be set in one operation.
listStyleImage		list-style-image	Defines the image used as a background for a list element.
listStylePosition		list-style-position	Defines the position of the bullets used in a list element.
listStyleType		list-style-type	Defines the design of the bullets used in a list element.

Property Name	Attribute Name	CSS Name	Description
margin		margin	Allows all four margins to be specified with a single attribute.
marginBottom		margin-bottom	Specifies the bottom margin for the page or text block.
marginLeft		margin-left	Specifies the left margin for the page or text block.
marginRight		margin-right	Specifies the right margin for the page or text block.
marginTop		margin-top	Specifies the top margin for the page or text block.
overflow		overflow	Defines how text that overflows the element is handled.
paddingBottom		padding-bottom	Sets the amount of space between the bottom border and content of an element.
paddingLeft		padding-left	Sets the amount of space between the left border and content of an element.
paddingRight		padding-right	Sets the amount of space between the right border and content of an element.
paddingTop		padding-top	Sets the amount of space between the top border and content of an element.
pageBreakAfter		page-break-after	Specifies if a page break should occur after the element.
pageBreakBefore		page-break-before	Specifies if a page break should occur after the element.
pixelHeight			Sets or returns the height style property of the element in pixels, as a pure number, rather than a string.
pixelLeft			Sets or returns the left style property of the element in pixels, as a pure number, rather than a string.
pixelTop			Sets or returns the top style property of the element in pixels, as a pure number, rather than a string.

Table Continued on Following Page

Property Name	Attribute Name	CSS Name	Description
pixelWidth			Sets or returns the width style property of the element in pixels, as a pure number, rather than a string.
posHeight			Returns the value of the height style property in its last specified units, as a pure number rather than a string.
position		position	Returns the value of the position style property, defining whether the element can be positioned.
posLeft			Returns the value of the left style property in its last specified units, as a pure number rather than a string.
posTop			Returns the value of the top style property in its last specified units, as a pure number rather than a string.
posWidth			Returns the value of the width style property in its last specified units, as a pure number rather than a string.
styleFloat		float	Specifies if the element will float above the other elements in the page, or cause them to flow round it.
textAlign		text-align	Indicates how text should be aligned within the element.
textDecoration		text-decoration	Specifies several font decorations (underline, overline, strikethrough) added to the text of an element.
textDecorationBlink			Specifies if the font should blink or flash. Has no effect in IE4.
textDecorationLineThrough			Specifies if the text is displayed as strikethrough, i.e. with a horizontal line through it.
textDecorationNone			Specifies if the text is displayed with no additional decoration.
textDecorationOverline			Denotes if the text is displayed as overline, i.e. with a horizontal line above it.

Property Name	Attribute Name	CSS Name	Description
textDecorationUnderline			Denotes if the text is displayed as underline, i.e. with a horizontal line below it.
textIndent		text-indent	Specifies the indent for the first line of text in an element, and may be negative.
textTransform		text-transform	Specifies how the text for the element should be capitalized.
top		top	Position of the top of the element, sets the **posTop** property. Also returns topmost window object.
verticalAlign		vertical-align	Sets or returns the vertical alignment style property for an element.
visibility		visibility	Indicates if the element or contents are visible on the page.
width	WIDTH	width	Specifies the width at which the element is to be drawn, and sets the **posWidth** property.
zIndex		z-index	Sets or returns the z-index for the element, indicating whether it appears above or below other elements.

MethodName	Description
getAttribute	Returns the value of an attribute defined in an HTML tag.
removeAttribute	Causes the specified attribute to be removed from the HTML element and the current page.
setAttribute	Adds and/or sets the value of an attribute in a HTML tag.

The StyleSheet Object

This object exposes all the styles within a single style sheet in the styleSheets collection

Property Name	Attribute Name	Description
disabled	DISABLED	Sets or returns whether an element is disabled.
href	HREF	The entire URL as a string.
id	ID	Identifier or name for an element in a page or style sheet, or as the target for hypertext links.

Table Continued on Following Page

Property Name	Attribute Name	Description
owningElement		Returns the style sheet that imported or referenced the current style sheet, usually through a `<LINK>` tag.
parentStyleSheet		Returns the style sheet that imported the current style sheet, or null for a non-imported style sheet.
readOnly	READONLY	Indicates that an element's contents are read only, or that a rule in a style sheet cannot be changed.
type	TYPE	Specifies the type of list style, link, selection, control, button, MIME-type, rel, or the CSS language.

Methods	Description
addImport	Adds a style sheet to the Imports collection for the given style sheet.
addRule	Loads the next URL in the browser's History list.

Collection	Description
imports	Collection of all the imported style sheets defined for a stylesheet object.

The TextRange Object

This object represents the text stream of the HTML document. It can be used to set and retrieve the text within the page.

Property Name	Description
htmlText	Returns the contents of a TextRange as text and HTML source.
text	The plain text contained within a block element, a TextRange or an `<OPTION>` tag.

Method Name	Description
collapse	Shrinks a TextRange to either the start or end of the current range.
compareEndPoints	Compares two text ranges and returns a value indicating the result.
duplicate	Returns a duplicate of a TextRange object.
execCommand	Executes a command over the document selection or range.
expand	Expands the range by a character, word, sentence or story so that partial units are completely contained.
findText	Sets the range start and end points to cover the text if found within the current document.

Method Name	Description
getBookmark	Sets String to a unique bookmark value to identify that position in the document.
inRange	Denotes if the specified range is within or equal to the current range.
isEqual	Denotes if the specified range is equal to the current range.
move	Changes the start and end points of a TextRange to cover different text.
moveEnd	Causes the range to grow or shrink from the end of the range.
moveStart	Causes the range to grow or shrink from the beginning of the range.
moveToBookmark	Moves range to encompass the range with a bookmark value previously defined in String.
moveToElementText	Moves range to encompass the text in the element specified.
moveToPoint	Moves and collapses range to the point specified in *x* and *y* relative to the document.
parentElement	Returns the parent element that completely encloses the current range.
pasteHTML	Pastes HTML and/or plain text into the current range.
queryCommandEnabled	Denotes if the specified command is available for a document or TextRange.
queryCommandIndeterm	Denotes if the specified command is in the indeterminate state.
queryCommandState	Returns the current state of the command for a document or TextRange object.
queryCommandSupported	Denotes if the specified command is supported for a document or TextRange object.
queryCommandValue	Returns the value of the command specified for a document or TextRange object.
scrollIntoView	Scrolls the element or TextRange into view in the browser, optionally at the top of the window.
select	Makes the active selection equal to the current object, or highlights the input area of a form element.
setEndPoint	Sets the end point of the range based on the end point of another range.

The Window Object

The **window** object refers to the current window. This can be a top-level window, or a window that is within a frame created by a **<FRAMESET>** in another document.

Property Name	AttributeName	CSS Name	Description
clientInformation			A reference that returns the navigator object for the browser.
closed			Indicates if a window is closed.
defaultStatus			The default message displayed in the status bar at the bottom of the window.
dialogArguments			Returns the arguments that were passed into a dialog window, as an array.
dialogHeight			Sets or returns the height of a dialog window.
dialogLeft			Sets or returns the x coordinate of a dialog window.
dialogTop			Sets or returns the y coordinate of a dialog window.
dialogWidth			Sets or returns the width of a dialog window.
document			Read-only reference to the window's document object.
event	EVENT		Read-only reference to the global event object.
history			Read-only reference to the window's history object.
length			Returns the number of elements in a collection.
location			Holds information on the current URL.
name	NAME		Specifies the name of the window, frame, element, control, bookmark, or applet.
navigator			Read-only reference to the window's navigator object.
offScreenBuffering			Specifies whether to use off-screen buffering for the document.
opener			Returns a reference to the window that created the current window.
parent			Returns the parent window or frame in the window/frame hierarchy.
returnValue			Allows a return value to be specified for the event or a dialog window.
screen			Read-only reference to the global screen object.

Property Name	AttributeName	CSS Name	Description
`self`			Provides a reference to the current window.
`status`			Text displayed in the window's status bar, or an alias for the value of an option button.
`top`		`top`	Position of the top of the element, sets the `posTop` property. Also returns topmost window object.

MethodName	Description
`alert`	Displays an Alert dialog box with a message and an OK button.
`blur`	Causes a control to lose focus and fire its `onblur` event.
`clearInterval`	Cancels an interval timer that was set with the `setInterval` method.
`clearTimeout`	Cancels a timeout that was set with the `setTimeout` method.
`close`	Closes a document forcing written data to be displayed, or closes the browser window.
`confirm`	Displays a Confirm dialog box with a message and OK and Cancel buttons.
`execScript`	Executes a script. The default language is JScript.
`focus`	Causes a control to receive the focus and fires its `onfocus` event.
`navigate`	Loads another page (VBScript only). Equivalent to changing the `window.location.href` property.
`open`	Opens the document as a stream to collect output of `write` or `writeln` methods.
`prompt`	Displays a Prompt dialog box with a message and an input field.
`scroll`	Scrolls the window to the specified x and y offset relative to the entire document.
`setInterval`	Denotes a code routine to execute repeatedly every specified number of milliseconds.
`setTimeout`	Denotes a code routine to execute a specified number of milliseconds after loading the page.
`showHelp`	Opens a window to display a Help file.
`showModalDialog`	Displays a HTML dialog window, and returns the `returnValue` property of its document when closed.

EventName	Description
onbeforeunload	Occurs just before the page is unloaded, allowing the unload event to be cancelled.
onblur	Occurs when the control loses the input focus.
onerror	Occurs when an error loading a document or image arises.
onfocus	Occurs when a control receives the input focus.
onhelp	Occurs when the user presses the *F1* or *Help* key.
onload	Occurs when the element has completed loading.
onresize	Occurs when the element or object is resized by the user.
onscroll	Occurs when the user scrolls a page or element.
onunload	Occurs immediately before the page is unloaded.

Collections	Description
frames	Collection of all the frames defined within a **<FRAMESET>** tag.

HTML and Form Controls Cross Reference

Dynamic HTML provides the same integral control types as HTML 3.2. However, there are many more different properties, methods and events available now for all the controls.

The following tables show those that are most relevant to controls.

Control Properties	checked	dataFld	dataFormatAs	dataSrc	defaultChecked	defaultValue	maxLength	readOnly	recordNumber	selectedIndex	size	status	type	value
HTML button	✗	✓	✓	✓	✗	✗	✗	✓	✓	✗	✗	✗	✓	✓
HTML checkbox	✓	✓	✗	✓	✓	✗	✗	✓	✓	✗	✓	✓	✓	✓
HTML file	✗	✗	✗	✗	✗	✓	✗	✓	✓	✗	✗	✗	✓	✓
HTML hidden	✗	✓	✗	✓	✗	✗	✗	✗	✗	✗	✗	✗	✓	✓
HTML image	✗	✗	✗	✗	✗	✗	✗	✗	✓	✗	✗	✗	✓	✗
HTML password	✗	✓	✗	✓	✗	✓	✓	✓	✗	✗	✓	✗	✓	✓
HTML radio	✓	✓	✗	✓	✓	✗	✗	✓	✓	✗	✓	✗	✓	✓
HTML reset	✗	✗	✗	✗	✗	✗	✗	✗	✓	✗	✗	✗	✓	✓
HTML submit	✗	✗	✗	✗	✗	✗	✗	✗	✓	✗	✗	✗	✓	✓
HTML text	✗	✓	✗	✓	✗	✓	✓	✓	✓	✗	✓	✗	✓	✓
BUTTON tag	✗	✓	✓	✓	✗	✗	✗	✗	✗	✗	✗	✓	✓	✓
FIELDSET tag	✗	✗	✗	✗	✗	✗	✗	✗	✓	✗	✗	✗	✗	✗
LABEL tag	✗	✗	✗	✗	✗	✗	✗	✗	✗	✗	✗	✗	✗	✗
LEGEND tag	✗	✗	✗	✗	✗	✗	✗	✗	✓	✗	✗	✗	✗	✗
SELECT tag	✗	✓	✗	✓	✗	✗	✗	✗	✓	✓	✗	✗	✓	✓
TEXTAREA tag	✗	✓	✗	✓	✗	✗	✗	✓	✗	✗	✗	✓	✓	✓

Control Methods	add	blur	click	createTextRange	focus	item	remove	select
HTML button	✗	✓	✓	✗	✓	✗	✗	✓
HTML checkbox	✗	✓	✓	✗	✓	✗	✗	✓
HTML file	✗	✓	✓	✗	✓	✗	✗	✓
HTML hidden	✗	✗	✗	✗	✗	✗	✗	✗
HTML image	✗	✓	✓	✗	✓	✗	✗	✓
HTML password	✗	✓	✓	✗	✓	✗	✗	✓
HTML radio	✗	✓	✓	✗	✓	✗	✗	✓
HTML reset	✗	✓	✓	✗	✓	✗	✗	✓
HTML submit	✗	✓	✓	✗	✓	✗	✗	✓
HTML text	✗	✓	✓	✓	✓	✗	✗	✓
BUTTON tag	✗	✓	✓	✓	✓	✗	✗	✗
FIELDSET tag	✗	✓	✓	✗	✓	✗	✗	✗
LABEL tag	✗	✗	✓	✗	✗	✗	✗	✗
LEGEND tag	✗	✓	✓	✗	✓	✗	✗	✗
SELECT tag	✓	✓	✓	✗	✓	✓	✓	✗
TEXTAREA tag	✗	✓	✓	✓	✓	✗	✗	✓

Control Events	onafterupdate	onbeforeupdate	onblur	onchange	onclick	ondblclick	onfocus	onrowenter	onrowexit	onselect
HTML button	✘	✘	✔	✘	✔	✔	✔	✘	✘	✔
HTML checkbox	✔	✔	✔	✔	✔	✔	✔	✘	✘	✔
HTML file	✘	✘	✔	✔	✔	✔	✔	✘	✘	✔
HTML hidden	✘	✘	✘	✘	✘	✘	✘	✘	✘	✘
HTML image	✘	✘	✔	✔	✘	✔	✔	✘	✘	✔
HTML password	✘	✘	✔	✔	✔	✔	✔	✘	✘	✔
HTML radio	✔	✔	✔	✔	✔	✔	✔	✘	✘	✔
HTML reset	✘	✘	✔	✘	✔	✔	✔	✘	✘	✔
HTML submit	✘	✘	✔	✘	✔	✔	✔	✘	✘	✔
HTML text	✔	✔	✔	✔	✔	✔	✔	✘	✘	✔
BUTTON tag	✔	✔	✔	✘	✔	✔	✔	✔	✔	✘
FIELDSET tag	✔	✔	✔	✘	✔	✔	✔	✔	✔	✘
LABEL tag	✘	✘	✘	✘	✔	✔	✘	✘	✘	✘
LEGEND tag	✔	✔	✔	✘	✔	✔	✔	✔	✔	✘
SELECT tag	✔	✔	✔	✔	✔	✔	✔	✔	✔	✘
TEXTAREA tag	✔	✔	✔	✔	✔	✔	✔	✔	✔	✔

Style Sheet Properties

APPENDIX E

There are over 70 properties defined for the implementation of CSS in Dynamic HTML, and they are broken up into several major 'groups'. We've listed all of the properties below (by group), with some of the crucial information for each. We start with a summary of the units of measurement which can be used in the properties.

Units of Measurement

There are two basic categories of unit: relative and absolute (plus percentages). As a general rule, relative measures are preferred, as using absolute measures requires familiarity with the actual mechanism of display (e.g. what kind of printer, what sort of monitor, etc.).

Relative Units

Values: em, en, ex, px

em, en and ex are typographic terms, and refer to the sizes of other characters on display.
px refers to a measurement in screen pixels, which is generally only meaningful for display on computer monitors and depends on the user's display resolution setting.
In IE4, em and ex are the same as pt, and en is the same as px.

Absolute Units

Values: in, cm, mm, pt, pc

in gives the measurement in inches, cm gives it in centimetres, mm in millimetres, pt is in typeface points (72 to an inch), and pc is in picas (1 pica equals 12 points). These units are generally only useful when you know what the output medium is going to be, since browsers are allowed to approximate if they must.

Percentage

Values: Numeric

This is given as a number (with or without a decimal point), and is relative to a length unit (which is usually the font size of the current element). You should note that child elements will inherit the computed value, not the percentage value (so a child will not be 20% of the parent, it will be the same size as the parent).

Listing of Properties

There follows a listing of all the properties for use in Dynamic HTML, together with their equivalent scripting property in IE4, possible values, defaults, and other useful information. The properties are divided up into categories–**font** properties, **color** and **background** properties, **text** properties, **size** and **border** properties, **printing** properties, **filter** properties and **other** properties.

Font Properties

font

Scripting Property:	`font`
Values:	`<font-size>, [/<line-height>], <font-family>`
Default:	Not defined
Applies to:	All elements
Inherited:	Yes
Percentage?:	Only on `<font-size>` and `<line-height>`

This allows you to set several font properties all at once, with the initial values being determined by the properties being used (e.g. the default for `font-size` is different to the default for `font-family`). This property should be used with multiple values separated by spaces, or a comma if specifying multiple font-families.

font-family

Scripting Property:	`fontFamily`
Values:	Name of a font family (e.g. New York) or a generic family (e.g. Serif)
Default:	Set by browser
Applies to:	All elements
Inherited:	Yes
Percentage?:	No

You can specify multiple values in order of preference (in case the browser doesn't have the font you want). To do so, simply specify them and separate multiple values with commas. You should end with a generic font-family (allowable values would then be `serif`, `sans-serif`, `cursive`, `fantasy`, or `monospace`). If the font name has spaces in it, you should enclose the name in quotation marks.

font-size

Scripting Property:	`fontSize`
Values:	`<absolute>, <relative>, <length>, <percentage>`
Default:	`medium`
Applies to:	All elements
Inherited:	Yes
Percentage?:	Yes, relative to parent font size

The values for this property can be expressed in several ways:

- Absolute size: legal values are `xx-small`, `x-small`, `small`, `medium`, `large`, `x-large`, `xx-large`
- Relative size: values are `larger`, `smaller`
- Length: values are in any unit of measurement, as described at the beginning of this Section.
- Percentage: values are a percentage of the parent font size

font-style

Scripting Property:	`fontStyle`
Values:	`normal`, `italic`, or `oblique`
Default:	`normal`
Applies to:	All elements
Inherited:	Yes
Percentage?:	No

This is used to apply styling to your font–if a pre-rendered font is available (e.g. New York Oblique) then that will be used if possible. If not, the styling will be applied electronically.

font-variant

Scripting Property:	`fontVariant`
Values:	`normal`, `small-caps`
Default:	`normal`
Applies to:	All elements
Inherited:	Yes
Percentage?:	No

`Normal` is the standard appearance, and is therefore set as the default. `Small-caps` uses capital letters that are the same size as normal lowercase letters.

font-weight

Scripting Property:	`fontWeight`
Values:	`normal`, `bold`, `bolder`, `lighter`–or numeric values from 100 to 900
Default:	`normal`
Applies to:	All elements
Inherited:	Yes
Percentage?:	No

Specifies the 'boldness' of text, which is usually expressed by stroke thickness. If numeric values are used, they must proceed in 100-unit increments (e.g. 250 isn't legal). `400` is the same as `normal`, and `700` is the same as `bold`.

Color and Background Properties

color

Scripting Property:	`color`
Values:	Color name or RGB value
Default:	Depends on browser
Applies to:	All elements
Inherited:	Yes
Percentage?:	No

Sets the text color of any element. The color can be specified by name (e.g. green) or by RGB-value. The RGB value can be expressed in several ways; in hex–"#FFFFFF"–, by percentage–"80%, 20%, 0%"–, or by value–"255,0,0".

background

Scripting Property:	`background`
Values:	`transparent, <color>, <URL>, <repeat>, <scroll>, <position>`
Default:	`transparent`
Applies to:	All elements
Inherited:	No
Percentage?:	Yes, will refer to the dimension of the element itself

Specifies the background of the document. `Transparent` is the same as no defined background. You can use a solid color, or you can specify the URL for an image to be used. The URL can be absolute or relative, but must be enclosed in parentheses and immediately preceded by `url`:

```
BODY { background: url(http://foo.bar.com/image/small.gif) }
```

It is possible to use a color and an image, in which case the image will be overlaid on top of the color. The color can be a single color, or two colors that will be blended together. Images can have several properties set:

- ▲ `<repeat>` can be `repeat`, `repeat-x` (where `x` is a number), `repeat-y` (where `y` is a number) and `no-repeat`. If no repeat value is given, then `repeat` is assumed.

- ▲ `<scroll>` determines whether the background image will remain fixed, or scroll when the page does. Possible values are `fixed` or `scroll`.

- ▲ `<position>` specifies the location of the image on the page. Values are by percentage (horizontal, vertical), by absolute distance (in a unit of measurement, horizontal then vertical), or by keyword (values are `top`, `middle`, `bottom`, `left`, `center`, `right`)

It is also possible to specify different parts of the background properties separately using these next five properties:

background-attachment

Scripting Property:	`backgroundAttachment`
Values:	`fixed, scroll`
Default:	`scroll`
Applies to:	All elements
Inherited:	No
Percentage?:	No

Determines whether the background will remain fixed, or scroll when the page does.

background-color

Scripting Property:	`backgroundColor`
Values:	`transparent, <color>`
Default:	`transparent`
Applies to:	All elements
Inherited:	No
Percentage?:	No

Sets a color for the background. This can be a single color, or two colors blended together. The colors can be specified by name (e.g. green) or by RGB-value (which can be stated in hex "#FFFFFF", by percentage "80%, 20%, 0%", or by value "255,0,0"). The syntax for using two colors is:

```
BODY { background-color: red / blue }
```

background-image

Scripting Property:	`backgroundImage`
Values:	`<URL>, none`
Default:	`none`
Applies to:	All elements
Inherited:	No
Percentage?:	No

You can specify the URL for an image to be used as the background. The **URL** can be absolute or relative, but must be enclosed in parentheses and immediately preceded by `url`:

background-position

Scripting Properties:	`backgroundPosition, backgroundPositionX, backgroundPositionY`
Values:	`<position> <length> top, center, bottom, left, right`
Default:	`top, left`
Applies to:	All elements
Inherited:	No
Percentage?:	No

Specifies the initial location of the background image on the page using two values, which are defined as a percentage (horizontal, vertical), an absolute distance (in a unit of measurement, horizontal then vertical), or using two of the available keywords.

background-repeat

Scripting Property:	`backgroundRepeat`
Values:	`repeat, repeat-x, repeat-y, no-repeat`
Default:	`repeat`
Applies to:	All elements
Inherited:	No
Percentage?:	No

Determines whether the image is repeated to fill the page or element. If **repeat-x** or **repeat-y** are used, the image is repeated in only one direction. The default is to repeat the image in both directions.

Text Properties

letter-spacing

Scripting Property:	`letterSpacing`
Values:	`normal, <length>`
Default:	`normal`
Applies to:	All elements
Inherited:	Yes
Percentage?:	No

Sets the distance between letters. The length unit indicates an addition to the default space between characters. Values, if given, should be in units of measurement.

line-height

Scripting Property:	`lineHeight`
Values:	`<number>, <length>, <percentage> normal`
Default:	Depends on browser
Applies to:	All elements
Inherited:	Yes
Percentage?:	Yes, relative to the font-size of the current element

Sets the height of the current line. Numerical values are expressed as the font size of the current element multiplied by the value given (for example, 1.2 would be valid). If given by length, a unit of measurement must be used. Percentages are based on the font-size of the current font, and should normally be more than 100%.

list-style

Scripting Property:	`listStyle`
Values:	`<keyword>, <position>, <url>`
Default:	Depends on browser
Applies to:	All elements
Inherited:	Yes
Percentage?:	No

Defines how list items are displayed. Can be used to set all the properties, or the individual styles can be set independently using the following styles.

list-style-image

Scripting Property:	`listStyleImage`
Values:	`none, <url>`
Default:	`none`
Applies to:	All elements
Inherited:	Yes
Percentage?:	No

Defines the URL of an image to be used as the 'bullet' or list marker for each item in a list.

list-style-position

Scripting Property:	`listStylePosition`
Values:	`inside, outside`
Default:	`outside`
Applies to:	All elements
Inherited:	Yes
Percentage?:	No

Indicates if the list marker should be placed indented or extended in relation to the list body.

list-style-type

Scripting Property:	`listStyleType`
Values:	`none, circle, disk, square, decimal, lower-alpha, upper alpha, lower-roman, upper-roman`
Default:	`disk`
Applies to:	All elements
Inherited:	Yes
Percentage?:	No

Defines the type of 'bullet' or list marker used to precede each item in the list.

text-align

Scripting Property:	`textAlign`
Values:	`left, right, center, justify`
Default:	Depends on browser
Applies to:	All elements
Inherited:	Yes
Percentage?:	No

Describes how text is aligned within the element. Essentially replicates the `<DIV ALIGN=>` tag.

text-decoration

Scripting Properties:	`textDecoration, textDecorationLineThrough, textDecorationUnderline, textDecorationOverline`
Values:	`none, underline, overline, line-through`
Default:	`none`
Applies to:	All elements
Inherited:	No
Percentage?:	No

Specifies any special appearance of the text. Open to extension by vendors, with unidentified extensions rendered as an underline. This property is not inherited, but will usually span across any 'child' elements.

text-indent

Scripting Property:	`textIndent`
Values:	`<length>, <percentage>`
Default:	Zero
Applies to:	All elements
Inherited:	Yes
Percentage?:	Yes, refers to width of parent element

Sets the indentation values, in units of measurement, or as a percentage of the parent element's width.

text-transform

Scripting Property:	`textTransform`
Values:	`capitalize, uppercase, lowercase, none`
Default:	`none`
Applies to:	All elements
Inherited:	Yes
Percentage?:	No

▲ `capitalize` will set the first character of each word in the element as uppercase.

▲ `uppercase` will set every character in the element in uppercase.

▲ `lowercase` will place every character in lowercase.

▲ `none` will neutralize any inherited settings.

vertical-align

Scripting Property:	`verticalAlign`
Values:	`baseline, sub, super, top, text-top, middle, bottom, text-bottom,` `<percentage>`
Default:	`baseline`
Applies to:	Inline elements
Inherited:	No
Percentage?:	Yes, will refer to the line-height itself

Controls the vertical positioning of any affected element.

▲ `baseline` sets the alignment with the base of the parent.

▲ `middle` aligns the vertical midpoint of the element with the baseline of the parent plus half of the vertical height of the parent.

▲ `sub` makes the element a subscript.

▲ `super` makes the element a superscript.

▲ `text-top` aligns the element with the top of text in the parent element's font.

▲ `text-bottom` aligns with the bottom of text in the parent element's font.

▲ `top` aligns the top of the element with the top of the tallest element on the current line.

▲ `bottom` aligns with the bottom of the lowest element on the current line.

Size and Border Properties

These values are used to set the characteristics of the layout 'box' that exists around elements. They can apply to characters, images, and so on.

border-top-color, border-right-color, border-bottom-color, border-left-color, border-color

Scripting Properties:	`borderTopColor`, `borderRightColor`, `borderBottomColor`, `borderLeftColor`, `borderColor`
Values:	`<color>`
Default:	`<none>`
Applies to:	Block and replaced elements
Inherited:	No
Percentage?:	No

Sets the color of the four borders. By supplying the URL of an image instead, the image itself is repeated to create the border.

border-top-style, border-right-style, border-bottom-style, border-left-style, border-style

Scripting Properties:	`borderTopStyle`, `borderRightStyle`, `borderBottomStyle`, `borderLeftStyle`, `borderStyle`
Values:	`none, solid, double, groove, ridge, inset, outset`
Default:	`none`
Applies to:	Block and replaced elements
Inherited:	No
Percentage?:	No

Sets the style of the four borders.

border-top, border-right, border-bottom, border-left, border

Scripting Properties:	`borderTop, borderRight, borderBottom, borderLeft, border`
Values:	`<border-width>, <border-style>, <color>`
Default:	`medium, none, <none>`
Applies to:	Block and replaced elements
Inherited:	No
Percentage?:	No

Sets the properties of the border element (box drawn around the effected element). Works roughly the same as the margin settings, except that it can be made visible.

▲ `<border-width>` can be `thin`, `medium`, `thick`, or as a unit of measurement.

▲ `<border-style>` can be `none`, `solid`.

The color argument is used to fill the background of the element while it loads, and behind any transparent parts of the element. By supplying the URL of an image instead, the image itself is repeated to create the border. It is also possible to specify values for attributes of the border property separately using the `border-width`, `border-style` and `border-color` properties.

border-top-width, border-right-width, border-bottom-width, border-left-width, border-width

Scripting Properties:	`borderTopWidth, borderRightWidth, borderBottomWidth,`
	`borderLeftWidth, borderWidth`
Values:	`thin, medium, thick <length>`
Default:	`medium`
Applies to:	Block and replaced elements
Inherited:	No
Percentage?:	No

Sets the width of the border for the element. Each side can be set individually, or the **border-width** property used to set all of the sides. You can also supply up to four arguments for the border-width property to set individual sides, in the same way as with the **margin** property.

clear

Scripting Property:	`clear`
Values:	`none, both, left, right`
Default:	`none`
Applies to:	All elements
Inherited:	No
Percentage?:	No

Forces the following elements to be displayed below an element which is aligned. Normally, they would wrap around it.

clip

Scripting Property:	`clip`
Values:	`rect(<top><right><bottom><left>) , auto`
Default:	`auto`
Applies to:	All elements
Inherited:	No
Percentage?:	No

Controls which part of an element is visible. Anything that occurs outside the clip area is not visible.

display

Scripting Property:	`display`
Values:	`" ", none`
Default:	`" "`
Applies to:	All elements
Inherited:	No
Percentage?:	No

This property indicates whether an element is rendered. If set to **none** the element is not rendered, if set to `" "` it is rendered.

float

Scripting Property:	`styleFloat`
Values:	`none, left, right`
Default:	`none`
Applies to:	`DIV`, `SPAN` and replaced elements
Inherited:	No
Percentage?:	No

Causes following elements to be wrapped to the left or right of the element, rather than being placed below it.

height

Scripting Properties:	`height, pixelHeight, posHeight`
Values:	`auto, <length>`
Default:	`auto`
Applies to:	`DIV`, `SPAN` and replaced elements
Inherited:	No
Percentage?:	No

Sets the vertical size of an element, and will scale the element if necessary. The value is returned as a string including the measurement type (**px**, **%**, etc.). To retrieve the value as a number, query the `posHeight` property.

left

Scripting Properties:	`left, pixelLeft, posLeft`
Values:	`auto, <length>, <percentage>`
Default:	`auto`
Applies to:	All elements
Inherited:	No
Percentage?:	Yes, refers to parent's width

Sets or returns the left position of an element when displayed in 2-D canvas mode, allowing accurate placement and animation of individual elements. The value is returned as a string including the measurement type (**px**, **%**, etc.). To retrieve the value as a number, query the `posLeft` property.

margin-top, margin-right, margin-bottom, margin-left, margin

Scripting Properties:	`marginTop, marginRight, marginBottom, marginLeft, margin`
Values:	`auto, <length>, <percentage>`
Default:	Zero
Applies to:	Block and replaced elements
Inherited:	No
Percentage?:	Yes, refers to parent element's width

Sets the size of margins around any given element. You can use **margin** as shorthand for setting all of the other values (as it applies to all four sides). If you use multiple values in **margin** but use less than four, opposing sides will try to be equal. These values all set the effective minimum distance between the current element and others.

overflow

Scripting Property:	`overflow`
Values:	`none, clip, scroll`
Default:	`none`
Applies to:	All elements
Inherited:	No
Percentage?:	No

This controls how a container element will display its content if this is not the same size as the container.

- ▲ `none` means that the container will use the default method. For example, as in an image element, the content may be resized to fit the container.

- ▲ `clip` means that the contents will not be resized, and only a part will be visible.

- ▲ `scroll` will cause the container to display scroll bars so that the entire contents can be viewed by scrolling.

padding-top, padding-right, padding-bottom, padding-left, padding

Scripting Properties:	`paddingTop, paddingRight, paddingBottom, paddingLeft, padding`
Values:	`auto, <length>, <percentage>`
Default:	`Zero`
Applies to:	Block and replaced elements
Inherited:	No
Percentage?:	Yes, refers to parent element's width

Sets the distance between the content and border of an element. You can use **padding** as shorthand for setting all of the other values (as it applies to all four sides). If you use multiple values in **padding** but use less than four, opposing sides will try to be equal. These values all set the effective minimum distance between the current element and others.

position

Scripting Property:	`position`
Values:	`absolute, relative, static`
Default:	`relative`
Applies to:	All elements
Inherited:	No
Percentage?:	No

Specifies if the element can be positioned directly on the 2D canvas.

- ▲ `absolute` means it can be fixed on the background of the page at a specified location, and move with it.

- ▲ `static` means it can be fixed on the background of the page at a specified location, but not move when the page is scrolled.

- ▲ `relative` means that it will be positioned normally, depending on the preceding elements.

top

Scripting Properties:	`top, pixelTop, posTop`
Values:	`auto, <percentage> <length>`
Default:	`auto`
Applies to:	All elements
Inherited:	No
Percentage?:	Yes, refers to parent's width

Sets or returns the vertical position of an element when displayed in 2-D canvas mode, allowing accurate placement and animation of individual elements. Value is returned as a string including the measurement type (`px`, `%`, etc.). To retrieve the value as a number, query the `posTop` property.

visibility

Scripting Property:	`visibility`
Values:	`visible, hidden, inherit`
Default:	`inherit`
Applies to:	All elements
Inherited:	No
Percentage?:	No

Allows the element to be displayed or hidden on the page. Elements which are hidden still take up the same amount of space, but are rendered transparently. Can be used to dynamically display only one of several overlapping elements

▲ `visible` means that the element will be visible.

▲ `hidden` means that the element will not be visible.

▲ `inherit` means that the element will only be visible when it's parent or container element is visible.

width

Scripting Properties:	`width, pixelWidth, posWidth`
Values:	`auto, <length>, <percentage>`
Default:	`auto`, except for any element with an intrinsic dimension
Applies to:	`DIV`, `SPAN` and replaced elements
Inherited:	No
Percentage?:	Yes, refers to parent's width

Sets the horizontal size of an element, and will scale the element if necessary. The value is returned as a string including the measurement type (`px`, `%`, etc.). To retrieve the value as a number, query the `posWidth` property.

z-index

Scripting Property:	`zIndex`
Values:	`<number>`
Default:	Depends on the HTML source
Applies to:	All elements
Inherited:	No
Percentage?:	No

Controls the ordering of overlapping elements, and defines which will be displayed 'on top'. Positive numbers are above the normal text on the page, and negative numbers are below. Allows a 2.5-D appearance by controlling the layering of the page's contents.

Printing Properties

page-break-after

Scripting Property:	`pageBreakAfter`
Values:	`<auto>`, `<always>`, `<left>`, `<right>`
Default:	`<auto>`
Applies to:	All elements
Inherited:	No
Percentage?:	No

Controls when to set a page break and on what page the content will resume, i.e. either the left or the right.

page-break-before

Scripting Property:	`pageBreakBefore`
Values:	`<auto>`, `<always>`, `<left>`, `<right>`
Default:	`<auto>`
Applies to:	All elements
Inherited:	No
Percentage?:	No

Controls when to set a page break and on what page the content will resume, i.e. either the left or the right.

Filter Properties

All filters are called with the keyword filter. There are two different types of filter, visual filters and transition filters. Transition filters are further divided into Blend Transition filters and Reveal Transition filters. All of these filters are called in the same way in cascading style sheets:

```
filter: filtername{fparameter1, fparameter2, etc}
```

There are 14 types of visual filter in all and two types of transition filter, all of them are documented.

Visual Filters

Scripting Property:	*object*.style.*filtername(fparameter1, etc)*
Values:	*filtername(fparameter1, fparameter2 etc)*
Default:	none
Applies to:	All elements
Inherited:	No
Percentage?:	No

Controls the manipulation of visible objects via any one of a set of predefined filters.

A list of possible filter names and what they do follows:

Filtername	Description
alpha	Sets a uniform transparency level
blur	Creates a movement effect
chroma	Makes one color transparent
dropshadow	Makes a silhouette of an object
fliph	Creates a horizontal mirror image
flipv	Creates a vertical mirror image
glow	Creates the effect that an object is glowing
grayscale	Changes an object to monochromatic colors
invert	Reverses all hue, saturation and brightness values
light	Shines a light source onto an object
mask	Creates a transparent mask from an object
shadow	Creates a silhouette of an object offset from the object
wave	Creates a sine wave distortion of an object along the x axis
xray	Shows just the outline of an object

revealtrans

Scripting Property:	*object*.style.**revealtrans**(duration = <duration>, transition = <transition shape>)
Values:	revealtrans(duration = <duration>, transition = <transition shape>)
Default:	none
Applies to:	All elements
Inherited:	No
Percentage?:	No

Allows you reveal or cover up visual objects using one of 23 predefined patterns, specified by a code.

▲ <duration> is the length of time that the transition will take to complete. This is specified in milliseconds.

▲ <transition shape> is determined by the integer value assigned to it. The following shapes have the following values.

<Shape>	<Value>	<Shape>	<Value>
Box In	0	Random Dissolve	12
Box Out	1	Split Vertical In	13
Circle In	2	Split Vertical Out	14
Circle Out	3	Split Horizontal In	15
Wipe Up	4	Split Horizontal Out	16
Wipe Down	5	Strips Left Down	17
Wipe Right	6	Strips Left Up	18
Wipe Left	7	Strips Right Down	19
Vertical Blinds	8	Strips Right Up	20
Horizontal Blinds	9	Random Bars Horizontal	21
Checkerboard Across	10	Random Bars Vertical	22
Checkerboard Down	11	Random	23

blendtrans

Scripting Property:	*object*.style.**revealtrans(duration = <duration>)**
Values:	**blendTrans(duration** = <duration>)
Default:	none
Applies to:	All elements
Inherited:	No
Percentage?:	No

Performs a fade in or fade out of selected visual objects.

▲ <duration> is the length of time the transition should take to complete.

Other Properties

cursor

Scripting Property:	cursor
Values:	auto, crosshair, default, hand, move, e-resize, ne-resize, nw-resize, n-resize, se-resize, sw-resize, s-resize, w-resize, text, wait, help
Default:	auto
Applies to:	All elements
Inherited:	No
Percentage?:	No

Specifies the type of cursor the mouse pointer should be.

Unsupported CSS Properties

Internet Explorer 4 doesn't support the following CSS properties:

- ▲ word-spacing
- ▲ !important
- ▲ first-letter pseudo
- ▲ first-line pseudo
- ▲ white-space

CDF and OSD Reference

Internet Explorer 4 uses two types of non-HTML file to control the installation and operation of Desktop Channels, Subscriptions, Active Desktop Items, and Software Installation Channels.

▲ **Channel Definition Format** (CDF) files are used to install and set up Active Desktop Items, Channels, Subscriptions and Active screensavers. They are also used to indicate to the browser that new or upgraded Software Channel content is available.

▲ **Open Software Distribution** (OSD) files are used to control the actual downloading and installation of new or upgraded software via a Software Channel.

The structure of the two types of files is different, but they use some common elements. The syntax of these elements is similar between the two file types.

CDF and OSD Element Syntax

There are two types of element tag (plus the special **XML** tag). Elements with an **opening and closing tag** can contain attributes within the opening tag, and are used to enclose other element tags. These work in a similar way to standard HTML tags. For example:

```
<ITEM HREF="http://www.wrox.com" LEVEL="3" PRECACHE="YES">
   <!-- other element tags go here. This is a comment tag -->
</ITEM>
```

Single, or **stand-alone** elements, have a forward slash "/" before the closing ">" bracket. This is different from the standard HTML element format, following the rules of XML (eXtensible Markup Language) instead. For example:

```
<LOGO HREF="mylogo.gif" STYLE="ICON" />
```

Unlike HTML, *all* attribute values (string or numeric) must be enclosed in quotation marks. Certain special characters cannot be used within attributes directly. These (and any other character) can be encoded using the normal URL-syntax. A full list of encodings is provided in Appendix **H**. Some of the popular ones are:

Character	Encoding	Character	Encoding	Character	Encoding
<	&lt	'	&apos	&	&amp
>	&gt	"	&quot	any*	&#nnn

* where *nnn* is the decimal ASCII character value, i.e. &#065 for 'A'.

CDF File Structure

Channel Definition Format (CDF) files provide the opportunity to install Active Channels, Active Desktop Items and Active Screensavers on the target machine. They can optionally be used to indicate that new or upgraded software items are available for download and installation.

The outline format of a CDF file is shown below, followed by a detailed breakdown of the **ITEM** and **SOFTDIST** elements. All of the available elements are shown, although with the exception of the **XML** and top-level **CHANNEL**, they are all optional.

The outline structure of a CDF file, showing all the top-level elements:

```
<?XML ?>                              <!-- format of the CDF file -->
<CHANNEL>                             <!-- top level channel element -->
    <A> ... </A>                      <!-- to replace HREF in CHANNEL only -->
    <ABSTRACT> ... </ABSTRACT>        <!-- description of channel -->
    <TITLE> ... </TITLE>              <!-- to display in Channels pane -->
    <DELETEONINSTALL />               <!-- remove channel after install -->
    <HTTP-EQUIV />                    <!-- can be repeated as required -->
    <LOG />                           <!-- not yet implemented at top level -->
    <LOGIN />                         <!-- use in top level channel only -->
    <LOGO />                          <!-- repeated for icon and logo -->
    <LOGTARGET>                       <!-- details of log to record hits -->
        <HTTP-EQUIV />                <!-- can be repeated as required -->
        <PURGETIME />                 <!-- specifies log file timing -->
    </LOGTARGET>
    <SCHEDULE>                        <!-- channel update interval -->
        <EARLIESTTIME />              <!-- earliest time to update -->
        <INTERVALTIME />              <!-- interval, must be non-zero -->
        <LATESTTIME />                <!-- latest time to update -->
    </SCHEDULE>
    <CHANNEL>                         <!-- define sub channel content -->
        ...                           <!-- details of sub channel go here -->
    </CHANNEL>                        <!-- repeated for each sub channel -->
    <ITEM>                            <!-- defines each item in channel -->
        ...                           <!-- details of ITEM shown below -->
    </ITEM>                           <!-- repeated for each item to include -->
    <SOFTPKG>                         <!-- software notifications in channel -->
        ...                           <!-- details of SOFTDIST shown below -->
    </SOFTPKG>                        <!-- repeated for each item to include -->
</CHANNEL>
```

The detail structure of the ITEM element, showing all the available elements:

```
    ...
    <ITEM>                              <!-- repeated for each item in channel -->
        <A> ... </A>                    <!-- to replace HREF in ITEM only -->
        <ABSTRACT> ... </ABSTRACT>      <!-- description of channel -->
        <TITLE> ... </TITLE>            <!-- to display in Channels pane -->
        <HTTP-EQUIV />                  <!-- can be repeated as required -->
        <LOG />                         <!-- details of how to log the item -->
        <LOGO />                        <!-- repeated for icon and logo -->
        <SCHEDULE>                      <!-- channel update interval -->
            <EARLIESTTIME />            <!-- earliest time to update -->
            <INTERVALTIME />            <!-- interval, must be non-zero -->
            <LATESTTIME />              <!-- latest time to update -->
        </SCHEDULE>
        <USAGE>                         <!-- details of how to use item -->
            <HEIGHT />                  <!-- height for display on desktop -->
            <WIDTH />                   <!-- width for display on desktop -->
            <CANRESIZE />               <!-- can be resized by the user -->
            <CANRESIZEX />              <!-- user can resize width only -->
            <CANRESIZEY />              <!-- user can resize height only -->
            <OPENAS />                  <!-- specifies how to show content -->
        </USAGE>
        <USAGE>                         <!-- can be repeated as required -->
            ...                         <!-- with various usage values -->
        </USAGE>
    </ITEM>
    ...
```

Note that ITEM-level scheduling is not yet supported in Internet Explorer

The detail structure of the SOFTPKG element, showing all the available elements:

```
    ...
    <SOFTPKG>                           <!-- repeated for each item in channel -->
        <ABSTRACT> ... </ABSTRACT>      <!-- description of software -->
        <TITLE> ... </TITLE>            <!-- to display while installing -->
        <LANGUAGE />                    <!-- languages supported by file -->
        <LOGO />                        <!-- logo for software item -->
        <USAGE ... </USAGE>             <!-- no child elements in SOFTDIST -->
        <IMPLEMENTATION>                <!-- repeated for each platform or OS -->
            <CODEBASE />                <!-- location of file to install -->
            <LANGUAGE />                <!-- languages supported by file -->
            <OS />                      <!-- operating system required -->
            <OSVERSION />               <!-- op.system version required -->
            <PROCESSOR />               <!-- processor type required -->
        </IMPLEMENTATION>
        <DEPENDENCY>                    <!-- can be repeated as required -->
            <LANGUAGE />                <!-- languages supported by file -->
            <OS />                      <!-- operating system required -->
            <OSVERSION />               <!-- op.system version required -->
            <PROCESSOR />               <!-- processor type required -->
        </DEPENDENCY>
    </SOFTPKG>
    ...
```

OSD File Structure

Open Software Distribution (OSD) files are used to specify in detail what the software items are, how they are to be installed, and the requirements of the system that they will be installed upon. In outline, the file has the following optional sections and elements.

The outline structure of an OSD file, showing all the top-level elements:

```
<SOFTPKG>
    <ABSTRACT> ... </ABSTRACT>          <!-- description of software -->
    <TITLE> ... </TITLE>                <!-- to display while installing -->
    <DELETEONINSTALL />                 <!-- remove channel after install -->
    <LANGUAGE />                        <!-- languages supported by file -->
    <LOGO />                            <!-- logo for software item -->
    <USAGE> ... </USAGE>                <!-- usage of the software -->
    <IMPLEMENTATION>                    <!-- system requirements -->
        <CODEBASE />                    <!-- location of software -->
        <LANGUAGE />                    <!-- languages it supports -->
        <OS />                          <!-- operating system required -->
        <OSVERSION />                   <!-- op.system version required -->
        <PROCESSOR />                   <!-- processor type required -->
    </IMPLEMENTATION>
    <JAVA>                              <!-- to install Java objects -->
        <PACKAGE>                       <!-- identifies a package -->
            ...                         <!-- package detail goes here -->
        </PACKAGE>                      <!-- can be repeated as required -->
    </JAVA>
    <NATIVECODE>                        <!-- install platform specific code -->
        <CODE>                          <!-- can be repeated as required -->
            ...                         <!-- code detail goes here -->
        </CODE>
    </NATIVECODE>
    <DEPENDENCY>                        <!-- existing software dependencies -->
        <SOFTPKG>                       <!-- can be repeated as required -->
            ...                         <!-- software detail goes here -->
        </SOFTPKG>
    </DEPENDENCY>
</SOFTPKG>
```

The detailed structure of the JAVA element, showing all the possible elements:

```
...
<JAVA>                                <!-- to install Java objects -->
   <PACKAGE>                          <!-- can be repeated as required -->
      <IMPLEMENTATION>                <!-- can be repeated as required -->
         <CODEBASE />                 <!-- location of software -->
         <LANGUAGE />                 <!-- languages it supports -->
         <NEEDSTRUSTEDSOURCE />       <!-- Java installations only -->
         <OS />                       <!-- operating system required -->
         <OSVERSION />                <!-- op.system version required -->
         <PROCESSOR />                <!-- processor type required -->
         <SYSTEM />                   <!-- Java installations only -->
      </IMPLEMENTATION>
      <CLASS>
         <ICON />                     <!-- icon file to associate -->
         <ISBEAN />                   <!-- only if is JavaBean object -->
         <TYPELIB />                  <!-- the type library file -->
      </CLASS>
   </PACKAGE>
</JAVA>
...
```

The detailed structure of the NATIVECODE element, showing all the possible elements:

```
...
<NATIVECODE>                          <!-- install platform specific code -->
   <CODE>                             <!-- can be repeated as required -->
      <IMPLEMENTATION>                <!-- can be repeated as required -->
         <CODEBASE />                 <!-- location of software -->
         <LANGUAGE />                 <!-- languages it supports -->
         <NEEDSTRUSTEDSOURCE />       <!-- Java installations only -->
         <OS />                       <!-- operating system required -->
         <OSVERSION />                <!-- op.system version required -->
         <PROCESSOR />                <!-- processor type required -->
         <SYSTEM />                   <!-- Java installations only -->
      </IMPLEMENTATION>
   </CODE>
</NATIVECODE>
...
```

The detailed structure of the DEPENDENCY element, showing all the possible elements:

```
...
<DEPENDENCY>                          <!-- existing software dependencies -->
   <SOFTPKG>                          <!-- can be repeated as required -->
      <IMPLEMENTATION>                <!-- can be repeated as required -->
         <CODEBASE />                 <!-- location of software -->
         <LANGUAGE />                 <!-- languages it supports -->
         <NEEDSTRUSTEDSOURCE />       <!-- Java installations only -->
         <OS />                       <!-- operating system required -->
         <OSVERSION />                <!-- op.system version required -->
         <PROCESSOR />                <!-- processor type required -->
         <SYSTEM />                   <!-- Java installations only -->
      </IMPLEMENTATION>
   </SOFTPKG>
</DEPENDENCY>
...
```

Elements used in CDF and/or OSD Files

This section provides a listing of all the elements that can be used in CDF and/or OSD files. It shows the element type (open and close tags or single-tag), and provides a list of the available attributes for the element.

<?XML ?>

This special tag defines the type of CDF file in use. It is the only one that doesn't follow the syntax rules outlined in the introduction to this section, using question marks as tag content 'start and end' delimiters.

Attribute	Values	Description
ENCODING	"*string*"	Character set of the file, i.e. "**UTF-8**" (the default).
VERSION	"*string*"	The version number, i.e. "**1.0**" (the default).

<A> ... </A>

Defines a hypertext link that is used in place of the **HREF** attribute in an associated **CHANNEL** or **ITEM** element. Allows Netscape browsers, which do not detect this **HREF** attribute, to access the channel contents. Used in CDF files only.

Attribute	Values	Description
HREF	"*string*"	The URL or address for the item. Required.

<ABSTRACT> ... </ABSTRACT>

A description of the associated **CHANNEL**, **ITEM** or software element, displayed in a tool-tip for the channel in the browser's Channel pane. The XML-SPACE attribute can also be included in any other CDF element tag, where it will apply to all child elements unless over-ridden with a different **XML-SPACE** setting. Used in CDF and OSD files.

Attribute	Values	Description
XML-SPACE	"**DEFAULT**" | "**PRESERVE**"	If "**PRESERVE**", white space characters (tabs, extra spaces, blank lines, etc.) are preserved. If "**DEFAULT**" they are treated like ordinary HTML and filtered out during file processing.

<CANRESIZE />

Specifies whether the user can resize the Active Desktop Item created by the parent **ITEM** element. Controls both the X and Y directions. Used in CDF files only.

Attribute	Values	Description
VALUE	"**YES**" | "**NO**"	The default if this element is omitted is "**YES**".

<CANRESIZEX />

Specifies whether the user can resize the Active Desktop Item created by the parent **ITEM** element. Controls only the X direction. Used in CDF files only.

Attribute	Values	Description
VALUE	"YES" | "NO"	The default if this element is omitted is "YES".

<CANRESIZEY />

Specifies whether the user can resize the Active Desktop Item created by the parent **ITEM** element. Controls only the Y direction. Used in CDF files only.

Attribute	Values	Description
VALUE	"YES" | "NO"	The default if this element is omitted is "YES".

<CHANNEL> ... </CHANNEL>

Defines a channel. This can be a sub channel, nested within another channel. The **SELF** attribute is optional, and can only be used in the top-level channel. This element is used only in CDF files.

Attribute	Values	Description
BASE	"*string*"	The base URL or address for the channel, used to resolve relative URLs specified in **ITEM** and **CHANNEL** elements within the channel
HREF	"*string*"	The URL or address for the channel. Required unless there is an **A** element for the channel.
LASTMOD	"*number*"	Specifies the date the item was last modified. Compared against cached item to allow download of new material. Format is *yyyy-mm-dd*T*hh:mm*
LEVEL	"*number*"	The number of levels below the page to pre-cache. Default is zero, but if the page contains frames, their contents will be fetched and cached.
PRECACHE	"YES|NO"	Specifies if content should be downloaded and cached on the client computer. Default is **YES**.
SELF	"*string*"	URL or address of the channel's CDF file. Included only for backward compatibility.

<CLASS> ... </CLASS>

Specifies the class information for a Java package distribution. Used only in OSD files.

Attribute	Values	Description
CLASSID	"*string*"	A unique platform-dependent format string that identifies the software. In IE4, this consists of sets of hex digits separated by hyphens and enclosed by braces, as: {*hhhhhhhh- hhhh- hhhh- hhhh- hhhhhhhhhhhh*}.
NAME	"*string*"	Name of the Java class. Must end in `.class`.

<CODE> ... </CODE>

Used to enclose a `NATIVECODE` element, and provides information about the version of the code for this software distribution. Used only in OSD files.

Attribute	Values	Description
CLASSID	"*string*"	A unique platform-dependent format string that identifies the software. In IE4, this consists of sets of hex digits separated by hyphens, and enclosed by braces, as: {*hhhhhhhh- hhhh- hhhh- hhhh- hhhhhhhhhhhh*}.
NAME	"*string*"	Name of the software or distribution unit.
VERSION	"*m, m, c, b*"	The major, minor, custom, and build version numbers of the software.

<CODEBASE />

The URL or address of the file or distribution unit to be installed. Used in CDF and OSD files.

Attribute	Values	Description
FILENAME	"*string*"	The name of the file if it is within the distribution unit.
HREF	"*string*"	The URL or address of the file if not within distribution unit.
SIZE	"*number*"	Maximum permitted size in KB for the file. If exceeded, the file or distribution unit will not be downloaded.
STYLE	"ActiveSetup" | "MSICD"	The system to use to download and install the files. "MSICD" is the Microsoft Internet Component Download system which looks at the Open Software Distribution (`.osd`) file for processing instructions.

<DELETEONINSTALL />

If present, specifies that the channel should delete itself once the software it specifies has been successfully installed. Used in CDF and OSD files.

<DEPENDENCY> ... </DEPENDENCY>

Defines a component that must be present on the client for the software distribution to be relevant. Used in CDF and OSD files, but the **ACTION** attribute is only available for an OSD file.

Attribute	Values	Description
ACTION	"Assert" | Install	Used if the files listed in the **DEPENDENCY** are not already installed. "**ASSERT**" causes the installation of the current distribution to be abandoned. "**INSTALL**" instructs the browser to fetch and install all the software listed in the **DEPENDENCY** as well as the installing the current distribution.

<EARLIESTTIME />

In a **SCHEDULE**, defines the earliest time that the update to the channel can occur. If not specified, the earliest time is the beginning of the **INTERVALTIME** value. Used only in CDF files.

Attribute	Values	Description
DAY	"*number*"	First day that the channel can be updated.
HOUR	"*number*"	First hour on this day that the channel can be updated.
MIN	"*number*"	First minute in this hour that the channel can be updated.

<HEIGHT />

Specifies the height that an Active Desktop Item should appear at. Used only in CDF files.

Attribute	Values	Description
VALUE	"*number*"	Height of the item in pixels for this **ITEM**.

<HTTP-EQUIV />

Used to add items to HTTP client response headers. For **CHANNEL** and **ITEM** elements, the context is of receiving files. For the **LOGTARGET** element, the context is of sending log files. Available HTTP header parameters include "**Charset**" for receiving files, and "**Encoding-Type**" for sending files. Used only in CDF files.

Attribute	Values	Description
NAME	"*string*"	The name of the HTTP header parameter. Required.
VALUE	"*string*"	The value for this parameter. Required.

<ICON />

Specifies an icon file (`.ico`) to associate with a Java Bean object. Used only in OSD files.

Attribute	Values	Description
FILENAME	"*string*"	Filename of an icon file.

<IMPLEMENTATION> ... </IMPLEMENTATION>

Used to define the operating system, platform and configuration required before the software distribution is valid. This element accepts no attributes. Used for both CDF and OSD files.

<ISBEAN />

Indicates that this software distribution item is a Java bean, rather than a regular Java class. This element accepts no attributes. Used only in OSD files.

<INTERVALTIME />

Specifies the intervals when the channel should be updated. The days, hours, and minutes are added together to determine the total value. Used only in CDF files.

Attribute	Values	Description
DAY	"*number*"	Number of days between channel updates.
HOUR	"*number*"	Number of hours between channel updates.
MIN	"*number*"	Number of minutes between channel updates.

<ITEM> ... </ITEM>

Defines an item within a channel, usually a Web page or Desktop Item. Used only in CDF files.

Attribute	Values	Description
HREF	"*string*"	The URL or address for the item. Required unless there is an **A** element for the item.
LASTMOD	"*string*"	Date the item was last modified. The client can determine if it has changed since the last time it was downloaded. Format is: *yyyy-mm-dd*T*hh:mm+hhmm*
LEVEL	"*number*"	The number of levels below the page to pre-cache. Default is zero, but if the page contains frames, their contents will be fetched and cached.
PRECACHE	"YES" | "NO"	Specifies if content should be downloaded and cached on the client computer.

<JAVA> ... </JAVA>

Identifies a section of the file that contains installation instructions for Java code. If it is not a Java package, the **NAMESPACE** attribute is used to create a name space for it. Used only in OSD files.

Attribute	Values	Description
NAMESPACE	"*string*"	The name space for non packaged code.

<LANGUAGE />

A list of ISO 639 language codes separated by semicolons, and used for internationalization of distribution items. Used in CDF and OSD files.

Attribute	Values	Description
VALUE	"*number*"	List of codes, such as "`en;de;it`".

<LATESTTIME />

In a **SCHEDULE**, defines the latest time that the update to the channel can occur. If not specified, the latest time is the beginning of the **INTERVALTIME** value. Used only in CDF files.

Attribute	Values	Description
DAY	"*number*"	Last day that the channel can be updated.
HOUR	"*number*"	Last hour on this day that the channel can be updated.
MIN	"*number*"	Last minute in this hour that the channel can be updated.

<LOG />

Indicates that the URL of the parent **CHANNEL** or **ITEM** element will be stored in a log file each time it is accessed on the client, acting as a page hit counter. Used only in CDF files.

Attribute	Values	Description
VALUE	"`document :view`"	The event that triggers logging. This is the only value currently supported in IE4.

<LOGIN />

Provides the login information required for retrieving channel content. Omitting all the attributes, using an empty element **<LOGIN/>**, means that the browser will prompt the user for the information. Used only in CDF files.

Attribute	Values	Description
DOMAIN	"*string*"	The URL or address of the domain to login to.
METHOD	"BASIC" | "DPA" | "MSN" | "NTLM" | "RPA"	Type of authentication. "BASIC" is base-64 encoding, the default. Distributed Password Authentication ("DPA") is a challenge-response scheme. "MSN" is the scheme used by the Microsoft Network. NT LAN Manager ("NTLM") is a challenge-response scheme based on the user name, and Remote Passphrase Authentication ("RPA") is CompuServe's authentication scheme.
PASS	"*string*"	The user password to log in with.
USER	"*string*"	The username or ID of the user.

<LOGO />

Specifies the image used to represent a channel or channel item in the user's Channel bar and Channels pane. IE4 accepts `.ico` files for the channel item icon only, or `.gif` and `.jpeg` (or `.jpg`) for both types of image. Animated GIF files are not supported, though image formats and styles are subject to change. Used in CDF and OSD files.

Attribute	Values	Description
HREF	"*string*"	The URL or address of the image to use.
STYLE	"ICON" | "IMAGE" | "IMAGE-WIDE"	For the channel icon, image must be 16 x 16 pixels. For the main channel image, the size must be 32H x 80W pixels. "IMAGE-WIDE" displays in the Channel Explorer bar and provides a link to the main channel page. 32H x 194W.

<LOGTARGET> ... </LOGTARGET>

Specifies where the client-based page hit count log is to be sent. Used only in CDF files.

Attribute	Values	Description
HREF	"*string*"	The URL or address to send the log file to.
METHOD	"POST"	HTTP method to be used for sending the file. IE4 only supports "POST" at present.
SCOPE	"ALL" | "OFFLINE" | "ONLINE"	Type of hits to be logged. Can be when the page is read from the local cache ("OFFLINE"), read from URL while browsing ("ONLINE"), or both ("ALL"–the default).

<NAMESPACE> ... </NAMESPACE>

Specifies a private name space to be used for a standalone Java application. There are no attributes for this element. Used only in OSD files.

<NATIVECODE> ... </NATIVECODE>

Encloses the CODE element, and indicates that this is an installation of platform-specific code. Supports no attributes. Used only in OSD files.

<NEEDSTRUSTEDSOURCE />

Indicates that only trusted (signed) code can be used to call the classes in this Java package. Supports no attributes. Used only in OSD files.

<OPENAS />

Defines how an Active Desktop Item will appear when displayed on the user's desktop, i.e. the content-type of the item file. Used in CDF files only.

Attribute	Values	Description
VALUE	"HTML" | "Image"	If "HTML" (the default)dg item will be displayed in an IFRAME element. If "Image", will be displayed inside an IMG element.

<OS />

Specifies the operating system that the software in a distribution supports. Used in CDF and OSD files.

Attribute	Values	Description
VALUE	"Mac" | "Win95" | "Winnt"	Name of the operating system.

<OSVERSION />

Specifies the version of the operating system that the software in a distribution supports. Used in CDF and OSD files.

Attribute	Values	Description
VALUE	"m, m, c, b"	The major, minor, custom, and build version numbers.

<PACKAGE> ... </PACKAGE>

Used inside the JAVA element to identify the software, either a Java package or a stand-alone Java application. Used only in OSD files.

Attribute	Values	Description
NAME	"$string$"	The name of the software package or application.
VERSION	"m, m, c, b"	The major, minor, custom, and build version numbers of the software.

<PROCESSOR />

Specifies the type of processor the software will run on. Used in CDF and OSD files.

Attribute	Values	Description
VALUE	"Alpha" | "MIPS" | "PPC" | "x86"	The processor type.

<PURGETIME />

Specifies the earliest date and time for entries included in the page hit count log file when uploaded. Earlier entries will not be reported. Used only in CDF files.

Attribute	Values	Description
DAY	"*number*"	Number of days in **PURGETIME** value.
HOUR	"*number*"	Number of hours in **PURGETIME** value.
MIN	"*number*"	Number of minutes in **PURGETIME** value.

<SCHEDULE> ... </SCHEDULE>

Specifies the schedule for the updating of the channel. The attributes define the first and last dates for updates, and the enclosed **EARLIESTTIME**, **INTERVALTIME** and **LATESTTIME** elements define the intervals within this period. The **TIMEZONE** attribute allows the channel provider to set the schedule's timescale to GMT for all users, by stating the difference between local time and GMT. Used only in CDF files.

Attribute	Values	Description
STARTDATE	"*string*"	Date when the schedule will start to apply, in the format *yyyy-mm-dd*. If omitted, starts on the current day.
ENDDATE	"*string*"	Date from which the schedule will no longer apply, in the format *yyyy-mm-dd*. If omitted, continues indefinitely.
TIMEZONE	"*string*"	Sets the difference between local time and GMT. Adjusts **EARLIESTTIME** and **LATESTTIME** accordingly. Format is +|-*hhmm*, with −|+ indicating that local time is earlier|later than GMT.

<SOFTPKG> ... </SOFTPKG>

Defines the parameters for a software distribution channel. Used in CDF and OSD files.

Attribute	Values	Description
AUTOINSTALL	`"NO"` | `"YES"`	`"YES"` tells the browser to download the distribution unit, install it, and then delete it upon successful installation. CDF files only.
HREF	`"string"`	URL for launching this installation. CDF files only.
NAME	`"string"`	Name of the software or distribution unit.
PRECACHE	`"NO"` | `"YES"`	Specifies if content should be downloaded and cached on the client computer. CDF files only.
STYLE	`"ActiveSetup"` | `"MSICD"`	The system to use to download and install the files. `"MSICD"` is the Microsoft Internet Component Download system which looks at the Open Software Distribution (`.osd`) file for processing instructions.
VERSION	`"m, m, c, b"`	The major, minor, custom, and build version of the software.

<SYSTEM />

Used to indicate that the software is a signed (trusted) Java package containing system classes that are not sand-boxed. Supports no attributes. Used only in OSD files.

<TITLE> ... </TITLE>

The title of the **CHANNEL**, **ITEM** or software element, displayed next to the icon in the browser's Channel pane. Supports **XML-SPACE**. Used in CDF and OSD files.

Attribute	Values	Description
XML-SPACE	`"DEFAULT"` | `"PRESERVE"`	If `"PRESERVE"`, white space characters (tabs, extra spaces, blank lines, etc.) are preserved. If `"DEFAULT"` they are treated like ordinary HTML and filtered out during file processing.

<TYPELIB />

Specifies the type library file (`.tlb`) for a Java Bean within this software distribution. Used only in OSD files.

Attribute	Values	Description
CLASSID	`"string"`	A unique platform-dependent format string that identifies the software. In IE4, this consists of sets of hex digits separated by hyphens, as: *hhhhhhhh-hhhh-hhhh-hhhh-hhhhhhhhhhhh*.

<USAGE> ... </USAGE>

Indicates how an element within a channel should be used. If the USAGE element appears within the main body of the CHANNEL tag, instead of within a ITEM element, the item will be assumed to be an Active Desktop Item, and any Channel information is disregarded. Used in CDF and OSD files.

Attribute	Values	Description
VALUE	"Channel" | "Email" | "Desktop_ Component" | "ScreenSaver" | "SmartScreen" | "NONE"	"Channel" is the default and indicates the item will appear in the browser's Channel pane. "Email" indicates items e-mailed when the channel content is updated. "DesktopComponent" indicates items displayed on the Active Desktop. "ScreenSaver" and "SmartScreen" indicate items used in the special Channels screen saver ("SmartScreen" is the PointCast™ format). "NONE" indicates items that will be cached but will not appear in the browser's Channel pane.

<WIDTH />

Specifies the width that an Active Desktop Item should appear at. Used only in CDF files.

Attribute	Values	Description
VALUE	"*number*"	Width of the item in pixels for this ITEM.

Remote Data Service Reference

This appendix provides reference material for section 2 on Databinding. It is divided into three parts; a discussion of the ADO recordset object, with listings of its methods and properties; an explanation of the ADC scripting constants file and, finally, an overview explanation of how ADC and RDS work.

Part 1 - The ADO Recordset Object

When writing Dynamic HTML scripts deploying the IE4 "intrinsic" data source object (either the TDC or the RDS/ADC), the script writer frequently has to interact with the **recordset** object exposed by the data source object. We saw several examples in Chapters 8 and 9. In reality, the recordset object is exposed by the ADO programming layer. The following is a list of properties and methods that are available on the standard ADO **recordset** object.

Methods of Recordset Object

Method	Description
`addNew`	Creates a new record in an updateable recordset.
`cancelBatch`	Cancels a pending batch update.
`cancelUpdate`	Cancels any changes made to a current or new record (or in the client-side cache in the case of the ADC).
`clone`	Creates a duplicate copy of the recordset.
`close`	Closes an open recordset and any dependent objects.
`delete`	Deletes the current record in an open recordset.
`getRows`	Retrieves multiple records into an array.
`move`	Moves the position of the current record.
`moveFirst, moveLast, moveNext, movePrevious`	Moves to the first, last, next or previous record in the recordset, and makes that the current record.
`open`	Opens a cursor on a recordset.
`requery`	Updates the data by re-executing the original query.
`resync`	Refreshes the data from the underlying database.
`supports`	Determines whether the recordset supports certain functions.
`update`	Saves any changes made to the current record.
`updateBatch`	Writes all pending batch updates to disk.

Properties of Recordset Object

Property	Description
absolutePage	The absolute 'page' on which the current record is located, or specifies the 'page' to move to.
absolutePosition	The ordinal position of the current record.
activeConnection	The **Connection** object that the recordset currently belongs to.
BOF	True if the current record position is before the first record.
bookmark	Returns a bookmark that uniquely identifies the current record, or sets the current record to the record identified by a valid bookmark.
cacheSize	The number of records that are cached locally in memory.
cursorType	The type of cursor used in the recordset.
editMode	The editing status of the current record.
EOF	True if the current record position is after the last record.
filter	Indicates whether a filter is in use.
lockType	The type of locks placed on records during editing.
maxRecords	The maximum number of records to return from a query.
pageCount	The number of 'pages' of data that the recordset contains.
pageSize	The number of records constituting one 'page'.
recordCount	The number of records currently in the recordset.
source	The source for the data in the recordset, i.e. **Command** object, SQL statement, table name, or stored procedure.
status	Status of the current record with respect to batch updates or other bulk operations.

Note that it is possible for a particular instance of a **recordset** object to have more exposed properties than listed above. This usually happens only on server-side ADO based scripting. In these cases, the actual set of properties available depends on the underlying OLE DB data provider involved. However, this subject matter is beyond the scope of this book.

Part 2 - "Adcvbs.inc" ADC Scripting Constants file

This file is by default installed in **\Program Files\Common Files\System\Msadc** and it contains various constants that may be useful when scripting with the RDS/ADC. Specifically, the set of constants highlighted below are used in our discussion of the "cancel" method and the "state" property of the ADC in Chapter 8. Whenever possible, these constants should be used during scripting instead of the actual numeric value. It is foreseeable that these numerical values may change in the future. To include the file, first copy it to the same directory as the web page containing the script, then include the following lines:

```
<!-- #include file="Adcvbs.inc" →
```

Here is the content of the "Adcvbs.inc" with the set constants describing ADC states highlighted.

```
<%
'-------------------------------------------------------------------
' Microsoft ADC
'
' (c) 1997 Microsoft Corporation.  All Rights Reserved.
'
' ADO constants include file for VBScript
'
'-------------------------------------------------------------------

'---- enum Values ----
Const adcExecSync = 1
Const adcExecAsync = 2

'---- enum Values ----
Const adcFetchUpFront = 1
Const adcFetchBackground = 2
Const adcFetchAsync = 3

'---- enum Values ----
Const adcStateClosed = &H00000000
Const adcStateOpen = &H00000001
Const adcStateConnecting = &H00000002
Const adcStateExecuting = &H00000004
Const adcStateFetching = &H00000008
%>
```

Part 3 - How ADC Works

RDS in a Nutshell

As previously promised, we will now examine how the ADC, and the underlying Remote Data Service works. At the beginning of chapter 8, we discovered that the RDS works on a three-tiered client/server basis.

On the first tier, we have the browser (sometimes called Universal Client) – IE4, with visual HTML elements bound to a data source object – the ADC. The ADC communicates with a web server extension living in the middle tier – this extension is called ADCISAPI. The ADC doesn't actually perform the communications itself; rather, it makes use of other components in the RDS client implementation to do so. The communication between the RDS client side implementation and the ADCISAPI extension (server side implementation) is completely tunneled through HTTP. The client-side implementation maintains a local cache of data to provide the browser with rapid access to data when user interacts with the data binding application.

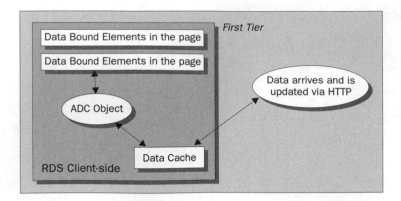

On the middle tier live the web server (IIS or PWS) and the ADCISAPI extension providing RDS server-side functionality. The extension talks to the client data provider and performs the requested operations and returns results tunneled in HTTP. It carries out its data operations through a set of server-side objects which implements the RDS server-side support. Through these RDS components, the ADCISAPI extension will access a third tier database server. This is done over a database independent access layer called OLE DB. Data provider components (essentially database drivers) can be written to the OLE DB specifications, the most popular and currently used provider is Microsoft's own ODBC provider for OLE DB. If the first tier client wants to perform custom data access instead of "standard" database access, the middle tier extension may also be replaced by a custom business object (a custom software component which implements data access and manipulation rules).

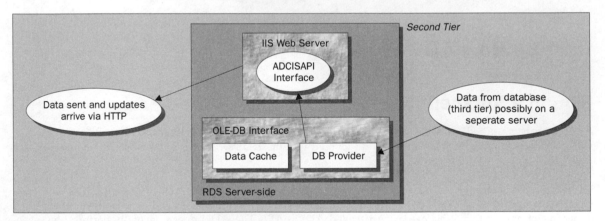

The third tier consists of the database server. The database server, besides servicing the client through the middle tier OLE DB provider, may execute "stored procedures" (code written to execute within the database server) to further optimize data access. This is often done in conjunction with a middle tier custom business object, or with specific first tier client scripting/programming.

RDS in Glorious Detail

We are about to take an in-depth look at the client and server implementation of the RDS. That is, components on the client and the middle tier supporting ADC data binding operations. The power and flexibility of the RDS transcends IE4 data binding and Dynamic HTML interworking. Microsoft hopes to replace the current heterogeneous mess of often inefficient data access technologies with a unified "Universal Data Access" solution based on RDS and associated technologies. This means that RDS based technology can also be used on all levels.

Level of Programming	Enabling Technology	Programming Language/Environment
High (little or no coding required)	ADC data binding	IE4, other browsers, other Rapid Application Development Environments/Tools which support ActiveX controls; especially the data binding extensions. e.g. VB, VJ++, Delphi
Medium (scripting or interpreted coding)	ActiveX Data Objects (an object based scriptable layer)	VBScript in all sort of clients, and the Windows 98 shell; also VBScript on the server (i.e. through Active Server Pages); other scripting languages; also any language which supports Automation (including Visual Basic, Visual J++, etc.)
Low (detailed system level coding)	OLE DB (a "COM" interface based layer – requires system programming according to Microsoft specified rules)	Typically system language such as C, C++. assembler, etc. Also possible through J++ and Visual Basic 5.

Obviously, someone using a lower level programming language can also access the RDS from middle and high level programming support. What we will realize shortly is that these three layers of access are actually built upon (and along side) each other. They are not at all mutually exclusive. This means that it is entirely possible to be simultaneously accessing the RDS stack at multiple levels. A case in point: in our TinyChat application, we used the high-level data binding facility to display the messages from other users, practically without coding. In the very same application, we also used scripting (medium level) when sending messages to the server-side database by manipulating the exposed ADO recordset property of the ADC.

By now, we know that the Remote Data Service is not a particular executable, DLL, or ActiveX control. Instead, it is a complete suite of client and server side components, which makes up the RDS. Specifically, for RDS 1.5, we have the following components:

Client Components (First Tier)	Server Components (Middle Tier)
Advanced Data Control	Advanced Data ISAPI (ADISAPI) component
Business Object Proxy	Business Object
Advanced Data Space	Advanced Data Factory
Data Cache (consisting of ActiveX Data Objects and Advanced Data Virtual Table Manager)	Data Cache (consisting of ActiveX Data Objects, Advanced Data Virtual Table Manager, and the Microsoft ODBC Data Provider for OLE DB)

The Client-Side RDS Components

Here is how the RDS client side components actually fit together.

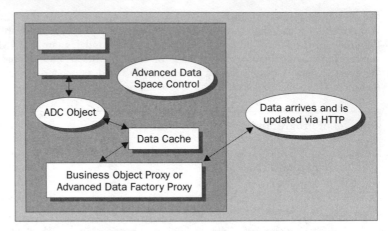

We will now take a more detailed look at each of the components and what they do

Advanced Data Control

There is no need to take a look at this component in detail, since we've already given it great coverage. We understand that its main purpose in life is to provide data binding capability to "bindable ActiveX controls", in our case they are certain IE4 visual HTML elements. What was not evident to us until now, however, is that it actually makes use of both the ActiveX Data Object (ADO) and the Advanced Data Space to perform most of the other work. For example, when we manipulated its "recordset" property in TinyChat, we were working with the data cache through the ADO access layer.

Advanced Data Space Control

The Advanced Data Space control is the parent of all programmatically created RDS objects on the client side. It is used to create the Advanced Data Factory Proxy and/or Business Object Proxy. A proxy makes a remote object (on the server–middle tier) appear as if it is on the local machine. This control is most useful in programming languages such as Visual Basic, but is of limited use in Dynamic HTML scripting. This is because we typically do not need to create objects programmatically. The ADC objects we use are typically embedded in the web page.

For our purpose, it is sufficient to know that the Advanced Data Space control is used to create custom business object proxy programmatically if we ever need to do so. The Advanced Data Space control has no accessible properties, and only one method.

Method	Description
CreateObject	Creates a client side proxy for any specified business object. The proxy of the default business object, Advanced Data Factory, can be created using this call.

Business Object Proxy and the Advanced Data Factory Proxy

In the TinyChat example in Chapter 8, we did not use any custom business object proxy on the client side. As a matter of fact, even with the more involved case study in Chapter 9, we did not need to create custom business object proxies. Instead, the default business object proxy, called the Advanced Data Factory proxy, is all that we need for most Dynamic HTML data binding programming.

This proxy allows us to access, from the client side, an ActiveX control located on the server. By default, this proxy will pass the command over (called command marshalling) to the server, execute them on the server-side Advanced Data Factory object, and then carry the results back (called recordset marshalling). The ADC handles all of this transparently. Because of this, we can code as if the Advanced Data Factory is right on the client. RDS 1.5 and beyond made it possible to access many of the methods of the Advanced Data Factory object right on the client-side via the ADC. This simplifies programming, and also reduces request traffic over the network. The following are the available methods for the Advanced Data Factory object (through the proxy) or from the server-side, you will notice significant similarity with those available from the ADC.

Method	Description
convertToString	Use this to encode a recordset when doing custom tunneling on the server side. It will encode the recordset in MIME using a non-compressed tablegram format.
createRecordset	Creates a disconnected, empty recordset. Typically used in custom tunneling.
query	Uses a SQL statement to make a query and return the corresponding recordset.
submitChanges	Send any pending changes in the local recordset to the third tier database.

Again, for our purposes, the default Advanced Data Factory proxy handles all the required query, command and recordset marshalling through HTTP for us. Furthermore, this is done transparently through the ADC, making the existence of the Advanced Data Factory object almost oblivious to us.

The Client Side Data Cache - ADO

At the data cache, where the "marshaled" recordsets from the server (by the Advanced Data Factory object) is stored for access, we see a prime benefit of object oriented technology: code reuse.

Here we will find a strata of software layers that is almost identical on the client side to the one on the server side. The layer on the very top is called Active Data Objects (ADO). It is the layer that allows us to use VBScript to program the ADC's recordset property.

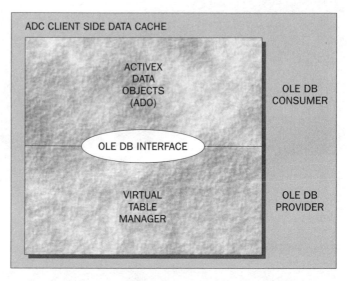

Notice how the ADO layer, along with the Virtual Table Manger implementation, is reused on the client as well as the server data cache. This is possible, thanks to a well-defined layer of interfaces known as OLE DB.

The Client-Side Data Cache - OLE DB

OLE DB is not software itself, but actually a set of interface specifications. The unique thing about the OLE DB specification is that all the interfaces described are completely COM based interfaces. COM is a system level programming standard defined by Microsoft. It is not considered a middleware layer because there need not be another layer of software above the "native" data source. As long as a data access "provider" (essentially driver) software is programmed to the OLE DB specifications, any OLE DB consumer (i.e. ADO) can access the native data without any additional layers of software.

The important thing to remember about OLE DB is that it is not a layer of middleware, but a published object based interface specification. In the client-side data-cache implementation of RDS, the actual in-memory recordset management is performed through an OLE DB provider called the Virtual Table Manager.

The Client-Side Data Cache - Virtual Table Manager

The virtual table manager is an OLE DB data provider. It provides a row set abstraction to data, managed in memory. Essentially, it manages multiple sets of data records, each consisting of multiple rows. By implementing the virtual table manager as an OLE DB data provider, the "caching" code can be re-used readily anywhere; and we have the flexibility of using higher level abstractions (such as ADO), as long as the abstraction layer is implemented as an OLE DB consumer.

This completes our examination of RDS client-side components. Let's take a quick look at the server side.

The Server-Side RDS Components

Here is how the server-side RDS components fit together.

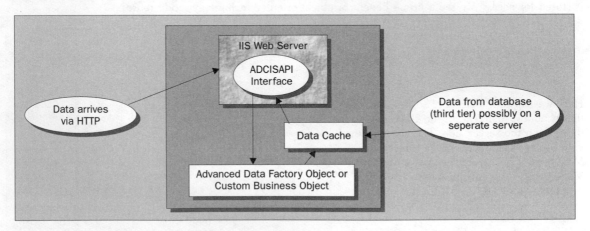

We will now take a more detailed look at each of the components. It will be much easier since we have seen most of the components from the client-side already.

ADCISAPI (Advanced Data Connector ISAPI)

This is an ISAPI (Information Server Application Programming Interface) extension DLL. It is loaded by the web server (typically IIS or PWS) during execution. It is this DLL which provides hooks to recognize requests from client-side RDS components and connect them to the appropriate server-side components. It runs inside the IIS process, and creates the required server-side components as necessary to perform the tasks requested by the RDS client.

Note that the "ADC" in "ADCISAPI" actually refers to "Advanced Data Connector" (and not Advanced Data Control). This is the 'former' name for Remote Data Service.

Business Objects or Advanced Data Factory

In our client-side coverage, we have mentioned that most Dynamic HTML data binding applications only need the default Advanced Data Factory object. This is the default server-side business object created by the client-side Advanced Data Space Control. It will perform the necessary data query, SQL execution, data fetch, command and recordset marshalling as required by the client-side ADC.

We will not go into the detail of creating a custom business object here, since it is beyond the scope of the book. The only thing we need to understand is that it is entirely possible to replace the functionality of the default Advanced Data Factory business object with one which does data access, manipulation, computation, and transportation using totally different means. For example, it is entirely possible to create a custom business object which uses DCOM instead of HTTP to provide these (and more) functionalities.

The Server Side Data-Cache

Here is what the server-side data cache looks like.

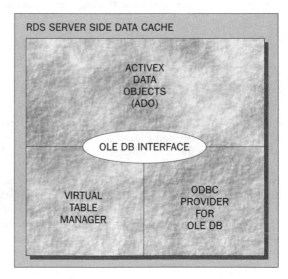

We know that the default Advanced Data Factory business object needs to access data from the actual third tier database. What is new here is an OLE DB data provider, which connects to an ODBC data source. This provider is called the ODBC data provider for OLE DB. It was formerly codenamed Kagera. The provider is essentially a thin mapping layer that maps the API centric programming style of ODBC programming to the new interface based COM style of programming

Just like the client-side data cache, we see here the reuse of both the ADO layer (providing server-side scripting from environment such as ASP), and the Virtual Table Manager (for server-side in-core caching).

Now, we have a very complete picture of how RDS actually works, and the actual components that make the magic possible. Let us now turn our attention to the reason for implementing this new way of data access.

The Promise of Universal Data Access

RDS, ADO, and OLE DB are the cornerstone for a "new wave" of technologies supporting what Microsoft calls "Universal Data Access". To fully understand why these new technologies are so necessary, we must go back in time and take a look at the evolution of the existing data access standards, including ODBC (Open Database Connectivity), DAO (Data Access Objects), and RDO (Remote Data Objects).

Open Database Connectivity (ODBC)

Since the days of Windows 3.1, ODBC has always been part of WOSA (Windows Open Software Architecture), which is Microsoft's word for Middleware. It specifies two layers of APIs, the layer on the bottom for database vendors to create drivers for their particular DBMS. The top layer API was designed for ODBC applications that can work with any vendor's RDBMS. An ODBC driver may access the database right on the client machine, such as the MS Access driver, or be communicating to a database server via custom protocol (such as the SQL Server driver).

After three major revisions, ODBC has finally appeared to achieve its goal. It has absorbed almost all of the quirks and idiosyncrasies that major relational database systems may have into its API specifications. The latest version is completely thread safe, and can even be running in a middle-tier server configuration and manage its own connections. The goal of making ODBC access as high performance as one provided by the native database system's API has been surpassed in many cases.

The only remaining "problems" with ODBC are:

▲   it is only good for dealing with relational databases

▲   the only "easy" way to program is using C or C++

▲   it is not easily accessible from script languages

Data Access Object

DAO provides access to data through Microsoft's Jet Engine. The Jet engine is the underlying database engine for the Microsoft Access product. It is a terrific implementation of standalone database. Multiple users can share the same database only through file sharing. Every single client must load the Jet Engine when accessing the data through DAO.

DAO provides an object-oriented abstraction to Jet engine based data access through a large set of interrelated objects. As a standard feature, the Jet engine can also work with non-Access databases. This includes ODBC data sources. Unfortunately, due to the intervening Jet engine layer, and the complex object abstraction, accessing ODBC data sources through DAO is a performance disaster. The most recent version of DAO (version 3.5) attempts to deal with this problem by offering ODBC direct implementation which by-passes the Jet engine altogether.

The problem with DAO as the main data access mechanism is:

▲   it is only good for dealing with relational data

▲   Jet engine layer makes efficient access difficult

▲   complex object model requires instantiation of many object to perform trivial data operation

▲   it prefers an intrinsically non-client/server architecture

▲   DAO access requires "fat client" because of the Jet engine's footprint

Remote Data Objects

For enterprise edition of Visual Basic and Visual C++, Microsoft has been including an object based data access mechanism programmed directly on top of ODBC. This very thin access layer is called Remote Data Objects (or RDO). Since the RDO object abstraction mirrors very closely the structure of ODBC, RDO can provide very high performance access to ODBC data. Furthermore, RDO operates exclusively in a client-server model, assuming a "remote data source". With the RDO abstraction layer, Microsoft also released a data binding control "controller" called the Remote Data Control (RDC). This is actually the predecessor of the RDS and ADC as we know them today.

The remaining problems, if you can call them problems, with RDO were:

▲   it is only good for dealing with ODBC data sources

▲   ODBC still needs to be installed at every client

▲   ODBC data source needs to be configured at every client

▲   very little third-party support for the RDC, making the coding of most data application rather complex

▲   communication between the client and the server is done through a proprietary protocol

▲   favors a two-tiered architecture

OLE DB and Universal Data Access

With the impending changeover to OLE DB as the database programming interface of choice, Microsoft is attempting to redefine the database middleware industry. It is an attempt to de-throne the API based ODBC standard in favor of the COM based OLE DB.

In real life, however, especially when dealing with established access standard like ODBC, the transition must be gradual. This means that the two standards must co-exist and work in harmony for the time being. For this to happen, another layer of software over ODBC is necessary to make it plug-and-play with OLE DB. Microsoft provides such a component. It is called the Microsoft ODBC provider for OLE DB, and we have seen it deployed at the RDS server-side data cache. It is essentially a thin mapping layer that maps the API centric programming style of ODBC programming to the new interface based COM style of programming. In the longer term, the Microsoft ODBC provider for OLE DB and the ODBC driver management layer below it will merge; and there will be an OLE DB provider for all relational database access. At this time, the standard ODBC APIs may be re-implemented on top of OLE DB for compatibility purposes.

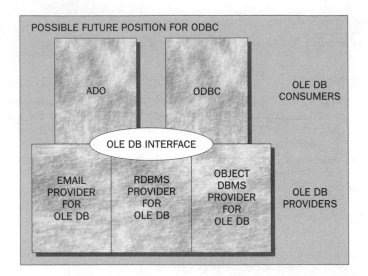

The key idea about OLE DB is that anyone can write new data access providers (drivers) that conform to the OLE DB specifications. These new providers can provide access to any arbitrary data sources, using past, present, or future technologies. The actual data can be structured and tabular, like the relational databases; or they can be totally unstructured. For example, it is entirely feasible to write an OLE DB provider for archived email data, another one for some photographic image banks, and yet another provider that will scour the Internet newsgroup for required data. The generic OLE DB specification does not favor specific data organization, technology, or implementation. Where or how the actual data is stored is totally irrelevant to OLE DB.

Conceptually, the engineers at Microsoft have abstracted the general data access problem, defined the roles of data consumers versus data/service providers, enumerated the interactions possible between these roles, and devised programmatic means of expressing these interactions in the form of object and interfaces. Theoretically, any data access problem, now or in the future, can fit into the OLE DB abstraction. This is why Microsoft is pushing the technology as "Universal Data Access".

Active Data Object (Reusable Medium Level Programmatic Access)

To provide an easily re-usable object based abstraction layer for data access, Microsoft has created ADO. ADO is an OLE DB consumer, meaning that it is programmed to OLE DB. This allows ADO to be used to manipulate any data from any source (relational or otherwise), that may support a rowset abstraction.

Learning from past experience with DAO and RDO, ADO is designed to have a very different design philosophy. Instead of having a complex object model requiring extensive navigation, most ADO objects can be created independently. The result is that there are fewer instantiations of 'dummy' hierarchy objects. In effect, an ADO object is allowed to perform work without creating any additional object until such time as the user actually requires it.

Although not strictly following object oriented design principles, this approach allows the ADO designers to keep both the storage and execution footprint of an ADO implementation very small. ADO is a tightly optimized, Automation compatible, object access layer over a new database access standard called OLE DB.

RDS and Instant Client Access

Last but not least, the final piece in the Universal Data Access puzzle–the RDS. Through its support for the three tiered client/server architecture, the RDS provides instantaneous data access from universal clients (IE4) without program download or ODBC setup. The approach maintains many of the high performance benefits of the older architecture, while leveraging on the flexibility of the new OLE DB layer. It also provides unparalleled ease of deployment and maintenance since both the data source and actual access methods are independent of the client.

Here is a table summarizing the various technology components:

Technology	Type	Characteristic	Performance
ODBC	Middleware specification; has associated code; API based	Best accessed through C or C++ Relational data Only	Can be very high, depending on driver
OLE DB	Middleware specification; no associated code; COM interface based	Best accessed through C or C++ For any data, structured or unstructured	Can be very high, depending on provider
DAO	Object based access layer; accessible through automation; works over Jet engine; favors local data source; large navigable object hierarchy; supports ODBC direct access	Best accessed through VB, VJ++, or scripting	High performance only for Jet databases low ODBC performance until by-pass used
RDO	Object based access layer; accessible through automation; works over ODBC; assumes remote data source; small object hierarchy; thin layer over ODBC	Best accessed through VB, VJ++ or scripting	Very high ODBC performance
ADO	Object based access layer; accessible through automation; works over OLE DB providers; assumes remote data source; no object hierarchy needed for operation; very thin layer and small footprint	Best access through scripting, but soon through VB and VJ++	Very high performance (for ODBC data source)
RDS	Data access infrastructure provides "zero download"; client access to databases through IE4; favors three-tiered client/server; extensible through custom business objects; change of data access application requires no client changes!	No programming necessary when using ADC data binding any level of programming	High performance for all OLE DB compatible data source

Special Characters in HTML

The following table gives you the codes you need to insert special characters into your HTML documents. Some characters have their own mnemonic names–for example, the registered trademark character can be written in HTML as `&reg`. Where there is no mnemonic name, you can insert the character simply by including its decimal code.

Character	Decimal Code	HTML	Description
"	`&#34;`	`&quot;`	Quotation mark
&	`&#38;`	`&amp;`	Ampersand
<	`&#60;`	`&lt;`	Less than
>	`&#62;`	`&gt;`	Greater than
	` `	` `	Non-breaking space
¡	`&#161;`	`&iexcl;`	Inverted exclamation
¢	`&#162;`	`&cent;`	Cent sign
£	`&#163;`	`&pound;`	Pound sterling
¤	`&#164;`	`&curren;`	General currency sign
¥	`&#165;`	`&yen;`	Yen sign
¦	`&#166;`	`&brvbar;`	Broken vertical bar
§	`&#167;`	`&sect;`	Section sign
¨	`&#168;`	`&uml;`	Diæresis/umlaut
©	`&#169;`	`&copy;`	Copyright
ª	`&#170;`	`&ordf;`	Feminine ordinal
«	`&#171;`	`&laquo;`	Left angle quote,
¬	`&#172;`	`&not;`	Not sign
-	`&#173;`	`&shy;`	Soft hyphen
®	`&#174;`	`&reg;`	Registered trademark
¯	`&#175;`	`&macr;`	Macron accent
°	`&#176;`	`&deg;`	Degree sign
±	`&#177;`	`&plusmn;`	Plus or minus
²	`&#178;`	`&sup2;`	Superscript two

Character	Decimal Code	HTML	Description
³	³	³	Superscript three
´	´	´	Acute accent
µ	µ	µ	Micro sign
¶	¶	¶	Paragraph sign
·	·	·	Middle dot
¸	¸	¸	Cedilla
¹	¹	¹	Superscript one
º	º	º	Masculine ordinal
»	»	»	Right angle quote
¼	¼	¼	Fraction one quarter
½	½	½	Fraction one half
¾	¾	¾	Fraction three-quarters
¿	¿	¿	Inverted question mark
À	À	À	Capital A, grave accent
Á	Á	Á	Capital A, acute accent
Â	Â	Â	Capital A, circumflex
Ã	Ã	Ã	Capital A, tilde
Ä	Ä	Ä	Capital A, diæresis / umlaut
Å	Å	Å	Capital A, ring
Æ	Æ	Æ	Capital AE, ligature
Ç	Ç	Ç	Capital C, cedilla
È	È	È	Capital E, grave accent
É	É	É	Capital E, acute accent
Ê	Ê	Ê	Capital E, circumflex
Ë	Ë	Ë	Capital E, diæresis / umlaut
Ì	Ì	Ì	Capital I, grave accent
Í	Í	Í	Capital I, acute accent
Î	Î	Î	Capital I, circumflex
Ï	Ï	Ï	Capital I, diæresis /umlaut
Ð	Ð	Ð	Capital Eth, Icelandic
Ñ	Ñ	Ñ	Capital N, tilde
Ò	Ò	Ò	Capital O, grave accent

Character	Decimal Code	HTML	Description
Ó	`&#211;`	`&Oacute;`	Capital O, acute accent
Ô	`&#212;`	`&Ocirc;`	Capital O, circumflex
Õ	`&#213;`	`&Otilde;`	Capital O, tilde
Ö	`&#214;`	`&Ouml;`	Capital O, diæresis / umlaut
×	`&#215;`	`&times;`	Multiplication sign
Ø	`&#216;`	`&Oslash;`	Capital O, slash
Ù	`&#217;`	`&Ugrave;`	Capital U, grave accent
Ú	`&#218;`	`&Uacute;`	Capital U, acute accent
Û	`&#219;`	`&Ucirc;`	Capital U, circumflex
Ü	`&#220;`	`&Uuml;`	Capital U, diæresis / umlaut
Ý	`&#221;`	`&Yacute;`	Capital Y, acute accent
Þ	`&#222;`	`&THORN;`	Capital Thorn, Icelandic
ß	`&#223;`	`&szlig;`	German sz
à	`&#224;`	`&agrave;`	Small a, grave accent
á	`&#225;`	`&aacute;`	Small a, acute accent
â	`&#226;`	`&acirc;`	Small a, circumflex
ã	`&#227;`	`&atilde;`	Small a, tilde
ä	`&#228;`	`&auml;`	Small a, diæresis / umlaut
å	`&#229;`	`&aring;`	Small a, ring
æ	`&#230;`	`&aelig;`	Small ae ligature
ç	`&#231;`	`&ccedil;`	Small c, cedilla
è	`&#232;`	`&egrave;`	Small e, grave accent
é	`&#233;`	`&eacute;`	Small e, acute accent
ê	`&#234;`	`&ecirc;`	Small e, circumflex
ë	`&#235;`	`&euml;`	Small e, diæresis / umlaut
ì	`&#236;`	`&igrave;`	Small i, grave accent
í	`&#237;`	`&iacute;`	Small i, acute accent
î	`&#238;`	`&icirc;`	Small i, circumflex
ï	`&#239;`	`&iuml;`	Small i, diæresis / umlaut
ð	`&#240;`	`&eth;`	Small eth, Icelandic
ñ	`&#241;`	`&ntilde;`	Small n, tilde
ò	`&#242;`	`&ograve;`	Small o, grave accent

Character	Decimal Code	HTML	Description
ó	ó	ó	Small o, acute accent
ô	ô	ô	Small o, circumflex
õ	õ	õ	Small o, tilde
ö	ö	ö	Small o, diæresis / umlaut
÷	÷	÷	Division sign
ø	ø	ø	Small o, slash
ù	ù	ù	Small u, grave accent
ú	ú	ú	Small u, acute accent
û	û	û	Small u, circumflex
ü	ü	ü	Small u, diæresis / umlaut
ý	ý	ý	Small y, acute accent
þ	þ	þ	Small thorn, Icelandic
ÿ	ÿ	ÿ	Small y, diæresis / umlaut

Remember, if you want to show HTML code in a browser, you have to use the special character codes for the angled brackets in order to avoid the browser interpreting them as start and end of tags.

Support and Errata

APPENDIX

One of the most irritating things about any programming book can be when you find that a bit of code you've just spent an hour typing simply doesn't work. You check it a hundred times to see if you've set it up correctly and then you notice the spelling mistake in the variable name on the book page. Grrrr! Of course, you can blame the authors for not taking enough care and testing the code, the editors for not doing their job properly, or the proofreaders for not being eagle-eyed enough but this doesn't get around the fact that mistakes do happen.

We try hard to ensure no mistakes sneak out into the real world, but we can't promise you that this book is 100% error free. What we can do is offer the next best thing by providing you with immediate support and feedback from experts who have worked on the book and try to ensure that future editions eliminate these gremlins. The following sections will take you step by step through how to post errata to our web site to get that help:

- ▲ Finding a list of existing errata on the web site
- ▲ Adding your own errata to the existing list
- ▲ What happens to your errata once you've posted it (why doesn't it appear immediately?)

and how to mail a question for technical support:

- ▲ What your e-mail should include
- ▲ What happens to your e-mail once it has been received by us

Finding an Errata on the Web Site

Before you send in a query, you might be able to save time by finding the answer to your problem on our web site, `http:\\www.wrox.com`. Each book we publish has its own page and its own errata sheet. You can get to any book's page by using the drop down list box on our web site's welcome screen.

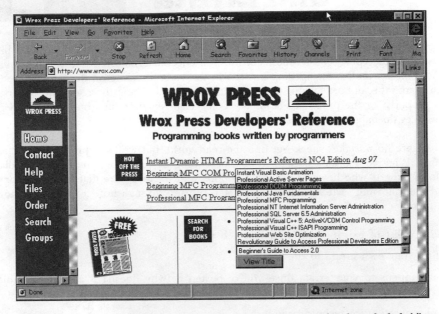

From this you can locate any book's home page on our site. Select your book and click View Title to get the individual title page:

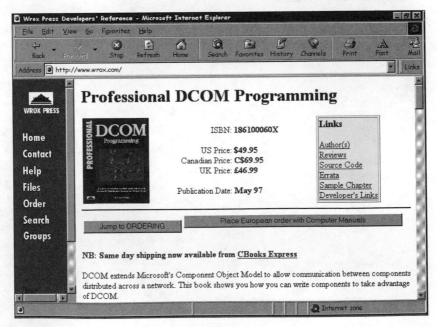

Each book has a set of links. If you click on the Errata link, you'll immediately be transported to the errata sheet for that book:

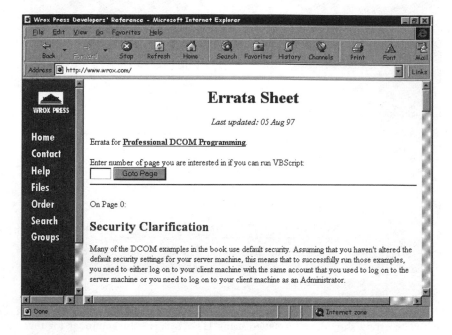

If you're using Internet Explorer 3.0 or later, you can jump to errors more quickly using the text box provided. The errata lists are updated on daily basis, ensuring that you always have the most up-to-date information on bugs and errors.

Adding an Errata to the Sheet Yourself

It's always possible that you may not find your error listed, in which case you can enter details of the fault yourself. It might be anything from a spelling mistake to a faulty piece of code in a book. Sometimes you'll find useful hints that aren't really errors on the listing. By entering errata you may save another reader some hours of frustration and, of course, you will be helping us to produce even higher quality information. We're very grateful for this sort of guidance and feedback. Here's how to do it:

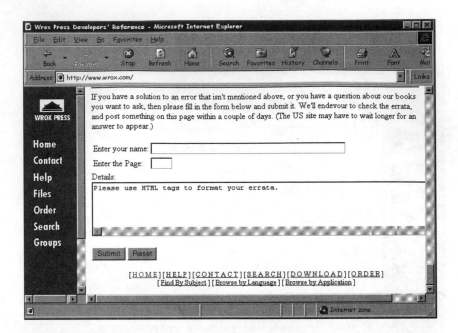

Find the errata page for the book, then scroll down to the bottom of the page, where you will see a space for you to enter your name (and e-mail address for preference), the page the errata occurs on and details of the errata itself. The errata should be formatted using HTML tags - the reminder for this can be deleted as you type in your error.

Once you've typed in your message, click on the Submit button and the message is forwarded to our editors. They'll then test your submission and check that the error exists, and that any suggestions you make are valid. Then your submission, together with a solution, is posted on the site for public consumption. Obviously this stage of the process can take a day or two, but we will endeavor to get a fix up sooner than that.

E-mail Support

If you wish to directly query a problem in the book with an expert who knows the book in detail then e-mail **support@wrox.com**, with the title of the book and the last four numbers of the ISBN in the Subject field of the e-mail. A typical e-mail should include the following things:

the title of the book

the last four numbers of the ISBN

the page number of the errata

the e-mail address

the snail mail address

the phone and fax numbers

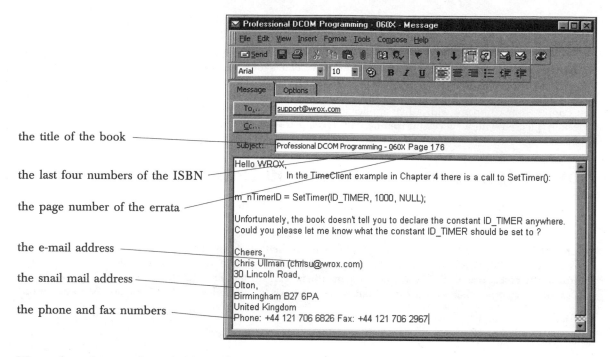

We won't send you junk mail. We need details to help save your time and ours. If we need to replace a disk or CD we'll be able to get it to you straight away. When you send an e-mail it will go through the following chain of support;

Customer Support

Your message is delivered to one of our customer support staff who are the first people to read it. They have files on the most frequently asked questions and will answer anything immediately. They answer general questions about the books and web site.

Editorial

Deeper queries are forwarded on the same day to the technical editor responsible for that book. They have experience with the programming language or particular product and are able to answer detailed technical questions on the subject. Once an issue has been resolved, the editor can post the errata to the web site.

The Author(s)

Finally, in the unlikely event that the editor can't answer your problem, he/she will forward the request to the author. We try to protect the author from any distractions from writing. However, we are quite happy to forward specific requests to them. All Wrox authors help with the support on their books. They'll mail the customer and editor with their response, and again, all readers should benefit.

What we can't answer

Obviously with an ever growing range of books and an ever-changing technology base, there is an increasing volume of data requiring support. While we endeavor to answer all questions about a book, we can't answer bugs in your own programs that you've adapted from our code. So, while you might have loved the help desk system examples in our Active Server Pages book, don't expect too much sympathy if you cripple your company with a live application you customized from chapter 12. But do tell us if you're especially pleased with a successful routine you developed with our help.

How to tell us exactly what you think!

We understand that errors can destroy the enjoyment of a book and can cause many wasted and frustrated hours, so we seek to minimize the distress that they can cause.

You might just wish to tell us how much you liked or loathed the book in question. Or you might have ideas about how this whole process could be improved. In which case you should e-mail `feedback@wrox.com`. You'll always find a sympathetic ear, no matter what the problem is. Above all you should remember that we do care about what you have to say and we will do our utmost to act upon it.

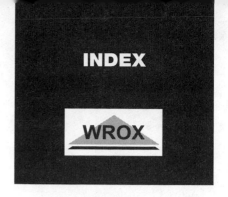

INDEX

WROX

Register Professional IE4 Programming and sign up for a free subscription to The Developer's Journal.

A bi-monthly magazine for software developers, The Wrox Press Developer's Journal features in-depth articles, news and help for everyone in the software development industry. Each issue includes extracts from our latest titles and is crammed full of practical insights into coding techniques, tricks, and research.

Fill in and return the card below to receive a free subscription to the Wrox Press Developer's Journal.

Professional IE4 Programming Registration Card

Name _____

Address _____

_____

_____

_____

City _____ State/Region _____

Country _____ Postcode/Zip _____

E-mail _____

Occupation _____

How did you hear about this book? _____

☐ Book review (name) _____

☐ Advertisement (name) _____

☐ Recommendation _____

☐ Catalog _____

☐ Other _____

Where did you buy this book? _____

☐ Bookstore (name) _____ City _____

☐ Computer Store (name) _____

☐ Mail Order _____

☐ Other _____

What influenced you in the purchase of this book?

☐ Cover Design

☐ Contents

☐ Other (please specify) _____

How did you rate the overall contents of this book?

☐ Excellent ☐ Good

☐ Average ☐ Poor

What did you find most useful about this book? _____

What did you find least useful about this book? _____

Please add any additional comments. _____

What other subjects will you buy a computer book on soon? _____

What is the best computer book you have used this year? _____

Note: This information will only be used to keep you updated about new Wrox Press titles and will not be used for any other purpose or passed to any other third party.

Check here if you DO NOT want a subscription to The Developer's Journal or further support for this book ☐

WROX PRESS INC.

Wrox writes books for you. Any suggestions, or
ideas about how you want information given in
your ideal book will be studied by our team.
Your comments are always valued at Wrox.

Free phone in USA 800-USE-WROX
Fax (312) 397 8990

UK Tel. (0121) 706 6826   Fax   (0121) 706 2967

Computer Book Publishers

NB. If you post the bounce back card below in the UK, please send it to:
Wrox Press Ltd. 30 Lincoln Road, Birmingham, B27 6PA